Class Diagram

Shows the existence of classes and their relationships in the logical view of a system.

Class icons

class name
attributes
operations()
{constraints}

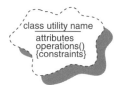

class utility name
attributes
operations()
{constraints}

class <u>category name</u>
classes

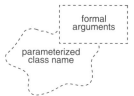

formal
arguments

parameterized
class name

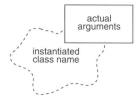

actual
arguments

instantiated
class name

metaclass name

Class relationships

———————	*association*	●———————	*has*	- - - - -▸	*instantiation*
——————▶	*inheritance*	○———————	*using*	——————▶	*metaclass*

Relationship adornments

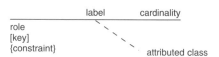

label   cardinality

role
[key]
{constraint}

 attributed class

Containment adornments

●————■ *by value*

●————□ *by reference*

Properties

⟨A⟩ *abstract class*   ⟨F⟩ *friend*

⟨S⟩ *static*   ⟨V⟩ *virtual*

Export control

public || *private*

| *protected* ||| *implementation*

Nesting

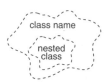

class name

nested
class

Notes

text

OBJECT-ORIENTED ANALYSIS AND DESIGN

with Applications
SECOND EDITION

The Benjamin/Cummings Series in Object-Oriented Software Engineering

Grady Booch, Series Editor

Booch, *Object-Oriented Analysis and Design with Applications, Second Edition* (1994)

Booch, *Object Solutions: A Sourcebook for Developers* (1994)

Booch/Bryan, *Software Engineering with Ada, Third Edition* (1994)

Collins, *Designing Object-Oriented User Interfaces* (1995)

LaLonde, *Discovering Smalltalk* (1994)

Pohl, *Object-Oriented Programming Using C++* (1993)

Tkach/Puttick, *Object Technology in Application Development* (1994)

Other Titles of Interest

Fischer/LeBlanc, *Crafting a Compiler in C* (1991)

Kelley/Pohl, *A Book on C, Second Edition* (1990)

Kelley/Pohl, *C by Dissection: The Essentials of C Programming, Second Edition* (1992)

Pohl, *C++ for C Programmers* (1994)

Sebesta, *Concepts of Programming Languages, Second Edition* (1993)

Sobell, *A Practical Guide to the Unix System, Third Edition* (1994)

Weiss, *Data Structures and Algorithm Analysis in C++* (1992)

OBJECT-ORIENTED ANALYSIS AND DESIGN
with Applications
SECOND EDITION

Grady Booch

Rational
Santa Clara, California

The Benjamin/Cummings Publishing Company, Inc.
Redwood City, California • Menlo Park, California
Reading, Massachusetts • New York • Don Mills, Ontario
Wokingham, U.K. • Amsterdam • Bonn • Sydney • Tokyo • Madrid • San Juan

To Jan
my friend, my lover, my wife

Sponsoring Editor: Dan Joraanstad   *Production Editor:* Wendy Earl
Editorial Assistant: Melissa Standen   *Cartoonist:* Tony Hall
Copy Editor: Nicholas Murray   *Proofreader:* Eleanor Renner Brown
Cover Designer: Yvo Riezebos Design   *Design Consultant:* David Granville Healy

Camera-ready copy for this book was prepared on a Macintosh with Microsoft Word and Adobe Illustrator. All C++ examples were developed using tools from Apple Computer, AT&T, Borland International, Centerline, Pure Software, and Sun Microsystems.

The notation and process described in this book is in the public domain, and its use by all is encouraged (but please acknowledge its source).

Library of Congress Cataloging-in-Publication Data
Booch, Grady.
    Object-oriented analysis and design with applications / Grady Booch. – 2nd ed.
       p.   cm.
    Includes bibliographical references and index.
    ISBN 0-8053-5340-2
    1. Object-oriented programming (Computer science) I. Title.
    QA76.64.B66 1994.
    005.1'1--dc20   93-28658
                                                                               CIP

1 2 3 4 5 6 7 8 9 10 – DO – 97 96 95 94 93

The Benjamin/Cummings Publishing Company, Inc.
390 Bridge Parkway
Redwood City, California 94065

Mankind, under the grace of God, hungers for spiritual peace,
esthetic achievements, family security, justice, and liberty,
none directly satisfied by industrial productivity. But productivity
allows the sharing of the plentiful rather than fighting over
scarcity; it provides time for spiritual, esthetic, and family
matters. It allows society to delegate special skills to
institutions of religion, justice, and the preservation of liberty.

HARLAN MILLS
DPMA and Human Productivity

As computer professionals, we strive to build systems that are useful and that work; as software engineers, we are faced with the task of creating complex systems in the presence of scarce computing and human resources. Over the past few years, object-oriented technology has evolved in diverse segments of the computer sciences as a means of managing the complexity inherent in many different kinds of systems. The object model has proven to be a very powerful and unifying concept.

Changes to the First Edition

Since the publication of the first edition of *Object-Oriented Design with Applications*, object-oriented technology has indeed moved into the mainstream of industrial-strength software development. We have encountered the use of the object-oriented paradigm throughout the world, for such diverse domains as the administration of banking transactions; the automation of bowling alleys; the management of public utilities; and the mapping of the human genome. Many of the next generation operating systems, database systems, telephony systems, avionics systems, and multimedia applications are being written using object-oriented techniques. Indeed, many such projects have chosen to use object-oriented technology simply because there appears to be no other way to economically produce an enduring and resilient programming system.

Over the past several years, hundreds of projects have applied the notation and process described in *Object-Oriented Design with Applications.*[*] Through our own work with several of these projects, as well as the kind contribution of many individuals who have taken the time to communicate with us, we have found ways to improve our method, in terms of better articulating the process, adding and clarifying certain semantics otherwise missing or difficult to express in the notation, and simplifying the notation where possible.

During this time, many other methods have also appeared, including the work of Jacobson, Rumbaugh, Coad and Yourdon, Constantine, Shlaer and Mellor, Martin and Odell, Wasserman, Goldberg and Rubin, Embley, Wirfs-Brock, Goldstein and Alger, Henderson-Sellers, Firesmith, and others. Rumbaugh's work is particularly interesting, for as he points out, our methods are more similar than they are different. We have surveyed many of these methods, interviewed developers and managers who have applied them, and where possible, tried these methods ourselves. Because we are more interested in helping projects succeed with object-oriented technology rather than dogmatically hanging on to practices solely for emotional or historical reasons, we have tried to incorporate the best from each of these methods in our own work. We gratefully acknowledge the fundamental and unique contributions each of these people has made to the field.

It is in the best interests of the software development industry, and object-oriented technology in particular, that there be standard notations for development. Therefore, this edition presents a unified notation that, where possible, eliminates the cosmetic differences between our notation and that of others, particularly Jacobson's and Rumbaugh's. As before, and to encourage the unrestricted use of the method, this notation is in the public domain.

The goals, audience, and structure of this edition remain the same as for the first edition. However, there are five major differences between this edition and the original publication.

First, Chapter 5 has been expanded to provide much more specific detail about the unified notation. To enhance the reader's understanding of this notation, we explicitly distinguish between its fundamental and advanced elements. In addition, we have given special attention to how the various views of the notation integrate with one another.

Second, Chapters 6 and 7, dealing with the process and pragmatics of object-oriented analysis and design, have been greatly expanded. We have also changed the title of this second edition to reflect the fact that our process does indeed encompass analysis as well as design.

Third, we have chosen to express all programming examples in the main text using C++. This language is rapidly becoming the de facto standard in

---

[*] Including my own projects. Ultimately, I'm a developer, not just a methodologist. The first question you should ask any methodologist is if he or she uses their own methods to develop software.

many application domains; additionally, most professional developers who are versed in other object-oriented programming languages can read C++. This is not to say that we view other languages – such as Smalltalk, CLOS, Ada, or Eiffel – as less important. The focus of this book is on analysis and design, and because we need to express concrete examples, we choose to do so in a reasonably common programming language. Where applicable, we describe the semantics unique to these other languages and their impact upon the method.

Fourth, this edition introduces several new application examples. Certain idioms and architectural frameworks have emerged in various application domains, and these examples take advantage of these practices. For example, client/server computing provides the basis of a revised application example.

Finally, almost every chapter provides references to and discussion of the relevant object-oriented technology that has appeared since the first edition.

Goals

This book provides practical guidance on the construction of object-oriented systems. Its specific goals are:

- To provide a sound understanding of the fundamental concepts of the object model
- To facilitate a mastery of the notation and process of object-oriented analysis and design
- To teach the realistic application of object-oriented development within a variety of problem domains

The concepts presented herein all stand on a solid theoretical foundation, but this is primarily a pragmatic book that addresses the practical needs and concerns of the software engineering community.

Audience

This book is written for the computer professional as well as for the student.

- For the practicing software engineer, we show you how to effectively use object-oriented technology to solve real problems.
- In your role as an analyst or architect, we offer you a path from requirements to implementation, using object-oriented analysis and design. We develop your ability to distinguish "good" object-oriented architectures from "bad" ones, and to trade off alternate designs when the perversity of the real world intrudes. Perhaps most important, we offer you fresh approaches to reasoning about complex systems.

- For the program manager, we provide insight on how to allocate the resources of a team of developers, and on how to manage the risks associated with complex software systems.

- For the tool builder and the tool user, we provide a rigorous treatment of the notation and process of object-oriented development as a basis for computer-aided software engineering (CASE) tools.

- For the student, we provide the instruction necessary for you to begin acquiring several important skills in the science and art of developing complex systems.

This book is also suitable for use in undergraduate and graduate courses as well as in professional seminars and individual study. Because it deals primarily with a method of software development, it is most appropriate for courses in software engineering and advanced programming, and as a supplement to courses involving specific object-oriented programming languages.

Structure

The book is divided into three major sections – Concepts, The Method, and Applications – with considerable supplemental material woven throughout.

Concepts

The first section examines the inherent complexity of software and the ways in which complexity manifests itself. We present the object model as a means of helping us manage this complexity. In detail, we examine the fundamental elements of the object model: abstraction, encapsulation, modularity, hierarchy, typing, concurrency, and persistence. We address basic questions such as "What is a class?" and "What is an object?" Because the identification of meaningful classes and objects is the key task in object-oriented development, we spend considerable time studying the nature of classification. In particular, we examine approaches to classification in other disciplines, such as biology, linguistics, and psychology, then apply these lessons to the problem of discovering classes and objects in software systems.

The Method

The second section presents a method for the development of complex systems based on the object model. We first present a graphic notation for object-oriented analysis and design, followed by its process. We also examine the pragmatics of object-oriented development – in particular, its place in the software development life cycle and its implications for project management.

Applications

The final section offers a collection of five complete, nontrivial examples encompassing a diverse selection of problem domains: data acquisition, application frameworks, client/server information management, artificial intelligence, and command and control. We have chosen these particular problem domains because they are representative of the kinds of complex problems faced by the practicing software engineer. It is easy to show how certain principles apply to simple problems, but because our focus is on building useful systems for the real world, we are more interested in showing how the object model scales up to complex applications. Some readers may be unfamiliar with the problem domains chosen, so we begin each application with a brief discussion of the fundamental technology involved (such as database design and blackboard system architecture). The development of software systems is rarely amenable to cookbook approaches; therefore, we emphasize the incremental development of applications, guided by a number of sound principles and well-formed models.

Supplemental Material

A considerable amount of supplemental material is woven throughout the book. Most chapters have boxes that provide information on important topics, such as the mechanics of method dispatch in different object-oriented programming languages. We also include an appendix on object-oriented programming languages, in which we consider the distinction between object-based and object-oriented programming languages and the evolution and essential properties of both categories of languages. For those readers who are unfamiliar with certain object-oriented programming languages, we provide a summary of the features of a few common languages, with examples. We also provide a glossary of common terms and an extensive classified bibliography that provides references to source material on the object model. Lastly, the end pages provide a summary of the notation and process of the object-oriented development method.

Available apart from the text, and new to the second edition, is an Instructor's Guide containing suggested exercises, discussion questions, and projects, which should prove very useful in the classroom as well as stimulating for the individual reader. The *Instructor's Guide with Exercises* (ISBN 0-8053-5341-0) has been developed by Mary Beth Rosson from IBM's Thomas J. Watson laboratory. For a free copy, please contact Benjamin/Cummings in Redwood City, California, or by Internet `bookinfo@bc.aw.com`. Questions, suggestions, and contributions to the Instructor's Guide may be sent by Internet to `rosson@watson.ibm.com`.

Tools and training that support the Booch method are available from a variety of sources. For further information, contact Rational at any of the numbers listed on the last page of this book. Additionally, Benjamin/Cummings can provide educational users with software that supports this notation.

Using this Book

This book may be read from cover to cover or it may be used in less structured ways. If you are seeking a deep understanding of the underlying concepts of the object model or the motivation for the principles of object-oriented development, you should start with Chapter 1 and continue forward in order. If you are primarily interested in learning the details of the notation and process of object-oriented analysis and design, start with Chapters 5 and 6; Chapter 7 is especially useful to managers of projects using this method. If you are most interested in the practical application of object-oriented technology to a specific problem domain, select any or all of Chapters 8 through 12.

Acknowledgments

This book is dedicated to my wife, Jan, for her loving support.

Through both the first and second editions, a number of individuals have shaped my ideas on object-oriented development. For their contributions, I especially thank Sam Adams, Mike Akroid, Glenn Andert, Sid Bailin, Kent Beck, Daniel Bobrow, Dick Bolz, Dave Bulman, Dave Bernstein, Kayvan Carun, Dave Collins, Steve Cook, Damian Conway, Jim Coplien, Brad Cox, Ward Cunningham, Tom DeMarco, Mike Devlin, Richard Gabriel, William Genemaras, Adele Goldberg, Ian Graham, Tony Hoare, Jon Hopkins, Michael Jackson, Ralph Johnson, James Kempf, Norm Kerth, Jordan Kreindler, Doug Lea, Phil Levy, Barbara Liskov, Cliff Longman, James MacFarlane, Masoud Milani, Harlan Mills, Robert Murray, Steve Neis, Gene Ouye, Dave Parnas, Bill Riddel, Mary Beth Rosson, Kenny Rubin, Jim Rumbaugh, Kurt Schmucker, Ed Seidewitz, Dan Shiffman, Dave Stevenson, Bjarne Stroustrup, Dave Thomas, Mike Vilot, Tony Wasserman, Peter Wegner, Iseult White, John Williams, Lloyd Williams, Mario Wolczko, Niklaus Wirth, and Ed Yourdon.

A large part of the pragmatics of this book derives from my involvement with complex software systems being developed around the world at companies such as Apple, Alcatel, Andersen Consulting, AT&T, Autotrol, Bell Northern Research, Boeing, Borland, Computer Sciences Corporation, Contel, Ericsson, Ferranti, General Electric, GTE, Holland Signaal, Hughes Aircraft Company, IBM, Lockheed, Martin Marietta, Motorola, NTT, Philips, Rockwell International, Shell Oil, Symantec, Taligent, and TRW. I have had the opportunity to interact with literally hundreds of professional software engineers and their managers, and I thank them all for their help in making this book relevant to real-world problems.

A special acknowledgment goes to Rational for their support of my work. Thanks also to my editor, Dan Joraanstad, for his encouragement during this project, and to Tony Hall, whose cartoons brighten what would otherwise be just another stuffy technical book. Finally, thanks to my three cats, Camy, Annie, and Shadow, who kept me company on many a late night of writing.

BRIEF CONTENTS

CONTENTS

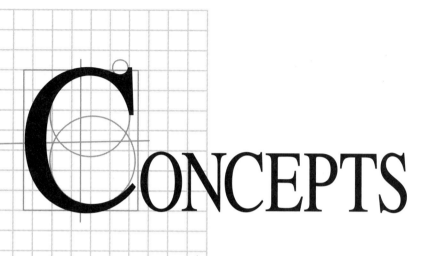

CONCEPTS

Sir Isaac Newton secretly admitted to some friends: He
understood how gravity *behaved*, but not how it *worked!*

LILY TOMLIN
The Search for Signs of Intelligent Life in the Universe

Complexity

A physician, a civil engineer, and a computer scientist were arguing about what was the oldest profession in the world. The physician remarked, "Well, in the Bible, it says that God created Eve from a rib taken out of Adam. This clearly required surgery, and so I can rightly claim that mine is the oldest profession in the world." The civil engineer interrupted, and said, "But even earlier in the book of Genesis, it states that God created the order of the heavens and the earth from out of the chaos. This was the first and certainly the most spectacular application of civil engineering. Therefore, fair doctor, you are wrong: mine is the oldest profession in the world." The computer scientist leaned back in her chair, smiled, and then said confidently, "Ah, but who do you think created the chaos?"

1.1 The Inherent Complexity of Software

The Properties of Simple and Complex Software Systems

A dying star on the verge of collapse, a child learning how to read, white blood cells rushing to attack a virus: these are but a few of the objects in the physical world that involve truly awesome complexity. Software may also involve elements of great complexity; however, the complexity we find here is of a fundamentally different kind. As Brooks points out, "Einstein argued that there must be simplified explanations of nature, because God is not capricious or arbitrary. No such faith comforts the software engineer. Much of the complexity that he must master is arbitrary complexity" [1].

We do realize that some software systems are not complex. These are the largely forgettable applications that are specified, constructed, maintained, and used by the same person, usually the amateur programmer or the professional developer working in isolation. This is not to say that all such systems are crude and inelegant, nor do we mean to belittle their creators. Such systems tend to have a very limited purpose and a very short life span. We can afford to throw them away and replace them with entirely new software rather than attempt to reuse them, repair them, or extend their functionality. Such applications are generally more tedious than difficult to develop; consequently, learning how to design them does not interest us.

Instead, we are much more interested in the challenges of developing what we will call *industrial-strength software*. Here we find applications that exhibit a very rich set of behaviors, as, for example, in reactive systems that drive or are driven by events in the physical world, and for which time and space are scarce resources; applications that maintain the integrity of hundreds of thousands of records of information while allowing concurrent updates and queries; and systems for the command and control of real-world entities, such as the routing of air or railway traffic. Software systems such as these tend to have a long life span, and over time, many users come to depend upon their proper functioning. In the world of industrial-strength software, we also find frameworks that simplify the creation of domain-specific applications, and programs that mimic some aspect of human intelligence. Although such applications are generally products of research and development they are no less complex, for they are the means and artifacts of incremental and exploratory development.

The distinguishing characteristic of industrial-strength software is that it is intensely difficult, if not impossible, for the individual developer to comprehend all the subtleties of its design. Stated in blunt terms, the complexity of such systems exceeds the human intellectual capacity. Alas, this complexity we speak of seems to be an essential property of all large software systems. By *essential* we mean that we may master this complexity, but we can never make it go away.

Certainly, there will always be geniuses among us, people of extraordinary skill who can do the work of a handful of mere mortal developers, the software engineering equivalents of Frank Lloyd Wright or Leonardo da Vinci. These are the people whom we seek to deploy as our systems architects: the ones who devise innovative idioms, mechanisms, and frameworks that others can use as the architectural foundations of other applications or systems. However, as Peters observes, "The world is only sparsely populated with geniuses. There is no reason to believe that the software engineering community has an inordinately large proportion of them" [2]. Although there is a touch of genius in all of us, in the realm of industrial-strength software we cannot always rely upon divine inspiration to carry us through. Therefore, we must consider more disciplined ways to master complexity. To better understand what we seek to control, let us next examine why complexity is an essential property of all software systems.

Why Software Is Inherently Complex

As Brooks suggests, "The complexity of software is an essential property, not an accidental one" [3]. We observe that this inherent complexity derives from four elements: the complexity of the problem domain, the difficulty of managing the developmental process, the flexibility possible through software, and the problems of characterizing the behavior of discrete systems.

The Complexity of the Problem Domain The problems we try to solve in software often involve elements of inescapable complexity, in which we find a myriad of competing, perhaps even contradictory, requirements. Consider the requirements for the electronic system of a multi-engine aircraft, a cellular phone switching system, or an autonomous robot. The raw functionality of such systems is difficult enough to comprehend, but now add all of the (often implicit) nonfunctional requirements such as usability, performance, cost, survivability, and reliability. This unrestrained external complexity is what causes the arbitrary complexity about which Brooks writes.

This external complexity usually springs from the "impedance mismatch" that exists between the users of a system and its developers: users generally find it very hard to give precise expression to their needs in a form that developers can understand. In extreme cases, users may have only vague ideas of what they want in a software system. This is not so much the fault of either the users or the developers of a system; rather, it occurs because each group generally lacks expertise in the domain of the other. Users and developers have different perspectives on the nature of the problem and make different assumptions regarding the nature of the solution. Actually, even if users had perfect knowledge of their needs, we currently have few instruments for precisely capturing these requirements. The common way of expressing requirements today is with large volumes of text, occasionally accompanied by a few drawings. Such documents are difficult to comprehend, are open to varying interpretations, and too often contain elements that are designs rather than essential requirements.

A further complication is that the requirements of a software system often change during its development, largely because the very existence of a software development project alters the rules of the problem. Seeing early products, such as design documents and prototypes, and then using a system once it is installed and operational, are forcing functions that lead users to better understand and articulate their real needs. At the same time, this process helps developers master the problem domain, enabling them to ask better questions that illuminate the dark corners of a system's desired behavior.

Because a large software system is a capital investment, we cannot afford to scrap an existing system every time its requirements change. Planned or not,

The task of the software development team is to engineer the illusion of simplicity.

large systems tend to evolve over time, a condition that is often incorrectly labeled *software maintenance*. To be more precise, it is *maintenance* when we correct errors; it is *evolution* when we respond to changing requirements; it is *preservation* when we continue to use extraordinary means to keep an ancient and decaying piece of software in operation. Unfortunately, reality suggests that an inordinate percentage of software development resources are spent on software preservation.

The Difficulty of Managing the Development Process The fundamental task of the software development team is to engineer the illusion of simplicity – to shield users from this vast and often arbitrary external complexity. Certainly, size is no great virtue in a software system. We strive to write less code by inventing clever and powerful mechanisms that give us this illusion of simplicity, as well as by reusing frameworks of existing designs and code. However, the sheer volume of a system's requirements is sometimes inescapable and forces us either to write a large amount of new software or to reuse existing software in novel ways. Just two decades ago, assembly language programs of only a few thousand lines of code stressed the limits of our software engineering abilities. Today, it is not unusual to find delivered systems whose size is measured in hundreds of thousands, or even millions of lines of code (and all of that in a high-order programming language, as well). No one person can ever understand such a system completely. Even if we decompose our implementation in meaningful ways, we still end up with hundreds and sometimes thousands of separate modules. This amount of work demands that we use a team of developers, and ideally we use as small a team as possible. However, no matter what its size, there are always significant challenges associated with team development. More developers means more complex communication and hence more difficult coordination, particularly if the team is geographically dispersed, as is often the case in very large projects. With a team of developers, the key management challenge is always to maintain a unity and integrity of design.

The Flexibility Possible Through Software A home-building company generally does not operate its own tree farm from which to harvest trees for lumber; it is highly unusual for a construction firm to build an on-site steel mill to forge custom girders for a new building. Yet in the software industry such practice is common. Software offers the ultimate flexibility, so it is possible for a developer to express almost any kind of abstraction. This flexibility turns out to be an incredibly seductive property, however, because it also forces the developer to craft virtually all the primitive building blocks upon which these higher-level abstractions stand. While the construction industry has uniform building codes and standards for the quality of raw materials, few such standards exist in the software industry. As a result, software development remains a labor-intensive business.

The Problems of Characterizing the Behavior of Discrete Systems If we toss a ball into the air, we can reliably predict its path because we know that under normal conditions, certain laws of physics apply. We would be very surprised if just because we threw the ball a little harder, halfway through its flight it suddenly stopped and shot straight up into the air.[*] In a not-quite-debugged software simulation of this ball's motion, exactly that kind of behavior can easily occur.

Within a large application, there may be hundreds or even thousands of variables as well as more than one thread of control. The entire collection of these variables, their current values, and the current address and calling stack of each process within the system constitute the present state of the application. Because we execute our software on digital computers, we have a system with discrete states. By contrast, analog systems such as the motion of the tossed ball are continuous systems. Parnas suggests that "when we say that a system is described by a continuous function, we are saying that it can contain no hidden surprises. Small changes in inputs will always cause

---

[*] Actually, even simple continuous systems can exhibit very complex behavior, because of the presence of chaos. Chaos introduces a randomness that makes it impossible to precisely predict the future state of a system. For example, given the initial state of two drops of water at the top of a stream, we cannot predict exactly where they will be relative to one another at the bottom of the stream. Chaos has been found in systems as diverse as the weather, chemical reactions, biological systems, and even computer networks. Fortunately, there appears to be underlying order in all chaotic systems, in the form of patterns called *attractors*.

correspondingly small changes in outputs" [4]. On the other hand, discrete systems by their very nature have a finite number of possible states; in large systems, there is a combinatorial explosion that makes this number very large. We try to design our systems with a separation of concerns, so that the behavior in one part of a system has minimal impact upon the behavior in another. However, the fact remains that the phase transitions among discrete states cannot be modeled by continuous functions. Each event external to a software system has the potential of placing that system in a new state, and furthermore, the mapping from state to state is not always deterministic. In the worst circumstances, an external event may corrupt the state of a system, because its designers failed to take into account certain interactions among events. For example, imagine a commercial airplane whose flight surfaces and cabin environment are managed by a single computer. We would be very unhappy if, as a result of a passenger in seat 38J turning on an overhead light, the plane immediately executed a sharp dive. In continuous systems this kind of behavior would be unlikely, but in discrete systems all external events can affect any part of the system's internal state. Certainly, this is the primary motivation for vigorous testing of our systems, but for all except the most trivial systems, exhaustive testing is impossible. Since we have neither the mathematical tools nor the intellectual capacity to model the complete behavior of large discrete systems, we must be content with acceptable levels of confidence regarding their correctness.

The Consequences of Unrestrained Complexity

"The more complex the system, the more open it is to total breakdown" [5]. Rarely would a builder think about adding a new sub-basement to an existing 100-story building; to do so would be very costly and would undoubtedly invite failure. Amazingly, users of software systems rarely think twice about asking for equivalent changes. Besides, they argue, it is only a simple matter of programming.

Our failure to master the complexity of software results in projects that are late, over budget, and deficient in their stated requirements. We often call this condition the *software crisis*, but frankly, a malady that has carried on this long must be called normal. Sadly, this crisis translates into the squandering of human resources – a most precious commodity – as well as a considerable loss of opportunities. There are simply not enough good developers around to create all the new software that users need. Furthermore, a significant number of the developmental personnel in any given organization must often be dedicated to the maintenance or preservation of geriatric software. Given the indirect as well as the direct contribution of software to the economic base of most industrialized countries, and considering the ways in which software can amplify the powers of the individual, it is unacceptable to allow this situation to continue.

How can we change this dismal picture? Since the underlying problem springs from the inherent complexity of software, our suggestion is to first study how complex systems in other disciplines are organized. Indeed, if we open our eyes to the world about us, we will observe successful systems of significant complexity. Some of these systems are the works of humanity, such as the Space Shuttle, the England/France tunnel, and large business organizations such as Microsoft or General Electric. Many even more complex systems appear in nature, such as the human circulatory system or the structure of a plant.

1.2 The Structure of Complex Systems

Examples of Complex Systems

The Structure of a Personal Computer A personal computer is a device of moderate complexity. Most of them are composed of the same major elements: a central processing unit (CPU), a monitor, a keyboard, and some sort of secondary storage device, usually either a floppy disk or a hard disk drive. We may take any one of these parts and further decompose it. For example, a CPU typically encompasses primary memory, an arithmetic/logic unit (ALU), and a bus to which peripheral devices are attached. Each of these parts may in turn be further decomposed: an ALU may be divided into registers and random control logic, which themselves are constructed from even more primitive elements, such as NAND gates, inverters, and so on.

Here we see the hierarchic nature of a complex system. A personal computer functions properly only because of the collaborative activity of each of its major parts. Together, these separate parts logically form a whole. Indeed, we can reason about how a computer works only because we can decompose it into parts that we can study separately. Thus, we may study the operation of a monitor independently of the operation of the hard disk drive. Similarly, we may study the ALU without regard for the primary memory subsystem.

Not only are complex systems hierarchic, but the levels of this hierarchy represent different levels of abstraction, each built upon the other, and each understandable by itself. At each level of abstraction, we find a collection of devices that collaborate to provide services to higher layers. We choose a given level of abstraction to suit our particular needs. For instance, if we were trying to track down a timing problem in the primary memory, we might properly look at the gate-level architecture of the computer, but this level of abstraction would be inappropriate if we were trying to find the source of a problem in a spreadsheet application.

The Structure of Plants and Animals In botany, scientists seek to understand the similarities and differences among plants through a study of their morphology, that is, their form and structure. Plants are complex multicellular organisms, and from the cooperative activity of various plant organ systems arise such complex behaviors as photosynthesis and transpiration.

Plants consist of three major structures (roots, stems, and leaves), and each of these has its own structure. For example, roots encompass branch roots, root hairs, the root apex, and the root cap. Similarly, a cross-section of a leaf reveals its epidermis, mesophyll, and vascular tissue. Each of these structures is further composed of a collection of cells, and inside each cell we find yet another level of complexity, encompassing such elements as chloroplasts, a nucleus, and so on. As with the structure of a computer, the parts of a plant form a hierarchy, and each level of this hierarchy embodies its own complexity.

All parts at the same level of abstraction interact in well-defined ways. For example, at the highest level of abstraction, roots are responsible for absorbing water and minerals from the soil. Roots interact with stems, which transport these raw materials up to the leaves. The leaves in turn use the water and minerals provided by the stems to produce food through photosynthesis.

There are always clear boundaries between the outside and the inside of a given level. For example, we can state that the parts of a leaf work together to provide the functionality of the leaf as a whole, and yet have little or no direct interaction with the elementary parts of the roots. In simpler terms, there is a clear separation of concerns among the parts at different levels of abstraction.

In a computer, we find NAND gates used in the design of the CPU as well as in the hard disk drive. Likewise, a considerable amount of commonality cuts across all parts of the structural hierarchy of a plant. This is God's way of achieving an economy of expression. For example, cells serve as the basic building blocks in all structures of a plant; ultimately, the roots, stems, and leaves of a plant are all composed of cells. Yet, although each of these primitive elements is indeed a cell, there are many different kinds of cells. For example, there are cells with and without chloroplasts, cells with walls that are impervious to water and cells with walls that are permeable, and even living cells and dead cells.

In studying the morphology of a plant, we do not find individual parts that are each responsible for only one small step in a single larger process, such as photosynthesis. In fact, there are no centralized parts that directly coordinate the activities of lower level ones. Instead, we find separate parts that act as independent agents, each of which exhibits some fairly complex behavior, and each of which contributes to many higher-level functions. Only through the mutual cooperation of meaningful collections of these agents do we see the higher-level functionality of a plant. The science of complexity calls this *emergent behavior:* The behavior of the whole is greater than the sum of its parts [6].

Turning briefly to the field of zoology, we note that multicellular animals exhibit a hierarchical structure similar to that of plants: collections of cells form tissues, tissues work together as organs, clusters of organs define systems (such as the digestive system), and so on. We cannot help but again notice God's awesome economy of expression: the fundamental building block of all animal matter is the cell, just as the cell is the elementary structure of all plant life. Granted, there are differences between these two. For example, plant cells are enclosed by rigid cellulose walls, but animal cells are not. Notwithstanding these differences, however, both of these structures are undeniably cells. This is an example of commonality that crosses domains.

A number of mechanisms above the cellular level are also shared by plant and animal life. For example, both use some sort of vascular system to transport nutrients within the organism, and both exhibit differentiation by sex among members of the same species.

The Structure of Matter The study of fields as diverse as astronomy and nuclear physics provides us with many other examples of incredibly complex systems. Spanning these two disciplines, we find yet another structural hierarchy. Astronomers study galaxies that are arranged in clusters, and stars, planets, and various debris are the constituents of galaxies. Likewise, nuclear physicists are concerned with a structural hierarchy, but one on an entirely different scale. Atoms are made up of electrons, protons, and neutrons; electrons appear to be elementary particles, but protons, neutrons, and other particles are formed from more basic components called *quarks*.

Again we find that a great commonality in the form of shared mechanisms unifies this vast hierarchy. Specifically, there appear to be only four distinct kinds of forces at work in the universe: gravity, electromagnetic interaction, the strong force, and the weak force. Many laws of physics involving these elementary forces, such as the laws of conservation of energy and of momentum, apply to galaxies as well as quarks.

The Structure of Social Institutions As a final example of complex systems, we turn to the structure of social institutions. Groups of people join together to accomplish tasks that cannot be done by individuals. Some organizations are transitory, and some endure beyond many lifetimes. As organizations grow larger, we see a distinct hierarchy emerge. Multinational corporations contain companies, which in turn are made up of divisions, which in turn contain branches, which in turn encompass local offices, and so on. If the organization endures, the boundaries among these parts may change, and over time, a new, more stable hierarchy may emerge.

The relationships among the various parts of a large organization are just like those found among the components of a computer, or a plant, or even a galaxy. Specifically, the degree of interaction among employees within an individual office is greater than that between employees of different offices. A mail clerk usually does not interact with the chief executive officer of a company but does interact frequently with other people in the mail room. Here too, these different levels are unified by common mechanisms. The clerk and the executive are both paid by the same financial organization, and both share common facilities, such as the company's telephone system, to accomplish their tasks.

The Five Attributes of a Complex System

Drawing from this line of study, we conclude that there are five attributes common to all complex systems. Building upon the work of Simon and Ando, Courtois suggests the following:

> 1. *"Frequently, complexity takes the form of a hierarchy, whereby a complex system is composed of interrelated subsystems that have in turn their own subsystems, and so on, until some lowest level of elementary components is reached"* [7].

Simon points out that "the fact that many complex systems have a nearly decomposable, hierarchic structure is a major facilitating factor enabling us to understand, describe, and even 'see' such systems and their parts" [8]. Indeed, it is likely that we can understand only those systems that have a hierarchic structure.

It is important to realize that the architecture of a complex system is a function of its components as well as the hierarchic relationships among these components. As Rechtin observes, "All systems have subsystems and all systems are parts of larger systems . . . The valued added by a system must come from the relationships between the parts, not from the parts per se" [9].

Regarding the nature of the primitive components of a complex system, our experience suggests that

> 2. *The choice of what components in a system are primitive is relatively arbitrary and is largely up to the discretion of the observer of the system.*

What is primitive for one observer may be at a much higher level of abstraction for another.

Simon calls hierarchic systems *decomposable*, because they can be divided into identifiable parts; he calls them *nearly decomposable*, because their parts are not completely independent. This leads us to another attribute common to all complex systems:

> 3. *"Intracomponent linkages are generally stronger than intercomponent linkages. This fact has the effect of separating the high-frequency dynamics of the components – involving the internal structure of the components – from the low-frequency dynamics – involving interaction among components"* [10].

This difference between intra- and intercomponent interactions provides a clear separation of concerns among the various parts of a system, making it possible to study each part in relative isolation.

As we have discussed, many complex systems are implemented with an economy of expression. Simon thus notes that

4. *"Hierarchic systems are usually composed of only a few different kinds of subsystems in various combinations and arrangements"* [11].

In other words, complex systems have common patterns. These patterns may involve the reuse of small components, such as the cells found in both plants and animals, or of larger structures, such as vascular systems, also found in both plants and animals.

Earlier, we noted that complex systems tend to evolve over time. As Simon suggests, "complex systems will evolve from simple systems much more rapidly if there are stable intermediate forms than if there are not" [12]. In more dramatic terms, Gall states that

5. *"A complex system that works is invariably found to have evolved from a simple system that worked. . . . A complex system designed from scratch never works and cannot be patched up to make it work. You have to start over, beginning with a working simple system"* [13].

As systems evolve, objects that were once considered complex become the primitive objects upon which more complex systems are built. Furthermore, we can never craft these primitive objects correctly the first time: we must use them in context first, and then improve them over time as we learn more about the real behavior of the system.

Organized and Disorganized Complexity

The Canonical Form of a Complex System The discovery of common abstractions and mechanisms greatly facilitates our understanding of complex systems. For example, with just a few minutes of orientation, an experienced pilot can step into a multi-engine jet aircraft he or she has never flown before and safely fly the vehicle. Having recognized the properties common to all such aircraft, such as the functioning of the rudder, ailerons, and throttle, the pilot primarily needs to learn what properties are unique to that particular aircraft. If the pilot already knows how to fly a given aircraft, it is far easier to know how to fly a similar one.

This example suggests that we have been using the term *hierarchy* in a rather loose fashion. Most interesting systems do not embody a single hierarchy; instead, we find that many different hierarchies are usually present within the same complex system. For example, an aircraft may be studied by decomposing it into its propulsion system, flight-control system, and so on. This decomposition represents a structural, or "part of" hierarchy. Alternately, we can cut across the system in an entirely orthogonal way. For example, a turbofan engine is a specific kind of jet engine, and a Pratt and Whitney TF30 is a specific kind of turbofan engine. Stated another way, a jet engine represents a generalization of the properties common to every kind of jet engine; a turbofan engine is simply a specialized kind of jet engine, with properties that distinguish it, for example, from ramjet engines.

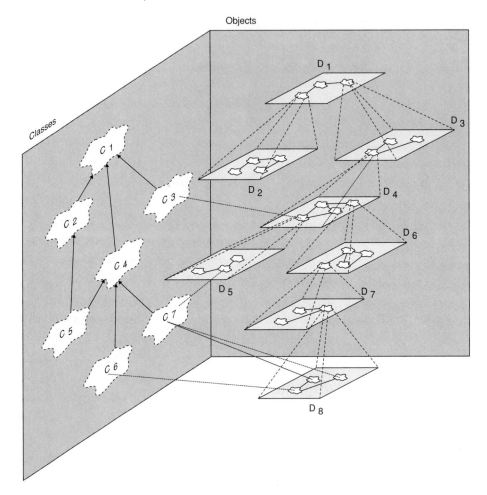

Figure 1-1
The Canonical Form of a Complex System

This second hierarchy represents an "is a" hierarchy. In our experience, we have found it essential to view a system from both perspectives, studying its "is a" hierarchy as well as its "part of" hierarchy. For reasons that will become clear in the next chapter, we call these hierarchies the *class structure* and the *object structure*, respectively.[*]

Combining the concept of the class and object structure together with the five attributes of a complex system, we find that virtually all complex systems take on the same (canonical) form, as we show in Figure 1-1. Here we see the

---

[*] Complex software systems embody other kinds of hierarchies as well. Of particular importance is its module structure, which describes the relationships among the physical components of the system, and the process hierarchy, which describes the relationships among the system's dynamic components.

two orthogonal hierarchies of the system: its class structure and its object structure. Each hierarchy is layered, with the more abstract classes and objects built upon more primitive ones. What class or object is chosen as primitive is relative to the problem at hand. Especially among the parts of the object structure, there are close collaborations among objects at the same level of abstraction. Looking inside any given level reveals yet another level of complexity. Notice also that the class structure and the object structure are not completely independent; rather, each object in the object structure represents a specific instance of some class. As the figure suggests, there are usually many more objects than classes of objects within a complex system. Thus, by showing the "part of" as well as the "is a" hierarchy, we explicitly expose the redundancy of the system under consideration. If we did not reveal a system's class structure, we would have to duplicate our knowledge about the properties of each individual part. With the inclusion of the class structure, we capture these common properties in one place.

Our experience is that the most successful complex software systems are those whose designs explicitly encompass a well-engineered class and object structure and whose structure embodies the five attributes of complex systems described in the previous section. Lest the importance of this observation be missed, let us be even more direct: we very rarely encounter software systems that are delivered on time, within budget, and that meet their requirements, unless they are designed with these factors in mind.

Collectively, we speak of the class and object structure of a system as its *architecture*.

The Limitations of the Human Capacity for Dealing with Complexity If we know what the design of complex software systems should be like, then why do we still have serious problems in successfully developing them? As we discuss in the next chapter, this concept of the organized complexity of software (whose guiding principles we call the *object model*) is relatively new. However, there is yet another factor that dominates: the fundamental limitations of the human capacity for dealing with complexity.

As we first begin to analyze a complex software system, we find many parts that must interact in a multitude of intricate ways, with little perceptible commonality among either the parts or their interactions: this is an example of disorganized complexity. As we work to bring organization to this complexity through the process of design, we must think about many things at once. For example, in an air traffic control system, we must deal with the state of many different aircraft at once, involving such properties as their location, speed, and heading. Especially in the case of discrete systems, we must cope with a fairly large, intricate, and sometimes nondeterministic state space. Unfortunately, it is absolutely impossible for a single person to keep track of all of these details at once. Experiments by psychologists, such as those of Miller, suggest that the maximum number of chunks of information that an individual can simultaneously comprehend is on the order of seven, plus or minus two [14]. This channel capacity seems to be related to the capacity of short-term

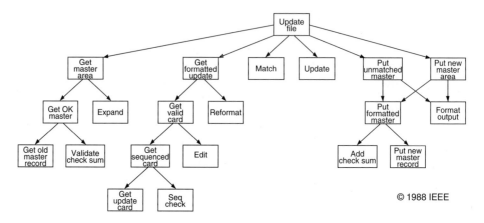

© 1988 IEEE

Figure 1-2
Algorithmic Decomposition

memory. Simon additionally notes that processing speed is a limiting factor: it takes the mind about five seconds to accept a new chunk of information [15].

We are thus faced with a fundamental dilemma. The complexity of the software systems we are asked to develop is increasing, yet there are basic limits upon our ability to cope with this complexity. How then do we resolve this predicament?

1.3 Bringing Order to Chaos

The Role of Decomposition

As Dijkstra suggests, "The technique of mastering complexity has been known since ancient times: *divide et impera* (divide and rule)" [16]. When designing a complex software system, it is essential to decompose it into smaller and smaller parts, each of which we may then refine independently. In this manner, we satisfy the very real constraint that exists upon the channel capacity of human cognition: to understand any given level of a system, we need only comprehend a few parts (rather than all parts) at once. Indeed, as Parnas observes, intelligent decomposition directly addresses the inherent complexity of software by forcing a division of a system's state space [17].

Algorithmic Decomposition Most of us have been formally trained in the dogma of top-down structured design, and so we approach decomposition as a simple matter of algorithmic decomposition, wherein each module in the system denotes a major step in some overall process. Figure 1-2 is an example of one of the products of structured design, a structure chart that shows the relationships among various functional elements of the solution. This particular structure chart illustrates part of the design of a program that updates the

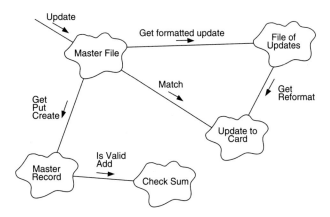

Figure 1-3
Object-Oriented Decomposition

content of a master file. It was automatically generated from a data flow diagram by an expert system tool that embodies the rules of structured design [18].

Object-Oriented Decomposition We suggest that there is an alternate decomposition possible for the same problem. In Figure 1-3, we have decomposed the system according to the key abstractions in the problem domain. Rather than decomposing the problem into steps such as *Get formatted update* and *Add check sum*, we have identified objects such as *Master File* and *Check Sum*, which derive directly from the vocabulary of the problem domain.

Although both designs solve the same problem, they do so in quite different ways. In this second decomposition, we view the world as a set of autonomous agents that collaborate to perform some higher level behavior. *Get formatted update* thus does not exist as an independent algorithm; rather, it is an operation associated with the object *File of Updates*. Calling this operation creates another object, *Update to Card*. In this manner, each object in our solution embodies its own unique behavior, and each one models some object in the real world. From this perspective, an object is simply a tangible entity which exhibits some well-defined behavior. Objects do things, and we ask them to perform what they do by sending them messages. Because our decomposition is based upon objects and not algorithms, we call this an *object-oriented* decomposition.

Algorithmic versus Object-Oriented Decomposition Which is the right way to decompose a complex system – by algorithms or by objects? Actually, this is a trick question, because the right answer is that both views are important: the algorithmic view highlights the ordering of events, and the object-oriented view emphasizes the agents that either cause action or are the subjects upon which these operations act. However, the fact remains that we cannot construct a

Categories of Analysis and Design Methods

We find it useful to distinguish between the terms *method* and *methodology*. A method is a disciplined process for generating a set of models that describe various aspects of a software system under development, using some well-defined notation. A methodology is a collection of methods applied across the software development life cycle and unified by some general, philosophical approach. Methods are important for several reasons. Foremost, they instill a discipline into the development of complex software systems. They define the products that serve as common vehicles for communication among the members of a development team. Additionally, methods define the milestones needed by management to measure progress and to manage risk.

Methods have evolved in response to the growing complexity of software systems. In the early days of computing, one simply did not write large programs, because the capabilities of our machines were greatly limited. The dominant constraints in building systems were then largely due to hardware: machines had small amounts of main memory, programs had to contend with considerable latency within secondary storage devices such as magnetic drums, and processors had cycle times measured in the hundreds of microseconds. In the 1960s and 1970s the economics of computing began to change dramatically as hardware costs plummeted and computer capabilities rose. As a result, it was more desirable and now finally economical to automate more and more applications of increasing complexity. High-order programming languages entered the scene as important tools. Such languages improved the productivity of the individual developer and of the development team as a whole, thus ironically pressuring us to create software systems of even greater complexity.

Many design methods were proposed during the 1960s and 1970s to address this growing complexity. The most influential of them was top-down structured design, also known as *composite design*. This method was directly influenced by the topology of traditional high-order programming languages, such as FORTRAN and COBOL. In these languages, the fundamental unit of decomposition is the subprogram, and the resulting program takes the shape of a tree in which subprograms perform their work by calling other subprograms. This is exactly the approach taken by top-down structured design: one applies algorithmic decomposition to break a large problem down into smaller steps.

Since the 1960s and 1970s, computers of vastly greater capabilities have evolved. The value of structured design has not changed, but as Stein observes, "Structured programming appears to fall apart when applications exceed 100,000 lines or so of code" [19]. More recently, dozens of design methods have been proposed, many of them invented to deal with the perceived shortcomings of top-down structured design. The more interesting and successful design methods are cataloged by Peters [20] and Yau and Tsai [21], and in a comprehensive survey by Teledyne-Brown Engineering [22]. Perhaps not surprisingly, many of these methods are largely variations upon a similar theme. Indeed, as Sommerville suggests, most methods can be categorized as one of three kinds [23]:

- Top-down structured design
- Data-driven design
- Object-oriented design

Top-down structured design is exemplified by the work of Yourdon and Constantine [24], Myers [25], and Page-Jones [26]. The foundations of this method derive from the work of Wirth [27, 28] and Dahl, Dijkstra, and Hoare [29]; an important variation on structured design is found in the design method of Mills, Linger, and Hevner [30]. Each of these variations applies algorithmic decomposition. More software has probably been written using these design methods than with any other. Nevertheless, structured design does not address the issues of data abstraction and information hiding, nor does it provide an adequate means of dealing with concurrency. Structured design does not scale up well for extremely complex systems, and this method is largely inappropriate for use with object-based and object-oriented programming languages.

Data-driven design is best exemplified by the early work of Jackson [31, 32] and the methods of Warnier and Orr [33]. In this method, the structure of a software system is derived by mapping system inputs to outputs. As with structured design, data-driven design has been successfully applied to a number of complex domains, particularly information management systems, which involve direct relationships between the inputs and outputs of the system, but require little concern for time-critical events.

Object-oriented analysis and design is the method we introduce in this book. Its underlying concept is that one should model software systems as collections of cooperating objects, treating individual objects as instances of a class within a hierarchy of classes. Object-oriented analysis and design directly reflects the topology of more recent high-order programming languages such as Smalltalk, Object Pascal, C++, the Common Lisp Object System (CLOS), and Ada.

complex system in both ways simultaneously, for they are completely orthogonal views.[*] We must start decomposing a system either by algorithms or by objects, and then use the resulting structure as the framework for expressing the other perspective.

Our experience leads us to apply the object-oriented view first because this approach is better at helping us organize the inherent complexity of software systems, just as it helped us to describe the organized complexity of complex

---

[*] Langdon suggests that this orthogonality has been studied since ancient times. As he states, "C. H. Waddington has noted that the duality of views can be traced back to the ancient Greeks. A passive view was proposed by Democritus, who asserted that the world was composed of matter called atoms. Democritus' view places things at the center of focus. On the other hand, the classical spokesman for the active view is Heraclitus, who emphasized the notion of process" [34].

systems as diverse as computers, plants, galaxies, and large social institutions. As we will discuss further in Chapters 2 and 7, object-oriented decomposition has a number of highly significant advantages over algorithmic decomposition. Object-oriented decomposition yields smaller systems through the reuse of common mechanisms, thus providing an important economy of expression. Object-oriented systems are also more resilient to change and thus better able to evolve over time, because their design is based upon stable intermediate forms. Indeed, object-oriented decomposition greatly reduces the risk of building complex software systems, because they are designed to evolve incrementally from smaller systems in which we already have confidence. Furthermore, object-oriented decomposition directly addresses the inherent complexity of software by helping us make intelligent decisions regarding the separation of concerns in a large state space.

Chapters 8 through 12 demonstrate these benefits through several complete applications, drawn from a diverse set of problem domains. The sidebar in this chapter further compares and contrasts the object-oriented view with more traditional approaches to design.

The Role of Abstraction

Earlier, we referred to Miller's experiments, from which he concluded that an individual can comprehend only about seven, plus or minus two, chunks of information at one time. This number appears to be independent of information content. As Miller himself observes, "The span of absolute judgment and the span of immediate memory impose severe limitations on the amount of information that we are able to receive, process and remember. By organizing the stimulus input simultaneously into several dimensions and successively into a sequence of chunks, we manage to break . . . this informational bottleneck" [35]. In contemporary terms, we call this process chunking, or *abstraction.*

As Wulf describes it, "We (humans) have developed an exceptionally powerful technique for dealing with complexity. We abstract from it. Unable to master the entirety of a complex object, we choose to ignore its inessential details, dealing instead with the generalized, idealized model of the object" [36]. For example, when studying how photosynthesis works in a plant, we can focus upon the chemical reactions in certain cells in a leaf, and ignore all other parts, such as the roots and stems. We are still constrained by the number of things that we can comprehend at one time, but through abstraction, we use chunks of information with increasingly greater semantic content. This is especially true if we take an object-oriented view of the world, because objects, as abstractions of entities in the real world, represent a particularly dense and cohesive clustering of information. Chapter 2 examines the meaning of abstraction in much greater detail.

The Role of Hierarchy

Another way to increase the semantic content of individual chunks of information is by explicitly recognizing the class and object hierarchies within a complex software system. The object structure is important because it illustrates how different objects collaborate with one another through patterns of interaction that we call *mechanisms*. The class structure is equally important, because it highlights common structure and behavior within a system. Thus, rather than study each individual photosynthesizing cell within a specific plant leaf, it is enough to study one such cell, because we expect that all others will exhibit similar behavior. Although we treat each instance of a particular kind of object as distinct, we may assume that it shares the same behavior as all other instances of that same kind of object. By classifying objects into groups of related abstractions (for example, kinds of plant cells versus animal cells), we come to explicitly distinguish the common and distinct properties of different objects, which further helps us to master their inherent complexity [37].

Identifying the hierarchies within a complex software system is often not easy, because it requires the discovery of patterns among many objects, each of which may embody some tremendously complicated behavior. Once we have exposed these hierarchies, however, the structure of a complex system, and in turn our understanding of it, becomes vastly simplified. Chapter 3 considers in detail the nature of class and object hierarchies, and Chapter 4 describes techniques that facilitate our identification of these patterns.

1.4 On Designing Complex Systems

Engineering as a Science and an Art

The practice of every engineering discipline – be it civil, mechanical, chemical, electrical, or software engineering – involves elements of both science and art. As Petroski eloquently states, "The conception of a design for a new structure can involve as much a leap of the imagination and as much a synthesis of experience and knowledge as any artist is required to bring to his canvas or paper. And once that design is articulated by the engineer as artist, it must be analyzed by the engineer as scientist in as rigorous an application of the scientific method as any scientist must make" [38]. Similarly, Dijkstra observes that "the programming challenge is a large-scale exercise in applied abstraction and thus requires the abilities of the formal mathematician blended with the attitude of the competent engineer." [39].

The role of the engineer as artist is particularly challenging when the task is to design an entirely new system. Frankly, this is the most common circumstance in software engineering. Especially in the case of reactive systems and systems for command and control, we are frequently asked to write software for an entirely unique set of requirements, often to be executed on a configuration of target processors constructed specifically for this system. In other cases, such as the creation of frameworks, tools for research in artificial intelligence, or even information management systems, we may have a well-defined, stable target environment, but our requirements may stress the software technology in one or more dimensions. For example, we may be asked to craft systems that are faster, have greater capacity, or have radically improved functionality. In all these situations, we try to use proven abstractions and mechanisms (the "stable intermediate forms," in Simon's words) as a foundation upon which to build new complex systems. In the presence of a large library of reusable software components, the software engineer must assemble these parts in innovative ways to satisfy the stated and implicit requirements, just as the painter or the musician must push the limits of his or her medium. Unfortunately, since such rich libraries rarely exist for the software engineer, he or she must usually proceed with a relatively primitive set of facilities.

The Meaning of Design

In every engineering discipline, design encompasses the disciplined approach we use to invent a solution for some problem, thus providing a path from requirements to implementation. In the context of software engineering, Mostow suggests that the purpose of design is to construct a system that

- "Satisfies a given (perhaps informal) functional specification
- Conforms to limitations of the target medium
- Meets implicit or explicit requirements on performance and resource usage
- Satisfies implicit or explicit design criteria on the form of the artifact
- Satisfies restrictions on the design process itself, such as its length or cost, or the tools available for doing the design" [40]

As Stroustrup suggests, "the purpose of design is to create a clean and relatively simple internal structure, sometimes also called an architecture. . . . A design is the end product of the design process" [41]. Design involves balancing a set of competing requirements. The products of design are models that enable us to reason about our structures, make trade-offs when requirements conflict, and in general, provide a blueprint for implementation.

The Importance of Model Building The building of models has a broad acceptance among all engineering disciplines, largely because model building appeals to the principles of decomposition, abstraction, and hierarchy [42]. Each model within a design describes a specific aspect of the system under consideration. As much as possible, we seek to build new models upon old models in which we already have confidence. Models give us the opportunity to fail under controlled conditions. We evaluate each model under both expected and unusual situations, and then alter them when they fail to behave as we expect or desire.

We have found that in order to express all the subtleties of a complex system, we must use more than one kind of model. For example, when designing a single-board computer, an electrical engineer must take into consideration the gate-level view of the system as well as the physical layout of integrated circuits on the board. This gate-level view forms a logical picture of the design of the system, which helps the engineer to reason about the cooperative behavior of the gates. The board layout represents the physical packaging of these gates, constrained by the board size, available power, and the kinds of integrated circuits that exist. From this view, the engineer can independently reason about factors such as heat dissipation and manufacturability. The board designer must also consider dynamic as well as static aspects of the system under construction. Thus, the electrical engineer uses diagrams showing the static connections among individual gates, as well as timing diagrams that show the behavior of these gates over time. The engineer can then employ tools such as oscilloscopes and digital analyzers to validate the correctness of both the static and dynamic models.

The Elements of Software Design Methods Clearly, there is no magic, no "silver bullet" [43], that can unfailingly lead the software engineer down the path from requirements to the implementation of a complex software system. In fact, the design of complex software systems does not lend itself at all to cookbook approaches. Rather, as noted earlier in the fifth attribute of complex systems, the design of such systems involves an incremental and iterative process.

Still, sound design methods do bring some much-needed discipline to the development process. The software engineering community has evolved dozens of different design methods, which we can loosely classify into three categories (see sidebar). Despite their differences, all of these methods have elements in common. Specifically, each method includes the following:

- Notation   The language for expressing each model
- Process   The activities leading to the orderly construction of the system's models
- Tools   The artifacts that eliminate the tedium of model building and enforce rules about the models themselves, so that errors and inconsistencies can be exposed

A sound design method is based upon a solid theoretical foundation, yet offers degrees of freedom for artistic innovation.

The Models of Object-Oriented Development Is there a "best" design method? No, there is no absolute answer to this question, which is actually just a veiled way of asking the earlier question: What is the best way to decompose a complex system? To reiterate, we have found great value in building models

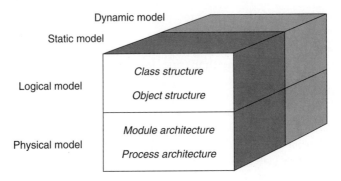

Figure 1-4
The Models of Object-Oriented Development

that are focused upon the "things" we find in the problem space, forming what we refer to as an *object-oriented decomposition.*

Object-oriented analysis and design is the method that leads us to an object-oriented decomposition. By applying object-oriented design, we create software that is resilient to change and written with economy of expression. We achieve a greater level of confidence in the correctness of our software through an intelligent separation of its state space. Ultimately, we reduce the risks that are inherent in developing complex software systems.

Because model building is so important to the construction of complex systems, object-oriented development offers a rich set of models, which we describe in Figure 1-4. The models of object-oriented analysis and design reflect the importance of explicitly capturing both the class and object hierarchies of the system under design. These models also cover the spectrum of the important design decisions that we must consider in developing a complex system, and so encourage us to craft implementations that embody the five attributes of well-formed complex systems.

Chapter 5 presents each of these four models in detail. Chapter 6 explains the process of object-oriented design, which provides an orderly set of steps for the creation and evolution of these models. Chapter 7 examines the pragmatics of managing a project using object-oriented design.

In this chapter, we have made a case for using object-oriented analysis and design to master the complexity associated with developing software systems. Additionally, we have suggested a number of fundamental benefits to be derived from applying this method. Before we present the notation and process of object-oriented design, however, we must study the principles upon which object-oriented development is founded, namely, abstraction, encapsulation, modularity, hierarchy, typing, concurrency, and persistence.

Summary

- Software is inherently complex; the complexity of software systems often exceeds the human intellectual capacity.
- The task of the software development team is to engineer the illusion of simplicity.
- Complexity often takes the form of a hierarchy; it is useful to model both the "is a" and the "part of" hierarchies of a complex system.
- Complex systems generally evolve from stable intermediate forms.
- There are fundamental limiting factors of human cognition; we can address these constraints through the use of decomposition, abstraction, and hierarchy.
- Complex systems can be viewed either by focusing upon things or processes; there are compelling reasons for applying object-oriented decomposition, in which we view the world as a meaningful collection of objects that collaborate to achieve some higher level behavior.
- Object-oriented analysis and design is the method that leads us to an object-oriented decomposition; object-oriented design defines a notation and process for constructing complex software systems, and offers a rich set of logical and physical models with which we may reason about different aspects of the system under consideration.

Further Readings

The challenges associated with developing complex software systems are articulately described in the classic works by Brooks in [H 1975] and [H 1987]. Glass [H 1982], the Defense Science Board [H 1987], and the Joint Service Task Force [H 1982] provide further information on contemporary software practices. Empirical studies on the nature and causes of software failures may be found in van Genuchten [H 1991], Guindon, et. al. [H 1987] and Jones [H 1992].

Simon [A 1962, 1982] are the seminal references on the architecture of complex systems; Courtois [A 1985] applies these ideas to the domain of software. Alexander's seminal work in [I 1979] provides a fresh approach to architecting physical structures. Peter [I 1986] and Petroski [I 1985] examine complexity in the context of social and physical systems, respectively. Similarly, Allen and Starr [A 1982] examine hierarchical systems in a number of domains. Flood and Carson [A 1988] offer a formal study of complexity as seen through the theory of systems science. Waldrop [A 1992] describes the emerging science of complexity and its study of complex adaptive systems, emergent behavior, and self-organization. The report by Miller [A 1956] provides empirical evidence for the fundamental limiting factors of human cognition.

There are a number of excellent references on the subject of software engineering. Ross, Goodenough, and Irvine [H 1980], and Zelkowitz [H 1978] are two of the classic papers summarizing the essential elements of software engineering. Extended works on the subject include Jensen and Tonies [H 1979], Sommerville [H 1985], Vick and Ramamoorthy [H 1984], Wegner [H 1980], Pressman [H 1992], Oman and Lewis [A

1990], Berzins and Luqi [H 1991], and Ng and Yeh [H 1990]. Other papers relevant to software engineering in general may be found in Yourdon [H 1979] and Freeman and Wasserman [H 1983]. Graham [F 1991] and Berard [H 1993] both present a broad treatment of object-oriented software engineering.

Gleick [I 1987] offers a very readable introduction to the science of chaos.

CHAPTER 2

The Object Model

Object-oriented technology is built upon a sound engineering foundation, whose elements we collectively call the *object model*. The object model encompasses the principles of abstraction, encapsulation, modularity, hierarchy, typing, concurrency, and persistence. By themselves, none of these principles are new. What is important about the object model is that these elements are brought together in a synergistic way.

Let there be no doubt that object-oriented analysis and design is fundamentally different than traditional structured design approaches: it requires a different way of thinking about decomposition, and it produces software architectures that are largely outside the realm of the structured design culture. These differences arise from the fact that structured design methods build upon structured programming, whereas object-oriented design builds upon object-oriented programming. Unfortunately, object-oriented programming means different things to different people. As Rentsch correctly predicted, "My guess is that object-oriented programming will be in the 1980s what structured programming was in the 1970s. Everyone will be in favor of it. Every manufacturer will promote his products as supporting it. Every manager will pay lip service to it. Every programmer will practice it (differently). And no one will know just what it is" [1]. Rentsch's predictions still apply to the 1990s.

In this chapter, we will show clearly what object-oriented development is and what it is not, and how it differs from other methods through its use of the seven elements of the object model.

2.1 The Evolution of the Object Model

Trends in Software Engineering

The Generations of Programming Languages As we look back upon the relatively brief yet colorful history of software engineering, we cannot help but notice two sweeping trends:

- The shift in focus from programming-in-the-small to programming-in-the-large
- The evolution of high-order programming languages

Most new industrial-strength software systems are larger and more complex than their predecessors were even just a few years ago. This growth in complexity has prompted a significant amount of useful applied research in software engineering, particularly with regard to decomposition, abstraction, and hierarchy. The development of more expressive programming languages has complemented these advances. The trend has been a move away from languages that tell the computer what to do (imperative languages) toward languages that describe the key abstractions in the problem domain (declarative languages).

Wegner has classified some of the more popular high-order programming languages in generations arranged according to the language features they first introduced:

- First-Generation Languages (1954–1958)

FORTRAN I	Mathematical expressions
ALGOL 58	Mathematical expressions
Flowmatic	Mathematical expressions
IPL V	Mathematical expressions

- Second-Generation Languages (1959–1961)

FORTRAN II	Subroutines, separate compilation
ALGOL 60	Block structure, data types
COBOL	Data description, file handling
Lisp	List processing, pointers, garbage collection

- Third-Generation Languages (1962–1970)

PL/1	FORTRAN + ALGOL + COBOL
ALGOL 68	Rigorous successor to ALGOL 60
Pascal	Simple successor to ALGOL 60
Simula	Classes, data abstraction

- The Generation Gap (1970–1980)

  Many different languages were invented, but few endured [2].

In successive generations, the kind of abstraction mechanism each language supported changed. First-generation languages were used primarily for scientific and engineering applications, and the vocabulary of this problem domain was almost entirely mathematics. Languages such as FORTRAN I were thus developed to allow the programmer to write mathematical formulas, thereby freeing the programmer from some of the intricacies of assembly or machine language. This first generation of high-order programming languages therefore represented a step closer to the problem space, and a step further away from the underlying machine. Among second-generation languages, the emphasis was upon algorithmic abstractions. By this time, machines were becoming more and more powerful, and the economics of the computer industry meant that more kinds of problems could be automated, especially for business applications. Now, the focus was largely upon telling the machine what to do: read these personnel records first, sort them next, and then print this report. Again, this new generation of high-order programming languages moved us a step closer to the problem space, and further away from the underlying machine. By the late 1960s, especially with the advent of transistors and then integrated circuit technology, the cost of computer hardware had dropped dramatically, yet processing capacity had grown almost exponentially. Larger problems could now be solved, but these demanded the manipulation of more kinds of data. Thus, languages such as ALGOL 60 and, later, Pascal evolved with support for data abstraction. Now a programmer could describe the meaning of related kinds of data (their type) and let the programming language enforce these design decisions. This generation of high-order programming languages again moved our software a step closer to the problem domain, and further away from the underlying machine.

The 1970s provided us with a frenzy of activity in programming language research, resulting in the creation of literally a couple of thousand different programming languages and their dialects. To a large extent, the drive to write larger and larger programs highlighted the inadequacies of earlier languages; thus, many new language mechanisms were developed to address these limitations. Few of these languages survived (have you seen a recent textbook on the languages Fred, Chaos, or Tranquil?); however, many of the concepts that they introduced found their way into successors of earlier languages. Thus, today we have Smalltalk (a revolutionary successor to Simula), Ada (a successor to ALGOL 68 and Pascal, with contributions from Simula, Alphard, and CLU),

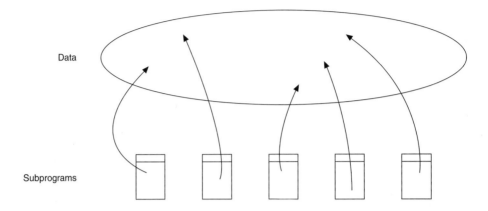

Data

Subprograms

Figure 2-1
The Topology of First- and Early Second-Generation Programming Languages

CLOS (which evolved from Lisp, LOOPS, and Flavors), C++ (derived from a marriage of C and Simula), and Eiffel (derived from Simula and Ada). What is of the greatest interest to us is the class of languages we call *object-based* and *object-oriented*. Object-based and object-oriented programming languages best support the object-oriented decomposition of software.

The Topology of First- and Early Second-Generation Programming Languages
To show precisely what we mean, let's study the structure of each generation of programming languages. In Figure 2-1, we see the topology of most first- and early second-generation programming languages. By topology, we mean the basic physical building blocks of the language and how those parts can be connected. In this figure, we see that for languages such as FORTRAN and COBOL, the basic physical building block of all applications is the subprogram (or the paragraph, for those who speak COBOL). Applications written in these languages exhibit a relatively flat physical structure, consisting only of global data and subprograms. The arrows in this figure indicate dependencies of the subprograms on various data. During design, one can logically separate different kinds of data from one another, but there is little in these languages that can enforce these design decisions. An error in one part of a program can have a devastating ripple effect across the rest of the system, because the global data structures are exposed for all subprograms to see. When modifications are made to a large system, it is difficult to maintain the integrity of the original design. Often, entropy sets in: after even a short period of maintenance, a program written in one of these languages usually contains a tremendous amount of cross-coupling among subprograms, implied meanings of data, and twisted flows of control, thus threatening the reliability of the entire system and certainly reducing the overall clarity of the solution.

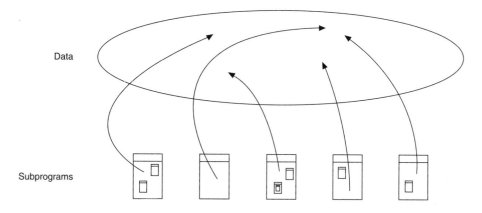

Figure 2-2
The Topology of Late Second- and Early Third-Generation Programming Languages

The Topology of Late Second- and Early Third-Generation Programming Languages By the mid-1960s, programs were finally being recognized as important intermediate points between the problem and the computer [3]. As Shaw points out, "The first software abstraction, now called the 'procedural' abstraction, grew directly out of this pragmatic view of software. . . . Subprograms were invented prior to 1950, but were not fully appreciated as abstractions at the time. . . . Instead, they were originally seen as labor-saving devices. . . . Very quickly though, subprograms were appreciated as a way to abstract program functions" [4]. The realization that subprograms could serve as an abstraction mechanism had three important consequences. First, languages were invented that supported a variety of parameter-passing mechanisms. Second, the foundations of structured programming were laid, manifesting themselves in language support for the nesting of subprograms and the development of theories regarding control structures and the scope and visibility of declarations. Third, structured design methods emerged, offering guidance to designers trying to build large systems using subprograms as basic physical building blocks. Thus, it is not surprising, as Figure 2-2 shows, that the topology of late second- and early third-generation languages is largely a variation on the theme of earlier generations. This topology addresses some of the inadequacies of earlier languages, namely, the need to have greater control over algorithmic abstractions, but it still fails to address the problems of programming-in-the-large and data design.

The Topology of Late Third-Generation Programming Languages Starting with FORTRAN II, and appearing in most late third-generation program languages, another important structuring mechanism evolved to address the growing issues of programming-in-the-large. Larger programming projects meant larger

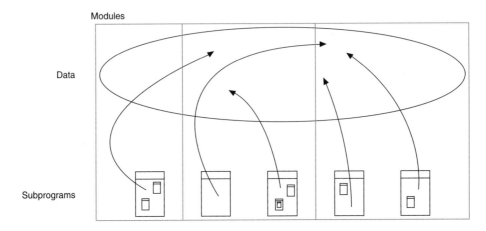

Figure 2-3
The Topology of Late Third-Generation Programming Languages

development teams, and thus the need to develop different parts of the same program independently. The answer to this need was the separately compiled module, which in its early conception was little more than an arbitrary container for data and subprograms, as Figure 2-3 shows. Modules were rarely recognized as an important abstraction mechanism; in practice they were used simply to group subprograms that were most likely to change together. Most languages of this generation, while supporting some sort of modular structure, had few rules that required semantic consistency among module interfaces. A developer writing a subprogram for one module might assume that it would be called with three different parameters: a floating-point number, an array of ten elements, and an integer representing a Boolean flag. In another module, a call to this subprogram might incorrectly use actual parameters that violated these assumptions: an integer, an array of five elements, and a negative number. Similarly, one module might use a block of common data which it assumed as its own, and another module might violate these assumptions by directly manipulating this data. Unfortunately, because most of these languages had dismal support for data abstraction and strong typing, such errors could be detected only during execution of the program.

The Topology of Object-Based and Object-Oriented Programming Languages
The importance of data abstraction to mastering complexity is clearly stated by Shankar: "The nature of abstractions that may be achieved through the use of procedures is well suited to the description of abstract operations, but is not particularly well suited to the description of abstract objects. This is a serious drawback, for in many applications, the complexity of the data objects to be manipulated contributes substantially to the overall complexity of the problem" [5]. This realization had two important consequences. First, data-driven design

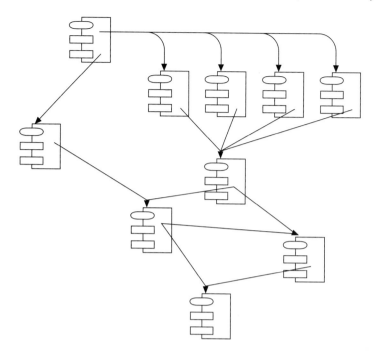

Figure 2-4
The Topology of Small- to Moderate-Sized Applications Using Object-Based
and Object-Oriented Programming Languages

methods emerged, which provided a disciplined approach to the problems of doing data abstraction in algorithmically oriented languages. Second, theories regarding the concept of a type appeared, which eventually found their realization in languages such as Pascal.

The natural conclusion of these ideas first appeared in the language Simula and was improved upon during the period of the language generation gap, resulting in the relatively recent development of several languages such as Smalltalk, Object Pascal, C++, CLOS, Ada, and Eiffel. For reasons that we will explain shortly, these languages are called *object-based* or *object-oriented.* Figure 2-4 illustrates the topology of these languages for small- to moderate-sized applications. The physical building block in these languages is the *module,* which represents a logical collection of classes and objects instead of subprograms, as in earlier languages. To state it another way, "If procedures and functions are verbs and pieces of data are nouns, a procedure-oriented program is organized around verbs while an object-oriented program is organized around nouns" [6]. For this reason, the physical structure of a small- to moderate-sized object-oriented application appears as a graph, not as a tree, which is typical of algorithmically oriented languages. Additionally, there is little or no global data. Instead, data and operations are united in such a way

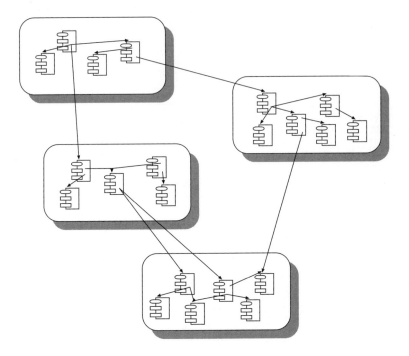

Figure 2-5
The Topology of Large Applications Using Object-Based and Object-Oriented
Programming Languages

that the fundamental logical building blocks of our systems are no longer
algorithms, but instead are classes and objects.

By now we have progressed beyond programming-in-the-large and must
cope with programming-in-the-colossal. For very complex systems, we find that
classes, objects, and modules provide an essential yet insufficient means of
abstraction. Fortunately, the object model scales up. In large systems, we find
clusters of abstractions built in layers on top of one another. At any given level
of abstraction, we find meaningful collections of objects that collaborate to
achieve some higher-level behavior. If we look inside any given cluster to view
its implementation, we unveil yet another set of cooperative abstractions. This
is exactly the organization of complexity described in Chapter 1; this topology
is shown in Figure 2-5.

Foundations of the Object Model

Structured design methods evolved to guide developers who were trying to
build complex systems using algorithms as their fundamental building blocks.
Similarly, object-oriented design methods have evolved to help developers
exploit the expressive power of object-based and object-oriented programming
languages, using the class and object as basic building blocks.

Actually, the object model has been influenced by a number of factors, not just object-oriented programming. Indeed, as the sidebar further discusses, the object model has proven to be a unifying concept in computer science, applicable not just to programming languages, but also to the design of user interfaces, databases, and even computer architectures. The reason for this widespread appeal is simply that an object orientation helps us to cope with the complexity inherent in many different kinds of systems.

Object-oriented analysis and design thus represents an evolutionary development, not a revolutionary one; it does not break with advances from the past, but builds upon proven ones. Unfortunately, most programmers today are formally and informally trained only in the principles of structured design. Certainly, many good engineers have developed and deployed countless useful software systems using these techniques. However, there are limits to the amount of complexity we can handle using only algorithmic decomposition; thus we must turn to object-oriented decomposition. Furthermore, if we try to use languages such as C++ and Ada as if they were only traditional, algorithmically oriented languages, we not only miss the power available to us, but we usually end up worse off than if we had used an older language such as C or Pascal. Give a power drill to a carpenter who knows nothing about electricity, and he would use it as a hammer. He will end up bending quite a few nails and smashing several fingers, for a power drill makes a lousy hammer.

OOP, OOD, and OOA

Because the object model derives from so many disparate sources, it has unfortunately been accompanied by a muddle of terminology. A Smalltalk programmer uses *methods*, a C++ programmer uses *virtual member functions*, and a CLOS programmer uses *generic functions*. An Object Pascal programmer talks of a *type coercion*; an Ada programmer calls the same thing a *type conversion*. To minimize the confusion, let's define what is object-oriented and what is not. The glossary provides a summary of all the terms described here, plus many others.

Bhaskar has observed that the phrase *object-oriented* "has been bandied about with carefree abandon with much the same reverence accorded 'motherhood,' 'apple pie,' and 'structured programming'" [7]. What we can agree upon is that the concept of an object is central to anything object-oriented. In the previous chapter, we informally defined an object as a tangible entity that exhibits some well-defined behavior. Stefik and Bobrow define objects as "entities that combine the properties of procedures and data since they perform computations and save local state" [8]. Defining *objects* as *entities* begs the question somewhat, but the basic concept here is that objects serve to unify the ideas of algorithmic and data abstraction. Jones further clarifies this term by noting that "in the object model, emphasis is placed on crisply characterizing the components of the physical or abstract system to be

Foundations of the Object Model

As Yonezawa and Tokoro point out, "The term 'object' emerged almost independently in various fields in computer science, almost simultaneously in the early 1970s, to refer to notions that were different in their appearance, yet mutually related. All of these notions were invented to manage the complexity of software systems in such a way that objects represented components of a modularly decomposed system or modular units of knowledge representation" [9]. Levy adds that the following events have contributed to the evolution of object-oriented concepts:

- "Advances in computer architecture, including capability systems and hardware support for operating systems concepts
- Advances in programming languages, as demonstrated in Simula, Smalltalk, CLU, and Ada
- Advances in programming methodology, including modularization and information hiding" [10]

We would add to this list three more contributions to the foundation of the object model:

- Advances in database models
- Research in artificial intelligence
- Advances in philosophy and cognitive science

The concept of an object had its beginnings in hardware over twenty years ago, starting with the invention of descriptor-based architectures and, later, capability-based architectures [11]. These architectures represented a break from the classical von Neumann architectures, and came about through attempts to close the gap between the high-level abstractions of programming languages and the low-level abstractions of the machine itself [12]. According to its proponents, the advantages of such architectures are many: better error detection, improved execution efficiency, fewer instruction types, simpler compilation, and reduced storage requirements. Computers that have an object-oriented architecture include the Burroughs 5000, the Plessey 250, and the Cambridge CAP [13], SWARD [14], the Intel 432 [15], Caltech's COM [16], the IBM System/38 [17], the Rational R1000, and the BiiN 40 and 60.

Closely related to developments in object-oriented architectures are object-oriented operating systems. Dijkstra's work with the THE multiprogramming system first introduced the concept of building systems as layered state machines [18]. Other pioneering object-oriented operating systems include the Plessey/System 250 (for the Plessey 250 multiprocessor), Hydra (for CMU's C.mmp), CALTSS (for the CDC 6400), CAP (for the Cambridge CAP computer), UCLA Secure UNIX (for the PDP 11/45 and 11/70), StarOS (for CMU's Cm*), Medusa (also for CMU's Cm*), and iMAX (for the Intel 432) [19]. The next generation of operating systems appears to follow this trend: Microsoft's Cairo project and Taligent's Pink project are both object-oriented operating systems.

Perhaps the most important contribution to the object model derives from the class of programming languages we call object-based and object-oriented. The fundamental ideas of classes and objects first appeared in the language Simula 67. The Flex system, followed by various dialects of Smalltalk, such as Smalltalk-72, -74, and -76, and finally the current version, Smalltalk-80, took Simula's object-oriented paradigm to its natural conclusion by making everything in the language an instance of a class. In the 1970s languages such as Alphard, CLU, Euclid, Gypsy, Mesa, and Modula were developed, which supported the then-emerging ideas of data abstraction. More recently, language research has led to the grafting of Simula and Smalltalk concepts onto traditional high-order programming languages. The unification of object-oriented concepts with C has lead to the languages C++ and Objective C. Adding object-oriented programming mechanisms to Pascal has led to the languages Object Pascal, Eiffel, and Ada. Additionally, there are many dialects of Lisp that incorporate the object-oriented features of Simula and Smalltalk, including Flavors, LOOPS, and more recently, the Common Lisp Object System (CLOS). The appendix discusses these and other programming language developments in greater detail.

The first person to formally identify the importance of composing systems in layers of abstraction was Dijkstra. Parnas later introduced the idea of information hiding [20], and in the 1970s a number of researchers, most notably Liskov and Zilles [21], Guttag [22], and Shaw [23], pioneered the development of abstract data type mechanisms. Hoare contributed to these developments with his proposal for a theory of types and subclasses [24].

Although database technology has evolved somewhat independently of software engineering, it has also contributed to the object model [25], primarily through the ideas of the entity-relationship (ER) approach to data modeling [26]. In the ER model, first proposed by Chen [27], the world is modeled in terms of its entities, the attributes of these entities, and the relationships among these entities.

In the field of artificial intelligence, developments in knowledge representation have contributed to an understanding of object-oriented abstractions. In 1975, Minsky first proposed a theory of frames to represent real-world objects as perceived by image and natural language recognition systems [28]. Since then, frames have been used as the architectural foundation for a variety of intelligent systems.

Lastly, philosophy and cognitive science have contributed to the advancement of the object model. The idea that the world could be viewed either in terms of objects or processes was a Greek innovation, and in the seventeenth century, we find Descartes observing that humans naturally apply an object-oriented view of the world [29]. In the twentieth century, Rand expanded upon these themes in her philosophy of objectivist epistemology [30]. More recently, Minsky has proposed a model of human intelligence in which he considers the mind to be organized as a society of otherwise mindless agents [31]. Minsky argues that only through the cooperative behavior of these agents do we find what we call *intelligence*.

modeled by a programmed system. . . . Objects have a certain 'integrity' which should not – in fact, cannot – be violated. An object can only change state, behave, be manipulated, or stand in relation to other objects in ways appropriate to that object. Stated differently, there exist invariant properties that characterize an object and its behavior. An elevator, for example, is characterized by invariant properties including [that] it only travels up and down inside its shaft. . . . Any elevator simulation must incorporate these invariants, for they are integral to the notion of an elevator" [32].

Object-Oriented Programming What then, is object-oriented programming (or *OOP*, as it is sometimes written)? We define it as follows:

> *Object-oriented programming is a method of implementation in which programs are organized as cooperative collections of objects, each of which represents an instance of some class, and whose classes are all members of a hierarchy of classes united via inheritance relationships.*

There are three important parts to this definition: object-oriented programming (1) uses *objects*, not algorithms, as its fundamental logical building blocks (the "part of" hierarchy we introduced in Chapter 1); (2) each object is an *instance* of some *class*; and (3) classes are related to one another via *inheritance* relationships (the "is a" hierarchy we spoke of in Chapter 1). A program may appear to be object-oriented, but if any of these elements is missing, it is not an object-oriented program. Specifically, programming without inheritance is distinctly not object-oriented; we call it *programming with abstract data types*.

By this definition, some languages are object-oriented, and some are not. Stroustrup suggests that "if the term 'object-oriented language' means anything, it must mean a language that has mechanisms that support the object-oriented style of programming well. . . . A language supports a programming style well if it provides facilities that make it convenient to use that style. A language does not support a technique if it takes exceptional effort or skill to write such programs; in that case, the language merely enables programmers to use the techniques" [33]. From a theoretical perspective, one can fake object-oriented programming in non-object-oriented programming languages like Pascal and even COBOL or assembly language, but it is horribly ungainly to do so. Cardelli and Wegner thus say "that a language is object-oriented if and only if it satisfies the following requirements:

- It supports objects that are data abstractions with an interface of named operations and a hidden local state.
- Objects have an associated type [class].
- Types [classes] may inherit attributes from supertypes [superclasses]" [34].

For a language to support inheritance means that it is possible to express "is a" relationships among types, for example, a red rose is a kind of flower, and a flower is a kind of plant. If a language does not provide direct support for inheritance, then it is not object-oriented. Cardelli and Wegner distinguish such languages by calling them *object-based* rather than *object-oriented.* Under this definition, Smalltalk, Object Pascal, C++, Eiffel, and CLOS are all object-oriented, and Ada is object-based. However, since objects and classes are elements of both kinds of languages, it is both possible and highly desirable for us to use object-oriented design methods for both object-based and object-oriented programming languages.

Object-Oriented Design The emphasis in programming methods is primarily on the proper and effective use of particular language mechanisms. By contrast, design methods emphasize the proper and effective structuring of a complex system. What then is object-oriented design? We suggest that

> *Object-oriented design is a method of design encompassing the process of object-oriented decomposition and a notation for depicting both logical and physical as well as static and dynamic models of the system under design.*

There are two important parts to this definition: object-oriented design (1) leads to an object-oriented decomposition and (2) uses different notations to express different models of the logical (class and object structure) and physical (module and process architecture) design of a system, in addition to the static and dynamic aspects of the system.

The support for object-oriented decomposition is what makes object-oriented design quite different from structured design: the former uses class and object abstractions to logically structure systems, and the latter uses algorithmic abstractions. We will use the term *object-oriented design* to refer to any method that leads to an object-oriented decomposition. We will occasionally use the acronym *OOD* to designate the particular method of object-oriented design described in this book.

Object-Oriented Analysis The object model has influenced even earlier phases of the software development life cycle. Traditional structured analysis techniques, best typified by the work of DeMarco [35], Yourdon [36], and Gane and Sarson [37], with real-time extensions by Ward and Mellor [38] and by Hatley and Pirbhai [39], focus upon the flow of data within a system. Object-oriented analysis (or *OOA,* as it is sometimes called) emphasizes the building of real-world models, using an object-oriented view of the world:

> *Object-oriented analysis is a method of analysis that examines requirements from the perspective of the classes and objects found in the vocabulary of the problem domain.*

How are OOA, OOD, and OOP related? Basically, the products of object-oriented analysis serve as the models from which we may start an object-oriented design; the products of object-oriented design can then be used as blueprints for completely implementing a system using object-oriented programming methods.

2.2 Elements of the Object Model

Kinds of Programming Paradigms

Jenkins and Glasgow observe that "most programmers work in one language and use only one programming style. They program in a paradigm enforced by the language they use. Frequently, they have not been exposed to alternate ways of thinking about a problem, and hence have difficulty in seeing the advantage of choosing a style more appropriate to the problem at hand" [40]. Bobrow and Stefik define a programming style as "a way of organizing programs on the basis of some conceptual model of programming and an appropriate language to make programs written in the style clear" [41]. They further suggest that there are five main kinds of programming styles, here listed with the kinds of abstractions they employ:

- Procedure-oriented   Algorithms
- Object-oriented   Classes and objects
- Logic-oriented   Goals, often expressed in a predicate calculus
- Rule-oriented   If-then rules
- Constraint-oriented   Invariant relationships

There is no single programming style that is best for all kinds of applications. For example, rule-oriented programming would be best for the design of a knowledge base, and procedure-oriented programming would be best suited for the design of computation-intense operations. From our experience, the object-oriented style is best suited to the broadest set of applications; indeed, this programming paradigm often serves as the architectural framework in which we employ other paradigms.

Each of these styles of programming is based upon its own conceptual framework. Each requires a different mindset, a different way of thinking about the problem. For all things object-oriented, the conceptual framework is the *object model*. There are four major elements of this model:

- Abstraction
- Encapsulation
- Modularity
- Hierarchy

By *major*, we mean that a model without any one of these elements is not object-oriented.

There are three minor elements of the object model:

- Typing
- Concurrency
- Persistence

By *minor*, we mean that each of these elements is a useful, but not essential, part of the object model.

Without this conceptual framework, you may be programming in a language such as Smalltalk, Object Pascal, C++, CLOS, Eiffel, or Ada, but your design is going to smell like a FORTRAN, Pascal, or C application. You will have missed out on or otherwise abused the expressive power of the object-oriented language you are using for implementation. More importantly, you are not likely to have mastered the complexity of the problem at hand.

Abstraction

The Meaning of Abstraction Abstraction is one of the fundamental ways that we as humans cope with complexity. Hoare suggests that "abstraction arises from a recognition of similarities between certain objects, situations, or processes in the real world, and the decision to concentrate upon these similarities and to ignore for the time being the differences" [42]. Shaw defines an abstraction as "a simplified description, or specification, of a system that emphasizes some of the system's details or properties while suppressing others. A good abstraction is one that emphasizes details that are significant to the reader or user and suppresses details that are, at least for the moment, immaterial or diversionary" [43]. Berzins, Gray, and Naumann recommend that "a concept qualifies as an abstraction only if it can be described, understood, and analyzed independently of the mechanism that will eventually be used to realize it" [44]. Combining these different viewpoints, we define an abstraction as follows:

> *An abstraction denotes the essential characteristics of an object that distinguish it from all other kinds of objects and thus provide crisply defined conceptual boundaries, relative to the perspective of the viewer.*

An abstraction focuses on the outside view of an object, and so serves to separate an object's essential behavior from its implementation. Abelson and Sussman call this behavior/implementation division an *abstraction barrier* [45] achieved by applying the principle of least commitment, through which the interface of an object provides its essential behavior, and nothing more [46]. We like to use an additional principle that we call the *principle of least astonishment*, through which an abstraction captures the entire behavior of some object, no more and no less, and offers no surprises or side effects that go beyond the scope of the abstraction.

Abstraction focuses upon the essential characteristics of some object, relative to the perspective of the viewer.

Deciding upon the right set of abstractions for a given domain is the central problem in object-oriented design. Because this topic is so important, the whole of Chapter 4 is devoted to it.

Seidewitz and Stark suggest that "there is a spectrum of abstraction, from objects which closely model problem domain entities to objects which really have no reason for existence" [47]. From the most to the least useful, these kinds of abstractions include the following:

• Entity abstraction	An object that represents a useful model of a problem-domain or solution-domain entity
• Action abstraction	An object that provides a generalized set of operations, all of which perform the same kind of function
• Virtual machine abstraction	An object that groups together operations that are all used by some superior level of control, or operations that all use some junior-level set of operations

• Coincidental abstraction   An object that packages a set of operations that have no relation to each other

We strive to build entity abstractions, because they directly parallel the vocabulary of a given problem domain.

A *client* is any object that uses the resources of another object (known as the *server*). We can characterize the behavior of an object by considering the services that it provides to other objects, as well as the operations that it may perform upon other objects. This view forces us to concentrate upon the outside view of an object, and leads us to what Meyer calls the *contract model* of programming [48]: the outside view of each object defines a contract upon which other objects may depend, and which in turn must be carried out by the inside view of the object itself (often in collaboration with other objects). This contract thus establishes all the assumptions a client object may make about the behavior of a server object. In other words, this contract encompasses the *responsibilities* of an object, namely, the behavior for which it is held accountable [49].

Individually, each operation that contributes to this contract has a unique signature comprising all of its formal arguments and return type. We call the entire set of operations that a client may perform upon an object, together with the legal orderings in which they may be invoked, its *protocol*. A protocol denotes the ways in which an object may act and react, and thus constitutes the entire static and dynamic outside view of the abstraction.

Central to the idea of an abstraction is the concept of invariance. An *invariant* is some Boolean (true or false) condition whose truth must be preserved. For each operation associated with an object, we may define *preconditions* (invariants assumed by the operation) as well as *postconditions* (invariants satisfied by the operation). Violating an invariant breaks the contract associated with an abstraction. If a precondition is violated, this means that a client has not satisfied its part of the bargain, and hence the server cannot proceed reliably. Similarly, if a postcondition is violated, this means that a server has not carried out its part of the contract, and so its clients can no longer trust the behavior of the server. An exception is an indication that some invariant has not been or cannot be satisfied. As we will describe later, certain languages permit objects to throw exceptions so as to abandon processing and alert some other object to the problem, who in turn may catch the exception and handle the problem.

As an aside, the terms *operation, method,* and *member function* evolved from three different programming cultures (Ada, Smalltalk, and C++, respectively). They all mean virtually the same thing, and so we will use them interchangeably.

All abstractions have static as well as dynamic properties. For example, a file object takes up a certain amount of space on a particular memory device; it has a name, and it has contents. These are all static properties. The value of each of these properties is dynamic, relative to the lifetime of the object: a file object may grow or shrink in size, its name may change, its contents may change. In a procedure-oriented style of programming, the activity that changes the dynamic value of objects is the central part of all programs: things happen when subprograms are called and statements are executed. In a rule-oriented style of programming, things happen when new events cause rules to fire, which in turn may trigger other rules, and so on. In an object-oriented style of programming, things happen whenever we operate upon an object (in Smalltalk terminology, when we *send a message* to an object). Thus, invoking an operation upon an object elicits some reaction from the object. What operations we can meaningfully perform upon an object and how that object reacts constitute the entire behavior of the object.

Examples of Abstraction Let's illustrate these concepts with some examples. Our purpose here is to show how we can concretely express abstractions, not so much how we find the right abstractions for the given problem. We defer a complete treatment of this latter topic to Chapter 4.

On a hydroponics farm, plants are grown in a nutrient solution, without sand, gravel, or other soils. Maintaining the proper greenhouse environment is a delicate job, and depends upon the kind of plant being grown and its age. One must control diverse factors such as temperature, humidity, light, pH, and nutrient concentrations. On a large farm, it is not unusual to have an automated system that constantly monitors and adjusts these elements. Simply stated, the purpose of an automated gardener is to efficiently carry out, with minimal human intervention, growing plans for the healthy production of multiple crops.

One of the key abstractions in this problem is that of a sensor. Actually, there are several different kinds of sensors. Anything that affects production must be measured, and so we must have sensors for air and water temperature, humidity, light, pH, and nutrient concentrations, among other things. Viewed from the outside, a temperature sensor is simply an object that knows how to measure the temperature at some specific location. What is a temperature? It is some numeric value, within a limited range of values and with a certain precision, that represents degrees in the scale of Fahrenheit, Centigrade, or Kelvin, whichever is most appropriate for our problem. What then is a location? It is some identifiable place on the farm at which we desire to measure the temperature; presumably, there are only a few such locations. What is important for a temperature sensor is not so much where it is located, but the fact that it has a unique location and identity from all other temperature sensors. Now we are ready to ask: What are the responsibilities of a temperature sensor? Our design decision is that a sensor is responsible for knowing the temperature at a given location, and reporting that temperature when asked. More concretely, what operations can a client perform upon a temperature sensor? Our design decision is that a client can calibrate it, as well as ask what the current temperature is.

Let's use C++ to capture these design decisions. For those readers who are not familiar with C++, or for that matter any of the other object-oriented programming languages we mention in this book, the appendix provides a brief overview of several languages, with examples. In C++, we might write the following declarations that capture our abstraction of a temperature sensor:

```
// Temperature in degrees Fahrenheit
typedef float Temperature;

// Number uniquely denoting the location of a sensor
typedef unsigned int Location;

class TemperatureSensor {
public:

  TemperatureSensor(Location);
  ~TemperatureSensor();

  void calibrate(Temperature actualTemperature);

  Temperature currentTemperature() const;

private:
  ...
};
```

The two typedefs, `Temperature` and `Location`, provide convenient aliases for more primitive types, thus letting us express our abstractions in the vocabulary of the problem domain.[*] `Temperature` is a floating-point type representing temperature in degrees Fahrenheit. The type `Location` denotes the places where temperature sensors may be deployed throughout the farm.

The class `TemperatureSensor` captures our abstraction of a sensor itself; its representation is hidden in the private part of the class.

`TemperatureSensor` is defined as a class, not a concrete object, and therefore we must first create an *instance* so that we have something upon which to operate. For example, we might write:

```
Temperature temperature;

TemperatureSensor greenhouse1Sensor(1);
TemperatureSensor greenhouse2Sensor(2);

temperature = greenhouse1Sensor.currentTemperature();
...
```

Consider the invariants associated with the operation `currentTemperature`: its preconditions include the assumption that the sensor has been elaborated with

---

[*] Unfortunately, however, typedefs do not introduce new types, and so offer little type safety. For example, in C++, the following declaration simply creates a synonym for the primitive type int:

```
typedef int Count;
```

As we will discuss in a later section, other languages, such as Ada and Eiffel, have more rigorous semantics regarding the strong typing of primitive types.

a valid location, and its postconditions include the assumption that the value returned is in degrees Fahrenheit.

The abstraction we have described thus far is passive; some client object must operate upon an air temperature sensor object to determine its current temperature. However, there is another legitimate abstraction that may be more or less appropriate depending upon the broader system design decisions we might make. Specifically, rather than the temperature sensor being passive, we might make it active, so that it is not acted upon but rather acts upon other objects whenever the temperature at its location changes a certain number of degrees from a given set point. This abstraction is almost the same as our first one, except that its responsibilities have changed slightly: a sensor is now responsible for reporting the current temperature when it changes, not just when asked. What new operations must this abstraction provide? A common programming idiom used in such circumstances is the callback, in which a client provides a function to the server (the callback function), and the server calls the client's function whenever the appropriate conditions are met. Thus, we might write the following:

```
class ActiveTemperatureSensor {
public:

   ActiveTemperatureSensor(Location,
                          void (*f)(Location, Temperature));
   ~ActiveTemperatureSensor();

   void calibrate(Temperature actualTemperature);
   void establishSetpoint(Temperature setpoint,
                          Temperature delta);

   Temperature currentTemperature() const;

private:
   ...
};
```

This class is a bit more complicated than the first, but it captures our new abstraction quite well. Whenever we create a sensor object, we must as before provide its location, but we must now also provide a callback function whose signature includes a Location parameter and a Temperature parameter. Additionally, a client of this abstraction may invoke the operation establishSetpoint to establish a critical range of temperatures. It is then the responsibility of the ActiveTemperatureSensor object to invoke the given callback function whenever the temperature at its location drops below or rises above the given setpoint. When the callback is invoked, the sensor provides its location and the current temperature, so that the client has sufficient information to respond to the condition.

Notice that a client can still inquire as to the current temperature of a sensor at any time. What if a client never establishes a setpoint? Our abstraction must make some reasonable assumption: one design decision might be to initially assume an infinite range of critical temperatures, and so the callback would never be invoked until some client finally established a setpoint.

How the `ActiveTemperatureSensor` class carries out its responsibilities is a function of its inside view, and is of no concern to outside clients. These then are the secrets of the class, which are implemented by the class' private parts together with the definition of its member functions.

Let's consider a different abstraction. For each crop, there must be a growing plan that describes how temperature, light, nutrients, and other factors should change over time to maximize the harvest. A growing plan is a legitimate entity abstraction, because it forms part of the vocabulary of the problem domain. Each crop has its own growing plan, but the growing plans for all crops take the same form. Basically, a growing plan is a mapping of time to action. For example, on day 15 in the lifetime of a certain crop, our growing plan might be to maintain a temperature of 78°F for 16 hours, turn on the lights for 14 of these hours, and then drop the temperature to 65°F for the rest of the day. We might also want to add certain extra nutrients in the middle of the day, while still maintaining a slightly acidic pH.

A growing plan is thus responsible for keeping track of all interesting actions associated with growing a crop, correlated with the times at which those actions should take place. Our decision is also that we will not require a growing plan to carry out its plan: we will leave this as the responsibility of a different abstraction. In this manner, we create a clear separation of concerns among the logically different parts of the system, so as to reduce the conceptual size of each individual abstraction.

From the perspective of the outside of each growing-plan object, a client must be able to establish the details of a plan, modify a plan, and inquire about a plan. For example, there might be an object that sits at the boundary of the human/machine interface and translates human input into plans. This is the object that establishes the details of a growing-plan, and so it must be able to change the state of a growing-plan object. There must also be an object that carries out the growing plan, and it must be able to read the details of a plan for a particular time.

As this example points out, no object stands alone; every object collaborates with other objects to achieve some behavior.[*] Our design decisions about how these objects cooperate with one another define the boundaries of each abstraction and thus the responsibilities and protocol of each object.

We might capture our design decisions for a growing plan as follows. First, we provide the following typedefs, so as to bring our abstractions closer to the vocabulary of the problem domain:

```
// Number denoting the day of the year
typedef unsigned int Day;

// Number denoting the hour of the day
typedef unsigned int Hour;
```

---

[*] Stated another way, with apologies to the poet John Donne, no object is an island (although an island may be abstracted as an object).

```
// Boolean type
enum Lights {OFF, ON};

// Number denoting acidity/alkalinity on a scale of 1 to 14
typedef float pH;

// Number denoting percent concentration from 0 to 100
typedef float Concentration;
```

Next, as a tactical design decision, we provide the following structure:

```
// Structure denoting relevant plan conditions
struct Condition {
  Temperature temperature;
  Lights lighting;
  pH acidity;
  Concentration concentration;
};
```

Here we have something less than an entity abstraction: a Condition is simply a physical aggregation of other things, with no intrinsic behavior. For this reason, we use a C++ record structure, rather than a C++ class, which has richer semantics.

Finally, we turn to the growing-plan class itself:

```
class GrowingPlan {
public:

  GrowingPlan(char* name);
  virtual ~GrowingPlan();

  void clear();
  virtual void establish(Day, Hour, const Condition&);

  const char* name() const;
  const Condition& desiredConditions(Day, Hour) const;

protected:
  ...
};
```

Notice that we have introduced one new responsibility to this abstraction: a growing plan has a name, which a client can set and inquire about. Also, note that we declare the operation establish as virtual, because we expect subclasses to override the default behavior provided by the class GrowingPlan.

In the declaration of this class, the public part exports *constructor* and *destructor member functions* (which provide for the birth and death of an object, respectively), two *modifiers* (the member functions clear and establish), and two *selectors* (the member functions name and desiredConditions). We have intentionally left out the private members (designated by the ellipses), because at this point in our design we wish to focus only upon the responsibilities of the class, not its representation.

Encapsulation hides the details of the implementation of an object.

Encapsulation

The Meaning of Encapsulation Although we earlier described our abstraction of the class GrowingPlan as a time/action mapping, its implementation is not necessarily a literal table or map data structure. Indeed, whichever representation is chosen is immaterial to the client's contract with this class, as long as that representation upholds the contract. Simply stated, the abstraction of an object should precede the decisions about its implementation. Once an implementation is selected, it should be treated as a secret of the abstraction and hidden from most clients. As Ingalls wisely suggests, "No part of a complex system should depend on the internal details of any other part" [50]. Whereas abstraction "helps people to think about what they are doing," encapsulation "allows program changes to be reliably made with limited effort" [51].

Abstraction and encapsulation are complementary concepts: abstraction focuses upon the observable behavior of an object, whereas *encapsulation* focuses upon the implementation that gives rise to this behavior. Encapsulation is most often achieved through *information hiding*, which is the process of hiding all the secrets of an object that do not contribute to its essential characteristics; typically, the structure of an object is hidden, as well as the implementation of its methods.

Encapsulation provides explicit barriers among different abstractions and thus leads to a clear separation of concerns. For example, consider again the structure of a plant. To understand how photosynthesis works at a high level of abstraction, we can ignore details such as the responsibilities of plant roots or the chemistry of cell walls. Similarly, in designing a database application, it is standard practice to write programs so that they don't care about the physical representation of data, but depend only upon a schema that denotes the data's logical view [52]. In both of these cases, objects at one level of abstraction are shielded from implementation details at lower levels of abstraction.

Liskov goes as far as to suggest that "for abstraction to work, implementations must be encapsulated" [53]. In practice, this means that each class must have two parts: an interface and an implementation. The *interface* of a class captures only its outside view, encompassing our abstraction of the behavior common to all instances of the class. The *implementation* of a class comprises the representation of the abstraction as well as the mechanisms that achieve the desired behavior. The interface of a class is the one place where we assert all of the assumptions that a client may make about any instances of the class; the implementation encapsulates details about which no client may make assumptions.

To summarize, we define *encapsulation* as follows:

> *Encapsulation is the process of compartmentalizing the elements of an abstraction that constitute its structure and behavior; encapsulation serves to separate the contractual interface of an abstraction and its implementation.*

Britton and Parnas call these encapsulated elements the "secrets" of an abstraction [54].

Examples of Encapsulation To illustrate the principle of encapsulation, let's return to the problem of the hydroponics gardening system. Another key abstraction in this problem domain is that of a heater. A heater is at a fairly low level of abstraction, and thus we might decide that there are only three meaningful operations that we can perform upon this object: turn it on, turn it off, and find out if it is running. We do not make it a responsibility of this abstraction to maintain a fixed temperature. Instead, we choose to give this responsibility to another object, which must collaborate with a temperature sensor and a heater to achieve this higher-level behavior. We call this behavior *higher-level* because it builds upon the primitive semantics of temperature sensors and heaters and adds some new semantics, namely, *hysteresis*, which prevents the heater from being turned on and off too rapidly when the temperature is near boundary conditions. By deciding upon this separation of responsibilities, we make each individual abstraction more cohesive.

We begin with another `typedef`:

```
// Boolean type
enum Boolean {FALSE, TRUE};
```

For the heater class, in addition to the three operations mentioned earlier, we must also provide metaoperations, namely, constructor and destructor operations that initialize and destroy instances of this class, respectively. Because our system might have multiple heaters, we use the constructor to associate each software object with a physical heater, similar to the approach we used with the TemperatureSensor class.. Given these design decisions, we might write the definition of the class Heater in C++ as follows:

```
class Heater {
public:

  Heater(Location);
  ~Heater();

  void turnOn();
  void turnOff();

  Boolean isOn() const;

private:
  ...
};
```

This interface represents all that a client needs to know about the class Heater.

Turning to the inside view of this class, we have an entirely different perspective. Suppose that our system engineers have decided to locate the computers that control each greenhouse away from the building (perhaps to avoid the harsh environment), and to connect each computer to its sensors and actuators via serial lines. One reasonable implementation for the heater class might be to use an electromechanical relay that controls the power going to each physical heater, with the relays in turn commanded by messages sent along these serial lines. For example, to turn on a heater, we might transmit a special command string, followed by a number identifying the specific heater, followed by another number used to signal turning the heater on.

Consider the following class, which captures our abstraction of a serial port:

```
class SerialPort {
public:

  SerialPort();
  ~SerialPort();

  void write(char*);
  void write(int);

  static SerialPort ports[10];

private:
  ...
};
```

Here we provide a class whose instances denote actual serial ports, to which we can write strings and integers. Additionally, we declare an array of serial ports, denoting all the different serial ports in our systems.

We complete the declaration of the class Heater by adding three attributes:

```
class Heater {
public:
  ...
protected:
  const Location repLocation;
  Boolean repIsOn;
  SerialPort* repPort;
};
```

These three attributes (repLocation, repIsOn, and repPort) form the encapsulated representation of this class. The rules of C++ are such that compiling client code that tries to access these member objects directly will result in a semantic error.

We may next provide the implementation of each operation associated with this class:

```
Heater::Heater(Location l)
  : repLocation(l),
    repIsOn(FALSE),
    repPort(&SerialPort::ports[l]) {}

Heater::~Heater() {}

void Heater::turnOn()
{
  if (!repIsOn) {
    repPort->write("*");
    repPort->write(repLocation);
    repPort->write(1);
    repIsOn = TRUE;
  }
}


void Heater::turnOff()
{
  if (repIsOn) {
    repPort->write("*");
    repPort->write(repLocation);
    repPort->write(0);
    repIsOn = FALSE;
  }
}

Boolean Heater::isOn() const
{
  return repIsOn;
}
```

This implementation is typical of well-structured object-oriented systems: the implementation of a particular class is generally small, because it can build upon the resources provided by lower-level classes.

Suppose that for whatever reason our system engineers choose to use memory-mapped I/O instead of serial communication lines. We would not need to change the interface of this class; we would only need to modify its implementation. Because of C++'s obsolescence rules, we would probably have to recompile this class and the closure of its clients, but because the functional behavior of this abstraction would not change, we would not have to modify any code that used this class unless a particular client depended upon the time or space semantics of the original implementation (which would be highly undesirable and so very unlikely, in any case).

Let's next consider the implementation of the class GrowingPlan. As we mentioned earlier, a growing plan is essentially a time/action mapping. Perhaps the most reasonable representation for this abstraction would be a dictionary of time/action pairs, using an open hash table. We need not store an action for every hour, because things don't change that quickly. Rather, we can store actions only for when they change, and have the implementation extrapolate between times.

In this manner, our implementation encapsulates two secrets: the use of an open hash table (which is distinctly a part of the vocabulary of the solution domain, not the problem domain), and the use of extrapolation to reduce our storage requirements (otherwise we would have to store many more time/action pairs over the duration of a growing season). No client of this abstraction need ever know about these implementation decisions, because they do not materially affect the outwardly observable behavior of the class.

Intelligent encapsulation localizes design decisions that are likely to change. As a system evolves, its developers might discover that in actual use, certain operations take longer than acceptable or that some objects consume more space than is available. In such situations, the representation of an object is often changed so that more efficient algorithms can be applied or so that one can optimize for space by calculating rather then storing certain data. This ability to change the representation of an abstraction without disturbing any of its clients is the essential benefit of encapsulation.

Ideally, attempts to access the underlying representation of an object should be detected at the time a client's code is compiled. How a particular language should address this matter is debated with great religious fervor in the object-oriented programming language community. For example, Smalltalk prevents a client from directly accessing the instance variables of another class; violations are detected at the time of compilation. On the other hand, Object Pascal does not encapsulate the representation of a class, so there is nothing in the language that prevents clients from referencing the fields of another object directly. CLOS takes an intermediate position; each *slot* may have one of the slot options :reader, :writer, or :accessor, which grant a client read access, write access, or read/write access, respectively. If none of these options are used, then the slot is fully encapsulated. By convention, revealing that some value is stored in a slot is considered a breakdown of the abstraction, and so good CLOS style requires that when the interface to a class is published, only its generic function names are documented, and the fact that a slot has accessor functions is not revealed [55]. C++ offers even more flexible control over the visibility of member objects and member functions. Specifically, members may be placed in the public, private, or protected parts of a class. Members declared in the public parts are visible to all clients; members declared in the private parts are fully encapsulated; and members declared in the protected parts are visible only to the class itself and its subclasses. C++ also supports the notion of *friends*: cooperative classes that are permitted to see each other's private parts.

Hiding is a relative concept: what is hidden at one level of abstraction may represent the outside view at another level of abstraction. The underlying representation of an object can be revealed, but in most cases only if the creator of the abstraction explicitly exposes the implementation, and then only if the client is willing to accept the resulting additional complexity. Thus, encapsulation cannot stop a developer from doing stupid things: as Stroustrup points out, "Hiding is for the prevention of accidents, not the prevention of fraud" [56]. Of course, no programming language prevents a human from literally seeing the implementation of a class, although an operating system might deny access to a particular file that contains the implementation of a class. In practice, there are times when one must study the implementation of a class to really understand its meaning, especially if the external documentation is lacking.

Modularity

The Meaning of Modularity As Myers observes, "The act of partitioning a program into individual components can reduce its complexity to some degree. . . . Although partitioning a program is helpful for this reason, a more powerful justification for partitioning a program is that it creates a number of well-defined, documented boundaries within the program. These boundaries, or interfaces, are invaluable in the comprehension of the program" [57]. In some languages, such as Smalltalk, there is no concept of a module, and so the class forms the only physical unit of decomposition. In many others, including Object Pascal, C++, CLOS, and Ada, the module is a separate language construct, and therefore warrants a separate set of design decisions. In these languages, classes and objects form the logical structure of a system; we place these abstractions in *modules* to produce the system's physical architecture. Especially for larger applications, in which we may have many hundreds of classes, the use of modules is essential to help manage complexity.

Liskov states that "modularization consists of dividing a program into modules which can be compiled separately, but which have connections with other modules. We will use the definition of Parnas: 'The connections between modules are the assumptions which the modules make about each other' " [58]. Most languages that support the module as a separate concept also distinguish between the interface of a module and its implementation. Thus, it is fair to say that modularity and encapsulation go hand in hand. As with encapsulation, particular languages support modularity in diverse ways. For example, modules in C++ are nothing more than separately compiled files. The traditional practice in the C/C++ community is to place module interfaces in files named with a *.h* suffix; these are called *header files*. Module implementations are placed in files named with a *.c* suffix.[*] Dependencies among files can then be asserted

---

[*] The suffixes .cp, .cp, and .cpp are commonly used for C++ programs.

Modularity packages abstractions into discrete units.

using the #include macro. This approach is entirely one of convention; it is neither required nor enforced by the language itself. Object Pascal is a little more formal about the matter. In this language, the syntax for *units* (its name for modules) distinguishes between module interface and implementation. Dependencies among units may be asserted only in a module's interface. Ada goes one step further. A package (its name for modules) has two parts: the package specification and the package body. Unlike Object Pascal, Ada allows connections among modules to be asserted separately in the specification and body of a package. Thus, it is possible for a package body to depend upon modules that are otherwise not visible to the package's specification.

Deciding upon the right set of modules for a given problem is almost as hard a problem as deciding upon the right set of abstractions. Zelkowitz is absolutely right when he states that "because the solution may not be known when the design stage starts, decomposition into smaller modules may be quite difficult. For older applications (such as compiler writing), this process may become standard, but for new ones (such as defense systems or spacecraft control), it may be quite difficult" [59].

Modules serve as the physical containers in which we declare the classes and objects of our logical design. This is no different than the situation faced by the electrical engineer designing a board-level computer. NAND, NOR, and NOT gates might be used to construct the necessary logic, but these gates must be physically packaged in standard integrated circuits, such as a 7400, 7402, or 7404. Lacking any such standard software parts, the software engineer has considerably more degrees of freedom – as if the electrical engineer had a silicon foundry at his or her disposal.

For tiny problems, the developer might decide to declare every class and object in the same package. For anything but the most trivial software, a better solution is to group logically related classes and objects in the same module, and expose only those elements that other modules absolutely must see. This kind of modularization is a good thing, but it can be taken to extremes. For example, consider an application that runs on a distributed set of processors and uses a message passing mechanism to coordinate the activities of different programs. In a large system, like that described in Chapter 12, it is common to have several hundred or even a few thousand kinds of messages. A naive strategy might be to define each message class in its own module. As it turns out, this is a singularly poor design decision. Not only does it create a documentation nightmare, but it makes it terribly difficult for any users to find the classes they need. Furthermore, when decisions change, hundreds of modules must be modified or recompiled. This example shows how information hiding can backfire [60]. Arbitrary modularization is sometimes worse than no modularization at all.

In traditional structured design, modularization is primarily concerned with the meaningful grouping of subprograms, using the criteria of coupling and cohesion. In object-oriented design, the problem is subtly different: the task is to decide where to physically package the classes and objects from the design's logical structure, which are distinctly different from subprograms.

Our experience indicates that there are several useful technical as well as nontechnical guidelines that can help us achieve an intelligent modularization of classes and objects. As Britton and Parnas have observed, "The overall goal of the decomposition into modules is the reduction of software cost by allowing modules to be designed and revised independently. . . . Each module's structure should be simple enough that it can be understood fully; it should be possible to change the implementation of other modules without knowledge of the implementation of other modules and without affecting the behavior of other modules; [and] the ease of making a change in the design should bear a reasonable relationship to the likelihood of the change being needed" [61]. There is a pragmatic edge to these guidelines. In practice, the cost of recompiling the body of a module is relatively small: only that unit need be recompiled and the application relinked. However, the cost of recompiling the *interface* of a module is relatively high. Especially with strongly typed languages, one must recompile the module interface, its body, all other modules that depend upon this interface, the modules that depend upon these modules, and so on. Thus, for very large programs (assuming that our development environment does not support incremental compilation), a change in a single module interface might result in many minutes if not hours of recompilation. Obviously, a development manager cannot often afford to allow a massive "big bang" recompilation to happen too frequently. For this reason, a module's interface should be as narrow as possible, yet still satisfy the needs of all using modules. Our style is to hide as much as we can in the implementation of a module. Incrementally shifting declarations from a module's implementation to its interface is far less painful and destabilizing than ripping out extraneous interface code.

The developer must therefore balance two competing technical concerns: the desire to encapsulate abstractions, and the need to make certain abstractions visible to other modules. Parnas, Clements, and Weiss offer the following guidance: "System details that are likely to change independently should be the secrets of separate modules; the only assumptions that should appear between modules are those that are considered unlikely to change. Every data structure is private to one module; it may be directly accessed by one or more programs within the module but not by programs outside the module. Any other program that requires information stored in a module's data structures must obtain it by calling module programs" [62]. In other words, strive to build modules that are cohesive (by grouping logically related abstractions) and loosely coupled (by minimizing the dependencies among modules). From this perspective, we may define modularity as follows:

Modularity is the property of a system that has been decomposed into a set of cohesive and loosely coupled modules.

Thus, the principles of abstraction, encapsulation, and modularity are synergistic. An object provides a crisp boundary around a single abstraction, and both encapsulation and modularity provide barriers around this abstraction.

Two additional technical issues can affect modularization decisions. First, since modules usually serve as the elementary and indivisible units of software that can be reused across applications, a developer might choose to package classes and objects into modules in a way that makes their reuse convenient. Second, many compilers generate object code in segments, one for each module. Therefore, there may be practical limits on the size of individual modules. With regard to the dynamics of subprogram calls, the placement of declarations within modules can greatly affect the locality of reference and thus the paging behavior of a virtual memory system. Poor locality happens when subprogram calls occur across segments and lead to cache misses and page thrashing that ultimately slow down the whole system.

Several competing nontechnical needs may also affect modularization decisions. Typically, work assignments in a development team are given on a module-by-module basis, and so the boundaries of modules may be established to minimize the interfaces among different parts of the development organization. Senior designers are usually given responsibility for module interfaces, and more junior developers complete their implementation. On a larger scale, the same situation applies with subcontractor relationships. Abstractions may be packaged so as to quickly stabilize the module interfaces as agreed upon among the various companies. Changing such interfaces usually involves much wailing and gnashing of teeth – not to mention a vast amount of paperwork – and so this factor often leads to conservatively designed interfaces. Speaking of paperwork, modules also usually serve as the unit of documentation and configuration management. Having ten modules where one would do sometimes means ten times the paperwork, and so, unfortunately, sometimes the documentation requirements drive the module design decisions (usually in the most negative way). Security may also be an issue: most code may be considered unclassified, but other code that might be classified secret or higher is best placed in separate modules.

Juggling these different requirements is difficult, but don't lose sight of the most important point: finding the right classes and objects and then organizing them into separate modules are *largely independent* design decisions. The identification of classes and objects is part of the logical design of the system, but the identification of modules is part of the system's physical design. One cannot make all the logical design decisions before making all the physical ones, or vice versa; rather, these design decisions happen iteratively.

Examples of Modularity Let's look at modularity in the hydroponics gardening system. Suppose that instead of building some special-purpose hardware, we decide to use a commercially available workstation, and employ an off-the-shelf graphical user interface (GUI). At this workstation, an operator could create new growing plans, modify old ones, and follow the progress of currently active ones. Since one of our key abstractions here is that of a growing plan, we might therefore create a module whose purpose is to collect all of the classes associated with individual growing plans. In C++, we might write the header file for this module (which we name gplan.h) as:

```
// gplan.h

#ifndef _GPLAN_H
#define _GPLAN_H 1

#include "gtypes.h"
#include "except.h"
#include "actions.h"

class GrowingPlan ...

class FruitGrowingPlan ...

class GrainGrowingPlan ...

    ...

#endif
```

Here we import three other header files (gtypes.h, except.h, and actions.h), upon whose interface we must rely.

The implementations of these growing-plan classes then appear in the implementation of this module, in a file we name (by convention) gplan.cpp.

We might also define a module whose purpose is to collect all of the code associated with application-specific dialog boxes. This unit most likely depends upon the classes declared in the interface of gplan.h, as well as files that encapsulate certain GUI interfaces, and so it must in turn include the header file gplan.h, as well as the appropriate GUI header files.

Our design will probably include many other modules, each of which imports the interface of lower level units. Ultimately, we must define some main program from which we can invoke this application from the operating system. In object-oriented design, defining this main program is often the least important decision, whereas in traditional structured design, the main program serves as the root, the keystone that holds everything else together. We suggest that the object-oriented view is more natural, for as Meyer observes, "Practical software systems are more appropriately described as offering a number of services. Defining these systems by single functions is usually possible, but yields rather artificial answers. . . . Real systems have no top" [63].

Hierarchy

The Meaning of Hierarchy Abstraction is a good thing, but in all except the most trivial applications, we may find many more different abstractions than we can comprehend at one time. Encapsulation helps manage this complexity by hiding the inside view of our abstractions. Modularity helps also, by giving us a way to cluster logically related abstractions. Still, this is not enough. A set of abstractions often forms a hierarchy, and by identifying these hierarchies in our design, we greatly simplify our understanding of the problem.

We define hierarchy as follows:

Hierarchy is a ranking or ordering of abstractions.

The two most important hierarchies in a complex system are its class structure (the "is a" hierarchy) and its object structure (the "part of" hierarchy).

Examples of Hierarchy: Single Inheritance Inheritance is the most important "is a" hierarchy, and as we noted earlier, it is an essential element of object-oriented systems. Basically, inheritance defines a relationship among classes, wherein one class shares the structure or behavior defined in one or more classes (denoting *single inheritance* and *multiple inheritance*, respectively). Inheritance thus represents a hierarchy of abstractions, in which a subclass inherits from one or more superclasses. Typically, a subclass augments or redefines the existing structure and behavior of its superclasses.

Semantically, inheritance denotes an "is-a" relationship. For example, a bear "is a" kind of mammal, a house "is a" kind of tangible asset, and a quick sort "is a" particular kind of sorting algorithm. Inheritance thus implies a generalization/specialization hierarchy, wherein a subclass specializes the more general structure or behavior of its superclasses. Indeed, this is the litmus test for inheritance: if B "is not a" kind of A, then B should not inherit from A.

Consider the different kinds of growing plans we might use in the hydroponics gardening system. An earlier section described our abstraction of a very generalized growing plan. Different kinds of crops, however, demand specialized growing plans. For example, the growing plan for all fruits is

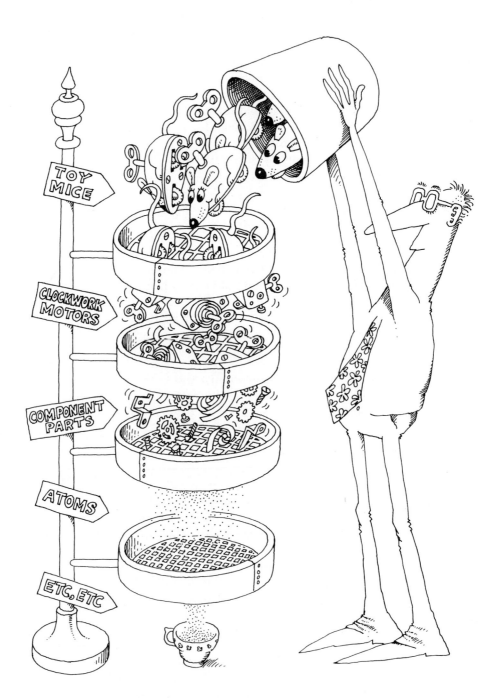

Abstractions form a hierarchy.

generally the same, but is quite different from the plan for all vegetables, or for all floral crops. Because of this clustering of abstractions, it is reasonable to define a standard fruit-growing plan that encapsulates the specialized behavior common to all fruits, such as the knowledge of when to pollinate or when to harvest the fruit. We can assert this "is a" relationship among these abstractions in C++ as follows:

```
// Yield type
typedef unsigned int Yield;

class FruitGrowingPlan : public GrowingPlan {
public:

  FruitGrowingPlan(char* name);
  virtual ~FruitGrowingPlan();

  virtual void establish(Day, Hour, Condition&);
  void scheduleHarvest(Day, Hour);

  Boolean isHarvested() const;
  unsigned daysUntilHarvest() const;
  Yield estimatedYield() const;

protected:
  Boolean repHarvested;
  Yield repYield;
};
```

This class declaration captures our design decision wherein a `FruitGrowingPlan` "is a" kind of `GrowingPlan`, with some additional structure (the member objects `repHarvested` and `repYield`) and behavior (the four new member functions, plus the overriding of the superclass operation `establish`). Using this class, we could declare even more specialized subclasses, such as the class `AppleGrowingPlan` .

As we evolve our inheritance hierarchy, the structure and behavior that are common for different classes will tend to migrate to common superclasses. This is why we often speak of inheritance as being a *generalization/specialization* hierarchy. Superclasses represent generalized abstractions, and subclasses represent specializations in which fields and methods from the superclass are added, modified, or even hidden. In this manner, inheritance lets us state our abstractions with an economy of expression. Indeed, neglecting the "is a" hierarchies that exist can lead to bloated, inelegant designs. As Cox points out, "Without inheritance, every class would be a free-standing unit, each developed from the ground up. Different classes would bear no relationship with one another, since the developer of each provides methods in whatever manner he chooses. Any consistency across classes is the result of discipline on the part of the programmers. Inheritance makes it possible to define new software in the same way we introduce any concept to a newcomer, by comparing it with something that is already familiar" [64].

There is a healthy tension among the principles of abstraction, encapsulation, and hierarchy. As Danforth and Tomlinson point out, "Data abstraction attempts to provide an opaque barrier behind which methods and state are hidden; inheritance requires opening this interface to some extent and may allow state as well as methods to be accessed without abstraction" [65]. For a given class, there are usually two kinds of clients: objects that invoke operations upon instances of the class, and subclasses that inherit from the class. Liskov therefore notes that, with inheritance, encapsulation can be violated in one of three ways: "The subclass might access an instance variable of its superclass, call a private operation of its superclass, or refer directly to superclasses of its superclass" [66]. Different programming languages trade off support for encapsulation and inheritance in different ways, but among the languages described in this book, C++ offers perhaps the greatest flexibility. Specifically, the interface of a class may have three parts: *private* parts, which declare members that are accessible only to the class itself, *protected* parts, which declare members that are accessible only to the class and its subclasses, and *public* parts, which are accessible to all clients.

Examples of Hierarchy: Multiple Inheritance The previous example illustrated the use of single inheritance: the subclass FruitGrowingPlan had exactly one superclass, the class GrowingPlan. For certain abstractions, it is useful to provide inheritance from multiple superclasses. For example, suppose that we choose to define a class representing a kind of plant. In C++, we might declare this class as follows:

```
class Plant {
public:

  Plant (char* name, char* species);
  virtual ~Plant();

  void setDatePlanted(Day);
  virtual establishGrowingConditions(const Condition&);

  const char* name() const;
  const char* species() const;
  Day datePlanted() const;

protected:
  char* repName;
  char* repSpecies;
  Day repPlanted;
private:
  ...
};
```

According to this class definition, each instance of the class Plant has a name, species, and date of planting. Additionally, optimal growing conditions may be established for each particular kind of plant. Because we expect this behavior to be specialized by subclasses, we declare this operation as *virtual* in C++.[*] Notice that the three member objects are declared as protected; thus, they are

---

[*] In CLOS, we use generic functions; in Smalltalk, all operations of a superclass may be specialized by a subclass, and so no special designation is required.

accessible only to the class itself and its subclasses. On the other hand, all members declared in the private part are accessible only to the class itself.

Our analysis of the problem domain might suggest that flowering plants and fruits and vegetables have specialized properties that are relevant to our application. For example, given a flowering plant, its expected time to flower and time to seed might be important to us. Similarly, the time to harvest might be an important part of our abstraction of all fruits and vegetables. One way we could capture our design decisions would be to make two new classes, a `Flower` class and a `FruitVegetable` class, both subclasses of the class Plant. However, what if we need to model a plant that both flowered and produced fruit? For example, florists commonly use blossoms from apple, cherry, and plum trees. For this abstraction, we would need to invent a third class, a `FlowerFruitVegetable`, that duplicated information from the `Flower` and `FruitVegetablePlant` classes.

A better way to express our abstractions and thereby avoid this redundancy is to use multiple inheritance. First, we invent classes that independently capture the properties unique to flowering plants and fruits and vegetables:

```
class FlowerMixin {
public:

  FlowerMixin(Day timeToFlower, Day timeToSeed);
  virtual ~FlowerMixin();

  Day timeToFlower() const;
  Day timeToSeed() const;

protected:
  ...
};

class FruitVegetableMixin {
public:

  FruitVegetableMixin(Day timeToHarvest);
  virtual ~FruitVegetableMixin();

  Day timeToHarvest() const;

protected:
  ...
};
```

Notice that these two classes have no superclass; they stand alone. These are called *mixin* classes, because they are meant to be mixed together with other classes to produce new subclasses. For example, we can define a `Rose` class as follows:

```
class Rose : public Plant, public FlowerMixin...
```

Similarly, a `Carrot` class can be declared as follows:

```
class Carrot : public Plant, public FruitVegetableMixin {};
```

In both cases, we form the subclass by inheriting from two superclasses. Instances of the subclass Rose thus include the structure and behavior from the class Plant together with the structure and behavior from the class FlowerMixin. Now, suppose we want to declare a class for a plant such as the cherry tree that has both flowers and fruit. We might write the following:

```
class Cherry : public Plant,
               public FlowerMixin,
               public FruitVegetableMixin...
```

Multiple inheritance is conceptually straightforward, but it does introduce some practical complexities for programming languages. Languages must address two issues: clashes among names from different superclasses, and repeated inheritance. Clashes will occur when two or more superclasses provide a field or operation with the same name or signature as a peer superclass. In C++, such clashes must be resolved with explicit qualification; in Smalltalk, the first occurrence of the name is used. Repeated inheritance occurs when two or more peer superclasses share a common superclass. In such a situation, the inheritance lattice will be diamond-shaped, and so the question arises, does the leaf class have one copy or multiple copies of the structure of the shared superclass? Some languages prohibit repeated inheritance, some unilaterally choose one approach, and others, such as C++, permit the programmer to decide. In C++, virtual base classes are used to denote a sharing of repeated structures, whereas nonvirtual base classes result in duplicate copies appearing in the subclass (with explicit qualification required to distinguish among the copies).

Multiple inheritance is often overused. For example, cotton candy is a kind of candy, but it is distinctly not a kind of cotton. Again, the litmus test for inheritance applies: if B is not a kind of A, then B should not inherit from A. Often, ill-formed multiple inheritance lattices can be reduced to a single superclass plus aggregation of the other classes by the subclass.

Examples of Hierarchy: Aggregation Whereas these "is a" hierarchies denote generalization/specialization relationships, "part of" hierarchies describe aggregation relationships. For example, consider the following class:

```
class Garden {
public:

  Garden();
  virtual ~Garden();

  ...

protected:
  Plant* repPlants[100];
  GrowingPlan repPlan;
};
```

Here we have the abstraction of a garden, consisting of a collection of plants together with a growing plan.

When dealing with hierarchies such as these, we often speak of *levels of abstraction*, a concept first described by Dijkstra [67]. In terms of its "is a" hierarchy, a high-level abstraction is generalized, and a low-level abstraction is specialized. Therefore, we say that a Flower class is at a higher level of abstraction then a Plant class. In terms of its "part of" hierarchy, a class is at a higher level of abstraction than any of the classes that make up its implementation. Thus, the class Garden is at a higher level of abstraction than the type Plant, upon which it builds.

Aggregation is not a concept unique to object-oriented programming languages. Indeed, any language that supports record-like structures supports aggregation. However, the combination of inheritance with aggregation is powerful: aggregation permits the physical grouping of logically related structures, and inheritance allows these common groups to be easily reused among different abstractions.

Aggregation raises the issue of ownership. Our abstraction of a garden permits different plants to be raised in a garden over time, but replacing a plant does not change the identity of the garden as a whole, nor does removing a garden necessarily destroy all of its plants (they are likely just transplanted). In other words, the lifetime of a garden and its plants are independent: We capture this design decision in the example above, by including pointers to Plant objects rather than values. In contrast, we have decided that a GrowingPlan object is intrinsically associated with a Garden object, and does not exist independently of the garden. For this reason, we use a value of GrowingPlan. Therefore, when we create an instance of Garden, we also create an instance of GrowingPlan; when we destroy the Garden object, we in turn destroy the GrowingPlan instance. We will discuss the semantics of ownership by value versus reference in more detail in the next chapter.

Typing

The Meaning of Typing The concept of a *type* derives primarily from the theories of abstract data types. As Deutsch suggests, "A type is a precise characterization of structural or behavioral properties which a collection of entities all share" [68]. For our purposes, we will use the terms *type* and *class* interchangeably.* Although the concepts of a type and a class are similar, we include typing as a separate element of the object model because the concept of a type places a very different emphasis upon the meaning of abstraction. Specifically, we state the following:

---

* A type and a class are not exactly the same thing; some languages actually distinguish these two concepts. For example, early versions of the language Trellis/Owl permitted an object to have both a class and a type. Even in Smalltalk, objects of the classes SmallInteger, LargeNegativeInteger, and LargePositiveInteger are all of the same type, Integer, although not of the same class [69]. For most mortals, however, separating the concepts of type and class is utterly confusing and adds very little value. It is sufficient to say that a class implements a type.

Strong typing prevents mixing abstractions.

> *Typing is the enforcement of the class of an object, such that objects of different types may not be interchanged, or at the most, they may be interchanged only in very restricted ways.*

Typing lets us express our abstractions so that the programming language in which we implement them can be made to enforce design decisions. Wegner observes that this kind of enforcement is essential for programming-in-the-large [70].

The idea of conformance is central to the notion of typing. For example, consider units of measurement in physics [71]. When we divide distance by time, we expect some value denoting speed, not weight. Similarly, multiplying temperature by a unit of force doesn't make sense, but multiplying mass by force does. These are both examples of strong typing, wherein the rules of our domain prescribe and enforce certain legal combinations of abstractions.

Examples of Typing: Strong and Weak Typing A given programming language may be strongly typed, weakly typed, or even untyped, yet still be called object-oriented. For example, Eiffel is strongly-typed, meaning that type conformance is strictly enforced: operations cannot be called upon an object unless the exact signature of that operation is defined in the object's class or superclasses. In strongly typed languages, violation of type conformance can be detected at the time of compilation. Smalltalk, on the other hand, is an untyped language: a client can send any message to any class (although a class may not know how to respond to the message). Violations of type conformance may not be known until execution, and usually manifest themselves as execution errors. Languages such as C++ are hybrid: they have tendencies toward strong typing, but it is possible to ignore or suppress the typing rules.

Consider the abstraction of the various kinds of storage tanks that might exist in a greenhouse. We are likely to have storage tanks for water as well as various nutrients; although one holds a liquid and the other a solid, these abstractions are sufficiently similar to warrant a hierarchy of classes, as the following example illustrates. First, we introduce another typedef:

```
// Number denoting level from 0 to 100 percent
typedef float Level;
```

In C++, typedefs do not introduce new types. In particular, the typedefs `Level` and `Concentration` are both floating-point numbers, and can be intermixed. In this aspect, C++ is weakly typed: values of primitive types such as `int` and `float` are indistinguishable within that particular type. In contrast, languages such as Ada and Object Pascal enforce strong typing among primitive types. In Ada, for example, the derived type and subtype constructs allow the developer to define distinct types, constrained by range or precision from more general types.

Next, we have the class hierarchy for storage tanks:

```
class StorageTank {
public:

    StorageTank();
    virtual ~StorageTank();

    virtual void fill();
    virtual void startDraining();
    virtual void stopDraining();

    Boolean isEmpty() const;
    Level level() const;

protected:
    ...
};

class WaterTank : public StorageTank {
public:

    WaterTank();
    virtual ~WaterTank();

    virtual void fill();
    virtual void startDraining();
    virtual void stopDraining();
    void startHeating();
    void stopHeating();

    Temperature currentTemperature() const;

protected:
    ...
};
```

```
class NutrientTank : public StorageTank {
public:

  NutrientTank();
  virtual ~NutrientTank();

  virtual void startDraining();
  virtual void stopDraining();

protected:
  ...
};
```

The class StorageTank is the base class in this hierarchy, and provides the structure and behavior common to all such tanks, such as the ability to fill and drain the tank. WaterTank and NutrientTank are both subclasses of StorageTank. Both subclasses redefine some of the behavior of the superclass, and the class WaterTank introduces some new behavior associated with temperature.

Suppose that we have the following declarations:

```
StorageTank s1, s2;
WaterTank w;
NutrientTank n;
```

Variables such as s1, s2, w, and n are not objects. To be precise, these are simply names we use to designate objects of their respective classes: when we say "the object s1," we really mean the instance of StorageTank denoted by the variable s1. We will explain this subtlety again in the next chapter.

With regard to type checking among classes, C++ is more strongly typed, meaning that expressions that invoke operations are checked for type correctness at the time of compilation. For example, the following statements are legal:

```
Level l = s1.level();
w.startDraining();
n.stopDraining();
```

In the first statement, we invoke the selector level, declared for the base class StorageTank. In the next two statements, we invoke a modifier (startDraining, and stopDraining) declared in the base class, but overridden in the subclass.

However, the following statements are not legal and would be rejected at compilation time:

```
s1.startHeating(); // Illegal
n.stopHeating();   // Illegal
```

Neither of these two statements is legal because the methods startHeating and stopHeating are not defined for the class of the corresponding variable, nor for any superclasses of its class. On the other hand, the following statement is legal:

```
n.fill()
```

Although `fill` is not defined in the class `NutrientTank`, it is defined in the superclass `StorageTank`, from which the class `NutrientTank` inherits its structure and behavior.

Strong typing lets us use our programming language to enforce certain design decisions, and so is particularly relevant as the complexity of our system grows. However, there is a dark side to strong typing. Practically, strong typing introduces semantic dependencies such that even small changes in the interface of a base class require recompilation of all subclasses. Also, in the absence of parameterized classes, which we will discuss further in the next chapter and in Chapter 9, it is problematic to have type-safe collections of heterogeneous objects. For example, suppose we need the abstraction of a greenhouse inventory, which collects all of the tangible assets associated with a particular greenhouse. A common C idiom applied to C++ is to use a container class that stores pointers to `void`, which represents objects of an indefinite type:

```
class Inventory {
public:

  Inventory );
  ~Inventory();

  void add(void*);
  void remove(void*);

  void* mostRecent() const;

  void apply(Boolean (*)(void*));

private:
  ...
};
```

The operation `apply` is an iterator, which allows us to apply an operation to every item in the collection. We will discuss iterators in more detail in the next chapter.

Given an instance of the class `Inventory`, we may add and remove pointers to objects of any class. However, this approach is not type-safe: we can legally add tangible assets such as storage tanks to an inventory, as well as nontangible assets, such as temperature or growing plans, which violates our abstraction of an inventory. Similarly, we might add a `WaterTank` object as well as a `TemperatureSensor` object, and unless we are careful, invoke the selector `mostRecent`, expecting to find a water tank when we are actually returned a storage tank.

There are two general solutions to these problems. First, we could use a type-safe container class. Instead of manipulating pointers to `void`, we might define an inventory class that manipulates only objects of the class `TangibleAsset`, which we would use as a mixin class for all classes that represent tangible assets, such as `WaterTank` but not `GrowingPlan`. This approach addresses the first problem, wherein objects of different types are incorrectly mingled. Second, we could use some form of runtime type identification; this addresses the second problem of knowing what kind of object you happen to be examining at the moment. In Smalltalk, for example, it is possible to query an object for its class. In C++, runtime type identification is not yet part of the language standard,[*] but a similar effect can be achieved pragmatically, by defining an operation in the base class that returns a string or enumeration type identifying the particular class of the object. In general, however, runtime type identification should be used only when there is a compelling reason, because it can represent a weakening of encapsulation. As we will discuss in the next section, the use of polymorphic operations can often (but not always) mitigate the need for runtime type identification.

A *strongly typed* language is one in which all expressions are guaranteed to be type-consistent. The meaning of type consistency is best illustrated by the following example, using the previously declared variables. The following assignment statements are legal:

```
s1 = s2;
s1 = w;
```

The first statement is legal because the class of the variable on the left side of the statement (StorageTank) is the same as the class of the expression on the right side. The second statement is also legal because the class of the variable on the left side (StorageTank) is a superclass of the variable on the right side (WaterTank). However, this assignment results in a loss of information (known in C++ as *slicing*). The subclass WaterTank introduces structure and behavior beyond that defined in the base class, and this information cannot be copied to an instance of the base class.

Consider the following illegal statements:

```
w = s1; // Illegal
w = n;  // Illegal
```

The first statement is not legal because the class of the variable on the left side of the assignment statement (WaterTank) is a subclass of the class of the variable on the right side (StorageTank). The second statement is illegal because the classes of the two variables are peers, and are not along the same line of inheritance (although they have a common superclass).

In some situations, it is necessary to convert a value from one type to another. For example, consider the following function:

```
void checkLevel(const StorageTank& s);
```

If and only if we are certain that the actual argument we are given is of the class WaterTank, then we may explicitly coerce the value of the base class to the subclass, as in the following expression:

```
if (((WaterTank&)s).currentTemperature() < 32.0) ...
```

---

[*] Runtime type identification has been adopted for future versions of C++.

This expression is type-consistent, although it is not completely type-safe. For example, if the variable s happened to denote an object of the class NutrientTank at runtime, then the coercion would fail with unpredictable results during execution. In general, type conversion is to be avoided, because it often represents a violation of abstraction.

As Tesler points out, there are a number of important benefits to be derived from using strongly typed languages:

- "Without type checking, a program in most languages can 'crash' in mysterious ways at runtime.
- In most systems, the edit-compile-debug cycle is so tedious that early error detection is indispensable.
- Type declarations help to document programs.
- Most compilers can generate more efficient object code if types are declared" [72].

Untyped languages offer greater flexibility, but even with untyped languages, as Borning and Ingalls observe, "In almost all cases, the programmer in fact knows what sorts of objects are expected as the arguments of a message, and what sort of object will be returned" [73]. In practice, the safety offered by strongly typed languages usually more then compensates for the flexibility lost by not using an untyped language, especially for programming-in-the-large.

Examples of Typing: Static and Dynamic Binding The concepts of strong typing and static typing are entirely different. Strong typing refers to type consistency, whereas static typing – also known as *static binding* or *early binding* – refers to the time when names are bound to types. Static binding means that the types of all variables and expressions are fixed at the time of compilation; *dynamic binding* (also called *late binding*) means that the types of all variables and expressions are not known until runtime. Because strong typing and binding are independent concepts, a language may be both strongly and statically typed (Ada), strongly typed yet support dynamic binding (Object Pascal and C++), or untyped yet support dynamic binding (Smalltalk). CLOS fits somewhere between C++ and Smalltalk, in that an implementation may either enforce or ignore any type declarations asserted by a programmer.

Let's again illustrate these concepts with an example from C++. Consider the following nonmember function:[*]

```
void balanceLevels(StorageTank& s1, StorageTank& s2);
```

---

[*] A nonmember function is a function not directly associated with a class. Nonmember functions are also called *free subprograms*. In a pure object-oriented language such as Smalltalk, there are no free subprograms; every operation must be associated with some class.

Calling the operation `balanceLevels` with instances of `StorageTank` or any of its subclasses is type-consistent because the type of each actual parameter is part of the same line of inheritance, whose base class is `StorageTank`.

In the implementation of this function, we might have the expression:

```
if (s1.level() > s2.level())
  s2.fill();
```

What are the semantics of invoking the selector `level`? This operation is declared only in the base `StorageTank`, and therefore, no matter what specific class or subclass instance we provide for the formal argument `s1`, the base class operation will be invoked. Here, the call to `level` is statically bound: at the time of compilation, we know exactly what operation will be invoked.

On the other hand, consider the semantics of invoking the modifier `fill`, which is dynamically bound. This operation is declared in the base class and then redefined only in the subclass `WaterTank`. If the actual argument to `s1` is a `WaterTank` instance, then `WaterTank::fill` will be invoked; if the actual argument to `s1` is a `NutrientTank` instance, then `StorageTank::fill` will be invoked.[*]

This feature is called *polymorphism*; it represents a concept in type theory in which a single name (such as a variable declaration) may denote objects of many different classes that are related by some common superclass. Any object denoted by this name is therefore able to respond to some common set of operations [74]. The opposite of polymorphism is *monomorphism*, which is found in all languages that are both strongly typed and statically bound, such as Ada.

Polymorphism exists when the features of inheritance and dynamic binding interact. It is perhaps the most powerful feature of object-oriented programming languages next to their support for abstraction, and it is what distinguishes object-oriented programming from more traditional programming with abstract data types. As we will see in the following chapters, polymorphism is also a central concept in object-oriented design.

Concurrency

The Meaning of Concurrency For certain kinds of problems, an automated system may have to handle many different events simultaneously. Other problems may involve so much computation that they exceed the capacity of any single processor. In each of these cases, it is natural to consider using a distributed set of computers for the target implementation or to use processors capable of multitasking. A single process – also known as a *thread of control* – is the root from which independent dynamic action occurs within a system. Every program has at least one thread of control, but a system involving concurrency may have many such threads: some that are transitory, and others that last the entire lifetime of the system's execution. Systems executing across multiple CPUs allow for truly concurrent threads of control, whereas systems

---

[*] `StorageTank::fill` is the syntax C++ uses to explicitly qualify the name of a declaration.

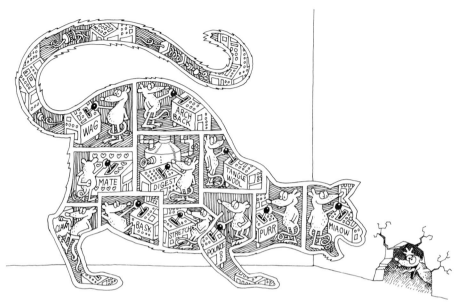

Concurrency allows different objects to act at the same time.

running on a single CPU can only achieve the illusion of concurrent threads of control, usually by means of some time-slicing algorithm.

We also distinguish between heavyweight and lightweight concurrency. A *heavyweight process* is one that is typically independently managed by the target operating system, and so encompasses its own address space. A *lightweight process* usually lives within a single operating system process along with other lightweight processes, which share the same address space. Communication among heavyweight processes is generally expensive, involving some form of interprocess communication; communication among lightweight processes is less expensive, and often involves shared data.

Many contemporary operating systems now provide direct support for concurrency, and so there is greater opportunity (and demand) for concurrency within object-oriented systems. For example, UNIX provides the system call *fork*, which spans a new process. Similarly, Windows/NT and OS/2 are multithreaded, and provide programmatic interfaces for creating and manipulating processes.

Lim and Johnson point out that "designing features for concurrency in OOP languages is not much different from [doing so in] other kinds of languages – concurrency is orthogonal to OOP at the lowest levels of abstraction. OOP or not, all the traditional problems in concurrent programming still remain" [75]. Indeed, building a large piece of software is hard enough; designing one that encompasses multiple threads of control is much harder because one must worry about such issues as deadlock, livelock, starvation, mutual exclusion, and race conditions. Fortunately, as Lim and Johnson also point out, "At the highest levels of abstraction, OOP can alleviate the concurrency problem for the majority of programmers by hiding the concurrency inside reusable abstractions" [76]. Black et al. therefore suggest that "an object model is appropriate for a distributed system because it implicitly defines (1) the units of distribution and movement and (2) the entities that communicate" [77].

Whereas object-oriented programming focuses upon data abstraction, encapsulation, and inheritance, concurrency focuses upon process abstraction and synchronization [78]. The object is a concept that unifies these two different viewpoints: each object (drawn from an abstraction of the real world) may represent a separate thread of control (a process abstraction). Such objects are called *active*. In a system based on an object-oriented design, we can conceptualize the world as consisting of a set of cooperative objects, some of which are active and thus serve as centers of independent activity. Given this conception, we define concurrency as follows:

> *Concurrency is the property that distinguishes an active object from one that is not active.*

Examples of Concurrency Our earlier discussion of abstraction introduced the class ActiveTemperatureSensor, whose behavior required periodically sensing the current temperature and then invoking the callback function of a client object whenever the temperature changed a certain number of degrees from a given setpoint. We did not explain how the class implemented this behavior. That fact is a secret of the implementation, but it is clear that some form of concurrency is required. In general, there are three approaches to concurrency in object-oriented design.

First, concurrency is an intrinsic feature of certain programming languages. For example, Ada's mechanism for expressing a concurrent process is the task. Similarly, Smalltalk provides the class Process, which we may use as the superclass of all active objects. There are a number of other concurrent object-oriented programming languages, such as Actors, Orient 84/K, and ABCL/1, that provide similar mechanisms for concurrency and synchronization. In each case, we may create an active object that runs some process concurrently with all other active objects.

Second, we may use a class library that implements some form of lightweight processes. This is the approach taken by the AT&T task library for C++, which provides the classes Sched, Timer, Task, and others. Naturally, the implementation of this library is highly platform-dependent, although the interface to the library is relatively portable. In this approach, concurrency is not an intrinsic part of the language (and so does not place any burdens upon nonconcurrent systems), but appears as if it were intrinsic, through the presence of these standard classes.

Third, we may use interrupts to give us the illusion of concurrency. Of course, this requires that we have knowledge of certain low-level hardware details. For example, in our implementation of the class ActiveTemperatureSensor, we might have a hardware timer that periodically interrupts the application, during which time all such sensors read the current temperature, then invoke their callback function as necessary.

No matter which approach to concurrency we take, one of the realities about concurrency is that once you introduce it into a system, you must consider how active objects synchronize their activities with one another as well as with objects that are purely sequential. For example, if two active objects try to send messages to a third object, we must be certain to use some means of mutual exclusion, so that the state of the object being acted upon is not corrupted when both active objects try to update its state simultaneously. This is the point where the ideas of abstraction, encapsulation, and concurrency interact. In the presence of concurrency, it is not enough simply to define the methods of an object; we must also make certain that the semantics of these methods are preserved in the presence of multiple threads of control.

Persistence

An object in software takes up some amount of space and exists for a particular amount of time. Atkinson *et al.* suggest that there is a continuum of object existence, ranging from transitory objects that arise within the evaluation of an expression, to objects in a database that outlive the execution of a single program. This spectrum of object persistence encompasses the following:

- "Transient results in expression evaluation
- Local variables in procedure activations
- Own variables [as in ALGOL 60], global variables, and heap items whose extent is different from their scope
- Data that exists between executions of a program
- Data that exists between various versions of a program
- Data that outlives the program" [79]

Traditional programming languages usually address only the first three kinds of object persistence; persistence of the last three kinds is typically the domain of database technology. This leads to a clash of cultures that sometimes results in very strange architectures: programmers end up crafting *ad hoc* schemes for storing objects whose state must be preserved between program executions, and database designers misapply their technology to cope with transient objects [80].

Unifying the concepts of concurrency and objects gives rise to concurrent object-oriented programming languages. In a similar fashion, introducing the concept of persistence to the object model gives rise to object-oriented databases. In practice, such databases build upon proven technology, such as sequential, indexed, hierarchical, network, or relational database models, but then offer to the programmer the abstraction of an object-oriented interface, through which database queries and other operations are completed in terms of

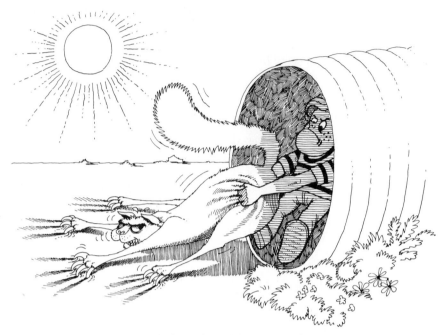

Persistence saves the state and class of an object across time or space.

objects whose lifetime transcends the lifetime of an individual program. This unification vastly simplifies the development of certain kinds of applications. In particular, it allows us to apply the same design methods to the database and nondatabase segments of an application, as we will see in Chapter 10.

Very few object-oriented programming languages provide direct support for persistence; Smalltalk is one notable exception, wherein there are protocols for streaming objects to and from disk (which must be redefined by subclasses). However, streaming objects to flat files is a naive solution to persistence that does not scale well. More commonly, persistence is achieved through a modest number of commercially available object-oriented databases [81]. Another reasonable approach to persistence is to provide an object-oriented skin over a relational database. This approach is most appealing when there is a large capital investment in relational database technology that would be risky or too expensive to replace. We will examine this very situation in Chapter 10.

Persistence deals with more than just the lifetime of data. In object-oriented databases, not only does the *state* of an object persist, but its *class* must also transcend any individual program, so that every program interprets this saved state in the same way. This clearly makes it challenging to maintain the integrity of a database as it grows, particularly if we must change the class of an object.

Our discussion thus far pertains to persistence in time. In most systems, an object, once created, consumes the same physical memory until it ceases to exist. However, for systems that execute upon a distributed set of processors, we must sometimes be concerned with persistence across space. In such systems, it is useful to think of objects that can move from machine to machine, and that may even have different representations on different machines. We examine this kind of persistence further in the application in Chapter 12.

To summarize, we define persistence as follows:

Persistence is the property of an object through which its existence transcends time (i.e. the object continues to exist after its creator ceases to exist) and/or space (i.e. the object's location moves from the address space in which it was created).

2.3 Applying the Object Model

Benefits of the Object Model

As we have shown, the object model is fundamentally different from the models embraced by the more traditional methods of structured analysis, structured design, and structured programming. This does not mean that the object model abandons all of the sound principles and experiences of these older methods. Rather, it introduces several novel elements that build upon these earlier models. Thus, the object model offers a number of significant benefits that other models simply do not provide. Most importantly, the use of the object model leads us to construct systems that embody the five attributes of well-structured complex systems. In our experience, there are five other practical benefits to be derived from the application of the object model.

First, the use of the object model helps us to exploit the expressive power of object-based and object-oriented programming languages. As Stroustrup points out, "It is not always clear how best to take advantage of a language such as C++. Significant improvements in productivity and code quality have consistently been achieved using C++ as 'a better C' with a bit of data abstraction thrown in where it is clearly useful. However, further and noticeably larger improvements have been achieved by taking advantage of class hierarchies in the design process. This is often called object-oriented design and this is where the greatest benefits of using C++ have been found" [82]. Our experience has been that, without the application of the elements of the object model, the more powerful features of languages such as Smalltalk, Object Pascal, C++, CLOS, and Ada are either ignored or greatly misused.

Next, the use of the object model encourages the reuse not only of software but of entire designs, leading to the creation of reusable application frameworks [83]. We have found that object-oriented systems are often smaller than equivalent non-object-oriented implementations. Not only does this mean less code to write and maintain, but greater reuse of software also translates into cost and schedule benefits.

Third, the use of the object model produces systems that are built upon stable intermediate forms, which are more resilient to change. This also means

Air traffic control
Animation
Avionics
Banking and insurance software
Business data processing
Chemical process control
Command and control systems
Computer aided design
Computer aided education
Computer integrated manufacturing
Databases
Document preparation
Expert systems
Film and stage storyboarding
Hypermedia
Image recognition

Investment strategies
Mathematical analysis
Medical electronics
Music composition
Office automation
Operating systems
Petroleum engineering
Reusable software components
Robotics
Software development environments
Space station software
Spacecraft and aircraft simulation
Telecommunications
Telemetry systems
User interface design
VLSI design

Figure 2-6
Applications of the Object Model

that such systems can be allowed to evolve over time, rather than be abandoned or completely redesigned in response to the first major change in requirements.

Chapter 7 explains further how the object model reduces the risks inherent in developing complex systems, primarily because integration is spread out across the life cycle rather than occurring as one major event. The object model's guidance in designing an intelligent separation of concerns also reduces development risk and increases our confidence in the correctness of our design.

Finally, the object model appeals to the workings of human cognition, for as Robson suggests, "Many people who have no idea how a computer works find the idea of object-oriented systems quite natural" [84].

Applications of the Object Model

The object model has proven applicable to a wide variety of problem domains. Figure 2-6 lists many of the domains for which systems exist that may properly be called object-oriented. The Bibliography provides an extensive list of references to these and other applications.

Object-oriented analysis and design may be the only method we have today that can be employed to attack the complexity inherent in very large systems. In all fairness, however, the use of object-oriented development may be ill-advised for some domains, not for any technical reasons, but for nontechnical ones, such as the absence of a suitably trained staff or a good development environment. We will discuss these issues in more detail in Chapter 7.

Open Issues

To effectively apply the elements of the object model, we must next address several open issues:

- What exactly are classes and objects?
- How does one properly identify the classes and objects that are relevant to a particular application?
- What is a suitable notation for expressing the design of an object-oriented system?
- What process can lead us to a well-structured object-oriented system?
- What are the management implications of using object-oriented design?

These issues are the themes of the next five chapters.

Summary

- The maturation of software engineering has led to the development of object-oriented analysis, design, and programming methods, all of which address the issues of programming-in-the-large.
- There are several different programming paradigms: procedure-oriented, object-oriented, logic-oriented, rule-oriented, and constraint-oriented.
- An abstraction denotes the essential characteristics of an object that distinguish it from all other kinds of objects and thus provide crisply defined conceptual boundaries, relative to the perspective of the viewer.
- Encapsulation is the process of compartmentalizing the elements of an abstraction that constitute its structure and behavior; encapsulation serves to separate the contractual interface of an abstraction and its implementation.
- Modularity is the property of a system that has been decomposed into a set of cohesive and loosely coupled modules.
- Hierarchy is a ranking or ordering of abstractions.
- Typing is the enforcement of the class of an object, such that objects of different types may not be interchanged, or at the most, be interchanged only in very restricted ways.
- Concurrency is the property that distinguishes an active object from one that is not active.
- Persistence is the property of an object through which its existence transcends time and/or space.

Further Readings

The concept of the object model was first introduced by Jones [F 1979] and Williams [F 1986]. Kay's Ph.D. thesis [F 1969] established the direction for much of the work in object-oriented programming that followed.

Shaw [J 1984] provides an excellent summary regarding abstraction mechanisms in high-order programming languages. The theoretical foundation of abstraction may be found in the work of Liskov and Guttag [H 1986], Guttag [J 1980], and Hilfinger [J 1982]. Parnas [F 1979] is the seminal work on information hiding. The meaning and importance of hierarchy are discussed in the work edited by Pattee [J 1973].

There is a wealth of literature regarding object-oriented programming. Cardelli and Wegner [J 1985] and Wegner [J 1987] provide an excellent survey of object-based and object-oriented programming languages. The tutorial papers of Stefik and Bobrow [G 1986], Stroustrup [G 1988], Nygaard [G 1986], and Grogono [G 1991] are good starting points on the important issues in object-oriented programming. The books by Cox [G 1986], Meyer [F 1988], Schmucker [G 1986], and Kim and Lochovsky [F 1989] offer extended coverage of these topics.

Object-oriented design methods were first introduced by Booch [F 1981, 1982, 1986, 1987, 1989]. Object-oriented analysis methods were first introduced by Shlaer and Mellor [B 1988] and Bailin [B 1988]. Since then, a variety of object-oriented analysis and design methods have been proposed, most notably Rumbaugh [F 1991], Coad and Yourdon [B 1991], Constantine [F 1989], Shlaer and Mellor [B 1992], Martin and Odell [B 1992], Wasserman [B 1991], Jacobson [F 1992], Rubin and Goldberg [B 1992], Embly [B 1992], Wirfs-Brock [F 1990], Goldstein and Alger [C 1992], Henderson-Sellers [F 1992], Firesmith [F 1992], and Fusion [F 1992].

Case studies of object-oriented applications may be found in Taylor [H 1990, C 1992], Berard [H 1993], Love [C 1993], and Pinson and Weiner [C 1990].

An excellent collection of papers dealing with all topics of object-oriented technology may be found in Peterson [G 1987], Schriver and Wegner [G 1987], and Khoshafian and Abnous [G 1990]. The proceedings of several yearly conferences on object-oriented technology are also excellent sources of material. Some of the more interesting forums include OOPSLA, ECOOP, TOOLS, Object World, and ObjectExpo.

Organizations responsible for establishing standards for object technology include the Object Management Group and the ANSI X3J7 committee.

The primary reference for C++ is Ellis and Stroustrup [G 1990]. Other useful references include Stroustrup [G 1991], Lippman [G 1991], and Coplien [G 1992].

CHAPTER 3

Classes and Objects

Both the engineer and the artist must be intimately familiar with the materials of their trade. When we use object-oriented methods to analyze or design a complex software system, our basic building blocks are classes and objects. Since we have thus far provided only informal definitions of these two elements, in this chapter we turn to a detailed study of the nature of classes, objects, and their relationships, and along the way provide several rules of thumb for crafting quality abstractions and mechanisms.

3.1 The Nature of an Object

What Is and What Isn't an Object

The ability to recognize physical objects is a skill that humans learn at a very early age. A brightly colored ball will attract an infant's attention, but typically, if you hide the ball, the child will not try to look for it; when the object leaves her field of vision, as far as she can determine, it ceases to exist. It is not until near the age of one that a child normally develops what is called the *object concept*, a skill that is of critical importance to future cognitive development. Show a ball to a one-year-old and then hide it, and she will usually search for it even though it is not visible. Through the object concept, a child comes to realize that objects have a permanence and identity apart from any operations upon them [1].

In the previous chapter, we informally defined an object as a tangible entity that exhibits some well-defined behavior. From the perspective of human cognition, an object is any of the following:

- A tangible and/or visible thing
- Something that may be apprehended intellectually
- Something toward which thought or action is directed

We add to our informal definition the idea that an object models some part of reality and is therefore something that exists in time and space. In software, the term *object* was first formally applied in the Simula language; objects typically existed in Simula programs to simulate some aspect of reality [2].

Real-world objects are not the only kinds of objects that are of interest to us during software development. Other important kinds of objects are inventions of the design process whose collaborations with other such objects serve as the mechanisms that provide some higher-level behavior [3]. This leads us to the more refined definition of Smith and Tockey, who suggest that "an object represents an individual, identifiable item, unit, or entity, either real or abstract, with a well-defined role in the problem domain" [4]. In even more general terms, we define an object as anything with a crisply defined boundary [5].

Consider for a moment a manufacturing plant that processes composite materials for making such diverse items as bicycle frames and airplane wings. Manufacturing plants are often divided into separate shops: mechanical, chemical, electrical, and so forth. Shops are further divided into cells, and in each cell we have some collection of machines, such as die stamps, presses, and lathes. Along a manufacturing line, we might find vats containing raw materials, which are used in a chemical process to produce blocks of composite materials, and which in turn are formed and shaped to produce end items such as bicycle frames and airplane wings. Each of the tangible things we have mentioned thus far is an object. A lathe has a crisply defined boundary that separates it from the block of composite material it operates upon; a bicycle frame has a crisply defined boundary that distinguishes it from the cell of machines that produced the frame itself.

Some objects may have crisp conceptual boundaries, yet represent intangible events or processes. For example, a chemical process in a manufacturing plant may be treated as an object, because it has a crisp conceptual boundary, interacts with certain other objects through a well-ordered collection of operations that unfolds over time, and exhibits a well-defined behavior. Similarly, consider a CAD/CAM system for modeling solids. Where two solids such as a sphere and a cube intersect, they may form an irregular line of intersection. Although it does not exist apart from the sphere or cube, this line is still an object with crisply defined conceptual boundaries.

An object has state, exhibits some well-defined behavior, and has a unique identity.

Some objects may be tangible, yet have fuzzy physical boundaries. Objects such as rivers, fog, and crowds of people fit this definition.[*] Just as the person holding a hammer tends to see everything in the world as a nail, so the developer with an object-oriented mindset begins to think that everything in the world is an object. This perspective is a little naive, because there are some things that are distinctly not objects. For example, attributes such as time, beauty, or color are not objects, nor are emotions such as love and anger. On the other hand, these things are all potentially properties of other objects. For example, we might say that a man (an object) loves his wife (another object), or that a particular cat (yet another object) is gray.

Thus, it is useful to say that an object is something that has crisply defined boundaries, but this is not enough to guide us in distinguishing one object from another, nor does it allow us to judge the quality of our abstractions. Our experience therefore suggests the following definition:

An object has state, behavior, and identity; the structure and behavior of similar objects are defined in their common class; the terms instance *and* object *are interchangeable.*

---

[*] This is true only at a sufficiently high level of abstraction. To a person walking through a fog bank, it is generally futile to distinguish "my fog" from "your fog." However, consider a weather map: a fog bank over San Francisco is a distinctly different object than a fog bank over London.

State

Semantics Consider a vending machine that dispenses soft drinks. The usual behavior of such objects is that when one puts coins in a slot and pushes a button to make a selection, a drink emerges from the machine. What happens if a user first makes a selection and then puts money in the slot? Most vending machines just sit and do nothing, because the user has violated the basic assumptions of their operation. Stated another way, the vending machine was playing a role (of waiting for coins) that the user ignored (by making a selection first). Similarly, suppose that the user ignores the warning light that says "Correct change only," and puts in extra money. Most machines are user-hostile; they will happily swallow the excess coins.

In each of these circumstances, we see how the behavior of an object is influenced by its history: the order in which one operates upon the object is important. The reason for this event- and time-dependent behavior is the existence of state within the object. For example, one essential state associated with the vending machine is the amount of money currently entered by a user but not yet applied to a selection. Other important properties include the amount of change available and the quantity of soft drinks on hand.

From this example, we may form the following low-level definition:

The state of an object encompasses all of the (usually static) properties of the object plus the current (usually dynamic) values of each of these properties.

Another property of a vending machine is that it can accept coins. This is a static (that is, fixed) property, meaning that it is an essential characteristic of a vending machine. In contrast, the actual quantity of coins accepted at any given moment represents the dynamic value of this property, and is affected by the order of operations upon the machine. This quantity increases as a user inserts coins, and then decreases when a salesperson services the machine. We say that values are "usually dynamic" because in some cases values are static. For example, the serial number of a vending machine is a static property and value.

A property is an inherent or distinctive characteristic, trait, quality, or feature that contributes to making an object uniquely that object. For example, one essential property of an elevator is that it is constrained to travel up and down and not horizontally. Properties are usually static, because attributes such as these are unchanging and fundamental to the nature of the object. We say "usually" static, because in some circumstances the properties of an object may change. For example, consider an autonomous robot that can learn about its environment. It may first recognize an object that appears to be a fixed barrier, only to learn later that this object is in fact a door that can be opened. In this case, the object created by the robot as it builds its conceptual model of the world gains new properties as new knowledge is acquired.

All properties have some value. This value might be a simple quantity, or it might denote another object. For example, part of the state of an elevator might have the value 3, denoting the current floor on which the elevator is located. In the case of the vending machine, the state of the vending machine encompasses many other objects, such as a collection of soft drinks. The individual drinks are in fact distinct objects; their properties are different from those of the machine (they can be consumed, whereas a vending machine cannot), and they can be operated upon in distinctly different ways. Thus, we distinguish between objects and simple values: simple quantities such as the number 3 are "atemporal, unchangeable, and non-instantiated," whereas objects "exist in time, are changeable, have state, are instantiated, and can be created, destroyed, and shared" [6].

The fact that every object has state implies that every object takes up some amount of space, be it in the physical world or in computer memory.

Example Consider the structure of a personnel record. In C++ we might write:

```
struct PersonnelRecord
{
  char  name[100];
  int   socialSecurityNumber;
  char  department[10];
  float salary;
};
```

Each part of this structure denotes a particular property of our abstraction of a personnel record. This declaration denotes a class, not an object, because it does not represent a specific instance.[*] To declare objects of this class, we write

```
PersonnelRecord deb, dave, karen, jim, tom, denise, kaitlyn, krista, elyse;
```

Here, we have nine distinct objects, each of which takes up some amount of space in memory. None of these objects shares its space with any other object, although each of them has the same properties; thus their states have a common representation.

It is good engineering practice to encapsulate the state of an object rather than expose it as in the preceding declaration. For example, we might rewrite that class declaration as follows:

```
class PersonnelRecord {
public:
  char* employeeName() const;
  int   employeeSocialSecurityNumber() const;
  char* employeeDepartment() const;
protected:
  char  name[100];
  int   socialSecurityNumber;
  char  department[10];
  float salary;
};
```

_____

[*] To be precise, this declaration denotes a structure, a lower-level C++ record construct whose semantics are the same as a class with all public members. Structures thus denote unencapsulated abstractions.

This declaration is slightly more complicated than the previous one, but it is superior for a number of reasons.[*] Specifically, we have written this class so that its representation is hidden from all other outside clients. If we change its representation, we will have to recompile some code, but semantically, no outside client will be affected by this change (in other words, existing code will not break). Also, we have captured certain decisions about the problem space by explicitly stating some of the operations that clients may perform upon objects of this class. In particular, we grant all clients the right to retrieve the name, social security number, and department of an employee. Only special clients (namely, subclasses of this class) have permission to modify the values of these properties. Furthermore, only these special clients may modify or retrieve the salary of an employee, whereas outside clients may not. Another reason why this declaration is better than the previous one has to do with reuse. As we will see in a later section, inheritance makes it possible for us to reuse this abstraction, and then refine it or specialize it in a variety of ways.

We may say that all objects within a system encapsulate some state, and that all of the state within a system is encapsulated by objects. However, encapsulating the state of an object is a start, but is not enough to allow us to capture the full intent of the abstractions we discover and invent during development. For this reason, we must also consider how objects behave.

Behavior

The Meaning of Behavior No object exists in isolation. Rather, objects are acted upon, and themselves act upon other objects. Thus, we may say that

> *Behavior is how an object acts and reacts, in terms of its state changes and message passing.*

In other words, the behavior of an object represents its outwardly visible and testable activity.

An operation is some action that one object performs upon another in order to elicit a reaction. For example, a client might invoke the operations `append` and `pop` to grow and shrink a queue object, respectively. A client might also invoke the operation `length`, which returns a value denoting the size of the queue object but does not alter the state of the queue itself. In pure object-oriented languages such as Smalltalk, we speak of one object passing a

---

[*] An issue of style: the `PersonnelRecord` class as we've declared it here is not a tremendously high-quality class, according to the metrics we describe later in this chapter – this example only serves to illustrate the semantics of a class's state. Having a member function return a value of `char*` is often dangerous, because this violates a memory-safe paradigm: if the method creates storage for which the client does not take responsibility, garbage will result In production systems, we prefer to use a parameterized variable-length string class, as we might find in a foundation class library such as described in Chapter 9. Also, classes are more than just C **struct** declarations wrapped up in C++ class syntax; as we explain in Chapter 4, classification requires an deliberate focus upon common structure and behavior.

m   AD's
r bookmark

nguages such as C++, which derive from more
)eak of one object invoking the member function of
age is simply an operation that one object performs
.e underlying dispatch mechanisms are different. For
peration and *message* are interchangeable.

ted programming languages, operations that clients
oject are typically declared as *methods*, which are part
a. C++ uses the term *member function* to denote the
ise the these terms interchangeably.

one part of the equation that defines the behavior of an
or behavior also notes that the state of an object affects
Consider again the vending machine example. We may
on to make a selection, but the vending machine will
lepending upon its state. If we do not deposit change
.ection, then the machine will probably do nothing. If we
nange, the machine will take our change and then give us
:by altering its state). Thus, we may say that the behavior of
tion of its state as well as the operation performed upon it,
tions having the side effect of altering the object's state. This
fect thus leads us to refine our definition of state:

object represents the cumulative results of its behavior.

Most interesting objects do not have state that is static; rather, their state has
properties whose values are modified and retrieved as the object is acted upon.

Example Consider the following declaration of a queue class in C++:

```
class Queue {
public:

  Queue();
  Queue(const Queue&);
  virtual ~Queue();

  virtual Queue& operator=(const Queue&);
  virtual int operator==(const Queue&) const;
  int operator!=(const Queue&) const;

  virtual void clear();
  virtual void append(const void*);
  virtual void pop();
  virtual void remove(int at);

  virtual int length() const;
  virtual int isEmpty() const;
  virtual const void* front() const;
  virtual int location(const void*);

protected:
  ...
};
```

This class uses the common C idiom of setting and getting items via `void*`, which provides the abstraction of a heterogeneous queue, meaning that clients can append objects of any class to a queue object. This approach is not particularly type-safe, because the client must remember the class of the objects placed in the queue. Also, the use of `void*` prevents the `Queue` object from "owning" its items, meaning that we cannot rely upon the action of the queue's destructor (`~Queue()`) to destroy the elements in the queue. In a later section we will study parameterized types, which mitigate these problems.

Since the declaration `Queue` represents a class, not an object, we must declare instances that clients can manipulate:

```
Queue a, b, c, d;
```

Continuing, we may operate upon these objects as in the following code:

```
a.append(&deb);
a.append(&karen);
a.append(&denise);
b = a;
a.pop();
```

After executing these statements, the queue denoted by `a` contains two items (with a pointer to the `karen` record at its front), and the queue denoted by `b` contain three items (with the `deb` record at its front). In this manner, each of these queue objects embodies some distinct state, and this state affects the future behavior of each object. For example, we may safely pop `b` three more times, but `a` may be safely popped only two more times.

Operations An operation denotes a service that a class offers to its clients. In practice, we have found that a client typically performs five kinds of operations upon an object.[*] The three most common kinds of operations are the following:

- Modifier   An operation that alters the state of an object
- Selector   An operation that accesses the state of an object, but does not alter the state
- Iterator   An operation that permits all parts of an object to be accessed in some well-defined order

Because these operations are so logically dissimilar, we have found it useful to apply a coding style that highlights their differences. For example, in our declaration of the class `Queue`, we first declare all modifiers as non-const member functions (the operations `clear`, `append`, `pop`, and `remove`), followed by all selectors as const functions (the operations `length`, `isEmpty`, `front`, and `location`). As we will

---

[*] Lippman suggests a slightly different categorization: manager functions, implementor functions, helping functions (all kinds of modifiers), and access functions (equivalent to selectors) [7].

illustrate in Chapter 9, our style is to define a separate class that acts as the agent responsible for iterating across queues.

Two other kinds of operations are common; they represent the infrastructure necessary to create and destroy instances of a class:

- Constructor   An operation that creates an object and/or initializes its state
- Destructor   An operation that frees the state of an object and/or destroys the object itself

In C++, constructors and destructors are declared as part of the definition of a class (the members `Queue` and `~Queue`), whereas in Smalltalk and CLOS, such operations are typically part of the protocol of a metaclass (that is, the class of a class).

In pure object-oriented programming languages such as Smalltalk, operations may only be declared as methods, since the language does not allow us to declare procedures or functions separate from any class. In contrast, languages such as Object Pascal, C++, CLOS, and Ada allow the developer to write operations as free subprograms; in C++, these are called nonmember functions. *Free subprograms* are procedures or functions that serve as nonprimitive operations upon an object or objects of the same or different classes. Free subprograms are typically grouped according to the classes upon which they are built; therefore, we call such collections of free subprograms *class utilities*. For example, given the preceding declaration of the package `Queue`, we might write the following nonmember function:

```
void copyUntilFound(Queue& from, Queue& to, void* item)
{
  while ((!from.isEmpty()) && (from.front() != item)) {
    to.append(from.front());
    from.pop();
  }
}
```

The purpose of this operation is to repeatedly copy and then pop the contents of one queue until the given item is found at the front of the queue. This operation is not primitive; it can be built from lower-level operations that are already a part of the `Queue` class.

It is common style in C++ (and Smalltalk) to collect all logically related free subprograms and declare them as part of a class that has no state. In particular, in C++, these become static.

Thus, we may say that all methods are operations, but not all operations are methods: some operations may be expressed as free subprograms. In practice, we are inclined to declare most operations as methods, although as we discuss in a later section, there are sometimes compelling reasons to do otherwise, such as when a particular operation affects two or more objects of different classes, and there is no particular benefit in declaring that operation in one class over the other.

Roles and Responsibilities Collectively, all of the methods and free subprograms associated with a particular object comprise its *protocol*. The protocol of an object thus defines the envelope of an object's allowable behavior, and so comprises the entire static and dynamic view of the object. For most nontrivial abstractions, it is useful to divide this larger protocol into logical groupings of behavior. These collections, which thus partition the behavior space of an object, denote the *roles* that an object can play. As Adams suggests, a role is a mask that an object wears [8], and so defines a contract between an abstraction and its clients.

Unifying our definitions of state and behavior, Wirfs-Brock defines the *responsibilities* of an object to "include two key items: the knowledge an object maintains and the actions an object can perform. Responsibilities are meant to convey a sense of the purpose of an object and its place in the system. The responsibilities of an object are all the services it provides for all of the contracts it supports" [9]. In other words, we may say that the state and behavior of an object collectively define the roles that an object may play in the world, which in turn fulfill the abstraction's responsibilities.

Indeed, most interesting objects play many different roles during their lifetime; for example [10]:

- A bank account may be in good or bad standing, and which role it is in affects the semantics of a withdrawal transaction.
- To a trader, a share of stock represents an entity with value that may be bought or sold; to a lawyer, the same share denotes a legal instrument encompassing certain rights.
- In the course of one day, the same person may play the role of mother, doctor, gardener, and movie critic.

In the case of the bank account, the roles that this object can play are dynamic yet mutually exclusive: a bank account can be either in good or bad standing, but not both. In the case of the share of stock, its roles overlap slightly, but each role is static relative to the client that interacts with the share. In the case of the person, her roles are quite dynamic, and may change from moment to moment.

As we will discuss further in Chapters 4 and 6, we often start our analysis of a problem by examining the various roles that an object plays. During design, we refine these roles by inventing the particular operations that carry out each role's responsibilities.

Objects as Machines The existence of state within an object means that the order in which operations are invoked is important. This gives rise to the idea that each object is like a tiny, independent machine [11]. Indeed, for some objects, this event- and time-ordering of operations is so pervasive that we can best formally characterize the behavior of such objects in terms of an equivalent finite state machine. In Chapter 5, we will show a particular notation for hierarchical finite state machines that we may use for expressing these semantics.

Continuing the machine metaphor, we may classify objects as either active or passive. An *active object* is one that encompasses its own thread of control, whereas a *passive object* does not. Active objects are generally autonomous, meaning that they can exhibit some behavior without being operated upon by another object. Passive objects, on the other hand, can only undergo a state change when explicitly acted upon. In this manner, the active objects in our system serve as the roots of control. If our system involves multiple threads of control, then we will usually have multiple active objects. Sequential systems, on the other hand, usually have exactly one active object, such as a main window object responsible for managing an event loop that dispatches messages. In such architectures, all other objects are passive, and their behavior is ultimately triggered by messages from the one active object. In other kinds of sequential system architectures (such as transaction processing systems), there is no obvious central active object, and so control tends to be distributed throughout the system's passive objects.

Identity

Semantics Khoshafian and Copeland offer the following definition:

> *"Identity is that property of an object which distinguishes it from all other objects"* [12].

They go on to note that "most programming and database languages use variable names to distinguish temporary objects, mixing addressability and identity. Most database systems use identifier keys to distinguish persistent objects, mixing data value and identity." The failure to recognize the difference between the name of an object and the object itself is the source of many kinds of errors in object-oriented programming.

Example Consider the following declarations in C++. First, we start with a simple structure that denotes a point in space:

```
struct Point {
  int x;
  int y;
  Point() : x(0), y(0) {}
  Point(int xValue, int yValue) : x(xValue), y(yValue) {}
};
```

Here, we have chosen to declare Point as a structure, not as a full-blown class. The rule of thumb we apply to make this distinction is simple. If our abstraction represents a simple record of other objects and has no really interesting behavior that applies to the object as a whole, make it a structure. However, if our abstraction requires behavior more intense than just simple puts and gets of largely independent record items, then make it a class. In the case of our Point abstraction, we define a point as representing an (x, y) coordinate in space. For convenience, we provide one constructor that provides a default (0, 0) value, and another constructor that initializes a point with an explicit (x, y) value.

Next, we provide a class that denotes a display item. A display item is a common abstraction in all GUI-centric systems: it represents the base class of all objects that have a visual representation on some window, and so captures the structure and behavior common to all such objects. Here we have an abstraction that is more than just a simple record of data. Clients expect to be able to draw, select, and move display items, as well as query their selection state and location. We may capture our abstraction in the following C++ declaration:

```
class DisplayItem {
public:

  DisplayItem();
  DisplayItem(const Point& location);
  virtual ~DisplayItem();

  virtual void draw();
  virtual void erase();
  virtual void select();
  virtual void unselect();
  virtual void move(const Point& location);

  int isSelected() const;
  Point location() const;
  int isUnder(const Point& location) const;

protected:
  ...
};
```

This declaration is incomplete: we have intentionally omitted all of the constructors and operators needed to handle copying, assignment, and tests for equality. We will consider these aspects of our abstraction in the next section.

Because we expect clients to declare subclasses of this class, we have declared its destructor and all of its modifiers as virtual. In particular, we expect concrete subclasses to redefine draw to reflect the behavior of drawing domain-specific items in a window. We have not declared any of its selectors as virtual, because we do not expect subclasses to refine this behavior. Note also that the one selector isUnder involves more than just retrieving a simple state value. Here, the semantics of this operation require the object to calculate if the given point falls anywhere within the frame of the display item.

To declare instances of this class, we might write the following:

```
DisplayItem item1;
DisplayItem* item2 = new DisplayItem(Point(75, 75));;
DisplayItem* item3 = new DisplayItem(Point(100, 100));
DisplayItem* item4 = 0;
```

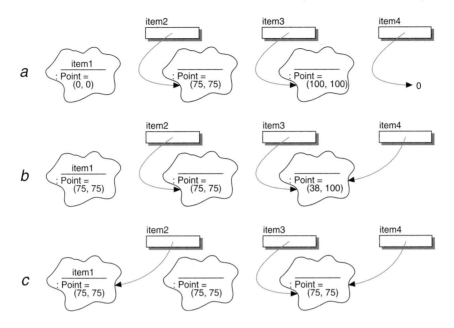

Figure 3-1
Object Identity

As Figure 3-1a shows, the elaboration of these declarations creates four names and three distinct objects. Specifically, elaboration sets aside four locations in memory whose names are item1, item2, item3, and item4, respectively. Also, item1 is the name of a distinct DisplayItem object, but the other three names each denote a *pointer* to a DisplayItem object. Only item2 and item3 actually point to distinct DisplayItem objects (because only their declarations allocate a new DisplayItem object); item4 designates no such object. Furthermore, the names of the objects pointed to by item2 and item3 are anonymous: we can only refer to these distinct objects indirectly, by dereferencing their pointer value. Thus, we may properly say that item2 points to a distinct DisplayItem object, whose name we may refer to indirectly as *item2. The unique identity (but not necessarily the name) of each object is preserved over the lifetime of the object, even when its state is changed. This is like the Zen question about a river: is a river the same river from one day to the next, even though the same water never flows through it? For example, consider the results of executing the following statements:

```
item1.move(item3->location());
item4 = item3;
item4->move(Point(38, 100));
```

Figure 3-1b illustrates these results. Here we see that item1 and the object designated by item2 both have the same location state, and that item4 now also designates the same object as does item3. Notice that we use the phrase "the object designated by `item2`" rather than saying "the object `item2`." The first phrase is more precise, although we will sometimes use these phrases interchangeably.

Although `item1` and the object designated by `item2` have the same state, they represent distinct objects. Also, note that we have changed the state of the object designated by `item3` by operating upon it through its new indirect name, `item4`. This is a situation we call *structural sharing*, meaning that a given object can be named in more than one way; in other words, there are aliases to the object. Structural sharing is the source of many problems in object-oriented programming. Failure to recognize the side effects of operating upon an object through aliases often leads to memory leaks, memory-access violations, and, even worse, unexpected state changes. For example, if we destroyed the object designated by `item3` using the expression `delete item3`, then `item4`'s pointer value would be meaningless: this is a situation we call a *dangling reference*.

Consider also Figure 3-1c, which illustrates the results of executing the following statements:

```
item2 = &item1;
item4->move(item2->location());
```

The first statement introduces an alias, for now `item2` designates the same object as `item1`; the second statement accesses the state of `item1` through the new alias. Unfortunately, we have introduced a memory leak: the object originally designated by `item2` can no longer be named, either directly or indirectly, and so its identity is lost. In languages such as Smalltalk and CLOS, such objects will be garbage-collected and their storage reclaimed automatically, but in languages such as C++, their storage will not be reclaimed until the program that created them finishes. Especially for long-running programs, memory leaks such as this are either bothersome or disastrous.[*]

Copying, Assignment, and Equality Structural sharing takes place when the identity of an object is aliased to a second name. In most interesting object-oriented applications, using aliases simply cannot be avoided. For example, consider the following two function declarations in C++:

```
void highlight(DisplayItem& i);
void drag(DisplayItem i);        // Dangerous
```

Invoking the first function with the argument `item1` creates an alias: the formal parameter `i` denotes a reference to the object designated by the actual parameter, and hence `item1` and `i` will name the same object at execution time. On the other hand, invoking the second function with the argument `item1` makes a copy of the actual parameter, and so there is no alias: `i` denotes a

---

[*] Consider the effects of a memory leak in software controlling a satellite or a pacemaker. Restarting the computer in a satellite several million miles away from earth is quite inconvenient. Similarly, the unpredictable occurrence of automatic garbage collection in a pacemaker's software is likely to be fatal. For these reasons, real-time system developers often steer away from the unrestrained allocation of objects on the heap.

completely different object (but with the same state) as does item1. In languages such as C++ where there is a distinction between passing arguments by reference versus by value, care must be taken to avoid operating upon a copy of an object, when the intent was to operate upon the original object itself.[*] Indeed, as we will discuss in a later section, passing objects by reference in C++ is essential to eliciting polymorphic behavior. In general, passing objects by reference is the most desirable practice for nonprimitive objects, for its semantics only involve copying references, not state, and hence is far more efficient for passing anything larger than simple values.

In some circumstances, however, copying is the intended semantics, and in languages such as C++, it is possible to control the semantics of copying. In particular, we may introduce a copy constructor to a class's declaration, as in the following code fragment, which we would declare as part of the declaration for DisplayItem:

```
DisplayItem(const DisplayItem&);
```

In C++, a copy constructor may be invoked either explicitly (as part of the declaration of an object) or implicitly (as when passing an object by value). Omitting this special constructor invokes the default copy constructor, whose semantics are defined as a memberwise copy. However, for objects whose state itself involves pointers or references to other objects, default memberwise copying is usually dangerous, for copying then implicitly introduces lower-level aliases. The rule of thumb we apply, therefore, is that we omit an explicit copy constructor only for those abstractions whose state consists of simple, primitive values; in all other cases, we usually provide an explicit copy constructor.

This practice distinguishes what some languages call *shallow* versus *deep* copying. Smalltalk, for example, provides the methods shallowCopy (which copies the object, but shares its state) and deepCopy (which copies the object as well as its state, and recursively so). Redefining these operations for aggregate classes permits a mixture of semantics: copying a higher-level object might copy most of its state, but introduce aliases for certain other lower-level elements.

Assignment is also generally a copying operation, and in languages such as C++, its semantics can be controlled as well. For example, we might add the following declaration to our declaration of DisplayItem:

```
virtual DisplayItem& operator=(const DisplayItem&);
```

We declare this operator as virtual, because we expect a subclass to redefine its behavior. As with the copy constructor, we may implement this operation to provide either shallow or deep copy semantics. Omitting this explicit declaration invokes the default assignment operator, whose semantics are defined as a memberwise copy.

Closely related to the issue of assignment is that of equality. Although it seems like a simple concept, equality can mean one of two things. First,

---

[*] In Smalltalk, the semantics of passing objects as arguments to methods is the moral equivalent to C++'s passing of arguments by reference.

equality can mean that two names designate the same object. Second, equality can mean that two names designate distinct objects whose states are equal. For example, in Figure 3-1c, both kinds of equality evaluate to true between item1 and item2. However, only the second kind of equality evaluates to true between item1 and item3.

In C++, these is no default equality operator, thus we must establish our own semantics by introducing the explicit operators for equality and inequality as part of the declaration for DisplayItem:

```
virtual int operator==(const DisplayItem&) const;
int operator!=(const DisplayItem&) const;
```

Our style is to declare the equality operator as virtual (because we expect subclasses to redefine its behavior) and to declare the inequality operator as nonvirtual (we always want inequality to mean the logical negation of equality: subclasses should not override this behavior).

In a similar manner, we may explicitly define the meaning of ordering operators, such as tests for less-than or greater-than orderings between two objects.

Object Life Span The lifetime of an object extends from the time it is first created (and thus first consumes space) until that space is reclaimed. To explicitly create an object, we must either declare it or allocate it.

Declaring an object (such as item1 in our earlier example) creates a new instance on the stack. Allocating an object (such as item3) creates a new instance on the heap. In C++, in either case, whenever an object is created, its constructor is automatically invoked, whose purpose is to allocate space for the object and establish an initial stable state. In languages such as Smalltalk, such constructor operations are actually a part of the object's metaclass, not the object's class – we will examine metaclass semantics later in this chapter.

Often, objects are created implicitly. For example, in C++ passing an object by value creates a new object on the stack that is a copy of the actual parameter. Furthermore, object creation is transitive: creating an aggregate object also creates any objects that are physically a part of the whole. Overriding the semantics of the copy constructor and assignment operator in C++ permits explicit control over when such parts are created and destroyed. Also, in C++ it is possible to redefine the semantics of the new operator (which allocates instances on the heap), so that each class can provide its own memory management policy.

In languages such as Smalltalk, an object is destroyed automatically as part of garbage collection when all references to it have been lost. In languages without garbage collection, such as C++, an object continues to exist and consume space even if all references to it are lost. Objects created on the stack are implicitly destroyed whenever control passes beyond the block in which the object was declared. Objects created on the heap with the new operator must be explicitly destroyed with the **delete** operator. Failure do to so leads to memory leaks, as we discussed earlier. Deallocating an object twice (usually because of an alias) is equally bad, and may manifest itself in memory corruption or a complete crash of the system.

In C++, whenever an object is destroyed either implicitly or explicitly, its destructor is automatically invoked, whose purpose is to deallocate space assigned to the object and its part, and to otherwise clean up after the object (such as, for example, closing files and releasing resources).*

Persistent objects have slightly different semantics regarding destruction. As we discussed in the previous chapter, certain objects may be persistent, meaning that their lifetime transcends the lifetime of the program that created them. Persistent objects are usually elements of some larger, object-oriented database framework, and so the semantics of destruction (and also creation) are largely a function of the policies of the particular database system. In such systems, the most common approach to providing persistence is the use of a persistent mixin class. All objects for which we desire persistence semantics thus have this mixin class as a superclass somewhere in their class's inheritance lattice.

3.2 Relationships Among Objects

Kinds of Relationships

An object by itself is intensely uninteresting. Objects contribute to the behavior of a system by collaborating with one another. As Ingalls suggests, "Instead of a bit-grinding processor raping and plundering data structures, we have a universe of well-behaved objects that courteously ask each other to carry out their various desires" [13]. For example, consider the object structure of an airplane, which has been defined as "a collection of parts having an inherent tendency to fall to earth, and requiring constant effort and supervision to stave off that outcome" [14]. Only the collaborative efforts of all the component objects of an airplane enable it to fly.

The relationship between any two objects encompasses the assumptions that each makes about the other, including what operations can be performed and what behavior results. We have found that two kinds of object hierarchies are of particular interest in object-oriented analysis and design, namely:

- Links
- Aggregation

Seidewitz and Stark call these *seniority* and *parent/child* relationships, respectively [15].

---

* Destructors do not automatically reclaim space allocated by the new operator; programmers must explicitly reclaim this space as part of destruction.

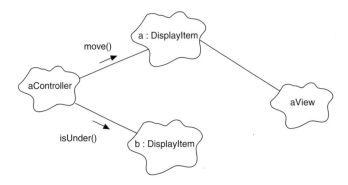

Figure 3-2
Links

Links

Semantics The term *link* derives from Rumbaugh, who defines it as a "physical or conceptual connection between objects" [16]. An object collaborates with other objects through its links to these objects. Stated another way, a link denotes the specific association through which one object (the client) applies the services of another object (the supplier), or through which one object may navigate to another.

Figure 3-2 illustrates several different links. In this figure, a line between two object icons represents the existence of a link between the two and means that messages may pass along this path. Messages are shown as directed lines representing the direction of the message, with a label naming the message itself. For example, here we see that the object aController has links to two instances of DisplayItem (the objects a and b). Although both a and b probably have links to the view in which they are shown, we have chosen to highlight only once such link, from a to aView. Only across these links may one object send messages to another.

Message passing between two objects is typically unidirectional, although it may occasionally be bidirectional. In our example, the object aController only invokes operations upon the two display objects (to move them and query their location), but the display objects do not themselves operate upon the controller object. This separation of concerns is quite common in well-structured object-oriented systems, as we discuss in Chapter 5.* Notice also that although message passing is initiated by the client (such as aController) and is directed toward the supplier (such as object a), data may flow in either direction across a link. For example, when aController invokes the operation move upon a, data

---

* In fact, this organization of controller, view, and display item object is so common, we can identify it as a design pattern, which we can then reuse. In Smalltalk, this is called an *MVC mechanism*, for model/view/controller. As we discuss in the next chapter, well-structured object-oriented system usually have many such identifiable patterns.

flows from the client to the supplier. However, when aController invokes the operation isUnder upon object b, the result passes from the supplier to the client.

As a participant in a link, an object may play one of three roles:

- Actor   An object that can operate upon other objects but is never operated upon by other objects; in some contexts, the terms *active object* and *actor* are interchangeable

- Server   An object that never operates upon other objects; it is only operated upon by other objects

- Agent   An object that can both operate upon other objects and be operated upon by other objects; an agent is usually created to do some work on behalf of an actor or another agent

Restricted to the context of Figure 3-2, aController represents an actor object, aView represents a server object, and a represents an agent that carries out the controller's request to draw the item in the view.

Example In many different kinds of industrial processes, certain reactions require a temperature ramp, wherein we raise the temperature of some substance, hold it at that temperature for a fixed period, and then let it cool to ambient temperature. Different processes require different profiles: some objects (such as telescope mirrors) must be cooled slowly, whereas other materials (such as steel) must be cooled rapidly. This abstraction of a temperature ramp has a sufficiently well-defined behavior that it warrants the creation of a class, such as the following. First, we introduce a typedef whose values represent elapsed time in minutes:

```
// Number denoting elapsed minutes
typedef unsigned int Minute;
```

This typedef is similar to that for Day and Hour, which we introduced in Chapter 2. Next, we provide the class TemperatureRamp, which is conceptually a time/temperature mapping:

```
class TemperatureRamp {
public:

  TemperatureRamp();
  virtual ~TemperatureRamp();

  virtual void clear();
  virtual void bind(Temperature, Minute);

  Temperature temperatureAt(Minute);

protected:
  ...
};
```

In keeping with our style, we have declared a number of operations as virtual, because we expect there to be subclasses of this class.

Actually, the behavior of this abstraction is more than just a literal time/temperature mapping. For example, we might set a temperature ramp that requires the temperature to be 250° F at time 60 (one hour into the temperature ramp) and 150° F at time 180 (three hours into the process), but then we would like to know what the temperature should be at time 120. This requires linear interpolation, which is therefore another behavior we expect of this abstraction.

One behavior we explicitly do not require of this abstraction is the control of a heater to carry out a particular temperature ramp. Rather, we prefer a greater separation of concerns, wherein this behavior is achieved through the collaboration of three objects: a temperature ramp instance, a heater, and a temperature controller. For example, we might introduce the following class:

```
class TemperatureController {
public:

  TemperatureController(Location);
  ~TemperatureController();

  void process(const TemperatureRamp&);

  Minute schedule(const TemperatureRamp&) const;

private:
  ...
};
```

This class uses the typedef Location introduced in Chapter 2. Notice that we do not expect there to be any subclasses of this class, and so have not made any of its operations virtual.

The operation process provides the central behavior of this abstraction; its purpose is to carry out the given temperature ramp for the heater at the given location. For example, given the following declarations:

```
TemperatureRamp growingRamp;
TemperatureController rampController(7);
```

We might then establish a particular temperature ramp, then tell the controller to carry out this profile:

```
growingRamp.bind(250, 60);
growingRamp.bind(150, 180);

rampController.process(growingRamp);
```

Consider the relationship between the objects growingRamp and rampController: the object rampController is an agent responsible for carrying out a temperature ramp, and so uses the object growingRamp as a server. This link manifests itself in the fact that the object rampController uses the object growingPlan as an argument to one of its operations.

A comment regarding our style: at first glance, it may appear that we have devised an abstraction whose sole purpose is to wrap a functional decomposition inside a class to make it appear noble and object-oriented. The operation `schedule` suggests that this is not the case. Objects of the class `TemperatureController` have sufficient knowledge to determine when a particular profile should be scheduled, and so we expose this operation as an additional behavior of our abstraction In some high-energy industrial processes (such as steel making), heating a substance is a costly event, and it is important to take into account any lingering heat from a previous process, as well as the normal cool-down of an unattended heater. The operation `schedule` exists so that clients can query a `TemperatureController` object to determine the next optimal time to process a particular temperature ramp.

Visibility Consider two objects, A and B, with a link between the two. In order for A to send a message to B, B must be visible to A in some manner. During our analysis of a problem, we can largely ignore issues of visibility, but once we begin to devise concrete implementations, we must consider the visibility across links, because our decisions here dictate the scope and access of the objects on each side of a link.

In the previous example, the object `rampController` has visibility to the object `growingRamp`, because both objects are declared within the same scope, and `growingRamp` is presented as an argument to an operation upon the object `rampController`. Actually, this is just one of the four different ways that one object may have visibility to another:

- The supplier object is global to the client.
- The supplier object is a parameter to some operation of the client.
- The supplier object is a part of the client object.
- The supplier object is a locally declared object in some operation of the client.

How one object is made visible to another is a tactical design issue.

Synchronization Whenever one object passes a message to another across a link, the two objects are said to be *synchronized*. For objects in a completely sequential application, this synchronization is usually accomplished by simple method invocation, as described in the sidebar. However, in the presence of multiple threads of control, objects require more sophisticated message passing in order to deal with the problems of mutual exclusion that can occur in concurrent systems. As we described earlier, active objects embody their own thread of control, and so we expect their semantics to be guaranteed in the presence of other active objects. However, when one active object has a link to a passive one, we must choose one of three approaches to synchronization:

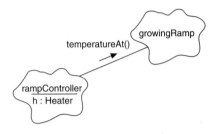

Figure 3-3
Aggregation

- Sequential   The semantics of the passive object are
                    guaranteed only in the presence of a single
                    active object at a time.

- Guarded   The semantics of the passive object are
                    guaranteed in the presence of multiple
                    threads of control, but the active clients must
                    collaborate to achieve mutual exclusion.

- Synchronous   The semantics of the passive object are
                    guaranteed in the presence of multiple
                    threads of control, and the supplier guarantees
                    mutual exclusion.

All the objects described thus far in this chapter are sequential. In Chapter 9, we will illustrate each of these other forms in greater detail.

Aggregation

Semantics Whereas links denote peer-to-peer or client/supplier relationships, aggregation denotes a whole/part hierarchy, with the ability to navigate from the whole (also called the *aggregate*) to its parts (also known as its *attributes*). In this sense, aggregation is a specialized kind of association. For example, as shown in Figure 3-3, the object rampController has a link to the object growingRamp as well as an attribute h whose class is Heater. The object rampController is thus the whole, and h is one of its parts. In other words, h is a part of the state of the object rampController. Given the object rampController, it is possible to find its corresponding heater h. Given an object such as h, it is possible to navigate to its enclosing object (also called its *container*) if and only if this knowledge is a part of the state of h.

Aggregation may or may not denote physical containment. For example, an airplane is composed of wings, engines, landing gear, and so on: this is a case of physical containment. On the other hand, the relationship between a shareholder and her shares is an aggregation relationship that does not require physical containment. The shareholder uniquely owns shares, but the shares are by no means a physical part of the shareholder. Rather, this whole/part relationship is more conceptual and therefore less direct than the physical aggregation of the parts that form an airplane.

There are clear trade-offs between links and aggregation. Aggregation is sometimes better because it encapsulates parts as secrets of the whole. Links are sometimes better because they permit looser coupling among objects. Intelligent engineering decisions require careful weighing of these two factors.

By implication, an object that is an attribute of another has a link to its aggregate. Across this link, the aggregate may send messages to its parts.

Example   To continue our declaration of the class `TemperatureController`, we might complete its private part as follows:

```
Heater h;
```

This declares `h` as a part of each instance of `TemperatureController`. According to our declaration of the class `Heater` in the previous chapter, we must properly create this attribute, because its class does not provide a default constructor. Thus, we might write the constructor for the `TemperatureController` as follows:

```
TemperatureController::TemperatureController(Location l)
  : h(l) {}
```

3.3 The Nature of a Class

What Is and What Isn't a Class

The concepts of a class and an object are tightly interwoven, for we cannot talk about an object without regard for its class. However, there are important differences between these two terms. Whereas an object is a concrete entity that exists in time and space, a class represents only an abstraction, the "essence" of an object, as it were. Thus, we may speak of the class `Mammal`, which represents the characteristics common to all mammals. To identify a particular mammal in this class, we must speak of "this mammal" or "that mammal."

In everyday terms, we may define a class as "a group, set, or kind marked by common attributes or a common attribute; a group division, distinction, or rating based on quality, degree of competence, or condition" [17].[*] In the context of object-oriented analysis and design, we define a class as follows:

A class is a set of objects that share a common structure and a common behavior.

A single object is simply an instance of a class.

---

[*] By permission. From *Webster's Third New International Dictionary* © 1986 by Merriam-Webster Inc., publisher of the Merriam-Webster ® dictionaries.

A class represents a set of objects that share a common structure and a common behavior.

What isn't a class? An object is not a class, although, curiously, as we will describe later, a class may be an object. Objects that share no common structure and behavior cannot be grouped in a class because, by definition, they are unrelated except by their general nature as objects.

It is important to note that the class – as defined by most programming languages – is a necessary but insufficient vehicle for decomposition. Sometimes abstractions are so complex that they cannot be conveniently expressed in terms of a single class declaration. For example, at a sufficiently high level of abstraction, a GUI framework, a database, and an entire inventory system are all conceptually individual objects, none of which can be expressed as a single class.[*] Instead, it is far better for us to capture these abstractions as a cluster of classes whose instances collaborate to provide the desired structure and behavior. Stroustrup calls such a cluster a *component* [18]. For reasons that we will explain in Chapter 5, we call each such cluster a *class category*.

---

[*] One might be tempted to express such abstractions in a single class, but the granularity of reuse and change is all wrong. Having a fat interface is bad practice, because most clients will want to reference only a small subset of the services provided. Furthermore, changing one part of a huge interface obsolesces every client, even those that don't care about the parts that changed. Nesting classes doesn't eliminate these problems; it only defers them.

Interface and Implementation

Meyer [19] and Snyder [20] have both suggested that programming is largely a matter of "contracting": the various functions of a larger problem are decomposed into smaller problems by subcontracting them to different elements of the design. Nowhere is this idea more evident than in the design of classes.

Whereas an individual object is a concrete entity that performs some role in the overall system, the class captures the structure and behavior common to all related objects. Thus, a class serves as a sort of binding contract between an abstraction and all of its clients. By capturing these decisions in the interface of a class, a strongly typed programming language can detect violations of this contract during compilation.

This view of programming as contracting leads us to distinguish between the outside view and the inside view of a class. The *interface* of a class provides its outside view and therefore emphasizes the abstraction while hiding its structure and the secrets of its behavior. This interface primarily consists of the declarations of all the operations applicable to instances of this class, but it may also include the declaration of other classes, constants, variables, and exceptions as needed to complete the abstraction. By contrast, the *implementation* of a class is its inside view, which encompasses the secrets of its behavior. The implementation of a class primarily consists of the implementation of all of the operations defined in the interface of the class.

We can further divide the interface of a class into three parts:

- Public   A declaration that is accessible to all clients
- Protected   A declaration that is accessible only to the
                    class itself, its subclasses, and its friends
- Private   A declaration that is accessible only to the
                    class itself and its friends

Different programming languages provide different mixtures of public, protected, and private parts, which developers can choose among to establish specific access rights for each part of a class's interface and thereby exercise control over what clients can see and what they can't see.

In particular, C++ allows a developer to make explicit distinctions among all three of these different parts.[*] The C++ friendship mechanism permits a class to distinguish certain privileged classes that are given the rights to see the class's protected and private parts. Friendships break a class's encapsulation, and so, as in life, must be chosen carefully. By contrast, Ada permits declarations to be public or private, but not protected. In Smalltalk, all instance variables are private, and all methods are public. In Object Pascal, both fields and operations are public and hence unencapsulated. In CLOS, generic

---

[*] The C++ **struct** is a special case, in the sense that a **struct** is a kind of class with all of its elements public.

functions are public, and slots may be made private, although their access can be broken via the function slot-value.

The state of an object must have some representation in its corresponding class, and so is typically expressed as constant and variable declarations placed in the protected or private part of a class's interface. In this manner, the representation common to all instances of a class is encapsulated, and changes to this representation do not functionally affect any outside clients.

The careful reader may wonder why the representation of an object is part of the interface of a class (albeit a nonpublic part), not of its implementation. The reason is one of practicality; to do otherwise requires either object-oriented hardware or very sophisticated compiler technology. Specifically, when a compiler processes an object declaration such as the following in C++:

```
DisplayItem item1;
```

it must know how much memory to allocate to the object item1. If we defined the representation of an object in the implementation of a class, we would have to complete the class's implementation before we could use any clients, thus defeating the very purpose of separating the class's outside and inside views.

The constants and variables that form the representation of a class are known by various terms, depending upon the particular language we use. For example, Smalltalk uses the term *instance variable*, Object Pascal uses the term *field*, C++ uses the term *member object*, and CLOS uses the term *slot*. We will use these terms interchangeably to denote the parts of a class that serve as the representation of its instance's state.

Class Life Cycle

We may come to understand the behavior of a simple class just by understanding the semantics of its distinct public operations in isolation. However, the behavior of more interesting classes (such as moving an instance of the class DisplayItem, or scheduling an instance of the class TemperatureController) involves the interaction of their various operations over the lifetime of each of their instances. As described earlier in this chapter, the instances of such classes act as little machines, and since all such instances embody the same behavior, we can use the class to capture these common event- and time-ordered semantics. As we discuss in Chapter 5, we may describe such dynamic behavior for certain interesting classes by using finite state machines.

3.4 Relationships Among Classes

Kinds of Relationships

Consider for a moment the similarities and differences among the following classes of objects: flowers, daisies, red roses, yellow roses, petals, and ladybugs. We can make the following observations:

- A daisy is a kind of flower.
- A rose is a (different) kind of flower.
- Red roses and yellow roses are both kinds of roses.
- A petal is a part of both kinds of flowers.
- Ladybugs eat certain pests such as aphids, which may be infesting certain kinds of flowers.

From this simple example we conclude that classes, like objects, do not exist in isolation. Rather, for a particular problem domain, the key abstractions are usually related in a variety of interesting ways, forming the class structure of our design [21].

We establish relationships between two classes for one of two reasons. First, a class relationship might indicate some sort of sharing. For example, daisies and roses are both kinds of flowers, meaning that both have brightly colored petals, both emit a fragrance, and so on. Second, a class relationship might indicate some kind of semantic connection. Thus, we say that red roses and yellow roses are more alike than are daisies and roses, and daisies and roses are more closely related than are petals and flowers. Similarly, there is a symbiotic connection between ladybugs and flowers: ladybugs protect flowers from certain pests, which in turn serve as a food source for the ladybug.

In all, there are three basic kinds of class relationships [22]. The first of these is generalization/specialization, denoting an "is a" relationship. For instance, a rose is a kind of flower, meaning that a rose is a specialized subclass of the more general class, flower. The second is whole/part, which denotes a "part of" relationship. Thus, a petal is not a kind of a flower; it is a part of a flower. The third is association, which denotes some semantic dependency among otherwise unrelated classes, such as between ladybugs and flowers. As another example, roses and candles are largely independent classes, but they both represent things that we might use to decorate a dinner table.

Several common approaches have evolved in programming languages to capture generalization/specialization, whole/part, and association relationships. Specifically, most object-oriented languages provide direct support for some combination of the following relationships:

- Association
- Inheritance
- Aggregation
- Using
- Instantiation
- Metaclass

An alternate approach to inheritance involves a language mechanism called *delegation*, in which objects are viewed as prototypes (also called *exemplars*) that delegate their behavior to related objects, thus eliminating the need for classes [23].

Of these six different kinds of class relationships, associations are the most general but also the most semantically weak. As we will discuss further in Chapter 6, the identification of associations among classes is often an activity of analysis and early design, at which time we begin to discover the general dependencies among our abstractions. As we continue our design and implementation, we will often refine these weak associations by turning them into one of the other more concrete class relationships.

Inheritance is perhaps the most semantically interesting of these concrete relationships, and exists to express generalization/specialization relationships. In our experience, however, inheritance is an insufficient means of expressing all of the rich relationships that may exist among the key abstractions in a given problem domain. We also need aggregation relationships, which provide the whole/part relationships manifested in the class's instances. Additionally, we need using relationships, which establish the links among the class's instances. For languages such as Ada, C++, and Eiffel, we also need instantiation relationships, which, like inheritance, support a kind of generalization, although in an entirely different way. Metaclass relationships are quite different and are only explicitly supported by languages such as Smalltalk and CLOS. Basically, a metaclass is the class of a class, a concept that allows us to treat classes as objects.

Association

Example In an automated system for retail point of sale, two of our key abstractions include products and sales. As shown in Figure 3-4, we may show a simple association between these two classes: the class `Product` denotes the products sold as part of a sale, and the class `Sale` denotes the transaction through which several products were last sold. By implication, this association suggests bidirectional navigation: given an instance of `Product`, we should be able to locate the object denoting its sale, and given an instance of `Sale`, we should be able to locate all the products sold during the transaction.

We may capture these semantics in C++ by using what Rumbaugh calls *buried pointers* [24]. For example, consider the highly elided declaration of these two classes:

```
class Product;
class Sale;

class Product {
public:
  ...
protected:
  Sale* lastSale;
};
```

Figure 3-4
Association

```
class Sale {
public:
  ...
protected:
  Product** productSold;
};
```

Here we show a one-to-many association: each instance of `Product` may have a pointer to its last sale, and each instance of `Sale` may have a collection of pointers denoting the products sold.

Semantic Dependencies As this example suggests, an association only denotes a semantic dependency and does not state the direction of this dependency (unless otherwise stated, an association implies bidirectional navigation, as in our example), nor does it state the exact way in which one class relates to another (we can only imply these semantics by naming the role each class plays in relationship with the other). However, these semantics are sufficient during the analysis of a problem, at which time we need only to identify such dependencies. Through the creation of associations, we come to capture the participants in a semantic relationship, their roles, and, as we will discuss, their cardinality.

Cardinality Our example introduced a one-to-many association, meaning that for each instance of the class `Sale`, there are zero or more instances of the class `Product`, and for each product, there is exactly one sale. This multiplicity denotes the *cardinality* of the association. In practice, there are three common kinds of cardinality across an association:

- One-to-one
- One-to-many
- Many-to-many

A one-to-one relationship denotes a very narrow association. For example, in retail telemarketing operations, we would find a one-to-one relationship between the class `Sale` and the class `CreditCardTransaction`: each sale has exactly one corresponding credit card transaction, and each such transaction corresponds to one sale. Many-to-many relationships are also common. For example, each instance of the class `Customer` might initiate a transaction with an instance of the class `SalesPerson`, and each such salesperson might interact with many different customers. As we will discuss further in Chapter 5, there are variations upon these three basic forms of cardinality.

Inheritance

Examples After space probes are launched, they report back to ground stations with information regarding the status of important subsystems (such as electrical power and propulsion systems) and different sensors (such as radiation sensors, mass spectrometers, cameras, micro meteorite collision detectors, and so on). Collectively, this relayed information is called *telemetry data.* Telemetry data is commonly transmitted as a bit stream consisting of a header, which includes a time stamp and some keys identifying the kind of information that follows, plus several frames of processed data from the various subsystems and sensors. Because this appears to be a straightforward aggregation of different kinds of data, we might be tempted to define a record type for each kind of telemetry data. For example, in C++, we might write

```
class Time...

struct ElectricalData {
  Time  timeStamp;
  int   id;
  float fuelCell1Voltage, fuelCell2Voltage;
  float fuelCell1Amperes, fuelCell2Amperes;
  float currentPower;
};
```

There are a number of problems with this declaration. First, the representation of ElectricalData is completely unencapsulated. Thus, there is nothing to prevent a client from changing the value of important data such as the timeStamp or currentPower (which is a derived attribute, directly proportional to the current voltage and amperes drawn from both fuel cells). Furthermore, the representation of this structure is exposed, so if we were to change the representation (for example, by adding new elements or changing the bit alignment of existing ones), every client would be affected. At the very least, we would certainly have to recompile every reference to this structure. More importantly, such changes might violate the assumptions that clients had made about this exposed representation and cause the logic in our program to break. Also, this structure is largely devoid of meaning: a number of operations are applicable to instances of this structure as a whole (such as transmitting the data, or calculating a check sum to detect errors during transmission), but there is no way to directly associate these operations with this structure. Lastly, suppose our analysis of the system's requirements reveals the need for several hundred different kinds of telemetry data, including other electrical data that encompassed the preceding information and also included voltage readings from various test points throughout the system. We would find that declaring these additional structures would create a considerable amount of redundancy, both in terms of replicated structures and common functions.

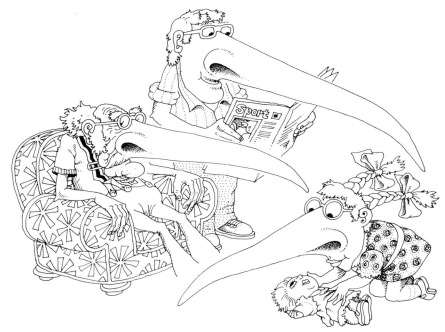

A subclass may inherit the structure and behavior of its superclass.

A slightly better way to capture our decisions would be to declare one class for each kind of telemetry data. In this manner, we could hide the representation of each class and associate its behavior with its data. Still, this approach does not address the problem of redundancy.

A far better solution, therefore, is to capture our decisions by building a hierarchy of classes, in which specialized classes inherit the structure and behavior defined by more generalized classes. For example:

```
class TelemetryData {
public:

  TelemetryData();
  virtual ~TelemetryData();

  virtual void transmit();

  Time currentTime() const;

protected:
  int id;
  Time timeStamp;
};
```

This declares a class with a constructor and a virtual destructor (meaning that we expect to have subclasses), as well as the functions transmit and currentTime, which are both visible to all clients. The protected member objects id and timeStamp are slightly more encapsulated, and so are accessible only to the class itself and its subclasses. Note that we have declared the function `currentTime` as a public selector, which makes it possible for a client to access the `timeStamp`, but not change it.

Next, let's rewrite our declaration of the class `ElectricalData`:

```
class ElectricalData : public TelemetryData {
public:

  ElectricalData(float v1, float v2, float a1, float a2);
  virtual ~ElectricalData();

  virtual void transmit();

  float currentPower() const;

protected:
  float fuelCell1Voltage, fuelCell2Voltage;
  float fuelCell1Amperes, fuelCell2Amperes;
};
```

This class inherits the structure and behavior of the class `TelemetryData`, but adds to its structure (the four new protected member objects), redefines its behavior (the function `transmit`), and adds to its behavior (the function `currentPower`).

Single Inheritance Simply stated, inheritance is a relationship among classes wherein one class shares the structure and/or behavior defined in one (*single inheritance*) or more (*multiple inheritance*) other classes. We call the class from which another class inherits its *superclass*. In our example, `TelemetryData` is a superclass of `ElectricalData`. Similarly, we call a class that inherits from one or more classes a *subclass*; `ElectricalData` is a subclass of `TelemetryData`. Inheritance therefore defines an "is a" hierarchy among classes, in which a subclass inherits from one or more superclasses. This is in fact the litmus test for inheritance. given classes A and B, if A "is not a" kind of B, then A should not be a subclass of B. In this sense, `ElectricalData` is a specialized kind of the more generalized class `TelemetryData`. The ability of a language to support this kind of inheritance distinguishes object-oriented from object-based programming languages.

A subclass typically augments or restricts the existing structure and behavior of its superclasses. A subclass that augments its superclasses is said to use inheritance for extension. For example, the subclass `GuardedQueue` might extend the behavior of its superclass `Queue` by providing extra operations that make instances of this class safe in the presence of multiple threads of control. In contrast, a subclass that constrains the behavior of its superclasses is said to use inheritance for restriction. For example, the subclass `UnselectableDisplayItem` might constrain the behavior of its superclass, `DisplayItem`, by prohibiting clients from selecting its instances in a view. In practice, it is not always so clear whether or not a subclass augments or restricts its superclass; in fact, it is common for a subclass to do both.

Figure 3-5 illustrates the single inheritance relationships deriving from the superclass `TelemetryData`. Each directed line denotes an "is a" relationship. For example, `CameraData` "is a" kind of `SensorData`, which in turn "is a" kind of

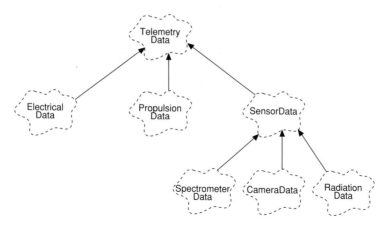

Figure 3-5
Single Inheritance

TelemetryData. This is identical to the hierarchy one finds in a semantic net, a tool often used by researchers in cognitive science and artificial intelligence to organize knowledge about the world [25]. Indeed, as we discuss further in Chapter 4, designing a suitable inheritance hierarchy among abstractions is largely a matter of intelligent classification.

We expect that some of the classes in Figure 3-5 will have instances and some will not. For example, we expect to have instances of each of the most specialized classes (also known as *leaf classes* or *concrete classes*), such as ElectricalData and SpectrometerData. However, we are not likely to have any instances of the intermediate, more generalized classes, such as SensorData or even TelemetryData. Classes with no instances are called *abstract classes.* An abstract class is written with the expectation that its subclasses will add to its structure and behavior, usually by completing the implementation of its (typically) incomplete methods. In fact, in Smalltalk, a developer may force a subclass to redefine the method introduced in an abstract class by using the method subclassResponsibility to implement a body for the abstract class's method. If the subclass fails to redefine it, then invoking the method results in an execution error. C++ similarly allows the developer to assert that an abstract class's method cannot be invoked directly by initializing its declaration to zero. Such a method is called a *pure virtual function,* and the language prohibits the creation of instances whose class exports such functions.

The most generalized class in a class structure is called the *base class.* Most applications have many such base classes, which represent the most generalized categories of abstractions within the given domain. In fact, especially in C++, well-structured object-oriented architectures generally have forests of inheritance trees, rather than one deeply rooted inheritance lattice. However, some languages require a topmost base class, which serves as the ultimate superclass of all classes. In Smalltalk, this class is called Object.

A given class typically has two kinds of clients [26]:

- Instances
- Subclasses

It is often useful to define different interfaces for these two kinds of clients [27]. In particular, we wish to expose only outwardly visible behaviors to instance clients, but we need to expose helping functions and representations only to subclass clients. This is precisely the motivation for the public, protected, and private parts of a class definition in C++: a designer can choose what members are accessible to instances, to subclasses, or to both clients. As we mentioned earlier, in Smalltalk the developer has less control over access: instance variables are visible to subclasses but not to instances, and all methods are visible to both instances and subclasses (one can mark a method as private, but this hiding is not enforced by the language).

There is a very real tension between inheritance and encapsulation. To a large degree, the use of inheritance exposes some of the secrets of an inherited class. Practically, this means that to understand the meaning of a particular class, you must often study all of its superclasses, sometimes including their inside views.

Inheritance means that subclasses inherit the structure of their superclass. Thus, in our earlier example, the instances of the class `ElectricalData` include the member objects of the superclass (such as `id` and `timeStamp`), as well as those of the more specialized classes (such as `fuelCell1Voltage`, `fuelCell2Voltage`, `fuelCell1Amperes`, and `fuelCell2Amperes`).[*]

Subclasses also inherit the behavior of their superclasses. Thus, instances of the class `ElectricalData` may be acted upon with the operations `currentTime` (inherited from its superclass), `currentPower` (defined in the class itself), and `transmit` (redefined in the subclass). Most object-oriented programming languages permit methods from a superclass to be redefined and new methods to be added. In Smalltalk, for example, any superclass method may be redefined in a subclass. In C++, the developer has a bit more control. Member functions that are declared as *virtual* (such as the function `transmit`) may be redefined in a subclass; members declared otherwise (the default) may not be redefined (such as the function `currentTime`).

Single Polymorphism For the class `TelemetryData`, we might implement the member function `transmit` as follows:

```
void TelemetryData::transmit()
{
  // transmit the id
  // transmit the timeStamp
}
```

---

[*] A few, mostly experimental, object-oriented programming languages allow a subclass to reduce the structure of its superclass.

We might implement the same member function for the class `ElectricalData` as follows:

```
void ElectricalData::transmit()
{
  TelemetryData::transmit();
  // transmit the voltages
  // transmit the amperes
}
```

In this implementation, we first invoke the corresponding superclass function (using the fully qualified name `TelemetryData::transmit`), which transmits the data's `id` and `timeStamp`, and then we transmit the data particular to the `ElectricalData` subclass.

Suppose that we have an instance of each of these two classes:

```
TelemetryData telemetry;
ElectricalData electrical(5.0, -5.0, 3.0, 7.0);
```

Now, given the following nonmember function,

```
void transmitFreshData(TelemetryData& d, const Time& t)
{
  if (d.currentTime() >= t)
    d.transmit();
}
```

what happens when we invoke the following two statements?

```
transmitFreshData(telemetry, Time(60));
transmitFreshData(electrical, Time(120));
```

In the first statement, we transmit a bit stream consisting of only an `id` and a `timeStamp`. In the second statement, we transmit a bit stream consisting of an `id`, a `timeStamp`, and four other floating-point values. How is this so? Ultimately, the implementation of the function `transmitFreshData` simply executes the statement `d.transmit()`, which does not explicitly distinguish the class of `d`.

The answer is that this behavior is due to polymorphism. Basically, *polymorphism* is a concept in type theory wherein a name (such as the parameter `d`) may denote instances of many different classes as long as they are related by some common superclass. Any object denoted by this name is thus able to respond to some common set of operations in different ways.

As Cardelli and Wegner note, "Conventional typed languages, such as Pascal, are based on the idea that functions and procedures, and hence operands, have a unique type. Such languages are said to be monomorphic, in the sense that every value and variable can be interpreted to be of one and only one type. Monomorphic programming languages may be contrasted with polymorphic languages in which some values and variables may have more than one type" [28]. The concept of polymorphism was first described by Strachey [29], who spoke of *ad hoc* polymorphism, by which symbols such as "+" could be defined to mean different things. Today, in modern programming languages, we call this concept *overloading*. For example, in C++, one may declare functions having the same names, as long as their invocations can be distinguished by their signatures, consisting of the number and types of their arguments (in C++, unlike Ada, the type of a function's returned value is not considered in overload resolution). Strachey also spoke of *parametric polymorphism*, which today we simply call *polymorphism*.

Without polymorphism, the developer ends up writing code consisting of large case or switch statements.[*] For example, in a non-object-oriented programming language such as Pascal, we cannot create a hierarchy of classes for the various kinds of telemetry data; rather, we have to define a single, monolithic variant record encompassing the properties associated with all the kinds of data. To distinguish one variant from another, we have to examine the tag associated with the record. Thus an equivalent procedure to transmitFreshData might be written in Pascal as follows:

```
const
  Electrical   = 1;
  Propulsion   = 2;
  Spectrometer = 3;
...
procedure Transmit_Fresh_Data(The_Data : Data; The_Time : Time);
begin
  if (The_Data.Current_Time >= The_Time) then
    case The_Data.Kind of
      Electrical: Transmit_Electrical_Data(The_Data);
      Propulsion: Transmit_Propulsion_Data(The_Data);
      ...
    end
end;
```

To add another kind of telemetry data, we would have to modify the variant record and add it to every case statement that operated upon instances of this record. This is particularly error-prone, and, furthermore, adds instability to the design.

In the presence of inheritance, there is no need for a monolithic type, since we may separate different kinds of abstractions. As Kaplan and Johnson note, "Polymorphism is most useful when there are many classes with the same protocols" [30]. With polymorphism, large case statements are unnecessary, because each object implicitly knows its own type.

Inheritance without polymorphism is possible, but it is certainly not very useful. This is the situation in Ada, in which one can declare derived types, but because the language is monomorphic, the actual operation being called is always known at the time of compilation.

Polymorphism and late binding go hand in hand. In the presence of polymorphism, the binding of a method to a name is not determined until execution. In C++, the developer may control whether a member function uses early or late binding. Specifically, if the method is declared as virtual, then late

---

[*] This is in fact the litmus test for polymorphism. The existence of a switch statement that selects an action based upon the type of an object is often an warning sign that the developer has failed to apply polymorphic behavior effectively.

binding is employed, and the function is considered to be polymorphic. If this virtual declaration is omitted, then the method uses early binding and thus can be resolved at the time of compilation. How an implementation selects a particular method for execution is described in the sidebar.

Inheritance and Typing Consider again the redefinition of the member `transmit`:

```
void ElectricalData::transmit()
{
  TelemetryData::transmit();
  // transmit the voltages
  // transmit the amperes
}
```

Most object-oriented programming languages permit the implementation of a subclass's method to directly invoke a method defined by some superclass. As this example shows, it is also quite common for the implementation of a redefined method to invoke the method of the same name defined by a parent class. In Smalltalk, one may invoke a method starting from the immediate ancestor class by using the keyword `super`; one may also refer to the object for which a method was invoked via the special variable `self`. In C++, one can invoke the method of any accessible ancestor by prefixing the method name with the name of the class, thus forming a *qualified name*, and one may refer to the object for which a method was invoked via the implicitly declared pointer named `this`.

In practice, a redefined method usually invokes a superclass method either before or after doing some other action. In this manner, subclass methods play the role of augmenting the behavior defined in the superclass.*

In Figure 3-5, all of the subclasses are also subtypes of their parent class. For example, instances of `ElectricalData` are considered to be subtypes as well as subclasses of `TelemetryData`. The fact that typing parallels inheritance relationships is common to most strongly typed object-oriented programming languages, including C++. Because Smalltalk is largely typeless, or at most weakly typed, this issue is less of a concern.

The parallel between typing and inheritance is to be expected when we view the generalization/specialization hierarchies created through inheritance as the means of capturing the semantic connection among abstractions. Again, consider the declarations in C++:

```
TelemetryData telemetry;
ElectricalData electrical(5.0, -5.0, 3.0, 7.0);
```

---

* In CLOS, these different method roles are made explicit by declaring a method with the qualifiers `:before` and `:after`, as well as `:around`. A method without a qualifier is considered a *primary* method and does the central work of the desired behavior. *Before* methods and *after* methods augment the behavior of a primary method; they are called before and after the primary method, respectively. *Around* methods form a wrapper around a primary method, which may be invoked at some place inside the method by the `call-next-method` function.

Invoking a Method

In traditional programming languages, invoking a subprogram is a completely static activity. In Pascal for example, for a statement that calls the subprogram P, a compiler will typically generate code that creates a new stack frame, places the proper arguments on the stack, and then changes the flow of control to begin executing the code associated with P. However, in languages that support some form of polymorphism, such as Smalltalk, and C++,, invoking an operation may require a dynamic activity, because the class of the object being operated upon may not be known until runtime. Matters are even more interesting when we add inheritance to the situation. The semantics of invoking an operation in the presence of inheritance without polymorphism is largely the same as for a simple static subprogram call, but in the presence of polymorphism, we must use a much more sophisticated technique.

Consider the class hierarchy in Figure 3-6, which shows the base class DisplayItem along with three subclasses named Circle, Triangle, and Rectangle. Rectangle also has one subclass, named SolidRectangle. In the class DisplayItem, suppose that we define the instance variable theCenter (denoting the coordinates for the center of the displayed item), along with the following operations as in our earlier example:

- draw   Draw the item.
- move   Move the item.
- location   Return the location of the item.

The operation location is common to all subclasses, and therefore need not be redefined, but we expect the operations draw and move to be redefined, since only the subclasses know how to draw and move themselves.

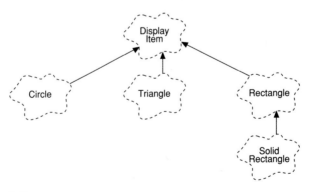

Figure 3-6
DisplayItem Class Diagram

The class Circle must include the instance variable theRadius and appropriate operations to set and retrieve its value. For this subclass, the redefined operation `draw` draws a circle of the given radius, centered on `theCenter`. Similarly, the class `Rectangle` must include the instance variables `theHeight` and `theWidth`, along with appropriate operations to set and retrieve their values. For this subclass, the operation `draw` draws a rectangle with the given height and width, again centered on `theCenter`. The subclass `SolidRectangle` inherits all characteristics of the class `Rectangle`, but again redefines the behavior of the operation `draw`. Specifically, the implementation of `draw` for the class `SolidRectangle` first calls `draw` as defined in its superclass `Rectangle` (to draw the outline of the rectangle) and then fills in the shape.

Consider now the following code fragment:

```
DisplayItem* items[10];
...
for (unsigned index = 0; index < 10; index++)
  items[index]->draw();
```

The invocation of `draw` demands polymorphic behavior. Here, we find a heterogeneous array of items, meaning that the collection may contain pointers to objects of any of the `DisplayItem` subclasses. Suppose now that we have some client object that wishes to draw all of the items found in this collection, as in the code fragment. Our approach is to iterate through the array and invoke the operation `draw` upon each object we encounter. In this situation, the compiler cannot statically generate code to invoke the proper `draw` operation, because the class of the object being operated upon is not known until runtime. Let's consider how various object-oriented programming languages deal with this situation.

Because Smalltalk is a typeless language, method dispatch is completely dynamic. When the client sends the message `draw` to an item found in the list, here is what happens:

- The item object looks up the message in its class's message dictionary.

- If the message is found, the code for that locally defined method is invoked.

- If the message is not found, the search for the method continues in the superclass.

This process continues up the superclass hierarchy until the message is found, or until we reach the topmost base class, `Object`, without finding the message. In the latter case, Smalltalk ultimately passes the message `doesNotUnderstand`, to signal an error.

The key to this algorithm is the message dictionary, which is part of each class's representation and is therefore hidden from the client. This dictionary is created when the class is created, and contains all the methods to which instances of this class may respond. Searching for the message is time-consuming; method lookup in Smalltalk takes about 1.5 times as long as a simple subprogram call. All production-quality Smalltalk implementations optimize method dispatch by supplying a cached message dictionary, so that commonly passed messages may be invoked quickly. Caching typically improves performance by 20%–30% [31].

The operation `draw` defined in the subclass `SolidRectangle` poses a special case. We said that its implementation of `draw` first calls `draw` as defined in the superclass `Rectangle`. In Smalltalk, we specify a superclass method by using the keyword `super`. Then, when we pass the message `draw` to `super`, Smalltalk uses the same method-dispatch algorithm as above, except that the search begins in the superclass of the object instead of its class.

Studies by Deutsch suggest that polymorphism is not needed about 85% of the time, so message passing can often be reduced to simple procedure calls [32]. Duff notes that in such cases, the developer often makes implicit assumptions that permit an early binding of the object's class [33]. Unfortunately, typeless languages such as Smalltalk have no convenient means for communicating these implicit assumptions to the compiler.

More strongly typed languages such as C++ do let the developer assert such information. Because we want to avoid method dispatch wherever possible but must still allow for the occurrence of polymorphic dispatch, invoking a method in these languages proceeds a little differently than in Smalltalk.

In C++, the developer can decide if a particular operation is to be bound late by declaring it to be `virtual`; all other methods are considered to be bound early, and thus the compiler can statically resolve the method call to a simple subprogram call. In our example, we declared `draw` as a virtual member function, and the method `location` as nonvirtual, since it need not be redefined by any subclass. The developer can also declare nonvirtual methods as inline, which avoids the subprogram call, and so trades off space for time.

To handle virtual member functions, most C++ implementations use the concept of a *vtable*, which is defined for each object requiring polymorphic dispatch, when the object is created (and thus when the class of the object is fixed). This table typically consists of a list of pointers to virtual functions. For example, if we create an object of the class `Rectangle`, then the vtable will have an entry for the virtual function `draw`, pointing to the closest implementation of `draw`. If, for example, the class `DisplayItem` included the virtual function `Rotate`, which was not redefined in the class `Rectangle`, then the vtable entry for `Rotate` would point to the implementation of `Rotate` in the class `DisplayItem`. In this manner, runtime searching is eliminated: referring to a virtual member function of an object is just an indirect reference through the appropriate pointer, which immediately invokes the correct code without searching [34].

The implementation of `draw` for the class `SolidRectangle` introduces a special case in C++ as well. To make the implementation of this method refer to the method `draw` in the superclass, C++ requires the use of the scope operator. Thus, one must write:

```
Rectangle::draw();
```

Studies by Stroustrup suggest that a virtual function call is just about as efficient as a normal function call [35]. In the presence of single inheritance, a virtual function call requires only about three or four more memory references than a normal function call; multiple inheritance adds only about five or six memory references.

Method dispatch in CLOS is complicated because of the presence of `:before`, `:after`, and `:around` methods. The existence of multiple polymorphism also complicates matters.

Method dispatch in CLOS normally uses the following algorithm:

- Determine the types of the arguments.
- Calculate the set of applicable methods.
- Sort the methods from most specific to most general, according to the object's class precedence list.
- Call all :before methods.
- Call the most specific primary method.
- Call all :after methods.
- Return the value of the primary method [36].

CLOS also introduces a metaobject protocol, whereby one may redefine the very algorithm used for generic dispatch (although in practice, one typically uses the predefined process). As Winston and Horn wisely point out, "The CLOS algorithm is complicated, however, and even wizard-level CLOS programmers try to get by without thinking about it, just as physicists try to get by with Newtonian mechanics rather than dealing with quantum mechanics" [37].

The following assignment statement is legal:

```
telemetry = electrical; // electrical is a subtype of telemetry
```

Although legal, this statement is also dangerous: any additional state defined for an instance of the subclass is sliced upon assignment to an instance of the superclass. In this example, the four member objects, fuelCell1Voltage, fuelCell2Voltage, fuelCell1Amperes, and fuelCell2Amperes, would not be copied, because the object denoted by the variable telemetry is an instance of the class TelemetryData, which does not have these members as part of its state.

The following statement is not legal:

```
electrical = telemetry; // Illegal: telemetry is not a subtype of electrical
```

To summarize, the assignment of object X to object Y is possible if the type of X is the same as the type or a subtype of Y.

Most strongly typed languages permit conversion of the value of an object from one type to another, but usually only if there is some superclass/subclass relationship between the two. For example, in C++ one can explicitly write conversion operators for a class using what are called *type casts*. Typically, as in our example, one uses implicit type conversion to convert an instance of a more specific class for assignment to a more general class. Such conversions are said to be *type-safe*, meaning that they are checked for semantic correctness at compilation time. We sometimes need to convert a variable of a more general class to one of a more specific class, and so must write an explicit type cast. However, such operations are not type-safe, because they can fail during execution time if the object being coerced is incompatible with the new type.[*] Such conversions are actually not rare (although they should be avoided unless there is compelling reason), since the developer often knows the real types of certain objects. For example, in the absence of parameterized types, it is common practice to build classes such as sets and bags that represent collections of objects, and because we want to permit collections of instances of arbitrary classes, we typically define these collection classes to operate upon instances of some base class (a style much safer than the void* idiom used earlier for the class Queue). Then, iteration operations defined for such a class would only know how to return objects of this base class. However, within a particular application, a developer might only place objects of some specific subclass of this base class in the collection. To invoke a class-specific operation upon objects visited during iteration, the developer would have to explicitly coerce each object visited to the expected type. Again, this operation would fail at execution time if an object of some unexpected type appeared in the collection.

Most strongly typed languages permit an implementation to better optimize method *dispatch* (lookup), often reducing the message to a simple subprogram call. Such optimizations are straightforward if the language's type hierarchy parallels its class hierarchy (as in C++). However, there is a dark side to unifying these hierarchies. Specifically, changing the structure or behavior of some superclass can affect the correctness of its subclasses. As Micallef states, "If subtyping rules are based on inheritance, then reimplementing a class such that its position in the inheritance graph is changed can make clients of that class type-incorrect, even if the external interface of the class remains the same" [38].

These issues lead us to the very foundations of inheritance semantics. As we noted earlier in this chapter, inheritance may be used to indicate sharing or to suggest some semantic connection. As stated another way by Snyder, "One can view inheritance as a private decision of the designer to 'reuse' code because it is useful to do so; it should be possible to easily change such a decision. Alternatively, one can view inheritance as making a public declaration that objects of the child class obey the semantics of the parent class, so that the child class is merely specializing or refining the parent class" [39]. In languages such as Smalltalk, and CLOS, these two views are indistinguishable. However, in C++ the developer has greater control over the implications of inheritance. Specifically, if we assert that the superclass of a given subclass is public (as in our example of the class ElectricalData), then we mean that the subclass is also a subtype of the superclass, since both share the same interface (and therefore the same structure and behavior). Alternately, in the declaration of a class, one may assert that a superclass is private, meaning that the structure and behavior

---

[*] Recent extensions to C++ for run-time type identification will help to mitigate this problem.

of the superclass are shared but the subclass is not a subtype of the superclass*. This means that for private superclasses, the public and protected members of the superclass become private members of the subclass, and hence inaccessible to lower subclasses. Furthermore, no subtype relationship between the subclass and its private superclass is formed, because the two classes no longer present the same interface to other clients.

Consider the following class declaration:

```
class InternalElectricalData : private ElectricalData {
public:

    InternalElectricalData(float v1, float v2, float a1, float a2);
    virtual ~InternalElectricalData();

    ElectricalData::currentPower;

};
```

In this declaration, methods such as `transmit` are not visible to any clients of this class, because `ElectricalData` is declared to be private superclass. Because `InternalElectricalData` is not a subtype of `ElectricalData`, this also means that we cannot assign instances of `InternalElectricalData` to objects of the superclass, as we can for classes using public superclasses. Lastly, note that we have made the member function `currentPower` visible by explicitly naming the function. Without this explicit naming, it would be treated as private. As you would expect, the rules of C++ prohibit one from making a member in a subclass more visible than it is in its superclass. Thus, the member object `timeStamp`, declared as a protected member in the class `TelemetryData`, could not be made public by explicit naming as done for `currentPower`.

In languages such as Ada, the equivalent of this distinction can be achieved by using derived types versus subtypes. Specifically, a subtype of a type defines no new type, but only a constrained subtype, while a derived type defines a new, incompatible type, which shares the same representation as its parent type.

As we discuss in a later section, there is great tension between inheritance for reuse and aggregation.

Multiple Inheritance With single inheritance, each subclass has exactly one superclass. However, as Vlissides and Linton point out, although single inheritance is very useful, "it often forces the programmer to derive from one of two equally attractive classes. This limits the applicability of predefined classes, often making it necessary to duplicate code. For example, there is no way to derive a graphic that is both a circle and a picture; one must derive from one or the other and reimplement the functionality of the class that was excluded" [40]. Multiple inheritance is supported directly by languages such as C++ and CLOS

---

* We may also declare a superclass as protected, which has the same semantics as a private superclass, except that the public and protected members of the protected superclass are made accessible to lower subclasses.

and, to a limited degree, by Smalltalk. The need for multiple inheritance in object-oriented programming languages is still a topic of great debate. In our experience, we find multiple inheritance to be like a parachute: you don't always need it, but when you do, you're really happy to have it on hand.

Consider for a moment how one might organize various assets such as savings accounts, real estate, stocks, and bonds. Savings accounts and checking accounts are both kinds of assets typically managed by a bank, so we might classify both of them as kinds of bank accounts, which in turn are kinds of assets. Stocks and bonds are managed quite differently than bank accounts, so we might classify stocks, bonds, mutual funds, and the like as kinds of securities which in turn are also kinds of assets.

However, there are many other equally satisfactory ways to classify savings accounts, real estate, stocks, and bonds. For example, in some contexts, it may be useful to distinguish insurable items such as real estate and certain bank accounts (which, in the United States, are insured up to certain limits by the Federal Depositors Insurance Corporation). It may also be useful to identify assets that return a dividend or interest, such as savings accounts, checking accounts, and certain stocks and bonds.

Unfortunately, single inheritance is not expressive enough to capture this lattice of relationships, so we must turn to multiple inheritance.[*] Figure 3-7 illustrates such a class structure. Here we see that the class `Security` is a kind of `Asset` as well as a kind of `InterestBearingItem`. Similarly, the class `BankAccount` is a kind of `Asset`, as well as a kind of `InsurableItem` and `InterestBearingItem`.

To capture these design decisions in C++, we might write the following (highly elided) declarations. First, we start with the base classes:

```
class Asset ...
class InsurableItem ...
class InterestBearingItem ...
```

Next we have various intermediate classes, each of which has multiple superclasses:

```
class BankAccount : public Asset,
                    public InsurableItem,
                    public InterestBearingItem ...
class RealEstate : public Asset,
                   public InsurableItem ...
class Security : public Asset,
                 public InterestBearingItem ...
```

---

[*] In fact, this is the litmus test for multiple inheritance. If we encounter a class lattice wherein the leaf classes can be grouped into sets denoting orthogonal behavior (such as insurable and interest-bearing items), *and* these sets overlap, this is an indication that, within a single inheritance lattice, no intermediate classes exist to which we can cleanly attach these behaviors without violating our abstraction of certain leaf classes by granting them behaviors that they should not have. We can remedy this situation by using multiple inheritance to mix in these behaviors only where we want them.

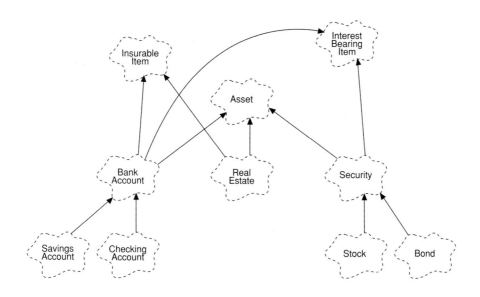

Figure 3-7
Multiple Inheritance

And finally, we have the remaining leaf classes:

```
class SavingsAccount : public BankAccount ...
class CheckingAccount : public BankAccount ...

class Stock : public Security ...
class Bond : public Security ...
```

Designing a suitable class structure involving inheritance, and especially involving multiple inheritance, is a difficult task. As we explain in Chapter 4, this is often an incremental and iterative process. Two problems present themselves when we have multiple inheritance: How do we deal with name collisions from different superclasses, and how do we handle repeated inheritance?

Name collisions are possible when two or more different superclasses use the same name for some element of their interfaces, such as instance variables and methods. For example, suppose that the classes InsurableItem and Asset both have attributes named presentValue, denoting the present value of the item. Since the class RealEstate inherits from both of these classes, what does it mean to inherit two operations with the same name? This in fact is the key difficulty with multiple inheritance: clashes may introduce ambiguity in the behavior of the multiply inherited subclass.

There are three basic approaches to resolving this kind of clash. First, the language semantics might regard such a clash as illegal, and reject the compilation of the class. This is the approach taken by languages such as Smalltalk and Eiffel. In Eiffel, however, it is possible to rename items so that there is no ambiguity. Second, the language semantics might regard the same name introduced by different classes as referring to the same attribute, which is the approach taken by CLOS. Third, the language semantics might permit the clash, but require that all references to the name fully qualify the source of its declaration. This is the approach taken by C++.[*]

The second problem is repeated inheritance, which Meyer describes as follows: "One of the delicate problems raised by the presence of multiple inheritance is what happens when a class is an ancestor of another in more than one way. If you allow multiple inheritance into a language, then sooner or later someone is going to write a class D with two parents B and C, each of which has a class A as a parent – or some other situation in which D inherits twice (or more) from A. This situation is called repeated inheritance and must be dealt with properly" [41]. As an example, suppose that we define the following (ill-conceived) class:

```
class MutualFind : public Stock,
                   public Bond ...
```

This class introduces repeated inheritance of the class Security, which is a superclass of both Stock and Bond.

There are three approaches to dealing with the problem of repeated inheritance. First, we can treat occurrences of repeated inheritance as illegal. This is the approach taken by Smalltalk and Eiffel (with Eiffel again permitting renaming to disambiguate the duplicate references). Second, we can permit duplication of superclasses, but require the use of fully qualified names to refer to members of a specific copy. This is one of the approaches taken by C++. Third, we can treat multiple references to the same class as denoting the same class. This is the approach taken by C++ when the repeated superclass is introduced as a virtual base class. A virtual base class exists when a subclass names another class as its superclass and marks that superclass as virtual, to indicate that it is a shared class. Similarly, in CLOS repeated classes are shared, using a mechanism called the *class precedence list*. This list, calculated whenever a new class is introduced, includes the class itself and all of its superclasses, without duplication, and is based upon the following rules:

- A class always has precedence over its superclass.
- Each class sets the precedence order of its direct superclasses [42].

---

[*] In C++, name collisions among member objects may be resolved by fully qualifying each member name. Member functions with identical names and signatures are semantically considered the same function..

In this approach, the inheritance graph is flattened, duplicates are removed, and the resulting hierarchy is resolved using single inheritance [43]. This is akin to the computation of a topological sorting of classes. If a total ordering of classes can be calculated, then the class that introduces the repeated inheritance is accepted. Note that this total ordering may be unique, or there may be several possible orderings (and a deterministic algorithm will always select one such ordering). If no ordering can be found (for example, when there are cycles in the class dependencies), the class is rejected.

The existence of multiple inheritance gives rise to a style of classes called *mixins*. Mixins derive from the programming culture surrounding the language Flavors: one would combine ("mix in") little classes to build classes with more sophisticated behavior. As Hendler observes, "A mixin is syntactically identical to a regular class, but its intent is different. The purpose of such a class is solely to . . . [add] functions to other flavors [classes] – one never creates an instance of a mixin" [44]. In Figure 3-7, the classes `InsurableItem` and `InterestBearingItem` are mixins. Neither of these classes can stand alone; rather, they are used to augment the meaning of some other class.[*] Thus, we may define a mixin as a class that embodies a single, focused behavior and is used to augment the behavior of some other class via inheritance. The behavior of a mixin is usually completely orthogonal to the behavior of the classes with which it is combined. A class that is constructed primarily by inheriting from mixins and does not add its own structure or behavior is called an *aggregate class*.

Multiple Polymorphism Consider again the following member function declared for the class `DisplayItem`:

```
virtual void draw();
```

The purpose of this operation is to draw the given object in some context. This operation is declared as `virtual` and is therefore polymorphic, meaning that whenever we invoke this operation for a particular object, the proper subclass's implementation of this operation will be called, using an algorithm for method dispatch as described in the sidebar. This is an example of single polymorphism, meaning that the method is specialized (is polymorphic) on exactly one parameter, namely, the object for which the operation is invoked.

Suppose now that we need a slightly different behavior, depending upon the exact display device we use. In one case, we would want the method `draw` to display a high-resolution graphical representation; in another, we would want it to print a representation quickly, and so would draw only a very coarse image. We could declare two distinct although very similar operations, such as `drawGraphic` and `drawText`. This is not entirely satisfying, however, because this solution does not scale very well: introducing yet another drawing context requires us to add a new operation to every class in the `DisplayItem` hierarchy.

---

[*] In CLOS, it is common practice to build a mixin using only `:before` and `:after` methods to augment the behavior of existing primary methods.

In languages such as CLOS, we can write operations called *multimethods* that are polymorphic on more than one parameter (such as the display item and the display device). In languages that support only single polymorphism (such as C++), we can fake this multiple polymorphic behavior by using an idiom called *double dispatching*.

First, we might define a hierarchy of display devices, rooted in the class `DisplayDevice`. Next, we would rewrite the `DisplayItem` operation as follows:

```
virtual void draw(DisplayDevice&);
```

In the implementation of this method, we would invoke drawing operations that are polymorphic on the given actual `DisplayDevice` parameter – thus the name double dispatch: `draw` first exhibits polymorphic behavior based upon the object's exactly subclass of `DisplayItem`, and then next exhibits polymorphic behavior based upon the argument's exact subclass of `DisplayDevice`.

This idiom can be extended to any degree of polymorphic dispatch.

Aggregation

Example Aggregation relationships among classes have a direct parallel to aggregation relationships among the objects corresponding to these classes. For example, consider again the declaration of the class `TemperatureController`:

```
class TemperatureController {
public:

  TemperatureController(Location);
  ~TemperatureController();

  void process(const TemperatureRamp&);

  Minute schedule(const TemperatureRamp&) const;

private:
  Heater h;
};
```

As we show in Figure 3-8, the class `TemperatureController` denotes the whole, and an instance of the class `Heater` is one of its parts. This corresponds exactly to the aggregation relationship among the instances of these classes, illustrated in Figure 3-3.

Physical Containment In the case of the class `TemperatureController`, we have aggregation as containment *by value*, a kind of physical containment meaning that the `Heater` object does not exist independently of its enclosing `TemperatureController` instance. Rather the lifetimes of these two objects are intimately connected: when we create an instance of `TemperatureController`, we also create an instance of the class `Heater`. When we destroy our `TemperatureController` object, by implication we also destroy the corresponding `Heater` object.

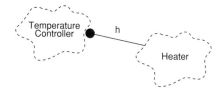

Figure 3-8
Aggregation

A less direct kind of aggregation is also possible, called containment *by reference*. For example, we might replace the private part of the class TemperatureController with the following declaration:[*]

Heater* h;

In this case, the class TemperatureController still denotes the whole, and an instance of the class Heater is still one of its parts, although that part must now be accessed indirectly. Hence, the lifetimes of these two objects are not so tightly coupled as before: we may create and destroy instances of each class independently. Furthermore, because it is possible for the part to be structurally shared, we must decide upon some policy whereby its storage is properly created and reclaimed by only one agent that shares references to that part.

Aggregation asserts a direction to the whole/part relationship. For example, the Heater object is a part of the TemperatureController object, and not vice versa. Containment by value may not be cyclic (that is, both objects may not physically be parts of one another), although containment by reference may be (each object may hold a pointer to the other).[**]

Of course, as we described in an earlier example, aggregation need not require physical containment, as implied through containment by value or by reference. For example, although shareholders own stocks, a shareholder does not physically contain the owned stocks. Rather, the lifetimes of these objects may be completely independent, although there is still conceptually a whole/part relationship (each share is always a part of the shareholder's assets), and thus our representation of this aggregation can be very indirect. For example, we might declare the class Shareholder, whose state includes a key to a database table that we may use to look up the shares owned by a particular shareholder. This is still aggregation, although not physical containment. Ultimately, the litmus test for aggregation is this: If and only if there exists a

---

[*] Alternately, we could have declared h as a reference to a heater object (in C++, Heater&), whose semantics regarding initialization and modification are quite different than for pointers.

[**] An association may be often replaced be cyclic aggregation or cyclic "using" relationships. More often than not, however, an association (which by definition implies bidirectional navigation) is refined during design to be a single aggregation or "using" relationship, thus denoting a constraint upon the direction of the association.

whole/part relationship between two objects, we must have an aggregation relationship between their corresponding classes.

Multiple inheritance is often confused with aggregation. In fact, in C++ `protected` or `private` inheritance can easily be replaced with protected or private aggregation of an instance of the superclass, with no loss in semantics. When considering inheritance versus aggregation, remember to apply the litmus test for each. If you can not honestly affirm that here is an "is a" relationship between two classes, then aggregation or some other relationship should be used instead of inheritance.

Using

Example Our earlier example of the `rampController` and `growingRamp` objects illustrated a link between the two objects, which we represented via a "using" relationship between their corresponding classes, `TemperatureController` and `TemperatureRamp`:

```
class TemperatureController {
public:

  TemperatureController(Location);
  ~TemperatureController();

  void process(const TemperatureRamp&);

  Minute schedule(const TemperatureRamp&) const;

private:
  Heater h;
};
```

The class `TemperatureRamp` appears as part of the signature in certain member functions, and thus we can say that `TemperatureController` uses the services of the class `TemperatureRamp`.

Clients and Suppliers "Using" relationships among classes parallel the peer-to-peer links among the corresponding instances of these classes. Whereas an association denotes a bidirectional semantic connection, a "using" relationship is one possible refinement of an association, whereby we assert which abstraction is the client and which is the supplier of certain services. We illustrate such a client/supplier "using" relationship in Figure 3-9.[*]

Actually, one class may use another in a variety of ways. In our example, the `TemperatureController` uses the `TemperatureRamp` in the signature of its interface. The `TemperatureController` might also use another class such as `Predictor` in its implementation of the member function `schedule`. This is not an assertion of a whole/part relationship: an instance of the `Predictor` class is only used by and is not a part of the `TemperatureController` instance. Typically, such a "using"

---

[*] As we stated earlier, a cyclic "using" relationship is equivalent to an association, although the reverse is not necessarily true.

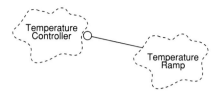

Figure 3-9
The "Using" Relationship

relationship manifests itself by the implementation of some operation declaring
a local object of the used class.

Strict "using" relationships are occasionally too confining because they
allow the client access only to the public interface of the supplier. Sometimes,
for tactical reasons, we must break our encapsulation of these abstractions,
which is the very purpose of the friend concept in C++.

Instantiation

Examples Our earlier declaration of the class Queue was not very satisfying
because its abstraction was not type-safe. We can vastly improve our
abstraction by using languages such as C++ and Eiffel that support genericity.

For example, we might rewrite our earlier class declaration using a
parameterized class in C++:

```
template<class Item>
class Queue {
public:

  Queue();
  Queue(const Queue<Item>&);
  virtual ~Queue();

  virtual Queue<Item>& operator=(const Queue<Item>&);
  virtual int operator==(const Queue<Item>&) const;
  int operator!=(const Queue<Item>&) const;

  virtual void clear();
  virtual void append(const Item&);
  virtual void pop();
  virtual void remove(int at);

  virtual int length() const;
  virtual int isEmpty() const;
  virtual const Item& front() const;
  virtual int location(const void*);

protected:
  ...
};
```

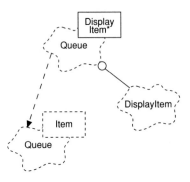

Figure 3-10
Instantiation

Note that in this declaration we no longer append and retrieve objects via void* (which is not type-safe); we do so via the class Item declared as a template argument.

A parameterized class cannot have instances unless we first instantiate it. For example, we might declare two concrete queue objects, a queue of integers, and a queue of display items:

```
Queue<int> intQueue;
Queue<DisplayItem*> itemQueue;
```

The objects intQueue and itemQueue are instances of distinctly different classes, and are not even united by any common superclass, although they both derive from the same parameterized class. For reasons that we describe further in Chapter 9, we use a pointer to the class DisplayItem in the second instantiation, so that objects of a DisplayItem subclass placed in the queue will not be sliced, but will preserve their polymorphic behavior.

These instantiations are type-safe. C++'s typing rules will reject any statements that attempt to append or retrieve anything other than integers from intQueue and anything but instances of DisplayItem or its subclasses from itemQueue.

Figure 3-10 illustrates the relationships among the parameterized class Queue, its instantiation for DisplayItem, and its corresponding instance itemQueue.

Genericity There are four basic ways to build classes such as the parameterized class Queue. First, we can use macros. This is the style one had to use in earlier versions of C++, but as Stroustrup observes, this "approach does not work well except on a small scale" [45] because maintaining macros is clumsy and outside the semantics of the language; furthermore, each instantiation results in a new copy of the code. Second, we can take the approach used by Smalltalk and rely upon inheritance and late binding [46]. With this approach, we may build only heterogeneous container classes, because there is no way to assert the specific class of the container's elements; every item is treated as if it were an instance of some distant base class. Third, we may take an approach commonly used in languages such as Object Pascal, which are strongly typed, support inheritance, but do not support any form of parameterized classes. Here, we build generalized container classes, as in Smalltalk, but then use explicit type-checking code to enforce the convention that the contents are all of the same class, which is asserted when the container object is created. This approach has significant runtime overhead. Fourth, we may take the approach first introduced by CLU and provide a direct mechanism for parameterizing classes, as in our example. A *parameterized class* (also known as a *generic class*) is one that serves as a template for other classes – a template that may be parameterized by other classes, objects, and/or operations. A parameterized class must be instantiated (that is, its parameters must be filled in) before objects can be created. C++ and Eiffel both support generic class mechanisms.

In Figure 3-10, note that to instantiate the class Queue, we must also use the class DisplayItem. Indeed, instantiation relationships almost always require some "using" relationships, which make visible the actual classes used to fill in the template.

Meyer has pointed out that inheritance is a more powerful mechanism than genericity and that much of the benefit of genericity can be achieved through inheritance, but not vice versa [47]. In practice, we find it helpful to use a language that supports both inheritance and parameterized classes.

Parameterized classes may be used for much more than building container classes. As Stroustrup points out, "Type parameterization will allow arithmetic functions to be parameterized over their basic number type so that programmers can (finally) get a uniform way of dealing with integers, single-precision floating-point numbers, double-precision floating point-numbers, etc." [48].

From a design perspective, parameterized classes are also useful in capturing certain design decisions about the protocol of a class. Whereas a class definition exports the operations that one may perform upon instances of that class, the arguments of a template serve to import classes (and values) that provide a specific protocol. In C++, this conformance checking is done at compilation time, when expanding the instantiation. For example, we might declare an ordered queue class that represents collections of objects that are sorted according to some criteria. This parameterized class must rely upon some class Item, as before, but also expects Item to provide some ordering operation. By parameterizing the class in this manner, we make it more loosely coupled: we can match the formal argument Item with any class that provides this ordering function. In this sense, we may define a parameterized class as one that denotes a family of classes whose structure and behavior are defined independently of their formal class parameters.

Metaclass

We have said that every object is an instance of some class. What if we treat a class itself as an object that can be manipulated? To do so, we must ask, What

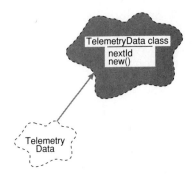

Figure 3-11
Metaclasses

is the class of a class? The answer is simply, a metaclass. To state it another way, a *metaclass* is a class whose instances are themselves classes. Languages such as Smalltalk and CLOS support the concept of a metaclass directly; C++ does not. Indeed, the idea of a metaclass takes the idea of the object model to its natural completion in pure object-oriented programming languages.

Robson motivates the need for metaclasses by noting that "in a system under development, a class provides an interface for the programmer to interface with the definition of objects. For this use of classes, it is extremely useful for them to be objects, so that they can be manipulated in the same way as all other descriptions" [49].

In languages such as Smalltalk, the primary purpose of a metaclass is to provide class variables (which are shared by all instances of the class) and operations for initializing class variables and for creating the metaclass's single instance [50]. By convention, a Smalltalk metaclass typically contains examples that show the use of the metaclass's class. For example, as shown in Figure 3-11, we might in Smalltalk define a class variable `nextID` for the metaclass of `TelemetryData`, whose purpose is to assist in generating distinct id's upon the creation of each instance of `TelemetryData`. Similarly, we might define an operation for creating new instances of the class, which perhaps generates them from some preallocated pool of storage.

Although C++ does not explicitly support metaclasses, its constructor and destructor semantics serve the purpose of metaclass creation operations. Also, C++ has provisions for class variables and metaclass operations. Specifically, in C++ one may declare a member object or a member function as *static*, meaning that the member is shared by all instances of the class. Static member objects in C++ are equivalent to Smalltalk's class variables, and static member functions are equivalent to metaclass operations in Smalltalk.

As we have mentioned, support for metaclasses in CLOS is even more powerful than in Smalltalk. Through the use of metaclasses, one may redefine the very semantics of elements such as class precedence, generic functions, and methods. The primary benefit of this facility is that it permits experimentation with alternate object-oriented programming paradigms and facilitates the construction of software development tools, such as browsers.

In CLOS, the predefined class named `standard-class` is the metaclass of all untyped classes defined via `defclass`. This metaclass defines the method `make-instance`, which implements the semantics of how instances are created. `Standard-class` also defines the algorithm for computing the class precedence list. CLOS allows the behavior of both of these methods to be redefined.

Methods and generic functions may also be treated as objects in CLOS. Because they are somewhat different than the usual kinds of objects, class objects, method objects, and generic function objects are collectively called *metaobjects*. Each method is an instance of the predefined class `standard-method`, and each generic function is treated as an instance of the class `standard-generic-function`. Because the behavior of these predefined classes may be redefined, it is possible to change the meanings of methods and generic functions.

3.5 The Interplay of Classes and Objects

Relationships Between Classes and Objects

Classes and objects are separate yet intimately related concepts. Specifically, every object is the instance of some class, and every class has zero or more instances. For practically all applications, classes are static; therefore, their existence, semantics, and relationships are fixed prior to the execution of a program. Similarly, the class of most objects is static, meaning that once an object is created, its class is fixed. In sharp contrast, however, objects are typically created and destroyed at a furious rate during the lifetime of an application.

For example, consider the classes and objects in the implementation of an air traffic control system. Some of the more important abstractions include planes, flight plans, runways, and air spaces. By their very definition, the meanings of these classes of objects are relatively static. They must be static, for otherwise one could not build an application that embodied knowledge of such commonsense facts as that planes can take off, fly, and then land, and that two planes should not occupy the same space at the same time. Conversely, the instances of these classes are dynamic. At a fairly slow rate, new runways are built, and old ones are deactivated. Faster yet, new flight plans are filed, and old ones are filed away. With great frequency, new planes enter a particular air space, and old ones leave.

The Role of Classes and Objects in Analysis and Design

During analysis and the early stages of design, the developer has two primary tasks:

- Identify the classes and objects that form the vocabulary of the problem domain.
- Invent the structures whereby sets of objects work together to provide the behaviors that satisfy the requirements of the problem.

Collectively, we call such classes and objects the *key abstractions* of the problem, and we call these cooperative structures the *mechanisms* of the implementation.

During these phases of development, the focus of the developer must be upon the outside view of these key abstractions and mechanisms. This view represents the logical framework of the system, and therefore encompasses the class structure and object structure of the system. In the later stages of design and then moving into implementation, the task of the developer changes: the focus is on the inside view of these key abstractions and mechanisms, involving their physical representation. We may express these design decisions as part of the system's module architecture and process architecture.

3.6 On Building Quality Classes and Objects

Measuring the Quality of an Abstraction

Ingalls suggests that "a system should be built with a minimum set of unchangeable parts; those parts should be as general as possible; and all parts of the system should be held in a uniform framework" [51]. With object-oriented development, these parts are the classes and objects that make up the key abstractions of the system, and the framework is provided by its mechanisms.

In our experience, the design of classes and objects is an incremental, iterative process. Frankly, except for the most trivial abstractions, we have never been able to define a class exactly right the first time. As Chapters 4 and 7 explain, it takes time to smooth the conceptual jagged edges of our initial abstractions. Of course, there is a cost to refining these abstractions, in terms of recompilation, understandability, and the integrity of the fabric of our system design. Therefore, we want to come as close as we can to being right the first time.

How can one know if a given class or object is well designed? We suggest five meaningful metrics:

- Coupling
- Cohesion
- Sufficiency
- Completeness
- Primitiveness

Coupling is a notion borrowed from structured design, but with a liberal interpretation it also applies to object-oriented design. Stevens, Myers, and Constantine define coupling as "the measure of the strength of association established by a connection from one module to another. Strong coupling complicates a system since a module is harder to understand, change, or correct by itself if it is highly interrelated with other modules. Complexity can be reduced by designing systems with the weakest possible coupling between modules" [52]. A counterexample to good coupling is given by Page-Jones, in his description of a modular stereo system in which the power supply is located in one of the speaker cabinets [53].

Coupling with regard to modules is still applicable to object-oriented analysis and design, but coupling with regard to classes and objects is equally important. However, there is tension between the concepts of coupling and inheritance, because inheritance introduces significant coupling. On the one hand, weakly coupled classes are desirable; on the other hand, inheritance – which tightly couples superclasses and their subclasses – helps us to exploit the commonality among abstractions.

The idea of cohesion also comes from structured design. Simply stated, cohesion measures the degree of connectivity among the elements of a single module (and for object-oriented design, a single class or object). The least desirable form of cohesion is coincidental cohesion, in which entirely unrelated abstractions are thrown into the same class or module. For example, consider a class comprising the abstractions of dogs and spacecraft, whose behaviors are quite unrelated. The most desirable form of cohesion is functional cohesion, in which the elements of a class or module all work together to provide some well-bounded behavior. Thus, the class Dog is functionally cohesive if its semantics embrace the behavior of a dog, the whole dog, and nothing but the dog.

Closely related to the ideas of coupling and cohesion are the criteria that a class or module should be sufficient, complete, and primitive. By *sufficient*, we mean that the class or module captures enough characteristics of the abstraction to permit meaningful and efficient interaction. To do otherwise renders the component useless. For example, if we are designing the class Set, it is wise to include an operation that removes an item from the set, but our wisdom is futile if we neglect an operation that adds an item. In practice, violations of this characteristic are detected very early; such shortcomings rise up almost every time we build a client that must use this abstraction. By *complete*, we mean that the interface of the class or module captures all of the meaningful characteristics of the abstraction. Whereas sufficiency implies a minimal interface, a complete interface is one that covers all aspects of the abstraction. A complete class or module is thus one whose interface is general enough to be commonly usable to any client. Completeness is a subjective matter, and it can be overdone. Providing all meaningful operations for a particular abstraction overwhelms the user and is generally unnecessary, since many high-level operations can be composed from low-level ones. For this reason, we also suggest that classes and modules be primitive. *Primitive* operations are those that can be efficiently implemented only if given access to the underlying representation of the abstraction. Thus, adding an item to a set is primitive, because to implement this operation Add, the underlying representation must be visible. On the other hand, an operation that adds four items to a set is not primitive, because it can be implemented just as efficiently upon the more primitive Add operation, without having access to the underlying representation. Of course, efficiency is also a subjective measure. An operation is indisputably primitive if we can implement it only through access to the underlying representation. An operation that could be implemented on top of existing primitive operations, but at the cost of significantly more computational resources, is also a candidate for inclusion as a primitive operation.

Choosing Operations

Functional Semantics Crafting the interface of a class or module is plain hard work. Typically, we make a first attempt at the design of a class, and then, as we and others create clients, we find it necessary to augment, modify, and further refine this interface. Eventually, we may discover patterns of operations or patterns of abstractions that lead us to invent new classes or to reorganize the relationships among existing ones.

Within a given class, it is our style to keep all operations primitive, so that each exhibits a small, well-defined behavior. We call such methods *fine-grained*. We also tend to separate methods that do not communicate with one another. In this manner, it is far easier to construct subclasses that can meaningfully redefine the behavior of their superclasses. The decision to contract out a behavior to one versus many methods may be made for two competing reasons: lumping a particular behavior in one method leads to a simpler interface but larger, more complicated methods; spreading a behavior across methods leads to a more complicated interface, but simpler methods. As Meyer observes, "A good designer knows how to find the appropriate balance between too much contracting, which produces fragmentation, and too little, which yields unmanageably large modules" [54].

It is common in object-oriented development to design the methods of a class as a whole, because all these methods cooperate to form the entire protocol of the abstraction. Thus, given some desired behavior, we must decide in which class to place it. Halbert and O'Brien offer the following criteria to be considered when making such a decision:

• Reusability	Would this behavior be more useful in more than one context?
• Complexity	How difficult is it to implement the behavior?
• Applicability	How relevant is the behavior to the type in which it might be placed?

- Implementation knowledge   Does the behavior's implementation
depend upon the internal details of a
type [55]?

We usually choose to declare the meaningful operations that we may perform
upon an object as methods in the definition of that object's class (or
superclass). In languages such as C++ and CLOS, however, we may also
declare such operations as free subprograms, which we then group in class
utilities. In C++ terminology, a *free subprogram* is a nonmember function.
Because free subprograms cannot be redefined as methods can, they are less
general. However, utilities are helpful in keeping a class primitive and in
reducing the coupling among classes, especially if these higher-level operations
involve objects of many different classes.

Time and Space Semantics Once we have established the existence of a
particular operation and defined its functional semantics, we must decide upon
its time and space semantics. This means that we must specify our decisions
about the amount of time it takes to complete an operation and the amount of
storage it needs. Such decisions are often expressed in terms of best, average,
and worst cases, with the worst case specifying an upper limit on what is
acceptable.

Earlier, we also mentioned that whenever one object passes a message to
another across a link, the two objects must be synchronized in some manner.
In the presence of multiple threads of control, this means that message passing
is much more than a subprogram-like dispatch. In most of the languages we
use, synchronization among objects is simply not an issue, because our
programs contain exactly one thread of control, meaning that all objects are
sequential. We speak of message passing in such situations as simple, because
its semantics are most akin to simple subprogram calls. However, in languages
that support concurrency,* we must concern ourselves with more sophisticated
forms of message passing, so as to avoid the problems created if two threads of
control act upon the same object in unrestrained ways. As we described earlier,
objects whose semantics are preserved in the presence of multiple threads of
control are either guarded or synchronized objects.

We have found it useful in some circumstances to express concurrency
semantics for each individual operation as well as for the object as a whole,
since different operations may require different kinds of synchronization.
Message passing may thus take one of the following forms:

- Synchronous   An operation commences only when the
sender has initiated the action and the
receiver is ready to accept the message; the

---

* Ada and Smalltalk have direct support for concurrency. Languages such as C++ do not,
but they can often provide concurrency semantics by extension through platform-
specific classes, such as the AT&T task library for C++.

	sender and receiver will wait indefinitely until both parties are ready to proceed.
• Balking	The same as synchronous, except that the sender will abandon the operation if the receiver is not immediately ready.
• Timeout	The same as synchronous, except that the sender will only wait for a specified amount of time for the receiver to be ready.
• Asynchronous	A sender may initiate an action regardless of whether the receiver is expecting the message.

The form can be selected on an operation-by-operation basis, but only after the functional semantics of the operation have been decided upon.

Choosing Relationships

Collaborations Choosing the relationships among classes and among objects is linked to the selection of operations. If we decide that object X sends message M to object Y, then either directly or indirectly, Y must be accessible to X; otherwise, we could not name the operation M in the implementation of X. By *accessible*, we mean the ability of one abstraction to see another and reference resources in its outside view. Abstractions are accessible to one another only where their scopes overlap and only where access rights are granted (for example, private parts of a class are accessible only to the class itself and its friends). Coupling is thus a measure of the degree of accessibility.

One useful guideline in choosing the relationships among objects is called the Law of Demeter, which states that "the methods of a class should not depend in any way on the structure of any class, except the immediate (top-level) structure of their own class. Further, each method should send messages to objects belonging to a very limited set of classes only" [56]. The basic effect of applying this law is the creation of loosely coupled classes, whose implementation secrets are encapsulated. Such classes are fairly unencumbered, meaning that to understand the meaning of one class, you need not understand the details of many other classes.

In looking at the class structure of an entire system, we may find that its inheritance hierarchy is either wide and shallow, narrow and deep, or balanced. Class structures that are wide and shallow usually represent forests of free-standing classes that can be mixed and matched [57]. Class structures that are narrow and deep represent trees of classes that are related by a common ancestor [58]. There are advantages and disadvantages to each approach. Forests of classes are more loosely coupled, but they may not exploit all the commonality that exists. Trees of classes exploit this commonality, so that individual classes are smaller than in forests. However, to understand a particular class, it is usually necessary to understand the meaning of all the classes it inherits from or uses. The proper shape of a class structure is highly problem-dependent.

We must make similar trade-offs among inheritance, aggregation, and using relationships. For example, should the class Car inherit, contain, or use the classes named Engine and Wheel? In this case, we suggest that an aggregation relationship is more appropriate than an inheritance relationship. Meyer states that between the classes A and B, "inheritance is appropriate if every instance of B may also be viewed as an instance of A. The client relationship is appropriate when every instance of B simply possesses one or more attributes of A" [59]. From another perspective, if the behavior of an object is more than the sum of its individual parts, then creating an aggregation relationship rather than an inheritance relationship between the appropriate classes is probably superior.

Mechanisms and Visibility Deciding upon the relationship among objects is mainly a matter of designing the mechanisms whereby these objects interact. The question the developer must ask is simply, Where does certain knowledge go? For example, in a manufacturing plant, materials (called *lots*) enter manufacturing cells to be processed. As they enter certain cells, we must notify the room's manager to take appropriate action. We now have a design choice: is the entry of a lot into a room an operation upon the room, an operation upon the lot, or an operation upon both? If we decide that it is an operation upon the room, then the room must be visible to the lot. If we decide that it is an operation upon the lot, then the lot must be visible to the room, because the lot must know what room it is in. Lastly, if we consider this to be an operation upon both the room and the lot, then we must arrange for mutual visibility. We must also decide on some visibility relationship between the room and the manager (and not the lot and the manager); either the manager must know the room it manages, or the room must know of its manager.

During the design process, it is occasionally useful to state explicitly how one object is visible to another. There are four fundamental ways that object X may be made visible to object Y:

- The supplier object is global to the client.
- The supplier object is a parameter to some operation of the client.
- The supplier object is a part of the client object.
- The supplier object is a locally declared object in the scope of the object diagram.

A variation upon each of these is the idea of shared visibility. For example, Y might be a part of X, but Y might also be visible to other objects in different ways. In Smalltalk, this kind of visibility usually represents a dependency between two objects. Shared visibility involves structural sharing, meaning that one object does not have exclusive access to another: the shared object's state may be altered via more than one path.

Choosing Implementations

Only after we stabilize the outside view of a given class or object do we turn to its inside view. This perspective involves two different decisions: a choice of representation for a class or object and the placement of the class or object in a module.

Representation The representation of a class or object should almost always be one of the encapsulated secrets of the abstraction. This makes it possible to change the representation (for example, to alter the time and space semantics) without violating any of the functional assumptions that clients may have made. As Wirth wisely states, "The choice of representation is often a fairly difficult one, and it is not uniquely determined by the facilities available. It must always be taken in light of the operations that are to be performed upon the data" [60]. For example, given a class whose objects denote a set of flight-plan information, do we optimize the representation for fast searching or for fast insertion and deletion? We cannot optimize for both, so our choice must be based upon the expected use of these objects. Sometimes it is not easy to choose, and we end up with families of classes whose interfaces are virtually identical but whose implementations are radically different, in order to provide different time and space behavior.

One of the more difficult trade-offs when selecting the implementation of a class is between computing the value of an object's state versus storing it as a field. For example, suppose we have the class Cone, which includes the method Volume. Invoking this method returns the volume of the object. As part of the representation of this class, we are likely to use fields for the height of the cone and the radius of its base. Should we have an additional field in which we store the volume of the object, or should the method Volume just calculate it every time [60]? If we want this method to be fast, we should store the volume as a field. If space efficiency is more important to us, we should calculate the value. Which representation is better depends entirely upon the particular problem. In any case, we should be able to choose an implementation independently of the class's outside view; indeed, we should even be able to change this representation without its clients caring.

Packaging Similar issues apply to the declaration of classes and objects within modules. For Smalltalk, this is a not an issue, because there is no concept of a module within the language. It is a different matter for languages such as Object Pascal, C++, CLOS, and Ada, which support the notion of the module as a separate language construct. The competing requirements of visibility and information hiding usually guide our design decisions about where to declare classes and objects. Generally, we seek to build functionally cohesive, loosely coupled modules. Many nontechnical factors influence these decisions, such as matters of reuse, security, and documentation. Like the design of classes and objects, module design is not to be taken lightly. As Parnas, Clements, and Weiss note with regard to information hiding, "Applying this principle is not always easy. It attempts to minimize the expected cost of software over its period of use and requires that the designer estimate the likelihood of changes. Such estimates are based on past experience and usually require knowledge of the application area as well as an understanding of hardware and software technology" [61].

Summary

- An object has state, behavior, and identity.
- The structure and behavior of similar objects are defined in their common class.
- The state of an object encompasses all of the (usually static) properties of the object plus the current (usually dynamic) values of each of these properties.
- Behavior is how an object acts and reacts in terms of its state changes and message passing.
- Identity is the property of an object that distinguishes it from all other objects.
- The two kinds of object hierarchies include links and aggregation relationships.
- A class is a set of objects that share a common structure and a common behavior.
- The six kinds of class hierarchies include association, inheritance, aggregation, "using," instantiation, and metaclass relationships.
- Key abstractions are the classes and objects that form the vocabulary of the problem domain.
- A mechanism is a structure whereby a set of objects work together to provide a behavior that satisfies some requirement of the problem.
- The quality of an abstraction may be measured by its coupling, cohesion, sufficiency, completeness, and primitiveness.

Further Readings

MacLennan [G 1982] discusses the distinction between values and objects. The work by Meyer [J 1987] proposes the idea of programming as contracting.

Much has been written on the topic of class hierarchies, with particular emphasis upon approaches to inheritance and polymorphism. The papers by Albano [G 1983], Allen [A 1982], Brachman [J 1983], Hailpern and Nguyen [G 1987], and Wegner and Zdonik [J 1988] provide an excellent theoretical foundation for all the important concepts and issues. Cook and Palsberg [J 1989] and Touretzky [G 1986] provide formal treatments of the semantics of inheritance. Wirth [J 1987] proposes a related approach for record type extensions, as used in the language Oberon. Ingalls [G 1986] provides a useful discussion on the topic of multiple polymorphism. Grogono [G 1989] studies the interplay of polymorphism and type checking, and Ponder and Buch [G 1992] warn of the dangers of unrestrained polymorphism. Practical guidance on the effective use of inheritance is offered by Meyer [G 1988] and Halberd and O'Brien [G 1988]. LaLonde and Pugh [J 1985] examine the problems of teaching the effective use of specialization and generalization.

The nature of an abstraction's roles and responsibilities are further detailed by Rubin and Goldberg [B 1992] and Wirfs-Brock, Wilkerson, and Wiener [F 1990]. Measures of goodness for class design are also considered by Coad [F 1991].

Meyer [G 1986] examines the relationships between genericity and inheritance, as viewed by the language Eiffel. Stroustrup [G 1988] proposes a mechanism for parameterized types in C++. CLOS's metaobject protocol is described in detail by Kiczales, Rivieres, and Bobrow [G 1991].

An alternative to class-based hierarchies is provided by delegation, using exemplars. This approach is examined in detail by Stein [G 1987].

CHAPTER 4

Classification

Classification is the means whereby we order knowledge. In object-oriented design, recognizing the sameness among things allows us to expose the commonality within key abstractions and mechanisms, and eventually leads us to smaller and simpler architectures. Unfortunately, there is no golden path to classification. To the reader accustomed to finding cookbook answers, we unequivocally state that there are no simple recipes for identifying classes and objects. There is no such thing as the "perfect" class structure, nor the "right" set of objects. As in any engineering discipline, our design choices are a compromise shaped by many competing factors.

At a conference on software engineering, several developers were asked what rules they applied to identify classes and objects. Stroustrup, the designer of C++, responded "It's a Holy Grail. There is no panacea." Gabriel, one of the designers of CLOS, stated, "That's a fundamental question for which there is no easy answer. I try things" [1]. Fortunately, there does exist a vast legacy of experience with classification in other disciplines. From more classical approaches, techniques of object-oriented analysis have emerged that offer several useful recommended practices and rules of thumb for identifying the classes and objects relevant to a particular problem. These heuristics are the focus of this chapter.

Classification is the means whereby we order knowledge.

4.1 The Importance of Proper Classification

Classification and Object-Oriented Development

The identification of classes and objects is the hardest part of object-oriented analysis and design. Our experience shows that identification involves both discovery and invention. Through discovery, we come to recognize the key abstractions and mechanisms that form the vocabulary of our problem domain. Through invention, we devise generalized abstractions as well as new mechanisms that specify how objects collaborate. Ultimately, discovery and invention are both problems of classification, and classification is fundamentally a problem of finding sameness. When we classify, we seek to group things that have a common structure or exhibit a common behavior.

Intelligent classification is actually a part of all good science. As Michalski and Stepp observe, "An omnipresent problem in science is to construct meaningful classifications of observed objects or situations. Such classifications facilitate human comprehension of the observations and the subsequent development of a scientific theory" [2]. The same philosophy applies to engineering. In the domain of building architecture and city planning, Alexander notes that, for the architect, "his act of design, whether humble, or gigantically complex, is governed entirely by the patterns he has in his mind at that moment, and his ability to combine these patterns to form a new design"

[3]. Not surprisingly, then, classification is relevant to every aspect of object-oriented design. Classification helps us to identify generalization, specialization, and aggregation hierarchies among classes. By recognizing the common patterns of interaction among objects, we come to invent the mechanisms that serve as the soul of our implementation. Classification also guides us in making decisions about modularization. We may choose to place certain classes and objects together in the same module or in different modules, depending upon the sameness we find among these declarations; coupling and cohesion are simply measures of this sameness. Classification also plays a role in allocating processes to processors. We place certain processes together in the same processor or different processors, depending upon packaging, performance, or reliability concerns.

The Difficulty of Classification

Examples of Classification In the previous chapter, we defined an object as something that has a crisply defined boundary. However, the boundaries that distinguish one object from another are often quite fuzzy. For example, look at your leg. Where does your knee begin, and where does it end? In recognizing human speech, how do we know that certain sounds connect to form a word, and are not instead a part of any surrounding words? Consider also the design of a word processing system. Do characters constitute a class, or are whole words a better choice? How do we treat arbitrary, noncontiguous selections of text? Also, what about sentences, paragraphs, or even whole documents: are these classes of objects relevant to our problem?

The fact that intelligent classification is difficult is hardly new information. Since there are parallels to the same problems in object-oriented design, consider for a moment the problems of classification in two other scientific disciplines: biology and chemistry.

Until the eighteenth century, the prevailing scientific thought was that all living organisms could be arranged from the most simple to the most complex, with the measure of complexity being highly subjective (not surprisingly, humans were usually placed at the top of this list). In the mid-1700s, however, the Swedish botanist Carolus Linnaeus suggested a more detailed taxonomy for categorizing organisms, according to what he called *genus* and *species*. A century later, Darwin proposed the theory that natural selection was the mechanism of evolution, whereby present-day species evolved from older ones. Darwin's theory depended upon an intelligent classification of species. As Darwin himself states, naturalists "try to arrange the species, genera, and families in each class, on what is called the natural system. But what is meant by this system? Some authors look at it merely as a scheme for arranging together those living objects which are most alike, and for separating those which are most unlike" [4]. In contemporary biology, classification denotes "the establishment of a hierarchical system of categories on the basis of presumed natural relationships among organisms" [5]. The most general category in a biological taxonomy is the kingdom, followed in order of increasing specialization, by phylum, subphylum, class, order, family, genus, and, finally, species. Historically, a particular organism is placed in a specific category according to its body structure, internal structural characteristics, and evolutionary relationships. More recently, classification has been approached by grouping organisms that share a common generic heritage: organisms that have similar DNA are grouped together. Classification by DNA is useful in distinguishing organisms that are structurally similar, but genetically very different. For example, contemporary research suggests that the lungfish and the cow are more closely related than the lungfish and the trout [6].

To a computer scientist, biology may seem to be a stodgily mature discipline, with well-defined criteria for classifying organisms. This is simply not the case. As the biologist May reports, "At the purely factual level, we do not know to within an order of magnitude how many species of plants and animals we share the globe with: fewer than 2 million are currently classified, and estimates of the total number range from under 5 million to more than 50 million" [7]. Furthermore, different criteria for classifying the same organisms yield different results. Martin suggests that "it all depends on what you want classification to do. If you want it to reflect precisely the genetic relatedness among species, that will give you one answer. But if you want it instead to say something about levels of adaptation, then you will get another" [8]. The moral here is that even in scientifically rigorous disciplines, classification is highly dependent upon the reason for the classification.

Similar lessons may be learned from chemistry [9]. In ancient times, all substances were thought to be some combination of earth, air, fire, and water. By today's standards (unless you are an alchemist), these do not represent very good classifications. In the mid-1600s, the chemist Robert Boyle proposed that elements were the primitive abstractions of chemistry, from which more complex compounds could be made. It wasn't until over a century later, in 1789, that the chemist Lavoisier published the first list of elements, containing some twenty-three items, some of which were later discovered not to be elements at all. The discovery of new elements continued and the list grew, but finally, in 1869, the chemist Mendeleyev proposed the periodic law that gave a precise criteria for organizing all known elements, and could predict the properties of those yet undiscovered. The periodic law was not the final story in the classification of the elements. In the early 1900s, elements with similar chemical properties but different atomic weights were discovered, leading to the idea of isotopes of elements.

The lesson here is simple: as Descartes states, "The discovery of an order is no easy task. . . . yet once the order has been discovered there is no difficulty at all in knowing it" [10]. The best software designs look simple, but as experience shows, it takes a lot of hard work to design a simple architecture.

The Incremental and Iterative Nature of Classification We have not said all this to defend lengthy software development schedules, although to the manager or end user, it does sometimes seem that software engineers need centuries to complete their work. Rather, we have told these stories to point out that

Different observers will classify the same object in different ways.

intelligent classification is intellectually hard work, and that it best comes about through an incremental and iterative process. This incremental and iterative nature is evident in the development of such diverse software technologies as graphical user interfaces, database standards, and even fourth-generation languages. As Shaw has observed in software engineering, "The development of individual abstractions often follows a common pattern. First, problems are solved *ad hoc*. As experience accumulates, some solutions turn out to work better than others, and a sort of folklore is passed informally from person to person. Eventually, the useful solutions are understood more systematically, and they are codified and analyzed. This enables the development of models that support automatic implementation and theories that allow the generalization of the solution. This in turn enables a more sophisticated level of practice and allows us to tackle harder problems – which we often approach *ad hoc*, starting the cycle over again" [11].

The incremental and iterative nature of classification directly impacts the construction of class and object hierarchies in the design of a complex software system. In practice, it is common to assert a certain class structure early in a design and then revise this structure over time. Only at later stages in the design, once clients have been built that use this structure, can we meaningfully evaluate the quality of our classification. On the basis of this experience, we may decide to create new subclasses from existing ones (derivation). We may split a large class into several smaller ones (factorization), or create one larger class by uniting smaller ones (composition). Occasionally, we may even discover previously unrecognized commonality, and proceed to devise a new class (abstraction) [12].

Why then, is classification so hard? We suggest that there are two important reasons. First, there is no such thing as a "perfect" classification, although certainly some classifications are better than others. As Coombs, Raffia, and Thrall state, "There are potentially at least as many ways of dividing up the world into object systems as there are scientists to undertake the task" [13]. Any classification is relative to the perspective of the observer doing the classification. Flood and Carson give the example that the United Kingdom "could be seen as an economy by economists, a society by sociologists, a threatened chunk of nature by conservationists, a tourist attraction by some Americans, a military threat by rulers of the Soviet Union, and the green, green grass of home to the more romantic of us Britons" [14]. Second, intelligent classification requires a tremendous amount of creative insight. Birtwistle, Dahl, Myhrhaug, and Nygard observe that "sometimes the answer is evident, sometimes it is a matter of taste, and at other times, the selection of suitable components is a crucial point in the analysis" [15]. This fact recalls the riddle, "Why is a laser beam like a goldfish? . . . because neither one can whistle" [16]. Only a creative mind can find sameness among such otherwise unrelated things.

4.2 Identifying Classes and Objects

Classical and Modern Approaches

The problem of classification has been the concern of countless philosophers, linguists, cognitive scientists, and mathematicians, even since before the time of Plato. It is reasonable to study their experiences and apply what we learn to object-oriented design. Historically, there have only been three general approaches to classification:

- Classical categorization
- Conceptual clustering
- Prototype theory [17]

Classical Categorization In the classical approach to categorization, "All the entities that have a given property or collection of properties in common form a category. Such properties are necessary and sufficient to define the category" [18]. For example, married people constitute a category: one is either married or not, and the value of this property is sufficient to decide to which group a particular person belongs. On the other hand, tall people do not form a category, unless we can agree to some absolute criteria for what distinguishes the property of tall from short.

A Problem of Classification

Figure 4-1 contains ten items, labeled *A* to *J*, each of which represents a train. Each train includes an engine (on the right) and from two to four cars, each shaped differently and holding different loads. Before reading further, spend the next few minutes arranging these trains into any number of groups you deem meaningful. For example, you might create three groups: one for trains whose engines have all black wheels, one for trains whose engines have all white wheels, and one for trains whose engines have black and white wheels.

This problem comes from the work by Stepp and Michalski on conceptual clustering [19]. As in real life, there is no "right" answer. In their experiments, subjects came up with some ninety-three different classifications. The most popular classification was by the length of the train, forming three groups (trains with two, three, and four cars). The second most popular classification was by engine wheel color, as we suggested. Of these ninety-three classifications, some forty of them were totally unique.

Our use of this example confirms Stepp and Michalski's study. Most of our subjects have used the two most popular classifications, although we have encountered some rather creative groupings. For example, one subject arranged these trains into two groups: one group represented trains labeled by letters containing straight lines *(A, E, F, H,* and *I)* and the other group representing trains labeled by letters containing curved lines. This is truly an example of nonlinear thinking: creative, albeit bizarre.

Once you have completed this task, let's change the requirements (again, as in real life). Suppose that circles represent toxic chemicals, rectangles represent lumber, and all other shapes of loads represent passengers. Try classifying the trains again, and see how this new knowledge changes your classification.

Among our subjects, the clustering of trains changed significantly. Most subjects classified trains according to whether or not they carried toxic loads. We conclude from this simple experiment that more knowledge about a domain, up to a point, makes it easier to achieve an intelligent classification.

Classical categorization comes to us first from Plato, and then from Aristotle through his classification of plants and animals, in which he uses a technique much akin to the contemporary children's game of Twenty Questions (Is it an animal, mineral, or vegetable? Does it have fur or feathers? Can it fly? Does is smell?) [20]. Later philosophers, most notably Aquinas, Descartes, and Locke, adopted this approach. As Aquinas stated, "We can name a thing according to the knowledge we have of its nature from its properties and effects" [21].

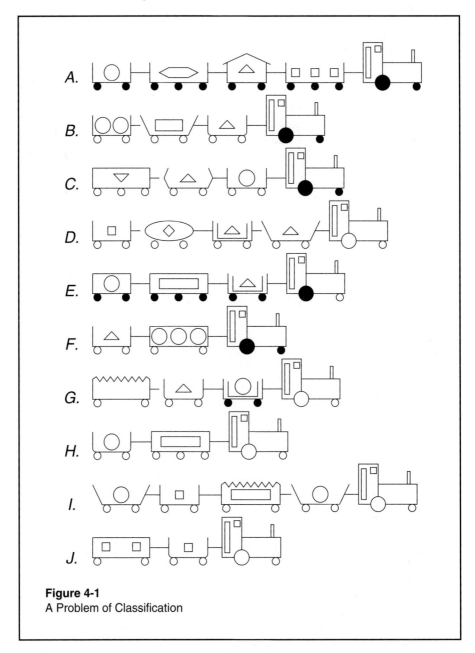

Figure 4-1
A Problem of Classification

The classical approach to categorization is also reflected in modern theories of child development. Piaget observed that around the age of one, a child typically develops the concept of object permanence; shortly thereafter, the child acquires skills in classifying these objects, first using basic categories such as dogs, cats, and toys [22]. Later, the child discovers more general categories (such as animals) and more specific ones (such as beagles) [23].

To summarize, the classical approach uses related properties as the criteria for sameness among objects. Specifically, one can divide objects into disjoint sets depending upon the presence or absence of a particular property. Minsky suggests that "the most useful sets of properties are those whose members do not interact too much. This explains the universal popularity of that particular combination of properties: size, color, shape, and substance. Because these attributes scarcely interact at all with one another, you can put them together in any combination whatsoever to make an object that is either large or small, red or green, wooden or glass, and having the shape of a sphere or a cube" [24]. In a general sense, properties may denote more than just measurable characteristics; they may also encompass observable behaviors. For example, the fact that a bird can fly but a fish cannot is one property that distinguishes an eagle from a salmon.

The particular properties that should be considered in a given situation are highly domain-specific. For instance, the color of a car may be important for the purposes of inventory control in an automobile manufacturing plant, but it is not at all relevant to the software that controls the traffic lights within a metropolitan area. This is in fact why we say that there are no absolute measures of classification, although a given class structure may be better suited to one application than another. As James suggests, "No one scheme of classification, more than any other, represents the real structure or order of nature. Nature indifferently submits to any and all divisions which we wish to make among existing things. Some classifications may be more significant than others, but only by reference to our interests, not because they represent reality more accurately or adequately" [25].

Classical categorization permeates much of contemporary Western thought, but, as our earlier example of classifying tall and short people suggests, this approach is not always satisfactory. Kosok observes that "natural categories tend to be messy: Most birds fly, but some do not. Chairs can consist of wood, plastic, or metal and can have almost any number of legs, depending on the whim of the designer. It seems practically impossible to come up with a property list for any natural category that excludes all examples that are not in the category and includes all examples that are in the category" [26]. These are indeed fundamental problems for classical categorization, which conceptual clustering and prototyping theory attempt to resolve.

Conceptual Clustering *Conceptual clustering* is a more modern variation of the classical approach, and largely derives from attempts to explain how knowledge is represented. As Stepp and Michalski state, "In this approach, classes (clusters of entities) are generated by first formulating conceptual descriptions of these classes and then classifying the entities according to the descriptions" [27]. For example, we may state a concept such as "a love song." This is a concept more than a property, for the "love songness" of any song is not something that may be measured empirically. However, if we decide that a certain song is more of a love song than not, we place it in this category. Thus, conceptual clustering represents more of a probabilistic clustering of objects.

Conceptual clustering is closely related to fuzzy (multivalue) set theory, in which objects may belong to one or more groups, in varying degrees of fitness. Conceptual clustering makes absolute judgments of classification by focusing upon the "best fit."

Prototype Theory Classical categorization and conceptual clustering are sufficiently expressive to account for most of the classifications we ever need in the design of complex software systems. However, there are still some situations in which these approaches are inadequate. This leads us to the more recent approach to classification, called *prototype theory*, which derives primarily from the work of Rosch and her colleagues in the field of cognitive psychology [28].

There are some abstractions that have neither clearly bounded properties nor concepts. As Lakoff explains the problem, "Wittgenstein pointed out that a category like game does not fit the classical mold, since there are no common properties shared by all games. . . . Though there is no single collection of properties that all games share, the category of games is united by what Wittgenstein calls family resemblances. . . . Wittgenstein also observed that there was no fixed boundary to the category game. The category could be extended and new kinds of games introduced, provided that they resembled previous games in appropriate ways" [29]. This is why the approach is called *prototype theory*: a class of objects is represented by a prototypical object, and an object is considered to be a member of this class if and only if it resembles this prototype in significant ways.

Lakeoff and Johnson apply prototype theory to the earlier problem of classifying chairs. They observe that "we understand beanbag chairs, barber chairs, and contour chairs as being chairs, not because they share some fixed set of defining properties with the prototype, but rather because they bear a sufficient family resemblance to the prototype. . . . There need be no fixed core of properties of prototypical chairs that are shared by both beanbag and barber chairs, yet they are both chairs because each, in its different way, is sufficiently close to the prototype. Interactional properties are prominent among the kinds of properties that count in determining sufficient family resemblance" [30].

This notion of interactional properties is central to the idea of prototype theory. In conceptual clustering, we group things according to distinct concepts. In prototype theory, we group things according to the degree of their relationship to concrete prototypes.

Applying Classical and Modern Theories To the developer in the trenches fighting changing requirements amidst limited resources and tight schedules, our discussion may seem to be far removed from the battlefields of reality. Actually, these three approaches to classification have direct application to object-oriented design.

In our experience, we identify classes and objects first according to the properties relevant to our particular domain. Here, we focus upon identifying the structures and behavior that are part of the vocabulary of our problem space. Many such abstractions are usually available for the picking [31]. If this approach fails to yield a satisfactory class structure, then we next consider clustering objects by concepts. Here, we focus our attention upon the behavior of collaborating objects. If either of these two approaches fails to capture our understanding of the problem domain, then we consider classification by association, through which clusters of objects are defined according to how closely each resembles some prototypical object.

More directly, these three approaches to classification provide the theoretical foundation of object-oriented analysis, which offers a number of pragmatic practices and rules of thumb that we may apply to identify classes and objects in the design of a complex software system.

Object-Oriented Analysis

The boundaries between analysis and design are fuzzy, although the focus of each is quite distinct. In analysis, we seek to model the world by *discovering* the classes and objects that form the vocabulary of the problem domain, and in design, we *invent* the abstractions and mechanisms that provide the behavior that this model requires.*

In the following sections, we examine a number of proven approaches for analysis that are relevant to object-oriented systems.

Classical Approaches A number of methodologists have proposed various sources of classes and objects, derived from the requirements of the problem domain. We call these approaches *classical* because they derive primarily from the principles of classical categorization.

For example, Shlaer and Mellor suggest that candidate classes and objects usually come from one of the following sources [32]:

- Tangible things   Cars, telemetry data, pressure sensors
- Roles   Mother, teacher, politician
- Events   Landing, interrupt, request
- Interactions   Loan, meeting, intersection

From the perspective of database modeling, Ross offers a similar list [33]:

- People   Humans who carry out some function
- Places   Areas set aside for people or things

---

* The notation and process described in this book are equally applicable to the traditional development phases of analysis and design, as we discuss further in Chapter 6. Indeed, it is for this reason that we renamed this second edition to be *Object-Oriented Analysis and Design.*

• Things	Physical objects, or groups of objects, that are tangible
• Organizations	Formally organized collections of people, resources, facilities, and capabilities having a defined mission, whose existence is largely independent of individuals
• Concepts	Principles or ideas not tangible *per se;* used to organize or keep track of business activities and/or communications
• Events	Things that happen, usually to something else at a given date and time, or as steps in an ordered sequence

Coad and Yourdon suggest yet another set of sources of potential objects [34]:

• Structure	"Is a" and "part of" relationships
• Other systems	External systems with which the application interacts
• Devices	Devices with which the application interacts
• Events remembered	An historical event that must be recorded
• Roles played	The different roles users play in interacting with the application
• Locations	Physical locations, offices, and sites important to the application
• Organizational units	Groups to which users belong

At a higher level of abstraction, Coad introduces the idea of subject areas, which are basically logical groups of classes that relate to some higher-level system function.

Behavior Analysis Whereas these classical approaches focus upon tangible things in the problem domain, another school of though in object-oriented analysis focuses upon dynamic behavior as the primary source of classes and objects.* These approaches are more akin to conceptual clustering: we form classes based upon groups of objects that exhibit similar behavior.

Wirfs-Brock, for example, emphasizes responsibilities, which denote "the knowledge an object maintains and the actions an object can perform. Responsibilities are meant to convey a sense of the purpose of an object and its place in the system. The responsibilities of an object are all the services it provides for all of the contracts it supports" [36]. In this manner, we group

---

* Shlaer and Mellor have extended their earlier work to focus on behavior as well. In particular, they study the life cycle of each object as a means of understanding the boundaries [35].

things that have common responsibilities, and form hierarchies of classes involving superclasses that embody general responsibilities and subclasses that specialize their behavior.

Rubin and Goldberg offer an approach to identifying classes and objects derived from system functions. As they suggest, "the approach we use emphasizes first understanding what takes place in the system. These are the system behaviors. We next assign these behaviors to parts of the system, and try to understand who initiates and who participates in these behaviors. . . . Initiators and participants that play significant roles are recognized as objects, and are assigned the behavioral responsibilities for these roles" [37].

Rubin's concept of system behavior is closely related to the idea of function points, first suggested in 1979 by Albrech. A function point is "defined as one end-user business function" [38]. A business function represents some kind of output, inquiry, input, file, or interface. Although the information-system roots of this definition show through, the idea of a function point generalizes to all kinds of automated systems: A function point is any relevant outwardly-visible and testable behavior of the system.

Domain Analysis The principles we have discussed thus far are typically applied to the development of single, specific applications. Domain analysis, on the other hand, seeks to identify the classes and objects that are common to all applications within a given domain, such as patient record tracking, bond trading, compilers, or missile avionics systems. If you are in the midst of a design and stuck for ideas as to the key abstractions that exist, a narrow domain analysis can help by pointing you to the key abstractions that have proven useful in other related systems. Domain analysis works well because, except for special situations, there are very few truly unique kinds of software systems.

The idea of domain analysis was first suggested by Neighbors. We define domain analysis as "an attempt to identify the objects, operations, and relationships [that] domain experts perceive to be important about the domain" [39]. Moore and Bailin suggest the following steps in domain analysis:

- "Construct a strawman generic model of the domain by consulting with domain experts.
- Examine existing systems within the domain and represent this understanding in a common format.
- Identify similarities and differences between the systems by consulting with domain experts.
- Refine the generic model to accommodate existing systems" [40].

Domain analysis may be applied across similar applications (vertical domain analysis), as well as to related parts of the same application (horizontal domain analysis). For example, when starting to design a new patient-monitoring system, it is reasonable to survey the architecture of existing systems to understand what key abstractions and mechanisms were previously employed and to evaluate which were useful and which were not. Similarly, an accounting system must provide many different kinds of reports. By considering these reports within the same application as a single domain, a domain analysis can lead the developer to an understanding of the key abstractions and mechanisms that serve all the different kinds of reports. The resulting classes and objects reflect a set of key abstractions and mechanisms generalized to the immediate report-generation problem; therefore, the resulting design is likely to be simpler than if each report had been analyzed and designed separately.

Who exactly is a domain expert? Often, a domain expert is simply a user, such as a train engineer or dispatcher in a railway system, or a nurse or doctor in a hospital. A domain expert need not be a software engineer; more commonly, he or she is simply a person who is intimately familiar with all the elements of a particular problem. A domain expert speaks the vocabulary of the problem domain.

Some managers may be concerned with the idea of direct communication between developers and end users (for some, even more frightening is the prospect of letting an end user see a developer!). For highly complex systems, domain analysis may involve a formal process, using the resources of multiple domain experts and developers over a period of many months. In practice, such a formal analysis is rarely necessary. Often, all it takes to clear up a design problem is a brief meeting between a domain expert and a developer. It is truly amazing to see what a little bit of domain knowledge can do to assist a developer in making intelligent design decisions. Indeed, we find it highly useful to have many such meetings throughout the design of a system. Domain analysis is rarely a monolithic activity; it is better focused if we consciously choose to analyze a little, then design a little.

Use-Case Analysis In isolation, the practices of classical analysis, behavior analysis, and domain analysis all depend upon a large measure of personal experience on the part of the analyst. For the majority of development projects, this is unacceptable, because such a process is neither deterministic nor predictably successful.

However, there is one practice that can be coupled with all three of these earlier approaches, to drive the process of analysis in a meaningful way. That practice is use-case analysis, first formalized by Jacobson. Jacobson defines a use case as "a particular form or pattern or exemplar of usage, a scenario that begins with some user of the system initiating some transaction or sequence of interrelated events" [41].

Briefly, we can apply use-case analysis as early as requirements analysis, at which time end users, other domain experts, and the development team enumerate the scenarios that are fundamental to the system's operation (we need not elaborate upon these scenarios at first, we can simply enumerate them). These scenarios collectively describe the system functions of the application. Analysis then proceeds by a study of each scenario, using storyboarding techniques similar to practices in the television and movie industry [42]. As the team walks through each scenario, they must identify the objects that participate in the scenario, the responsibilities of each object, and how those objects collaborate with other objects, in terms of the operations each invokes upon the other. In this manner, the team is forced to craft a clear separation of concerns among all abstractions. As the development process continues, these initial scenarios are expanded to consider exceptional conditions as well as secondary system behaviors (what Goldstein and Alger speak of as peripheral topics [43]). The results from these secondary scenarios either introduce new abstractions or add, modify, or reassign the responsibilities of existing abstractions. As we will discuss further in Chapter 6, scenarios also serve as the basis of system tests.

CRC Cards CRC cards have emerged as a simple yet marvelously effective way to analyze scenarios.* First proposed by Beck and Cunningham as a tool for teaching object-oriented programming [44], CRC cards have proven to be a useful development tool that facilitates brainstorming and enhances communication among developers. A CRC card is nothing more than a 3x5 index card,** upon which the analyst writes – in pencil – the name of a class (at the top of the card), its responsibilities (on one half of the card) and its collaborators (on the other half of the card). One card is created for each class identified as relevant to the scenario. As the team walks through the scenario, they may assign new responsibilities to an existing class, group certain responsibilities to form a new class, or (most commonly) divide the responsibilities of one class into more fine-grained ones, and perhaps distribute these responsibilities to a different class.

CRC cards can be spatially arranged to represent patterns of collaboration. As viewed from the dynamic semantics of the scenario, the cards are arranged to show the flow of messages among prototypical instances of each class; as viewed from the static semantics of the scenario, the cards are arranged to represent generalization/specialization or aggregation hierarchies among the classes.

Informal English Description A radical alternative to classical object-oriented analysis was first proposed by Abbott, who suggests writing an English description of the problem (or a part of a problem) and then underlining the nouns and verbs [45]. The nouns represent candidate objects, and the verbs represent candidate operations upon them. This technique lends itself to automation, and such a system has been built at the Tokyo Institute of Technology and at Fujitsu [46].

Abbott's approach is useful because it is simple and because it forces the developer to work in the vocabulary of the problem space. However, it is by

---

* CRC stands for Class/Responsibilities/Collaborators
** If your software development budget can handle it, buy 5x7 cards. Cards with lines are nice, a sprinkling of colored cards shows that you are a very cool developer.

no means a rigorous approach, and it definitely does not scale well to anything beyond fairly trivial problems. Human language is a terribly imprecise vehicle of expression, so the quality of the resulting list of objects and operations depends upon the writing skill of its author. Furthermore, any noun can be verbed, and any verb can be nouned; therefore, it is easy to skew the candidate list to emphasize either objects or operations.

Structured Analysis A second alternative to classical object-oriented analysis uses the products of structured analysis as a front end to object-oriented design. This technique is appealing only because a large number of analysts are skilled in structured analysis, and many CASE tools exist that support the automation of these methods. Personally, we discourage the use of structured analysis as a front end to object-oriented design, but for some organizations, it is the only pragmatic alternative.

In this approach, we start with an essential model of the system, as described by data flow diagrams and the other products of structured analysis. These diagrams provide us with a reasonably formal model of the problem. From this model, we may proceed to identify the meaningful classes and objects in our problem domain in three different ways.

McMenamin and Palmer suggest starting with an analysis of the data dictionary and proceeding to analyze the model's context diagram. As they state, "With your list of essential data elements, think about what they tell you or what they describe. If they were adjectives in a sentence, for instance, what nouns would they modify? The answers to this question make up the list of candidate objects" [47]. These candidate objects typically derive from the surrounding environment, from the essential inputs and outputs, and from the products, services, and other resources managed by the system.

The next two techniques involve analyzing individual data flow diagrams. Given a particular data flow diagram (using the terminology of Ward/Mellor [48]), candidate objects may be derived from the following:

- External entities
- Data stores
- Control stores
- Control transformations

Candidate classes derive from two sources:

- Data flows
- Control flows

This leaves us with data transformations, which we assign either as operations upon existing objects or as the behavior of an object we invent to serve as the agent responsible for this transformation.

Seidewitz and Stark suggest another technique, which they call *abstraction analysis*. Abstraction analysis focuses upon the identification of central entities, which are similar in nature to central transforms in structured design. As they state, "In structured analysis, input and output data are examined and followed inwards until they reach the highest level of abstraction. The processes between the inputs and the outputs form the central transform. In abstraction analysis a designer does the same, but also examines the central transform to determine which processes and states represent the best abstract model of what the system does" [49]. After identifying the central entity in a particular data flow diagram, abstraction analysis proceeds to identify all the supporting entities by following the afferent and efferent data flows from the central entity, and grouping the processes and states encountered along the way. In practice, Seidewitz and Stark have found abstraction analysis a difficult technique to apply successfully, and as an alternative recommend object-oriented analysis methods [50].

We must emphasize that structured design, as normally coupled with structured analysis, is entirely orthogonal to the principles of object-oriented design. Our experience indicates that using structured analysis as a front end to object-oriented design often fails when the developer is unable to resist the urge of falling back into the abyss of the structured design mindset. Another very real danger is the fact that many analysts tend to write data flow diagrams that reflect a design rather than an essential model of the problem. It is tremendously difficult to build an object-oriented system from a model that is so obviously biased towards algorithmic decomposition. This is why we prefer object-oriented analysis as the front end to object-oriented design: there is simply less danger of polluting the design with preconceived algorithmic notions.

If you must use structured analysis as a front end, for whatever honorable reasons,* we suggest that you stop writing data flow diagrams as soon as they start to smell of a design instead of an essential model. Also, it is a healthy practice to walk away from the products of structured analysis once the design is fully underway. Remember that the products of development, including data flow diagrams, are not ends in themselves; they should be viewed simply as tools along the way that aid the developer's intellectual comprehension of the problem and its implementation. One typically writes a data flow diagram and then invents the mechanisms that implement the desired behavior. Practically speaking, the very act of design changes the developer's understanding of the problem, making the original model somewhat obsolete. Keeping the original model up to date with the design is terribly labor intensive, is not amenable to automation, and, frankly, doesn't add a lot of value. Thus, only the products of structured analysis that are at a sufficiently high level of abstraction should be retained. They capture an essential model of the problem, and so lend themselves to any number of different designs.

---

* Political and historical reasons are distinctly not honorable.

4.3 Key Abstractions and Mechanisms

Identifying Key Abstractions

Finding Key Abstractions A *key abstraction* is a class or object that forms part of the vocabulary of the problem domain. The primary value of identifying such abstractions is that they give boundaries to our problem; they highlight the things that are in the system and therefore relevant to our design, and suppress the things that are outside the system and therefore superfluous. The identification of key abstractions is highly domain-specific. As Goldberg states, the "appropriate choice of objects depends, of course, on the purposes to which the application will be put and the granularity of information to be manipulated" [51].

As we mentioned earlier, the identification of key abstractions involves two processes: discovery and invention. Through discovery, we come to recognize the abstractions used by domain experts; if the domain expert talks about it, then the abstraction is usually important [52]. Through invention, we create new classes and objects that are not necessarily part of the problem domain, but are useful artifacts in the design or implementation. For example, a customer using an automated teller speaks in terms of accounts, deposits, and withdrawals; these words are part of the vocabulary of the problem domain. A developer of such a system uses these same abstractions, but must also introduce new ones, such as databases, screen managers, lists, queues, and so on. These key abstractions are artifacts of the particular design, not of the problem domain.

Perhaps the most powerful way to identify key abstractions is to look at the problem or design and see if there are any abstractions that are similar to the classes and objects that already exist. As we will discuss further in Chapter 6, in the absence of such reusable abstractions, we recommend the use of scenarios to drive the process of identifying classes and objects.

Refining Key Abstractions Once we identify a certain key abstraction as a candidate, we must evaluate it according to the metrics described in the previous chapter. As Stroustrup suggests, "Often this means that the programmer must focus on the questions: how are objects of this class created? can objects of this class be copied and/or destroyed? what operations can be done on such objects? If there are no good answers to such questions, the concept probably wasn't 'clean' in the first place, and it might be a good idea to think a bit more about the problem and the proposed solution instead of immediately starting to 'code around' the problems" [53].

Given a new abstraction, we must place it in the context of the existing class and object hierarchies we have designed. Practically speaking, this is

LOOK AT THE QUADRUPED RECLINING ON THE VERANDA

Classes and objects should be at the right level of abstraction: neither too high nor too low.

neither a top-down nor a bottom-up activity. As Halbert and O'Brien observe, "You do not always design types in a type hierarchy by starting with a supertype and then creating the subtypes. Frequently, you create several seemingly disparate types, realize they are related, and then factor out their common characteristics into one or more supertypes. . . . several passes up and down are usually required to produce a complete and correct program design" [54]. This is not a license to hack, but an observation, based upon experience, that object-oriented design is both incremental and iterative. Stroustrup makes a similar observation when he notes that "the most common reorganizations of a class hierarchy are factoring the common part of two classes into a new class and splitting a class into two new ones" [55].

Placing classes and objects at the right levels of abstraction is difficult. Sometimes we may find a general subclass, and so may choose to move it up in the class structure, thus increasing the degree of sharing. This is called *class promotion* [56]. Similarly, we may find a class to be too general, thus making inheritance by a subclass difficult because of the large semantic gap. This is called a *grainsize conflict* [57]. In either case, we strive to identify cohesive and loosely coupled abstractions, so as to mitigate these two situations.

Naming things properly – so that they reflect their semantics – is often treated lightly by most developers, yet is important in capturing the essence of the abstractions we are describing. Software should be written as carefully as English prose, with consideration given to the reader as well as to the computer

[58]. Consider for a moment all the names we may need just to identify a single object: we have the name of the object itself, the name of its class, and the name of the module in which that class is declared. Multiply this by thousands of objects and possibly hundreds of classes, and you have a very real problem.

We offer the following suggestions:

- Objects should be named with proper noun phrases, such as `theSensor` or just simply `shape`.

- Classes should be named with common noun phrases, such as `Sensors` or `Shapes`.

- Modifier operations should be named with active verb phrases, such as `draw` or `moveLeft`.

- Selector operations should imply a query or be named with verbs of the form "to be," such as `extentOf` or `isOpen`.

- The use of underscores and styles of capitalization are largely matters of personal taste. No matter which cosmetic style you use, at least have your programs be self-consistent.

Identifying Mechanisms

Finding Mechanisms In the previous chapter, we used the term *mechanism* to describe any structure whereby objects collaborate to provide some behavior that satisfies a requirement of the problem. Whereas the design of a class embodies the knowledge of how individual objects behave, a mechanism is a design decision about how collections of objects cooperate. Mechanisms thus represent patterns of behavior.

For example, consider a system requirement for an automobile: pushing the accelerator should cause the engine to run faster, and releasing the accelerator should cause the engine to run slower. How this actually comes about is absolutely immaterial to the driver. Any mechanism may be employed as long as it delivers the required behavior, and thus which mechanism is selected is largely a matter of design choice. More specifically, any of the following designs might be considered:

- A mechanical linkage from the accelerator to the carburetor (the most common mechanism).

- An electronic linkage from a pressure sensor below the accelerator to a computer that controls the carburetor (a drive-by-wire mechanism).

- No linkage exists; the gas tank is placed on the roof of the car, and gravity causes fuel to flow to the engine. Its rate of flow is regulated by a clip around the fuel line; pushing on the accelerator pedal eases tension on the clip, causing the fuel to flow faster (a low-cost mechanism).

Mechanisms are the means whereby objects collaborate to provide some higher-level behavior.

Which mechanism a developer chooses from a set of alternatives is most often a result of other factors, such as cost, reliability, manufacturability, and safety.

Just as it is rude for a client to violate the interface of another object, so it is socially unacceptable for objects to step outside the boundaries of the rules of behavior dictated by a particular mechanism. Indeed, it would be surprising for a driver if stepping on an accelerator turned on the car's lights instead of causing the engine to run faster.

Whereas key abstractions reflect the vocabulary of the problem domain, mechanisms are the soul of the design. During the design process, the developer must consider not only the design of individual classes, but also how instances of these classes work together. Again, the use of scenarios drives this analysis process. Once a developer decides upon a particular pattern of collaboration, the work is distributed among many objects by defining suitable methods in the appropriate classes. Ultimately, the protocol of an individual class encompasses all the operations required to implement all the behavior and all the mechanisms associated with each of its instances.

Mechanisms thus represent strategic design decisions, as does the design of a class structure. In contrast, however, the interface of an individual class is more of a tactical design decision. These strategic decisions must be made explicitly; otherwise we will end up with a mob of relatively uncooperative objects, all pushing and shoving to do their work with little regard for other objects. The most elegant, lean, and fast programs embody carefully engineered mechanisms.

Mechanisms are actually one in a spectrum of patterns we find in well-structured software systems. At the low end of the food chain, we have idioms. An *idiom* is an expression peculiar to a certain programming language or application culture, representing a generally accepted convention for use of the language.* For example, in CLOS, no programmer would use underscores in function or variable names, although this is common practice in Ada [59]. Part of the effort in learning a programming language is learning its idioms, which are usually passed down as folklore from programmer to programmer. However, as Coplien points out, idioms play an important role in codifying low-level patterns. He notes that, "many common programming tasks [are] idiomatic" and therefore identifying such idioms allows "using C++ constructs to express functionality outside the language proper, while giving the illusion of being part of the language" [60].

At the high end of the food chain, we have frameworks. A *framework* is collection of classes that provide a set of services for a particular domain; a framework thus exports a number of individual classes and mechanisms which clients can use or adapt. As we will discuss in Chapter 9, frameworks represent reuse in the large.

Whereas idioms are part of a programming culture, frameworks are often the product of commercial ventures. For example, Apple's MacApp (and its successor, Bedrock) are both application frameworks, written in C++, for building applications that conform to Macintosh user interface standards. Similarly, the Microsoft Foundation Library and Borland's ObjectWindows library are frameworks for building applications that conform to the Windows user interface standards.

Examples of Mechanisms Consider the drawing mechanism commonly used in graphical user interfaces. Several objects must collaborate to present an image to a user: a window, a view, the model being viewed, and some client that knows when (but not how) to display this model. The client first tells the window to draw itself. Since it may encompass several subviews, the window next tells each of its subviews to draw themselves. Each subview in turn tells its model to draw itself, ultimately resulting in an image shown to the user. In this mechanism, the model is entirely decoupled from the window and view in which it is presented: views can send messages to models, but models cannot send messages to views. Smalltalk uses a variation of this mechanism, and calls it the *model-view-controller (MVC)* paradigm [61]. A similar mechanism is employed in almost every object-oriented graphical user interface framework.

Mechanisms thus represent a level of reuse that is higher than the reuse of individual classes. For example, the MVC paradigm is used extensively in the

---

* One defining characteristic of an idiom is that ignoring or violating the idiom has immediate social consequences: you are branded as a yahoo or, worse, an outsider, unworthy of respect.

Smalltalk user interface. The MVC paradigm in turn builds on another mechanism, the dependency mechanism, which is embodied in the behavior of the Smalltalk base class `Model`, and thus pervades much of the Smalltalk class library.

Examples of mechanisms may be found in virtually every domain. For example, the structure of an operating system may be described at the highest level of abstraction according to the mechanism used to dispatch programs. A particular design might be monolithic (such as MS-DOS), or it may employ a kernel (such as UNIX) or a process hierarchy (as in the THE operating system) [62]. In artificial intelligence, a variety of mechanisms have been explored for the design of reasoning systems. One of the most widely used paradigms is the blackboard mechanism, in which individual knowledge sources independently update a blackboard. There is no central control in such a mechanism, but any change to the blackboard may trigger an agent to explore some new problem-solving path [63]. Coad has similarly identified a number of common mechanisms in object-oriented systems, including patterns of time association, event logging, and broadcasting [64]. In each case, these mechanisms manifest themselves not as individual classes, but as the structure of collaborating classes.

This completes our study of classification and of the concepts that serve as the foundation of object-oriented design. The next three chapters focus on the method itself, including its notation, process, and pragmatics.

Summary

- The identification of classes and objects is the fundamental issue in object-oriented design; identification involves both discovery and invention.

- Classification is fundamentally a problem of clustering.

- Classification is an incremental and iterative process, made difficult because a given set of objects may be classified in many equally proper ways.

- The three approaches to classification include classical categorization (classification by properties), conceptual clustering (classification by concepts), and prototype theory (classification by association with a prototype).

- Scenarios are a powerful tool of object-oriented analysis; and can be used to drive the process of classical analysis, behavior analysis, and domain analysis.

- Key abstractions reflect the vocabulary of the problem domain and may either be discovered from the problem domain, or invented as part of the design.

- Mechanisms denote strategic design decisions regarding the collaborative activity of many different kinds of objects.

Further Readings

The problem of classification is timeless. In his work titled *Statesman*, Plato introduces the classical approach to categorization, through which objects with similar properties are grouped. In *Categories*, Aristotle picks up this theme and analyzes the differences between classes and objects. Several centuries later, Aquinas, in *Summa Theologica*, and then Descartes, in *Rules for the Direction of the Mind*, ponder the philosophy of classification. Contemporary objectivist philosophers include Rand [I 1979].

Alternatives to the objectivist view of the world are discussed in Lakoff [I 1980] and Goldstein and Alger [C 1992]

Classification is an essential human skill. Theories regarding its acquisition during early childhood development were pioneered by Piaget, and are summarized by Maier [A 1969]. Lefrancois [A 1977] offers a very readable introduction to these ideas and provides an excellent discourse on children's acquisition of the object concept.

Cognitive scientists have explored the problems of classification in great detail. Newell and Simon [A 1972] provide an unmatched source of material regarding human classification skills. More general information may be found in Simon [A 1982], Hofstadter [I 1979], Siegler and Richards [A 1982], and Stillings, Feinstein, Garfield, Rissland, Rosenbaum, Weisler, and Baker-Ward [A 1987]. Lakoff [A 1987], a linguist, offers insights into the ways different human languages have evolved to cope with the problems of classification and what this reveals about the mind. Minksy [A 1986] approaches this subject from the opposite direction, starting with a theory regarding the structure of the mind.

Conceptual clustering, an approach to knowledge representation through classification, is described in detail by Michalski and Stepp [A 1983, 1986], Peckham and Maryanski [J 1988], and Sowa [A 1984]. Domain analysis, an approach to finding key abstractions and mechanisms by examining the vocabulary of the problem domain, is described in the comprehensive collection of papers by Prieto-Diaz and Arango [A 1991]. Iscoe [B 1988] has made several important contributions to this field. Additional information may be found in Iscoe, Browne, and Weth [B 1989], Moore and Bailin [B 1988], and Arango [B 1989].

Intelligent classification often requires looking at the world in innovative ways, and these skills can be taught (or, at least, encouraged). VonOech [I 1990] suggests some paths to creativity. Coad [A 1993] has a developed a board game (the *Object Game*) that fosters skills in class and object identification.

Although the field is still in its infancy, some very promising work is being carried out in the cataloging of patterns in software systems, giving rise to a taxonomy of idioms, mechanisms, and frameworks. Interesting references include Coplien [G 1992], Coad [A 1992], Johnson [A 1992], Shaw [A 1989, 1990, 1991], Wirfs-Brock [C 1991]. Alexander's influential work [I 1979] applies patterns to the field of building architecture and city planning.

Mathematicians have attempted to devise empirical approaches to classification, leading to what is called *measurement theory*. Stevens [A 1946] and Coombs, Raiffa, and Thrall [A 1954] provide the seminal work on this topic.

The Classification Society of North America publishes a journal twice a year, containing a variety of papers on the problems of classification.

THE METHOD

Which innovation leads to a successful design and which to a failure is not completely predictable. Each opportunity to design something new, either bridge or airplane or skyscraper, presents the engineer with choices that may appear countless. The engineer may decide to copy as many seemingly good features as he can from existing designs that have successfully withstood the forces of man and nature, but he may also decide to improve upon those aspects of prior designs that appear to be wanting.

HENRY PETROSKI
To Engineer is Human

CHAPTER 5

The Notation

The act of drawing a diagram does not constitute analysis or design. A diagram simply captures a statement of a system's behavior (for analysis), or the vision and details of an architecture (for design). If you follow the work of any engineer – software, civil, mechanical, chemical, architectural, or whatever – you will soon realize that the one and only place that a system is conceived is in the mind of the designer. As this design unfolds over time, it is often captured on such high-tech media as white boards, napkins, and the backs of envelopes [1].

Still, having a well-defined and expressive notation is important to the process of software development. First, a standard notation makes it possible for an analyst or developer to describe a scenario or formulate an architecture and then unambiguously communicate those decisions to others. Draw an electrical circuit, and the symbol for a transistor will be understood by virtually every electrical engineer in the world. Similarly, if an architect in New York City drafts the plans for a house, a builder in San Francisco will have little trouble understanding where to place doors, windows, and electrical outlets from the details of the blueprints. Second, as Whitehead states in his seminal work on mathematics, "By relieving the brain of all unnecessary work, a good notation sets it free to concentrate on more advanced problems" [2]. Third, an

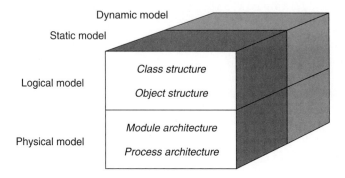

Figure 5-1
The Models of Object-Oriented Development

expressive notation makes it possible to eliminate much of the tedium of checking the consistency and correctness of these decisions by using automated tools. As a report by the Defense Science Board states, "Software development is and always will be a labor-intensive technology. . . . Although our machines can do the dog-work and can help us keep track of our edifices, concept development is the quintessentially human activity. . . . The part of software development that will not go away is the crafting of conceptual structures; the part that can go away is the labor of expressing them" [3].

5.1 Elements of the Notation

The Need for Multiple Views

It is impossible to capture all the subtle details of a complex software system in just one view. As Kleyn and Gingrich observe, "One must understand both the structure and the function of the objects involved. One must understand the taxonomic structure of the class objects, the inheritance mechanisms used, the individual behaviors of objects, and the dynamic behavior of the system as a whole. The problem is somewhat analogous to that of viewing a sports event such as tennis or a football game. Many different camera angles are required to provide an understanding of the action taking place. Each camera reveals particular aspects of the action that could not be conveyed by one camera alone" [4].

First introduced in Chapter 1, Figure 5-1 indicates the different models we have found to be important in object-oriented development. For a given project, the products of analysis and design are expressed through these models. Collectively, these different models are semantically rich: they are expressive enough to allow a developer to capture all of the interesting strategic and tactical decisions one must make during the analysis of a system as well as during the formulation of its architecture, and they are complete enough to serve as blueprints for implementation in almost any object-oriented programming language.

The fact that this notation is detailed does not mean that every aspect of it must be used at all times. In fact, a proper subset of this notation is sufficient to express the semantics of a large percentage of analysis and design issues; one of our colleagues refers to this subset as the *Booch Lite* notation. We will highlight this subset during our presentation of the notation in this chapter. Why then bother with the detail beyond this subset? Quite simply, such detail is necessary to express certain important tactical decisions; additionally, some detail exists to facilitate the creation of forward-engineering and reverse-engineering tools, which provide integration of front-end CASE tools that support this notation together with software development environments that focus upon manipulating the products of the object-oriented programming language.

As Weinberg notes, "In other design fields, such as architecture, the rough sketch is the most frequently used graphic device, and precise detailed drawings are rarely used at all until the creative part of the design work is finished" [5]. Remember, a notation is only a vehicle for capturing the reasoning about the behavior and architecture of a system; a notation is not an end in itself. Therefore, one should apply only those elements of the notation that are necessary to convey the intended meaning, and nothing more. Just as it is dangerous to overspecify a set of requirements, so it is dangerous to overspecify a solution to a problem. For example, on a blueprint, an architect may show the general location of a light switch in a room, but its exact location will not be established until the construction manager and owner do an electrical walk-through, after the house has been framed. It would be foolish to specify the precise three-dimensional coordinates of the light switch on the blueprint (unless, of course, this was a detail that was functionally important to the owner: perhaps the owner's family is significantly taller or shorter than average). Thus, if the analysts, designers, and implementors of a software-intensive system are highly skilled and have already established a close working relationship, then rough sketches may suffice (although it will still be necessary to leave a legacy of the architectural vision for the sake of the system's maintainers). If, on the other hand, the implementors are not quite so skilled, or if the developers are separated geographically, in time, or by contract, then more detail will be required during the development process. The notation we present in this chapter covers each of these situations.

Different programming languages sometimes use different terms to express the same concept. The notation we present in this chapter is largely language-independent, as any good development notation should be. Of course, some elements of the notation have no parallel in certain languages and thus should be avoided if that language is to be used for implementation. For example, free subprograms cannot be declared in Smalltalk, and therefore class utilities will not in general be used in a system implemented in Smalltalk. Similarly, C++ does not support metaclasses, and therefore this element of the notation may be ignored. Also, there is nothing wrong with tailoring this notation in language-specific ways. For example, the qualification associated with an operation might be tailored for CLOS to identify primary methods, as well as :before, :after, and :around methods. Similarly, a tool for C++ might ignore the notation's class specification, and use C++ header files directly.

The only purpose of this chapter is to describe the syntax and semantics of our notation for object-oriented analysis and design. We will provide a few small examples of this notation, using the problem of the hydroponics gardening system that we introduced in Chapter 2. This current chapter does not explain the process by which we derived these figures; that is the topic of Chapter 6. In Chapter 7, we discuss the pragmatics of this process, and in Chapters 8 through 12, we demonstrate the practical application of this notation through a series of extended application examples.

Models and Views

In Chapter 3, we explained the meaning of classes and objects and their relationships. As Figure 5-1 suggests, we may capture our analysis and design decisions regarding these classes and objects and their collaborations according to two dimensions: their logical/physical view, and their static/dynamic view. Both dimensions are necessary to specify the structure and behavior of an object-oriented system.

For each dimension, we define a number of diagrams that denote a view of a system's models. In this sense, the system's models denote the "whole truth" about its classes, relationships, and other entities, and each diagram represents a projection of these models. In the steady state, all such diagrams must be consistent with the model and therefore among themselves.

For example, consider an application comprising several hundred classes; the classes form part of the application's model. It is impossible and in fact unnecessary to produce a single diagram that shows all of these classes and all of their relationships. Rather, we might view this model through several class diagrams, each of which presents one view of the model. One diagram might show the inheritance lattice of certain key classes; another might show the transitive closure of all classes used by one particular class. At times when the model is stable (what we speak of as a *steady state*), all such diagrams remain semantically consistent with one another and with the model. For example, if in a given scenario (which we describe in an object diagram), object A passes the message M to object B, then M must be defined for B's class either directly or indirectly. In a corresponding class diagram, there must be an appropriate relationship between the classes of A and B, such that instances of A's class can in fact invoke message M.

For simplicity, across all diagrams, all entities with the same name and within the same scope are considered to be references to the same model item. For example, if class C appears in two different diagrams for the same system, both are references to the same class C. The exception to this rule is for operations, whose names may be overloaded.

To distinguish one diagram from another, we must provide a name whose purpose is to indicate the focus or intent of the diagram. Other labels and notes may be attached to a diagram to further elucidate its contents, as we will describe in a later section; such notes in general have no additional semantics.

Logical Versus Physical Models

The logical view of a system serves to describe the existence and meaning of the key abstractions and mechanisms that form the problem space or that define the system's architecture. The physical model of a system describes the concrete software and hardware composition of the system's context or implementation.

During analysis, we must address the following central questions:

- What is the desired behavior of the system?
- What are the roles and responsibilities of the objects that carry out this behavior?

As we described in the previous chapter, we use scenarios to express our decisions about the behavior of a system. In the logical model, object diagrams serve as the primary vehicles for describing scenarios. During analysis, we may also use class diagrams to capture our abstraction of these objects in terms of their common roles and responsibilities.

During design, we must address the following central questions relative to the system's architecture:

- What classes exist, and how are those classes related?
- What mechanisms are used to regulate how objects collaborate?
- Where should each class and object be declared?
- To what processor should a process be allocated, and for a given processor, how should its multiple processes be scheduled?

We use the following diagrams, respectively, to answer to these questions:

- Class diagrams
- Object diagrams
- Module diagrams
- Process diagrams

Static Versus Dynamic Semantics

The four diagrams we have introduced thus far are largely static. However, events happen dynamically in all software-intensive systems: objects are created and destroyed, objects send messages to one another in an orderly fashion, and in some systems, external events trigger operations upon certain objects. Not surprisingly, describing a dynamic event in a static medium such as a sheet of paper is a difficult problem, but it confronts virtually every scientific discipline. In object-oriented development, we express the dynamic semantics of a problem or its implementation through two additional diagrams:

- State transition diagrams
- Interaction diagram

Each class may have an associated state transition diagram that indicates the event-ordered behavior of the class's instances. Similarly, in conjunction with an object diagram representing a scenario, we may provide a script or interaction diagram to show the time or event-ordering of messages as they are evaluated.

The Role of Tools

Given automated support for any notation, one of the things that tools can do is help bad designers create ghastly designs much more quickly than they ever could in the past. Great designs come from great designers, not from great tools. Tools simply empower the individual, freeing him or her to concentrate upon the truly creative aspects of analysis or design. Thus, there are some things that tools can do well and some things that tools cannot do at all. For example, when we use an object diagram to show a scenario with a message being passed from one object to another, a tool can ensure that the message is in fact part of the object's protocol; this is an example of consistency checking. When we state invariants, such as "there are no more than three instances of this class," we expect that a tool can enforce these conventions; this is an example of constraint checking. Similarly, a tool can tell us if certain classes or methods of a given class are never used; this is an example of completeness checking. Additionally, a sophisticated tool might tell us how long it takes to complete a certain operation, or whether or not a certain state in a state transition diagram is reachable; this is an example of analysis. On the other hand, a tool cannot tell us that we ought to invent a new class so as to simplify our class structure; that takes human insight. We might consider trying to use some expert system as such a tool, but this requires (1) a person who is an expert both in object-oriented development and in the problem domain and (2) the ability to articulate classification heuristics, as well as a great deal of common-sense knowledge. We don't expect such tools to emerge in the near future; in the meantime, we have real systems to create.

5.2 Class Diagrams

Essentials: Classes and Their Relationships

A *class diagram* is used to show the existence of classes and their relationships in the logical view of a system. A single class diagram represents a view of the

Figure 5-2
Class Icon

class structure of a system. During analysis, we use class diagrams to indicate the common roles and responsibilities of the entities that provide the system's behavior. During design, we use class diagrams to capture the structure of the classes that form the system's architecture.

The two essential elements of a class diagram are classes and their basic relationships.

Classes Figure 5-2 shows the icon we use to represent a class in a class diagram. Its shape is that of a cloud; some call it an amorphous blob.[*]

A name is required for each class; if the name is particularly long, it can either be elided or the icon magnified. Every class name must be unique to its enclosing class category. For certain languages, most notably C++ and

---

[*] The selection of icons for any notation is a difficult task, and is not to be taken lightly. Indeed, icon design is largely an art, not a science, and requires a careful balance between the demands for expressiveness and simplicity. Our choice of the cloud icon derives from work by Intel in documenting their original object-oriented architecture, the iAPX432 [6]. The intent of this icon is to suggest the boundaries of an abstraction, a concept that does not necessarily have plain or simple edges. The dashed lines that form the outline of the class icon indicate that clients generally only operate upon instances of a class, not the class itself. An acceptable alternative to this shape is a rectangle:

This follows the practice of Rumbaugh [7]. Although simpler to sketch by hand, rectangles are intensely overused symbols and hence do not intuitively denote anything. Additionally, Rumbaugh's choices of rectangles for classes and rounded rectangles for objects clash with other symbols in his notation (rectangles are used for actors in data flow diagrams, and rounded rectangles are used for states in state transition diagrams). In practice, the cloud icon lends itself more to adornments such as those required for abstract classes or for parameterized classes, which we discuss later in this chapter. For these reasons, the cloud is the preferred shape for use in class and object diagrams. Especially in the presence of automated support for the notation, the argument for the simplicity of drawing rectangles is moot. However, to facilitate drawing diagrams by hand, and to offer a bridge to Rumbaugh's work, we do allow the rectangle as an acceptable alternative for representing classes and the rounded rectangle for representing objects.

Smalltalk, we may further constrain these semantics to require that every class name be unique to the system.

For certain class diagrams, it is useful to expose some of the attributes and operations associated with a class. We say "some" because for all but the most trivial class, it is clumsy and indeed unnecessary to show all such members in a diagram, even when using a rectangular icon. In this sense, the attributes and operations that we show represent an elided view of the class's entire specification, which serves as the single point of declaration for all of its members. If we need to show many such members, we may magnify the class icon; if we choose to show no such members at all, we may drop the separating line and show only the class name.

As we described in Chapter 3, an attribute denotes a part of an aggregate object, and so is used during analysis as well as design to express a singular property of the class.[*] Using the following language-independent syntax, an attribute may have a name, a class, or both, and optionally a default value:

- A   Attribute name only
- : C   Attribute class only
- A : C   Attribute name and class
- A : C = E   Attribute name, class, and default expression

An attribute name must be unambiguous in the context of the class.

As we also described in Chapter 3, an operation denotes some service provided by the class. Operations are usually just named when shown inside a class icon, and are distinguished from attributes by appending parentheses or, where necessary for the purposes of the diagram, by providing the operation's complete signature:

- N()   Operation name only
- R N(Arguments)   Operation return class, name, and formal
                             arguments (if any)

Operation names must be unambiguous in the context of the class, according to the rules for overloading in the chosen implementation language.

As a general principle for the notation, the syntax for items such as attributes and operations may be tailored to use the syntax for the chosen implementation language. This simplifies the notation by isolating the peculiarities of various languages. For example, in C++, we may wish to declare certain attributes as static or certain operations as virtual or pure virtual;[**] in CLOS, we may wish to designate certain operations as :around methods. In

---

[*] To be precise, an attribute is equivalent to an aggregation association with physical containment, whose label is the attribute name and whose cardinality is exactly one.
[**] In C++, *static* denotes a class member; *virtual* denotes a polymorphic operation, and *pure virtual* denotes an operation whose implementation is a subclass responsibility.

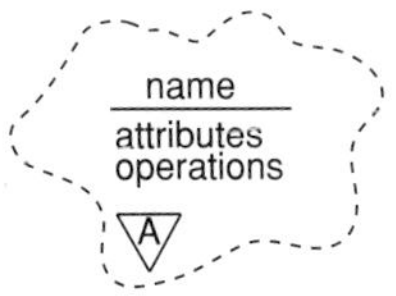

Figure 5-3
Abstract Class Adornment

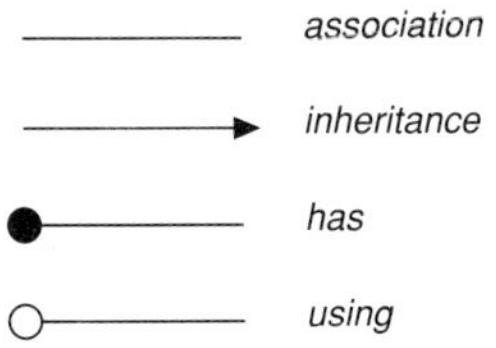

Figure 5-4
Class Relationship Icons

either case, we use the specific syntax of the given language to show these details. As we described in Chapter 3, an abstract class is one for which no instances may be created. Because such classes are so important to engineering good class lattices, we introduce a special adornment to designate a class as abstract, as shown in Figure 5-3. Specifically, we adorn the class icon with the letter *A* (for abstract) placed inside a triangle anywhere inside the class icon. This adornment follows a general principle for the notation: adornments are secondary pieces of information about some entity in a system's model. All similar kinds of adornments use the same triangle icon consistently.

Class Relationships Classes rarely stand alone; instead, as Chapter 3 explained, they collaborate with other classes in a variety of ways. The essential connections among classes include association, inheritance, "has," and "using" relationships, whose icons we summarize in Figure 5-4. Each such relationship may include a textual label that documents the name of the relationship or suggests its purpose. Relationship names need not be global, but must be unique within their context.

The association icon connects two classes and denotes a semantic connection. Associations are often labeled with noun phrases, such as Employment, denoting the nature of the relationship. A class may have an association to itself (called a *reflexive* association). It is also possible to have more than one association between the same pair of classes. Associations may be further adorned with their cardinality, as described in Chapter 3, using the syntax in the following examples:

- 1   Exactly one
- N   Unlimited number (zero or more)
- 0 .. N   Zero or more
- 1 .. N   One or more
- 0 .. 1   Zero or one
- 3 .. 7   Specified range
- 1 .. 3, 7   Specified range or exact number

The cardinality adornment is applied to the target end of an association, and denotes the number of links between each instance of the source class and instances of the target class. Unless explicitly adorned, the cardinality of a relationship is considered unspecified.

The remaining three essential class relationships are drawn as refinements of the more general association icon. Indeed, during development, this is exactly how relationships tend to evolve. We first assert the existence of a semantic connection between two classes and then, as we make tactical decisions about the exact nature of their relationship, often refine them into inheritance, has, or using relationships.

The inheritance icon denotes a generalization/specialization relationship (the "is a" relationship, described in Chapter 3), and appears as an association with an arrowhead. The arrowhead points to the superclass, and the opposite end of the association designates the subclass. According to the rules of the chosen implementation language, the subclass inherits the structure and behavior of its superclass. Also according to these rules, a class may have one (single inheritance) or more (multiple inheritance) superclasses; name clashes among the superclasses are also resolved according to the rules of the chosen language. In general, there may be no cycles among inheritance relationships. Also, inheritance relationships may not have cardinality adornments.

The "has" icon denotes a whole/part relationship (the "has a" relationship, also known as *aggregation.*), and appears as an association with a filled circle at the end denoting the aggregate. The class at the other end denotes the part whose instances are contained by the aggregate object. Reflexive and cyclic aggregation is possible; aggregation does not require physical containment.

The "using" icon denotes a client/supplier relationship, and appears as an association with an open circle at the end denoting the client. As described in Chapter 3, this relationship indicates that the client in some manner depends upon the supplier to provide certain services. It is typically used to indicate the decision that operations of the client class invoke operations of the supplier class, or have signatures whose return class or arguments are instances of the supplier class.

Example The icons described thus far constitute the essential elements of all class diagrams. Collectively, they provide the developer with a notation sufficient to describe the fundamentals of a system's class structure.

In Figure 5-5, we provide an example of this notation, drawn from the problem of the hydroponics gardening system. This diagram describes only a small part of the hydroponics system class structure. Here we see the class GardeningPlan, which includes an attribute named crop together with one modifier operation, execute, and one selector operation, canHarvest. There is an association between this class and the class EnvironmentController, wherein instances of the plan define the climate that instances of the controller monitor and modify.

This diagram also indicates that the class EnvironmentController is an aggregate, whose instances contain exactly one heater, one cooler, and any number of lights. The Heater and Cooler classes in turn are both subclasses of the abstract

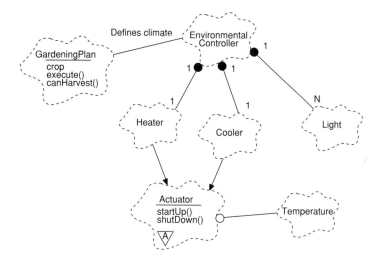

Figure 5-5
Hydroponics Gardening System Class Diagram

class Actuator, which provides the protocol startUp and shutDown, and which uses the class Temperature.

Essentials: Class Categories

As we explained in Chapter 3, the class is a necessary but insufficient vehicle for decomposition. Once our system grows to include more than a dozen or so abstractions, we may begin to identify clusters of classes that are themselves cohesive, but are loosely coupled relative to other clusters. We represent these clusters as class categories.

Most object-oriented programming languages do not have any linguistic support for class categories. Therefore, providing a notation for class categories allows us to express an important architectural element that cannot otherwise be expressed directly in our implementation language.[*]

Classes and class categories may appear in the same diagram. More commonly, to represent the high-level logical architecture of our system, we provide some class diagrams that contain only class categories.

Class Categories Class categories serve to partition the logical model of a system. A class category is an aggregate containing classes and other class

---

[*] The Smalltalk programming environment does support the concept of class categories. In fact, this was one of the inspirations for introducing categories into the notation. However, in Smalltalk, class categories have no semantic content: they exist solely as a convenience for organizing the Smalltalk class library. In C++, class categories are related to Stroustrup's concept of components, which are not yet a feature of the language, although namespace semantics are being considered for adoption [8].

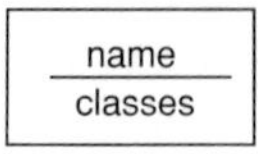

Figure 5-6
Class Category Icon

categories, in the same sense that a class is an aggregate containing operations and other classes. Each class in the system must live in a single class category or at the top level of the system. Unlike a class, a class category does not directly contribute state or operations to the model; it does so only indirectly, through its contained classes.

Figure 5-6 shows the icon we use to represent a class category. As for a class, a name is required for each class category; if the name is particularly long, it can either be elided or the icon magnified. As in the C++ rules for naming classes, every class category name in the logical model must be unique and distinct from all other class names.

For certain class diagrams, it is useful to expose some of the classes contained in a particular class category. Again, we say "some" because most class categories contain more than a handful of classes, and so it would be clumsy to enumerate all of their classes. Thus, as with the attributes and operations shown in the class icon, we may list the names of interesting classes contained in a class category. In this sense, this list of classes represents an elided view of the class category's specification, which serves as the single point of declaration of all of its classes. If we need to show many such classes, we may magnify the class category icon; if we choose to show no such classes at all, we may drop the separating line and show only the class category name.

A class category represents an encapsulated name space. As in C++ name qualification, we may use the name of a class category to unambiguously qualify the name of any class contained in a category. For example, given the class C contained in class category A, its fully qualified name is A::C. Since classes and class categories may be nested, as we will discuss later, we may extend this qualification to whatever depth necessary.

Some of the classes enclosed by a class category may be public, meaning that they are exported from the class category and hence usable outside the class category. Other classes may be part of the implementation, meaning that they are not usable by any other class outside of the class category. During analysis and architectural design, this distinction is quite important, because it lets us specify a clear separation of concerns between the exported classes that provide the services of the class category and those classes that implement these services. In fact, during analysis, we may typically ignore the private details of a class category. By convention, every class in a class category is considered public, unless explicitly defined otherwise. Restricting access is an advanced concept, which we discuss in a later section.

A class category can use another non-nested class category or class, and a class can use a class category. For consistency, we apply the same "using"

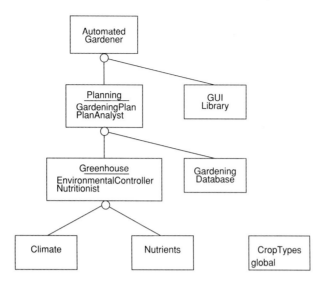

Figure 5-7
Hydroponics Gardening System Top-Level Class Diagram

relationship icon shown in Figure 5-4 to indicate such importing connections among class categories. For example, consider a "using" relationship from class category A to B. This relationship means that the classes contained in A can inherit from, contain instances of, use, and otherwise associate with only the classes exported from B.

A practical problem arises when a class category contains a number of common classes, such as foundation container classes or other pervasive base classes, such as the class Object in Smalltalk. Such classes end up being used by virtually every other class category in the system, and therefore cause top-level class diagrams to become cluttered. To deal with this problem, we permit a class category to be adorned with the key word global placed in its lower left corner, indicating that this category may be used by all others.

Top-level class diagrams containing only class categories represent the high-level architecture of our system. Such diagrams are extremely useful in visualizing the layers and partitions of our system. A layer denotes the collection of class categories at the same level of abstraction. Thus, layers represent groupings of class categories, just as class categories represent clusters of classes. A common use of layers is to insulate higher layers from lower layer details. In contrast, a partition denotes each of the peer class categories that live at the same level of abstraction. In this regard, layers represent horizontal slices through the architecture, and partitions represent vertical slices.

Example Figure 5-7 shows an example of a top-level class diagram for the hydroponics gardening system. This is a typical layered system in which

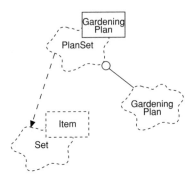

Figure 5-8
Parameterized Classes

abstractions that are close to the boundaries of the physical system (namely, the climate and nutrient sensors and actuators) are at the lowest levels, and user-centric abstractions are closest to the top. The class category named CropTypes is global, indicating that its services are available to all other class categories. Note also that the class category Planning exposes two of its interesting classes, GardeningPlan (which we saw in Figure 5-5) and PlanAnalyst. If we zoom in to any of the eight class categories shown here, we will find all of their corresponding classes.

Advanced Concepts

The elements we have presented thus far constitute the essential parts of the notation.[*] However, there are often a number of strategic and tactical decisions that we must capture that require us to extend this basic notation. As a general rule, stick to the essential elements of the notation, and apply only those advanced concepts necessary to express analysis or design details that are essential to visualizing or understanding the system.

Parameterized Classes Some object-oriented programming languages, most notably C++, Eiffel, and Ada, provide parameterized classes. As we discussed in Chapter 3, a parameterized class denotes a family of classes whose structure and behavior are defined independent of its formal class parameters. We must match these formal parameters with actual ones (the process of instantiation) to form a concrete class in this family; by *concrete* class, we mean one that may have instances.

Parameterized classes are sufficiently different than plain classes to warrant a special adornment. As the example in Figure 5-8 shows, a parameterized class is visualized as a simple class, but with a dashed-line box in the upper right corner denoting its formal parameters. An instantiated class is adorned with a

---

[*] Collectively, all essential elements form the "Booch Lite" form of the notation.

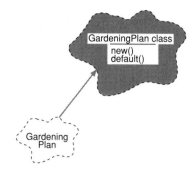

Figure 5-9
Metaclasses

solid-line box denoting its actual parameters, matched positionally to the corresponding formal parameters. In either case, we may optionally supply the formal and actual parameters as text inside the box.

The instantiation relationship between a parameterized class and its instantiated class is shown as a dashed line, pointing to the parameterized class. Most often, the instantiated class requires a "using" relation to other concrete classes (such as GardeningPlan in this example) for use as an actual parameter.

A parameterized class may not have any instances and may not itself be used as a parameter. An instantiated class defines a new class distinct from all other concrete classes in the same family whose actual parameters differ.

Metaclasses Languages such as Smalltalk and CLOS provide metaclasses. As we discussed in Chapter 3, a metaclass is the class of a class. In Smalltalk, the most common use of metaclasses is to provide class instance variables and operations, similar to the C++ practice of static members, or to define factory operations that generate instances of the corresponding class. In CLOS, metaclasses play an important role in the ability to tailor that language's semantics [9].

Metaclasses are also sufficiently different than plain classes to warrant a special adornment. As we show in Figure 5-9, a metaclass is visualized as a simple class, but with a gray-filled icon. The meta relationship is shown as a directed thick gray line, and points from a class to its metaclass. In this example, the metaclass provides the factory operations new and default for generating new instances of the class GardeningPlan.

A metaclass may not itself have any instances, but may inherit from, contain instances of, use, and otherwise associate with other classes.

Meta relationships have one other use. On certain class diagrams, it is useful to show an object that serves as a static member for some class. To show the class of this object, we may draw a meta relationship from the object to its class. This is consistent with the earlier use: a meta relationship shows the connection between some entity (either an object or a class) and its class.

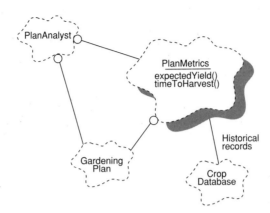

Figure 5-10
Class Utilities

Class Utilities Due to their heritage, hybrid languages such as C++, Object Pascal, and CLOS permit the developer to apply a procedural as well as an object-oriented style of programming. This is in contrast to Smalltalk, where everything in the language is ultimately organized around classes. In hybrid languages, it is possible to write nonmember functions, also known as *free subprograms*. Free subprograms often show up during analysis and design at the boundary of the object-oriented system with its procedural interfaces to real world entities.

Class utilities manifest themselves in one of two ways. First, a class utility may denote one or more free subprograms; the name of the class utility then has no semantic content other than to provide a convenient way to name a logical group of such nonmember functions. Second, a class utility may name a class that only has class instance variables and operations; in C++, this would denote a class with only static members.* Such classes have no meaningful instances, mainly because there can be no state associated with any instances. In a sense, the class itself acts as the sole instance that can be operated upon.

As shown in Figure 5-10, a class utility is represented as an icon for a plain class and adorned with a shadow. In this example, the class utility PlanMetrics provides two interesting operations, expectedYield and timeToHarvest. The class utility constructs these two operations upon the services of the lower-level classes GardeningPlan and CropDatabase. As the diagram indicates, PlanMetrics depends upon CropDatabase for retrieving historical information on certain interesting crops. In turn, the class PlanAnalyst uses the services of PlanMetrics.

Figure 5-10 illustrates a common motivation for class utilities: here we have a class utility that provides some common algorithmic services built upon two disparate lower-level abstractions. Rather than associating these operations with

---

* This idiom is also commonly used by Smalltalk programmers to achieve the same effect as in C++.

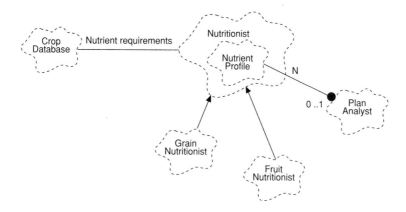

Figure 5-11
Nesting

a higher-level class such as PlanAnalyst, we choose to collect them in a class utility so that there is a clear separation of concerns between these simpler procedural utilities and the more complicated abstraction of the analyst. In addition, collecting these free subprograms into one logical structure increases their chance of reuse, because this provides a finer granularity of abstraction.

As the example shows, classes may associate with and use but not inherit from or contain an instance of a class utility. Similarly, a class utility may associate with, use, or contain static instances of other classes, but not inherit from them.

Just as for plain classes, class utilities may be parameterized and in turn instantiated. To denote such class utilities, we may apply the same adornments for parameterized and instantiated classes as shown in Figure 5-8. We may also use the same instantiation relationship shown in that figure to denote the relationship between a parameterized class utility and its instantiation.

Nesting Classes may be physically nested in other classes, and categories may be nested in other categories as well, to any depth of nesting, typically to achieve some control over the namespace. In each case, this nesting corresponds to the declaration of the nested entity occurring in the enclosing context. As shown in Figure 5-11, we indicate nesting by physically nesting icons; the qualified name of the nested class isNutritionist::NutrientProfile. According to the rules of the chosen implementation language, classes may contain instances of or use a nested class. Typically, languages do not permit inheritance from the nested class.

The nesting of classes tends to be a tactical design decision. The nesting of class categories, however, is typically a strategic architectural decision. In either case, there is rarely a compelling reason to nest classes or class categories to depths much greater than one or two levels.

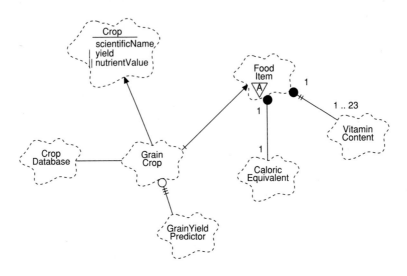

Figure 5-12
Export Control

Export Control All interesting object-oriented programming languages provide a clear separation between the interface and implementation of a class. As we described in Chapter 3, most also permit the developer to specify finer-grained access to the interface as well. For example, in C++, members may be public (accessible to all clients), protected (accessible only to subclasses, friends, or the class itself), or private (accessible only to the class itself or its friends). Certain elements might also be a part of a class's implementation, and thus inaccessible even to friends of the class.[*] Similarly, in Ada, elements of a class may be either public or private. In Smalltalk, all instance variables are private by default, and all operations are public. Access is granted explicitly by the class itself, not taken forcibly by the client.

We may specify access by adorning the appropriate relationship with the following symbols:

- <no adornment>   Public access (the default)
- | Protected access
- || Private access
- ||| Implementation access

We place these hash marks at the source end of a relationship. For example, in Figure 5-12, we note that the class `GrainCrop` multiply inherits from the class `Crop` (a public superclass) and the abstract class `FoodItem` (a protected superclass).

---

[*] For example, consider an object or a class declared in a .cpp file, and thus accessible only to the member functions implemented therein.

FoodItem in turn contains from 1 to 23 private instances of the class VitaminContent, and one public instance of the class CaloricEquivalent. Note that CaloricEquivalent could have been written as an attribute to the class FoodItem, because attributes are equivalent to aggregation whose cardinality is exactly 1:1. Continuing, we see that the class GrainCrop uses the class GrainYieldPredictor as part of its implementation. This typically means that some method of the class GrainCrop uses the services of GrainYieldPredictor in its implementation.

In addition to the cases shown in this example, plain associations may also be adorned with access symbols. Instantiation and metaclass relationships may not be so adorned.

These access symbols also apply to nested entities in all their forms. Specifically, in a class icon we may indicate the accessibility of attributes, operations, and nested classes by prefixing one of the access symbols to the name of the nested item. For example, in Figure 5-12, we see that the class Crop has one public attribute (scientificName), one protected attribute (yield), and one private attribute (nutrientValue). This same notation applies to classes and class categories nested inside other class categories. By default, all such nested classes and class categories are public, but we may indicate restricted access by attaching the adornment denoting implementation access.

Properties For certain languages, some relationship qualifications are so pervasive and their semantics so fundamental, that they warrant the use of special symbols. In C++ for example, there are three such properties:

- static   The designation of a class member object or function
- virtual   The designation of a shared base class in a diamond-shaped inheritance lattice
- friend   The designation of a class that grants rights to another to access its nonpublic parts

For consistency, we draw these adornments using the same triangle-shaped icon used for the abstract class adornment, but with the symbols S, V, and F, respectively.

Consider the example in Figure 5-13, which provides a different view of the classes shown in the previous figure. Here, we see that the base class OrganicItem contains one instance of the class ItemDictionary, and that this instance is owned by the class itself, not by its individual instances. In general, we may apply the static adornment to either end of an association or to the part end of a "has" relationship.

Observing the class GrainCrop, we see that its inheritance lattice takes on a diamond (fork-join) shape. By default in C++, a diamond lattice generates for the leaf class duplicates of the state from the shared base class. In order to have the class GrainCrop share a single copy of the multiply-inherited state from

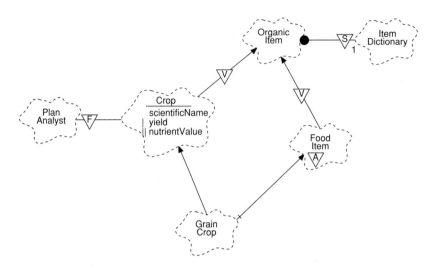

Figure 5-13
Properties

OrganicItem, we must specify virtual inheritance, as shown in the figure. We may apply the virtual adornment only to an inheritance relationship.

Friendship may be applied to the supplier of any relationship, denoting that the supplier has granted the right of friendship to the client. For example, in Figure 5-13, we see that the class PlanAnalyst is a friend of the class Crop, and therefore has access to its nonpublic members, including both the attributes yield and scientificname.

Physical Containment As noted in Chapter 3, aggregation, as manifested in the "has" relationship, is a constrained form of the more general association relationship. Aggregation denotes a whole/part hierarchy, and also implies the ability to navigate from the aggregate to its parts. This whole/part hierarchy does not necessarily mean physical containment: a professional society has a number of members, but by no means does the society "own" its members. On the other hand, an individual record of crop history does physically contain subordinate information, such as crop name, yield, and as-applied nutrient schedules.

The choice of aggregation is usually an analysis or architectural design decision; the choice of aggregation as physical containment is usually a detailed, tactical issue. However, distinguishing physical containment is important for two reasons: first, physical containment has semantics that play a role in the construction and destruction of an aggregate's parts, and second, the specification of physical containment is necessary for meaningful code generation from the design and reverse-engineering from the implementation.

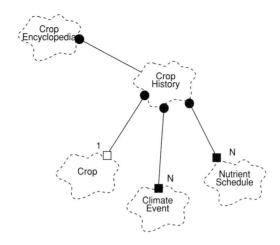

Figure 5-14
Physical Containment

Physical containment is indicated as an adornment on the part end of a "has" relationship; the absence of this adornment means that the decision regarding physical containment is unspecified. In hybrid languages, we distinguish between two types of physical containment:

- By value   Denotes physical containment of a value of the part
- By reference   Denotes physical containment of a pointer or a reference to the part

In pure object-oriented programming languages, most notably Smalltalk, all containment is by reference.

Because physical containment and its corresponding notions of structural sharing are sufficiently different from the semantics of properties discussed earlier, we choose a slightly different style of adornment. Specifically, we use a filled box to denote aggregation by value and an open box to denote aggregation by reference. As we will discuss in a later section, this style of adornment is consistent with adornments representing similar physical semantics in object diagrams.

Consider the example in Figure 5-14. Here we see the class CropHistory, whose instances physically contain N instances of the class NutrientSchedule and N instances of the class ClimateEvent. Containment by value implies that the construction and destruction of these parts occurs as a consequence of the construction and destruction of the aggregate. Specifically, containment by value ensures that the lifetimes of the aggregate and its parts are equal. By contrast, each instance of CropHistory physically contains only a reference or pointer to one instance of Crop. This means that the lifetimes of the two objects

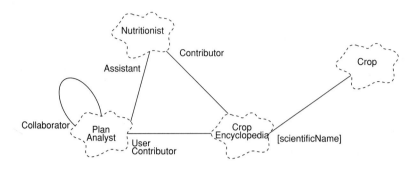

Figure 5-15
Roles and Keys

are independent, although the one is still considered physically a part of the other. This is also in contrast with the aggregation relationship shown between the classes CropEncyclopedia and CropHistory. Here, we have not specified physical containment. The semantics of this part of the diagram tells us that these two classes do indeed participate in a whole/part relationship, and that it is possible to navigate from an instance of CropEncyclopedia to an instance of CropHistory, although this may not be the result of physical containment. Instead, there may be some much more elaborate mechanism that implements this association; for example, it may be necessary for the CropEncyclopedia to initiate a search upon some other agent, such as a database actor, to look up the appropriate instance of CropHistory and return a shared reference to it.

Roles and Keys In the previous chapter, we described the importance of identifying the various roles an object plays in its collaboration with other objects; in the next chapter, we will study how role identification helps drive the process of analysis.

Briefly, the role of an abstraction is the face it presents to the world at a given moment. A role denotes the purpose or capacity wherein one class associates with another. As the example in Figure 5-15 shows, we name the role of a class as a textual adornment to any association, placed adjacent to the class offering the role. Here we see that instances of the class PlanAnalyst and Nutritionist are both contributors to the CropEncyclopedia object (meaning that they both add information to the encyclopedia), and that PlanAnalyst objects are users as well (meaning that they look up information in the encyclopedia). In each case, the client's role identifies the particular behavior and protocol that it uses with its supplier while acting in that role. Note also the reflexive association for the class PlanAnalyst: here we show that multiple instances of this class may collaborate with one another, and that they have a particular protocol they use when collaborating, which is distinguished from their behavior in their association with, for instance, CropEncyclopedia.

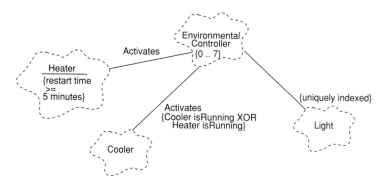

Figure 5-16
Constraints

Our example also shows an association between the classes CropEncyclopedia and Crop, but with a different kind of adornment, this one representing a key, shown as an identifier surrounded by brackets. A key is an attribute whose value uniquely identifies a single target object. In this example, the class CropEncyclopedia uses the attribute scientificName as a key to navigate to individual entries in the set of items managed by instances of CropEncyclopedia. In general, a key must be an attribute of the object that is a part of the aggregate object at the target end of the association. Multiple keys are possible, but key values must be unique.

Constraints As we discussed in Chapter 3, a constraint is the expression of some semantic condition that must be preserved. Stated another way, a constraint is an invariant of a class or relationship that must be preserved while the system is in a steady state. We emphasize *steady state* because there may be transitory circumstances wherein the state of the system is changing (and thus is temporarily in a self-inconsistent state), during which time it is impossible to preserve all the system's constraints. Constraints are guarantees that apply only when the state of the system is stable.

Notationally, we use an adornment for constraints similar to that for roles and keys: specifically, we place an expression, surrounded by braces, adjacent to the class or relationship for which the constraint applies. As the example in Figure 5-16 indicates, we may apply constraints to individual classes, whole associations, and participants in an association.

In this diagram, we see a cardinality constraint upon the class EnvironmentalController, stating that there may be no more than 7 instances of this class in the system. In the absence of a cardinality constraint, a class may have zero or more instances. The abstract class adornment described earlier is a special case (denoting a cardinality of zero), but because it occurs so often in class lattices, it is given a special symbol (the triangular adornment).

The class `Heater` has a different kind of constraint. Here we see a statement of hysteresis in the heater's operation: a heater may not be restarted sooner than five minutes after it was last shut down. We attach this constraint to the class `Heater`, because we mean this to be an invariant preserved by instances of the class themselves.

In this diagram we also find two different kinds of association constraints. In the association between the classes `EnvironmentalController` and `Light`, we require that individual lights be uniquely indexed with respect to one another in the context of this association. We also have a constraint that spans the controller's association with the `Heater` and `Cooler` classes, stating the invariant that the `EnvironmentalController` may not activate the heater and the cooler at the same time. We place this as a constraint upon the association rather than as a constraint upon the class `Heater` or the class `Cooler`, because it is an invariant that cannot be preserved by heaters or coolers themselves.

If necessary, we may write constraint expressions that name other associations, using the syntax for qualified names used elsewhere in the notation. For example, `Cooler:::Activates` uniquely names one of the controller's associations. In the notation, such expressions are often used in circumstances wherein one class has an association (such as aggregation) with two or more other classes, but its instances may associate with only one of these target instances at any given time.

Constraints are also useful for the expression of secondary classes, attributes, and associations.[*] For example, consider the classes `Adult` and `Child`, both of which might be subclasses of the abstract class `Person`. For the class `Person`, we might provide the attribute `dateofbirth`, and we might also include an attribute named `age`, perhaps because age is important in our model of the real world. However, the `age` attribute is secondary: it can be computed from `dateofbirth`. Thus, in our model, we might include both attributes, but include an attribute constraint that states this derivation. It is a tactical decision as to which attribute derives from the other, but our constraint can record whatever decision we make.

Similarly, we might have an association between the `Adult` and `Child` classes named `Parent`. We might also include another association named `Caretaker`, because it suits the purposes of our model (perhaps we are modeling the legal relationships between parent and child in the analysis of a social welfare system). `Caretaker` is secondary; it derives from the consequences of the `Parent` association, and we might state this invariant as a constraint upon the `Caretaker` association.

---

[*] In Rumbaugh's terms, these are called *derived entities*, for which he supplies a unique adornment. Our general approach to constraints is sufficient for expressing the semantics of derived classes, attributes, and associations, and has the advantages of reusing an existing notational element, as well as unambiguously identifying the entity from which the derivation occurs.

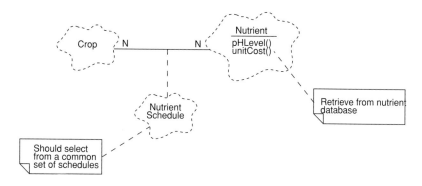

Figure 5-17
Attributed Associations and Notes

Attributed Associations and Notes The final advanced concept specific to class diagrams concerns itself with the problem of modeling properties of associations; the notational solution to this specific problem generalizes to a diagram element that may be applied to every diagram in the notation.

Consider the example in Figure 5-17. Here we see a many-to-many association between Crop and Nutrient, meaning that every crop depends upon N nutrients, and each nutrient may be applied to N different crops. The class NutrientSchedule is really a property of this many-to-many relationship, whose instances denote a specific mapping of a crop and its nutrients. To indicate this semantic fact, we draw a dashed line from the Crop/Nutrient association (the attributed association) to its property, the class NutrientSchedule (the association's attribute). A given unique association may have at most one such attribute, and the name of such an association must match the name of the class used as its attribute.

The very idea of attributing associations has a generalization. Specifically, during analysis and design, there are a myriad of seemingly random assumptions and decisions that each developer may collect; these insights are often lost, because there is usually no convenient place to collect them, save for keeping them in the head of the developer – a decidedly unreliable practice. Thus, it is useful to add arbitrary notes to any element of any diagram, whose text captures these assumptions and decisions. In Figure 5-17, we have two such notes. One note attached to the class NutrientSchedule tells us something about the expected uniqueness of its instances. The other note attached to a specific operation of the class Nutrient captures our expectation of how this operation will be implemented.

For such notes we use a distinctive note-shaped icon and connect it to the element it affects using a dashed line as before. Largely a tool issue, notes may contain any information, including plain text, fragments of code, or references to other documents. A note may be unconnected, meaning that it applies to the diagram as a whole.[*]

Specifications

A specification is a nongraphical form used to provide the complete definition of an entity in the notation, such as a class, an association, an individual operation, or even an entire diagram. Browsing through class diagrams lets the reader visualize a large system with relative ease; however, this graphical view alone is not enough: we must have some substance behind the pictures, and this is the motivation for specifications in general.

As we stated earlier, a diagram is simply a view into a model of the system under development. A specification thus serves as the nongraphical foundation model for each entity in the notation. The set of syntactic and semantic facts stated in each diagram is therefore a subset of, yet must be consistent with, the facts stated in the model's specifications. Obviously, tools that support the notation can play an important role in keeping diagrams and specifications in sync with one another.

In this section, we will first examine the essential elements of the two important specifications in the notation, and then consider their advanced properties. We will not concern ourselves with the exact presentation of each specification – that is a matter of the look and feel of particular tools that support the notation – nor need we present the specification of every element, such as the specifications for metaclasses or for individual kinds of relationships. Most such specifications are obvious subsets of the more central specifications, such as those for classes, or add no information beyond what we have already described in their graphical counterparts. What is particularly important in the following paragraphs is the exposition of those specification elements that have no analog in the diagrams; specifications contain some information that is best expressed textually, and so have no graphical representation.

Common Elements All specifications have at least the following entries:

```
Name:          identifier
Definition:    text
```

The meaning of the entity's name is obvious; its uniqueness depends upon the semantics of the item itself. For example, class names must at least be unique to their enclosing class category, whereas operation names have a scope that is local to their enclosing class.

---

[*] The icon we use is similar to the note icon used in a variety of windowing systems, especially those including the Macintosh look and feel. Our specific inspiration for this notational element derives from the suggestions of Gamma, Help, Johnson, and Vlissides [10].

A definition is text that identifies the concept or function represented by the entity, and is appropriate for inclusion in the data dictionary, as we will discuss in the next chapter.

There are the minimal entries for every specification. Tools may certainly define their own entries, to meet the needs of their particular computing environment. Also, it is important to state that although certain specifications may have a number of different entries, there is no obligation for developers to use every entry, or to follow the foolish rule that development cannot proceed to the next phase until all parts of a specification are filled in. Notations are an aid to development, not an end in themselves, and so must be used only when they add value to the activities of analysis and design.

Class Specifications Each class in the model has exactly one class specification that provides at least the following entries:

```
Responsibilities:   text
Attributes:         list of attributes
Operations:         list of operations
Constraints:        list of constraints
```

As we discussed in the previous chapter, the responsibilities of a class are its statements of obligation to provide certain behavior. The next chapter explains how we use this entry as a placeholder for a class's responsibilities, which we discover or invent during development.

The various attribute, operation, and constraint entries parallel their graphical counterparts. Individual operations are sufficiently interesting to warrant their own specifications, which we present in the next section.

These first essential elements may be provided in terms of the given implementation language. In particular, it may be sufficient to write C++ class declarations or Ada package specifications to capture this information.

As we discussed in Chapter 3, the behavior of certain interesting classes is often best expressed using state machines, and so we add another essential entry to such classes:

```
State machine:     reference to state machine
```

Advanced uses of the notation require the following additional entries to class specifications:

```
Export control:   public | implementation
Cardinality:      expression
```

These items parallel their advanced graphical counterparts.

Parameterized classes and instantiated classes must include the following entry:

```
Parameters:       list of formal or actual generic parameters
```

The following very advanced entries have no graphical counterparts; they serve to capture certain functional aspects of a class:

```
Persistence:        transient | persistent
Concurrency:        sequential | guarded | synchronous | active
Space complexity:   expression
```

The first of these three elements captures the property denoting whether or not the class's instances are persistent. As we discussed in Chapter 2, a persistent entity is one whose state transcends the lifetime of the enclosing object, whereas a transitory entity is one whose state and lifetime are identical.

As we also noted in Chapter 2, the concurrency of a class is a statement about its semantics in the presence of multiple threads of control. A sequential object is the default, and denotes a class whose semantics are guaranteed only in the presence of a single thread of control. A guarded class is one whose semantics are guaranteed in the presence of multiple threads of control, but that requires collaboration among all client threads to achieve mutual exclusion. A synchronized class is the same, except that mutual exclusion is provided by the class itself. Finally, an active class embodies its own thread of control.

The space complexity of a class is a statement about the relative or absolute storage consumed by each object of the class. We may use this entry to budget a size for each class, or to record the as-built space complexity of the class's instances.

Operation Specifications   For each operation that is a member of a class, and for all free subprograms, we define one operation specification that provides at least the following entries:

```
Return class:    reference to class
Arguments:       list of formal arguments
```

These elements may be written in the given implementation language. Depending upon the tailoring of the notation to specific languages, we may also include the following essential element:

```
Qualification:    text
```

In C++, for example, qualification would include a statement of the operation's static, virtual, pure virtual, and const properties.

Advanced uses of the notation require the following additional entry for operation specifications:

```
Export control:    public | protected | private | implementation
```

The values that are meaningful for export control are language-dependent. In Object Pascal, for example, attributes and operations are always public; in Ada, operations may be public or private, but in C++, all four values may apply.

Advanced use of the notation also includes the following element:

```
Protocol:    text
```

This element follows the practice in Smalltalk: the protocol of an operation has no semantic impact, but simply serves to name a logical grouping of operations, such as `initialize-release` or `model access`.

The following very advanced entries have no graphical counterparts, and serve to formally capture the semantics of an operation:

```
Preconditions:    text | reference to source code | reference to object diagram
Semantics:        text | reference to source code | reference to object diagram
Postconditions:   text | reference to source code | reference to object diagram
Exceptions        list of exceptions
```

The preconditions, semantics, and postconditions of an operation may be stated in any of a number of forms, including text (comprising either informal or formal expressions), references to potentially executable source code or assertion statements, or references to object diagrams that serve as scenarios of the given semantics. The exceptions entry lists the exceptions that can be raised (*thrown* in C++ terms) by the operation; each element in this list is the name of a class naming the exception.

The final very advanced entries serve to capture certain functional aspects of an operation:

```
Concurrency:       sequential | guarded | synchronous
Space complexity:  expression
Time complexity:   expression
```

The first two elements are the same as for class specifications. The time complexity of an operation is a statement about the relative or absolute time required to complete an operation. We may use this entry to budget a time for each operation or to record the as-built time complexity in terms of actual, average, and/or worst case performance.

5.3 State Transition Diagrams

Essentials: States and State Transitions

A *state transition diagram* is used to show the state space of a given class, the events that cause a transition from one state to another, and the actions that result from a state change. We have adopted the notation used by Harel [11] for state transition diagrams; his work provides a simple yet highly expressive approach that is far superior to conventional flat finite state machines[*]. A single state transition diagram represents a view of the dynamic model of a single class or of the entire system. Not every class has significant event-ordered behavior, and so we supply state transition diagrams only for those classes that exhibit such behavior; we may also provide state transition diagrams that show

---

[*] We supplement his work with the contributions by Rumbaugh [12] and Bear, Allen, Coleman, and Hayes [13], who all adapt Harel's work to the domain of object-oriented computing.

Figure 5-18
State Icon

the event-ordered behavior of the system as a whole. During analysis, we use state transition diagrams to indicate the dynamic behavior of the system. During design, we use state transition diagrams to capture the dynamic behavior of individual classes or of collaborations of classes.

The two essential elements of a state transition diagram are states and state transitions.

States The state of an object represents the cumulative results of its behavior. For example, when a telephone is first installed, it is in the idle state, meaning that no previous behavior is of great interest and that the phone is ready to initiate or receive calls. When someone picks up the handset, we say that the phone is now off-hook and in the dialing state; in this state, we do not expect the phone to ring; we expect to be able to initiate a conversation with a party or parties on other telephones. When the phone is on-hook, if it rings and then we pick up the handset, the phone is now in the receiving state, and we expect to be able to converse with the party that initiated the conversation.

At any given point in time, the state of an object encompasses all of its (usually static) properties, together with the current (usually dynamic) values of each of these properties. By properties, we mean the totality of the object's attributes and relationships with other objects. We can generalize the concept of an individual object's state to apply to the object's class, because all instances of the same class live in the same state space, which encompasses an indefinite yet finite number of possible (although not always desirable nor expected) states. Figure 5-18 shows the icon we use to represent a specific state.

A name is required for each state; if the name is particularly long, it can either be elided or the icon magnified. Every state name must be unique to its enclosing scope, namely, the enclosing class. States associated with the system as a whole have a global scope, and the scope of a nested state (an advanced concept) extends to its enclosing state. All state icons with the same name in a given diagram are considered to refer to the same state.

For certain states, it is useful to expose the actions associated with a state. As shown in the figure, for consistency we use same notation as for viewing the attributes and operations associated with a class. If necessary, we may

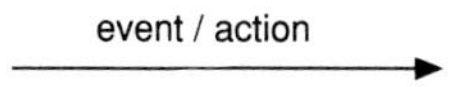

event / action

Figure 5-19
State Transition Icon

magnify the state icon; if there are no actions at all, we may drop the separating line.[*] Associating actions with a state is an advanced concept, which we will discuss in a later section.

State Transitions An event is some occurrence that may cause the state of a system to change. This change of state is called a *state transition*, which we draw using the icon shown in Figure 5-19. Each state transition connects two states. A state may have a state transition to itself, and it is common to have many different state transitions from the same state, although each such transition must be unique, meaning that there will never be any circumstances that would trigger more than one state transition from the same state.

For example, in the hydroponics gardening system, the following events play a role in the system's behavior:

- A new crop is planted.
- A crop becomes ready to harvest.
- The temperature in a greenhouse drops because of inclement weather.
- A cooler fails.
- Time passes.

As we will discuss in the next chapter, the identification of events such as these helps us to define the boundaries of a system's behavior and to assign responsibilities to individual classes that carry out the system's behavior.

Each of the first four events above is likely to trigger some action, such as starting or stopping the execution of a specific gardening plan, turning on a heater, or sounding an alarm to the gardener. The passage of time is another issue: although the passing of seconds or minutes may not be significant to our system (observable plant growth is generally on much longer scales of time), the passage of hours or days may be a signal to our system to turn lights on or off or to change the temperature in the greenhouse, in order to create an artificial day necessary for plant growth.

An action is an operation that, for all practical purposes, takes zero time. For example, sounding an alarm to the gardener is an action. An action typically denotes the invocation of a method, the triggering of another event, or the starting or stopping of an activity. An activity, on the other hand, is some operation that takes some time to complete. For example, heating the

---

[*] For consistency with Harel's notation, the separating line may be dropped altogether.

greenhouse is an activity, triggered by turning on the heater which may stay on for some indefinite time until explicitly turned off.

Although conceptually pure, Harel's model of broadcasting events must be tailored to fit into the object model. During analysis, we may name events and actions broadly, in order to capture our understanding of the problem space. However, once we begin to map these concepts to classes, we must impose a particular strategy for their implementation.

An event may be a symbolic name (or a named object), a class, or the name of some operation. For example, the event `cooler failure` might denote either a literal or the name of an object. We may take the strategy that all events are just symbolic names and that each class with interesting event-ordered behavior provides an operation that can consume such names and carry out the appropriate action. This is the strategy often taken in Smalltalk model-view-controller architectures, where events are symbolic names that are processed by update methods. For more generality, we may treat events as objects, and so define a hierarchy of event classes that provide our abstraction of specific events. For example, we might define a general class of events called `DeviceFailure` and specialized subclasses such as `CoolerFailure` and `HeaterFailure`. When we then post an event, we might post an instance of a leaf class (such as `CoolerFailure`) or a more general superclass (such as `DeviceFailure`). If we then specify the action of our system only in the presence of a `CoolerFailure` event, then we would intentionally ignore all other kinds of device failures. On the other hand, if we specify the action of our system in the presence of a `DeviceFailure` event, then we would trigger the same action no matter what specific device failure was posted. In this manner, we can make state transitions exhibit polymorphic behavior upon the class of the event that triggered the transition. Lastly, we might define an event simply as an operation, such as `GardeningPlan::execute()`. This approach is similar to that of treating events as symbolic names, except that we no longer require an explicit event-dispatching operation.

Which of these three strategies we choose is immaterial to the method, as long as one is chosen and used consistently in each part of the system. Typically, we use a note to indicate which strategy each finite state machine applies.

An action may be written using the syntax shown in the following examples:

- `heater.startUp()`   An operation
- `DeviceFailure`   Triggering of an event
- `start Heating`   Begin some activity
- `stop Heating`   Terminate some activity

In the case of an operation or event, the name must be in the scope of the diagram and, where necessary, may be qualified with the appropriate class or object name. In the case of starting and stopping an activity, an activity may

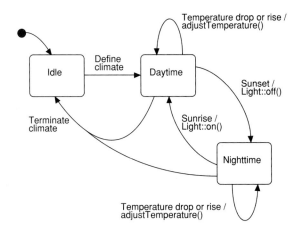

Figure 5-20
EnvironmentalController State Transition Diagram

denote an operation (such as `Actuator::shutDown()`) or a symbolic name (as for events). We typically use symbolic names when the activity corresponds to some system function, such as `harvest crop`.

In every state transition diagram, there must be exactly one default start state, which we designate by writing an unlabeled transition to the state from a special icon, shown as a filled circle. Less often, we need to designate a stop state. Usually, a state machine associated with a class or the system as a whole never reaches a stop state; the state machine just goes out of existence when the enclosing object is destroyed. We designate a stop state by drawing an unlabeled state transition from the state to a special icon, shown as a filled circle inside a slightly larger unfilled circle.

Example The icons described thus far constitute the essential elements of all state transition diagrams. Collectively, they provide the developer with a notation sufficient to describe simple, flat, finite state machines, suitable for applications with a limited number of states. Systems that have a large number of states or that exhibit particularly complicated event-ordered behavior involving conditional transitions or transitions based upon previously entered states require the use of the more advanced concepts for state transition diagrams.

In Figure 5-20, we provide an example of this essential notation, again drawn from the problem of the hydroponics gardening system. Here, we see a state transition diagram for the class `EnvironmentalController`, first introduced in Figure 5-5.

In this diagram, we have chosen a strategy in which events are designated as symbolic names. Here, we see that objects of this class start in the `Idle` state; then they change state upon receipt of the event `Define climate`, for which there is no explicit action (for the purposes of this diagram, we have made the simplifying assumption that this event will occur only during daytime). The dynamic behavior of this class then toggles between the states `Daytime` and `Nighttime`, triggered by the events `Sunset` and `Sunrise`, respectively, whose action is to change the lighting accordingly. In either state, a drop or rise in temperature event invokes an action to adjust the temperature (the operation `adjustTemperature()`, which is local to this class). We return to the `Idle` state whenever we receive a `Terminate climate` event.

Advanced Concepts

The elements of state transition diagrams we have described thus far are insufficient for many kinds of complex systems, and for this reason we expand our notation to include the semantics of Harel's statecharts.

State Actions and Conditional State Transitions As shown in Figure 5-18, actions may be associated with states. In particular, we may specify some action that is to be carried out upon entry or exit of a state, using the syntax in the following examples:

- `entry start Alarm`   Start an activity upon entry.
- `exit shutDown()`   Invoke an operation upon exit.

As for state transitions, we may specify any action after the keywords `entry` and `exit`.

Activities may be associated with a state, using the syntax in the following example:

- `do Cooling`   Carry out an activity while in the state.

This syntax is largely a shorthand for explicitly starting the activity upon entry to the state and explicitly stopping the activity upon exit.

In Figure 5-21, we see an example of this advanced concept. Here we see that upon entering the `Cooling` state, we invoke the operation `Cooler::startUp()`, and upon exiting this state, we invoke the operation `Cooler::shutDown()`. In the case of entering and exiting the state `Failure`, we start and stop an alarm, respectively.

Consider also the state transition from `Idle` to `Heating`. Here, we transition if the temperature is too cool, but only if it has been more than five minutes since we last shut down the heater. This is an example of a conditional (or guarded) state transition; we represent a condition as a Boolean expression placed inside brackets.

Generally, a given state transition will either have an event or an event and a condition. We also permit a state transition to have no associated event. In such a case, the transition is triggered immediately after the action of the source state has completed; exit actions are also carried out as a consequence. If the

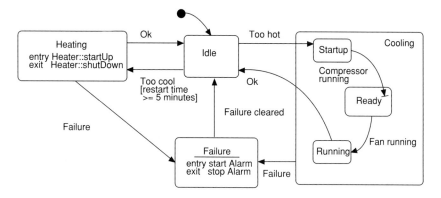

Figure 5-22
Nested States

state transition is conditional, then the transition will be triggered only if the expression evaluates true.

The order of evaluation in conditional state transitions is important. Given state S with transition T upon event E with condition C and action A, the following order applies:

- Event E occurs
- Condition C is evaluated
- If C evaluates true, then T is triggered and action A is invoked

This means that if a condition evaluates false, the state transition may not be triggered until the event occurs again and the condition is re-evaluated. Side effects in evaluating the condition or in carrying out an exit action will not affect the triggering of a state transition. For example, suppose that event E occurs, condition C evaluates true, and then the execution of the exit action changes the world so that C no longer evaluates true: the state transition will still be triggered.

We may include expressions that use the following syntax:

- in Cooling   Expression of current state

Here, we provide a state name (which may be qualified); this expression evaluates true if and only if the system is in the current state. This kind of expression is especially useful when an outer state needs to trigger a state transition conditionally based upon some lower-level nested state.

We may also write conditional expressions denoting time restrictions, as in the following example:

- timeout(Heating, 30)   Expression of time restriction

This condition evaluates true if the system was in the Heating state and had been in that state for more than 30 seconds. This kind of expression is common with eventless state transitions in many real-time systems, because it protects against settling in one state for too long. We can also use this expression to establish a lower bound for the time in a state. If we attach the same time restriction to every state transition with an event leading out of the state, then this is tantamount to requiring that the system be in the given state for at least the time specified by the time restriction.[*]

What happens if an event arrives but the current state has no transitions that lead to a new state, either because no such transition exists for the given event, or none of the proper conditions evaluate true? By default, this should be considered a failure: silently ignoring events is usually an indication of an incomplete analysis of the problem. In general, a state should document the events that it intentionally ignores.

Nested States The ability to nest states gives depth to state transition diagrams; this is the key feature of Harel's statecharts that mitigates the combinatorial explosion of states and state transitions that often occurs in complex systems.

In Figure 5-22, we have expanded the Cooling state to reveal its nested states; for simplicity, we have omitted all actions, including the state's entry and exit actions, as shown in Figure 5-21.

Enclosing states such as Cooling are called *superstates*, and its nested states, such as Running, are called *substates*. Nesting may be to any depth, and thus substates may be superstates to other lower-level substates. Given the superstate Cooling with its three substates, the semantics of nesting implies an xor (exclusive or) relationship: if the system is in the Cooling state (the superstate), then it must also be in exactly one of the three substates, Startup, Ready, or Running.

For simplicity in drawing state transition diagrams with depth, we may zoom in or zoom out relative to a particular state. Zooming out elides substates, and zooming in reveals substates. When we zoom out, state transitions to and from substates are shown with a stubbed arrow, as in the case of the state transition to the substate Ready.[**]

State transitions are allowed to originate and terminate at any level. Consider then the different forms of state transition:

- Transitioning from one state to a peer state (such as from Failure to Idle or from Ready to Running) is the simplest form of transition; it follows the semantics described in the previous section on state actions and conditional state transitions.

---

[*] Harel suggests a generalized "squiggle" notation for expressing both upper and lower bounds on time restrictions, but we will not discuss his generalization here, because timeout expressions are sufficiently expressive.
[**] In Figure 5-21, to be precise, the state transitions for Too hot and Ok relative to the Cooling state should be shown with stubs as well, because they transition to and from substates.

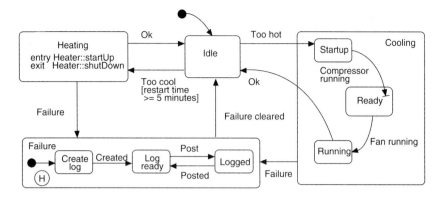

Figure 5-23
History

- One may transition directly to a substate (such as from Idle to Startup) or directly from a substate (such as the transition from Running to Idle) or both.

- Specifying a transition directly from a superstate (such as from Cooling to Failure via the Failure event) means that the state transition applies to every substate of the superstate. The transition is passed through all levels, until overridden. These semantics greatly reduce the clutter of common state transitions from substates.

- Specifying a transition directly to a state with substates (such as perhaps to Failure) indeed moves to the new state, but also implies moving to this superstate's default substate.

History Often when transitioning directly to a state with substates, we wish to return to the most recently visited state; these semantics may be indicated by the history icon, shown as the letter H inside a circle and placed anywhere directly inside the state. For example, in Figure 5-23, we have expanded the Failure state to reveal its substates. The very first time we transition into this state, we also move to its default start state Create log, indicated by the unlabeled transition from the filled circle; ultimately, the log is created, and we move into the Log ready state. After posting the failure, we return to this state. The next time we transition to the Failure state, we don't want to create the log again; rather, we want to begin in the Log ready state. Since this was the last state visited, and since we included the history icon, these are precisely the semantics we will get at all subsequent times when we enter the Failure state.

History applies only to the given level in which it appears. It may be made to apply all the way down to the lowest depth of nested states by attaching an asterisk to the history icon. It is possible to achieve intermediate kinds of history transition by applying history only to individual substates.

Orthogonal States Harel's statecharts introduce the concept of orthogonal states, which represent an "and" decomposition of states. Given a system in state A with orthogonal substates B and C, this means that the system is in state A as well as in both states B and C.

These semantics are largely unnecessary once we have mapped statecharts to the object model, as we have already done in this section. Specifically, peer objects whose classes have event-ordered behavior implicitly represent an "and" decomposition: the system is in the state denoted by both objects simultaneously. For this reason, we omit Harel's notion of orthogonal states.

Specifications

As for class diagrams, each entity in a state transition diagram may have a specification that provides its complete definition. Unlike the specification for classes, however, specifications for states and state transitions add no information beyond what we have already described in this section, and so we need not discuss their textual specification.

5.4 Object Diagrams

Essentials: Objects and Their Relationships

An *object diagram* is used to show the existence of objects and their relationships in the logical design of a system. Stated another way, an object diagram represents a snapshot in time of an otherwise transitory stream of events over a certain configuration of objects. Object diagrams are thus prototypical: each one represents the interactions or structural relationships that may occur among a given set of class instances, no matter what specifically named objects participate in the collaboration. In this sense, a single object diagram represents a view of the object structure of a system. During analysis, we use object diagrams to indicate the semantics of primary and secondary scenarios that provide a trace of the system's behavior. During design, we use object diagrams to illustrate the semantics of mechanisms in the logical design of a system.

The two essential elements of an object diagram are objects and their relationships.

Objects Figure 5-24 shows the icon we use to represent an object in an object diagram. As is our practice in class diagrams, we may optionally draw a horizontal line to partition the text inside the icon into two regions, one denoting the object's name, and another providing an optional view of the object's attributes.

Figure 5-24
Object Icon

The name of an object follows the syntax for attributes, and may be written in any of the three following forms, or using the syntax of the chosen implementation language:

- A   Object name only
- : C   Object class only
- A : C   Object name and class

If this text is particularly long, it can either be elided or the icon magnified. If several object icons in the same diagram use the same unqualified object name, then they all denote the same object; otherwise, each object icon denotes a distinct object occurrence.[*] If several object icons in different diagrams use the same name, then they denote different objects, unless their name is explicitly qualified.

The meaning of unqualified names depends upon the context of the object diagram. Specifically, object diagrams defined at the highest level of the system have a global scope; other object diagrams may be defined for class categories, individual classes, or individual methods, and so have the corresponding scope. Qualification may also be used as necessary to explicitly refer to global objects, class instance variables (in C++, static member objects), method parameters, attributes, and locally defined objects in the same scope.

If we never specify the class of an object, either explicitly using the above syntax, or implicitly through the object's specification, then the object's class is considered anonymous, and there can be no semantic checks as to the meaning of operations performed upon or by the object, nor of the object's relationship to any other objects in the diagram. If we only specify a class name, the object is said to be anonymous; each such icon without an object name denotes a distinct anonymous object.

In any case, the name given for an object's class must be that of the actual class (or any of its superclasses) in the scope of the diagram used to instantiate the object, even if such classes happen to be abstract. These rules make it

---

[*] Object icons with the same unqualified name but with different classes may appear on the same diagram, as long as these classes are related through some common superclass ancestor. This makes it possible to represent the propagation of operations from a subclass to a superclass and vice versa.

messages
—————————————————

Figure 5-25
Object Relationship Icon

possible to write scenarios that refer to objects without knowing the precise subclass in question.

For some objects, it is useful to expose some of their attributes. Again we say "some" because object icons only represent a view of the object's structure. The syntax for attributes follows that described in the earlier section on classes and their attributes, and includes the ability to specify a default expression for each attribute. Attribute names must refer to an attribute defined in the object's class or any of its superclasses. The syntax for items may be tailored to use the syntax for the chosen implementation language.

An object diagram may also include icons that denote class utilities and metaclasses, since both of these entities denote object-like things that may be operated upon and that operate upon other objects.

Object Relationships As explained in Chapter 3, objects interact through their links to other objects, represented by the icon in Figure 5-25. A link is an instance of an association, analogous to an object being an instance of a class.

A link may exist between two objects (including class utilities and metaclasses) if and only if there is an association between their corresponding classes. This class association may manifest itself in any way, meaning that the class relationship could be a plain association, an inheritance relationship, or a "has" relationship, for example. The existence of an association between two classes therefore denotes a path of communication (that is, a link) between instances of the classes, whereby one object may send messages to another. All classes implicitly have an association to themselves, and hence it is possible for an object to send a message to itself.

Given object A with a link L to object B, A may invoke any operation that is applicable to B's class and that is accessible to A; the reverse is true for operations invoked by B upon A. Whichever object invokes the operation is known as the *client*; whichever object provides the operation is known as the *supplier*. In general, the sender of a message knows the receiver, but the receiver does not necessarily know the sender.

In the steady state, there must be consistency between the class structure and the object structure of a system. If we show an operation M being invoked across link L upon object B, then B's specification (or the specification of an appropriate superclass) must contain the declaration of M.

As we show in Figure 5-25, we may adorn a link with a collection of messages. Each message consists of the following three elements:

- D   A synchronization symbol denoting the
                              direction of the invocation
- M   An operation invocation or event dispatch
- S   Optionally, a sequence number

We indicate the direction of a message by adorning it with a directed line, pointing to the supplier object. This particular symbol denotes the simplest form of message passing, whose semantics are guaranteed only in the presence of a single thread of control. As we will discuss in a later section, there are more advanced forms of synchronization that are appropriate to multiple threads of control.

An operation invocation is the most common kind of message. An operation invocation follows the syntax for operations as defined earlier, except that we may include actual parameters that match the signature of the operation:

- N()   Operation name only
- R N(arguments)   Operation return object, name, and actual
                              arguments

Matching actual arguments to formal arguments is done by position. If the operation return object and actual arguments use unqualified names that match other unqualified names in the object diagram, they are meant to denote the same object, and so their respective classes must be appropriate to the signature of the operation. In this manner, we can represent interactions that involve objects passed by parameter to or returned by certain operations.

A message denoting the dispatch of an event is also possible. An event dispatch follows the syntax for events as defined earlier, and so may represent a symbolic name, an object, or the name of some operation. In each case, the event name must be defined for the state transition diagrams appropriate to the class of the supplier object. Event dispatches as operations may include actual parameters as above.

In the absence of an explicit sequence number, messages may be passed at any time relative to all other messages represented in a particular object diagram. To show an explicit ordering of events, we may optionally prefix a sequence number (starting at one) to an operation invocation or event dispatch. This sequence number is used to indicate the relative ordering of messages. Messages with the same sequence number are unordered relative to each other; messages with lower sequence numbers are dispatched before messages with higher sequence numbers. Duplicate sequence numbers and missing sequence numbers allow a partial ordering of messages.

Example Figure 5-26 shows an example of an object diagram for the hydroponics gardening system, whose context is the class category Planning,, first described in Figure 5-7. The intent of this diagram is to illustrate a scenario that

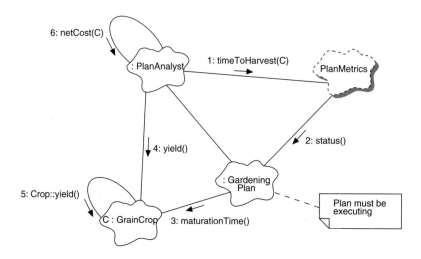

Figure 5-26
Hydroponics Gardening System Object Diagram

traces the execution of a common system function, namely, the determination of a predicted net cost-to-harvest for a specific crop.

Carrying out this system function requires the collaboration of several different objects. We see from this diagram that the action of the scenario begins with some PlanAnalyst object invoking the operation timeToHarvest() upon the class utility PlanMetrics. Note that the object C is passed as an actual argument to this operation. Subsequently, the PlanMetrics class utility calls status() upon a certain unnamed GardeningPlan object; our diagram includes a development note indicating that we must check that the given plan is in fact executing. The GardeningPlan object in turn invokes the operation maturationTime() upon the selected GrainCrop object, asking for the time the crop is expected to mature. After this selector operation completes, control then returns to the PlanAnalyst object, which then calls C.yield() directly, which in turn propagates this operation to the crop's superclass (the operation Crop::yield()). Control again returns to the PlanAnalyst object, which completes the scenario by invoking the operation netCost() upon itself.

This diagram indicates a link between the PlanAnalyst and GardeningPlan objects. Although no messages are passed, the presence of this link serves to highlight the existence of a semantic dependency between the two objects.

Advanced Concepts

The elements we have presented thus far constitute the essential parts of the notation for object diagrams. However, a number of particularly knotty development issues require that we extend this basic notation slightly. As we warned in our discussion on class diagrams, we must again emphasize that

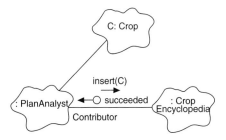

Figure 5-27
Roles

these advanced features should be applied only as necessary to capture the intended semantics of a scenario.

Roles, Keys, and Constraints In an earlier section, we noted that associations in a class diagram may be adorned with a role denoting the purpose or capacity wherein one class associates with another. For certain object diagrams, it is useful to restate this role on the corresponding link between two objects. Often, this adornment helps to explain why one object is operating upon another.

Figure 5-27 provides an example of this advanced feature. Here we see that some PlanAnalyst object inserts a specific crop into an anonymous CropEncyclopedia object, and does so while acting in the role of Contributor.

Using the same notation we introduced in class diagrams, we may indicates the keys or constraints associated with an object or a link.

Data Flow As we described in Chapter 3, data may flow with or against the direction of a message. Occasionally, explicitly showing the direction of a data flow helps to explain the semantics of a particular scenario. Borrowing from the notation for structured design, we use the icon shown in Figure 5-27 to show that the value succeeded returns upon completion of the message insert.

We may use either an object or a value in a data flow.

Visibility In certain complicated scenarios, it is useful to keep track of exactly how one object has visibility to another. Although associations in class diagrams denote the semantic dependencies that may exist among the classes of two objects, they do not dictate exactly how those instances can see one another. For this reason, we may adorn the links in our object diagrams with icons that represent the visibility of one object to another. This adornment is also important for tools that support forward code generation and reverse engineering.

Figure 5-28 is a refinement of Figure 5-26, and includes some of these adornments, which are similar to the icons we used to represent physical

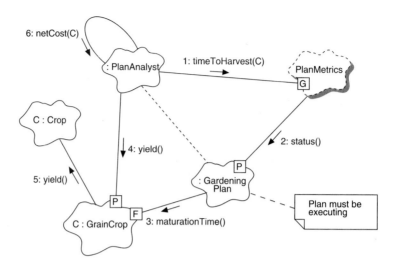

Figure 5-28
Visibility

containment in class diagrams, but with the addition of a letter designating the kind of visibility. For example, the G adornment shown on the link from the PlanAnalyst object to the PlanMetrics class utility denotes that the class utility is global to the declaration of the analyst object. The object C is visible to the PlanAnalyst object and the GardeningPlan object through two different paths. From the perspective of the PlanAnalyst object, the GrainCrop object C is visible as a parameter to some analyst operation (the P adornment); from the perspective of the GardeningPlan object, the GrainCrop object C is visible as a field (that is, as a part of the plan aggregate object).

To generalize, the following adornments may be used to indicate visibility:

- G   The supplier object is global to the client.
- P   The supplier object is a parameter to some operation of the client.
- F   The supplier object is a part of the client object.
- L   The supplier object is a locally declared object in the scope of the object diagram.

Consistent with the adornments for physical containment in class diagrams, these adornments may be written as an open box with a letter (representing that the object's identity is shared) or as a filled box with a letter (representing that the object's identity is not structurally shared).

The absence of a visibility adornment means that the precise visibility between the two objects is left unspecified. In practice, it is common to adorn

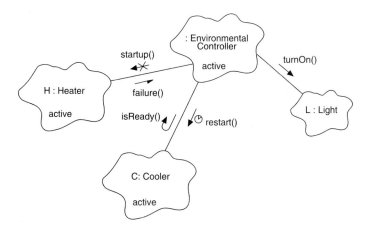

Figure 5-29
Active Objects and Synchronization

only a few key links in an object diagram with these visibility symbols. The most common use of these symbols is to represent whole/part (aggregation) relationships between two objects; the second most common use is to represent transitory objects that are passed into the object diagram's scenario as parameters.

Active Objects and Synchronization As noted in Chapter 3, certain objects may be active, meaning that they embody their own thread of control. Other objects may have only purely sequential semantics, while yet others might not be active, yet still guarantee their semantics in the presence of multiple threads of control.

In each of these circumstances, we must address two issues: how to signify the active objects that denote roots of control in a scenario, and how to represent different forms of synchronization among such objects.

In our earlier discussion on the advanced features of class specifications, we noted that classes may have one of four concurrency semantics: sequential, guarded, synchronous, and active. By implication, all instances of a class take on the concurrency semantics of their class; all objects are sequential unless otherwise stated. We may explicitly reveal the concurrency semantics of an object in an object diagram by adorning its object icon with the names `sequential`, `guarded`, `synchronous`, or `active`, placed in the lower left of the icon. For example, in Figure 5-29, we see that H, C, and the anonymous instance of the EnviornmentalController class are all active objects and thus embody their own thread of control. Unadorned objects (such as L) are assumed to be sequential.

The message synchronization symbol we introduced earlier (the simple directed line) represents simple sequential message passing. In the presence of multiple threads of control, however, we must specify other forms of synchronization.

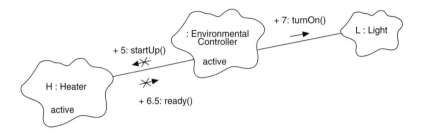

Figure 5-30
Time Budgets

Albeit slightly contrived, the example in Figure 5-29 illustrates the different kinds of message synchronization that may appear in an object diagram. The message turnOn() is an example of simple message passing, and is represented with the directed line. The semantics of simple message passing are guaranteed only in the presence of a single thread of control. In contrast, all the other messages involve some form of process synchronization; all such advanced forms of synchronization apply only to suppliers that are nonsequential.

For example, the message startUp() is synchronous, meaning that the client will wait forever until the supplier accepts the message. Synchronous message passing is equivalent to Ada's rendezvous mechanism among tasks. The isReady() message denotes balking message passing, meaning that the client will abandon the message if the supplier cannot immediately service the message. The restart() message denotes a timeout synchronization: the client will abandon the message if the supplier cannot service the message within a specified amount of time.

In each of these last three cases, the client must wait for the supplier to completely process the message (or abandon the message) before control can resume. In the case of the message failure(), the semantics are different. This is an example of an asynchronous message, which means that the client sends the event to the supplier for processing, the supplier queues the message, and the client then proceeds without waiting for the supplier. Asynchronous message passing is akin to interrupt handling.

Time Budgets For certain time-critical applications, it is important to trace scenarios in terms of exact time relative to the start of the scenario. To designate relative time, we use sequence numbers that denote time (in seconds), prefixed by the plus symbol. For example, in Figure 5-30, we see that the message startUp() is first invoked 5 seconds after the start of the scenario, followed by the message ready() 6.5 seconds after the start of the scenario, and then followed by the message turnOn() after 7 seconds.

Specifications

As for class diagrams, each entity in an object diagram may have a specification, which provides its complete definition. Because the specifications for objects and object relationships add no information beyond what we have already described in this section, we need not discuss their textual specification here.

On the other hand, the specifications for object diagrams as a whole do have one significant piece of nongraphical information that we must consider. As we described at the beginning of this section, every object diagram must designate a context. We do so in the diagram's specification, as follows:

```
Context:  global | category | class | operation
```

In particular, the scope of an object diagram may be global, or in the context of a named class category, class, or operation (including both methods and free subprograms).

5.5 Interaction Diagrams

Essentials: Objects and Interactions

An *interaction diagram* is used to trace the execution of a scenario in the same context as an object diagram.[*] Indeed, to a large degree, an interaction diagram is simply another way of representing an object diagram. For example, in Figure 5-31, we provide an interaction diagram that duplicates most of the semantics of the object diagram shown in Figure 5-26. The advantage of using an interaction diagram is that it is easier to read the passing of messages in relative order. The advantage of using an object diagram is that it scales well to many objects with complex invocations, and permits the inclusion of other information, such as links, attribute values, roles, data flow, and visibility. Because each diagram has compelling benefit we include both of them in the method.[**]

Interaction diagrams introduce no new concepts or icons; rather, they take most of the essential elements of object diagrams and restructure them. As Figure 5-31 indicates, an interaction diagram appears in tabular form. The entities of interest (which are the same as for object diagrams) are written horizontally across the top of the diagram. A dashed vertical line is drawn below each object. Messages (which may denote events or the invocation of operations) are shown horizontally using the same syntax and synchronization symbols as for object diagrams. The endpoints of the message icons connect

---

[*] These diagrams are generalizations of Rumbaugh's event trace diagrams [14] and Jacobson's interaction diagrams [15].

[**] Object diagrams and interaction diagrams are sufficiently close in terms of their semantics that it is possible for tools to generate one diagram from the other, with minimal loss of information.

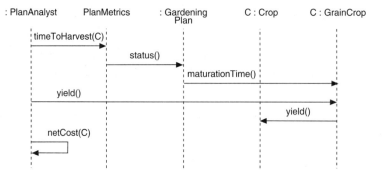

Figure 5-31
Hydroponics Gardening System Interaction Diagram

with the vertical lines that connect with the entities at the top of the diagram and are drawn from the client to the supplier. Ordering is indicated by vertical position, with the first message shown at the top of the diagram, and the last message shown at the bottom. As a result, it is unnecessary to use sequence numbers.

Interaction diagrams are often better than object diagrams for capturing the semantics of scenarios early in the development life cycle, before the protocols of individual classes have been identified. As we explain in the next chapter, early interaction diagrams tend to focus on events as opposed to operations, because events help to define the boundaries of a system under development. As development proceeds and the system's class structure is refined, the emphasis tends to migrate to object diagrams, whose semantics are more expressive.

Advanced Concepts

Interaction diagrams are conceptually very simple; however, there are two straightforward elements that can be added to make them more expressive in the presence of certain complicated patterns of interaction.

Scripts For complex scenarios that involve conditions or iterations, interaction diagrams can be enhanced by the use of scripts. As we see in the example in Figure 5-32, a script may be written to the left of an interaction diagram, with the steps of the script aligning with the message invocations. Scripts may be written using free-form or structured English text, or using the syntax of the chosen implementation language.

Focus of Control Neither simple object diagrams nor interaction diagrams indicate the focus of control as messages are passed. For example, if object A sends messages X and Y to other objects, it is not clear if X and Y are independent messages from A or if they have been invoked as part of the same

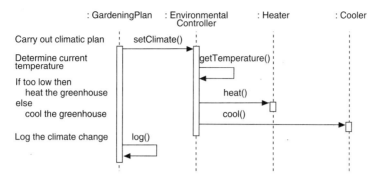

Figure 5-32
Scripts and Focus of Control

enclosing message Z. As we show in Figure 5-32, we may adorn the vertical lines descending from each object in an interaction diagram with a box representing the relative time that the flow of control is focused in that object. For example, here we see that the anonymous instance of the GardeningPlan is the ultimate focus of control, and its behavior of carrying out a climatic plan invokes other methods, which in turn call other methods that eventually return control back to the GardeningPlan object.

5.6 Module Diagrams

Essentials: Modules and Their Dependencies

A module diagram is used to show the allocation of classes and objects to modules in the physical design of a system. A single module diagram represents a view of the module structure of a system. During development, we use module diagrams to indicate the physical layering and partitioning of our architecture.

Certain languages, most notably Smalltalk, have no concept of a physical architecture formed of modules; in such cases, module diagrams are unnecessary.

The two essential elements of a module diagram are modules and their dependencies.

Modules Figure 5-33 shows the icons we use to represent various kinds of modules. The first three icons denote files, distinguished by their function. The main program icon denotes a file that contains the root of a program. In C++ for example, this would likely be some .cpp file that contains the definition of the privileged nonmember function called main. Typically, there is exactly one such module per program. The specification icon and the body icon denote files that contain the declaration and definition of entities, respectively. In C++,

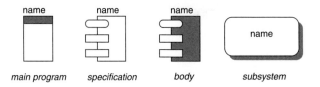

Figure 5-33
Module and Subsystem Icons

for example, specification modules denote .h files, and body modules denote .cpp files.

We will explain the meaning of the subsystem icon in a later section.

A name is required for each module; this name typically denotes the simple name of the corresponding physical file in the development directory. We usually write such names without their suffixes, which would be redundant when associated with a particular module icon. If the name is particularly long, it can either be elided or the icon magnified. Every full file name must be unique according to its enclosing subsystem. Depending upon the needs of our particular development environments, we may impose other constraints upon names, such as requiring distinctive prefixes or requiring unique names across the entire system.

Each module encompasses the declaration or definition of classes, objects, and other language details. Conceptually, we can zoom in to a module to see the physical contents of its corresponding file.

Dependencies The only relationship we may have between two modules is a compilation dependency, represented by a directed line pointing to the module upon which the dependency exists. In C++ for example, we indicate a compilation dependency by #include directives. Similarly in Ada, compilation dependencies are indicated by with clauses. In general, there may be no cycles within a set of compilation dependencies. Performing a topological sort upon all the dependencies of a system's module structure is sufficient to calculate a partial ordering of compilation.

Example In Figure 5-34, we provide an example of this notation, drawn from the physical architecture of the hydroponics gardening system. Here we see six modules. Two of them, climatedefs and cropdefs, are only specifications, and serve to provide common types and constants. The remaining four modules are shown with their specification and bodies grouped together: this is a typical style of drawing module diagrams, since the specification and body of a module are so intimately related. Because we have overlaid the two parts, the dependency of the body upon the corresponding specification is hidden, although it in fact exists. Similarly, the name of the body is hidden, which is not a problem because our convention is to name specifications and bodies the same except for a distinguishing suffix (such as .h and .cpp, respectively).

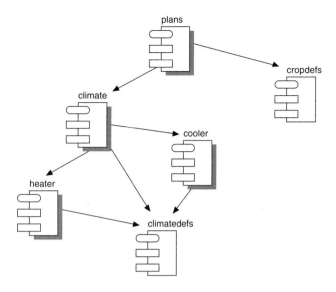

Figure 5-34
Hydroponics Gardening System Module Diagram

The dependencies in this diagram suggest a partial ordering of compilation. For example, the body of `climate` depends upon the specification of `heater`, which in turn depends upon the specification of `climatedefs`.

Essentials: Subsystems

As explained in Chapter 2, a large system may be decomposed into many hundreds, if not a few thousand, modules. Trying to comprehend the physical architecture of such a system is impossible without further chunking. In practice, developers tend to use informal conventions to collect related modules in directory structures. For similar reasons, we introduce the notion of a subsystem for module diagrams, which parallels the role played by the class category for class diagrams. Specifically, subsystems represent clusters of logically related modules.

Subsystems Subsystems serve to partition the physical model of a system. A subsystem is an aggregate containing other modules and other subsystems. Each module in the system must live in a single subsystem or at the top level of the system.

Figure 5-33 shows the icon we use to represent a subsystem. As for a module, a name is required for each subsystem. The rules for naming subsystems follow the rules for naming individual modules, although full subsystem names do not typically include distinctive suffixes.

Some of the modules enclosed by a subsystem may be public, meaning that they are exported from the subsystem and hence usable outside the

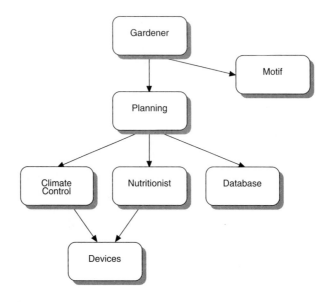

Figure 5-35
Hydroponics Gardening System Top-Level Module Diagram

subsystem. Other modules may be part of the subsystem's implementation, meaning that they are not intended to be used by any other module outside of the subsystem. By convention, every module in a subsystem is considered public, unless explicitly defined otherwise. Restricting access to implementation modules is achieved by using the same advanced concepts as for restricting access in class categories.

A subsystem can have dependencies upon other subsystems or modules, and a module can have dependencies upon a subsystem. For consistency, we apply the same dependency icon as described earlier.

In practice, a large system has one top-level module diagram, consisting of the subsystems at the highest level of abstraction. Through this diagram a developer comes to understand the general physical architecture of a system.

Example Figure 5-35 shows an example of a top-level module diagram for the hydroponics gardening system. If we zoom into any of the seven subsystems shown here, we will find all of their corresponding modules.

Notice how this physical architecture maps to the logical architecture of the hydroponics gardening system shown in Figure 5-7. These structures are largely isomorphic, although there are small differences. In particular, we have made the decision to separate the low-level device classes from the `Climate` and `Nutrients` class categories and place their corresponding modules into one subsystem called `Devices`. We have also split the `Greenhouse` class category into the two subsystems called `ClimateControl` and `Nutritionist`.

Advanced Concepts

Language Tailoring Certain languages, most notably Ada, define other kinds of modules than the simple ones provided for by Figure 5-33. In particular, Ada defines generic packages, generic subprograms, and tasks as separate compilation units. It is therefore reasonable to augment the essential icons of module diagrams to include icons that represent language-specific kinds of modules.

Segmentation Especially for platforms that have severely constrained memory models, the decision to generate code in different segments, or even to produce a scheme for overlays, is an important one. Module diagrams can be extended to help visualize this segmentation by including language-specific adornments to each module in a module diagram that denote its corresponding code or data segment.

Specifications

As with class and object diagrams, each entity in a module diagram may have a specification, which provides its complete definition. Because the specifications for modules and their dependencies add no information beyond what we have already described in this section, we need not discuss their textual specification here.

Given some degree of integration between tools that support this notation and tools for programming environments, it is reasonable to use module diagrams as a means of visualizing the modules managed by the programming environment. Zooming into a specific module or subsystem in a module diagram is therefore equivalent to navigating to the corresponding physical file or directory, and vice versa.

5.7 Process Diagrams

Essentials: Processors, Devices, and Connections

A process diagram is used to show the allocation of processes to processors in the physical design of a system. A single process diagram represents a view into the process structure of a system. During development, we use process diagrams to indicate the physical collection of processors and devices that serve as the platform for execution of our system.

The three essential elements of a process diagram are processors, devices, and their connections.

Processors Figure 5-36 shows the icon we use to represent a processor. A processor is a piece of hardware capable of executing programs. A name is

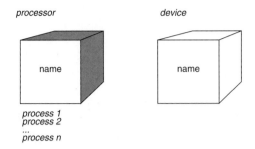

Figure 5-36
Processor and Device Icons

required for each processor; there are no particular constraints upon processor names, because they denote hardware, not software, entities.

We may adorn a processor icon with a list of processes. A process in this list denotes the root of a main program (from a module diagram) or the name of an active object (from an object diagram).

Devices Figure 5-36 shows the icon we use to represent a device. A device is a piece of hardware incapable of executing programs (as least as far as our logical model is concerned). As for processors, a name is required for each device. There are no particular constraints upon device names, and in fact, their names may be quite generic, such as `modem` or `terminal`.

Connections Processors and devices must communicate with one another. Using an undirected line, we may indicate the connection between a device and a processor, a processor and a processor, or a device and a device. A connection usually represents some direct hardware coupling, such as an RS232 cable, an Ethernet connection, or perhaps even a path to shared memory. A connection may also represent more indirect couplings, such as satellite-to-ground communications. Connections are usually considered to be bi-directional, although if a particular connection is unidirectional, an arrow may be added to show the direction. Each connection may include an optional label that names the connection.

Example In Figure 5-37, we provide an example of this notation, drawn from the physical architecture of the hydroponics gardening system. Here we see that our system architects have decided to decompose our system into a network of three computers, one assigned to a gardener workstation, and the others allocated to individual greenhouses. Processes running on the greenhouse computers cannot communicate directly with one another, although they can communicate with processes running on the gardener workstation. For simplicity, we have chosen not to show any devices in this diagram, although we expect there to be quite a few actuators and sensors in the system.

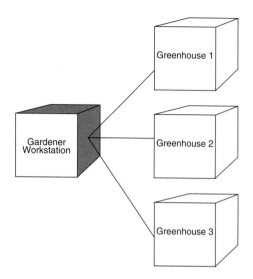

Figure 5-37
Hydroponics Gardening System Process Diagram

Advanced Concepts

Tailoring Figure 5-36 shows the standard icons we use to represent processors and devices, but it is reasonable and in fact desirable to allow alternate representations. For example, we might define specific icons to graphically represent an embedded microcomputer (a processor), a disk, a terminal, and an A/D converter (all devices), and then use these icons in a process diagram instead of the standard icons. By doing so, we offer a visualization of the physical platform of our implementation that speaks directly to our hardware and systems architects, as well as to the end users of the system, who are probably not experts in software development.

Nesting The hardware configuration of a system is sometimes very complex, and may involve complex hierarchies of processors and devices. In some circumstances, therefore, it is useful to be able to represent groups of processors, devices, and connections, much as class categories represent logical groupings of classes and objects. We may indicate such hardware groups with a named icon shaped as a rounded rectangle with dashed lines. Each such icon denotes a distinct group of processors, devices, and connections, and so zooming into a group reveals these nested entities. We may define connections between groups, as well as among processors, devices, and groups.

Process Scheduling We must have some policy for how to schedule the execution of processes within a processor. There are basically five general approaches to scheduling, and we may document which of these is used by adorning each processor icon with one of the names:

- Preemptive

  Higher-priority processes that are ready to execute may preempt lower-priority ones that are currently executing; typically, processes with equal priority are given a time slice in which to execute, so that computational resources are fairly distributed.

- Nonpreemptive

  The current process continues to execute until it relinquishes control.

- Cyclic

  Control passes from one process to another, and each process is given a fixed amount of processing time, usually called a *frame*; processes may be allocated time in frames or subframes.

- Executive

  Some algorithm controls process scheduling.

- Manual

  Processes are scheduled by a user outside of the system.

To further explain the scheduling used by a specific processor, it is sometimes useful to include an object diagram or an interaction diagram, particularly if executive scheduling is used.

Specifications

As with all other diagrams, each processor, device, and connection may have a specification, which provides its complete definition. Because the specifications for these entities add no information beyond what we have already described in this section, we need not discuss their textual specification here.

5.8 Applying the Notation

The Products of Object-Oriented Development

Typically, the analysis of a system will include sets of object diagrams (to express the behavior of the system through scenarios), class diagrams (to express the roles and responsibilities of agents that provide the system's behavior), and state transition diagrams (to show the event-ordered behavior of these agents). Similarly, the design of a system, encompassing its architecture and implementation, will include sets of class diagrams, object diagrams, module diagrams, and process diagrams, as well as their corresponding dynamic views.

End-to-end connectivity exists among these diagrams, permitting us to trace requirements from implementation back to specification. Starting with a process diagram, a processor may designate a main program, which is defined in some module diagram. This module diagram may encompass the definition of a collection of classes and objects, whose definitions we will find in the appropriate class or object diagrams. Finally, the definitions of individual classes point to our requirements, because these classes in general directly reflect the vocabulary of the problem space.

The notation described in this chapter can be used manually, although for larger applications it cries out for automated tool support. Tools can provide consistency checking, constraint checking, completeness checking, and analysis, and they can help a developer browse through the products of analysis and design in unconstrained ways. For example, while looking at a module diagram, a developer might want to study a particular mechanism; he or she can use a tool to locate all the classes allocated to a particular module. While looking at an object diagram describing a scenario that uses one of these classes, the developer might want to see its place in the inheritance lattice. Lastly, if this scenario involved an active object, the developer might use a tool to find the processor to which this thread of control is allocated, and then view an animation of its class's state machine on that processor. Using tools in this manner frees developers from the tedium of keeping all the details of the analysis and design consistent, allowing them to focus upon the creative aspects of the development process.

Scaling Up and Scaling Down

We have found this notation and its variants applicable both to small systems consisting of just a dozen or so classes, to ones consisting of a several thousand classes. As we will see in the next two chapters, this notation is particularly applicable to an incremental, iterative approach to development. One does not create a diagram and then walk away from it, treating it as some sacred, immutable artifact. Rather, these diagrams evolve during the design process as new design decisions are made and more detail is established.

We have also found this notation to be largely language-independent. It is applicable to any of a wide spectrum of object-oriented programming languages.

This chapter has described the essential products of object-oriented development, including their syntax and semantics. The next two chapters will describe the process that leads us to these products. The remaining five chapters demonstrate the practical application of this notation and process to a variety of problems.

Summary

- Designing is not the act of drawing a diagram; a diagram simply captures a design.
- In the design of a complex system, it is important to view the design from multiple perspectives: namely, its logical and physical structure, and its static and dynamic semantics.

- The notation for object-oriented development includes four basic diagrams (class diagrams, object diagrams, module diagrams, and process diagrams) and two supplementary diagrams (state transition diagrams and interaction diagrams).

- A class diagram is used to show the existence of classes and their relationships in the logical design of a system. A single class diagram represents a view of the class structure of a system.

- An object diagram is used to show the existence of objects and their relationships in the logical design of a system. A single object diagram is typically used to represent a scenario.

- A module diagram is used to show the allocation of classes and objects to modules in the physical design of a system. A single module diagram represents a view of the module architecture of a system.

- A process diagram is used to show the allocation of processes to processors in the physical design of a system. A single process diagram represents a view of the process architecture of a system.

- A state transition diagram is used to show the state space of an instance of a given class, the events that cause a transition from one state to another, and the actions that result from a state change.

- An interaction diagram is used to trace the execution of a scenario in the same context as an object diagram.

Further Readings

Since the publication of the first edition of this book, I have unilaterally tried to incorporate the best notational elements from many other methodologists, especially Rumbaugh and Jacobson, into the Booch method, and have cast away or simplified elements of the original Booch notation that proved to be clumsy, inconsistent, or of marginal utility, while at the same time striving to maintain a conceptual integrity in the notation. This chapter is the culmination of this unification effort.

A tremendous amount has been written about notations for software analysis and design; the book by Martin and McClure [H 1988] is a general reference to many of the more traditional approaches. Graham [F 1991] surveys a number of notations specific to object-oriented methods.

An early form of the notation described in this chapter was first documented by Booch [F 1981]. This notation later evolved to incorporate the expressive power of semantic nets (Stillings et al. [A 1987] and Barr and Feigenbaum [J 1981]), entity-relationship diagrams (Chen [E 1976]), entity models (Ross [F 1987]), Petri nets (Peterson [J 1977], Sahraoui [F 1987], and Bruon and Balsamo [F 1986]), associations (Rumbaugh [F 1991]) and statecharts (Harel [F 1987]). Rumbaugh's work is particularly interesting, for as he observes, our methods are more similar than they are different.

The icons representing objects and packages were inspired by the iAPX 432 [D 1981]. The notation for object diagrams derives from Seidewitz [F 1985]. The notation for concurrency semantics is adapted from the work of Buhr [F 1988, 1989].

Chang [G 1990] provides a good survey on the more general topic of visual languages.

CHAPTER 6

The Process

The amateur software engineer is always in search of magic, some sensational method or tool whose application promises to render software development trivial. It is the mark of the professional software engineer to know that no such panacea exists. Amateurs often want to follow cookbook steps; professionals know that right approaches to development usually lead to inept design products, born of a progression of lies, and behind which developers can shield themselves from accepting responsibility for earlier misguided decisions. The amateur software engineer either ignores documentation all together, or follows a process that is documentation-driven, worrying more about how these paper products look to the customer than about the substance they contain. The professional acknowledges the importance of creating certain documents, but never does so at the expense of making sensible architectural innovations.

The process of object-oriented analysis and design cannot be described in a cookbook, yet it is sufficiently well-defined as to offer a predictable and repeatable process for the mature software development organization. In this chapter, we examine this incremental, iterative process in detail, and consider the purpose, products, activities, and measures of its various phases.

6.1 First Principles

Traits of Successful Projects

A successful software project is one whose deliverables satisfy and possibly exceed the customer's expectations, was developed in a timely and economical fashion, and is resilient to change and adaptation. By this measure, we have observed two traits that are common to virtually all of the successful object-oriented systems we have encountered, and noticeably absent from the ones that we count as failures:

- The existence of a strong architectural vision
- The application of a well-managed iterative and incremental development life cycle

Architectural Vision A system that has a sound architecture is one that has conceptual integrity and, as Brooks firmly states, "conceptual integrity is *the* most important consideration in system design" [1]. As we described in Chapters 1 and 5, the architecture of an object-oriented software system encompasses its class and object structure, organized in terms of distinct layers and partitions. In some ways, the architecture of a system is largely irrelevant to its end users. However, as Stroustrup points out, having a "clean internal structure" is essential to constructing a system that is understandable, can be extended and reorganized, and is maintainable and testable [2]. Furthermore, it is only through having a clear sense of a system's architecture that it becomes possible to discover common abstractions and mechanisms. Exploiting this commonality ultimately leads to the constructions of systems that are simpler, and therefore smaller and more reliable.

Just as there is no "right" way to classify abstractions, there is no "right" way to craft the architecture of a given system. For any application domain, there are certainly some profoundly stupid ways, and occasionally some very elegant ways, to design the architecture of a solution. How then do we distinguish a good architecture from a bad one?

Fundamentally, good architectures tend to be object-oriented. This is not to say that all object-oriented architectures are good, nor that only object-oriented architectures are good. However, as we discussed in Chapters 1 and 2, it can be shown that the application of the principles that underlie object-oriented decomposition tend to yield architectures that exhibit the desirable properties of organized complexity.

Good software architectures tend to have several attributes in common:

- They are constructed in well-defined layers of abstraction, each layer representing a coherent abstraction, provided through a well-defined and controlled interface, and built upon equally well-defined and controlled facilities at lower levels of abstraction.

- There is a clear separation of concerns between the interface and implementation of each layer, making it possible to change the implementation of a layer without violating the assumptions made by its clients.
- The architecture is simple: common behavior is achieved through common abstractions and common mechanisms.

We make a distinction between strategic and tactical architectural decisions. A *strategic decision* is one that has sweeping architectural implications, and so involves the organization of the architecture's higher-level structures. Mechanisms for error detection and recovery, user interface paradigms, policies for memory management and object persistence, and approaches to process synchronization in real-time applications all represent strategic architectural decisions. In contrast, a *tactical decision* has only local architectural implications, and so usually only involves the details of an abstraction's interface and implementation. The protocol of a class, the signature of a method, and the choice of a particular algorithm to implement a method all represent tactical decisions.

A fundamental part of holding on to a strong architectural vision is maintaining a balance between these strategic and tactical decisions. In the absence of good strategic decisions, even the most cunningly designed class will never fit in quite right. A collection of the most profoundly engineered strategic decisions will be ruined by not paying careful attention to the design of individual classes. In either case, neglecting an architectural vision leaves us with the software equivalent of sludge.

Iterative and Incremental Life Cycle Consider two extremes: an organization that has no well-defined development life cycle, and one that has very rigid and strictly-enforced policies that dictate every aspect of development. In the former case, we have anarchy: through the hard work and individual contributions of a few developers, the team may eventually produce something of value, but we can never reliably predict anything: not progress to date, not work remaining, and certainly not quality. The team is likely to be very inefficient and, in the extreme, may never reach closure and so never deliver a software product that satisfies its customer's current or future expectations. This is an example of a project in free fall.[*] In the second case, we have a dictatorship, in which creativity is punished, experimentation that could yield a more elegant architecture is discouraged, and the customer's real expectations are never correctly communicated to the lowly developer who is hidden behind a veritable paper wall erected by the organization's bureaucracy.

The successful object-oriented projects we have encountered follow neither anarchic nor draconian development life cycles. Rather, we find that the process that leads to the successful construction of object-oriented architectures

---

[*] There is an outside chance that a project in free fall will eventually land intact, but you would not want to bet your company's future on it.

tends to be both iterative and incremental. Such a process is iterative in the sense that it involves the successive refinement of an object-oriented architecture, from which we apply the experience and results of each release to the next iteration of analysis and design. The process is incremental in the sense that each pass through an analysis/design/evolution cycle leads us to gradually refine our strategic and tactical decisions, ultimately converging upon a solution that meets the end user's real (and usually unstated) requirements, and yet is simple, reliable, and adaptable.

An iterative and incremental development life cycle is the antithesis of the traditional waterfall life cycle, and so represents neither a strictly top-down nor a bottom-up process. It is reassuring to note that there are precedents in the hardware and software communities for this style of development [3, 4]. For example, assume that we are faced with the problem of staffing an organization to design and implement a fairly complex multiboard device or some custom VLSI chip. We might use traditional horizontal staffing, in which we have a waterfall progression of products, with systems architects feeding logic designers feeding circuit designers. This is an example of top-down design, and requires designers who are "tall, skinny men" because of the narrow yet deep skills that each must possess [5]. Alternately, we might use vertical staffing, in which we have good all-around designers who take slices of the entire project, from architectural conception through circuit design. This style of development is much more iterative and incremental, and the skills that these designers must have leads us to call them "short, fat men" because of the broad architectural vision that each must possess.

Our experience indicates that object-oriented development is neither strictly top-down, nor strictly bottom-up. Instead, as Druke suggests, well-structured complex systems are best created through the use of "round-trip gestalt design." This style of design emphasizes the incremental and iterative development of a system through the refinement of different yet consistent logical and physical views of the system as a whole. Round-trip gestalt design is the foundation of the process of object-oriented design.

For a few limited application domains, the problem being solved may already be well-defined, with many different implementations currently fielded. Here, it is possible to almost completely codify the development process: the designers of a new system in such a domain already understand what the important abstractions are; they already know what mechanisms ought to be employed, and they generally know the range of behavior that is expected of such a system. Creativity is still important in such a process, but here the problem is sufficiently constrained as to already address most of the system's strategic decisions. In such circumstances, it is possibly to achieve radically high rates of productivity, because most of the development risk has been eliminated [6]. The more we know about the problem to be solved, the easier it is to solve.

Most industrial-strength software problems are not like this: most involve the balancing of a unique set of functional and performance requirements, and this task demands the full creative energies of the development team.

Furthermore, any human activity that requires creativity and innovation demands an iterative and incremental process that relies upon the experience, intelligence, and talent of each team member.* It is therefore impossible to provide any cookbook recipes.

Towards a Rational Design Process

Clearly, however, we desire to be prescriptive; otherwise, we will never secure a mature, repeatable development process for any organization. It is for this reason that we spoke earlier of having a well-managed incremental and iterative life cycle: well-managed in the sense that the process can be controlled and measured, yet not so rigid that it fails to provide sufficient degrees of freedom to encourage creativity and innovation.

Having a prescriptive process is fundamental to the maturity of a software organization. As described by Humphrey, there are five distinct levels of process maturity [7]:

- Initial   The development process is *ad hoc* and often chaotic. Organizations can progress by introducing basic project controls.

- Repeatable   The organization has reasonable control over its plans and commitments. Organizations can progress by institutionalizing a well-defined process.

- Defined   The development process is reasonably well-defined, understood, and practiced; it serves as a stable foundation for calibrating the team and predicting progress. Organizations can progress by instrumenting their development practices.

- Managed   The organization has quantitative measures of its process. Organizations can progress by lowering the cost of gathering this data, and instituting practices that permit this data to influence the process.

- Optimizing   The organization has in place a well-tuned process that consistently yields products of high quality in a predictable, timely, and cost-effective manner.

---

* The experiments by Curtis and his colleagues reinforce these observations. Curtis studied the work of professional software developers by videotaping them in action and then analyzing the different activities they undertook (analysis, design, implementation, etc.) and when they applied them. From these studies, he concluded that "software design appears to be a collection of interleaved, iterative, loosely ordered processes under opportunistic control. . . . Top-down balanced development appears to be a special case occurring when a relevant design schema is available or the problem is small. . . . Good designers work at multiple levels of abstraction and detail simultaneously" [8].

Unfortunately, as Parnas and Clements observe, "we will never find a process that allows us to design software in a perfectly rational way," because of the need for creativity and innovation during the development process. However, as they go on to say, "the good news is that we can fake it. . . . [Because] designers need guidance, we will come closer to a rational process if we try to follow the process rather than proceed on an *ad hoc* basis. When an organization undertakes many software projects, there are advantages to having a standard procedure. . . . If we agree on an ideal process, it becomes much easier to measure the progress that the project is making" [9].

As we move our development organizations to higher levels of maturity, how then do we reconcile the need for creativity and innovation with the requirement for more controlled management practices? The answer appears to lie in distinguishing the micro and macro elements of the development process. The micro process is more closely related to Boehm's spiral model of development, and serves as the framework for an iterative and incremental approach to development [10]. The macro process is more closely related to the traditional waterfall life cycle, and serves as the controlling framework for the micro process. By reconciling these two disparate processes, we end up "faking" a fully rational development process, and so have a foundation for the defined level of software process maturity.

We must emphasize that every project is unique, and hence developers must strike a balance between the informality of the micro process and the formality of the macro process. For exploratory applications, developed by a tightly knit team of highly experienced developers, too much formality would stifle innovation; for very complex projects, developed by a large team of developers who are likely to be distributed geographically as well as in time, too little formality will lead to chaos.

The remainder of this chapter provides an overview and then a detailed description of the purpose, products, activities, and measures that make up the micro and macro development processes. In the next chapter, we examine the practical implications of this process, primarily from the perspective of managers who must supervise object-oriented projects.

6.2 The Micro Development Process

Overview

The micro process of object-oriented development is largely driven by the stream of scenarios and architectural products that emerge from and that are successively refined by the macro process. To a large extent, the micro process represents the daily activities of the individual developer or a small team of developers.

The micro process applies equally to the software engineer and the software architect. From the perspective of the engineer, the micro process offers guidance in making the myriad tactical decisions that are part of the daily

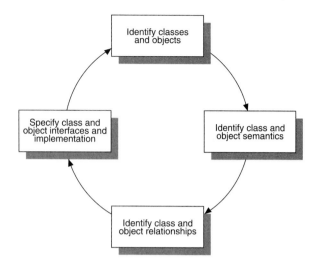

Figure 6-1
The Micro Development Process

fabrication and adaptation of the architecture; from the perspective of the architect, the micro process offers a framework for evolving the architecture and exploring alternative designs.

In the micro process, the traditional phases of analysis and design are intentionally blurred, and the process is under opportunistic control. As Stroustrup observes, "There are no 'cookbook' methods that can replace intelligence, experience, and good taste in design and programming. . . . The different phases of a software project, such as design, programming, and testing, cannot be strictly separated" [11].

As Figure 6-1 illustrates, the micro process tends to track the following activities:

- Identify the classes and objects at a given level of abstraction.
- Identify the semantics of these classes and objects.
- Identify the relationships among these classes and objects.
- Specify the interface and then the implementation of these classes and objects.

Let's examine each of these activities in detail.

Identifying Classes and Objects

Purpose The purpose of identifying classes and objects is to establish the boundaries of the problem at hand. Additionally, this activity is the first step in devising an object-oriented decomposition of the system under development.

As part of analysis, we apply this step to discover those abstractions that form the vocabulary of the problem domain, and by so doing, we begin to constrain our problem by deciding what is and what is not of interest. As part of design, we apply this step to invent new abstractions that form elements of the solution. As implementation proceeds, we apply this step in order to invent lower-level abstractions that we can use to construct higher-level ones, and to discover commonality among existing abstractions, which we can then exploit in order to simplify the system's architecture.

Products The central product of this step is a data dictionary that is updated as development proceeds. Initially, it may be sufficient to accumulate a "list of things" consisting of all significant classes and objects, using meaningful names that imply their semantics [12]. As development proceeds, and especially as the dictionary grows, it becomes necessary to formalize the repository, perhaps by using a simple *ad hoc* database to manage the list, or a more focused tool that supports the method directly.[*] In its more formal variations, a data dictionary serves as an index into all the other products of the development process, including the various diagrams and specifications of the object-oriented development notation.

The data dictionary thus serves as a central repository for the abstractions relevant to the system. Initially, it is permissible to keep the dictionary open-ended: some things in this repository might turn out to be classes, some objects, and others simply attributes of or synonyms for other abstractions. Over time, this dictionary will be refined by adding new abstractions, eliminating irrelevant ones, and consolidating similar ones.

There are three essential benefits to creating a data dictionary as part of this activity. First, maintaining a dictionary helps to establish a common and consistent vocabulary that can be used throughout the project. Second, a dictionary can serve as an efficient vehicle for browsing through all the elements of a project in arbitrary ways. This feature is particularly useful as new members are added to the development team, who must quickly orient themselves to the solution already under development. Third, a data dictionary permits architects to take a global view of the project, which may lead to the discovery of commonalities that otherwise might be missed.

Activities As we described in Chapter 4, the identification of classes and objects involves two activities: discovery and invention.

Not every developer has to be skilled in these activities. Analysts, usually working in conjunction with domain experts, must be good at discovering abstractions, capable of looking at the problem domain and finding meaningful classes and objects. Similarly, architects and the more senior developers must be skilled in crafting new classes and objects that derive from the solution domain. We will discuss the nature of this work breakdown in more detail in the next chapter.

---

[*] Formally, a data dictionary for object-oriented development encompasses the specification of each element in the architecture.

In each case, we carry out these activities by applying any of the various approaches to classification described in Chapter 4. A typical order of events might be the following:

- Apply the classical approach to object-oriented analysis (page 155) to generate a set of candidate classes and objects. Early in the life cycle, tangible things and the roles they play are good starting points. Later in the life cycle, following events will yield other first- and second-order abstractions: for each event, we must have some object that is ultimately responsible for detecting and/or reacting to the event.

- Apply the techniques of behavior analysis (page 156) to identify abstractions that are directly related to system function points. The system's function points, as we will discuss later in this chapter, fall out from the macro process, and represent distinct, outwardly visible and testable behaviors. As with events, for each behavior, we must have entities that initiate and participate in each behavior.

- From the relevant scenarios generated as part of the macro process, apply the techniques of use-case analysis (page 158). Early in the life cycle, we follow initial scenarios that describe broad behaviors of the system. As development proceeds, we examine more detailed scenarios as well as peripheral scenarios in order to explore the dark corners of the system's desired behavior.

For each of these approaches, the use of CRC cards is an effective catalyst for the brainstorming process, and has the added benefit of helping to jell the team by encouraging them to communicate.[*]

Some of the classes and objects we identify early in the life cycle will be wrong, but that is not necessarily a bad thing. Many of the tangible things and roles that we encounter early in the life cycle will carry through all the way to implementation, because they are so fundamental to our conceptual model of the problem. As we learn more about the problem, we will probably change the boundaries of certain abstractions by reallocating responsibilities, combining similar abstractions, and – quite often – dividing larger abstractions into groups of collaborating ones, thus forming some of the mechanisms of our solution.

Milestones and Measures We successfully complete this phase when we have a reasonably stable data dictionary. Because of the iterative and incremental nature of the micro process, we don't expect to complete or freeze this dictionary until very late in the development process. Rather, it is sufficient that we have a dictionary containing an ample set of abstractions, consistently named and with a sensible separation of responsibilities.

---

[*] It's a terrible stereotype, but some software developers are not particularly known for being great communicators.

A measure of goodness, therefore, is that the dictionary is not changing wildly each time we iterate through the micro process. A rapidly changing dictionary is a sign either that the development team has not yet achieved focus, or that the architecture is in some way flawed. As development proceeds, we can track stability in lower-level parts of the architecture by following the local changes in collaborative abstractions.

Identifying the Semantics of Classes and Objects

Purpose The purpose of identifying the semantics of classes and objects is to establish the behavior and attributes of each abstraction identified in the previous phase. Here we refine our candidate abstractions through an intelligent and measurable distribution of responsibilities.

As part of analysis, we apply this step to allocate the responsibilities for different system behaviors. As part of design, we apply this step to achieve a clear separation of concerns among the parts of our solution. As implementation proceeds, we move from free-form descriptions of roles and responsibilities to specifying a concrete protocol for each abstraction, eventually culminating in a precise signature for each operation.

Products There are several products that flow from this step. The first is a refinement of the data dictionary, whereby we initially attach responsibilities to each abstraction. As development proceeds, we may create specifications for each abstraction (as described in Chapter 5), which state the named operations that form the protocol of each class. As soon as possible, we will want to formally capture these decisions by writing the interface for each class in our particular implementation language. For C++, this means delivering *.h* files; for Ada, this means delivering package specifications; for CLOS, this means writing the generic functions for each class; for Smalltalk, this means declaring but not implementing the methods of each class. If we are dealing with the database elements of our problem, and especially if we are using an object-oriented database, we can produce the rudiments of our schema.

In addition to these products, which are more tactical in nature, we may also produce object diagrams and interaction diagrams that begin to capture the semantics of the scenarios that derive from the macro process. These diagrams serve to formally capture our storyboarding of each scenario, and so reflect an explicit distribution of responsibilities among collaborating objects. At this point, we may also begin to introduce finite state machines for certain abstractions.

As in the previous step, we may use an *ad hoc* database or a method-specific tool to keep track of each abstraction's responsibilities, so that the team can evolve a consistent language of expression. Once we produce formal class interfaces, we can begin to use our programming tools to test and enforce our design decisions.

The primary benefit of the more formal products of this step is that they force the developer to consider the pragmatics of each abstraction's protocol.

The inability to specify clear semantics is a sign that the abstractions themselves are flawed.

Activities There are three activities associated with this step: storyboarding, isolated class design, and pattern scavenging.

The primary and peripheral scenarios generated by the macro process are the main drivers of storyboarding. This activity represents a top-down identification of semantics and, where it concerns system function points, addresses strategic issues. A typical order of events might be the following:

- Select one scenario or a set of scenarios related to a single function point; from the previous step, identify those abstractions relevant to the scenario.

- Walk though the activity of the scenario, assigning responsibilities to each abstraction sufficient to accomplish the desired behavior. As needed, assign attributes that represent structural elements required to carry out certain responsibilities.

- As the storyboarding proceeds, reallocate responsibilities so that there is a reasonably balanced distribution of behavior. Where possible, reuse or adapt existing responsibilities. Splitting large responsibilities into smaller ones is a very common action; less often, but still not rarely, trivial responsibilities are assembled into larger behaviors.

Informally, we may use CRC cards for storyboarding. More formally, the development team may write object diagrams or interaction diagrams. During analysis, this storyboarding is typically accomplished by a team including, but not limited to, the analyst, the domain expert, the architect, and a quality-assurance person. During design and later into implementation, storyboarding is accomplished by the architects and senior developers for the purpose of refining strategic decisions, and by individual developers for refining tactical decisions. Having additional team members participate in storyboarding is a highly effective way of teaching more junior developers, and of communicating the architectural vision.

Early in the development process, we may specify the semantics of classes and objects by writing the responsibilities for each abstraction in free-form text. Usually a phrase or a single sentence is sufficient; anything more suggests that a given responsibility is overly complex and ought to be divided into smaller ones. Later in the development process, as we begin to refine the protocol of individual abstractions, we may name specific operations, ignoring their full signatures. As soon as practical, we may attach full signatures for each operation. In this manner, we have tractability: a specific responsibility is satisfied by a set of cooperative operations, and each operation contributes in some way to an abstraction's responsibilities. At this point, we may introduce finite state machines for certain classes, especially those whose responsibilities involve event-driven or state-ordered behavior, so as to capture the dynamic semantics of their protocols.[*]

It is important to focus upon behavior, not structure, in this step. Attributes represent structural elements, and so there is a danger, especially early in analysis, of binding implementation decisions too early by requiring the presence of certain attributes. Attributes should be identified at this point only insofar as they are essential to building a conceptual model of the scenario.

Isolated class design represents a bottom-up identification of semantics. Here, we focus our attention upon a single abstraction and, applying the heuristics for class design described in Chapter 3, consider the operations that complete our abstraction. This activity is more tactical in nature, because here we are concerned about good class design, not architectural design. A typical order of events might be the following:

- Select one abstraction and enumerate its roles and responsibilities.

- Devise a sufficient set of operations that satisfy these responsibilities. Where possible, try to reuse operations for conceptually similar roles and responsibilities.

- Consider each operation in turn, and ensure that it is primitive. If not, isolate and expose its more primitive operations. Composite operations may be retained in the class itself (if it is sufficiently common, or for reasons of efficiency) or be migrated to a class utility (especially if it is likely to change often). Where possible, consider a minimal set of primitive operations.

- Particularly later in the development cycle, consider the needs for construction, copying, and destruction [13]. It is better to have a common strategic policy for these behaviors, rather than allowing individual classes to follow their own idiom, unless there is compelling reason to do so.

- Consider the need for completeness: add other primitive operations that are not necessarily required for the immediate clients, but whose presence rounds out the abstraction, and therefore would probably be used by future clients. Realizing that it is impossible to have perfect completeness, lean more toward simplicity than complexity.

It is important to avoid looking for inheritance relationships too soon: introducing inheritance prematurely often leads to loss of type integrity.

In the early stages of development, class design is indeed isolated. However, once we have in place inheritance lattices, this step must address placement of operations in the hierarchy. As we consider the operations associated with a given abstraction, we must then decide at what level of

---

[*] As we described in Chapter 3, a protocol specifies that certain operations are to be invoked in a specific order. For all but the most trivial classes, operations rarely stand alone; each has preconditions that must be satisfied, often by invoking other operations.

abstraction it is best placed. Operations that may be used by a set of peer classes should be migrated to a common superclass, possibly by introducing a new intermediate abstract class. Operations that may be used by a disjoint set of classes should be encapsulated in a mixin class.

The third activity, pattern scavenging, recognizes the importance of commonality. As we identify the semantics of our classes and objects, we must be sensitive to patterns of behavior, which represent opportunities for reuse. A typical order of events might be the following:

- Given the complete set of scenarios at this level of abstraction, look for patterns of interaction among abstractions. Such collaborations may represent implicit idioms or mechanisms, which should be examined to ensure that there are no gratuitous differences among each invocation. Patterns of collaboration that are nontrivial should be explicitly documented as a strategic decision, so that they can be reused rather than reinvented. This activity preserves the integrity of the architectural vision.

- Given the set of responsibilities generated at this level of abstraction, look for patterns of behavior. Common roles and responsibilities should be unified in the form of common base, abstract, or mixin classes.

- Particularly later in the life cycle, as concrete operations are being specified, look for patterns within operation signatures. Remove any gratuitous differences, and introduce mixin classes or utility classes when such signatures are found to be repetitious.

Please realize that the activities of identifying and specifying the semantics of classes and objects apply to individual classes as well as to class categories. The semantics of a class as well as a class category encompass its roles and responsibilities as well as its operations. In the case of an individual class, these operations may eventually be expressed as concrete member functions; in the case of a class category, these operations represent the services exported from the category, and are ultimately provided by a collaborative set of classes, not just a single class. In this manner, the activities described above apply equally well to class design and architectural design.

Milestones and Measures We successfully complete this phase when we have a reasonably sufficient, primitive, and complete set of responsibilities and/or operations for each abstraction. Early in the development process, it is sufficient to have an informal statement of responsibilities. As development proceeds, we must have more precisely stated semantics.

Measures of goodness include all of the class heuristics described in Chapter 3. Responsibilities and operations that are neither simple nor clear suggest that the given abstraction is not yet well defined. An inability to express a concrete header file or other kinds of formal class interfaces also suggests that the abstraction is ill formed, or that the wrong person is doing the abstracting.[*]

During the walkthroughs of each scenario, expect there to be lively debates. Such activities help to communicate the architectural vision, and help to develop skills in abstraction. The unexamined abstraction is not worth writing.

Identifying the Relationships Among Classes and Objects

Purpose The purpose of identifying the relationships among classes and objects is to solidify the boundaries of and to recognize the collaborators with each abstraction identified earlier in the micro process. This activity formalizes the conceptual as well as physical separations of concern among abstractions begun in the previous step.

As part of analysis, we apply this step to specify the associations among classes and objects (including certain important inheritance and aggregation relationships). Expressing the existence of an association identifies some semantic dependency between two abstractions, as well as some ability to navigate from one entity to another. As part of design, we apply this step to specify the collaborations that form the mechanisms of our architecture, as well as the higher-level clustering of classes into categories and modules into subsystems. As implementation proceeds, we refine relationships such as associations into more implementation-oriented relationships, including instantiation and use.

Products Class diagrams, object diagrams, and module diagrams are the primary products of this step. Although we must ultimately express our analysis and design decisions concerning relationships in a concrete form (namely, through our programming languages), diagrams offer a broader view of the architecture, and additionally let us express relationships that are not enforced by the linguistics of our programming systems.

During analysis, we produce class diagrams that state the associations among abstractions, and add details from the previous step (the operations and attributes for certain abstractions) as needed to capture the important subtleties of our decisions. During design, we refine these diagrams to show the tactical decisions we have made about inheritance, aggregation, instantiation, and use.

It is not desirable, nor is it possible, to produce a comprehensive set of diagrams that express every conceivable view of the relationships among our abstractions. Rather, we must focus on the "interesting" ones, where our measure of *interesting* encompasses any set of related abstractions whose relationships are an expression of some fundamental architectural decision, or that express a detail necessary to complete a blueprint for implementation.

---

[*] Beware of analysts or architects who are unwilling or unable to concretely express the semantics of their abstractions: this is a sign of arrogance or ineptness.

As architectural design proceeds, we also generate class diagrams containing class categories that identify the clustering of abstractions into layers and partitions. These products serve to document our architectural framework.

During analysis, we also produce object diagrams that complete the walkthrough of scenarios begun in the previous step. What is different here is that we can now consider the interplay between classes and objects, and so may discover previously hidden patterns of interaction, which we would seek to exploit. This typically leads to a local tweaking of the inheritance lattice. During design, we use object diagrams together with more detailed finite state machines to show the dynamic action of our mechanisms. Indeed, an explicit product of this step is a set of diagrams that identify the collaborations that serve as the mechanisms of our design.

As implementation proceeds, we must make decisions about the physical packaging of our system into modules, and the allocation of processes to processors. These are both decisions of relationships, which we can express in module and process diagrams.

Our data dictionary is updated as part of this step as well, to reflect the allocation of classes and objects to categories and modules to subsystems.

The primary benefit of these products is that they help us visualize and reason about relationships that may cross entities that are conceptually and physically distant.

Activities There are three activities associated with this step: the specification of associations, the identification of various collaborations, and the refinement of associations.

The identification of associations is primarily an analysis and early design activity. As we explained in Chapter 3, associations are semantically weak: they only represent some sort of semantic dependency, the role and cardinality of each participant in the relationship, and possibly a statement of navigability. However, during analysis and early design, this is often sufficient, for it captures enough interesting details about the relationship between two abstractions, yet prevents us from making premature statements of detailed design. A typical order of events for this activity might be the following:

- Collect a set of classes at a given level of abstraction, or associated with a particular family of scenarios; populate the diagram with each abstraction's important operations and attributes as needed to illustrate the significant properties of the problem being modeled.

- Consider the presence of a semantic dependency between any two classes, and establish an association if such a dependency exists. The need for navigation from one object to another and the need to elicit some behavior from an object are both cause for introducing associations. Indirect dependencies are cause for introducing new abstractions that serve as agents or intermediaries. Some associations may immediately be identified as specialization/generalization or aggregation relationships.

- For each association, specify the role of each participant, as well as any relevant cardinality or other kind of constraint.
- Validate these decisions by walking through scenarios and ensuring that associations are in place that are necessary and sufficient to provide the navigation and behavior among abstractions required by each scenario.

Class diagrams are the primary model generated by this activity.

The identification of collaborations is primarily a design activity, and it is also largely a problem of classification, as described in Chapter 4. As such, this step requires creativity and insight. Depending upon where we are in the macro process, there are a number of different kinds of collaborations that we must consider:

- As part of the formulation of our strategic decisions, we must specify the mechanisms identified in the previous step by producing an object diagram for each, illustrating its dynamic semantics. Validate each mechanism by walking through primary and peripheral scenarios. Where there are opportunities for concurrency, specify the actors, agents, and servers, and the means of synchronization among them. Along the way, we may discover the need to introduce new paths among objects, as well as to eliminate or consolidate unused or redundant ones.
- As we encounter commonality among classes, we must place these classes in a generalization/specialization hierarchy. As described in Chapter 3, it is usually best to create forests of classes rather than a single tree of classes. From the previous step, we will have already identified candidate base, abstract, and mixin classes, which we may now place in an inheritance lattice. Attach significant concrete classes to the resulting class diagram, and review it to consider its goodness, according to the heuristics in Chapter 3. In particular, be sensitive to balance (the lattice should not be too tall or too short, and neither too wide nor too skinny). Where patterns of structure or behavior appear among these classes, reorganize the lattice to maximize commonality (but not at the expense of simplicity).
- As part of architectural design, we must consider the clustering of classes into categories and the organization of modules into subsystems. These decisions have strategic implications. Architects may use class diagrams to specify the hierarchy of class categories that form the layers and partitions of the system under development. Typically, this is done from the top down, by taking a global view of the system and partitioning it into abstractions that denote major system services that are logically cohesive and/or likely to change independently. This architecture may also be refined from the bottom up, as clusters of classes that are semantically close are

identified in each pass through the micro process. As development proceeds, we must also make decisions about the allocation of each class to a category. As existing categories become bloated, or as new clusters become evident, we may choose to introduce new class categories or reorganize the allocation of existing ones. The organization of modules to subsystems follows a similar set of activities, except that here we are focused upon elements of the physical model, and so generate module diagrams to capture our decisions.

- The allocation of classes and objects to modules is somewhat of a local decision, and is most often a reflection of the visibility relationships among abstractions. As we described in Chapter 5, mapping from the logical to the physical model offers opportunity for the developer to either open or restrict the access of each abstraction, as well as to package logically related abstractions that are likely to change together. As we will discuss in the next chapter, the work breakdown structure of the development team will also color these logical to physical mappings. In any case, we may capture our decisions in the form of module diagrams.

The third activity of this phase of the micro process, the refinement of associations, is both an analysis and a design activity. During analysis, we may evolve certain associations into other more semantically precise relationships to reflect our increasing understanding of the problem domain. During design, we similarly transform associations as well as add new concrete relationships in order to provide a blueprint for implementation.

Inheritance, containment, instantiation, and use are the main kinds of relationships of interest, together with other properties such as labels, roles, cardinality, and so on. A typical order of events for this activity might be the following:

- Given a collection of classes already clustered by some set of associations, look for patterns of behavior that represent opportunities for specialization/generalization. Place the classes in the context of an existing inheritance lattice, or fabricate a lattice if an appropriate one does not already exist.
- If there are patterns of structure, consider creating new classes that capture this common structure, and introduce them either through inheritance as mixin classes or through aggregation.
- Look for behaviorally similar classes that are either disjoint peers in an inheritance lattice or not yet part of an inheritance lattice, and consider the possibility of introducing common parameterized classes.

- Consider the navigability of existing associations, and constrain them as possible. Replace with simple using relationships if bidirectional navigation is not a desired property.

- As development proceeds, introduce tactical details such as statements of role, keys, cardinality, friendship, stances, and so on. It is not desirable to state every detail: just include information that represents an important analysis or design position, or that is necessary for implementation.

Milestones and Measures We successfully complete this phase when we have specified the semantics and relationships among certain interesting abstractions sufficiently to serve as a blueprint for their implementation.

Measures of goodness include cohesion, coupling, and completeness. In reviewing the relationships we discover or invent during this phase, we seek to have logically cohesive and loosely coupled abstractions. In addition, we seek to identify all of the important relationships at a given level of abstraction, so that implementation does not require us to introduce new significant relationships, or perform unnatural acts to use the ones we have already specified. In the next step, finding that our abstractions are awkward to implement is an indication that we have not yet devised a meaningful set of relationships among our abstractions.

Implementing Classes and Objects

Purpose During analysis, the purpose of implementing classes and objects is to provide a refinement of existing abstractions sufficient to unveil new classes and objects at the next level of abstraction, which we then feed into the following iteration of the micro process. During design, the purpose of this activity is to create tangible representations of our abstractions in support of the successive refinement of the executable releases in the macro process.

The ordering of this step is intentional: the micro process focuses first upon behavior, and defers decisions about representation until as late as possible. This strategy avoids premature implementation decisions that can ruin opportunities for smaller, simpler architectures, and also allows for the freedom to change representations as needed for reasons of efficiency, while limiting the disruption to the existing architecture.

Products Decisions about the representation of each abstraction and the mapping of these representations to the physical model drive the products from this step. Early in the development process, we may capture these tactical representation decisions in the form of refined class specifications. Where these decisions are of general interest or represent opportunities for reuse, we also document them in class diagrams (showing their static semantics) and finite state machines or interaction diagrams (showing their dynamic semantics). As development proceeds, and as we make further bindings to the given implementation language, we begin to deliver pseudo- or executable code.

To show the logical to physical bindings in our implementation, we also deliver module diagrams, which we can then use to visualize the mapping of our architecture on to its realization in code. As development proceeds, we may use method-specific tools that automatically forward-engineer code from these diagrams, or reverse engineer them from the implementation.

As part of this step, we also update our data dictionary, including the new classes and objects that we discovered or invented in formulating the implementation of existing abstractions. These new abstractions are part of the input into the next round of the micro process.

Activities There is one primary activity associated with this step: the selection of the structures and algorithms that provide the semantics of the abstractions we identified earlier in the micro process. Whereas the first three phases of the micro process focus upon the outside view of our abstractions, this step focuses upon their inside view.

During analysis, the results of this activity are relatively abstract: we are not so concerned about making representation decisions; rather, we are more interested in discovering the new abstractions to which we can delegate responsibility. During design, and especially in later stages of class design, we must increasingly make concrete decisions.

A typical order of events for this activity might be the following:

- For each class, consider again its protocol. Identify the patterns of use among clients, in order to determine which operations are central, and hence should be optimized. As implementation proceeds, develop precise signatures for all significant operations.

- Before choosing a representation from scratch, consider the use of protected or private inheritance for implementation, or the use of parameterized classes.. Select the appropriate abstract or mixin classes (or create new ones, if the problem is sufficiently general), and adjust the inheritance lattice as required.

- Consider the objects to which we might delegate responsibility. For an optimal fit, this may require a minor readjustment of the responsibilities and/or protocol of the lower-level abstraction.

- If the abstraction's semantics cannot be provided through inheritance, instantiation, or delegation, consider a suitable representation from primitives in the language. Keep in mind the importance of operations from the perspective of the abstraction's clients, and select a representation that optimizes for the expected patterns of use. Remember that it is not possible to optimize for every use, however. As we gain empirical information from successive releases, we can identify which abstractions are not time- and/or space-efficient, and alter their implementation locally, with little concern that we will violate the assumptions clients make of our abstraction.

- Select a suitable algorithm for each operation. Introduce helper operations to divide complex algorithms into less complicated, reusable parts. Consider the trade-offs of storing versus calculating certain states of an abstraction.

Milestones and Measures During analysis, we successfully complete this phase once we have identified all the interesting abstractions necessary to satisfy the responsibilities of higher-level abstractions identified during this pass through the micro process. During design, we successfully complete this phase when we have an executable or near-executable model of our abstractions.

The primary measure of goodness for this phase is simplicity. Implementations that are complex, awkward, or inefficient are an indication that the abstraction itself is lacking, or that we have chosen a poor representation.

6.3 The Macro Development Process

Overview

The macro process serves as the controlling framework for the micro process. This broader procedure dictates a number of measurable products and activities that permit the development team to meaningfully assess risk and make early corrections to the micro process, so as to better focus the team's analysis and design activities. The macro process represents the activities of the entire development team on the scale of weeks to months at a time.

Many elements of the macro process are simply sound software management practice, and so apply equally to object-oriented as well as non-object-oriented systems. These include basic practices such as configuration management, quality assurance, code walkthroughs, and documentation. In the next chapter, we will address a number of these pragmatic issues in the context of object-oriented software development. Our focus in this chapter will be to describe a core process that is tuned to the construction of object-oriented systems. Using Parnas' terms, this is how we shall fake a rational design process for building object-oriented systems.

The macro process is primarily the concern of the development team's technical management, whose focus is subtly different than that of the individual developer. Both are interested in delivering quality software that satisfies the customer's needs.[*] However, end users could generally care less about the fact that the developers used parameterized classes and polymorphic functions in clever ways; customers are much more concerned about schedules, quality, and completeness, and rightfully so. For this reason, the macro process

---

[*] Well, most of them. Unfortunately, some managers are more interested in building empires than in building software. See also the footnote on page 242: I expect Dante might propose a place for both these groups of people.

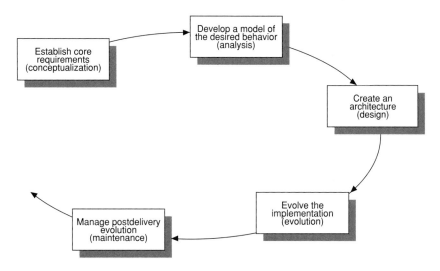

Figure 6-2
The Macro Development Process

focuses upon risk and architectural vision, the two manageable elements that have the greatest impact upon schedules, quality, and completeness.

In the macro process, the traditional phases of analysis and design are to a large extent retained, and the process is reasonably well-ordered. As Figure 6-2 illustrates, the macro process tends to track the following activities:

- Establish the core requirements for the software (conceptualization).
- Develop a model of the system's desired behavior (analysis).
- Create an architecture for the implementation (design).
- Evolve the implementation through successive refinement (evolution).
- Manage postdelivery evolution (maintenance).

For all interesting software, the macro process repeats itself after major product releases. This is particularly true for organizations that focus upon building families of programs, which often represent a significant capital investment.

The basic philosophy of the macro process is that of incremental development. As Vonk defines it, "in the case of incremental development, the system as a whole is built up step by step, and each successive version consists of the previous version unchanged plus a number of new functions" [14]. This approach is extremely well-suited to the object-oriented paradigm, and offers a number of benefits relative to risk management. As Gilb so aptly states, "evolutionary delivery is devised to give us early warning signals to impending unpleasant realities" [15].

Let's examine each of the activities of the macro process in detail. Of course, one of the characteristics of a mature development organization is knowing when to break these rules, and so we will point out these degrees of freedom along the way.

Conceptualization

Purpose Conceptualization seeks to establish the core requirements for the system. For any truly new piece of software, or even for the novel adaptation of an existing system, there exists some moment in time where, in the mind of the developer, the architect, the analyst, or the end user, there springs forth an idea for some application. This idea may represent a new business venture, a new complementary product in an existing product line, or perhaps a new set of features for an existing software system. It is not the purpose of conceptualization to completely define these ideas. Rather, the purpose of conceptualization is to establish the vision for the idea and validate its assumptions.

Products Prototypes are the primary products of conceptualization. Specifically, for every significant new system, there should be some proof of concept, manifesting itself in the form of a quick-and-dirty prototype. Such prototypes are by their very nature incomplete and only marginally engineered. However, by keeping around the interesting (although perhaps rejected) prototypes, the organization maintains a corporate memory of its original visions, and thus preserves the assumptions that were made when applications were first conceived. As development of production systems proceeds, this repository provides a place for unrestricted experimentation, to which analysts and architects may return to try out new ideas.

Obviously, for applications on a massive scale (such as ones of national significance, or ones that have multinational implications), the prototyping effort itself may be a large undertaking. That is to be expected, and in fact encouraged. It is far better to discover during proof of concept that assumptions of functionality, performance, size, or complexity were wrong, rather than later, where abandoning the current development path would prove to be financially or socially disastrous.

It must be emphasized that all such prototypes are meant to be thrown away. Prototypes should not be allowed to directly evolve into the production system, unless there is a strongly compelling reason. Convenience for the sake of meeting a short-term schedule is distinctly not a compelling reason: this decision represents a false economy that optimizes for short-term development, and ignores the cost of ownership of the software.

Activities Conceptualization is by its very nature an intensely creative activity, and therefore should not be fettered by rigid development rules. What is perhaps most important is for the development organization to set in place a structure that provides sufficient resources for new ideas to be explored.* New ideas can spring from virtually any source: end users, user groups, developers, analysts, the marketing team, and so on. It is wise for management to maintain a log of such new ideas, so that they can be prioritized, and scarce resources intelligently allocated to explore the more promising ones. Once a particular avenue has been selected for exploration, a typical order of events is the following:

- Establish a set of goals for the proof of concept, including criteria for when the effort is to be finished.

- Assemble an appropriate team to develop the prototype. Often, this may be a team of one (who is usually the original visionary). The best thing the development organization can do to facilitate the team's efforts is to stay out of its way.

- Evaluate the resulting prototype, and make an explicit decision for product development or further exploration. A decision to develop a product should be made with a reasonable assessment of the potential risks, which the proof of concept should uncover.

There is nothing inherently object-oriented about conceptualization. Any and all programming paradigms should be allowed to develop proofs of concept. However, it is often the case that, in the presence of a reasonably rich object-oriented application framework, developing prototypes is often faster than alternatives.

It is not unusual to see proofs of concept developed in one language (such as Smalltalk, for example) and product development to proceed in another (such as C++).

Milestones and Measures It is important that explicit criteria be established for completion of a prototype. Proofs of concept are often schedule-driven (meaning that the prototype must be delivered on a certain date) rather than feature-driven. This is not necessarily bad, for it artificially limits the prototyping effort, and discourages the tendency to deliver a production system prematurely.

Upper management can often measure the health of the software development organization by measuring its response to new ideas. Any organization that is not itself producing new ideas is dead, or in a moribund business. The most prudent action is usually to diversify or abandon the business. In contrast, any organization that is overwhelmed with new ideas and yet is unable to make any intelligent prioritization of them is out of control. Such organizations often waste significant development resources by jumping

---

* If the organization itself does not, then individual developers will do so anyway, in spite of the company they work for. This is how new software companies get started. This is often great for the industry as a whole, but usually represents a net loss for the organization.

to product development too early, without exploring the risks of the effort though a proof of concept. The most prudent action here is to formalize the production process, and make explicit the leap from concept to product.

Analysis

Purpose As Mellor states, "the purpose of analysis is to provide a description of a problem. The description must be complete, consistent, readable, and reviewable by diverse interested parties, [and] testable against reality" [16]. In our terms, the purpose of analysis is to provide a model of the system's behavior.

We must emphasize that analysis focuses upon behavior, not form. It is inappropriate to pursue issues of class design, representation, or other tactical decisions during this phase. Rather, analysis must yield a statement of what the system does, not how it does it. Any intentional statements of "how" during analysis should be viewed as useful only for the purpose of exposing the behavior of the system, and not as testable requirements of the design.

In this regard, the purposes of analysis and design are quite different. In analysis, we seek to model the world by identifying the classes and objects (and their roles, responsibilities, and collaborations) that form the vocabulary of the problem domain. In design, we invent the artifacts that provide the behavior that the analysis model requires. In this sense, analysis is the phase that first brings together the users and developers of a system, uniting them with a common vocabulary drawn from the problem domain.

By focusing upon behavior, we come to identify the function points of a system. Function points, first described by Allan Albrecht, denote the outwardly observable and testable behaviors of a system [17]. From the perspective of the end user, a function point represents some primary activity of a system in response to some event.* Function points often (but not always) denote the mapping of inputs to outputs, and so represent the transformations the system makes to its environment. From the perspective of the analyst, a function point represents a distinct quantum of behavior. Indeed, function points provide a measure of complexity: the greater the number of function points, the more complex the system. During analysis, we capture the semantics of a system's function points through scenarios.

Analysis never stands alone. During this phase, we do not expect to devise an exhaustive understanding of the system's behavior. Indeed, we claim that it is neither possible nor desirable to carry out a complete analysis before allowing design to commence. The very act of building a system raises questions of behavior that no reasonable amount of analysis can efficiently uncover. It is sufficient that we accomplish an analysis of all the primary behaviors of the system, with a sprinkling of secondary behaviors considered as well to ensure that no essential patterns of behavior are missed.

---

* In the domain of management information systems, Dreger notes that a function point represents one end-user business function [18].

A reasonably complete and formal analysis is essential to serve the needs of traceability. Traceability is largely a problem of accountability, through which we ensure that no function points are neglected. Traceabilty is also essential to risk management. As development proceeds in any nontrivial system, management will have to make difficult trade-offs in allocating resources, or in resolving some unpleasant tactical issue. By having traceability from function points to the implementation, it is far easier to assess the impact of disturbing the architecture when such knotty problems arise.

Products DeChampeaux suggests that the output of analysis is a description of the function of the system, along with statements about performance and resources required [19]. In object-oriented development, we capture these descriptions through scenarios, where each scenario denotes some particular function point. We use primary scenarios to illustrate key behaviors, and secondary scenarios to show behavior under exceptional conditions.

As we described in previous chapters, we use CRC-card techniques to storyboard scenarios, then use object diagrams to illustrate the semantics of each scenario more precisely. Such diagrams must show the objects that collaborate to achieve the function, as well as the process of collaboration (that is, the well-ordered way in which the objects interact by passing messages). In addition to object diagrams, we will also include class diagrams (to show the associations among the object's classes) and finite state machines (to show the life cycle of certain important objects).

Often, these analysis products will be assembled into a formal requirements analysis document, which states the system's behavioral requirements as illustrated by the diagrams, plus an analysis of all the nonbehavioral aspects of the system, such as efficiency, reliability, security, and portability [20].

A secondary product of analysis is a risk assessment that identifies the known areas of technical risk that may impact the design process. Facing up to the presence of risks early in the development process makes it far easier to make pragmatic architectural trade-offs later in the development process.

Activities Two primary activities are associated with analysis: domain analysis and scenario planning.

As we described in Chapter 4, domain analysis seeks to identify the classes and objects that are common to a particular problem domain. Before setting out to implement an entirely new system, it is often wise to study existing ones. In this way, we benefit from the experience of other projects that had to make similar development decisions. In the best case, the results of a domain analysis may lead us to discover that we do not need to develop any new software, but can reuse or adapt existing frameworks.

Scenario planning is the central activity of analysis. Interestingly, there appears to be a confluence of thought about this activity among other methodologists, especially Rubin and Goldberg, Adams, Wirfs-Brock, Coad, and Jacobson. A typical order of events for this activity follows:

- Identify all the primary function points of the system and, if possible, group them into clusters of functionally related behaviors. Consider also clustering according to hierarchies of functions, wherein certain high-level functions build upon more primitive ones.

- For each interesting set of function points, storyboard a scenario, using the techniques of use-case and behavior analysis described in Chapter 4.* CRC card techniques are effective in brainstorming about each scenario. As the semantics of each scenario become clearer, document them using object diagrams that illustrate the objects that are initiators or contributors of behavior, and that collaborate to carry out the activities of the scenario. Include a script that shows the events that trigger the scenario and the resulting ordering of actions. In addition, document any assumptions, constraints, or performance issues for each scenario [21].

- As needed, generate secondary scenarios that illustrate behavior under exceptional conditions.

- Where the life cycle of certain objects is significant or essential to a scenario, develop a finite state machine for the class of objects.

- Scavenge for patterns among scenarios, and express these patterns in terms of more abstract, generalized scenarios, or in terms of class diagrams showing the associations among key abstractions.

- Update the evolving data dictionary to include the new classes and objects identified for each scenario, along with their roles and responsibilities.

As described further in the next chapter, scenario planning is carried out by analysts, in conjunction with the domain expert and architect. Additionally, quality-assurance personnel should participate in scenario planning, since scenarios represent behaviors that can be tested. Involving quality-assurance personnel early in the process helps to institutionalize a commitment to quality. Involving other development team members during scenario planning is also an effective way to get them invested in the development process, and to foster their understanding of the system's vision.

Milestones and Measures We successfully complete this phase when we have developed and signed off on scenarios for all fundamental system behaviors. By *signed off* we mean that the resulting analysis products have been validated by the domain expert, end user, analyst, and architect; by *fundamental* we refer to behaviors that are central to the application's purpose. Again, we neither expect nor desire a complete analysis. It is sufficient that only primary and some secondary behaviors be considered.

---

* Jacobson [22] and Rubin and Goldberg [23] provide comprehensive treatments of this subject.

Measures of goodness include completeness and simplicity. A good analysis will cover all primary activities and a statistically interesting set of secondary ones. A good analysis will also carry out walkthroughs of all strategically important scenarios, so as to help communicate a vision of the system to the entire development team. In addition, a good analysis will also discover patterns of behavior, yielding a simple class structure that exploits all that is common among different scenarios.

Another important milestone of analysis is delivery of a risk assessment, which helps the team to manage future strategic and tactical tradeoffs.

Design

Purpose The purpose of design is to create an architecture for the evolving implementation, and to establish the common tactical policies that must be used by disparate elements of the system. We begin the design process as soon as we have some reasonably complete model of the behavior of the system. It is important to avoid premature designs, wherein development begins before analysis reaches closure. It is equally important to avoid delayed designing, wherein the organization thrashes while trying to complete a perfect and hence unachievable analysis model.[*]

Products There are two primary products of design: a description of the architecture, and descriptions of common tactical policies.

We may describe an architecture through diagrams as well as architectural releases of the system. As described in earlier chapters, the architecture of an object-oriented system encompasses its class and object structure, and so we may use class and object diagrams to show these strategic organizations. At the architectural level, it is most important to show the clustering of classes into class categories (for the logical architecture) and the clustering of modules into subsystems (for the physical architecture). We may deliver these diagrams as part of a formal architecture document, which should be reviewed with the entire team and updated as the architecture evolves.

We use architectural releases as tangible manifestations of the architecture design itself. An architectural release denotes a vertical slice through the entire architecture, capturing important (but incomplete) semantics of all significant categories and subsystems. An architectural release should be executable, thus allowing the architecture to be instrumented, studied, and evaluated precisely. As we will discuss in the next section, these architectural releases become the foundation of the evolving production system.

Common tactical policies include localized mechanisms that appear throughout the system. These encompass design artifacts such as policies for error detection and handling, memory management, data storage management, and generalized approaches to control. It is important to explicitly design these policies; otherwise we will see developers invent *ad hoc* solutions to common problems, thus ruining our strategic architecture through software rot.

---

[*] This condition is commonly diagnosed as analysis paralysis.

We capture descriptions of common policies through scenarios and executable releases of each mechanism.

Activities There are three activities associated with design: architectural planning, tactical design, and release planning.

Architectural planning involves devising the layers and partitions of the over-all system. Architectural planning encompasses a logical decomposition, representing a clustering of classes, as well as a physical decomposition, representing a clustering of modules and the allocation of functions to different processors. A typical order of events for this activity is as follows:

- Consider the clustering of function points from the products of analysis, and allocate these to layers and partitions of the architecture. Functions that build upon one another should fall into different layers; functions that collaborate to yield behaviors at a similar level of abstraction should fall into partitions, which represent peer services.

- Validate the architecture by creating an executable release that partially satisfies the semantics of a few interesting system scenarios as derived from analysis.

- Instrument that architecture and assess its weakness and strengths. Identify the risk of each key architectural interface so that resources can be meaningfully allocated as evolution commences.

The focus of architectural planning is to create very early in the life cycle a domain-specific application framework that we may successively refine.

Tactical design involves making decisions about the myriad of common policies. As we describe earlier in this chapter, poor tactical design can ruin even the most profound architecture, and so we mitigate this risk by explicitly identifying tactical policies, and putting in place incentives to adhere to these policies. A typical order of events for this activity is as follows:

- Relative to the given application domain, enumerate the common policies that must be addressed by disparate elements of the architecture. Some such policies are foundational, meaning that they address domain-independent issues such as memory management, error handling, and so on. Other policies are domain-specific, and include idioms and mechanisms that are germane to that domain, such as control policies in real-time systems, or transaction and database management in information systems.

- For each common policy, develop a scenario that describes the semantics of that policy. Further capture its semantics in the form of an executable prototype that can be instrumented and refined.

- Document each policy and carry out a peer walkthrough, so as to broadcast its architectural vision.

Release planning sets the stage for architectural evolution. Taking the required function points and risk assessment generated during analysis, release planning serves to identify a controlled series of architectural releases, each growing in its functionality, ultimately encompassing the requirements of the complete production system. A typical order of events for this activity is as follows:

- Given the scenarios identified during analysis, organize them in order of foundational to peripheral behaviors. Prioritizing scenarios can best be accomplished with a team including a domain expert, analysis, architect, and quality-assurance personnel.

- Allocate the related function points to a series of architectural releases whose final delivery represents the production system.

- Adjust the goals and schedules of this stream of releases so that delivery dates are sufficiently separated to allow adequate development time, and so that releases are synchronized with other development activities, such as documentation and field testing.

- Begin task planning, wherein a work breakdown structure is identified, and development resources are identified that are necessary to achieve each architectural release.

A natural by-product of release planning is a formal development plan, which identifies the stream of architectural releases, team tasks, and risk assessments

Milestones and Measures We successfully complete this phase when we have validated the architecture through a prototype and through formal review. In addition, we must have sign-off on the design of all primary tactical policies, and a plan for successive releases..

The primary measure of goodness is simplicity. A good architecture is one that embodies the characteristics of organized complex systems, as described in Chapter 1.

The main benefits of this activity is the early identification of architectural flaws and the establishment of common policies that yield a simpler architecture.

Evolution

Purpose The purpose of the evolutionary phase is to grow and change the implementation through successive refinement, ultimately leading to the production system.

The evolution of an architecture is largely a matter of trying to satisfy a number of competing constraints, including functionality, time, and space: one is always limited by the largest constraint. For example, if the weight of the computer is a critical factor (as it is in spacecraft design), then the weight of individual memory chips must be considered, and in turn the amount of memory permitted by the weight allowance limits the size of the program that may be loaded. Relax any given constraint, and other design alternatives become possible; tighten any constraint, and certain designs become intractable. By evolving the implementation of a software system rather than taking a more monolithic approach to development, we can identify which constraints are really important and which are delusions. For this reason, evolutionary development focuses upon designing for functionality first and for local performance second. Early in the design, we typically do not know enough to understand where the performance bottlenecks will arise in the system. By analyzing the behavior of incremental releases via histogramming or other such techniques, the development team can better understand how to tune the system over time.

Evolution is thus essentially the process of product development. As Andert observes, design "is a time of innovation, improvement, and unrestricted freedom to modify code to achieve the product goals. Production is a controlled methodological process of raising product quality to the point where the product can be shipped" [24].

Pages-Jones suggests a number of advantages to this kind of incremental development:

- "Important feedback to the users is provided when it's most needed, most useful, and most meaningful.
- Users can use several skeleton system versions to allow them to make a smooth transition from their old system to their new system.
- The project is less likely to be axed if it falls behind schedule.
- Major system interfaces are tested first and most often.
- Testing resources are distributed more evenly.
- Implementors can see early results from a working system, so their morale is improved.
- If time is short, coding and testing can begin before the design is finished" [25].

Products The primary product of evolution is a stream of executable releases representing successive refinements to the initial architectural release. Secondary products include behavioral prototypes that are used to explore alternative designs or to further analyze the dark corners of the systems' functionality.

These executable releases follow the schedule established in the earlier activity of release planning. For a modest sized project involving 12–18 months of end-to-end development time, this might mean a release every two to three months. For more complex projects that require much greater development effort, this might mean a release every six months or so. More extended release schedules are suspect, because they do not force closure of the micro process, and may hide areas of risk that are being intentionally or unintentionally ignored.

To whom is an executable release delivered? Early in the development process, major executable releases are turned over by the development team to quality-assurance personnel, who can begin to test the release against the scenarios established during analysis, and in so doing gather information on the completeness, correctness, and robustness of the release. This early data-gathering aids in identifying problems of quality, which are more easily addressed during evolution of the subsequent release. Later in the development process, executable releases are turned over to select end users (the alpha and beta customers) in a controlled manner. By controlled, we mean that the development team carefully sets expectations for each release, and identifies aspects that it wishes to have evaluated.

The needs of the micro process dictate that many more internal releases to the development team will be accomplished, with only a few executable releases turned over to external parties. These internal releases represent a sort of continuous integration of the system, and exist to force closure of the micro process.

Between each successive external release, the development team may also produce behavioral prototypes. A behavioral prototype serves to explore some isolated element of the system, such as a new algorithm, a user interface model, or a database schema. Its purpose is the rapid exploration of design alternatives, so that areas of risk can be resolved early without endangering the production releases. Behavioral prototypes are indeed prototypes, and so are meant to be thrown away after they have served their purposes. Typically, a team will use behavioral prototypes to storyboard user interface semantics and present them to end users for early feedback, or to do performance trade-offs for the implementation of tactical policies.

By implication, the documentation of the system evolves along with the architectural releases. Rather than treating the production of documentation as a major milestone, it is generally better to have it as a natural, semiautomatically generated artifact of the evolutionary process.

Activities Two activities are associated with evolution: application of the micro process, and change management.

The work that is caried out between executable releases represents a compressed development process, and so is essentially one spin of the micro process. This activity begins with an analysis of the requirements for the next release, proceeds to the design of an architecture, and continues with the invention of classes and objects necessary to implement this design. A typical order of events for this activity is as follows:

- Identify the function points to be satisfied by this executable release, as well as the areas of highest risk, especially those identified through evaluation of the previous release.

- Assign tasks to the team to carry out this release, and initiate one spin of the micro process. Supervise the micro process by establishing appropriate reviews of the design, and by managing against intermediate milestones that take on the order of a few days or a week or two to accomplish.

- As needed to understand the semantics of the system's desired behavior, assign developers to produce behavioral prototypes. Establish clear criteria for the goals and completion of each prototype. Upon completion, decide upon an approach to integrate the results of the prototyping effort into this or subsequent releases.

- Force closure of the micro process by integrating and releasing the executable release.

After each release, it is important to revisit the original release plan, and adjust the requirements and schedules for subsequent releases as necessary. Often, this involves small adjustments to dates, or migration of functionality from one release to another.

Change management exists in recognition of the incremental and iterative nature of object-oriented systems. It is tempting to allow undisciplined change to class hierarchies, class protocols, or mechanisms, but unrestrained change tends to rot the strategic architecture and leads to thrashing of the development team.

In practice, we find that the following kinds of changes are to be expected during the evolution of a system:

- Adding a new class or a new collaboration of classes
- Changing the implementation of a class
- Changing the representation of a class
- Reorganizing the class structure
- Changing the interface of a class

Each kind of change comes about for different reasons, and each has a different cost.

A developer will add new classes as new key abstractions are discovered or new mechanisms are invented. The cost of making such changes is usually inconsequential in terms of computing resources and management overhead. When a new class is added, consideration must be given to where it fits in the existing class structure. When a new collaboration is invented, a small domain analysis should be conducted to see if this is actually one of a pattern of collaborations.

Changing the implementation of a class is also generally not costly. In object-oriented design, we usually create the interface of a class first and then stub out its implementation (that is to say, the implementation of its member functions). Once the interface stabilizes to a reasonable extent, we can choose a representation for that class and complete the implementation of its methods. The implementation of a particular method may be changed later, usually to fix a bug or improve its performance. We might also change the implementation of a method to take advantage of new methods defined in an existing or newly added superclass. In any case, changing the implementation of a method is not generally costly, especially if one has previously encapsulated the class's implementation.

In a similar vein, one might alter the representation of a class (in C++, the protected and private members of a class). Usually, this is done to make instances of the class more space-efficient or to create more time-efficient methods. If the representation of the class is encapsulated, as is possible in Smalltalk, C++, CLOS, and Ada, then a change in representation will not logically disrupt how clients interact with instances of that class (unless, of course, this new representation does not provide the behavior expected of the class). On the other hand, if the representation of the class is not encapsulated, as is also possible in any language, then a change in representation is much more dangerous, because clients may have been written that depend upon a particular representation. This is especially true in the case of subclasses: changing the representation of a superclass affects the representation of all of its subclasses. In any case, changing the representation of a class incurs a cost: one must recompile its interface, its implementation, all of its clients (namely, its subclasses and instances), all of its client's clients, and so on.

Reorganizing the class structure of a system is common, although less so than the other kinds of changes we have mentioned. As Stefik and Bobrow observe, "Programmers often create new classes and reorganize their classes as they understand the opportunities for factoring parts of their programs" [26]. The reorganization of a class structure usually takes the form of changing inheritance relationships, adding new abstract classes, and shifting the responsibilities and implementation of common methods to classes higher in the class structure. In practice, reorganizing the class structure of a system usually happens frequently at first, and then stabilizes over time as its developers better understand how all the key abstractions work together. Reorganizing the class structure is to be encouraged in early stages of design because it can result in great economy of expression, meaning that we have smaller implementations and fewer classes to comprehend and maintain. However, reorganization of the class structure does not come without a cost. Typically, changing the location of a class high in the hierarchy makes all the classes below it obsolete and requires their recompilation (and thus the recompilation of the classes that depend on them, and so on).

An equally important kind of change that occurs during the evolution of a system is a change to the interface of a class. A developer usually changes the interface of a class either to add some new behavior, to satisfy the semantics of some new role for its objects, or to add an operation that was always part of the abstraction but was initially not exported and is now needed by some client. In practice, using the heuristics for building quality classes that we discussed in Chapter 3 (specifically, the concepts of building primitive, sufficient, and complete interfaces) reduces the likelihood of such changes. However, our experience is that such changes are inevitable. We have never written a nontrivial class whose interface was exactly right the first time.

It is rare but not unthinkable to remove an existing method; this is typically done only to better encapsulate an abstraction. More commonly, we add a new method or override a method defined in some superclass. In all three cases, the change is costly, because it logically affects all clients, making them obsolete and forcing their recompilation. Fortunately, these latter kinds of changes – adding and overriding methods – are upwardly compatible. In fact, we find in practice that the majority of all interface changes made to well-defined classes during the evolution of a system are upwardly compatible. This makes it possible to apply sophisticated compiler technology, such as incremental compilation, to reduce the impact of these changes. Incremental compilation allows us to recompile single declarations and statements one at a time, instead of entire modules, meaning that the recompilation of most clients can be optimized away.

Why is recompilation cost even an issue? For small systems, it is not an issue, because recompiling an entire program might take only a few minutes. However, for large systems, it is an entirely different matter. Recompiling a hundred-thousand line program might take as much as a half a day of computer time. Can you imagine making a change to the software for a shipboard computer system and then telling the captain that she cannot put to sea because you are still recompiling? In the extreme, recompilation costs may be so high as to inhibit developers from making changes that are reasonable improvements. Recompilation is a particularly important issue with object-oriented programming languages, because inheritance introduces compilation dependencies [27]. For strongly typed object-oriented programming languages, recompilation costs may be even higher; in such languages, one trades off compilation time for safety.

The kinds of changes we have discussed thus far are the easy ones: the greatest risk is major architectural change, which can sink a project. Often, this change results from bright engineers with too many good ideas [28].

Milestones and Measures We successfully complete this phase when the functionality and quality of the releases are sufficient to ship the product. The releases of intermediate executable forms are the major milestones we use to manage the development of the final product. The primary measure of goodness is therefore to what degree we satisfy the function points allocated to each intermediate release, and how well we met the schedules established during release planning.

Two other essential measures of goodness include tracking defect-discovery rates, and measuring the rate of change of key architectural interfaces and tactical policies.

Briefly, defect-discovery rate is a measure of how rapidly new errors are being detected [29]. By investing in quality assurance early in the development process, it is possible to establish measures for quality for each release, which the management team can use to identify areas of risk and also to calibrate the development team. After each release, the defect-discovery rate generally surges. A stagnant defect-discovery rate usually indicates undiscovered errors.

An off-scale defect-discovery rate is an indication that the architecture has not yet stabilized, or that there are new elements in a given release that are incorrectly designed or implemented. These measures are used to adjust the focus of subsequent releases.

Measuring the rate of change of architectural interfaces and tactical policies is the primary measure of architectural stability [30]. Localized changes are to be expected during evolution, but if inheritance lattices or the boundaries between class categories or subsystems are being changed often, this is an indication of architectural problems, and so should be recognized as an area of risk when planning the next release.

Maintenance

Products Maintenance is the activity of managing postdelivery evolution. This phase is largely a continuation of the previous phase, except that architectural innovation is less of an issue. Instead, more localized changes are made to the system as new requirements are added and lingering bugs stamped out.

Lehman and Belady have made a number of cogent observations regarding the maturation of a deployed software system:

- "A program that is used in a real-world environment necessarily must change or become less and less useful in that environment (the law of continuing change).

- As an evolving program changes, its structure becomes more complex unless active efforts are made to avoid this phenomenon (the law of increasing complexity)" [31].

We distinguish the preservation of a software system from its maintenance. During maintenance, developers will be asked to make continual improvements to an existing system; these maintainers are often a different group of people than the original developers. Preservation, on the other hand, involves using excessive development resources to shore up an aging system that often has a poorly designed architecture and is therefore hard to understand and modify. A business decision must be made: if the cost of ownership of this software is greater than the cost of developing a new system, the most merciful course of action is to metaphorically put the aging system out to pasture or, if conditions dictate, abandon it or shoot it.

Products Since maintenance is in a sense the continued evolution of a system, its products are similar to those of the previous phase. In addition, maintenance involves managing a punch list of new tasks. Immediately upon release of the production system, its developers and end users will probably already have a set of improvements or modifications they would like to carry out in subsequent production releases, which for business reasons did not make it into the initial production release. Additionally, as more users exercise the system, new bugs and patterns of use will be uncovered that quality assurance could not anticipate.* A punch list serves as the vehicle for collecting bugs and enhancement requirements, so that they can be prioritized for future releases.

Activities Maintenance involves activities that are little different than those required during the evolution of a system. Especially if we have done a good job in the original architecture, adding new functionality or modifying some existing behavior will come naturally.

In addition to the usual activities of evolution, maintenance involves a planning activity that prioritizes tasks on the punch list. A typical order of events for this activity is as follows:

- Prioritize requests for major enhancement or bug reports that denote systemic problems, and assess the cost of redevelopment.
- Establish a meaningful collection of these changes and treat them as function points for the next evolution.
- If resources allow it, add less intense, more localized enhancements (the so-called low-hanging fruit) to the next release.
- Manage the next evolutionary release.

Milestones and Measures The milestones of maintenance involve continued production releases, plus intermediate bug releases.

We know that we are still maintaining a system if the architecture remains resilient to change; we know we have entered the stage of preservation when responding to new enhancements begins to require excessive development resources.

Summary

- Successful projects are usually characterized by a strong architectural vision and a well-managed iterative and incremental development life cycle.
- A completely rational design process is not possible, but can be faked by reconciling the micro and macro process of development.
- The micro process of object-oriented development is driven by the stream of scenarios and architectural products that emerge from the macro process; the micro process represents daily activities of the development team.
- The first step in the micro process involves identifying the classes and objects at a given level of abstraction; primary activities include discovery and invention.

---

* Users are amazingly creative when it comes to exercising a system in unexpected ways.

- The second step in the micro process involves identifying the semantics of these classes and objects; primary activities include storyboarding, isolated class design, and pattern scavenging.

- The third step in the micro process involves identifying the relationships among these classes and objects; primary activities include the specification of associations, the identification of collaborations, and the refinement of associations.

- The fourth step in the micro process involves the implementation of these classes and objects; the primary activity is the selection of data structures and algorithms.

- The macro process of object-oriented development serves as the controlling framework for the micro process and defines a number of measurable products and activities for managing risk.

- The first step in the macro process is conceptualization, which establishes the core requirements for the system; its activity serves as a proof of concept, and so is largely uncontrolled, so as to allow unrestrained innovation.

- The second step in the macro process is analysis, which provides a model of the system's behavior; primary activities include domain analysis and scenario planning.

- The third step in the macro process is design, which creates an architecture for the implementation and establishes common tactical policies; primary activities include architectural planning, tactical design, and release planning.

- The fourth step in the macro process is evolution, which uses successive refinement to ultimately lead to the production system; primary activities include application of the micro process and change management.

- The fifth step in the macro process is maintenance, which is essentially the management of postdelivery evolution; primary activities are similar to those of the fourth step, with the addition of managing a punch list.

Further Readings

An early form of the process described in this chapter was first documented by Booch [F 1982]. Berard later elaborated upon this work in [F 1986]. Related approaches include GOOD (General Object-Oriented Design) by Seidewitz and Stark [F 1985, 1986, 1987], SOOD (Structured Object-Oriented Design) by Lockheed [C 1988], MOOD (Multiple-view Object-Oriented Design) by Kerth [F 1988], and HOOD (Hierarchical Object-Oriented Design) by CISI Ingenierie and Matra for the European Space Station [F 1987]. More recent related works include Stroustrup [G 1991] and Microsoft [G 1992], who suggest substantially similar processes.

In addition to the works cited in the further readings for Chapter 2, a number of other methodologists have proposed specific object-oriented development processes, for which the bibliography provides an extensive set of references. Some of the more interesting contributions come from Alabios [F 1988], Boyd [F 1987], Buhr [F 1984], Cherry [F 1987, 1990], deChampeaux [F 1992], Felsinger [F 1987], Firesmith [F 1986, 1993], Hines and Unger [G 1986], Jacobson [F 1985], Jamsa [F 1984], Kadie [F 1986], Masiero and Germano [F 1988], Nielsen [F 1988], Nies [F 1986], Rajlich and Silva [F 1987], and Shumate [F 1987].

Comparisons of various object-oriented development processes may be found in Arnold [F 1991], Boehm-Davis and Ross [H 1984], deChampeaux [B 1991], Cribbs, Moon and Roe [F 1992], Fowler [F 1992], Kelly [F 1986], Mannino [F 1987], Song [F 1992], and Webster [F 1988]. Brookman [F 1991] and Fichman [F 1992] provide a comparison of structured and object-oriented methods.

Empirical studies of software processes may be found in Curtis [H 1992] as well as the Software Process Workshop [H 1988]. Another interesting reference is Guindon [H 1987], who studies the exploratory processes used by developers early in the development process. Rechtin [H 1992] offers pragmatic guidance to the software architect who must drive the development process.

Humphrey [H 1989] is the seminal reference on software process maturity. Parnas [H 1986] is the classical reference on how to fake such a mature process.

CHAPTER 7

Pragmatics

Software development today remains a very labor-intensive business; to a large extent, it is still best characterized as a cottage industry [1]. A report by Kishida, Teramoto, Torri, and Urano notes that, even in Japan, the software industry "still relies mainly on the informal paper-and-pencil approach in the upstream development phases" [2].

Compounding matters is the fact that designing is not an exact science. Consider the design of a complex database using entity-relationship modeling, one of the foundations of object-oriented design. As Hawryszkiewycz observes, "Although this sounds fairly straightforward, it does involve a certain amount of personal perception of the importance of various objects in the enterprise. The result is that the design process is not deterministic: different designers can produce different enterprise models of the same enterprise" [3].

We may reasonably conclude that no matter how sophisticated the development method, no matter how well-founded its theoretical basis, we cannot ignore the practical aspects of designing systems for the real world. This means that we must consider sound management practices with regard to such issues as staffing, release management, and quality assurance. To the technologist, these are intensely dull topics; to the professional software engineer, these are realities that must be faced if one wants to be successful in building complex software systems. Thus, this chapter focuses upon the pragmatics of object-oriented development, and examines the impact of the object-model on various management practices.

7.1 Management and Planning

In the presence of an iterative and incremental life cycle, it is of paramount importance to have strong project leadership that actively manages and directs a project's activities. Too many projects go astray because of a lack of focus, and the presence of a strong management team mitigates this problem.

Risk Management

Ultimately, the responsibility of the software development manager is to manage technical as well as nontechnical risk. Technical risks in object-oriented systems include problems such as the selection of an inheritance lattice that offers the best compromise between usability and flexibility, or the choice of mechanisms that yield acceptable performance while simplifying the system's architecture. Nontechnical risks encompass issues such as supervising the timely delivery of software from a third-party vendor, or managing the relationship between the customer and the development team, so as to facilitate the discovery of the system's real requirements during analysis.

As we described in the previous chapter, the micro process of object-oriented development is inherently unstable, and requires active management to force closure. Fortunately, the macro process of object-oriented development is designed to lead to closure by providing a number of tangible products that management can study to ascertain the health of the project, together with controls that permit management to redirect the team's resources as necessary. The macro process's evolutionary approach to development means that there are opportunities to identify problems early in the life cycle and meaningfully respond to these risks before they jeopardize the success of the project.

Many of the basic practices of software development management, such as task planning and walkthroughs, are unaffected by object-oriented technology. What is different about managing an object-oriented project, however, is that the tasks being scheduled and the products being reviewed are subtly different than for non-object-oriented systems.

Task Planning

In any modest- to large-sized project, it is reasonable to have weekly team meetings to discuss work completed and activities for the coming week. Some minimal frequency of meetings is necessary to foster communication among team members; too many meetings destroy productivity, and in fact are a sign that the project has lost its way. Object-oriented software development requires that individual developers have unscheduled critical masses of time in which they can think, innovate, and develop, and meet informally with other team members as necessary to discuss detailed technical issues. The management team must plan for this unstructured time.

Such meetings provide a simple yet effective vehicle for fine-tuning schedules in the micro process, as well as for gaining insight into risks looming on the horizon. These meetings may result in small adjustments to work assignments, so as to ensure steady progress: no project can afford for any of its developers to sit idle while waiting for other team members to stabilize their part of the architecture. This is particularly true for object-oriented systems, wherein class and mechanism design pervades the architecture. Development can come to a standstill if certain key classes are in flux.

On a broader scale, task planning involves scheduling the deliverables of the macro process. Between evolutionary releases, the management team must assess the imminent risks to the project, focus development resources as necessary to attack those risks,[*] and then manage the next iteration of the micro process that yields a stable system satisfying the required scenarios scheduled for that release. Task planning at this level most often fails because of overly optimistic schedules [4]. Development that was viewed as a "simple matter of programming" expands to days of work; schedules are thrown out the window when developers working on one part of the system assume certain protocols from other parts of the system, but are then blindsided by delivery of incompletely or incorrectly fabricated classes. Even more insidious, schedules may be mortally wounded by the appearance of performance problems or compiler bugs, both of which must be worked around, often by corrupting certain tactical design decisions.

The key to not being at the mercy of overly optimistic planning is the calibration of the development team and its tools. Typically, task planning goes like this. First, the management team directs the energies of a developer to a specific part of the system, say, for example, the design of a set of classes for interfacing to a relational database. The developer considers the scope of the effort, and returns with an estimate of time to complete, which management then relies upon to schedule other developer's activities. The problem is that these estimates are not always reliable, because they usually represent best-case conditions. One developer might quote a week of effort for some task, whereas another developer might quote one month for the same task. When the work is actually carried out, it might take both developers three weeks: the first developer having underestimated the effort (the common problem of most developers), and the second developer having set much more realistic estimates (usually because he or she understood the difference between actual work time versus calendar time, which often gets filled with a multitude of nonfunctional activities). In order to develop schedules in which the team can have confidence, it is therefore necessary for the management team to devise multiplicative factors for each developer's estimates. This is not an indication of management not trusting its developers: it is a simple acknowledgment of the reality that most developers are focused upon technical issues, not planning issues. Management must help its developers learn to do effective planning, a skill that is only acquired through battlefield experience.

The process of object-oriented development explicitly helps to develop these calibration factors. Its iterative and incremental life cycle means that there

---

[*] Gilb notes that "if you do not actively attack the risks, they will actively attack you" [5].

are many intermediate milestones established early in the project, which management can use to gather data on each developer's track record for setting and meeting schedules. As evolutionary development proceeds, this means that management over time will gain a better understanding of the real productivity of each of its developers, and individual developers can gain experience in estimating their own work more accurately. The same lesson applies to tools: with the emphasis upon early delivery of architectural releases, the process of object-oriented development encourages the early use of tools, which leads to the identification of their limitations before it is too late to change course.

Walkthroughs

Walkthroughs are another well-established practice that every development team should employ. As with task planning, the conduct of software reviews is largely unaffected by object-oriented technology. However, relative to non-object-oriented systems, what is reviewed is a different matter.

Management must take steps to strike a balance between too many and too few walkthroughs. In all but the most human-critical systems, it is simply not economical to review every line of code. Therefore, management must direct the scarce resources of its team to review those aspects of the system that represent strategic development issues. For object-oriented systems, this suggests conducting formal reviews upon scenarios as well as the system's architecture, with many more informal reviews focused upon smaller tactical issues.

As described in the previous chapter, scenarios are a primary product of the analysis phase of object-oriented development, and serve to capture the desired behavior of the system in terms of its function points. Formal reviews of scenarios are led by the team's analysts, together with domain experts or other end users, and are witnessed by other developers. Such reviews are best conducted throughout the analysis phase, rather than waiting to carry out one massive review at the end of analysis, when it is already too late to do anything useful to redirect the analysis effort. Experience with the method shows that even nonprogrammers can understand scenarios presented through scripts or the formalisms of object diagrams.[*] Ultimately, such reviews help to establish a common vocabulary among a system's developers and its users. Letting other members of the development team witness these reviews exposes them to the real requirements of the system early in the development process.

Architectural reviews should focus upon the overall structure of the system, including its class structure and mechanisms. As with scenario reviews, architectural reviews should be conducted throughout the project, led by the project's architect or other designers. Early reviews will focus upon sweeping architectural issues, whereas later reviews may focus upon a certain class category or specific pervasive mechanisms. The central purpose of such

---

[*] We have encountered use of the notation in reviews involving such diverse non-programmer groups as astronomers, biologists, meteorologists, physicists, and bankers.

reviews is to validate designs early in the life cycle. In so doing, we also help to communicate the vision of the architecture. A secondary purpose of such reviews is to increase the visibility of the architecture so as to create opportunities for discovering patterns of classes or collaborations of objects, which may then be exploited over time to simplify the architecture.

Informal reviews should be carried out weekly, and generally involve the peer review of certain clusters of classes or lower-level mechanisms. The purpose of such reviews is to validate these tactical decisions; their secondary purpose is to provide a vehicle for more senior developers to instruct junior members of the team.

7.2 Staffing

Resource Allocation

One of the more delightful aspects of managing object-oriented projects is that, in the steady state, there is usually a reduction in the total amount of resources needed and a shift in the timing of their deployment relative to more traditional methods. The operative phrase here is "in the steady state." Generally speaking, the first object-oriented project undertaken by an organization will require slightly more resources than for non-object-oriented methods, primarily because of the learning curve inherent in adopting any new technology. The essential resource benefits of the object model will not show themselves until the second or third project, at which time the development team is more adept at class design and harvesting common abstractions and mechanisms, and the management team is more comfortable with driving the iterative and incremental development process.

For analysis, resource requirements do not typically change much when employing object-oriented methods. However, because the object-oriented process places an emphasis upon architectural design, we tend to accelerate the deployment of architects and other designers to much earlier in the development process, sometimes even engaging them during later phases of analysis to begin architectural exploration. During evolution, fewer resources are typically required, mainly because the ongoing work tends to leverage off of common abstractions and mechanisms invented earlier during architectural design or previous evolutionary releases. Testing may also require fewer resources, primarily because adding new functionality to a class or mechanism is achieved mainly by modifying a structure that is known to behave correctly in the first place. Thus, testing tends to begin earlier in the life cycle, and manifests itself as a cumulative rather than a monolithic activity. Integration usually requires vastly fewer resources as compared with traditional methods, mainly because integration happens incrementally throughout the development life cycle, rather than occurring in one big bang event. Thus, in the steady state, the net of all the human resources required for object-oriented development is typically less than that required for traditional approaches. Furthermore, when we consider the cost of ownership of object-oriented software, the total life cycle costs are often less, because the resulting product tends to be of far better quality, and so is much more resilient to change.

Development Team Roles

It is important to remember that software development is ultimately a human endeavor. Developers are not interchangeable parts, and the successful deployment of any complex system requires the unique and varied skills of a focused team of people.

Experience suggests that the object-oriented development process requires a subtly different partitioning of skills as compared with traditional methods. We have found the following three roles to be central to an object-oriented project:

- Project architect
- Subsystem lead
- Application programmer

The project architect is the visionary, and is responsible for evolving and maintaining the system's architecture. For small- to medium-sized systems, architectural design is typically the responsibility of one or two particularly insightful individuals. For larger projects, this may be the shared responsibility of a larger team. The project architect is not necessarily the most senior developer, but rather is the one best qualified to make strategic decisions, usually as a result of his or her extensive experience in building similar kinds of systems. Because of this experience, such developers intuitively know the common architectural patterns that are relevant to a given domain, and what performance issues apply to certain architectural variants. Architects are not necessarily the best programmers either, although they should have adequate programming skills. Just as a building architect should be skilled in aspects of construction, it is generally unwise to employ a software architect who is not also a reasonably decent programmer. Project architects should also be well-versed in the notation and process of object-oriented development, because they must ultimately express their architectural vision in terms of clusters of classes and collaborations of objects.

It is generally bad practice to hire an outside architect who, metaphorically speaking, storms in on a white horse, proclaims some architectural vision, then rides away while others suffer the consequences of these decisions. It is far better to actively engage an architect during the analysis process and then retain that architect throughout most if not all of the system's evolution. Thus, the architect will become more familiar with the actual needs of the system, and over time will be subject to the implications of his or her architectural decisions. In addition, by keeping responsibility for architectural integrity in the hands of one person or a small team of developers, we increase our chances of developing a small and more resilient architecture.

Subsystem leads are the primary abstractionists of the project. A subsystem lead is responsible for the design of an entire class category or subsystem. In conjunction with the project architect, each lead must devise, defend, and negotiate the interface of a specific class category or subsystem, and then direct its implementation. A subsystem lead is therefore the ultimate owner of a cluster of classes and its associated mechanisms, and is also responsible for its testing and release during the evolution of the system.

Subsystem leads must be well-versed in the notation and process of object-oriented development. They are usually faster and better programmers than the project architect, but lack the architect's broad experience. On the average, subsystem leads constitute about a third to a half of the development team.

Application engineers are the less senior developers in a project, and carry out one of two responsibilities. Certain application engineers are responsible for the implementation of a category or subsystem, under the supervision of its subsystem lead. This activity may involve some class design, but generally involves implementing and then unit testing the classes and mechanisms invented by other designers on the team. Other application engineers are then responsible for taking the classes designed by the architect and subsystem leads and assembling them to carry out the function points of the system. In a sense, these engineers are responsible for writing small programs in the domain-specific language defined by the classes and mechanisms of the architecture.

Application engineers are familiar with but not necessarily experts in the notation and process of object-oriented development; however, application engineers are very good programmers who understand the idioms and idiosyncrasies of the given programming languages. On the average, half or more of the development team consists of application engineers.

This breakdown of skills addresses the staffing problem faced by most software development organizations, which usually have only a handful of really good designers and many more less experienced ones. The social benefit of this approach to staffing is that it offers a career path to the more junior people on the team: specifically, junior developers work under the guidance of more senior developers in a mentor/apprentice relationship. As they gain experience in using well-designed classes, over time they learn to design their own quality classes. The corollary to this arrangement is that not every developer needs to be an expert abstractionist, but can grow in those skills over time.

In larger projects, there may be a number of other distinct development roles required to carry out the work of the project. Most of these roles (such as the toolsmith) are indifferent to the use of object-oriented technology, although some of them are especially relevant to the object model (such as the reuse engineer):

• Project manager	Responsible for the active management of the project's deliverables, tasks, resources, and schedules
• Analyst	Responsible for evolving and interpreting the end user's requirements; must be an expert in the problem domain, yet must not be isolated from the rest of the development team
• Reuse engineer	Responsible for managing the project's repository of components and designs; through participation in reviews and other activities, actively seeks opportunities for commonality, and causes them to be exploited; acquires, produces, and adapts components for general use within the project or the entire organization
• Quality assurance	Responsible for measuring the products of the development process; generally directs system-level testing of all prototypes and production releases
• Integration manager	Responsible for assembling compatible versions of released categories and subsystems in order to form a deliverable release; responsible for maintaining the configurations of released products
• Documenter	Responsible for producing end-user documentation of the product and its architecture
• Toolsmith	Responsible for creating and adapting software tools that facilitate the production of the project's deliverables, especially with regard to generated code
• System administrator	Responsible for managing the physical computing resources used by the project

Of course, not every project requires all of these roles. For small projects, many of these responsibilities may be shared by the same person; for larger projects, each role may represent an entire organization.

Experience indicates that object-oriented development makes it possible to use smaller development teams as compared with traditional methods. Indeed, it is not impossible for a team of roughly 30-40 developers to produce several hundred thousand lines of production-quality code in a single year. However, we agree with Boehm, who observes that "the best results occur with fewer and better people" [6]. Unfortunately, trying to staff a project with fewer people than traditional folklore suggests are needed may produce resistance. As we suggested in the previous chapter, such an approach infringes upon the attempts of some managers to build empires. Other managers like to hide behind the large numbers of employees, because more people represent more power. Furthermore, if a project fails, there are more subordinates upon whom to heap the blame.

Just because a project applies the most sophisticated design method or the latest fancy tool doesn't mean a manager has the right to abdicate responsibility for hiring designers who can think or to let a project run on autopilot [7].

7.3 Release Management

Integration

Industrial-strength projects require the development of families of programs. At any given time in the development process, there will be multiple prototypes and production releases, as well as development and test scaffolding. Most often, each developer will have his or her own executable view of the system under development.

As explained in the previous chapter, the nature of the interactive and incremental process of object-oriented development means that there should rarely if ever be a single "big bang" integration event. Instead, there will generally be many smaller integration events, each marking the creation of another prototype or architectural release. Each such release is generally incremental in nature, having evolved from an earlier stable release. As Davis et al. observe, "when using incremental development, software is deliberately built to satisfy fewer requirements initially, but is constructed in such a way as to facilitate the incorporation of new requirements and thus achieve higher adaptability" [8]. From the perspective of the ultimate user of the system, the macro process generates a stream of executable releases, each with increasing functionality, eventually evolving into the final production system. From the perspective of those inside the organization, many more releases are actually constructed, and only some are frozen and baselined to stabilize important system interfaces. This strategy tends to reduce development risk, because it accelerates the discovery of architectural and performance problems early in the development process.

For larger projects, an organization may produce an internal release of the system every few weeks and then release a running version to its customers for review every few months, according to the needs of the project. In the steady state, a release consists of a set of compatible subsystems along with their associated documentation. Building a release is possible whenever the major subsystems of a project are stable enough and work together well enough to provide some new level of functionality.

Configuration Management and Version Control

Consider this stream of releases from the perspective of an individual developer, who might be responsible for implementing a particular subsystem. He or she must have a working version of that subsystem, that is, a version under development. In order to proceed with further development, at least the interfaces of all imported subsystems must be available. As this working version becomes stable, it is released to an integration team, responsible for collecting a set of compatible subsystems for the entire system. Eventually, this collection of subsystems is frozen and baselined, and made part of an internal release. This internal release thus becomes the current operational release, visible to all active developers who need to further refine their particular part of its implementation. In the meantime, the individual developer can work on a newer version of his or her subsystem. Thus, development can proceed in parallel, with stability possible because of well-defined and well-guarded subsystem interfaces.

Implicit in this model is the idea that a cluster of classes, not the individual class, is the unit of version control. Experience suggests that managing versions of classes is too fine a granularity, since no class tends to stand alone. Rather, it is better to version related groups of classes. Practically speaking, this means versioning subsystems, since groups of classes (forming class categories in the logical view of the system) map to subsystems (in the physical view of the system).

At any given point in the evolution of a system, multiple versions of a particular subsystem may exist: there might be a version for the current release under development, one for the current internal release, and one for the latest customer release. This intensifies the need for reasonably powerful configuration management and version-control tools.

Source code is not the only development product that should be placed under configuration management. The same concepts apply to all the other products of object-oriented development, such as requirements, class diagrams, object diagrams, module diagrams, and process diagrams.

Testing

The principle of continuous integration applies as well to testing, which should also be a continuous activity during the development process. In the context of object-oriented architectures, testing must encompass at least three dimensions:

- Unit testing   Involves testing individual classes and mechanisms; is the responsibility of the application engineer who implemented the structure

- Subsystem testing   Involves testing a complete category or subsystem; is the responsibility of the subsystem lead; subsystem tests can be used

as regression tests for each newly released
version of the subsystem

- System testing   Involves testing the system as a whole; is the
responsibility of the quality-assurance team;
system tests are also typically used as
regression tests by the integration team when
assembling new releases

Testing should focus upon the system's external behavior; a secondary purpose
of testing is to push the limits of the system in order to understand how it fails
under certain conditions.

7.4 Reuse

Elements of Reuse

Any artifact of software development can be reused, including code, designs,
scenarios, and documentation. As noted in Chapter 3, in object-oriented
programming languages, classes serve as the primary linguistic vehicle for
reuse: classes may be subclassed to specialize or extend the base class. Also, as
explained in Chapter 4, we can reuse patterns of classes, objects, and designs
in the form of idioms, mechanisms, and frameworks. Pattern reuse is at a
higher level of abstraction than the reuse of individual classes, and so provides
greater leverage (but is harder to achieve).

It is dangerous and misleading to quote figures for levels of reuse [9]. In
successful projects, we have encountered reuse factors as high as 70%
(meaning that almost three-fourths of the software in the system was taken
intact from some other source) and as low as 0%. The degree of reuse should
not be viewed as a quota to achieve, because potential reuse appears to vary
wildly by domain and is affected by many nontechnical factors, including
schedule pressure, the nature of subcontractor relationships, and security
considerations.

Ultimately, any amount of reuse is better that none, because reuse
represents a savings of resources that would otherwise be needed to reinvent
some previously solved problem in abstraction.

Institutionalizing Reuse

Reuse within a project or even an entire organization doesn't just happen, it
must be institutionalized. This means that opportunities for reuse must be
actively sought out and rewarded. Indeed, this is why we include pattern
scavenging as an explicit activity in the macro process.

An effective reuse program is best achieved by making specific individuals
responsible for the reuse activity. As we described in the previous chapter, this
activity involves identifying opportunities for commonality, usually discovered

through architectural reviews, and exploiting these opportunities, usually by producing new components or adapting existing ones, and championing their reuse among developers. This approach requires the explicit rewarding of reuse. Even simple rewards are highly effective in fostering reuse: for example, peer recognition of the author or reuser is often useful. For something more tangible, it may be effective to offer a free dinner or weekend away to the developer (and his or her significant other) whose code was most often reused, or who reused the most code within a certain time period.[*]

Ultimately, reuse costs resources in the short term, but pays off in the long term. A reuse activity will only be successful in an organization that takes a long-term view of software development and optimizes resources for more than just the current project.

7.5 Quality Assurance and Metrics

Software Quality

Schulmeyer and McManus define software quality as "the fitness for use of the total software product" [10]. Software quality doesn't just happen: it must be engineering into the system. Indeed, the use of object-oriented technology doesn't automatically lead to quality software: it is still possible to write very bad software using object-oriented programming languages.

This is why we place such an emphasis upon software architecture in the process of object-oriented development. A simple, adaptable architecture is central to any quality software; its quality is made complete by carrying out simple and consistent tactical design decisions.

Software quality assurance involves "the systematic activities providing evidence of the fitness for use of the total software product" [11]. Quality assurance seeks to give us quantifiable measures of goodness for the quality of a software system. Many such traditional measures are directly applicable to object-oriented systems.

As we described earlier, walkthroughs and other kinds of inspections are important practices even in object-oriented systems, and provide insights into the software's quality. Perhaps the most important quantifiable measure of goodness is the defect-discovery rate. During the evolution of the system, we track software defects according to their severity and location. The defect-discovery rate is thereby a measure of how quickly errors are being discovered, which we plot against time. As Dobbins observes, "the actual number of errors is less important than the slope of the line" [12]. A project that is under control will have a bell-shaped curve, with the defect-discovery rate peaking at around the midpoint of the test period and then falling off to zero. A project that is out of control will have a curve that tails off very slowly, or not at all.

---

[*] This is often a welcome reward to the developer's significant other, who has likely not seen much of him or her during the final throes of software development.

One of the reasons that the macro process of object-oriented development works so well is that it permits the early and continuous collection of data about the defect-discovery rate. For each incremental release, we can perform a system test and plot the defect-discovery rate versus time. Even though early releases will have less functionality, we still expect to see a bell-shaped curve for every release in a healthy project.

Defect density is another relevant quality measure. Measuring defects per thousand source lines of code (KSLOC) is the traditional approach, and is still generally applicable to object-oriented systems. In healthy projects, defect density tends to "reach a stable value after approximately 10,000 lines of code have been inspected and will remain almost unchanged no matter how large the code volume is thereafter" [13].

In object-oriented systems, we have also found it useful to measure defect density in terms of the numbers of defects per class category or per class. With this measure, the 80/20 rule seems to apply: 80% of the software defects will be found in 20% of the system's classes [14].

In addition to the more formal approaches to gathering defect information through system testing, we have also found it useful to institute project- or company-wide "bug hunts" during which anyone may exercise a release over a given limited period of time. Prizes are then awarded to the person who finds the most defects, as well as to the person who finds the most obscure defect. Prizes need not be extravagant: coffee mugs, certificates for dinner or movies, or even T-shirts are appropriate to reward the fearless bug hunter.

Object-Oriented Metrics

Perhaps the most dreadful way for a manager to measure progress is to measure the lines of code produced. The number of line feeds in a fragment of source code has absolutely no correlation to its completeness or complexity. Contributing to the shortcomings of this Neanderthal approach is the ease of playing games with the numbers, resulting in productivity figures that may differ from one another by as much as two orders of magnitude. For example, what exactly is a line of code (especially in Smalltalk)? Does one count physical lines, or semicolons? What about counting multiple statements that appear on one line or statements that cross line boundaries? Similarly, how does one measure the labor involved? Are all personnel counted, or perhaps just the programmers? Is the workday measured as an eight-hour day, or is the time a programmer spends working in the wee hours of the morning also counted? Traditional complexity measures, better suited to early generation programming languages, also have minimal correlation with completeness and complexity in object-oriented systems, and are therefore largely useless when applied to the system as a whole.

For example, the McCabe Cyclomatic metric, when applied to an object-oriented system as a whole, does not give a very meaningful measure of complexity, because it is blind to the system's class structure and mechanisms. However, we have found it useful to generate a cyclomatic metric per class.

This gives some indication of the relative complexity of individual classes, and can then be used to direct inspections to the most complex classes, which are most likely to contain the greatest numbers of defects.

We tend to measure progress by counting the classes in the logical design, or the modules in the physical design, that are completed and working. As we described in the previous chapter, another measure of progress is the stability of key interfaces (that is, how often they change). At first, the interfaces of all key abstractions will change daily, if not hourly. Over time, the most important interfaces will stabilize first, the next most important interfaces will stabilize second, and so on. Towards the end of the development life cycle, only a few insignificant interfaces will need to be changed, since most of the emphasis is on getting the already designed classes and modules to work together. Occasionally, a few changes may be needed in a critical interface, but such changes are usually upwardly compatible. Even so, such changes are made only after careful thought about their impact. These changes can then be incrementally introduced into the production system as part of the usual release cycle.

Chidamber and Kemerer suggest a number of metrics that are directly applicable to object-oriented systems [15]:

- Weighted methods per class
- Depth of inheritance tree
- Number of children
- Coupling between objects
- Response for a class
- Lack of cohesion in methods

Weighted methods per class gives a relative measure of the complexity of an individual class; if all methods are considered to be equally complex, this becomes a measure of the number of methods per class. In general, a class with significantly more methods than its peers is more complex, tends to be more application-specific, and often hosts a greater number of defects.

The depth of the inheritance tree and number of children are measures of the shape and size of the class structure. As we described in Chapter 3, well-structured object-oriented systems tend to be architected as forests of classes, rather than as one very large inheritance lattice. As a rule of thumb, we tend to build lattices that are balanced and that are generally no deeper than 7±2 classes and no wider than 7±2 classes.

Coupling between objects is a measure of their connectedness to other objects, and thus is a measure of its class's encumbrance. As with traditional measures of coupling, we seek to design loosely coupled objects, which have a greater potential for reuse.

Response for a class is a measure of the methods that its instances can call; cohesion in methods is a measure of the unity of the class's abstraction. In general, a class that can invoke significantly more methods than its peers is more complex. A class with low cohesion among its methods suggests an accidental or inappropriate abstraction: such a class should generally be re-abstracted into more than one class, or its responsibilities delegated to other existing classes.

7.6 Documentation

Development Legacy

The development of a software system involves much more than the writing of its raw source code. Certain products of development offer ways to give its management team and users insight into the progress of the project. We also seek to leave behind a legacy of analysis and design decisions for the eventual maintainers of the system. As noted in Chapter 5, the products of object-oriented development in general include sets of class diagrams, object diagrams, module diagrams, and process diagrams. Collectively, these diagrams offer traceability back to the system's requirements. Process diagrams denote programs, which are the root modules found in module diagrams. Each module represents the implementation of some combination of classes and objects, which are in turn found in class diagrams and object diagrams, respectively. Finally, object diagrams denote scenarios specified by the requirements, and class diagrams represent key abstractions that form the vocabulary of the problem domain.

Documentation Contents

The documentation of a system's architecture and implementation is important, but the production of such documents should never drive the development process: documentation is an essential, albeit secondary, product of the development process. It is also important to remember that documents are living products that should be allowed to evolve together with the iterative and incremental evolution of the project's releases. Together with the generated code, delivered documents serve as the basis of most formal and informal reviews.

What must be documented? Obviously, end-user documentation must be produced, instructing the user on the operation and installation of each release.[*] In addition, analysis documentation must be produced to capture the semantics of the system's function points as viewed through scenarios. We must also generate architectural and implementation documentation, to communicate the vision and details of the architecture to the development team and to

---

[*] It is an unwritten rule that for personal productivity software, a system that requires a user to constantly refer to a manual is user-hostile. Object-oriented user interfaces in particular should be designed so that their use is intuitive and self-consistent, in order to minimize or eliminate the need for end-user documentation.

preserve information about all relevant strategic decisions, so that the system can readily be adapted and evolved over time.

In general, the essential documentation of a system's architecture and implementation should include the following:

- Documentation of the high-level system architecture
- Documentation of the key abstractions and mechanisms in the architecture
- Documentation of scenarios that illustrate the as-built behavior of key aspects of the system

The worst possible documentation to create for an object-oriented system is a stand-alone description of the semantics of each method on a class-by-class basis. This approach tends to generate a great deal of useless documentation that no one reads or trusts, and fails to document the more important architectural issues that transcend individual classes, namely, the collaborations among classes and objects. It is far better to document these higher-level structures, which can be expressed in diagrams of the notation but have no direct linguistic expression in the programming language, and then refer developers to the interfaces of certain important classes for tactical details.

7.7 Tools

With early generation languages, it was enough for a development team to have a minimal tool set: an editor, a compiler, a linker, and a loader were often all that were needed (and often all that existed). If the team were particularly lucky, they might even get a source-level debugger. Complex systems change the picture entirely: trying to build a large software system with a minimal tool set is equivalent to building a multistory building with stone hand tools.

Object-oriented development practices change the picture as well. Traditional software development tools embody knowledge only about source code, but since object-oriented analysis and design highlight key abstractions and mechanisms, we need tools that can focus on richer semantics. In addition, the rapid development of releases defined by the macro process of object-oriented development requires tools that offer rapid turnaround, especially for the edit/compile/execute/debug cycle.

It is important to choose tools that scale well. A tool that works for one developer writing a small stand-alone application will not necessarily scale to production releases of more complex applications. Indeed, for every tool, there will be a threshold beyond which the tool's capacity is exceeded, causing its benefits to be greatly outweighed by its liabilities and clumsiness.

Kinds of Tools

We have identified at least seven different kinds of tools that are applicable to object-oriented development. The first tool is a graphics-based system supporting the object-oriented notation presented in Chapter 5. Such a tool can be used during analysis to capture the semantics of scenarios, as well as early in the development process to capture strategic and tactical design decisions, maintain control over the design products, and coordinate the design activities of a team of developers. Indeed, such a tool can be used throughout the life cycle, as the design evolves into a production implementation. Such tools are also useful during systems maintenance. Specifically, we have found it possible to reverse-engineer many of the interesting aspects of an object-oriented system, producing at least the class structure and module architecture of the system as built. This feature is quite important: with traditional CASE tools, developers may generate marvelous pictures, only to find that these pictures are out of date once the implementation proceeds, because programmers fiddle with the implementation without updating the design. Reverse engineering makes it less likely that design documentation will ever get out of step with the actual implementation.

The next tool we have found important for object-oriented development is a browser that knows about the class structure and module architecture of a system.[*] Class hierarchies can become so complex that it is difficult even to find all of the abstractions that are part of the design or are candidates for reuse [16]. While examining a program fragment, a developer may want to see the definition of the class of some object. Upon finding this class, he or she might wish to visit some of its superclasses. While viewing a particular superclass, the developer might want to browse through all uses of that class before installing a change to its interface. This kind of browsing is extremely clumsy if one has to worry about files, which are an artifact of the physical, not the logical, design decisions. For this reason, browsers are an important tool for object-oriented analysis and design. For example, the standard Smalltalk environment allows one to browse all the classes of a system in the ways we have described. Similar facilities exist in environments for other object-oriented programming languages, although to different degrees of sophistication.

Another tool we have found to be important, if not absolutely essential, is an incremental compiler. The kind of evolutionary development that goes on in object-oriented development cries out for an incremental compiler that can compile single declarations and statements. Meyrowitz notes that "UNIX as it stands, with its orientation towards the batch compilation of large program files into libraries that are later linked with other code fragments, does not provide the support that is necessary for object-oriented programming. It is largely unacceptable to require a ten-minute compile and link cycle simply to change the implementation of a method and to require a one hour compile and link cycle simply to add a field to a high-level superclass! Incrementally compiled

---

[*] By integrating the first kind of tool with the host's software development environment, browsing between the design and its implementation becomes possible.

methods and incrementally compiled. . . . field definitions are a must for quick debugging" [17]. Incremental compilers exist for many of the languages described in the appendix; unfortunately, most implementations consist of traditional, batch-oriented compilers.

Next, we have found that nontrivial projects need debuggers that know about class and object semantics. When debugging a program, we often need to examine the instance variables and class variables associated with an object. Traditional debuggers for non-object-oriented programming languages do not embody knowledge about classes and objects. Thus, trying to use a standard C debugger for C++ programs, while possible, doesn't permit the developer to find the really important information needed to debug an object-oriented program. The situation is especially critical for object-oriented programming languages that support multiple threads of control. At any given moment during the execution of such a program, there may be several active processes. These circumstances require a debugger that permits the developer to exert control over all the individual threads of control, usually on an object-by-object basis.

Also in the category of debugging tools, we include tools such as stress testers, which stress the capacity of the software, usually in terms of resource utilization, and memory-analysis tools, which identify violations of memory access, such as writing to deallocated memory, reading from uninitialized memory, or reading and writing beyond the boundaries of an array.

Next, especially for larger projects, one must have configuration management and version-control tools. As mentioned earlier, the category or subsystem is the best unit of configuration management.

Another tool we have found important with object-oriented development is a class librarian. Most of the languages mentioned in this book have predefined class libraries, or commercially available class libraries. As a project matures, this library grows as domain-specific reusable software components are added over time. It does not take long for such a library to grow to enormous proportions, which makes it difficult for a developer to find a class or module that meets his or her needs. One reason that a library can become so large is that a given class commonly has multiple implementations, each of which has different time and space semantics. If the perceived cost (usually inflated) of finding a certain component is higher then the perceived cost (usually underestimated) of creating that component from scratch, then all hope of reuse is lost. For this reason, it is important to have at least some minimal librarian tool that allows developers to locate classes and modules according to different criteria and add useful classes and modules to the library as they are developed.

The last kind of tool we have found useful for certain object-oriented systems is a GUI builder. For systems that involve a large amount of user interaction, it is far better to use such a tool to interactively create dialogs and other windows than to create these artifacts from the bottom up in code. Code generated by such tools can then be connected to the rest of the object-oriented system and, where necessary, fine-tuned by hand.

Organizational Implications

This need for powerful tools creates a demand for two specific roles within the development organization: a reuse engineer and a toolsmith. Among other things, the duties of the reuse engineer are to maintain the class library for a project. Without active effort, such a library can become a vast wasteland of junk classes that no developer would ever want to walk through. Also, it is often necessary to be proactive to encourage reuse, and the reuse engineer can facilitate this process by scavenging the products of current design efforts. The duties of a toolsmith are to create domain-specific tools and tailor existing ones for the needs of a project. For example, a project might need common test scaffolding to test certain aspects of a user interface, or it might need a customized class browser. A toolsmith is in the best position to craft these tools, usually from components already in the class library. Such tools can also be used for later developmental efforts.

A manager already faced with scarce human resources may lament that powerful tools, as well as designated reuse engineers and toolsmiths, are an unaffordable luxury. We do not deny this reality for some resource-constrained projects. However, in many other projects, we have found that these activities go on anyway, usually in an *ad hoc* fashion. We advocate explicit investments in tools and people to make these *ad hoc* activities more focused and efficient, which adds real value to the overall development effort.

7.8 Special Topics

Domain-Specific Issues

We have found that certain application domains warrant special architectural consideration.

The design of an effective user interface is still much more of an art than a science. For this domain, the use of prototyping is absolutely essential. Feedback must be gathered early and often from end users, so as to evaluate the gestures, error behavior, and other paradigms of user interaction. The generation of scenarios is highly effective in driving the analysis of the user interface.

Some applications involve a major database component; other applications may require integration with databases whose schemas cannot be changed, usually because large amounts of data already populate the database (the problem of legacy data). For such domains, the principle of separation of concerns is directly applicable: it is best to encapsulate the access to all such databases inside the confines of well-defined class interfaces. This principle is particularly important when mixing object-oriented decomposition with relational database technology. In the presence of an object-oriented database, the interface between the database and the rest of the application can be much more seamless, but we must remember that object-oriented databases are more effective for object persistence and less so for massive data stores.

Consider also real-time systems. *Real-time* means different things in different contexts: real-time might denote sub-second response is user-centered systems, and sub-microsecond response in data acquisition and control applications. It is important to realize that even for hard-real-time systems, not every component of the system must (or can) be optimized. Indeed, for most complex systems, the greater risk is whether or not the system can be completed, not whether it will perform within its performance requirements. For this reason, we warn against premature optimization. Focus upon producing simple architectures, and the evolutionary generation of releases will illuminate the performance bottlenecks of the system early enough to take corrective action.

The term *legacy systems* refers to applications for which there is a large capital investment in software that cannot economically or safely be abandoned. However, such systems may have intolerable maintenance costs, which require that they be replaced over time. Fortunately, coping with legacy systems is much like coping with databases: we encapsulate access to the facilities of the legacy system within the context of well-defined class interfaces, and over time, migrate the coverage of the object-oriented architecture to replace certain functionality currently provided by the legacy system. Of course, it is essential to begin with an architectural vision of what the final system will look like, so that the incremental replacement of the legacy system will not end up as an inconsistent patchwork of software.

Technology Transfer

As Kempf reports, "Learning object-oriented programming may well be a more difficult task than learning 'just' another programming language. This may be the case because a different style of programming is involved rather than a different syntax within the same framework. That means that not a new language but a new way of thinking about programming is involved" [18].

How do we develop this object-oriented mindset? We recommend the following:

- Provide formal training to both developers and managers in the elements of the object model.
- Use object-oriented development in a low-risk project first, and allow the team to make mistakes; use these team members to seed other projects and act as mentors for the object-oriented approach.
- Expose the developers and managers to examples of well-structured object-oriented systems.

Good candidate projects include software development tools or domain-specific class libraries, which can then be used as resources in later projects.

In our experience, it takes only a few weeks for a professional developer to master the syntax and semantics of a new programming language. It may take several more weeks for the same developer to begin to appreciate the importance and power of classes and objects. Finally, it may take as many as six months of experience for that developer to mature into a competent class designer. This is not necessarily a bad thing, for in any discipline, it takes time to master the art.

We have found that learning by example is often an efficient and effective approach. Once an organization has accumulated a critical mass of applications written in an object-oriented style, introducing new developers and managers to object-oriented development is far easier. Developers start as application programmers, using the well-structured abstractions that already exist. Over time, developers who have studied and used these components under the supervision of a more experienced person gain sufficient experience to develop a meaningful conceptual framework of the object model and become effective class designers.

7.8 The Benefits and Risks of Object-Oriented Development

The Benefits of Object-Oriented Development

The adopters of object-oriented technology usually embrace these practices for one of two reasons. First, they seek a competitive advantage, such as reduced time to market, greater product flexibility, or schedule predictability. Second, they may have problems that are so complex that don't seem to have any other solution.

In Chapter 2, we suggested that the use of the object model leads us to construct systems that embody the five attributes of well-structured complex systems. The object model forms the conceptual framework for the notation and process of object-oriented development, and thus these benefits are true of the method itself. In that chapter, we also noted the benefits that flow from the following characteristics of the object model (and thus from object-oriented development):

- Exploits the expressive power of all object-oriented programming languages
- Encourages the reuse of software components
- Leads to systems that are more resilient to change
- Reduces development risk
- Appeals to the working of human cognition

A number of case studies reinforce these findings; in particular, they point out that the object-oriented approach can reduce development time and the size of the resulting source code [19, 20, 21].

The Risks of Object-Oriented Development

On the darker side of object-oriented design, we find that two areas of risk must be considered: performance and start-up costs.

Relative to procedural languages, there is definitely a performance cost for sending a message from one object to another in an object-oriented programming language. As we pointed out in Chapter 3, for method invocations that cannot be resolved statically, an implementation must do a dynamic lookup in order to find the method defined for the class of the receiving object. Studies indicate that in the worst case, a method invocation may take from 1.75 to 2.5 times as long as a simple subprogram call [22, 23]. On the positive side, let's focus on the operative phrase, "cannot be resolved statically." Experience indicates that dynamic lookup is really needed in only about 20 percent of most method invocations. With a strongly typed language, a compiler can often determine which invocations can be statically resolved and then generate code for a subprogram call rather than a method lookup.

Another source of performance overhead comes not so much from the nature of object-oriented programming languages as from the way they are used in conjunction with object-oriented development. As we have stated many times, object-oriented development leads to the creation of systems whose components are built in layers of abstraction. One implication of this layering is that individual methods are generally very small, since they build on lower-level methods. Another implication of this layering is that sometimes methods must be written to gain protected access to the otherwise encapsulated fields of an object. This plethora of methods means that we can end up with a glut of method invocations. Invoking a method at a high level of abstraction usually results in a cascade of method invocations; high-level methods usually invoke lower-level ones, and so on. For applications in which time is a limited resource, so many method invocations may be unacceptable. On the positive side again, such layering is essential for the comprehension of a system; it may be impossible ever to get a complex system working without starting with a layered design. Our recommendation is to design for functionality first, and then instrument the running system to determine where the timing bottlenecks actually exist. These bottlenecks can often be removed by declaring the appropriate methods as inline (thus trading off space for time), flattening the class hierarchy, or breaking the encapsulation of a class's attributes.

A related performance risk derives from the encumbrance of classes: a class deep in an inheritance lattice may have many superclasses, whose code must be included when linking in the most specific class. For small object-oriented applications, this may practically mean that deep class hierarchies are to be avoided, because they require an excessive amount of object code. This problem can be mitigated somewhat by using a mature compiler and linker that can eliminate all dead code.

Yet another source of performance bottlenecks in the context of object-oriented programming languages derives from the paging behavior of running applications. Most compilers allocate object code in segments, with the code for each compilation unit (often a single file) placed in one or more segments. This model presumes a high locality of reference: subprograms within one segment call subprograms in the same segment. However, in object-oriented systems, there is rarely such locality of reference. For large systems, classes are usually declared in separate files, and since the methods of one class usually build upon those of other classes, a single method invocation may involve code from many different segments. This violates the assumptions that most computers make about the runtime behavior of programs, particularly for computers with pipelined CPUs and paging memory systems. Again on the positive side, this is why we separate logical and physical design decisions. If a running system thrashes during execution owing to excessive segment swapping, then fixing the problem is largely a matter of changing the physical allocation of classes to modules. This is a design decision in the physical model of the system, which has no effect upon its logical design.

One remaining performance risk with object-oriented systems comes from the dynamic allocation and destruction of objects. Allocating an object on a heap is a dynamic action as opposed to statically allocating an object either globally or on a stack frame, and heap allocation usually costs more computing resources. For many kinds of systems, this property does not cause any real problems, but for time-critical applications, one cannot afford the cycles needed to complete a heap allocation. There are simple solutions for this problem: either preallocate such objects during elaboration of the program, instead of during any time-critical algorithms, or replace the system's default memory allocator with one tuned to the behavior of the specific system

One other positive note: certain properties of object-oriented systems often overshadow all these sources of performance overhead. For example, Russo and Kaplan report that the execution time of a C++ program is often faster than that of its functionally equivalent C program [24]. They attribute this difference to the use of virtual functions, which eliminate the need for some kinds of explicit type checking and control structures. Indeed, in our experience, the code sizes of object-oriented systems are commonly smaller than their functionally equivalent non-object-oriented implementations.

For some projects, the start-up costs associated with object-oriented development may prove to be a very real barrier to adopting the technology. Using any such new technology requires the capitalization of software development tools. Also, if a development organization is using a particular object-oriented programming language for the first time, they usually have no established base of domain-specific software to reuse. In short, they must start from scratch or at least figure out how to interface their object-oriented applications with existing non-object-oriented ones. Finally, a first attempt to use object-oriented development will surely fail without the appropriate training. An object-oriented programming language is not "just another programming language" that can be learned in a three-day course or by reading a book. As we have noted, it takes time to develop the proper mindset for object-oriented design, and this new way of thinking must be embraced by both developers and their managers alike.

Summary

- The successful development and deployment of a complex software system involves much more than just generating code.
- Many of the basic practices of software development management, such as walkthroughs, are unaffected by object-oriented technology.
- In the steady state, object-oriented projects typically require a reduction in resources during development; the roles required of these resources are subtly different than for non-object-oriented systems.
- In object-oriented analysis and design, there is never a single "big-bang" integration event; the unit of configuration management for releases should be the category or subsystem, not the individual file or class.
- Reuse must be institutionalized to be successful.
- Defect-discovery rate and defect density are useful measures for the quality of an object-oriented system. Other useful measures include various class-oriented metrics.
- Documentation should never drive the development process.
- Object-oriented development requires subtly different tools than do non-object-oriented systems.
- The transition by an organization to the use of the object model requires a change in mindset; learning an object-oriented programming language is more than learning "just another programming language."
- There are many benefits to object-oriented technology as well as some risks; experience indicates that the benefits far outweigh the risks.

Further Readings

van Genuchten [H 1991] and Jones [H 1992] examine common software risks. To understand the mind of the individual programmer, see Weinberg [J 1971, H 1988]. Abdel-Hamid and Madnick [H 1991] study the dynamics of development teams.

Gilb [H 1988] and Charette [H 1989] are primary references for software engineering management practices. The work by Aron [H 1974] offers a comprehensive look at managing the individual programmer and teams of programmers. For a realistic study of what really goes on during the development, when pragmatics chases theory out the window, see the works by Glass [G 1982], Lammers [H 1986], and Humphrey [H 1989]. DeMarco and Lister [H 1987], Yourdon [H 1989], Rettig [H 1990], and Thomsett [H 1990] offer a number of recommendations to the development manager.

Details on how to conduct software walkthroughs may be found in Weinberg and Freedman [H 1990] and Yourdon [H 1989a].

Schulmeyer and McManus [H 1992] provide an excellent general reference on software quality assurance. Chidamber and Kemerer [H 1991] and Walsh [H 1992, 1993] study quality assurance and metrics in the context of object-oriented systems.

Suggestions on how to transition individuals and organizations to the object model are described by Goldberg [C 1978], Goldberg and Kay [G 1977], and Kempf [G 1987].

APPLICATIONS

To build a theory, one needs to know a lot about the basic phenomena of the subject matter. We simply do not know enough about these, in the theory of computation, to teach the subject very abstractly. Instead, we ought to teach more about the particular examples we now understand thoroughly, and hope that from this we will be able to guess and prove more general principles.

MARVIN MINSKY
Form and Content in Computer Science

CHAPTER 8

Data Acquisition: Weather Monitoring Station

Methods are a wonderful thing, but from the perspective of the practicing engineer, the most elegant notation or process ever devised is entirely useless if it does not help us build systems for the real world. The last seven chapters have been but a prelude to this section of the book, in which we now apply object-oriented analysis and design to the pragmatic construction of software systems. In this and the remaining four chapters, we start with a set of system requirements and then use the notation and process of object-oriented development to lead us to an implementation. We have chosen a set of applications from widely varying domains, encompassing data acquisition, frameworks, information management systems, artificial intelligence, and command and control, each of which involves its own unique set of problems. Because our focus is on analysis and design rather than programming, we do not present the complete implementation of any one problem, although we will supply enough details to show the mapping from analysis through design to implementation, and to highlight particularly interesting aspects of the system's architecture.

Weather Monitoring Station Requirements

This system shall provide automatic monitoring of various weather conditions. Specifically, it must measure:

- Wind speed and direction
- Temperature
- Barometric pressure
- Humidity

The system shall also provide the following derived measurements:

- Wind chill
- Dew point temperature
- Temperature trend
- Barometric pressure trend

The system shall have a means of determining the current time and date, so that it can report the highest and lowest values of any of the four primary measurements during the previous 24 hour period.

The system shall have a display that continuously indicates all eight primary and derived measurements, as well as the current time and date. Through the use of a keypad, the user may direct the system to display the 24-hour high or low value of any one primary measurement, together with the time of the reported value.

The system shall allow the user to calibrate its sensors against known values, and to set the current time and date.

8.1 Analysis

Defining the Boundaries of the Problem

The sidebar provides the requirements for a weather monitoring system. This is a simple application, encompassing only a handful of classes. Indeed, at first glance, the object-oriented novice might be tempted to tackle this problem in an inherently non-object-oriented manner, by considering the flow of data and the various input/output mappings involved. However, as we shall see, even a system as small as this one lends itself well to an object-oriented architecture, and in so doing exposes some of the basic principles of the object-oriented development process.

We begin our analysis by considering the hardware on which our software must execute. This is inherently a problem of systems analysis, involving manufacturability and cost issues that are far beyond the scope of this text. To bound our problem and thus allow us to expose the issues of its software analysis and design, we will make the following strategic assumptions:

- We will use a single-board computer (SBC) with a 486-class processor.[*]
- Time and date are supplied by an on-board clock, accessible via memory-mapped I/O.
- Temperature, barometric pressure, and humidity are measured by on-board circuits (with remote sensors), also accessible via memory-mapped I/O.
- Wind direction and speed are measured from a boom encompassing a wind vane (capable of sensing wind from any of 16 directions) and cups (which advance a counter for each revolution).
- User input is provided through an off-the-shelf telephone keypad, managed by an on-board circuit supplying audible feedback for each key press. Last user input is accessible via memory mapped I/O.
- The display is an off-the-shelf LCD graphic device, managed by an on-board circuit capable of processing a simple set of graphics primitives, including messages for drawing lines and arcs, filling regions, and displaying text.
- An on-board timer interrupts the computer every 1/60 second.

Figure 8-1 provides a process diagram that illustrates this hardware platform.

We have chosen to throw some hardware at this problem, so that we might better focus upon the system's software. Obviously, we could require more of our software by doing less in hardware (such as by eliminating some of the hardware for the user input and LCD device), but as it turns out, changing the hardware/software boundary is largely immaterial to our object-oriented architecture. Indeed, one of the characteristics of an object-oriented system is that it tends to speak in the vocabulary of its problem space, and so represents a virtual machine that parallels our abstraction of the problem's key entities. Changing the details of the system's hardware only impacts our abstraction of the lower layers of the system.

The use of memory-mapped I/O is quite common for embedded systems such as this one, but obviously, we'd like to hide the secrets of this particular system decision, because these details are so implementation-dependent and therefore subject to change. We can easily insulate our software abstractions from these gnarly details by wrapping a class around each such interface. For example, we might devise a simple class for accessing the current time and

---

[*] This may seem like overkill, but the economies of scale are such that a 486-based SBC is only modestly more expensive than a computer based upon an earlier-generation processor. Specifying hardware with excess capacity means that we can manufacture a family of systems that use the same hardware, and whose family members are distinguished largely by their software.

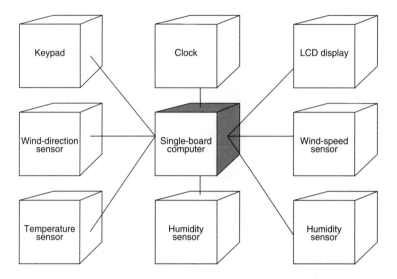

Figure 8-1
Weather Monitoring System Hardware

date: we begin by doing a little isolated class analysis, in which we consider what roles and responsibilities this abstraction should encompass.* Thus, we might decide that this class is responsible for keeping track of the current time in hours, minutes, and seconds, as well as the current month, day, and year. Our analysis might decide to turn these responsibilities into two services, denoted by the operations currentTime and currentDate, respectively. The operation currentTime returns a string in the following format:

13:56:42

showing the current hour, minute, and second. The operation currentDate returns a string in the following format:

6-10-93

showing the current month, day, and year.

Further analysis suggests that a more complete abstraction would allow a client to chose either a 12- or 24-hour format for the time, which we may provide in the form of an additional modifier named setFormat.

By specifying the behavior of this abstraction from the perspective of its public clients, we have devised a clear separation between its interface and implementation. The basic idea here is to build the outside view of each class

---

* Actually, instead of first setting out to design a new class from scratch, we should start by looking for an existing class that already satisfies our needs. A time and data class is certainly a good candidate for reuse: the abstraction is so common, it is likely that someone has already developed and tested such a class. For the purposes of this chapter, we will assume that no such class could be found.

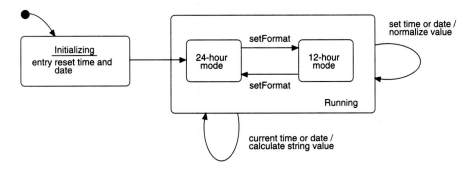

Figure 8-2
TimeDate Life Cycle

as if we had complete control over its underlying platform, then implement the class as a bridge to its real inside view. Thus, the implementation of a class at the system's hardware/software boundary serves to bolt the outside view of the abstraction to its underlying platform, which is often constrained by system decisions that are out of the hands of the software engineer. Of course, the gap between an abstraction's outside and inside views must not be so wide as to require a thick and inefficient implementation to glue the two views together.

Our memory-mapped I/O model might only provide access to the time and date as a 16-bit integer, representing the number of seconds since the system was powered on.* One responsibility of our time and date class must therefore include translating this raw data to some meaningful value. Carrying out this responsibility requires a new set of services to set the time and date, which we provide via the operations setHour, setMinute, setSecond, setDay, setMonth, and setYear.

We may summarize our abstraction of a time/date class as follows:

```
Name:
   TimeDate
Responsibilities:
   Keep track of the current time and date.
Operations:
   currentTime
   currentDate
   setFormat
   setHour
   setMinute
   setSecond
   setMonth
   setDay
   setYear
Attributes:
   time
   date
```

---

* A simple implementation might use a hardware timer that advances a counter every second. A more sophisticated implementation might use a time/date chip with a battery backup. In either case, the outside view of our class presents the same contract to its clients. Our implementation is then responsible for tying this contract to the hardware.

Instances of this class have a dynamic life cycle, which we can express in the state transition diagram shown in Figure 8-2. Here we see that upon initialization, an instance of this class resets its time and date attributes, and then unconditionally enters the `Running` state, where it begins in `24-hour mode`. Once in the `Running` state, receipt of the operation `setFormat` might toggle the object between 12- and 24-hour mode. No matter what its nested state, however, setting the time or date causes the object to renormalize its attributes. Similarly, requesting its time or date causes the object to calculate a new string value.

We have specified the behavior of this abstraction in enough detail so that we can offer it for use in scenarios with other clients we might discover during analysis. Before we consider these scenarios, let's specify the behavior of the other tangible objects in our system.

The class `TemperatureSensor` serves as an analog to the hardware temperature sensors in our system. Isolated class analysis yields the following first cut at this abstraction's outside view:

```
Name:
  TemperatureSensor
Responsibilities:
  Keep track of the current temperature.
Operations:
  currentTemperature
  setLowTemperature
  setHighTemperature
Attributes:
  temperature
```

The operation `currentTemperature` is self-explanatory. The other two operations derive directly from our requirements, which obligate us to provide a mechanism for calibrating each sensor. For the moment, we will assume that each temperature sensor value is represented by a fixed-point number, whose low and high points can be calibrated to fit known actual values. We translate intermediate numbers to their actual temperatures by simple linear interpolation between these two points, as we illustrate in Figure 8-3.

The careful reader may wonder why we have proposed a class for this abstraction, when our requirements imply that there is exactly one temperature sensor in the system. That is indeed true, but in anticipation of reusing this abstraction, we choose to capture it as a class, thereby decoupling it from the particulars of this one system. In fact, the number of temperature sensors monitored by a particular system is largely immaterial to our architecture, and by devising a class, we make it simple for other programs in this family of systems to manipulate any number of sensors.

We can express our abstraction of the barometric pressure sensor in the following specification:

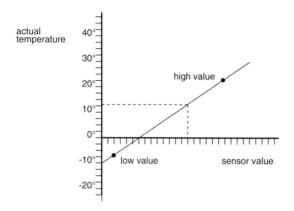

Figure 8-3
TemperatureSensor Calibration

```
Name:
  PressureSensor
Responsibilities:
  Keep track of the current barometric pressure.
Operations:
  currentPressure
  setLowPressure
  setHighPressure
Attributes:
  pressure
```

A review of the system's requirements reveals that we may have missed one important behavior for this and the previous class, `TemperatureSensor`. Specifically, our requirements compel us to provide a means for reporting the temperature and pressure trends. For the moment (because we are doing analysis, not design), we will be content to focus on the nature of this behavior and, most important, on deciding which abstraction we should make responsible for this behavior.

For both the `TemperatureSensor` and the `PressureSensor`, we can express the trends as floating point numbers between -1 and 1, representing the slope of a line fitting a number of values over some interval of time.[*] Thus, we may add the following responsibility and its corresponding operation to both these classes:

```
Responsibilities:
  Report the temperature or pressure trend as the slope of a line fitting the
  past values over the given interval.
Operations:
  trend
```

---

[*] A value of 0 means that the temperature or pressure is stable. A value of 0.1 denotes a modest rise; a value of -0.3 denotes rapidly declining values. A value approaching -1 or 1 suggests an environmental cataclysm, which is beyond the scope of the scenarios our system is expected to handle properly.

Because this behavior is common to both the temperature and pressure sensor classes, our analysis suggests the invention of a common superclass, which we will call `TrendSensor`, responsible for providing this common behavior.

For completeness, we should point out that there is an alternative view of the world that we might have chosen in our analysis. Our decision was to make this common behavior a responsibility of the sensor class itself. We could have decided to make this behavior a part of some external agent that periodically queried the particular sensor and calculated its trend, but we rejected this approach, because it was unnecessarily complex. Our original specification of the temperature and pressure sensor classes suggested that each abstraction had sufficient knowledge to carry out this trend-reporting behavior, and by combining responsibilities (albeit in the form of a superclass), we end up with a simple and conceptually cohesive abstraction.

Our abstraction of the humidity sensor can be expressed in the following specification:

```
Name:
  HumiditySensor
Responsibilities:
  Keep track of the current humidity, expressed as a percentage of
  saturation from 0% to 100%.
Operations:
  currentHumidity
  setLowHumidity
  setHighHumidity
Attributes:
  pressure
```

The `HumiditySensor` has no responsibility for calculating its trend and is therefore not a subclass of `TrendSensor`.

A review of the system's requirements suggests some behavior common to the classes `TemperatureSensor`, `PressureSensor`, and `HumiditySensor`. In particular, our requirements compel us to provide a means of reporting the highest and lowest values of each of these sensors during a 24-hour period. We might capture this behavior in the following specification, common to all three classes:

```
Responsibilities:
  Report the highest and lowest value over a 24-hour period.
Operations:
  highValue
  lowValue
  timeOfHighValue
  timeOfLowValue
```

We defer deciding how to carry out this responsibility, because that is an issue of design, not analysis. However, because this behavior is common to all three sensor classes, our analysis suggests the invention of a common superclass, which we call `HistorySensor`, responsible for providing this common behavior. `HumiditySensor` is a direct subclass of `HistorySensor`, as is `TrendSensor`, which serves as an intermediate abstract class, bridging our abstractions of `HistorySensor` and the concrete classes `TemperatureSensor` and `PressureSensor`.

Our abstraction of the wind-speed sensor can be expressed in the following specification:

```
Name:
  WindSpeedSensor
Responsibilities:
  Keep track of the current wind speed.
Operations:
  currentSpeed
  setLowSpeed
  setHighSpeed
Attributes:
  speed
```

Our requirements suggest that we cannot detect the current wind speed directly; rather, we must calculate its value by taking the number of revolutions of the cups on the boom, dividing by the interval over which those revolutions were counted, and then applying a scaling value appropriate to the particular boom assembly. Needless to say, this calculation is one of the secrets of this class; clients could care less how `currentSpeed` is calculated, as long as this operation satisfies its contract and delivers meaningful values.

A quick domain analysis of the last four concrete classes (`TemperatureSensor`, `PressureSensor`, `HumiditySensor`, and `WindSpeedSensor`) reveals yet another behavior in common: each of these classes knows how to calibrate itself by providing a linear interpolation against two known data points. Rather than replicating this behavior in all four classes, we instead choose to make this behavior the responsibility of an even higher superclass, which we call `CalibratingSensor`, whose specification includes the following:

```
Responsibilities:
  Provide a linear interpolation of values, given two known data points.
Operations:
  currentValue
  setHighValue
  setLowValue
```

`CalibratingSensor` is an immediate superclass of `HistoricalSensor`.[*]

Our final concrete sensor for wind direction is a bit different, because it requires neither calibration nor history. We may express our abstraction of this entity in the following specification:

```
Name:
  WindDirectionSensor
Responsibilities:
  Keep track of the current wind direction, in terms of points along a compass rose.
Operations:
  currentDirection
Attributes:
  direction
```

---

[*] This hierarchy passes our litmus test for inheritance: a `TemperatureSensor` is a kind of `TrendSensor`, which is also a kind of `HistoricalSensor`, which in turn is a kind of `CalibratingSensor`.

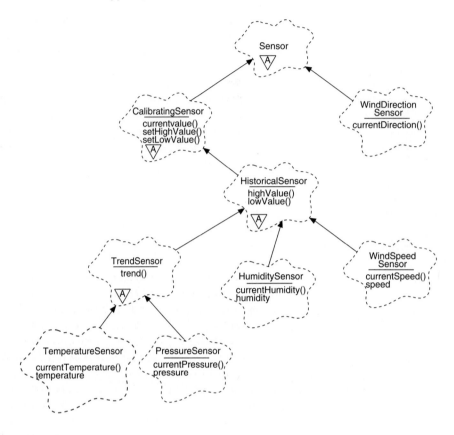

Figure 8-4
Sensor Class Hierarchy

To unify our sensor abstractions, we generate the abstract base class Sensor, which serves as the immediate superclass to both the classes WindDirectionSensor and CalibratingSensor. Figure 8-4 illustrates this complete hierarchy.

Although not part of the sensor hierarchy, our abstraction of the keypad for user input has a simple specification:

```
Name:
  Keypad
Responsibilities:
  Keep track of the last user input.
Operations:
  lastKeyPress
Attributes:
  key
```

Notice that this class has no knowledge of the meaning of any particular key: instances of this class only know that one of several keys was pressed. We delegate responsibility for interpreting the meaning of these keys to a different

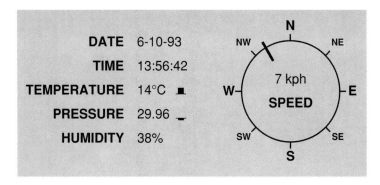

Figure 8-5
Weather Monitoring System Display

class, which we will identify when we apply these concrete boundary classes to our scenarios.

Our abstraction of an LCDDevice class serves to insulate our software from the particular hardware we might use. For workstations and personal computers, there have emerged widespread (albeit conflicting) standards for graphics programming, such as programmatic interfaces for Motif and Microsoft Windows. Unfortunately, for embedded controllers, no such common standards prevail. To decouple our software from the particular graphics hardware we might use, our analysis leads us to prototype some common displays for the weather monitoring system, and then determine our interface needs.

Figure 8-5 provides such a prototype. Here, we have omitted the display of wind chill and dew point as our requirements demand, as well as details such as how to display the 24-hour high or low value of primary measurements. Nonetheless, some patterns emerge: we only need to display text (in two different sizes and two different styles), circles, and lines (of varying thickness). Additionally, we note that some elements of our display are static (such as the label TEMPERATURE), while others are dynamic (such as the wind direction). We choose to display both static and dynamic elements via software. In this manner, we lessen the burden on our hardware by eliminating the need for special labels on the LCD itself, but require slightly more of our software.

We can translate these requirements into the following class specification:

```
Name:
  LCDDevice
Responsibilities:
  Manage the LCD device and provide services for displaying certain graphics elements.
Operations:
  drawText
  drawLine
  drawCircle
  setTextSize
  setTextStyle
  setPenSize
```

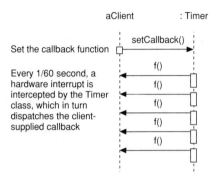

Figure 8-6
Timer Interaction Diagram

As with the class `Keypad`, the class `LCDDevice` has no knowledge of the meaning of the elements it manipulates. Instances of this class know only how to display text and lines, but do not know what these figures represent. This separation of concerns leaves us with loosely coupled abstractions (which is what we desire), but it does require that we find some agent responsible for mediating between the raw sensors and the display. We defer the invention of this new abstraction until we study some scenarios applicable to this system.

The final boundary class we need to consider is that of the timer. We will make the simplifying assumption that there is exactly one timer per system, whose behavior is to interrupt the computer ever 1/60 of a second and in so doing, invoke an interrupt service routine. Now, this is a particularly grungy detail, and it would be best if we could hide this implementation detail from the rest of our software abstractions. We can do so by devising a class that uses a callback function and that exports only static members (so that we constrain our system to have exactly one timer).

Figure 8-6 provides an interaction diagram that illustrates a use case for this abstraction. Here we see how the timer and its client collaborate: the client begins by supplying a callback function, and every 0.1 second, the timer calls that function. In this manner, we decouple the client from knowing about how to intercept timed events, and decouple the timer from knowing what to do when such an event occurs. The primary responsibility that this protocol places upon the client is simply that the execution of its callback function must always take less then 0.1 second, otherwise, the timer will miss an event.

By intercepting time events, the `Timer` class serves as an active abstraction, meaning that it is at the root of a thread of control. We may express our abstraction of this class in the following specification:

```
Name:
  Timer
Responsibilities:
  Intercept all timed events and dispatch a callback function accordingly.
Operations:
  setCallback()
```

Scenarios

Now that we have established the abstractions at the boundaries of our system, we continue our analysis by studying several scenarios of its use. We begin by enumerating a number of primary use cases, as viewed from the clients of this system:

- Monitoring basic weather measurements including wind speed and direction, temperature, barometric pressure, and humidity.
- Monitoring derived measurements including wind chill, dew point, temperature trend, and barometric pressure trend.
- Displaying the highest and lowest value of a selected measurement.
- Setting the time and date.
- Calibration of a selected sensor.
- Powering up the system.

We add to this list two secondary use cases:

- Power failure.
- Sensor failure.

Let's examine a number of these scenarios in order to illuminate the behavior – but not the design – of the system.

Monitoring basic weather measurements is the principle function point of the weather monitoring system. One of our system constraints is that we cannot take measurements any faster than 60 times a second. Fortunately, most interesting weather conditions change much more slowly. Our analysis suggests that the following sampling rates are sufficient to capture changing conditions:

- Every 0.1 second   wind direction
- Every 0.5 seconds   wind speed
- Every 5 minutes   temperature, barometric pressure, and humidity

Earlier, we decided that the classes representing each primary sensor should have no responsibility for dealing with timed events. Our analysis therefore requires that we devise an external agent that collaborates with these sensors to carry out this scenario. For the moment, we will defer our specification of the behavior of this agent (how it knows when to initiate a sample is an issue of design, not analysis). The interaction diagram in Figure 8-7 illustrates this scenario. Here, we see that when the agent begins sampling, it polls each sensor in turn, but intentionally skips certain sensors in order to sample them at a slower rate. By polling each sensor rather than letting each sensor act as a

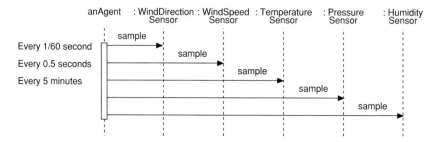

Figure 8-7
Scenario for Monitoring Basic Measurements

thread of control, the execution of our system is more predictable, because our agent can control the flow of events. Because this name reflects its place in the behavior of the system, we will make this agent an instance of the class Sampler.

We must continue this scenario by asking which of these objects in the interaction diagram is then responsible for displaying the sampled values on the one instance of our LCDDevice class. Ultimately, we have one of two choices: we can have each sensor be responsible for displaying itself (the common pattern used in MVC-like architectures), or we can have a separate object be responsible for this behavior. For this particular problem, we choose the latter, because it allows us to encapsulate all our design decisions about the layout of our display in one class.* Thus, we add the following class specification to our products of analysis:

```
Name:
  DisplayManager
Responsibilities:
  Manage layout or items on the LCD device.
Operations:
  drawStaticItems
  displayTime
  displayDate
  displayTemperature
  displayHumidity
  displayPressure
  displayWindChill
  displayDewPoint
  displayWindSpeed
  displayWindDirection
  displayHighLow
```

---

* The dominant problem here is *where* we display each item, not *how* each item looks. Because this is a decision that is likely to change (and we do not assume the existence of any general resource management mechanism as is common for GUIs such as Motif and Windows), it is best for us to encapsulate in one class all the knowledge about where to display each item on the LCD device. Changing our assumptions about front panel layout therefore requires that we only touch one class instead of many.

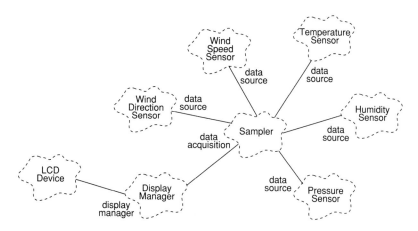

Figure 8-8
Sample and Display Classes

The operation `drawStaticItems` exists to draw the unchangeable parts of the display, such as the compass rose used for indicating the wind direction. We will also assume that the operations `displayTemperature` and `displayPressure` are responsible for displaying their corresponding trends (therefore, as we move into implementation, we must provide a suitable signature for these operations).

Figure 8-8 provides a class diagram illustrating the abstractions that must collaborate to carry out this scenario. Note that we also indicate the role that each abstraction plays in its association with other classes.

There is one important side effect from our decision to include the class `DisplayManager`.[*] Specifically, internationalizing our software, that is, adapting it to different countries and languages, becomes much easier given this design decision, because the knowledge about how elements are named (such as `TEMPERATURE` or `SPEED`) is part of the secrets of this one class.

Internationalization leads us to consider an issue about which the requirements are silent: should the system display temperature in Centigrade or Fahrenheit? Similarly, should the system display wind speed in kilometers per hour (KPH) or miles per hour (MPH)? Ultimately, our software should not constrain us. Because we seek end-user flexibility, we must add an operation `setMode` to both the classes `TemperatureSensor` and `WindSpeedSensor`. We must also add a new responsibility to each of these classes, which makes their instances construct themselves in a known stable state. Finally, we must modify the signature of the operation `DisplayManager::drawStaticItems` accordingly, so that when

---

[*] Is this an analysis decision or a design decision? The question can be argued in either direction, although such arguments are largely academic in the face of having to deliver production software. If a decision advances our understanding of the system's desired behavior and in addition leads us to an elegant architecture, then we don't really care what it is called.

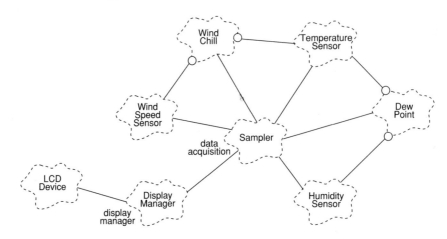

Figure 8-9
Derived Measurements

we change units of measurement, the display manager can update the front panel display if need be.

This discovery leads us to add one more scenario for consideration in our analysis, namely:

- Setting the unit of measurement for temperature and wind speed.

We will defer considering this scenario until we study the other use cases that deal with user interaction.

Monitoring the derived measurements for temperature and pressure trends can be achieved through the protocol we have already established for the classes TemperatureSensor and PressureSensor. However, to complete this scenario for all derived measurements, we are now led to discover two new classes, which we call WindChill and DewPoint, responsible for calculating their respective values. Neither of these abstractions represent sensors, because they do not denote any tangible device in the system. Rather, each one acts as an agent that collaborates with two other classes to carry out its responsibilities. Specifically, the class WindChill conspires with the classes TemperatureSensor and WindSpeedSensor, and the class DewPoint conspires with the classes TemperatureSensor and HumiditySensor. In turn, the classes WindChill and DewPoint collaborate with the class Sampler, using the same mechanism as Sampler uses to monitor all the primary weather measurements. Figure 8-9 illustrates the classes involved in this scenario; basically, this class diagram is just a slightly different view of the system than the one shown in Figure 8-8.

Why do we define WindChill and DewPoint as classes, instead of just carrying out their calculation through a simple nonmember function? The answer is that this situation passes our litmus test for object-oriented abstractions: instances of both WindChill and DewPoint provide some behavior (namely, the calculation of their respective values), encapsulate some state (each must maintain an association with a particular instance of two different concrete sensors), and each has a unique identity (each particular wind-speed sensor/temperature sensor association must have its own WindChill object). By "objectifying" these seemingly algorithmic abstractions, we also end up with a more reusable architecture: both WindChill and DewPoint can be lifted from this particular application, because each presents a clear contract to its clients, and each offers a clear separation of concerns relative to all the other abstractions.

Moving on, we next consider the various scenarios that relate to user interaction with the weather monitoring system. Deciding upon the proper user gestures for interacting with an embedded controller such as this one is still as much of an art as is designing a graphical user interface. A full treatment of how to devise such user interfaces is beyond the scope of this text, but the basic message for the software analyst is that prototyping works, and indeed is fundamental in helping to mitigate the risks involved in user-interface design. Furthermore, by implementing our decisions in terms of an object-oriented architecture, we make it relatively easy to change these user-interface decisions without rending the fabric of our design.

Consider some possible scripts that storyboard scenarios of user interaction:

Displaying the highest and lowest value of a selected measurement.
1. User presses the SELECT key.
2. System displays SELECTING.
3. User presses any one of the keys WIND SPEED, TEMPERATURE, PRESSURE or HUMIDITY; any other key press (except RUN) is ignored.
4. System flashes the corresponding label.
5. User presses the UP or DOWN key to select display of the highest or lowest 24-hour value, respectively; any other key press (except RUN) is ignored.
6. System displays the selected value, together with its time of occurrence.
7. Control passes back to step 3 or 5.
Note: the user may press the RUN key to commit or abandon the operation, at which time the flashing display, the selected value, and the SELECTING message are removed.

This scenario leads us to enhance the class DisplayManager by adding the both the operations flashLabel (which causes the identified label to flash or stop flashing, according to an appropriate operation argument) and displayMode (which displays a text message on the LCD device).

Setting the time and date follows a similar scenario:

Setting the time and date.
1. User presses the SELECT key.
2. System displays SELECTING.
3. User presses any one of the keys TIME or DATE; any other key press (except RUN and the keys listed in step 3 of the previous scenario) is ignored.
4. System flashes the corresponding label; display also flashes the first field of the selected item (namely, the hours field for the time and the month field for the date).
5. User presses the LEFT or RIGHT keys to select another field (selection wraps around); user presses the UP or DOWN keys to raise or lower the value of the selected field.
6. Control passes back to step 3 or 5.
Note: the user may press the RUN key to commit or abandon the operation, at which time the flashing display and the SELECTING message are removed, and the time or date are reset.

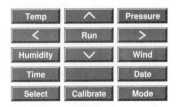

Figure 8-10
Weather Monitoring System User Keypad

Calibrating a particular sensor follows a related pattern of user gestures:

```
Calibrating a sensor.
  1. User presses the CALIBRATE key.
  2. System displays CALIBRATING.
  3. User presses any one of the keys WIND SPEED, TEMPERATURE, PRESSURE or HUMIDITY; any other
     key press (except RUN) is ignored.
  4. System flashes the corresponding label.
  5. User presses the UP or DOWN keys to select the high or low calibration point.
  6. Display flashes the corresponding value.
  7. User presses the UP or DOWN keys to adjust the selected value.
  8. Control passes back to step 3 or 8.
  Note: the user may press the RUN key to commit or abandon the operation, at which
        time the flashing display and the CALIBRATING message are removed, and the calibration
        function is reset.
```

While calibrating, instances of the class Sampler must be told to not sample the selected item, otherwise, erroneous information would be displayed to the user. This scenario therefore requires that we introduce two new operations for the class Sampler, namely inhibitSample and resumeSample, both of which have a signature that specifies a particular measurement.

Our last primary scenario involving the user interface concerns setting units of measurement:

```
Setting the unit of measurement for temperature and wind speed.
  1. User presses the MODE key.
  2. System displays MODE.
  3. User presses any one of the keys WIND SPEED or TEMPERATURE; any other key press (except
     RUN) is ignored.
  4. System flashes the corresponding label.
  5. User presses the UP or DOWN keys to toggle the current unit of measurement.
  6. System updates the unit of measurement for the selected item.
  7. Control passes back to step 3 or 5.
  Note: the user may press the RUN key to commit or abandon the operation, at which
        time the flashing display and the MODE message are removed, and the current unit of
        measurement for the item is set.
```

A study of these scenarios leads us to decide upon an arrangement for buttons on the keypad (a system decision), which we illustrate in Figure 8-10.

Each of these user interface scenarios involves some form of modality or event-ordered behavior, and so is well suited to expression through the use of state transition diagrams. Because these scenarios are so tightly coupled, we

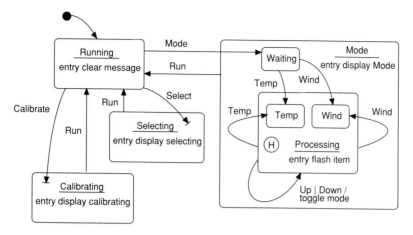

Figure 8-11
InputManager State Transition Diagram

choose to devise a new class, `InputManager`, which is responsible for carrying out the following contractual specification:

```
Name:
  InputManager
Responsibilities:
  Manage and dispatch user input.
Operations:
  processKeyPress
```

The sole operation, `processKeyPress`, animates the state machine that lives behind instances of this class.

As we see in Figure 8-11, the outermost state transition diagram for this class encompasses four states: `Running`, `Calibrating`, `Selecting`, and `Mode`. These states correspond directly to the earlier scenarios. We transition to the respective states based upon the first key press intercepted while `Running`, and we return to the `Running` state when the last key press is again `Run`. Each time we enter `Running`, we clear the message on the display.

We have expanded the `Mode` state to show how we might more formally express the dynamic semantics of our scenario. As we first enter this state, our entry action is to display an appropriate message on the display. We begin in the `Waiting` state, and transition out of this state if we intercept a user key press of the `Temperature` or `Wind Speed` keys, which causes us to enter a nested state of `Processing`, or a user key press of `Run`, which transitions us back to the outermost `Running` state. Each time we enter `Processing`, we flash the appropriate item; in subsequent entries to this state, we enter the previously entered nested state, `Temp` or `Wind`.

While in the `Temp` or `Wind` state, we may intercept one of five key presses: `Up` or `Down` (which toggles the corresponding mode), `Temp` or `Wind` (which reenters the appropriate nested state) or `Run` (which ejects us from the outer `Mode` state).

The `Selecting` and `Calibrating` states similarly expand out to reveal more nested states. We will not show their expanded state transition diagrams here, because their presentation does not reveal anything particularly interesting about the problem at hand.[*]

Our final primary scenario involves powering up the system, which requires that we bring all of its objects to life in an orderly fashion, ensuring that each one starts in a stable initial state. We may write a script for our analysis of this scenario as follows:

```
Powering up the system
   1. Power is applied.
   2. Each sensor is constructed; historical sensors clear their history, and trend sensors
      prime their slope-calculating algorithms.
   3. The user input buffer is initialized, causing garbage key presses (due to noise upon
      power up) to be discarded.
   4. The static elements of the display are drawn.
   5. The sampling process is initiated.
Postconditions: The past high/low values of each primary measurement is set to the value and
                   time of their first sample.
                The temperature and pressure trends are flat.
                The InputManager is in the Running state.
```

Notice the use of postconditions in our script to specify the expected state of the system after this scenario completes. As we shall see, there is no one agent in the system that carries out this scenario; rather, this behavior results from the collaboration of a number of objects, each of which is given the responsibility to bring itself to a stable initial state.

This completes our study of the weather monitoring system's primary scenarios. To be utterly complete, we might want to walk through the various secondary scenarios. At this point, however, we have exposed a sufficient number of the system's function points, and we want to proceed with architectural design, so that we might begin to validate our strategic decisions.

8.2 Design

Architectural Framework

Every software system needs to have a simple yet powerful organizational philosophy (think of it as the software equivalent of a sound bite that describes the system's architecture), and the weather monitoring system is no exception. The next step in our development process is to articulate this architectural framework, so that we might have a stable foundation upon which to evolve the system's function points.

---

[*] Of course, for a production product, a comprehensive analysis would complete the exposition of this state transition diagram. We can defer this task here, because it is more tedious than not, and in fact does not reveal anything we do not already know about the system under construction.

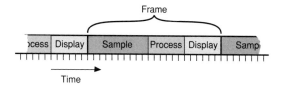

Figure 8-12
Time-Frame Processing

In data acquisition and process-control domains, there are many possible architectural patterns we might follow, but the two most common alternatives involve either the synchronization of autonomous actors or time-frame-based processing.

In the first pattern, our architecture encompasses a number of relatively independent objects, each of which serves as a thread of control. For example, we might invent several new sensor objects that build upon more primitive hardware/software abstractions, with each such object responsible for taking its own sample and reporting back to some central agent that processes these samples. This architecture has its merits; it is about the only meaningful framework if we have a distributed system in which we must collect samples from many remote locations. This architecture also allows for more local optimization of the sampling process (each sampling actor has the knowledge to adjust itself to changing conditions, perhaps by increasing or decreasing its sampling rate as conditions warrant).

However, this architectural pattern is generally not well suited to hard-real-time systems, wherein we must have complete predictability over when events take place. Now, the weather monitoring system is not hard-real-time, but it does require some modicum of predictable, ordered behavior. For this reason, we turn to an alternative pattern, that of time-frame-based processing.

As we illustrate in Figure 8-12, this model takes time and divides it into several (usually fixed-length) frames, which we further divide into subframes, each of which encompasses some functional behavior. The activity from one frame to another may be different. For example, we might sample the wind direction every 10 frames, but sample the wind speed only every 30 frames.[*] The primary merit of this architectural pattern is that we can more rigorously control the order of events.

Figure 8-13 provides a class diagram that expresses this architecture for the weather monitoring system. Here we find most of the classes we discovered earlier during analysis, the main difference here being that we now show how all the key abstractions collaborate with one another. As is typical in class diagrams for production systems, we do not (and cannot) show every class and

---

[*] For example, if each frame is allocated to be 1/60 second, 30 frames represents 0.5 second.

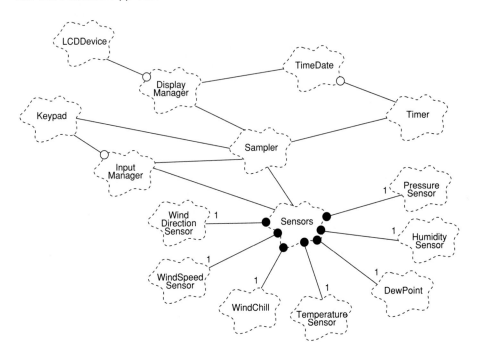

Figure 8-13
Weather Monitoring System Architecture

every relationship. For example, we have omitted the class hierarchy regarding all of the sensors.

We have invented one new class in this architecture, namely the class Sensors, whose responsibility is to serve as the collection of all the physical sensors in the system. Because at least two other agents in the system (Sampler and InputManager) must associate with the entire collection of sensors, bundling them in one container class allows us to treat our system's sensors as a logical whole.

Frame Mechanism

The central behavior of this architecture is carried out by a collaboration of the Sampler and Timer classes, and so we would be wise during architectural design to concretely prototype these classes, so that we might validate our assumptions.

We begin by refining the interface of the class Timer which dispatches a callback function. We may express these design decisions in the following C++ class declarations. First, we introduce a typedef that allows us to name clock ticks in the vocabulary of our problem space:

```
// Clock ticks, measures in 1/60 second
typedef unsigned int Tick;
```

Next, we present the Timer class:

```
class Timer {
public:

  static setCallback(void (*)(Tick));
  static startTiming();

  static Tick numberOfTicks();

private:
  ...
};
```

This is an unusual class, but remember that it holds some unusual secrets. We use the first member function setCallback to attach a callback function to the timer. We launch the timer's behavior by invoking startTiming, after which time the one Timer entity dispatches the callback function every 1/60 of a second. Notice that we introduce an explicit starting operation, because we cannot rely upon any particular implementation-dependent ordering in the elaboration of declarations.

Before we turn to the Sampler class, we introduce a new declaration that serves to name the various sensors in this particular system:

```
// Enumeration of sensor names
enum SensorName {Direction, Speed, WindChill, Temperature, DewPoint, Humidity, Pressure};
```

We may express the interface of the Sampler class as follows:

```
class Sampler {
public:

  Sampler();
  ~Sampler();

  void setSamplingRate(SensorName, Tick);
  void sample(Tick);

  Tick samplingRate() const;

protected:
  ...
};
```

We have introduced the modifier setSamplingRate and its selector samplingRate so that clients can dynamically alter the behavior of the sampling objects.

To tie the Timer and Sampler classes together, we just need a little bit of glue code. First we declare an instance of Sampler and a nonmember function:

```
Sampler sampler;

void acquire(Tick t)
{
  sampler.sample(t);
}
```

And now we can write a fragment of our main function, which simply attaches the callback function to the timer and starts the sampling process:

```
main() {

  Timer::setCallback(acquire);
  Timer::startTiming();

  while(1) {
    ;
  }

  return 0;

}
```

This is a fairly typical main program for object-oriented systems: it is short (because the real work is delegated to key objects in the system), and it involves a dispatch loop (which in this case does nothing, because we have no background processing to complete).*

To continue this thread of the system's architecture, we next provide an interface for the class Sensors. For the moment, we assume the existence of the various concrete sensor classes:

```
class Sensors : protected Collection {
public:

  Sensors();
  virtual ~Sensors();

  void addSensor(const Sensor& SensorName, unsigned int id = 0);

  unsigned int numberOfSensors() const;
  unsigned int numberOfSensors(SensorName);
  Sensor& sensor(SensorName, unsigned int id = 0);

protected:
  ...
};
```

This is basically a collection class, and for this reason we make Sensors a subclass of the foundation class Collection.** We make Collection a protected superclass, because we don't want to expose most of its operations to clients of the Sensors class. Our declaration of Sensors provides only a sparse set of operations, because our problem is sufficiently constrained that we know sensors are only added and never removed from the collection.

We have invented a generalized sensor collection class that can hold multiple instances of the same kind of sensor, with each instance within its class distinguished by a unique id, numbered starting at zero.

---

* This is yet another common architectural pattern: dispatch loops appear in most GUI systems, wherein the loop serves to intercept external or internal events and then dispatch them to the appropriate agents.
** Foundation classes are discussed in detail in the following chapter.

We must revise our specification of the `Sampler` class in order to carry out its association with the `Sensors` and `DisplayManager` classes:

```
class Sampler {
public:

  Sampler(Sensors&, DisplayManager&);

  ...
protected:
  Sensors& repSensors;
  DisplayManager& repDisplayManager;
};
```

We must also revise our declaration of the one instance of the `Sampler` class:

```
Sensors sensors;
DisplayManager display;

Sampler sampler(sensors, display);
```

The construction of the `sampler` object connects this agent with the specific collection of sensors and the particular display manager used in the system.

Now, we can implement the `Sampler` class's key operation, `sample`:

```
void Sampler::sample(Tick t)
{
  for (SensorName name = Direction; name <= Pressure; name++)
    for (unsigned int id = 0; id < repSensors.numberOfSensors(name); id++)
      if (!(t % samplingRate(name)))
        repDisplayManager.display(repSensors.sensor(name, id).currentValue(), name, id);
}
```

The action of this member function is to iterate through each kind of sensor and, in turn, each unique sensor of that kind in the collection. For each sensor it encounters, `sample` checks to see if it is time to sample its value and if so, references the sensor from the collection, takes its current value, and delivers this value to the display manager associated with the `Sampler` instance.[*]

The semantics of this operation relies upon the polymorphic behavior of one operation, namely:

```
virtual float currentValue();
```

defined for the base class `Sensor`. This operation also relies upon the following operation:

```
void display(float, SensorName, unsigned int id = 0);
```

defined for the class `DisplayManager`.

---

[*] An alternate approach would be to have each sensor provide a member function that returns its sampling rate and another member function that draws the sensor on the LCD. This design would make the implementation of the **Sampler** class simpler and more extensible, although it would shift more responsibilities to the sensor classes.

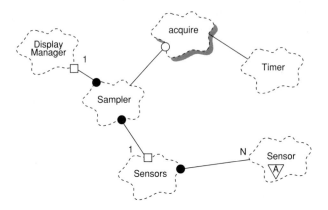

Figure 8-14
Frame Mechanism

Now that we have refined this element of our architecture, we present a new class diagram in Figure 8-14 that highlights this frame mechanism.

8.3 Evolution

Release Planning

Now that we have validated our architecture by walking through several scenarios, we can proceed with the incremental development of the system's function points. We start this process by proposing a sequence of releases, each of which builds upon the previous release:

- Develop a minimal functionality release, which monitors just one sensor.
- Complete the sensor hierarchy.
- Complete the classes responsible for managing the display.
- Complete the classes responsible for managing the user interface.

We could have ordered these releases in just about any manner, but we choose this one in order of highest to lowest risk, thereby forcing our development process to directly attack the hard problems first.

Developing the minimal functionality release forces us to take a vertical slice through our architecture, and implement small parts of just about every key abstraction. This activity addresses the highest risk in the project, namely, whether we have the right abstractions with the right roles and responsibilities. This activity also gives us early feedback, because we can now play with an executable system. Indeed, as we discussed in Chapter 7, forcing early closure like this has a number of technical and social benefits. On the technical side, it forces us to begin to bolt the hardware and software parts of our system together, thereby identifying any impedance mismatches early. On the social side, it allows us to get early feedback about the look and feel of the system, from the perspective of real users.

Because completing this release is largely a manner of tactical implementation (the so-called daily blocking and tackling that every development team must do), we will not bother with exposing any more of its structure. However, we will now turn to elements of later releases, because they reveal some interesting insights about the development process.

Sensor Mechanism

In inventing the architecture for this system, we have already seen how we had to iteratively and incrementally evolve our abstraction of the sensor classes, which we began during analysis. In this evolutionary release, we expect to build upon the earlier completion of a minimal functional system, and finish the details of this class hierarchy.

At this point in our development cycle, the class hierarchy we first presented in Figure 8-4 remains stable, although, not surprisingly, we had to adjust the location of certain polymorphic operations, in order to extract greater commonality. Specifically, in an earlier section we noted the requirement for the `currentValue` operation, declared in the abstract base class `Sensor`. We may complete our design of this class by writing the following C++ declaration:

```
class Sensor {
public:

  Sensor(SensorName, unsigned int id = 0);
  virtual ~Sensor();

  virtual float currentValue() = 0;
  virtual float rawValue() = 0;

  SensorName name() const;
  unsigned int id() const;

protected:
  ...
};
```

This is an abstract class because it includes pure virtual member functions.

Notice that through the class constructor, we gave the instances of this class knowledge of their name and id. This is essentially a kind of runtime type identification, but providing this information in unavoidable here, because per the requirements, each sensor instance must have a mapping to a particular memory-mapped I/O address. We can hide the secrets of this mapping by making this address a function of a sensor name and id.

Now that we have added this new responsibility, we can now go back and simplify the signature of `DisplayManager::display` to take only a single argument, namely, a reference to a `Sensor` object. We can eliminate the other arguments to this member function, because the display manager can now ask the sensor object its name and id.

Making this change is advisable, because it simplifies certain cross-class interfaces. Indeed, if we fail to keep up with small, rippling changes such as this one, then our architecture will eventually suffer software rot, wherein the protocols among collaborating classes becomes inconsistently applied.

The declaration of the immediate subclass `CalibratingSensor` builds upon this base class:

```
class CalibratingSensor : public Sensor {
public:

  CalibratingSensor(SensorName, unsigned int id = 0);
  virtual ~CalibratingSensor();

  void setHighValue(float, float);
  void setLowValue(float, float);

  virtual float currentValue();
  virtual float rawValue() = 0;

protected:
  ...
};
```

This class introduces two new operations (`setHighValue` and `setLowValue`), and implements the previously declared pure function `currentValue`.

Next, consider the declaration of the subclass `HistoricalSensor`, which builds upon the class `CalibratingSensor`:

```
class HistoricalSensor : public CalibratingSensor {
public:

  HistoricalSensor(SensorName, unsigned int id = 0);
  virtual ~HistoricalSensor();

  float highValue() const;
  float lowValue() const;
  const char* timeOfHighValue() const;
  const char* timeOfLowValue() const;

protected:
  ...
};
```

This class introduces four new operations, whose implementation requires collaboration with the `TimeDate` class. Note that `HistoricalSensor` is still an abstract class, because we have not yet completed the definition of the pure virtual function `rawValue`, which we defer to be a concrete subclass responsibility.

The class `TrendSensor` inherits from `HistoricalSensor`, and adds one new responsibility:

```
class TrendSensor : public HistoricalSensor {
public:

  TrendSensor(SensorName, unsigned int id = 0);
  virtual ~TrendSensor();

  float trend() const;

protected:
  ...
};
```

This class introduces one new member function. As with some of the other new operations that certain intermediate classes have added, we declare trend as non-virtual, because we do not desire that subclasses change their behavior.

Ultimately, we reach concrete subclasses such as TemperatureSensor:

```
class TemperatureSensor : public TrendSensor {
public:

  TemperatureSensor(unsigned int id = 0);
  virtual ~TemperatureSensor();

  virtual float rawValue();
  float currentTemperature();

protected:
  ...
};
```

Notice that the signature of this class's constructor is slightly different than its superclasses, simply because at this level of abstraction, we know the specific name of the class. Also, notice that we have introduced the operation currentTemperature, which follows from our earlier analysis. This operation is semantically the same as the polymorphic function currentValue, but we choose to include both of them, because the operation currentTemperature is slightly more type-safe.

Once we have successfully completed the implementation of all classes in this hierarchy and integrated them with the previous release, we may proceed to the next level of the system's functionality.

Display Mechanism

Implementing the next release, which completes the functionality of the classes DisplayManager and LCDDevice, requires virtually no new design work, just some tactical decisions about the signature and semantics of certain member functions. Combining the decisions we made during analysis with our first architectural prototype, wherein we made some important decisions about the protocol for displaying sensor values, we derive the following concrete interface in C++:

```
class DisplayManager {
public:

  DisplayManager();
  ~DisplayManager();

  void clear();
  void refresh();
  void display(Sensor&);
  void drawStaticItems(TemperatureScale, SpeedScale);
  void displayTime(const char*);
  void displayDate(const char*);
  void displayTemperature(float, unsigned int id = 0);
  void displayHumidity(float, unsigned int id = 0);
  void display Pressure(float, unsigned int id = 0);
  void displayWindChill(float, unsigned int id = 0);
  void displayDewPoint(float, unsigned int id = 0);
  void displayWindSpeed(float, unsigned int id = 0);
  void displayWindDirection(unsigned int, unsigned int id = 0);
  void displayHighLow(float, const char*, SensorName, unsigned int id = 0);
  void setTemperatureScale(TemperatureScale);
  void setSpeedScale(SpeedScale);

protected:
  // ...
};
```

None of these operations are virtual, because we neither expect nor desire any subclasses.

Notice that this class exports several primitive operations (such as `displayTime` and `refresh`), but also exposes the composite operation `display`, whose presence greatly simplifies the action of clients who must interact with instances of the `DisplayManager`.

The `DisplayManager` ultimately uses the resources of the class `LCDDevice`, which as we described earlier, serves as a skin over the underlying hardware. In this manner, the `DisplayManager` raises our level of abstraction by providing a protocol that speaks more directly to the nature of the problem space.

User-Interface Mechanism

The focus of our last major release is the tactical design and implementation of the classes `Keypad` and `InputManager`. Similar to the `LCDDevice` class, the class `KeyPad` serves as a skin over the underlying hardware, which thereby relieves the `InputManager` of the nasty details of talking directly to the hardware. Decoupling these two abstractions also makes it far easier to replace the physical input device without destabilizing our architecture.

We start with a declaration that names the physical keys in the vocabulary of our problem space:

```
enum Key {kRun, kSelect, kCalibrate, kMode,
          kUp, kDown, kLeft, kRight,
          kTemperature, kPressure, kHumidity, kWind, kTime, kDate, kUnassigned};
```

We use the `k` prefix to avoid name clashes with literals defined in `SensorName`.

Continuing, we may capture our abstraction of the `Keypad` class as follows:

```
class Keypad {
public:

  Keypad();
  ~Keypad();

  int inputPending() const;
  Key lastKeyPress() const;

protected:
  ...
};
```

The protocol of this class derives from our earlier analysis. We have added the operation `inputPending` so that clients can query if user input exists that has not yet been processed.

The class `InputManager` has a similarly sparse interface:

```
class InputManager {
public:

  InputManager(Keypad&);
  ~InputManager();

  void processKeyPress();

protected:
  Keypad& repKeypad;
};
```

As we will see, most of the interesting work of this class is carried out in the implementation of its finite state machine.

As we illustrated in Figure 8-13, instances of the class `Sampler`, `InputManager`, and `Keypad` collaborate to respond to user input. To integrate these three abstractions, we must subtly modify the interface of the class `Sampler` to include a new member object, `repInputManager`:

```
class Sampler {
public:

  Sampler(Sensors&, DisplayManager&, InputManager&);

  ...

protected:
  Sensors& repSensors;
  DisplayManager& repDisplayManager;
  InputManager& repInputManager;
};
```

Through this design decision, we establish an association among instances of the classes `Sensors`, `DisplayManager`, and `InputManager` at the time we construct an instance of `Sampler`. By using references, we assert that instances of `Sampler` must always have a collection of sensors, a display manager, and an input manager.

An alternate representation that used pointers would provide a looser association by allowing a `Sampler` to omit one or more of its components.

We must also incrementally modify the implementation of the key member function `Sampler::sample`

```
void Sampler::sample(Tick t)
{
  repInputManager.processKeyPress();
  for (SensorName name = Direction; name <= Pressure; name++)
    for (unsigned int id = 0; id < repSensors.numberOfSensors(name); id++)
      if (!(t % samplingRate(name)))
        repDisplayManager.display(repSensors.sensor(name, id));
}
```

Here we have added an invocation to `processKeyPress` at the beginning of every time frame.

The operation `processKeyPress` is the entry point to the finite state machine that drives the instances of this class. Ultimately, there are two approaches we can take to implement this or any other finite state machine: we can explicitly represent states as objects (and thereby depend upon their polymorphic behavior), or we can use enumeration literals to denote each distinct state.

For modest-sized finite state machines such as the one embodied by the class `InputManager`, it is sufficient for us to use the latter approach. Thus, we might first introduce the names of the class's outermost states:

```
enum InputState {Running, Selecting, Calibrating, Mode};
```

Next, we introduce some protected helper functions:

```
class InputManager {
public:
  ...
protected:
  Keypad& repKeypad;
  InputState repState;

  void enterSelecting();
  void enterCalibrating();
  void enterMode();
};
```

Finally, we can begin to implement the state transitions we first introduced in Figure 8-11:

```
void InputManager::processKeyPress()
{
  if (repKeypad.inputPending()) {
    Key key = repKeypad.lastKeyPress();
    switch (repState) {
      case Running:
        if (key == kSelect)
          enterSelecting();
        else if (key == kCalibrate)
          enterCalibrating();
        else if (key == kMode)
          enterMode();
```

```
            break;
        case Selecting:
            ...
            break;
        case Calibrating:
            ...
            break;
        case Mode:
            ...
            break;
        }
    }
}
```

The implementation of this member function and its associated helper functions thus parallels the state transition diagram in Figure 8-11.

8.4 Maintenance

The complete implementation of this basic weather monitoring system is of modest size, encompassing only about 20 classes. However, for any truly useful piece of software, change is inevitable. Let's consider the impact of two enhancements to the architecture of this system.

Our system thus far provides for the monitoring of many interesting weather conditions, but we may soon discover that users want to measure rainfall as well. What is the impact of adding a rain gauge?

Happily, we do not have to radically alter our architecture; we must merely augment it. Using the architectural view of the system from Figure 8-13 as a baseline, to implement this new feature, we must

- Create a new class `RainFallSensor` and insert it in the proper place in the sensor class hierarchy (a `RainFallSensor` is a kind of `HistoricalSensor`).
- Update the enumeration `SensorName`.
- Update the `DisplayManager` so that it knows how to display values of this sensor.
- Update the `InputManager` so that it knows how to evaluate the newly-defined key `RainFall`.
- Properly add instances of this class to the system's `Sensors` collection.

We must deal with a few other small tactical issues needed to graft in this new abstraction, but ultimately, we need not disrupt the system's architecture nor its key mechanisms.

Let's consider a totally different kind of functionality: suppose we desire the ability to download a day's record of weather conditions to a remote computer. To implement this feature, we must make the following changes:

- Create a new class `SerialPort`, responsible for managing an RS232 port used for serial communication.

- Invent a new class `ReportManager` responsible for collecting the information required for the download. Basically, this class must use the resources of the collection class `Sensors` together with its associated concrete sensors.

- Modify the implementation of `Sampler::sample` to periodically service the serial port.

It is the mark of a well-engineered object-oriented system that making this change does not rend our existing architecture, but rather, reuses and then augments its existing mechanisms.

Further Readings

The problems of process synchronization, deadlock, livelock, and race conditions are discussed in detail in Hansen [H 1977], Ben-Ari [H 1982], and Holt et al. [H 1978]. Mellichamp [H 1983], Glass [H 1983], and Foster [H 1981] offer general references on the issues of developing real-time applications. Concurrency as viewed by the interplay of hardware and software may be found in Lorin [H 1972].

CHAPTER 9

Frameworks: Foundation Class Library

A major benefit of object-oriented programming languages such as C++ and Smalltalk is the degree of reuse that can be achieved in well-engineered systems. A high degree of reuse means that far less code must be written for each new application; consequently, that is far less code to maintain.

Ultimately, software reuse can take on many forms: we can reuse individual lines of code, specific classes, or logically related societies of classes. Reusing individual lines of code is the simplest form of reuse (what programmer has not used an editor to copy the implementation of some algorithm and paste it into another application?) but offers the fewest benefits (because the code must be replicated across applications). We can do far better when using object-oriented programming languages by taking existing classes and specializing or augmenting them through inheritance. We can achieve even greater leverage by reusing whole groups of classes organized into a framework. As we discussed in Chapter 4, a framework is a collection of classes that provide a set of services for a particular domain; a framework thus exports a number of individual classes and mechanisms that clients can use or adapt.

Frameworks may actually be domain-neutral, meaning that they apply to a wide variety of applications. General foundation class libraries, math libraries, and libraries for graphical user interfaces fall into this category. Frameworks may also be specific to a particular vertical application domain, as for hospital patient records, securities and bonds trading, general business management, and telephone switching systems. Wherever there exists a family of programs that all solve substantially similar problems, there is an opportunity for an application framework.

In this chapter, we apply object-oriented technology to the creation of a foundation class library.[*] In the previous chapter, the heart of the problem turned out to involve the issues of real-time control and the intelligent distribution of behavior among several autonomous and relatively static objects. In the current problem, two very different issues dominate: the desire for an adaptable architecture that offers a range of time and space alternatives, and the need for general mechanisms for storage management, and synchronization.

9.1 Analysis

Defining the Boundaries of the Problem

The sidebar provides the detailed requirements for this foundation class library. Unfortunately, these requirements are rather open-ended: a library that provides abstractions for all the foundation classes required by all possible applications would be huge. The task of the analyst, therefore, requires judicious pruning of the problem space, so as to leave a problem that is solvable. A problem such as this one could easily suffer from analysis paralysis, and so we must focus upon providing library abstractions and services that are of the most general use, rather than trying to make this a framework that is everything for everybody (which would likely turn out to provide nothing useful for anyone). We begin with a domain analysis, first surveying the theory of data structures and algorithms, and then harvesting abstractions found in production programs.

To pursue its theoretical underpinnings, we can seek out domain expertise, such as that reflected in the seminal work by Knuth [2], as well as by other practitioners in the field, most notably Aho, Hopcroft, and Ullman [3], Kernighan and Plauger [4], Sedgewick [5], Stubbs and Webre [6], Tenenbaum and Augenstein [7], and Wirth [8]. As we continue our study, we can collect specific instances of foundational abstractions, such as queues, stacks, and graphs, as well as algorithms for quick sorting, regular expression pattern matching, and in-order tree searching.

One discovery we make in this analysis is the clear separation of structural abstractions (such as queues, stacks, and graphs) versus algorithmic abstractions (such as sorting, pattern matching, and searching). The first category of entities are obvious candidates for classes. The second category may not at first glance seem amenable to an object-oriented decomposition. However, with the proper mind-set, we can objectify these algorithms: we will

---

[*] The framework architecture described in this chapter is that of the C++ Booch Components [1].

Foundation Class Library Requirements

This class library must provide a collection of domain-independent data structures and algorithms sufficient to cover the needs of most production-quality C++ applications. In addition, this library must be

- Complete
  The library must provide a family of classes, united by a shared interface but each employing a different representation, so that developers can select the ones with the time and space semantics most appropriate to their given application.

- Adaptable
  All platform-specific aspects must be clearly identified and isolated, so that local substitutions may be made. In particular, developers must have control over storage management policies, as well as the semantics of process synchronization.

- Efficient
  Components must be easily assembled (efficient in terms of compilation resources), must impose minimal run-time and memory overhead (efficient in execution resources), and must be more reliable than hand-built mechanisms (efficient in developer resources).

- Safe
  Each abstraction must be type-safe, so that static assumptions about the behavior of a class may be enforced by the compilation system. Exceptions should be used to identify conditions under which a class's dynamic semantics are violated; raising an exception must not corrupt the state of the object that threw the exception.

- Simple
  The library must use a clear and consistent organization that makes it easy to identify and select appropriate concrete classes.

- Extensible
  Developers must be able to add new classes independently, while at the same time preserving the architectural integrity of the framework.

This library must also be small; all things being equal, developers are much more likely to build their own class rather than reuse one that is hard to understand.

We assume the existence of C++ compilers that support both parameterized classes and exceptions. For reasons of portability, this library must not depend upon any operating system services.

devise classes whose instances are agents responsible for carrying out these actions. As we will discuss later in this chapter, by objectifying these algorithmic abstractions, we can reap the benefits of commonality by forming a generalization/specialization hierarchy.

As our first analysis decision, therefore, we choose to bound our problem by organizing our abstractions into one of two major categories:

• Structures	Contains all structural abstractions
• Tools	Contains all algorithmic abstractions

As we will see shortly, there is a "using" relationship between these two categories: certain tools build upon the more primitive services provided by some of the structures.

For the second phase of our domain analysis, we study the foundation classes used by production systems in a variety of application areas (the wider the spectrum the better). Along the way, we may discover common abstractions that overlap with that we encountered in the first phase of analysis: this is a good indication that we have discovered truly general abstractions, so we will definitely keep these within the boundary of our problem. We may also find certain domain-biased abstractions, such as currency, astronomical coordinates, and measures of mass and size. We choose to reject these abstractions for our library, because they are either difficult to generalize (such as currency), highly domain-specific (such as astronomical coordinates), or so primitive that it is hard to find compelling reason to turn them into first-class citizens (such as measures of mass and size).

On the basis of this analysis, we may settle upon the following kinds of structures:

• Bags	Collection of (possibly duplicate) items
• Collections	Indexable collection of items
• Deques	Sequence of items in which items may be added and removed from either end
• Graphs	Unrooted collection of nodes and arcs, which may contain cycles and cross-references; structural sharing is permitted
• Lists	Rooted sequence of items; structural sharing is permitted
• Maps	Dictionary of item/value pairs
• Queues	Sequence of items in which items may be added from one end and removed from the opposite end
• Rings	Sequence of items in which items may be added and removed from the top of a circular structure

- Sets   Collection of (unduplicated) items
- Stacks   Sequence of items in which items may be
                       added and removed from the same end
- Strings   Indexable sequence of items, with behaviors
                       involving the manipulation of substrings
- Trees   Rooted collection of nodes and arcs, which
                       may not contain cycles or cross-references;
                       structural sharing is permitted.

As we discussed in Chapter 4, organizing the abstractions represented by this list is a problem of classification. We choose this particular organization because it offers a clear separation of behavior among each category of abstractions.

Notice the patterns of behavior we find spanning this decomposition: some structures behave like collections (such as bags and sets), while others behave like sequences (such as deques and stacks). Also, some structures permit structural sharing (such as graphs, lists, and trees), whereas others are more monolithic, and so do not permit the structural sharing of their parts. As we will see, we can take advantage of these patterns in order to form a simpler architecture during design.

Our analysis also reveals some desirable functional variations for certain of these classes. In particular, we find the need for ordered collections, deques, and queues (the latter are often called *priority queues*).[*] Additionally, we may distinguish between directed and undirected graphs, singly and doubly linked lists, as well as binary, multiway, and AVL trees. These specialized abstractions are similar enough to one another that we choose to make them further refinements of the categorization we listed above, rather than make them separate categories of abstractions.

Although we have discovered significant patterns of common behaviors, we explicitly choose not to organize these classes into an inheritance lattice at this time. It is sufficient during analysis to articulate the roles of each of these various abstractions; deciding upon inheritance relationships at this point would be premature, so we defer this issue to architectural design.

We may also settle upon the following kinds of tools, based upon our domain analysis:

- Date/Time   Operations for manipulating date and time
- Filters   Input, process, and output transformations
- Pattern matching   Operations for searching for sequences
                       within other sequences

---

[*] Simple queues are ordered according to the order in which items are added to the queue; priority queues are ordered according to some ordering function of the items themselves.

- Searching   Operations for searching for items within structures
- Sorting   Operations for ordering structures
- Utilities   Common composite operations that build upon more primitive structural operations

There are obvious functional variations for many of these abstractions. For example, we may distinguish among many different kinds of sorting agents (such as agents responsible for quick sorting, bubble sorting, heap sorting, and so on), as well as among different kinds of searching agents (such as agents responsible for sequential searching, binary searching, and pre-, in-, and post-order tree searching. As before, we choose to defer our decisions about inheritance lattices among these abstractions.

Patterns

We have now identified the major functional elements of this library, but a heap of isolated abstractions does not constitute a framework. As Wirfs-Brock suggests, "A framework provides a model of interaction among several objects belonging to classes defined by the framework. . . . To use a framework, you first study the collaborations and responsibilities of several classes" [9]. This then is the litmus test for distinguishing frameworks from simple class lattices: a framework consists of a collection of classes together with a number of patterns of collaboration among instances of these classes.

Analysis reveals that there are a number of important patterns essential to this foundation class library, encompassing the following issues:

- Time and space semantics
- Storage management policies
- Response to exceptional conditions
- Idioms for iteration
- Synchronization in the presence of multiple threads of control

As this list suggests, the design of this foundation class library demands the delicate balance of competing technical requirements.[*] If we try to tackle these issues in complete isolation from one another, we will surely end up with little sharing of protocols, policies, or implementation. Such a naive approach will in fact lead to an abundance of concepts that will intimidate the eventual clients of this library, and so inhibit its reuse.

Consider the perspective of the developer who must use this library. What do its classes represent? How do they work together? How can they be tailored to meet domain-specific needs? Which classes are really important, and which

---

[*] Indeed, as Stroustrup observes, "designing a general library is much harder than designing an ordinary program" [10].

can be ignored? These are the questions that we must answer before we can expect developers to use this library for any nontrivial application. Fortunately, it is not necessary for the developer to comprehend the entire subtlety of a library as large as this one, just as it is not necessary to understand how a microprocessor works in order to program a computer in a high-order language. In both cases, however, the raw power of the underlying implementation can be exposed if necessary, but only if the developer is willing to absorb the additional complexity.

Consider the protocol of each abstraction in this library from the perspective of its two kinds of clients: the clients that use an abstraction by declaring instances of it and then manipulating those instances, and clients that subclass an abstraction to specialize or augment its behavior. Designing in favor of the first client leads us to hide implementation details and focus upon the responsibilities of the abstraction in the real world; designing in favor of the second client requires us to expose certain implementation details, but not so many that we allow the fundamental semantics of the abstraction to be violated. This represents a very real tension of competing requirements in the design of such a library.

The truly hard part of living with any large, integrated class library is learning what mechanisms it embodies. The patterns we have enumerated above serve as the soul of this library's architecture; the more one knows about these mechanisms, the easier it is to discover innovative ways to use existing components rather than fabricate new ones from scratch. In practice, we observe that developers generally start by using the most obvious classes in a library. As they grow to trust certain abstractions, they move incrementally to the use of more sophisticated classes. Eventually, developers may discover a pattern in their own tailoring of a predefined class, and so add it to the library as a primitive abstraction. Similarly, a team of developers may realize that certain domain-specific classes keep showing up across systems; these too get introduced into the class library. This is precisely how class libraries grow over time: not overnight, but from smaller, stable, intermediate forms.

Indeed, this is precisely how we will expand this library: we will first invent an architecture that addresses each of the five patterns above, and then we will populate the library by evolving its implementation.

9.2 Design

Tactical Issues

Coggins's Law of Software Engineering states that "pragmatics must take precedence over elegance, for Nature cannot be impressed" [11]. A corollary of this law is that design can never be entirely language-independent. The particular features and semantics of a given language influence our architectural decisions, and to ignore these influences would leave us with abstractions that do not take advantage of the language's unique facilities, or with mechanisms that cannot be efficiently implemented in any language.

As we discussed in Chapter 3, object-oriented programming languages offer three basic facilities for organizing a rich collection of classes: inheritance, aggregation, and parameterization. Inheritance is certainly the most visible (and most popular) aspect of object-oriented technology; however, it is not the only structuring principle that we should consider. Indeed, as we will see, parameterization combined with inheritance and aggregation can lead us to a very powerful yet small architecture.

Consider this elided declaration of a domain-specific queue class in C++:

```
class NetworkEvent...

class EventQueue {
public:

  EventQueue();
  virtual ~EventQueue ();

  virtual void clear();
  virtual void add(const NetworkEvent&);
  virtual void pop();

  virtual const NetworkEvent& front() const;
  ...
};
```

Here we have the concrete realization of the abstraction of a queue of events: a structure in which we can add event objects to the tail of the queue, and remove them from the front of the queue. C++ encourages our abstraction by allowing us to state the intended public behavior of a queue (expressed via the operations clear, add, pop, and front), while hiding its exact representation.

Certain uses of this abstraction may demand slightly different semantics; specifically, we may need a priority queue, in which events are added to the queue in order of their urgency. We can take advantage of the work we have already done by subclassing the base queue class and specializing its behavior:

```
class PriorityEventQueue : public EventQueue {
public:

  PriorityEventQueue ();
  virtual ~PriorityEventQueue ();

  virtual void add(const NetworkEvent&);
  ...
};
```

Virtual functions encourage abstraction by allowing us to redefine the semantics of concrete operations (such as add) from a more generalized abstraction.

In combination with parameterized classes, we can craft even more general abstractions. The semantics of queues are the same, no matter if we have a queue of cabbages or a queue of kings. Using template classes, we may restate our original base class as follows:

```
template<class Item>
class Queue {
public:

  Queue();
  virtual ~Queue();

  virtual void clear();
  virtual void add(const Item&);
  virtual void pop();

  virtual const Item& front() const;

  ...
};
```

This is a very common strategy when applying parameterized classes: take an existing concrete class, identify the ways in which its semantics are invariant according to the items it manipulates, and extract these items as template arguments.

Note that we can combine inheritance and parameterization in some very powerful ways. For example, we may restate our original subclass as follows:

```
template<class Item>
class PriorityQueue : public Queue<Item> {
public:

  PriorityQueue ();
  virtual ~PriorityQueue ();

  virtual void add(const Item&);
  ...
};
```

Type safety is the key advantage offered by this approach. We may instantiate any number of concrete queue classes, such as the following:

```
Queue<char> characterQueue;
typedef Queue<NetworkEvent> EventQueue;
typedef PriorityQueue<NetworkEvent> PriorityEventQueue;
```

The language will enforce our abstractions, so that we cannot add events to the character queue, nor floating-point values to the event queue.

Figure 9-1 illustrates this design by showing the relationships among a parameterized class (Queue), its subclass (PriorityQueue), one of its instantiations (PriorityEventQueue), and one of its instances (mailQueue).

This example leads us to assert our first architectural principle for this library: Except for a few cases, the classes we provide should be parameterized. This decision supports the library's requirement for safety.

Macro Organization

As we discussed in earlier chapters, the class is a necessary but insufficient vehicle for decomposition. This observation certainly applies to this class

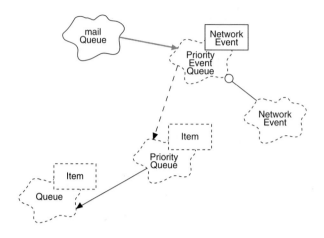

Figure 9-1
Inheritance and Parameterization

library. One of the worst organizations we could devise would be to form a flat collection of classes, through which developers would have to navigate to find the classes needed. We can do far better by placing each cluster of classes into its own category, as shown in Figure 9-2. This decision helps to satisfy the library's requirement for simplicity.

A quick domain analysis suggests that there is an opportunity for exploiting the representations common among the classes in this library. For this reason, we assert the existence of the globally accessible category named Support, whose purpose is to organize such lower-level abstractions. We will also use this category to collect the classes needed in support of the library's common mechanisms.

This leads us to state our second architectural principle for this library: We choose to make a clear distinction between policy and implementation. In a sense, abstractions such as queues, sets, and rings represent particular policies for using lower-level structures such as linked lists or arrays. For example, a queue defines the policy whereby items can only be added to one end of a structure, and removed from the other. A set, on the other hand, enforces no such policy requiring an ordering of items. A ring does enforce an ordering, but sets the policy that the front and the back of its items are connected. We will therefore use the support category for those more primitive abstractions upon which we can formulate different policies.

By exposing this category to library builders, we support the library's requirement for extensibility. In general, application developers need only concern themselves with the classes found in the categories for structures and tools. Library developers and power users, however, may wish to make use of the more primitive abstractions found in Support, from which new classes may be constructed, or through which the behavior of existing classes may be modified.

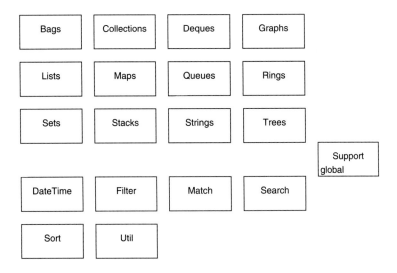

Figure 9-2
Foundation Class Library Class Categories

As Figure 9-2 suggests, we organize this library as a forest of classes, rather than as a tree; there exists no single base class, as we would find with languages such as Smalltalk.

Although not shown in this figure, the classes in the Graphs, Lists, and Trees categories are subtly different from the other structural classes. Earlier, we noted that abstractions such as deques and stacks are monolithic. A *monolithic* structure is one that is always treated as a single unit: there are no identifiable, distinct components, and thus referential integrity is guaranteed. Alternatively, a *polylithic* structure (such as a graph) is one in which structural sharing is permitted. For example, we may have objects that denote a sublist of a longer list, a branch of a larger tree, or individual vertices and arcs of a graph. The fundamental distinction between monolithic and polylithic structures is that, in monolithic structures, the semantics of copying, assignment, and equality are deep, whereas in polylithic structures, copying, assignment, and equality are all shallow operations (meaning that aliases may share a reference to a part of a larger structure).

Class Families

A third principle central to the design of this library is the concept of building families of classes, related by lines of inheritance. For each kind of structure, we will provide several different classes, united by a shared interface (such as the abstract base class Queue), but with several concrete subclasses, each having a slightly different representation, and therefore having different time and space semantics. In this manner, we thus support the library's requirement for completeness. A developer can select the one concrete class whose time and space semantics best fit the needs of a given application, yet still be confident that, no matter which concrete class is selected, it will be functionally the same as any other concrete class in the family. This intentional and clear separation of concerns between an abstract base class and its concrete classes allows a developer to initially select one concrete class and later, as the application is being tuned, replace it with a sibling concrete class with minimal effort (the only real cost is the recompilation of all uses of the new class). The developer can be confident that the application will still work, because all sibling concrete classes share the same interface and the same central behavior. Another implication of this organization is that it makes it possible to copy, assign, and test for equality among objects of the same family of classes, even if each object has a radically different representation.

In a very simple sense, an abstract base class thus serves to capture all of the relevant public design decisions about the abstraction. Another important use of abstract base classes is to cache common state that might otherwise be expensive to compute. This can convert an $O(n)$ computation to an $O(1)$ retrieval. The cost of this style is the required cooperation between the abstract base class and its subclasses, to keep the cached result up to date.

The various concrete members of a family of classes represent the *forms* of an abstraction. In our experience, there are two fundamental forms of most abstractions that every developer must consider when building a serious application. The first of these is the form of representation, which establishes the concrete implementation of an abstract base class. Ultimately, there are only two meaningful choices for in-memory structures: the structure is stored on the stack, or it is stored on the heap. We call these variations the *bounded* and *unbounded* forms of an abstraction, respectively:

- Bounded   The structure is stored on the stack and thus has a static size at the time the object is constructed.

- Unbounded   The structure is stored on the heap, and thus may grow to the limits of available memory.

Because the bounded and unbounded forms of an abstraction share a common interface and behavior, we choose to make them direct subclasses of the abstract base class for each structure. We will discuss these and other variations in more detail in later sections.

The second important variation concerns synchronization. As we discussed in Chapter 2, many useful applications involve only a single process. We call them *sequential* systems, because they involve only a single thread of control. Certain applications, especially those involving real-time control, may require the synchronization of several simultaneous threads of control within the same system. We call such systems *concurrent*. The synchronization of multiple threads of control is important because of the issues of mutual exclusion. Simply stated, it is improper to allow two or more threads of control to directly act upon the same object at the same time, because they may interfere with the

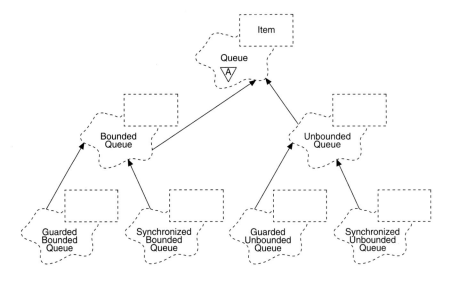

Figure 9-3
Class Families

state of the object, and ultimately corrupt its state. For example, consider two active agents that both try to add an item to the same Queue object. The first agent might start to add the new item, be preempted, and so leave the object in an inconsistent state for the second agent.

As we described in Chapter 3, there are fundamentally only three design alternatives possible, requiring different degrees of cooperation among the agents that interact with a shared object:

- Sequential
- Guarded
- Synchronous

We will discuss these variations in more detail in a later section.

The interactions among the abstract base class, the representation forms, and the synchronization forms yield the same family of classes for every structure as shown in Figure 9-3. This architecture explains why we have chosen to organize our library as a family of classes rather than having a singly rooted tree:

- It accurately reflects the regular structure of the various component forms.
- It involves less complexity and overhead when selecting one component from the library.

- It avoids the endless ontological debates engendered by a "pure object-oriented" approach.
- It simplifies integrating the library with other libraries.

Micro Organization

In support of the library's requirement for simplicity, we choose to follow a consistent style for every structure and tool in the library:

```
template<...>
class Name : public Superclass {
public:

  // constructors
  // virtual destructor

  // operators

  // modifiers

  // selectors

protected:

  // member objects

  // helper functions

private:

  // friends

};
```

For example, the definition of the abstract base class `Queue` begins as follows:

```
template<class Item>
class Queue {
```

The template signature serves to state the arguments whereby the class may be parameterized. Note that in C++, templates are deliberately underspecified, which leaves a degree of flexibility (and responsibility) in the hands of the developers who instantiate templates.

Next, we provide the usual set of constructors and destructors:

```
Queue();
Queue(const Queue<Item>&);
virtual ~Queue();
```

Notice that we have declared the destructor to be virtual, since we want polymorphic behavior when an object of this class is destroyed. Next, we have the declaration of all operators:

```
virtual Queue<Item>& operator=(const Queue<Item>&);
virtual int operator==(const Queue<Item>&) const;
int operator!=(const Queue<Item>&) const;
```

We define `operator=` (assignment) and `operator==` (the test for equality) as `virtual` for reasons of type safety. It is the responsibility of subclasses to overload these two member functions, using functions whose signature takes an argument of its own specialized class. In this manner, subclasses can take advantage of their knowledge of their instances' representation to provide a very efficient implementation. When the exact, concrete subclass of a queue is not known (such as when we pass an object by reference to the base class), then the base class's operations are invoked, using slightly less efficient but more general algorithms. This idiom has the side effect of permitting queue objects with different representations to be assigned and tested without a type clash.

If we wish to restrict certain objects from being copied, assigned, or tested, we may declare these operators as `protected` or `private`.

We next provide all modifiers, which are operations that may alter the state of the object:

```
virtual void clear() = 0;
virtual void append(const Item&) = 0;
virtual void pop() = 0;
virtual void remove(unsigned int at) = 0;
```

We declare these operations as pure virtual, meaning that it is the responsibility of subclasses to provide for their real implementation. By virtue of these pure virtual functions, the class `Queue` is defined to be abstract.

We use the `const` qualifier to indicate (and let the language enforce) the use of selector functions that observe, but do not modify, the state of an object.

```
virtual unsigned int length() const = 0;
virtual int isEmpty() const = 0;
virtual const Item& front() const = 0;
virtual int location(const Item&) const = 0;
```

These operations are also declared as pure virtual, because the class `Queue` has insufficient authority to carry out these particular responsibilities.

In our style, the protected part of every class begins with those member objects that form its representation and that we wish to make accessible to subclasses.[*] The abstract base class `Queue` has no such members, although its concrete subclasses do, as we will see in a later section.

We follow any such member objects with those helper functions required by the base class and polymorphically implemented by all concrete subclasses. The class `Queue` provides a typical set of these member functions:

---

[*] Unless there is compelling reason to do otherwise, we typically declare all member objects as `private`. Here, however, there is compelling reason to make them `protected`: subclasses need access to these members.

```
virtual void purge() = 0;
virtual void add(const Item&) = 0;
virtual unsigned int cardinality() const = 0;
virtual const Item& itemAt(unsigned int) const = 0;

virtual void lock();
virtual void unlock();
```

The reason we supply these particular helper functions will become clear in a later section.

Lastly, we provide a private part, which typically contains only friend declarations and the declaration of those member objects that we wish to make inaccessible to subclasses. In the case of the class `Queue`, we have only friend declarations:

```
friend class QueueActiveIterator<Item>;
friend class QueuePassiveIterator<Item>;
```

As we will describe in a later section, these friend declarations are needed in support of our iterator idioms.

Time and Space Semantics

Of the five patterns that permeate the architecture of this framework, perhaps the most important is the mechanism that provides the client with alternative time and space semantics within each family of classes.

Consider the range of semantics that a general library such as this one must cover. On a workstation that provides a large virtual address space, clients will often sacrifice space for faster abstractions. On the other hand, in certain embedded systems, such as deep space satellites or automobile engines, memory resources are often at a premium, and so clients must choose abstractions that conserve scarce memory resources (for example, by using stack-based rather than heap-based representations). Earlier, we distinguished these two alternatives as unbounded, and bounded, respectively.

Unbounded forms are applicable in those cases where the ultimate size of the structure cannot be predicted, and where allocating and deallocating storage from the heap is neither too costly nor unsafe (as it may be in certain time-critical applications).* Alternatively, bounded forms are better suited to smaller structures, whose average and maximum sizes are predictable, and where heap usage is deemed insecure.

All of the structures in this library require this range of alternatives, and for this reason we invent two lower-level support classes, `Unbounded` and `Bounded`, to provide this behavior. The responsibility of the class `Unbounded` is to provide a

---

* Certain critical requirements may ban the use of heap-based storage altogether. Consider software for a pacemaker, and the potentially fatal results if garbage collection took place at an inopportune time. Consider also a long-running reservation system, where even a tiny memory leak could have serious cumulative effects; having to reboot the system because of out-of-memory conditions might result in an unacceptable loss of service.

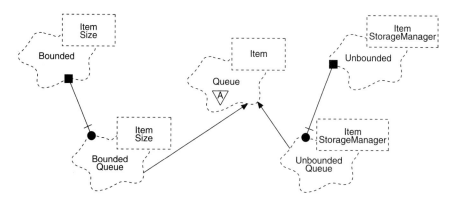

Figure 9-4
Bounded and Unbounded Forms

very efficient linked-list structure that uses items allocated from the heap; this representation is time-efficient, but less space-efficient, because for each item, we must also save storage for a pointer to the next item. The responsibility of the class Bounded is to provide a very efficient, optimally packed array-array-base class; this representation is space-efficient, but less time-efficient, because when adding new items in the middle of the container, items at one end must be moved down by copying.

As shown in Figure 9-4, we use aggregation to place these lower-level classes in our family of classes. Specifically, the diagram shows that we use physical containment by value with protected access, meaning that this lower-level representation is accessible only to subclasses and friends. In an earlier design, we tried a mixin style, whereby the Unbounded and Bounded classes were introduced as protected superclasses. We ultimately rejected this design, because it proved to be conceptually difficult for clients, and also violated our litmus test for inheritance: a BoundedQueue is not a kind of Bounded, in the sense that we desire to treat them as the same type.

Notice that these various forms introduce a second template argument. The bounded form requires an unsigned integer Size, denoting the static size of each instance. In contrast, the unbounded form requires a StorageManager class, whose responsibility is to provide a particular storage management policy, as we will discuss in the next section.

The protocol provided by both of the lower-level classes must be sufficient to implement the responsibilities of the concrete queue classes in particular, and complete enough to implement the responsibilities of all the other structures in the library. For reasons of efficiency, we choose to use no virtual functions in either of these classes. This has two implications: we cannot meaningfully unify Unbounded and Bounded with a common superclass, although they do have a common protocol; and we cannot properly create any subclasses. In a sense, we have chosen to trade off flexibility for blinding speed and reasonable memory use. As part of this trade-off, we also choose to inline certain functions for speed; selectors are usually good candidates for inlining, especially when they only involve returning a simple value.

For example, consider the declaration of the class `Bounded`:

```
template<class Item, unsigned int Size>
class Bounded {
public:

  Bounded();
  Bounded(const Bounded<Item, Size>&);
  ~Bounded();

  Bounded<Item, Size>& operator=(const Bounded<Item, Size>&);
  int operator==(const Bounded<Item, Size>&) const;
  int operator!=(const Bounded<Item, Size>&) const;
  const Item& operator[](unsigned int index) const;
  Item& operator[](unsigned int index);

  void clear();
  void insert(const Item&);
  void insert(const Item&, unsigned int before);
  void append(const Item&);
  void append(const Item&, unsigned int after);
  void remove(unsigned int at);
  void replace(unsigned int at, const Item&);

  unsigned int available() const;
  unsigned int length() const;
  const Item& first() const;
  const Item& last() const;
  const Item& itemAt(unsigned int) const;
  Item& itemAt(unsigned int);
  int location(const Item&) const;

  static void* operator new(size_t);
  static void operator delete(void*, size_t);

protected:

  Item rep[Size];
  unsigned int start;
  unsigned int stop;

  unsigned int expandLeft(unsigned int from);
  unsigned int expandRight(unsigned int from);
  void shrinkLeft(unsigned int from);
  void shrinkRight(unsigned int from);

};
```

This class declaration follows the style we described earlier. How exactly did we come to choose this particular interface? The honest answer is that isolated class design, as we explained in Chapter 6, got us to an 80% solution, but then we evolved this interface to the final form shown above, after having used this class to implement three or four of the structural families of classes. The hard part of this evolution was identifying suitably primitive operations that could be used to carry out all the different policies required of all the structures.

Notice the ultimate representation of this class, namely, the protected member object `rep`, declared to be an array of items with a static length `Size`. Consider the following declaration:

```
Bounded<char, 100U> charSequence;
```

Elaboration of this declaration creates a fixed-size, 100-element array on the stack. The protected member objects `start` and `stop` are used as indices into this array, denoting the beginning and the ending of the sequence, respectively. In this manner, we implement our abstraction by using a circular buffer. Adding items to the front and back of a sequence does not require any movement of items already in the sequence; adding items in the middle of the sequence only requires on average the copying of half of the existing items.

The design of both the unbounded and bounded support classes raises some subtle issues concerning the use of references, which we alluded to in Chapter 3. We explore these issues further here, not only because they impact the interface of every template class in the library, but also because they are fundamental issues that must be faced by the architect of any nontrivial class library. Indeed, this is a classic example of how particular language semantics can affect architectural decisions.

In C++, references provide an aliasing mechanism that can improve performance. However, references must be used carefully to avoid creating unsafe situations at runtime. In this library, we use references to improve the performance of passing arguments to member functions. Note, for example, the declaration of `Bounded`, in which we pass instances of `Bounded` and `Item` by reference. As a general rule, we do not pass primitive objects (such as integers, in the declaration of the member function `itemAt`) by reference, because it is likely to make the code slower, and additionally, C++ semantics introduce some potentially dangerous problems when temporary objects are used.

However, we do choose to have all structures store *values*, not references, in their respective concrete forms. This style prevents creating references to transient objects on the runtime stack. For the same reason, we rejected an alternative design involving storing pointers to items, because this approach exhibits very undesirable behavior when instantiating a template with built-in types. These issues are significant when designing the interface to a framework involving template classes, since clients can instantiate the templates with arbitrary types. There are three cases to consider, and we must design the library so that it strikes a balance among all three.

First, built-in types can be passed by reference and copied into concrete representations with no difficulty. Declaring the argument types as constant references avoids warnings due to temporaries involved in type conversion [12].

Second, user-defined types can be passed by reference and copied, but only if they provide copy constructors and the assignment operator. Although the references permit polymorphic operations (passing an object of a derived class instead of the declared class supplied in the instantiation), the copying will not be polymorphic. Assigning the object of the representation will "slice" the object to an instance of the base class [13].

Third, polymorphic uses of the library will have to instantiate the templates with pointers to the base classes involved. Although passing the pointers by reference does not necessarily improve performance, copying pointers into the representation preserves the polymorphism of the derived objects involved.

For example, given the class BoundedQueue, we can write the following:

```
class Event ...
typedef Event* EventPtr;

BoundedQueue<int, 10U> intQueue;
BoundedQueue<Event, 50U> eventQueue1;
BoundedQueue<EventPtr, 100U> eventQueue2;
```

With the object eventQueue1, clients may safely build queues of events, although adding instances of any Event subclasses will introduce slicing, and hence the polymorphic behavior of such items will be lost. On the other hand, the object eventQueue2 contains pointers to objects of class Event, and so we may store and retrieve objects of class Event or its subclasses without the danger of slicing.

Our decision to store values instead of references or pointers to items places certain responsibilities on the construction and destruction of items in a structure. In particular, the item classes used to instantiate a structure must provide at least a default constructor, a copy constructor, and an assignment operator. Additionally, items may not be destroyed immediately upon removal from a structure. For example, in bounded forms, items (which are ultimately stored in arrays) are not destroyed until the structure itself is destroyed.

Consider now how we use the class Bounded to form a concrete class such as BoundedQueue. As we see in the following declaration, BoundedQueue has a protected member object rep of the class Bounded:

```
template<class Item, unsigned int Size>
class BoundedQueue : public Queue<Item> {
public:

  BoundedQueue();
  BoundedQueue(const BoundedQueue<Item, Size>&);
  virtual ~BoundedQueue();

  virtual Queue<Item>& operator=(const Queue<Item>&);
  virtual Queue<Item>& operator=(const BoundedQueue<Item, Size>&);
  virtual int operator==(const Queue<Item>&) const;
  virtual int operator==(const BoundedQueue<Item, Size>&) const;
  int operator!=(const BoundedQueue<Item, Size>&) const;

  virtual void clear();
  virtual void append(const Item&);
  virtual void pop();
  virtual void remove(unsigned int at);

  virtual unsigned int available() const;
  virtual unsigned int length() const;
  virtual int isEmpty() const;
  virtual const Item& front() const;
  virtual int location(const Item&) const;
```

```
protected:

  Bounded<Item, Size> rep;

  virtual void purge();
  virtual void add(const Item&);
  virtual unsigned int cardinality() const;
  virtual const Item& itemAt(unsigned int) const;

  static void* operator new(size_t);
  static void operator delete(void*, size_t);

};
```

The primary responsibility of this class is to complete the protocol defined in the base class. Often, this involves little more than delegating the responsibility to the lower-level Bounded class, as suggested by the following implementation:

```
template<class Item, unsigned int Size>
unsigned int BoundedQueue<Item, Size>::length() const
{
  return rep.length();
}
```

Notice that the class BoundedQueue introduces some additional operations over those defined in its superclass. In particular, we add the selector available, which returns the number of free items in the structure (calculated as Size - length()). We did not include this operation in the base class, primarily because calculating the amount of available space on the heap is not so clear an operation. We also overloaded the operators for assignment and test for equality. As we mentioned earlier, this idiom permits subclasses to provide more efficient implementations of these operations than can the base class, because the subclasses have detailed knowledge of their own representation. Lastly, we added the operators new and delete, but declared them as protected members, which effectively prevents clients from allocating instances of BoundedQueue (which is consistent with the static storage semantics of this concrete form).

The class Unbounded, has substantially the same protocol as the class Bounded, although its implementation is radically different.

```
template<class Item, class StorageManager>
class Unbounded {
public:
  ...
protected:

  Node<Item, StorageManager>* rep;
  Node<Item, StorageManager>* last;
  unsigned int size;

  Node<Item, StorageManager>* cache;
  unsigned int cacheIndex;

};
```

The Unbounded form provides the implementation of a linked list of nodes, where Node is declared as follows:

```
template<class Item, class StorageManager>
class Node {
public:

    Node(const Item& i,
        Node<Item, StorageManager>* previous,
        Node<Item, StorageManager>* next);

    Item item;
    Node<Item, StorageManager>* previous;
    Node<Item, StorageManager>* next;

    static void* operator new(size_t);
    static void operator delete(void*, size_t);

};
```

The main responsibility of this class is to manage a single item together with pointers to the next and previous nodes. Because this is a support class and hence is not used by clients outside of the library, we have decided to relax our usual strict rules of encapsulation and expose all of its state as public members, thus trading off safety for efficiency.

Because the classes Bounded and Unbounded supply virtually the same public protocol, we know that they are functionally the same, and hence the implementation of all the bounded and unbounded concrete structures will look very much the same as well. However, the representation of these two support classes is what leads to radically different time and space semantics. In particular, for the linked-list representation, manipulating nodes is very fast, but finding particular items can be slow (on the order of $O(n)$). For this reason, our implementation caches the last referenced node, in the expectation that it or its neighbors are likely to be touched next. For the array-based implementation, manipulating items is can be slow, the worst case being $O(n/2)$, when inserting or deleting in the middle of a sequence, whereas finding a particular items is very fast (on the order of $O(1)$).

Storage Management

Storage management is an issue for all unbounded forms, because the library designer must consider specific policies for allocating and deallocating nodes from the heap. A naive approach will simply use the global new and delete functions, but this strategy will often exhibit very poor runtime performance. Furthermore, storage management on certain platforms can be quite complex (as with segmented address spaces under certain personal computer operating systems), and so requires that all of our classes use a policy tailored to the platform, rather than using a general one assumed by the library designer to work for all circumstances. By clearly isolating these patterns of storage management, we can construct a robust yet adaptable library.

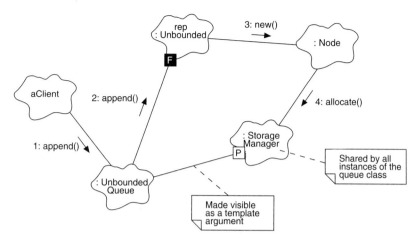

Figure 9-5
Storage Management Mechanism

Figure 9-5 illustrates the mechanism we have chosen to provide storage management for this library.* Let's walk through the scenario described in this object diagram:

- aClient invokes the operation append upon an instance of UnboundedQueue (more precisely, upon an instance of an instantiation of UnboundedQueue).

- The UnboundedQueue object in turn delegates responsibility for this operation to its member object rep, an instance of the class Unbounded.

- Unbounded allocates a new instance of Node by invoking its static member function new.

- The Node instance in turn delegates the responsibility of allocation to its storage manager, which is made visible to the class UnboundedQueue (and in turn to the classes Unbounded and Node) as a template argument. This storage manager is shared by all instances of the class, and so serves to provide a consistent class-wide storage management policy.

By treating the storage manager as an argument to all the unbounded concrete structures, we effectively decouple storage management policy from its implementation, and make it possible for library users to insert their own storage management policy without changing the library. This is a classic example of extensibility through instantiation instead of inheritance.

---

* An historical note: it took about four iterations of the library's architecture to evolve to this mechanism, which – not surprisingly – turned out to be the simplest of the lot. Earlier alternatives, which we ultimately rejected, proved to be not as adaptable as well as hard to explain, because they tended to expose the bones of our implementation to uncaring clients.

The only requirement we place upon our storage managers is that they provide the same well-defined protocol. Specifically, we require that all storage managers export the member functions `allocate` and `deallocate`, which dispense and release memory, respectively. For example, consider the simplest (and most naive) storage management policy:

```
class Unmanaged {
public:

  static void* allocate(size_t s)
    {return ::operator new(s);}
  static void deallocate(void* p, size_t)
    {::operator delete(p);}

private:

  Unmanaged() {}
  Unmanaged(Unmanaged&) {}
  void operator=(Unmanaged&) {}
  void operator==(Unmanaged&) {}
  void operator!=(Unmanaged&) {}

};
```

Notice the idiom we use to prevent clients from copying, assigning, or testing instances of this class.

We implement the protocol for the class `Unmanaged` by inline calls to the global operators `new` and `delete`. We call this policy *unmanaged*, because it effectively does nothing beyond the default policy provided by the language. A far better policy is called *managed*. Under this policy, nodes are allocated and deallocated from a common pool of memory. Unused nodes of any kind are returned to a free list, and allocation takes nodes from this free list unless it is empty, in which case another chunk of free memory is allocated from the heap. In this manner, we vastly reduce the number of times we must reach out to the operating system's storage management services: allocation now involves manipulating some pointers, which is far faster.[*]

With a little thought about its semantics, we can make our pool abstraction even better. For example, we might provide operations that permit a client to preallocate a chunk of memory, in advance of its use. Similarly, we might permit a client to defragment its chunks, and possibly return unused chunks back to the heap. We might also provide operations that permit a client to choose the chunk size, so as to tune storage allocation to the needs of the implementation (for example, to set a chunk size optimal for the size of the classes being allocated, and to make chunks align with word boundaries).

Given these design decisions, we might express our pool abstraction in the following nontemplate support class:

---

[*] In C++, the global operator `new` ultimately invokes some kind of `malloc` service, which is a relatively expensive operation..

```
class Pool {
public:

  Pool(size_t chunkSize);
  ~Pool();

  void* allocate(size_t);
  void deallocate(void*, size_t);

  void preallocate(unsigned int numberOfChunks);
  void reclaimUnusedChunks();
  void purgeUnusedChunks();

  size_t chunkSize() const;
  unsigned int totalChunks() const;
  unsigned int numberOfDirtyChunks() const;
  unsigned int numberOfUnusedChunks() const;

protected:

  struct Element ...
  struct Chunk ...

  Chunk* head;
  Chunk* unusedChunks;
  size_t repChunkSize;
  size_t usableChunkSize;

  Chunk* getChunk(size_t s);

};
```

This class uses two nested classes `Element` and `Chunk`. Each instance of the class `Pool` manages a linked list of `Chunk` objects which are actually raw chunks of memory, but are treated as if they were themselves linked lists of `Element` instances (this is one of the important secrets managed by the `Pool` class). Each chunk may manage elements of a different size, and so for efficiency, we sort our list of chunks from smallest to largest.

Our managed storage management class can now be written as follows:

```
class Managed {
public:

  static Pool& pool;

  static void* allocate(size_t s)
    {return pool.allocate(s);}
  static void deallocate(void* p, size_t s)
    {pool.deallocate(p, s);}

private:

  Managed() {}
  Managed(Managed&) {}
  void operator=(Managed&) {}
  void operator==(Managed&) {}
  void operator!=(Managed&) {}

};
```

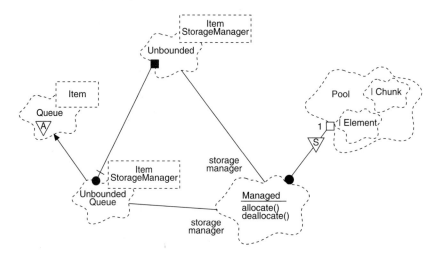

Figure 9-6
Storage Management Classes

This class provides the same public protocol as the class `Unmanaged`. Because of C++'s intentional underspecification of template semantics, conformance with this protocol is only checked when we compile an instantiation of a class such as `UnboundedQueue`, at which time we match a concrete class with the formal template argument `StorageManager`.

Notice that the class `Managed` has a static member object of the class `Pool`. In this manner, it is possible to have several unmanaged concrete structures share the same pool of storage. Different unmanaged structures can of course define their storage manager and hence their own pool, thus giving the developer complete control over storage management policy.

Figure 9-6 provides a class diagram illustrating the various classes that collaborate to provide a managed storage policy. We show only an association between the classes `Managed` and its clients `Unbounded` and `UnboundedQueue`, because this association will only be manifested in a specific instantiation of the classes.

Part of our architectural decisions must involve the physical packaging of these support classes. In Figure 9-7, we illustrate the module architecture of these classes. The particular partitioning we chose isolates those classes that are most likely to change.

Exceptional Conditions

Although we may use the C++ language itself to enforce most static assumptions about an abstraction (violations of these assumptions may be detected at compilation time), we must use some other mechanism for reporting any dynamic violations, such as trying to add an item to an already full bounded queue, or removing an item from an empty queue. In this library, we chose to apply C++'s exception facilities [14]. Our architecture uses a

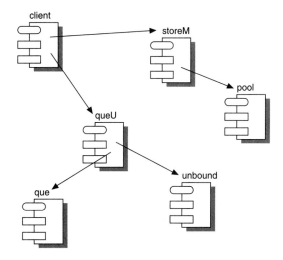

Figure 9-7
Storage Management Modules

hierarchy of exception classes, and separates them from the mechanisms involved in reporting them.

We start with a base exception class, whose protocol is straightforward:

```
class Exception {
public:

  Exception(const char* name, const char* who, const char* what);

  void display() const;

  const char* name() const;
  const char* who() const;
  const char* what() const ;

protected:

  ...

};
```

For every exceptional condition, we may attach its name, who threw it, and why it was thrown. Additionally, we provide a means for displaying an exception on some output stream hidden from the client.

A domain analysis of the various classes in the library reveals the following exceptional conditions, which we declare as subclasses to the base class Exception:

- ContainerError

- Duplicate

- IllegalPattern
- IsNull
- LexicalError
- MathError
- NotFound
- NotNull
- NotRoot
- Overflow
- RangeError
- StorageError
- Underflow

For example, the declaration of the exception Overflow appears as follows:

```
class Overflow : public Exception {
public:

  Overflow(const char* who, const char* what)
    : Exception("Overflow", who, what) {}

};
```

The responsibility of this class only requires that it knows its name, which it passes on to its superclass's constructor.

Under this mechanism, member functions in library classes only *throw* exceptions; none of them catch exceptions, mainly because there is nothing that any of them can do to respond meaningfully to an exceptional condition. By convention, we only throw exceptions as part of an assertion about some condition. An *assertion* is simply a Boolean expression of some condition whose truth must be preserved. To simplify the library's implementation, we thus introduce the following nonmember function:

```
inline void _assert(int expression, const Exception& exception)
{
  if (!expression)
    throw(exception);
}
```

We declare this function as inline for efficiency.

The advantage of providing this function is that it localizes all throws (in C++, throw has the syntax of a function call). Thus, for compilers that do not yet support exceptions, we can use a compiler directive (-D for most C++ compilers) to redefine this one mention of throw to be a call to some other nonmember function that displays the exception and then terminates the program:

```
void _catch(const Exception& e)
{
  cerr << "EXCEPTION: ";
  e.display();
  exit(1);
}
```

Now, consider the implementation of the Bounded member function insert:

```
template<class Item, unsigned int Size>
void Bounded<Item, Size>::insert(const Item& item)
{
  unsigned int count = length();
  _assert((count < Size), Overflow("Bounded::Insert", "structure is full"));
  if (!count)
    start = stop = 1;
  else {
    start--;
    if (!start)
      start = Size;
  }
  rep[start - 1] = item;
}
```

In this implementation, we assert that the current length of the structure must be less than its bounded size. If this condition evaluates false, then we throw the exception Overflow.

One very important aspect of our use of exceptions is that they are guaranteed not to corrupt the state of any object that throws an exception, except in the case of out-of-memory conditions (in which case all bets are usually off, anyway). In our design, member functions always make an assertion before any changes to the state of the object are made. For example, in the implementation of the member function insert above, we first call a selector (which by design is guaranteed to preserve the state of the object), then we check that all preconditions to the function are satisfied, and only then do we alter the state of the object. This is a style that we follow carefully and consistently, and should be preserved by any subclasses derived from this library.

Figure 9-8 illustrates the classes that collaborate to form this mechanism.

Iteration

Iteration is another architectural pattern found in this library. As we defined it in Chapter 3, an iterator is an operation that permits all parts of an object to be accessed in some well-defined order. As it turns out, not only do clients of the library need this behavior, but we also need iterators in the implementation of the library itself, to carry out certain responsibilities of each base class.

When introducing iterators, we have two design choices: we can define iteration as part of an object's protocol, or we can invent separate objects that act as agents responsible for iterating across a structure. We choose the second alternative for two compelling reasons:

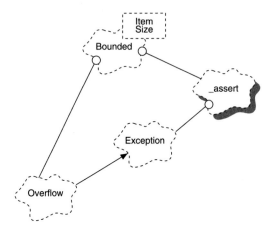

Figure 9-8
Exception Classes

- By providing separate iterator classes, we make it possible to have several iterator objects working upon the same object.
- Iteration slightly breaks the encapsulation of an object's state; by separating the behavior of iteration from the rest of an abstraction's protocol, we provide a much clearer separation of concerns.

For each structure, we provide two forms of iteration. Specifically, an *active* iterator requires that clients explicitly advance the iterator; in one logical expression, a *passive* iterator applies a client-supplied function, and so requires less collaboration on the part of the client.* For reasons of type safety, we define different iterators for each kind of structure.

For example, consider the active iterator for the class Queue:

```
template <class Item>
class QueueActiveIterator {
public:

    QueueActiveIterator(const Queue<Item>&);
    ~QueueActiveIterator();

    void reset();
    int next();

    int isDone() const;
    const Item* currentItem() const;
```

---

* Passive iterators implement an "apply" function, an idiom commonly used in functional programming languages.

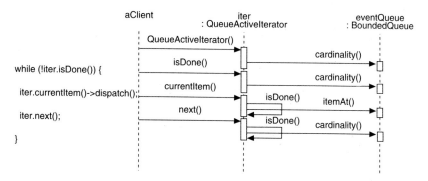

Figure 9-9
Iteration Mechanism

```
protected:

  const Queue<Item>& queue;
  int index;

};
```

At the time of its construction, every iterator is bound to a particular object. Iteration begins at the "top" of a structure, whatever that might mean for the given abstraction.

A client obtains a pointer to the current item through the member function currentItem; the pointer is null if iteration is complete or if the structure is empty. A client advances the iterator to the next successive item through the member function next (which returns 0 if the iterator could not be advanced, perhaps because iteration had already been completed). The selector isDone allows the client to query the progress of iteration, and returns 0 if the iteration is complete or if the structure is empty. The reset member function allows multiple traversals over the same object.

As an example, given the following declarations:

```
BoundedQueue<NetworkEvent> eventQueue;
```

the following code fragment uses an active iterator to visit each item in the queue, from front to back:

```
QueueActiveIterator<NetworkEvent> iter(eventQueue);

while (!iter.isDone()) {
  iter.currentItem()->dispatch();
  iter.next();
}
```

The interaction diagram in Figure 9-9 illustrates this scenario, and in addition, reveals some of the secrets of the iterator's implementation. In fact, let's consider the implementation of this mechanism in more detail.

The constructor for the class `QueueActiveIterator` binds itself to the given queue and calls the protected member function `cardinality` to determine how many items are in the queue. Thus, we may write:

```
template<class Item>
QueueActiveIterator<Item>::QueueActiveIterator(const Queue<Item>& q)
  : queue(q),
    index(q.cardinality() ? 0 : -1) {}
```

The class `QueueActiveIterator` is a friend of the class `Queue`, which is why the iterator can invoke the protected member function `cardinality`.

The iterator operation `isDone` checks that its index is currently within the extent of the queue object to which it is bound:

```
template<class Item>
int QueueActiveIterator<Item>::isDone() const
{
  return ((index < 0) || (index >= queue.cardinality()));
}
```

`currentItem` returns a pointer to the item upon which the iterator is focused. By implementing the iterator class as an index into a queue object, it is possible to safely add and delete items from the queue during iteration.

```
template<class Item>
const Item* QueueActiveIterator<Item>::currentItem() const
{
  return isDone() ? 0 : &queue.itemAt(index);
}
```

Here again, the iterator class invokes a protected member function exported from the queue. Notice that this operation is efficient when used either with a bounded or an unbounded queue. For bounded queues, `itemAt` is simply an indexing operation. For unbounded queues, `itemAt` in the worst case could involve traversing its entire linked-list representation. Remember, moreover, that our design of the class `Unbounded` caches the last referenced item, which means that finding the next item (which happens when the iterator advances) is a simple pointer operation.

The iterator operation `next`, in fact, just advances its index and then checks to see if it has fallen off the end of the queue:

```
template<class Item>
int QueueActiveIterator<Item>::next()
{
  index++;
  return !isDone();
}
```

The design of the iterator class thus motivates two of the protected member functions we provided for the abstract base class `Queue`, namely, `cardinality` and `itemAt`. By making these members pure virtual, we make it the responsibility of each concrete queue class to provide an implementation consistent with and optimal for its representation.

Earlier, we indicated that one important implication of our architectural decisions is that a client may copy, assign, and test for equality among instances of the same abstract base class, even though each has a different representation. We achieve this capability through an elegant use of iterators and helper functions. This style allows us, in the abstract base class, to traverse any structure in a representation-independent manner. For example, in the class Queue we find:

```
template<class Item>
Queue<Item>& Queue<Item>::operator=(const Queue<Item>& q)
{
  if (this == &q)
    return *this;
  ((Queue<Item>&)q).lock();
  purge();
  QueueActiveIterator<Item> iter(q);
  while (!iter.isDone()) {
    add(*iter.currentItem());
    iter.next();
  }
  ((Queue<Item>&)q).unlock();
  return *this;
}
```

This algorithm uses an idiom for locking and unlocking the queue object, which we will explain in the next section.

Assignment proceeds by traversing the structure of the argument q, using an active queue iterator. We apply the protected helper function purge to initially clear the queue, and then we add new items to the structure via the protected helper function add. The fact that iteration depends upon the polymorphic behavior of the base class's helper functions is what makes it possible for structures to copy, assign, and test for equality among objects that have the same structure, but with different representations.

A passive iterator is an *applicator,* meaning that it applies some function to every item in the structure. The following declaration provides the iterator for the class Queue:

```
template <class Item>
class QueuePassiveIterator {
public:

  QueuePassiveIterator(const Queue<Item>&);
  ~QueuePassiveIterator();

  int apply(int (*)(const Item&));

protected:

  const Queue<Item>& queue;

};
```

Passive iterators operate on all items in a structure in a (logically) single operation. The apply function visits each item in the structure and invokes the supplied function on each. It continues until it reaches the last item, or until the supplied function returns a result of 0 (in which case `apply` itself returns 0, indicating that the iteration was incomplete).

Synchronization

Any general framework must consider the problems of concurrency. Under operating systems such as UNIX, OS/2, and Windows/NT, for example, applications may be formed using multiple lightweight processes.[*] Unless special consideration is given, most classes will simply not work in such an environment: when two more tasks interact with the same object, active objects must in some manner cooperate to avoid corrupting the state of the shared object. As we described earlier, there are basically two approaches to process management, as represented by the guarded and synchronized forms of a class.

The design of this library makes the following assumption: Developers that care about concurrency will have ported or implemented at least a `Semaphore` class for synchronizing lightweight processes. Other clients won't care, and won't miss not having the guarded or synchronized forms of structures (and will appreciate not having to pay the overhead). The guarded and synchronized forms are thus an independent, layered part of the library, and rely upon local implementations of this concurrency mechanism. The library's only dependencies upon the local implementation are intentionally isolated in the implementation of the class `Semaphore`, whose interface appears as follows:

```
class Semaphore {
public:

  Semaphore ();
  Semaphore (const Semaphore &);
  Semaphore (unsigned int count);
  ~Semaphore ();

  void seize();
  void release();

  unsigned int nonePending() const;

protected:

  ...

};
```

Just as we did for storage management, we choose to separate the policies of process synchronization from its implementation. For this reason, the template

---

[*] A lightweight process is one that executes in the same address space as its peers. In contrast, the UNIX `fork` function produces heavyweight processes that require special operating system services for interprocess communication. For C++, the AT&T task library provides a semiportable abstraction of lightweight processes under UNIX. Lightweight processes are also directly available under OS/2 and Windows/NT. The Smalltalk class library provides the class `Process` in support of its model for lightweight processes.

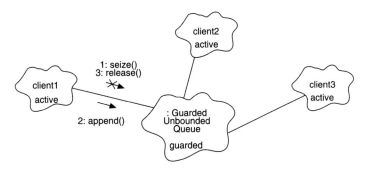

Figure 9-10
Guarded Process Mechanism

signature of every guarded form imports a *guard*, which is responsible for providing a binding to the local implementation of a semaphore or its equivalent. Similarly, the template signature of every synchronized form imports a *monitor*, which is similar to a semaphore but, as we will discuss, permits a higher degree of concurrency.

As we illustrated in Figure 9-3, a guarded class is a direct subclass of its concrete bounded or unbounded class; a guarded class contains a guard as a member object. All guarded classes introduce the member functions `seize` and `release`, which allow an active agent to gain exclusive access to the object. For example, consider the class `GuardedUnboundedQueue`, which is a kind of `UnboundedQueue`:

```
template<class Item, class StorageManager, class Guard>
class GuardedUnboundedQueue : public UnboundedQueue<Item, StorageManager> {
public:

  GuardedUnboundedQueue ();
  virtual ~GuardedUnboundedQueue ();

  virtual void seize();
  virtual void release();

protected:

  Guard guard;
};
```

For this library, we provide the interface of one predefined guard: the class `Semaphore`. Users of this library must complete the implementation of this class, according to the needs of the local definition of lightweight processes.

As we illustrate in Figure 9-10, clients who use guarded objects must follow the simple protocol of first seizing the object, operating upon it, and then releasing it (especially in the face of any exceptions thrown). To do otherwise is considered socially inappropriate, because aberrant behavior on the part of one agent denies the fair use by other agents. Seizing a guarded object and then failing to release it blocks the object indefinitely; releasing an object never first seized by the agent is subversive. Lastly, ignoring the seize/release protocol altogether is simply irresponsible, because interleaved tasks may corrupt the state of the shared object.

The primary benefit offered by the guarded form is its simplicity, although it does require the fair collective action of all agents that manipulate the same object. Another key feature of the guarded form is that it permits agents to form critical regions, in which several operations performed upon the same object are guaranteed to be treated as an atomic transaction.

Similar to the mechanism of storage management, the template signature of guarded forms imports the guard rather than making it an immutable feature. This makes it possible for library developers to introduce new synchronization policies. Using the predefined class Semaphore as a guard, the library's default policy is to give every object of the class its own semaphore. This policy is acceptable only up to the point where the total number of processes reaches some practical limit set by the local implementation.

An alternate policy involves having several guarded objects share the same semaphore. A developer need only produce a new guard class that provides the same protocol as Semaphore (but is not necessarily a subclass of Semaphore). This new guard might then contain a Semaphore as a static member object, meaning that the semaphore is shared by all its instances. By instantiating a guarded form with this new guard, the library developer introduces a different policy, whereby all objects of that instantiated class share the same guard, rather than there being one guard per object. The power of this policy comes about when the new guard class is used to instantiate other structures: all such objects ultimately share the same guard. The policy shift is subtle, but very powerful: not only does it reduce the number of processes in the application, but it also permits a client to globally lock a group of otherwise unrelated objects. Seizing one such object blocks all other objects that share this new guard, even if those objects are entirely different types.

A synchronized class is also a direct subclass of its concrete bounded or unbounded class. A synchronized class contains a monitor as a member object, whose protocol is defined by the following abstract base class:

```
class Monitor {
public:

  Monitor();
  Monitor(const Monitor&);
  virtual ~Monitor();

  virtual void seizeForReading() = 0;
  virtual void seizeForWriting() = 0;
  virtual void releaseFromReading() = 0;
  virtual void releaseFromWriting() = 0;

protected:

  ...

};
```

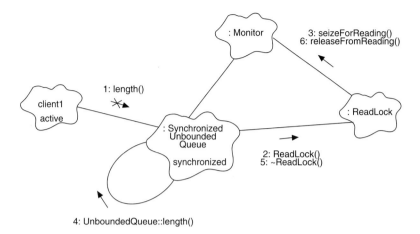

Figure 9-11
Synchronized Process Mechanism

There exist two basic kinds of process synchronization via monitors of this sort:

- Single   Guarantees the semantics of a structure in the presence of multiple threads of control, with a single reader or writer.

- Multiple   Guarantees the semantics of a structure in the presence of multiple threads of control, with multiple simultaneous readers or a single writer.

A *writer* is an agent that alters the state of an object; writers are those agents that invoke modifier member functions. A *reader* is an agent that operates upon an object, yet preserves its state; readers are those objects that only invoke selector functions. The multiple form therefore provides the greatest amount of real parallelism. We can implement these two policies as subclasses of the abstract base class Monitor. Both the single and multiple forms may be built upon the Semaphore class.

Unlike the guarded form, synchronized classes do not introduce any new member functions; rather, they redefine every virtual member function inherited from their superclass. The semantics added by a synchronized class cause every member function to be treated as an atomic transaction. Whereas clients of guarded forms must explicitly seize and release an object to achieve exclusive access, synchronized forms provide this exclusivity without requiring any special action on the part of their clients.

We achieve this exclusivity by means of a locking mechanism, as illustrated in Figure 9-11. Monitors collaborate with instances of the predefined classes ReadLock and WriteLock to achieve exclusive invocation of each individual member function. In this mechanism, a lock contains a semaphore or a monitor as the agent responsible for process synchronization, and the lock is responsible for seizing this agent upon construction and releasing it upon destruction. For example, consider the declaration of the class `ReadLock`:

```
class ReadLock {
public:

  ReadLock (const Monitor& m)
    : monitor(m) {monitor.seizeForReading();}
  ~ReadLock ()
    {monitor.releaseFromReading();}

private:

  Monitor& monitor;

};
```

By separating the abstractions of the lock and its monitor, our design permits a client to attach a different policy to the mechanism of locking. The declaration of the class `WriteLock` is just as simple, except that uses the monitor's protocol for reading.

The definition of each member function in a synchronized form uses locks to wrap around the corresponding operation inherited from its superclass. For example, consider the implementation of the member function `length` for the synchronized and unbounded queue:

```
template<class Item, class StorageManager, class Monitor>
unsigned int SynchronizedUnboundedQueue<Item, StorageManager, Monitor>::length() const
{
  ReadLock lock(monitor);
  return UnboundedQueue<Item, StorageManager>::length();
}
```

This code directly implements the mechanism described in Figure 9-11. In general, we use instances of the class `ReadLock` for all synchronized selectors, and we use instances of the class `WriteLock` for all synchronized modifiers. The simple elegance of this design is that it guarantees that every member function represents an atomic action, even in the face of exceptions and without any explicit action on the part of a reader or writer.

Indeed, clients who use synchronized objects need not follow any special protocol, because the mechanism of process synchronization is handled implicitly, and so is less prone to the deadlocks and livelocks that may result from incorrect usage of guarded forms. A developer should choose a guarded form instead of a synchronized form, however, if it is necessary to invoke several member functions together as one atomic transaction; the synchronized form only guarantees that individual member functions are atomic.

Our architecture renders synchronized forms relatively free of any circumstances that might lead to a deadly embrace. For example, assigning an object to itself or testing an object for equality with itself is potentially dangerous because in concept it requires locking the left and right elements of such expressions, which in these cases is the same object. Once constructed, an object cannot change its identity, thus, these tests for self-identify are performed first, before either object is locked. This is precisely why our earlier implementation of the `operator=` included a test for self-identity, as the following elided version indicates:

```
template<class Item>
Queue<Item>& Queue<Item>::operator=(const Queue<Item>& q)
{
  if (this == &q)
    return *this;
  ...
}
```

Even then, member functions that have instances of the class itself as arguments must be carefully designed to ensure that such arguments are properly locked. Our solution relies upon the polymorphic behavior of two helper functions, `lock` and `unlock`, defined in every abstract base class. Each abstract base class provides a default implementation of these two functions that does nothing; synchronized forms provide an implementation that seizes and releases the argument. This is precisely why our earlier implementation of the `operator=` included calls to these two functions, as the following elided version indicates:

```
template<class Item>
Queue<Item>& Queue<Item>::operator=(const Queue<Item>& q)
{
  ...
  ((Queue<Item>&)q).lock();
  ...
  ((Queue<Item>&)q).unlock();
  return *this;
}
```

Here we use the idiom of applying an explicit type cast to cast away the `const` property of the argument.

9.3 Evolution

Class Interface Design

In a framework such as this one, once we have selected the patterns that make up its architecture, the remaining work is relatively simple, although perhaps tedious. Our next step is to take three or four families of classes (such as the queue, set, and tree), implement them against this architecture, and then test them against real client applications.[*]

The hard part of this activity is deciding upon a suitable interface for each base class. This involves isolated class design, as we described in Chapter 6,

---

[*] Wirfs-Brock has observed that it takes at least three applications of a framework to validate its strategic and tactical decisions [15].

but it also requires that the designer keep a global perspective to ensure consistency. For example, we might select the following protocol for `Set`:

• setHashFunction	Sets a hash function for the set's items.
• clear	Empties the set.
• add	Adds an item to the set.
• remove	Removes an item from the set.
• setUnion	Performs a set union.
• intersection	Takes the intersection with the given set.
• difference	Removes the items in the given set.
• extent	Returns the number of items in the set.
• isEmpty	Returns 1 if there are no items in the set.
• isMember	Returns 1 if the given item is in the set.
• isSubset	Returns 1 if the set is a subset of the given set.
• isProperSubset	Returns 1 if the set is a proper subset of the given set.

Similarly, we might select the following protocol for the class `BinaryTree`:

• clear	Destroys the tree and its children.
• insert	Adds a node to the top of the tree.
• append	Adds a child to the tree.
• remove	Removes a child from the tree.
• share	Structurally shares the given tree.
• swapChild	Swaps the child with the given tree.
• child	Returns the given child.
• leftChild	Returns the left child.
• rightChild	Returns the right child.
• parent	Returns the parent of the tree.
• setItem	Sets the item associated with the tree.
• hasChildren	Returns 1 if the tree has children.
• isNull	Returns 1 if the tree is null.
• isShared	Returns 1 if the tree is structurally shared.
• isRoot	Returns 1 if the tree is rooted.
• itemAt	Returns the item associated with the tree.

Notice that we use similar names for similar kinds of operations. We also use the quality measures of sufficiency, completeness, and primitiveness (as described in Chapter 3) to guide our design of each family's interface.

Support Classes

Our implementation of the string class reveals that the range of time and space semantics offered by the support classes `Bounded` and `Unbounded` is insufficient for our purposes. Specifically, the bounded form is space-inefficient for strings, because we must instantiate this form for the longest expected string, thereby wasting a tremendous amount of storage in all shorter strings. Similarly, the unbounded form is time-inefficient for strings, because searching for an item or inserting an item in the middle of the string may require traversing its entire underlying linked-list structure. For this reason, we introduce a third form of representation, which we call `dynamic`, with the following responsibilities:

- Dynamic   The structure is stored on the heap as an array whose length may shrink or grow.

In this manner, the support class `Dynamic` offers a middle ground between the time efficiency of the bounded form (since items may be indexed directly) and the space efficiency of the unbounded form (since we only allocate storage for as many items as necessary).

Because the protocol of this class is identical to that of the classes `Bounded` and `Unbounded`, it is trivial to add this new behavior to the library. Specifically, we must add three new classes to each family (for example, `DynamicString`, `GuardedDynamicString`, and `SynchronizedDynamicString`). We thus include the support class `Dynamic`, whose elided declaration appears as follows:

```
template<class Item, class StorageManager>
class Dynamic {
public:

  Dynamic(unsigned int chunkSize);

  ...

protected:

  Item* rep;
  unsigned int size;
  unsigned int totalChunks;
  unsigned int chunkSize;
  unsigned int start;
  unsigned int stop;

  void resize(unsigned int currentLength, unsigned int newLength, int preserve = 1);

  unsigned int expandLeft(unsigned int from);
  unsigned int expandRight(unsigned int from);
  void shrinkLeft(unsigned int from);
  void shrinkRight(unsigned int from);
};
```

Sequences are sized in multiples of the constructor argument `chunkSize`. In this manner, a client can tailor each instance of this class to a size optimal to its use.

As this declaration suggests, the implementation of the class Dynamic shares many of the same characteristics as that of the Bounded and Unbounded classes. In fact, because all three of these classes have substantially the same public protocol, the implementation of each of the concrete classes in a family is largely the same as well.

Our implementation of the map class also reveals that the bounded, dynamic, and unbounded forms need tuning to satisfy the map's semantics. Specifically, searching for an item's membership in a map is unacceptably expensive if we have to search a long sequence sequentially . We can vastly improve performance it we use an open hash table instead.

The abstraction of an open hash table is straightforward. Basically, such a table consists of an array of sequences; each sequence is called a *bucket*. When we place an item in the table, we first generate a hash value from the item itself, which we then use to select a specific bucket. We enter the item in that bucket, just as with the bounded, dynamic, and unbounded forms. In this manner, an open hash table divides a long sequence into several smaller ones, thereby greatly accelerating searches.

We can capture these semantics in the following elided declaration:

```
template<class Item, class Value, unsigned int Buckets, class Container>
class Table {
public:

  Table(unsigned int (*hash)(const Item&))

  ...

  void setHashFunction(unsigned int (*hash)(const Item&));
  void clear();
  int bind(const Item&, const Value&);
  int rebind(const Item&, const Value&);
  int unbind(const Item&);
  Container* bucket(unsigned int bucket);

  unsigned int extent() const;
  int isBound(const Item&) const;
  const Value* valueOf(const Item&) const;
 const Container *const bucket(unsigned int bucket) const;

protected:

  Container rep[Buckets];

  ...

};
```

Notice the use of Container as a template argument, which allows us to define our abstraction of an open hash table independently of the particular concrete sequence we use. For example, consider the highly elided declaration of the unbounded map, which builds upon the classes Table and Unbounded:

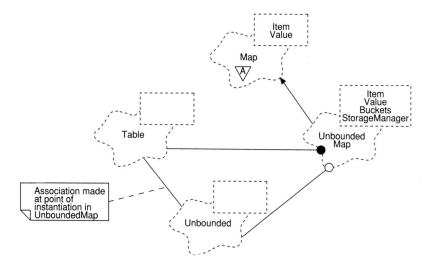

Figure 9-12
Support Classes

```
template<class Item, class Value, unsigned int Buckets, class StorageManager>
class UnboundedMap : public Map<Item, Value> {
public:

  UnboundedMap();

  ...

  virtual int bind(const Item&, const Value&);
  virtual int rebind(const Item&, const Value&);
  virtual int unbind(const Item&);

  ...

protected:

  Table<Item, Value, Buckets, Unbounded<Pair<Item, Value>, StorageManager> > rep;

  ...

};
```

Here, we instantiate the class `Table` with an `Unbounded` container. Figure 9-12 illustrates the collaboration of these classes.

As a measure of the general applicability of this abstraction, we may apply the class `Table` to our implementation of the `Set` and `Bag` classes as well.

Tools

In this library, the primary use of templates is to parameterize each structure with the kind of item it contains; this is why such structures are often called *container classes.* As the declaration of the class `Table` illustrates, templates may also be used to provide certain implementation information to a class.

An even more sophisticated situation involves tools that operate upon other structures. As we explained earlier, we can objectify algorithms by inventing classes whose instances act as agents responsible for carrying out the algorithm. This approach follows Jacobson's idea of a *control object*, whose behavior provides the glue whereby other objects collaborate within a use-case [16]. The advantage of this approach is that it lets us take advantage of patterns within certain families of algorithms, by forming inheritance lattices. This not only simplifies their implementation, but provides a way to conceptually unify similar algorithms from the perspective of their clients.

For example, consider the algorithms that search for patterns within a sequence. A number of such algorithms exist, with varying time semantics:

- Simple   The structure is searched sequentially for the given pattern; in the worst case, this algorithm has a time complexity on the order of $O(pn)$, where p is the length of the pattern, and n is the length of the sequence.

- Knuth-Morris-Pratt   The structure is searched for the given pattern, with a time complexity of $O(p + n)$; searching requires no backup, which makes this algorithm suitable for streams.

- Boyer-Moore   The structure is searched for the given pattern, with a sublinear time complexity of $O(c * (p + n))$, where $c < 1$ and is inversely proportional to p.

- Regular expression   The structure is searched for the given regular expression pattern.

There are at least three common features of these algorithms: they all operate upon sequences (and hence expect certain protocols from the objects they are searching), they all require the existence of an equality function for the items being searched (because the default equality operation may be insufficient), and they all have substantially the same signature for their invocation (they require a target, a pattern, and a starting index).

The need for an equality operation requires some explanation. Suppose, for example, we have an ordered collection of personnel records. We might wish to search this sequence for a certain pattern of records, such as groups of three records all from the same department. Using the `operator==` for the class `PersonnelRecord` won't work, because this operator probably tests for equality based upon some unique id. Instead, we must supply a special test for equality to our algorithm that queries the department of each person (by invoking a suitable selector). Because each pattern-matching agent requires an equality function, we can provide a common protocol for setting the function as part of some abstract base class. For example, we might use the following declaration:

```
template<class Item, class Sequence>
class PatternMatch {
public:

  PatternMatch();
  PatternMatch(int (*isEqual)(const Item& x, const Item& y));
  virtual ~PatternMatch();

  virtual void setIsEqualFunction(int (*)(const Item& x, const Item& y));
  virtual int
    match(const Sequence& target, const Sequence& pattern, unsigned int start = 0) = 0;
  virtual int
    match(const Sequence& target, unsigned int start = 0) = 0;

protected:

  Sequence rep;

  int (*isEqual)(const Item& x, const Item& y);

private:

  void operator=(const PatternMatch&) {}
  void operator==(const PatternMatch&) {}
  void operator!=(const PatternMatch&) {}

};
```

Notice that we again use the idiom for assignment and test for equality, which prevents objects of this class or its subclasses from being assigned or compared to one another. We do so because these operations have no real meaning when applied to such agent abstractions.

We can next devise concrete subclasses such as for the Boyer-Moore algorithm:

```
template<class Item, class Sequence>
class BMPatternMatch : public PatternMatch<Item, Sequence> {
public:

  BMPatternMatch();
  BMPatternMatch(int (*isEqual)(const Item& x, const Item& y));
  virtual ~BMPatternMatch();

  virtual int
    match(const Sequence& target, const Sequence& pattern, unsigned int start = 0);
  virtual int
    match(const Sequence& target, unsigned int start = 0);

protected:

  unsigned int length;
  unsigned int* skipTable;

  void preprocess(const Sequence& pattern);
  unsigned int itemsSkip(const Sequence& pattern, const Item& item);

};
```

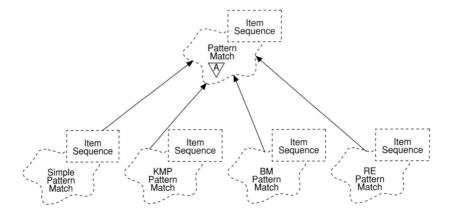

Figure 9-13
Pattern Matching Classes

The public protocol of this class implements that of its superclass. In addition, we provide two member objects and two member helper functions. One of the secrets of this class is the creation of a temporary table that it uses to skip over long, unmatched sequences; these members serve to implement this secret.

As figure 9-13 illustrates, we may build a hierarchy of pattern matching classes. In fact, this kind of hierarchy applies to all of the tools in our library, giving it a regular structure that makes it far easier for clients to find the abstractions that best fit their time and space semantics.

9.4 Maintenance

One fascinating characteristic of frameworks is that – if well-engineered – they tend to reach a sort of a critical mass of functionality and adaptability. In other words, if we have selected the right abstractions, and if we have populated the library with a set of mechanisms that work together well, then we will find that clients soon discover means to build upon the library in ways its designers never imagined or expected. As we discover patterns in the ways that clients use our framework, then it makes sense to codify these patterns by formally making them a part of the library. A sign of a well-designed framework is that we can introduce these new patterns during maintenance by reusing existing mechanisms and thus preserving its design integrity.

One such pattern of use for this library involves the problem of persistence. We might find clients who don't want or need the full power of an object-oriented database, but who from time to time need to save the state of structures such as queues and sets, and then reconstruct these objects in a later invocation of the program, or perhaps from a different program altogether. Because this pattern of use is so common, it makes sense for us to augment our library with a simple persistence mechanism.

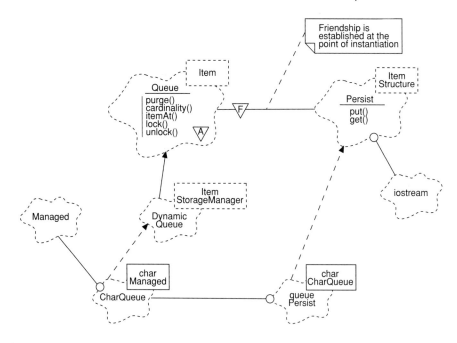

Figure 9-14
Persistence Classes

We will make two assumptions about this facility. First, clients are made responsible for providing a stream to which items are put and from which items are restored. Second, clients are responsible for ensuring that items have the behavior necessary for them to be streamed.

Two alternate designs for this facility come to mind. We could devise a mixin class that supplied persistence semantics; this is the approach used by many object-oriented databases. Alternately, we could devise a class whose instances act as agents responsible for streaming various structures. As part of our exploration, we might try both approaches, to see which is a better fit.

As it turns out, the mixin style doesn't work well for this particular simple form of persistence (although it is well suited for full-functioned object-oriented databases). Using a mixin style requires that clients who mix in an abstraction plug it together with their user-defined class, often by redefining certain mixin helper functions For such a simple agent, however, clients would end up writing more code than if they crafted the mechanism by hand. This is clearly not acceptable, and so we turn to the second approach, which requires little more than an instantiation on the part of the client.

Figure 9-14 illustrates our design for this mechanism, in which we provide persistence through the behavior of a separate agent. The class Persist is a friend of the class Queue, but we can defer this association by introducing the following friend declaration in the Queue class:

```
friend class Persist<Item, Queue<Item> >;
```

In this manner, friendship is established only at the time we instantiate the `Queue` class. In fact, by introducing a similar friend declaration in every abstract base class, we can reuse the class `Persist` for every structure in the library.

The parameterized class `Persist` provides the operations `put` and `get`, as well as operations for setting its input and output streams. We may capture this abstraction in the following declaration:

```
template<class Item, class Structure>
class Persist {
public:

  Persist();
  Persist(iostream& input, iostream& output);
  virtual ~Persist();

  virtual void setInputStream(iostream&);
  virtual void setOutputStream(iostream&);
  virtual void put(Structure&);
  virtual void get(Structure&);

protected:

  iostream* inStream;
  iostream* outStream;


  ...
};
```

The implementation of this class depends upon its friendship with the class `Structure`, which is imported as a template argument. Specifically, `Persist` depends upon the existence of the structure's helper functions: `purge`, `cardinality`, `itemAt`, `lock`, and `unlock`. Here the regularity of our library pays off: since every `Structure` base class provides these helper functions, we can use the class `Persist` without any change to the library's existing architecture.

Consider for example, the implementation of `Persist::put`:

```
template<class Item, class Structure>
void Persist<Item, Structure>::put(Structure& s)
{
  s.lock();
  unsigned int count = s.cardinality();
  (*outStream) << count << endl;
  for (unsigned int index = 0; index < count; index++)
    (*outStream) << s.itemAt(index);
  s.unlock();
}
```

This operation uses our earlier locking mechanism, so that its semantics work for both the guarded and synchronized forms. The algorithm proceeds by streaming out the size of the structure and then its individual elements in order. Similarly, the implementation of `Persist::get` reverses this action:

```
template<class Item, class Structure>
void Persist<Item, Structure>::get(Structure& s)
{
  s.lock();
  unsigned int count;
  Item item;
  if (!inStream->eof()) {
    (*inStream) >> count;
    s.purge();
    for (unsigned int index = 0; (index < count) && (!inStream->eof()); index++) {
      (*inStream) >> item;
      s.add(item);
    }
  }
  s.unlock();
}
```

To use this simple form of persistence consistency across the library, the client thus has only to instantiate one additional class per structure.

Building frameworks is hard. In crafting general class libraries, one must balance the needs for functionality, flexibility, and simplicity. Strive to build flexible libraries, because you can never know exactly how programmers will use your abstractions. Furthermore, it is wise to build libraries that make as few assumptions about their environment as possible, so that programmers can easily combine them with other class libraries. The architect must also devise simple abstractions, so that they are efficient, and so that programmers can understand them. The most profoundly elegant framework will never be reused, unless the cost of understanding it and then using its abstractions is lower than the programmer's perceived cost of writing them from scratch. The real payoff comes when these classes and mechanisms get reused over and over again, indicating that others are gaining leverage from the developer's hard work, allowing them to focus on the unique parts of their own particular problem.

Further Readings

Biggerstaff and Perlis [H 1989] provide a comprehensive treatment of software reuse. Wirfs-Brock [C 1988] offers a good introduction to object-oriented frameworks. Johnson [G 1992] examines approaches to documenting the architecture of frameworks through the recognition of their patterns.

MacApp [G 1989] offers an example of one specific, well-engineered, object-oriented application framework for the Macintosh. An introduction to an early version of this class library may be found in Schmucker [G 1986]. In a more recent work, Goldstein and Alger [C 1992] discuss the activities of developing object-oriented software for the Macintosh.

Other examples of frameworks abound, covering a variety of problem domains, including hypermedia (Meyrowitz [C 1986]), pattern recognition (Yoshida [C 1988]), interactive graphics (Young [C 1987]), and desktop publishing (Ferrel [K 1989]). General application frameworks include ET++ (Weinand, [K 1989]) and event-driven

MVC architectures (Shan [G 1989]). Coggins [C 1990] studies the issues concerning the development of C++ libraries in particular.

An empirical study of object-oriented architectures and their effects upon reuse may be found in Lewis [C 1992].

CHAPTER 10

Client/Server Computing: Inventory Tracking

For many business applications, a company will use an off-the-shelf database management system (DBMS) to furnish a generic solution to the problems of persistent data storage, concurrent database access, data integrity, security, and backups. Of course, any DBMS must be adapted to the given business enterprise, and organizations have traditionally approached this problem by separating it into two different ones: the design of the data is given over to database experts, and the design of the software for processing transactions against the database is given over to application developers. This technique has certain advantages, but it does involve some very real problems. Frankly, there are cultural differences between database designers and programmers, which reflect their different technologies and skills. Database designers tend to see the world in terms of persistent, monolithic tables of information, whereas application developers tend to see the world in terms of its flow of control.

It is impossible to achieve integrity of design in a complex system unless the concerns of these two groups are reconciled. In a system in which data issues dominate, we must be able to make intelligent trade-offs between a database and its applications. A database schema designed without regard for its use is both inefficient and clumsy. Similarly, applications developed in isolation place unreasonable demands upon the database and often result in serious problems of data integrity due to the redundancy of data.

In the past, traditional mainframe computing raised some very real walls around a company's database assets. However, given the advent of low-cost computing, which places personal productivity tools in the hands of a multitude of workers, together with networks that serve to link the ubiquitous personal computer across offices as well as across nations, the face of information management systems has been irreversibly changed. Clearly a major part of this fundamental change is the application of client/server architectures. As Mimno points out, "The rapid movement toward downsizing and client-server computing is being driven by business imperatives. In the face of rapidly increasing competition and shrinking product cycles, business managers are looking for ways to get products to market faster, increase services to customers, respond faster to competitive challenges, and cut costs" [1]. In this chapter, we tackle a management information system (MIS) application and show how object-oriented technology can address the issues of database and application design in a unified manner, in the context of a client/server architecture.

10.1 Analysis

Defining the Boundaries of the Problem

The sidebar provides the requirements for an inventory-tracking system. This is a highly complex application whose use touches virtually every aspect of the workflow within a warehouse. The physical warehouse exists to store products, but it is this software that serves as the warehouse's soul, for without it, the warehouse would cease to function as an efficient distribution center.

Part of the challenge in developing such a comprehensive system is that it requires planners to rethink their entire business process, yet balance this with the capital investment they already have in legacy code, as we discussed in Chapter 7. While productivity gains can sometimes be made simply by automating existing manual processes, radical gains are usually only achieved when we challenge some of our basic assumptions about how the business should be run. How we reengineer this business is a system-planning activity, and so is outside the scope of this text. However, just as our software architecture bounds our implementation problem, so too does our business vision bound our entire software problem. We therefore begin by considering an operational plan for running the warehouse. Systems analysis suggests that there are seven major functional activities in this business:

- Order entry   Responsible for taking customer orders and
                            for responding to customer queries about the
                            status of an order

Inventory-Tracking System Requirements

As part of its expansion into several new and specialized markets, a mail-order catalog company has decided to establish a number of relatively autonomous regional warehouses. Each such warehouse retains local responsibility for inventory management and order processing. To target niche markets efficiently, each warehouse is tasked with maintaining inventory that is best suited to the local market. The specific product line that each warehouse manages may differ from region to region; furthermore, the product line managed by any one region tends to be updated almost yearly to keep up with changing consumer tastes. For reasons of economies of scale, the parent company desires to have a common inventory- and order-tracking system across all its warehouses.

The key functions of this system include:

- Tracking inventory as it enters the warehouse, shipped from a variety of suppliers.
- Tracking orders as they are received from a central but remote telemarketing organization; orders may also be received by mail, and are processed locally.
- Generating packing slips, used to direct warehouse personnel in assembling and then shipping an order.
- Generating invoices and tracking accounts receivable.
- Generating supply requests and tracking accounts payable.

In addition to automating much of the warehouse's daily workflow, the system must provide a general and open-ended reporting facility, so that the management team can track sales trends, identify valued and problem customers and suppliers, and carry out special promotional programs.

- Accounting   Responsible for sending invoices and tracking customer payments (accounts receivable) as well as for paying suppliers for orders from purchasing (accounts payable)

- Shipping   Responsible for assembling packages for shipment in support of filling customer orders

- Stocking   Responsible for placing new inventory in stock as well as for retrieving inventory in support of filling customer orders

- Purchasing   Responsible for ordering stock from suppliers and tracking supplier shipments

- Receiving   Responsible for accepting stock from suppliers

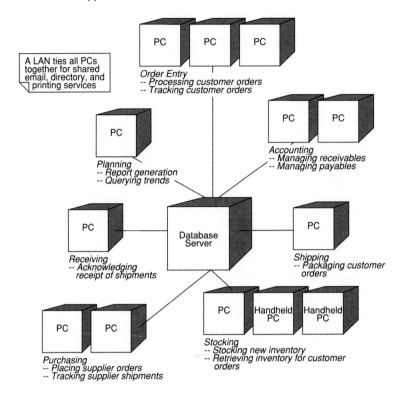

Figure 10-1
Inventory-Tracking System Network

• Planning   Responsible for generating reports to
                              management and studying trends in inventory
                              levels and customer activity

Not surprisingly, our system architecture is isomorphic to these functional units.
Figure 10-1 provides a process diagram that illustrates all of the major
computational elements in our network. This network is actually quite a
common MIS structure: banks of personal computers feed a central database
server, which in turn serves as a central repository for all of the enterprise's
interesting data.

A few details about this network are in order. First, although we show a
number of distinct PCs each tied to a particular functional unit, this is merely an
operational consideration. There should be nothing in our software architecture
that constrains a specific PC to only one activity: the accounting team should be
able to perform general queries, and the purchasing department should be able
to query accounting records concerning supplier payments. In this manner, as
changing business conditions dictate, management can add or reallocate
computing resources as needed to balance the daily workflow. Of course,

security requirements dictate that some management discipline is needed: a stockperson should not be allowed to send out checks. We delegate responsibility for these kinds of constraints as an operational consideration, carried out by general network access-control mechanisms that either constrain or grant rights to certain data and applications.

As part of this system architecture, we also assume the existence of a local area network (LAN) that ties all of our computing resources together, and serves to provide common network services such as electronic mail, shared directory access, printing, and communications. From the perspective of our inventory tracking system software, the choice of a particular LAN is largely immaterial, as long as it provides these services reliably and efficiently.

The presence of the handheld PCs as part of the stocking function adds a novel wrinkle to this network. The economies of notepad and specialized PCs carried on a belt together with wireless communications, make it possible to consider an operational plan that takes advantage of these technologies to increase productivity. Basically, our plan will be to give each stockperson a handheld PC. As new inventory is placed in the warehouse, they use these devices to report the fact that the stock is now in place, and also notify the system where it is located; as orders for the day are assigned to be filled, packing orders are transmitted to these devices, directing workers where to find certain stock, as well as how many of each to retrieve to pass on to shipping.

Now, none of this technology is exactly rocket science – everything in our network is essentially off-the-shelf hardware. Indeed, we expect to use more than a little off-the-shelf software as well. It makes considerable business sense to buy rather than build commercial spreadsheets, groupware products, and accounting packages. However, what brings this system to life is its inventory-tracking software, which serves as the glue to operationally tie everything together.

Applications such as this one perform very little computational work. Instead, large volumes of data must be stored, retrieved, and moved about. Most of our architectural work therefore will involve decisions about declarative knowledge (what entities exist, what they mean, and where they are located) rather than procedural knowledge (how things happen). The soul of our design will be found in the central concerns of object-oriented development: the key abstractions that form the vocabulary of the problem domain and the mechanisms that manipulate them.

Business demands require that our inventory-tracking system must be, by its very nature, open-ended. During analysis, we will come to understand the key abstractions that are important to the enterprise at that time: we will identify the kinds of data that must be stored, the reports to be generated, the queries to be processed, and all the other transactions demanded by the business procedures of the company. The operative phrase here is *at that time*, because businesses are not static entities. They must act and react to a changing marketplace, and their information management systems must keep pace with these changes. An obsolete software system can result in lost business or a squandering of precious human resources. Therefore, we must design the inventory-tracking system expecting that it will change over time. Our observation shows that two elements are most likely to change over the lifetime of this system:

- The kinds of data to be stored
- The hardware upon which the application executes

Over time, new product lines will be managed by each warehouse, new customers and suppliers will be added, and old ones removed. Operational use of this system may reveal the unanticipated need to capture additional information about a customer.[*] Also, hardware technology is still changing at a rate faster than software technology, and computers still become obsolete within a matter of a few years. However, it is simply neither affordable nor wise to frequently replace a large, complex software system. It is not affordable because the time and cost of developing the software can often outweigh the time and cost of procuring the hardware. It is not wise because introducing a new system every time an old one begins to look jaded adds risk to the business; stability and maturity are valuable features of the software that plays such an important role in the day-to-day activities of an organization.

A corollary to this second factor is the likelihood that the user interface of our application will need to change over time. In the past for many MIS applications, simple line- or screen-oriented interfaces proved to be adequate. However, falling hardware costs and stunning improvements in graphic user interfaces have made it practical and desirable to incorporate more sophisticated technology. To put things in perspective, the user interface of the inventory management system is only a small (albeit critical) part of the application. The core of this system involves its database; its user interface is largely a skin around this core. In fact, it is possible (and highly desirable) to permit a variety of user interfaces for this system. For example, a simple, interactive, menu-oriented interface is most likely adequate for customers who submit their own orders. Modern, window-based interfaces are likely best for the planning, purchasing, and accounting functions. Hardcopy reports may best be generated in a batch environment, although some managers may wish to

---

[*] Consider, for example, the impact of emerging technologies that will bring interactive video services to each household. It would not be unreasonable to think that in the future, customers would be able to electronically place orders to the mail-order company, and debit their bank accounts directly. Because standards for these domains are changing almost daily as companies position themselves to become the dominant purveyors of such services, it is impossible for the end-user application developer to accurately predict the protocol for interacting with such systems. The best we can hope to do as systems architects is to make intelligent assumptions and encapsulate these decisions in our software so that we can adapt when the dust finally settles in the battle for information highway domination – a battle in which the individual application developer is largely a pawn with minimal influence. This indeed leads us to a primary motivation for using object-oriented technology: as we have seen, object-oriented development helps us craft resilient, adaptable architectures, features that are essential to our survival in this marketplace.

use a graphic interface to view trends interactively. Stockpersons need an interface that is simple; mouse-driven windowing systems don't work well in the industrial environment of a warehouse, and furthermore, training costs are an issue to consider. For the purposes of our application, we will not dwell upon the nature of the user interface; just about any kind of interface may be employed without altering the fundamental architecture of the inventory-tracking system.

On the basis of this discussion, we choose to make two strategic system decisions. First, we choose to use an off-the-shelf relational database (RDBMS) around which to build our application. Designing an *ad hoc* database doesn't make any sense in this situation; the nature of our application would lead us to implement most of the functionality of a commercial DBMS at a vastly greater cost and with much less flexibility in the resulting product. An off-the-shelf RDBMS also has the advantage of being reasonably portable. Most popular RDBMS have implementations that run on a spectrum of hardware platforms, from personal computers to mainframes, thus transferring from the developer to the vendor the responsibility of porting the generic RDBMSs. Second, as we have shown in Figure 10-1, we choose to have the inventory tracking execute on a distributed network. For simplicity, we will plan for a centralized database that resides on one machine. However, we will allow applications to be targeted to a variety of machines from which they can access this database. This design represents a client/server model; the machine dedicated to the database acts as the server, and it may have many clients. The particular machine on which a client executes (even if it is the local database machine itself) is entirely immaterial to the server. Thus, our application can operate upon a heterogeneous network and allow new hardware technology to be incorporated with minimal impact upon the operation of the system.

Client/Server Computing

Although it is not the purpose of this chapter to provide a comprehensive survey of client/server computing, some observations are in order, because they influence our architectural decisions.

What client/server computing is and is not is a hotly debated topic.[*] For our purposes, it is sufficient to state that client/server computing encompasses "a decentralized architecture that enables end users to gain access to information transparently within a multivendor environment. Client-server applications couple a GUI to a server-based RDBMS" [2]. The very nature of client/server applications suggests a form of cooperative processing, wherein the responsibility for carrying out the system's functions is distributed among various nearly independent computational elements that exist as part of an open system. Berson further notes that each client/server application can typically be divided into one of four components:

---

[*] Not unlike the question of what is and what isn't object-oriented.

- Presentation logic   The part of an application that interacts with an end-user device such as a terminal, a bar code reader, or a handheld computer. Functions include "screen formatting, reading, and writing of the screen information, window management, keyboard, and mouse handling."

- Business logic   The part of an application that uses information from the user and from the database to carry out transactions as constrained by the rules of the business.

- Database logic   The part of an application that "manipulates data within the application. . . . Data manipulation in relational DBMSs is done using some dialect of the Structured Query Language (SQL)."

- Database processing   The "actual processing of the database data that is performed by the DBMS. . . . Ideally, the DBMS processing is transparent to the business logic of the application." [3].

The fundamental issue for the architect is how and where to distribute these computational elements across an open network. Greatly complicating the decision process is the fact that client/server standards and tools are evolving at a dizzying pace. The architect must find his or her way through an array of proposals such as POSIX (Portable Operating System Interface), the Open Systems Interconnection (OSI) reference model, the Object Management Group common object request broker (CORBA), and object-oriented extensions to SQL (SQL3), as well as vendor-specific solutions such as Microsoft's object linking and embedding (OLE) mechanism.[*]

Not only do standards impact the architect's decisions, but issues such as security, performance, and capacity must be weighed as well. Berson goes on to suggest some rules of thumb for the client/server architect:

- In general, a presentation logic component with its screen input-output facilities is placed on a client system.

- Given the available power of the client workstations, and the fact that the presentation logic resides on the client system, it makes sense to also place some part of the business logic on a client system.

---

[*] It is for this reason that good information systems architects tend to be paid vast sums of money for their skills, or alternately, at least get to have a lot of fun trying to piece together so many disparate technologies to form a coherent whole.

- If the database processing logic is embedded into the business logic, and if clients maintain some low-interaction, quasi-static data, then the database processing logic can be placed on the client system.

- Given the fact that a typical LAN connects clients within a common-purpose workgroup, and assuming that the workgroup shares a database, all common, shared fragments of the business and database processing logic and DBMS itself should be placed on the server. [4].

If we make the right architectural decisions and succeed in carrying out the tactical details of its implementation, the client/server model offers a number of benefits, as Berson observes:

- It allows corporations to leverage emerging desktop computing technology better.

- It allows the processing to reside close to the source of data being processed. . . . Therefore, network traffic (and response time) can be greatly reduced.

- It facilitates the use of graphical user interfaces available on powerful workstations.

- It allows for and encourages the acceptance of open systems [5].

Of course, there are risks:

- If a significant portion of application logic is moved to a server, the server may become a bottleneck in the same fashion as a mainframe in a master-slave architecture.

- Distributed applications . . . are more complex than nondistributed applications [6].

We mitigate these risks through the use of an object-oriented architecture and development process.

Scenarios

Now that we have established the scope of our system, we continue our analysis by studying several scenarios of its use. We begin by enumerating a number of primary use cases, as viewed from the various functional elements of the system:

- A customer phones the remote telemarketing organization to place an order.

- A customer mails in an order.

- A customer calls to find out about the status of an order.

- A customer calls to add items to or remove items from an existing order.
- A stockperson receives a packing order to retrieve stock for a customer order.
- Shipping receives an assembled order and prepares it for mailing.
- Accounting prepares a customer invoice.
- Purchasing places an order for new inventory.
- Purchasing adds or removes a new supplier.
- Purchasing queries the status of an existing supplier order.
- Receiving accepts a shipment from a supplier, placed against a standing purchase order.
- A stockperson places new stock into inventory.
- Accounting cuts a check against a purchase order for new inventory.
- The planning department generates a trend report, showing the sales activity for various products.
- For tax-reporting purposes, the planning department generates a summary showing current inventory levels.

For each of these primary scenarios, we can envision a number of secondary ones:

- An item a customer requested is out of stock or on backorder.
- A customer's order is incomplete, or mentions incorrect or obsolete product numbers.
- A customer calls to query about or change an order, but can't remember what exactly was ordered, by whom, or when.
- A stockperson receives a packing order to retrieve stock, but the item cannot be found.
- Shipping receives an incompletely assembled order.
- A customer fails to pay an invoice.
- Purchasing places an order for new inventory, but the supplier has gone out of business or no longer carries the item.
- Receiving accepts an incomplete shipment from a supplier.
- Receiving accepts a shipment from a supplier for which no purchase order can be found.
- A stockperson places new stock into inventory, only to discover that there is no space for the item.
- Business tax code changes, requiring the planning department to generate a number of new inventory reports.

For a system of this complexity, we would expect to identify dozens of primary scenarios and many more secondary ones. In fact, this part of the analysis

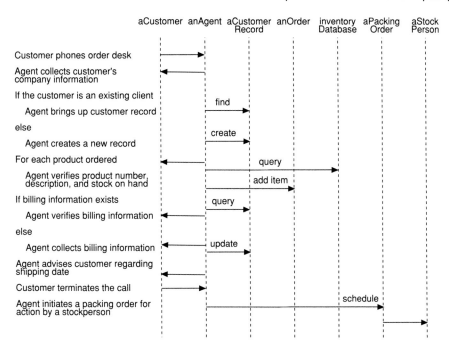

Figure 10-2
Order Scenario

process would probably take several weeks to complete to any reasonable level of detail.[*] For this reason, we strongly suggest applying the 80% rule of thumb: don't wait to generate a complete list of scenarios (no amount of time will be sufficient), but rather, study some 80% of the interesting ones, and if possible, try a quick-and-dirty proof of concept to see if this part of analysis is on the right track. For the purposes of this chapter, let's elaborate upon two of the system's primary scenarios.

Figure 10-2 provides a primary use case for a customer placing an order with the remote telemarketing organization. Here we see that a number of different objects collaborate to carry out this system function. Although control centers around the customer/agent interaction, three other key objects (namely, `aCustomerRecord`, the `inventoryDatabase`, and `aPackingOrder`, all of which are artifacts of the inventory tracking system) play a pivotal role. We add these abstractions to our "list of things" that fall out of the scenario planning process.

Figure 10-3 continues this scenario with an elaboration upon the packing order/stockperson interaction, another critical system behavior. Here we see that the stockperson is at the center of this scenario's activity, and collaborates with other objects, namely, `shipping`, which did not play a role in the previous

---

[*] But beware of analysis paralysis: if the software analysis cycle takes longer than the window of opportunity for the business, then abandon hope, all ye who follow this path, for you will eventually be out of business.

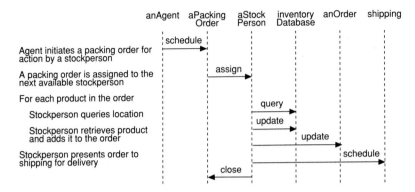

Figure 10-3
Packing Order Scenario

scenario. In fact, most of the objects that collaborate in Figure 10-3 are the same ones that showed up in Figure 10-2, although it is important to realize that these common objects play very different roles. For example, in the order scenario, we use anOrder to track a customer's requests, but in the packing scenario, we use anOrder as a check and balance against our packing orders.

As we walk through each of these scenarios, we must continually ask ourselves a number of questions. What object should be responsible for a certain action? Does an object have sufficient knowledge to carry out an operation directed to it, or must it delegate the behavior? Is the object trying to do too much? What could go wrong? That is to say, what happens if certain preconditions are violated, or if postconditions cannot be satisfied?

By anthropromorphizing our abstractions in this manner, for each of the system's function points we eventually come to discover many of the interesting high-level objects within our system. Specifically, our analysis leads us to discover the following abstractions. First, we list the various people that interact with the system:

- Customer
- Supplier
- OrderAgent
- Accountant
- ShippingAgent
- StockPerson
- PurchasingAgent
- ReceivingAgent
- Planner

It is important for us to identify these classes of people, because they represent the different roles that people play when interacting with the system. If we desire to track the who, when, and why of certain events that took place within our system, then we must formalize these roles. For example, when resolving a complaint, we might like to identify what people within the company had recently interacted with the unhappy customer, and only by making this a part of our enterprise model do we retain enough information to make an intelligent analysis. In addition to serving an outwardly visible role, it is important for us to distinguish among these classes of people for the purpose of operationally restricting or granting access to parts of the system's functionality. With an open network, this form of centralized control is a reasonably effective way to control accidental or malicious misuse.

Our analysis also reveals the following key abstractions, each of which represents some information manipulated by the system:

- CustomerRecord
- ProductRecord
- SupplierRecord
- Order
- PurchaseOrder
- Invoice
- PackingOrder
- StockingOrder
- ShippingLabel

The classes CustomerRecord, ProductRecord, and SupplierRecord parallel the abstractions Customer, Product, and Supplier, respectively. We retain both sets of abstractions because, as we will see, each plays a subtly different role in the system.

Note that there may be two kinds of invoices: those sent by the company to customers seeking payment for an order, and those received by the company for inventory ordered from suppliers. Both are materially the same kind of thing, although each plays a very different role in the system.

Our abstraction of the classes PackingOrder and StockingOrder require a bit more explanation. As our discussion concerning the first two scenarios described, the next action an OrderAgent takes after accepting an Order from a Customer is to schedule a StockPerson to carry out the Order. Our system decision is to formally capture this transaction as an instance of the class PackingOrder. The responsibility of this class is to collect all the information necessary to direct a stock person to fill a customer's order. Operationally, this means that our system schedules and then transmits this order to the handheld computer of the next available stockperson. Such information would, as a minimum, include the identification of some order number and the items to be retrieved from inventory. It is not difficult to think how we could vastly improve upon this simple scenario: our enterprise contains sufficient information for us to transmit the location of each

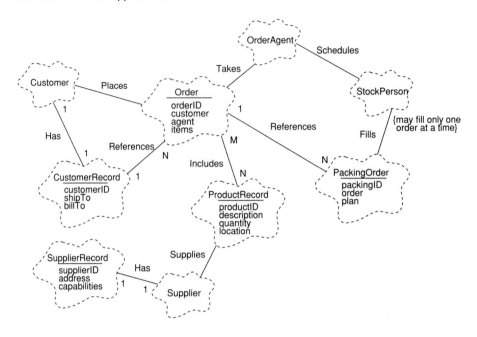

Figure 10-4
Key Classes for Taking and Filling Orders

such item to the stockperson, and perhaps even offer suggestions as to the order in which the stockperson should travel through the warehouse to retrieve these items most efficiently.* Sufficient information is also available in our system even to provide help to the newly hired stock person, perhaps by projecting a picture of the item to be retrieved on the display of the handheld computer. This general help facility would also be of use to the experienced stock person, in the face of a changing product line.

Figure 10-4 provides a class diagram that captures our understanding of the associations among certain of these abstractions, relative to the system function for taking and filling orders. We have further adorned this diagram with some of the attributes that are relevant to each class.

Much of what drives the particular concerns of this class structure is the requirement for navigating among instances of these classes. Given an order, we'd like to generate a shipping label for the associated customer; to do so, we navigate from the order back to the customer. Given a packing order, we'd like to navigate back to the customer and ordering agent, to report the fact that

---

* Of course, in the most general case, this is akin to the traveling salesperson problem, which is *np-complete*. However, it is possible to sufficiently constrain the problem so that a reasonable solution can be calculated. For example, business rules might dictate a partial ordering: we pack all heavy items first, and then the lighter ones. Also, we might retrieve related items together: pants go with shirts, hammers go with nails, tires go with hubcaps (we did say that this is a general-purpose inventory-tracking system!)

some items are on backorder; this requires that we navigate from the packing order back to the order and then back to the customer and ordering agent. Given a customer, we'd like to determine what products that customer most commonly orders during certain times of the year. This query requires that we navigate from the customer back to all pending and previous orders.

A few other details of this diagram are worth explaining. Why do we have a 1:N relationship between the classes `Order` and `PackingOrder`? Our business rules state that each packing order is unique to a given order (the 1 part of the cardinality expression). However, suppose that the warehouse is out of stock for certain items referenced in the original order: we have to schedule a second packing order once these items are back in stock.

Notice also the constraint upon the association of a `StockPerson` and a `PackingOrder`: for reasons of quality control, our business rules dictate that a stock person may fill only one order at a time.

To complete this phase of our analysis, we introduce two final key classes:

- `Report`
- `Transaction`

We include the abstraction `Report` to denote the base class of all the various kinds of hardcopy and online queries users might generate. Our detailed analysis by scenario will probably discover many of the concrete kinds of reports that our workflow demands, but because of the open-ended nature of our system, we are best advised to develop a more general reporting mechanism, so that new reports can be added in a consistent fashion. Indeed, by identifying the commonality among reports, we make it possible for all such reports to share common behavior and structure, thereby simplifying our architecture as well as allowing our system to present a homogeneous look and feel to its users.

Our list of things in the system is by no means complete, but we have sufficient information at this point to begin to move on to architectural design. Before we proceed, however, we must consider some principles that will influence our design decisions about the structure of data within our system.

Database Models

As described by Date, a database "is a repository for stored data. In general, it is both integrated and shared. By 'integrated' we mean that the database may be thought of as a unification of several otherwise distinct data files, with any redundancy among those files partially or wholly eliminated. . . . By 'shared' we mean that individual pieces of data in the database may be shared among several different users" [7]. With centralized control over a database, "inconsistency can be reduced, standards can be enforced, security restrictions can be applied, and database integrity can be maintained" [8].

Designing an effective database is a difficult task because there are so many competing requirements. The database designer must not only satisfy the functional requirements of the application, but must also address time and space factors. A time-inefficient database that retrieves data long after it is needed is pretty much useless. Similarly, a database that requires a building full of computers and a swarm of people to support it is not very cost-effective.

Database design has many parallels with object-oriented development. In database technology, design is often viewed as an incremental and iterative process involving both logical and physical decisions [9]. As Wiorkowski and Kull point out, "Objects that describe a database in the way that users and developers think about it are called logical objects. Those that refer to the way data are actually stored in the system are called physical objects" [10]. In a process not unlike that of object-oriented design, database designers bounce between logical and physical design throughout the development of the database. Additionally, the ways in which we describe the elements of a database are very similar to the ways in which we describe the key abstractions in an application using object-oriented design. Database designers often use notations such as entity-relationship diagrams to aid them in analyzing their problem. As we have seen, class diagrams can be written that map directly to entity-relationship diagrams, but have even greater expressive power.

As Date suggests, every kind of generalized database must address the following question: "What data structures and associated operators should the system support?" [11]. The different answers to this question bring us to three distinctly different database models:

- Hierarchical

- Network

- Relational

Recently, a fourth kind of database model has emerged, namely, *object-oriented databases* (*OODBMS*). An OODBMS represents a merging of traditional database technology and the object model. OODBMSs have proven to be particularly useful in domains such as computer-aided engineering (CAE) and computer-aided software engineering (CASE) applications, for which we must manipulate significant amounts of data with a rich semantic content. For certain applications, object-oriented databases can offer significant performance improvements over traditional relational databases. Specifically, in those circumstances where we must perform multiple joins over many distinct tables, object-oriented databases can be much faster than comparable relational databases. Furthermore, object-oriented databases provide a coherent, nearly seamless model for integrating data with business rules. To achieve much the same semantics, RDBMS usually require complex triggering functions, generated through a combination of third- and fourth-generation languages – not a very clean model at all.

However, for a variety of reasons, many companies may find that sticking with an RDBMS in the context of an object-oriented architecture reduces our development risk. Relational database technology is much more mature, available across a wider variety of platforms, and often more complete, offering solutions to the issues of security, versioning, and referential integrity. Furthermore, a company may have significant capital investment in people and tools supporting the relational model, and so for next-generation systems, simply cannot afford to transform their entire organization overnight.

The relational database model has indeed proven to be very popular. Because its use is so widespread, because an extensive infrastructure of products and standards support it, and because it satisfies the functional requirements of the inventory-tracking system, we choose to employ a relational database in our architecture; this is a strategic system decision. Thus, we have selected a hybrid architecture: we shall build an object-oriented skin over a traditional relational database, thereby deriving the benefits from both paradigms. Briefly, let's consider some general principles for relational database design, which will guide us in crafting this object-oriented skin.

The basic elements of a relational database "are tables in which columns represent things and the attributes that describe them and rows represent specific instances of the things described. . . . The model also provides for operators for generating new tables from old, which is the way users manipulate the database and retrieve information from it" [12].

Consider for a moment a database of products for a version of the inventory-tracking system tailored to manage a warehouse of electronic parts such as resistors, capacitors, and integrated circuits. In accordance with our previous class diagram, we have products uniquely identified by a product id, along with a descriptive part name. An example follows:

Products

productId	description
0081735	Resistor, 100 æ 1/4 watt
0081736	Resistor, 140 æ 1/4 watt
3891043	Capacitor, 100 pF
9074000	7400 IC quad NAND
9074001	74LS00 IC quad NAND

Here we have a table with two columns, each representing a different attribute. In a relation such as this, the order of rows and columns is insignificant; there may be any number of rows, but no duplicate rows. The heading `productID` represents a primary key, meaning that we may use its value to uniquely identify a particular part.

Products come from suppliers, so for each supplier we must maintain a unique id, a company name, an address, and perhaps a telephone number. Thus, we may write the following:

Suppliers

supplierID	company	address	telephone
00056	Interstate Supply	2222 Fannin, Amarillo, TX	806-555-0036
03107	Interstate Supply	3320 Scott, Santa Clara, CA	408-555-3600
78829	Universal Products	2171 Parfet Ct, Lakewood, CO	303-555-2405

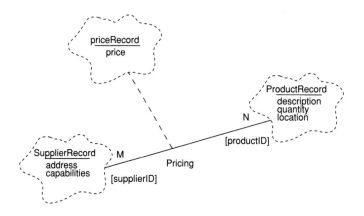

Figure 10-5
Attributed Association

supplierID is a primary key, meaning that its value may be used to uniquely identify a supplier. Notice that each row in this table is unique, although two rows have the same supplier name.

Different suppliers provide various products at different prices, and so we might also keep a table of prices. For a given product/supplier combination, this table includes the current price:

Prices

productID	supplierID	Price
0081735	03107	$0.10
0081735	78829	$0.09
0156999	78829	$367.75
7775098	03107	$10.90
6889655	00056	$0.09
9074001	03107	$1.75

This table has no single primary key. Rather, we must use a combination of the keys productID and supplierID to uniquely identify a row in this table. A key formed by combining column values is called a *composite key*. Notice that we do not include part and supplier names because they would be redundant; this information can be found by tracing from productID or supplierID back to the part or supplier table. productID and supplierID are therefore called *foreign keys*, because their values represent the primary keys of other tables.

Figure 10-5 illustrates the class structure that corresponds to this table. Here we use an attributed association to denote records that have meaning only in association with instances of two other records. Note that we also use our notation's key adornment to indicate the primary key of each class.

Continuing, we can track inventory via a table containing the quantity of all products currently on hand:

Inventory

productID	quantity
0081735	1000
0097890	2000
0156999	34
7775098	46
6889655	1
9074001	192

This table illustrates the fact that our object-oriented view of the system's data may differ from its database view. Whereas our schema in Figure 10-4 placed quantity as an attribute of the class ProductRecord, here we have chosen to keep quantity in a separate table, for performance reasons. Specifically, the description of a product tends to change very rarely, but we expect the quantity of a product to change constantly, as orders are filled and new stock is placed in the warehouse. Operationally, these are very different concepts, and we can optimize for quantity access and update by generating a separate table.

In the presence of an object-oriented schema such as we show in Figure 10-4, this implementation secret is hidden from all application clients. It therefore becomes the responsibility of the ProductRecord class to provide the illusion of quantity as being an integral part of the abstraction.

The simplest yet most important goal in database design is the concept that each fact should be stored in exactly one place. This eliminates redundancy, simplifies the process of updating the database, facilitates the maintenance of database integrity (that is, self-consistency and correctness), and reduces storage requirements. Achieving this goal is not particularly easy (and, as it turns out, not always important). Nevertheless, it is the most desirable characteristic we seek in our design.

Normalization theory has evolved as a technique for achieving this goal (although it is not the only relevant principle [13]). Normalization is a property of a table; we say that a particular table is in *normal form* if it satisfies certain properties. There are several levels of normal forms, each of which builds upon the other [14]:

- First normal form (1NF)   Each attribute represents an atomic value (nondecomposable attributes).

- Second normal form (2NF)   Table is in 1NF, and each attribute depends entirely upon the key (functionally independent attributes).

- Third normal form (3NF)   Table is in 2NF, and no attribute represents a fact about another attribute (mutually independent attributes).

Tables in 3NF "consist of 'properties of the key, the whole key, and nothing but the key' " [15].

The tables we have shown as examples are all in 3NF. There are higher forms of normalization, mainly relating to multivalued facts, but these are not of great importance to us here.

In bridging the semantic gap from object-oriented schema to a relational view, sometimes we may intentionally denormalize tables, meaning that we explicitly design them with some redundancy. This requires more effort to keep the redundant data in synch, but is worth the computational expense if access performance is a dominant issue.

SQL

Especially given our object-oriented view of the world, wherein we unite the data and behavioral aspects of our abstractions, a user might wish to perform a variety of common transactions upon these tables. For example, we might want to add new suppliers, delete products, or update quantities in the inventory. We also might want to query these tables in a variety of ways. For instance, we might want a report that lists all the products that we can order from a particular supplier. We might also want a report listing the products whose inventory is either too low or too high, according to some criteria we give it. Finally, we might want a comprehensive report giving us the cost to restock the inventory to certain levels, using the most inexpensive sources of products. These kinds of transactions are common to almost every application of an RDBMS, and so a standard language called SQL (Structured Query Language) has emerged for interacting with relational databases. SQL may be used either interactively or programmatically.

The most important construct in SQL is the select clause, which takes the following form:

```
SELECT <attribute>
FROM   <relation>
WHERE  <condition>
```

For example, to retrieve product numbers for which inventory is less than 100 items, we might write

```
SELECT PRODUCTID, QUANTITY
FROM   INVENTORY
WHERE  QUANTITY < 100
```

Much more complicated selection is possible. For example, we might want the same report to include the part name instead of the part number:

```
SELECT NAME, QUANTITY
FROM   INVENTORY, PRODUCTS
WHERE  QUANTITY < 100
AND    INVENTORY.PRODUCTID = PRODUCTS.PRODUCTID
```

This clause represents a *join*, whereby we combine two or more relations into a single relation. The select clause above doesn't generate a new table, but returns a set of rows. Since a single selection might return some arbitrarily large number of rows, we must have some means of visiting each row at a time. The mechanism SQL uses is the cursor, whose semantics are similar to the iteration operations we spoke of in Chapter 3. For example, one might declare a cursor as follows:

```
DECLARE C CURSOR
    FOR SELECT NAME, QUANTITY
        FROM   INVENTORY, PRODUCTS
        WHERE  QUANTITY < 100
        AND    INVENTORY.PRODUCTID = PRODUCTS.PRODUCTID
```

To cause evaluation of this join, we write

```
OPEN C
```

Then, to visit each row from the join, we write

```
FETCH C INTO NAME, AMOUNT
```

Finally, when we are done, we close the cursor by executing

```
CLOSE C
```

Instead of using a cursor, we may generate a virtual table that holds the result of the selection. Such a virtual table is called a *view*, and we may operate upon it just as if it were a real table. For example, to create a view containing the part name, supplier name, and cost, we might write:

```
CREATE VIEW V (NAME, COMPANY, COST)
    AS SELECT PRODUCTS.NAME, SUPPLIERS.COMPANY, PRICES.PRICE
        FROM   PRODUCTS, SUPPLIERS, PRICES
        WHERE  PRODUCTS.PRODUCTID = PRICES.PRODUCTID
        AND    SUPPLIERS.SUPPLIERID = PRICES.SUPPLIERID
```

Views are particularly important, because they make it possible for different users to have different views upon the database. Views may be quite different from the underlying relations in the database, and so permit a degree of data independence. Access rights may also be granted to users on a view-by-view basis, thus permitting the writing of secure transactions. Views are a little different from base tables, however, in that views representing joins may not be updated directly.

For our purposes, SQL represents a low level of abstraction. We don't expect end users to be SQL-literate; SQL is not directly a part of the vocabulary of the problem domain. Instead, we will use SQL within the implementation of our application, exposing it only to sophisticated tool builders, but hiding it from the mere mortals who must interact with the system on a daily basis.

Consider the following problem: Given an order, we'd like to determine the company name of the customer that placed the order. From the perspective of its implementation, carrying out this thread requires a modest amount of SQL; from the outside perspective, the application client would prefer to stay in the context of C++, and write expressions such as the following:

```
currentOrder.customer().name()
```

From our object-oriented perspective of the world, this expression invokes the selector customer to reference the order's customer; we then invoke the selector name to return the name of that customer. No great surprises here for the outside client, except that what is really happening is a database query, such as:

```
SELECT NAME
FROM    ORDERS, CUSTOMERS
WHERE   ORDERS.CUSTOMERID = CURRENTORDER.CUSTOMERID
AND     ORDERS.CUSTOMERID = CUSTOMERS.CUSTOMERID
```

Hiding this secret from the application client allows us to hide all the nasty details of working with SQL.

Mapping an object-oriented view of the world into a relational one is conceptually straightforward, although it in practice involves a lot of tedious details.* As Rumbaugh observes, "Mapping an object model into a relational database is simple except for the handling of generalization" [16]. Rumbaugh continues by offering some rules of thumb for mapping classes and associations (including aggregation relationships) to tables:

- Each class maps to one or more tables.
- Each many-to-many association maps to a distinct table.
- Each one-to-many association maps to a distinct table or may be buried as a foreign key [17].

He further suggests one of three alternatives for mapping superclass/subclass hierarchies to tables:

- The superclass and each subclass map to a table.
- Superclass attributes are replicated for each table (and each subclass maps to a distinct table).
- Bring all subclass attributes up to the superclass level (and have one table for the entire superclass/subclass hierarchy) [18].

Not surprisingly, there are limitations to using SQL in the underlying implementation.** In particular, SQL defines only a very limited set of data

---

* Much of the value of an object-oriented database derives from the fact that it hides these nasty details of SQL from the developer. The mapping of classes to tables is sufficiently codifiable that an alternate approach to using an OODBMS is possible: tools exist that take C++ class declarations and automatically generate the RDBMS schema and SQL code needed to bridge this semantic gap. Then, for example, as an application tries to access the attribute of a given object, this generated code transparently issues the necessary SQL statements to the off-the-shelf RDBMS, scrapes out the important data, and delivers it back to the client in a form consistent with the C++ interface.

** Recently, the SQL3 standard has been proposed, which offers object-oriented extensions. These extensions greatly reduce the semantic gap between an object-types, namely, characters, fixed-length strings, integers, and fixed- and floating-point numbers. Implementations occasionally extend this set of types; nonetheless, the representation of data such as pictures or long fragments of text is not supported directly.

Schema Analysis

As Date asks, "Given a body of data to be represented in a database, how do we decide on a suitable logical structure for that data? In other words, how do we decide what relations are needed and what their attributes should be? This is the database design problem" [19]. As it turns out, identifying the key abstractions of a database is much like the process of identifying classes and objects in object-oriented development. For this reason, in data-intensive applications such as the inventory-tracking system, we start with an object-oriented analysis and use its process to drive our design of the database, rather then the reverse of focusing upon the database schema first and deriving an object-oriented architecture from that.

The "list of things" we have assembled thus far in our analysis is a start. Taking this list and applying Rumbaugh's rules of thumb, we provide the following tables for our application's database. First we have tables that parallel the roles of various groups that interact with the system:

- CustomerTable
- SupplierTable
- OrderAgentTable
- AccountantTable
- ShippingAgentTable
- StockPersonTable
- ReceivingAgentTable
- PlannerTable

Next, we have some tables that deal with products and inventory:

- ProductTable
- InventoryTable

Finally, we have some tables that deal with the warehouse's workflow artifacts:

- OrderTable
- PurchaseOrderTable
- InvoiceTable

---

oriented view of the world and the relational view; these extensions also help to mitigate many of SQL's other limitations.

- PackingOrderTable
- StockingOrderTable
- ShippingLabelTable

We do not include tables for the classes Report or Transaction, because our analysis reveals that their instances are transitory, meaning that there is no requirement for making them persistent.

The next phase in our analysis would be to decide upon the attributes applicable to each of the above tables. We will not discuss these issues here, because we have already exposed some of the more interesting attributes of these abstractions (as, for example, in Figure 10-4), and the remaining attributes offer us no architectural insight into the system.

10.2 Design

In formulating the architecture of the inventory-tracking system, we must address three organizational elements: the split in client/server functionality, a mechanism for controlling transactions, and a strategy for building client applications.

Client/Server Architecture

The interesting issue here is not so much exactly *where* we draw the line between client and server responsibilities, but rather, *how* we intelligently make such a decision. Returning to first principles gives us the answer as to how: focus upon the behavior of each abstraction first, as derived from a use-case analysis of each entity, and only then decide where to allocate each abstraction's behavior. Once we have done this for a few interesting objects, some patterns of behavior will emerge, and we can then codify these patterns to guide us in allocating functionality for all the remaining abstractions.

For example, let's consider the behavior of the two classes Order and ProductRecord. Further analysis of the first class, together with some isolated class design, suggests that the following operations are applicable:

- construct
- setCustomer
- setOrderAgent
- addItem
- removeItem
- orderID
- customer
- orderAgent

- numberOfItems

- itemAt

- quantityOf

- totalValue

These services can be mapped directly to a C++ class declaration, such as the following. We start with two typedefs that bring in our vocabulary of the problem space:

```
// ID types
typedef unsigned int OrderID;

// Type denoting money in local currency
typedef float Money;
```

Next we provide a declaration for the Order class:

```
class Order {
public:

  Order();
  Order(OrderID);
  Order(const Order&);
  ~Order();

  Order& operator=(const Order&);
  int operator==(const Order&) const;
  int operator!=(const Order&) const;

  void setCustomer(Customer&);
  void setOrderAgent(OrderAgent&);
  void addItem(Product&, unsigned int quantity = 1);
  void removeItem(unsigned int index, unsigned int quantity = 1);

  OrderID orderID() const;
  Customer& customer() const;
  OrderAgent& orderAgent() const;
  unsigned int numberOfItems() const;
  Product& itemAt(unsigned int) const;
  unsigned int quantityOf(unsigned int) const;
  Money totalValue() const;

protected:
  ...
};
```

Notice the various constructors we provide, each with subtly different semantics. The default constructor (Order()) creates a new order object and assigns it a new unique OrderID value. The copy constructor also creates a new order object with a new OrderID value, but in addition copies the rest of its state from the given argument.

The remaining constructor takes an OrderID argument denoting an existing order object, and then retrieves the given uniquely numbered object. In other words, this particular constructor causes us to reach into the order database and

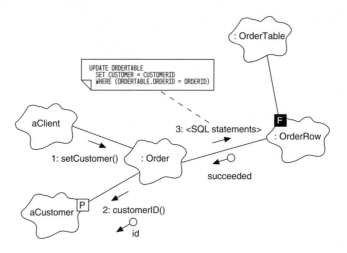

```
UPDATE ORDERTABLE
    SET CUSTOMER = CUSTOMERID
    WHERE (ORDERTABLE.ORDERID = ORDERID)
```

Figure 10-6
SQL Mechanism

(transparently) rematerialize the corresponding object. This of course requires a little bit of work below the surface: if some earlier activity in the same or another application had previously reconstructed the same order object, then our underlying SQL mechanism would have to make certain that these two objects either shared the same underlying state, or at least kept their states synchronized. This detail is, of course, a secret of the class's implementation, and therefore of little concern to clients who actually use the object from the perspective of its object-oriented interface.

Fortunately, implementing this strategy is not as bad as it sounds. If we define the class `Order` so that its only interesting state is a value of `OrderID`, then all operations largely involve dispatching SQL statements that read or write through to the database. Copies of the same object stay in synchronization, because the corresponding database table serves as the one repository of state for all views into the same object.

The object diagram in Figure 10-6 illustrates this SQL mechanism, with a scenario showing a client setting the customer for an order. Our scenario follows this order of events:

- `aClient` invokes `setCustomer` upon some instance of `Order`; an instance of the class `Customer` is provided as a parameter to this method function.
- The order object invokes the selector `customerID` upon the customer parameter, to retrieve its corresponding primary key.
- The order object dispatches an SQL `UPDATE` statement to set the customer id in the order database.

This mechanism also means that we can rely upon existing database mechanisms for locking and mutual exclusion (for example, consider two applications simultaneously trying to update an order's customer). If we need to make these locking mechanisms visible to clients, we can expose similar idioms for process synchronization as we use in the foundation class library in Chapter 9. As we will see later, our transaction strategy offers a unified way of updating a number of database objects at once, so as to preserve the database's self-consistency.

With this mechanism in place, it largely becomes a tactical issue of deciding where to place the logic that enforces our business rules for the application. This situation is no different than if we were to have used a non-object-oriented architecture, but by wrapping up our abstractions into classes, we make it possible to defer these decisions and, when we do make them, hide their details from clients. In this manner, clients are made insensitive to any changes we might make as we tune our system.

Let's consider two separate cases. First, adding or removing a product from the product database is clearly an action that requires significant rule checking, and thus we'd probably allocate most of the business-rule enforcement to the server. Adding a new product requires checking that we have uniquely defined and described this item; we might also have to broadcast the existence of the new product to various clients, so that they might update any cached tables they retain for reasons of performance. Similarly, removing an existing product requires checking that we don't invalidate any pending orders, and if we do, broadcasting the change to the appropriate clients who would be made obsolete by this action.[*]

In contrast, the rules surrounding the calculation of the total value of a new order apply to a much more local activity, and therefore are perhaps best allocated to enforcement by the client. With this action, we must query the current price of each item in the order, make conversions to local currency as necessary, and check against local rules for discounts, credit limits, and the like.

To summarize, we apply two rules of thumb in choosing the allocation of client/server responsibilities: first, place the enforcement of business rules according to which part of the system has the most knowledge regarding the impact of those rules, and second, hide these decisions below an object-oriented layer, so that if we change our mind, it doesn't matter.

Continuing our example, let's turn to our abstraction of a different class, namely `Product`. Further analysis, together with some isolated class design, suggests that the following operations are applicable:

- `construct`
- `setDescription`

---

[*] These kinds of semantics are exactly what triggers are all about: they represent the attachment of an action to some significant database event. By taking an object-oriented view of the world, we formalize this convention of using triggers by encapsulating them as part of the semantics of operating upon a database object.

- setQuantity
- setLocation
- setSupplier
- productID
- description
- quantity
- location
- supplier

These operations are common to every kind of product. However, use-case analysis reveals that these semantics are not sufficient for certain kinds of products. For example, given the open-ended nature of our inventory-tracking system together with the fact that product lines may change, our application may have to deal with the following kinds of products, which have their own unique behavior:

- Plants and food products that are perishable and therefore require special handling and shipping.
- Chemical products that also require special handling because they are caustic or toxic.
- Distinct products, such as radio transmitters and receivers, that should be shipped in matched sets and are therefore dependent upon one another.
- High-tech components, whose shipping is constrained by the local country's export laws.

These variations suggest the need for a hierarchy of product classes. However, as it turns out, the properties represented by the examples above are orthogonal, and therefore do not lend themselves to a strict hierarchy. Instead, as we show in Figure 10-7, a far more flexible strategy is to use a mixin style of design. Note that in this diagram we have used our notation's constraint adornment to capture our understanding of the particular semantics of each abstraction.

What value does an inheritance lattice offer for classes that in effect are higher-level abstractions of relational database entities? There is a tremendous amount of value: by formulating such hierarchies, we extract common behavior and elevate it to common superclasses, which are then responsible for providing this behavior consistently for all instances, unless those instances specialize that behavior (through an intermediate superclass) or augment that behavior (through a mixin superclass). This strategy simplifies our architecture and makes it more resilient to change, because it reduces redundancy and localizes common structure and behavior.

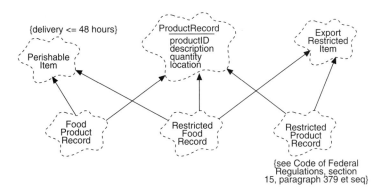

Figure 10-7
Product Classes

Transaction Mechanism

Client/server computing implies a collaboration between client and server, and so we must have some common mechanism whereby disparate parts of the system communicate with one another. As Berson notes, "There are three basic types of cooperative processing communications techniques that a client/server architecture can use" [20]:

- Pipes
- Remote procedure calls
- Client/server SQL interactions

Thus far, we have implied the use only of the third pattern, namely all SQL interactions. However, for a system as diverse as this one, it is likely that we will need to use all of these three patterns at one time or another for reasons of performance or, more pragmatically, because that is the convention that certain third-party software that we purchase requires us to use. For the sake of maintaining a clear and consistent architectural vision, we would be better served by devising a higher-level abstraction that hides our choice of communications patterns.

Earlier, we introduced the concept of a transaction class, but didn't elaborate upon its semantics. As Berson defines it, a transaction is "a unit of processing and information exchange between a local and a remote program that accomplishes a particular action or result" [21]. This is precisely the abstraction we need: a transaction object serves as the agent responsible for carrying out some remote action, and in so doing provides a clear separation of concerns between the action itself and the mechanisms for delivering that action.

Indeed, transactions are *the* central high-level communications pattern between client and server and among clients. Transactions tend to fall out of a use-case analysis. Each major business function in the inventory-tracking system can, in general, be abstracted as a transaction against the system. For example, placing an order, acknowledging receipt of new inventory, and updating supplier information are all transactions applicable to the system.

From the outside, we observe that the following operations capture our core abstraction of a transaction's behavior:

- `attachOperation`
- `dispatch`
- `commit`
- `rollback`
- `status`

For each transaction, we identify a complete set of operations it is to perform. Programatically, this means that we must provide member functions such as `attachOperation` for the class `Transaction` that allow other objects to package a collection of SQL statements for execution as a single unit.

It is pleasing to note that this object-oriented view of the world is conceptually in harmony with the way the database world views transactions. As Date states, "A transaction is a sequence of SQL (and possibly other) operations that is guaranteed to be atomic for the purposes of recovery and concurrency control" [22].

The concept of atomicity is an important part of a transaction's semantics. If the action of a particular transaction requires that we manipulate several rows of a table, then we must lump these operations together; otherwise we may leave the database in an inconsistent state. Therefore, when we `dispatch` a transaction, we mean to execute its associated operations as one mutually exclusive whole.

If a transaction completes normally, we must then `commit` it, causing all of its updates to take effect. However, dispatching a transaction may fail for a variety of reasons, perhaps because of a network failure that made it impossible to open a particular database, or perhaps because another client had locked certain critical records needed for updating. Under these conditions, we `rollback` the transaction, causing it to abandon any updates that the transaction began. The selector `status` returns a value reporting whether or not a dispatch completed normally.

Dispatching a transaction is far more complicated in the presence of distributed databases. The simple commit/rollback protocol works well if we have to update just one local database, but what if we have to update several databases on distinct servers? The general solution is to use what is called a *two-phase commit protocol* [23]. Under this protocol, an agent (in our design, an instance of the class `Transaction`) first assigns the various parts of the transaction's operations to their appropriate distributed servers; this is the *prepare phase*. If all these participants report that they are ready to commit, then the central transaction that started this action broadcasts a `commit` action; this is called the

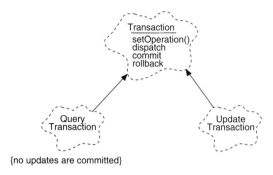

{no updates are committed}

Figure 10-8
Transaction Classes

commit phase. If instead any one server reports back after the prepare phase that it was not ready to commit, then we broadcast a `rollback` so as to back out of the entire distributed transaction. This is largely possible because each instance of `Transaction` encapsulates enough knowledge of its behavior to be able to turn back its original action.

Figure 10-8 shows a class diagram that illustrates our abstraction of transactions. Here we find a hierarchy of transactions. The base class `Transaction` above captures the structure and behavior common to all transactions, whereas the subclasses carry out the semantics of certain specialized transactions. We distinguish between `UpdateTransaction` and `QueryAction`, for example, because each provides very disjoint semantics: the former class modifies the state of the server, whereas the second class does not. By distinguishing among these and other kinds of transactions, we elevate common behavior to common classes, and in addition bring in more of our problem's vocabulary.

As we continue the development of our system, we are likely to find other patterns of transactions that make for suitable subclasses. For example, if we find that adding and removing items from certain databases have substantially the same semantics, we might want to invent both an `AddTransaction` and `DeleteTransaction` operation, so as to capture this common behavior.

Ultimately, the existence of the base class `Transaction` provides us an open-ended way of constructing and dispatching any kind of atomic action. For example, in C++ we might write:

```
class Transaction {
public:

    Transaction();
    virtual ~Transaction();

    virtual void setOperation(const UnboundedCollection<SQLStatement>&);
    virtual int dispatch();
    virtual void commit();
    virtual void rollback();
```

```
    virtual int status() const;

protected:
    ...
};
```

Notice how this class builds upon one of the foundation classes we discussed in Chapter 9. Here, our abstraction views a transaction as responsible for managing an indexable collection of statements. Operations for manipulating this collection are delegated to the parameterized class UnboundedCollection.

Ultimately, this architectural pattern allows sophisticated client applications to dispatch raw SQL statements. Transaction subclasses hide this power (and its associated complexity) from simpler clients who only need to perform certain common transactions.

Building Client Applications

To a large degree, building a client application is a problem of building a GUI-intensive program. Building an intuitive and friendly user interface is, however, as much an art as it is a science. In client/server applications such as this one, it is often the look and feel of the user interface that makes the difference between a wildly popular system and one that is quickly discarded. Human factors, technical constraints, historical reasons, and the personal preferences of the development team conspire to make crafting a useful, expressive, and self-consistent human/machine interface a very difficult task indeed.

As architects of the inventory-tracking system, we thus have two key development risks that confront us when crafting client applications. First, how do we evolve the "right" user interface?. Second, what common architecture can we use to build a family of client applications?

The first question has a simple answer, although its execution is tedious and requires active management direction: prototype, prototype, and prototype. This means using whatever facilities are available to get early releases of executable user-interface prototypes in the hands of real users, so that the development team can get quality feedback as to the look and feel of the system. Our object-oriented process helps us greatly in this matter, because it encourages this kind of incremental and iterative development. Using an object-oriented architecture also goes a long way in facilitating this kind of prototyping, because it allows us to tune our user interface without rending the fabric of our system.

The second question, that of devising a common client architecture, is ultimately a strategic design decision, but fortunately, it is one for which we can leverage off of GUI frameworks. Commercially, there exist products such as MIT's X Window System, Open Look, Microsoft's Windows, Apple's MacApp, Next's NextStep, and IBM's Presentation Manager. Each of these windowing systems is different: some are network-based, and others are kernel-based; some treat individual pixels as the most primitive graphical element, and others manipulate higher-level abstractions, such as rectangles, ovals, and arcs. In any case, all of these products have a common objective: they exist to simplify the task of implementing that part of an application that forms the human/machine interface. We should point out that none of these products sprang up overnight. Rather, the most useful windowing systems evolved over time, from proven, smaller systems. It has taken years of failures and successes for sufficient consensus to emerge in the industry on a meaningful set of abstractions for the problem of building user interfaces. We see many different windowing models because there is no single right answer to the problem of user interface design.

As we discuss in Chapter 9, the truly hard part of living with any large, integrated class library especially those for user interfaces, is learning what mechanisms it embodies. Perhaps the most important mechanisms we must understand, at least in the context of cooperative client/server computing, is how a GUI application responds to events. As Berson notes, GUI clients have to contend with the following kinds of events [24]:

- Mouse events
- Keyboard events
- Menu events
- Window update events
- Resizing events
- Activation/deactivation events
- Initialize/terminate events

We add to this list network events.* This last category is central in our approach to cooperative processing: client applications may receive network events from other applications, either asking them to take some action or providing them with some data. These semantics integrate well with our earlier invention of the Transaction class, for now we can view transactions as agents that send events from one application to another. In the context of each client application, the beauty of treating a network event as just another kind of event is that it permits us to use a consistent mechanism for reacting to any kind of event.

Berson goes on to observe that there are several architectural models for dealing with events [25]:

- Event-loop model   The event loop checks for pending events and dispatches an appropriate event-handling routine.
- Event-callback model   The application registers a callback function for each GUI widget that knows how to respond to a certain event; the callback is invoked when the widget detects an event.

---

* For example, Microsoft's DDE (Dynamic Data Exchange) and OLE (Object Linking and Embedding) are both peer-to-peer message-based protocols that provide Windows applications with a means of exchanging information.

- Hybrid model   A combination of the event loop and event callback models.

Although it is a bit of a simplification to say so, we observe that in general, MacApp uses the event loop model, Motif follows the event callback model, and Microsoft Windows applies the hybrid model.

In addition to this primary mechanism, we must follow a number of other common GUI mechanisms, including those for drawing, scrolling, tracking and responding to a mouse action, responding to a menu command, saving and restoring the state of an application, printing, editing (including cutting, copying, clearing, and pasting), dialog management, failure recovery, and memory management. Obviously, a complete discussion of each of these mechanisms is far beyond the scope of this text, for each GUI framework has its own conventions for these mechanisms.

A rule of thumb we offer to the developer of client applications is to select an appropriate GUI framework, learn its patterns, and apply them consistently.

10.3 Evolution

Release Management

Now that we have established an architectural framework for the inventory-tracking system, we can proceed with the system's incremental development. We start this process by first selecting a small number of interesting transactions, taking a vertical slice through our architecture, and then implementing enough of the system to produce an executable product that at least simulates the execution of these transactions.

For example, we might select just three simple transactions: adding a customer, adding a product, and taking an order. Together, the implementation of these three transactions requires us to touch almost every critical architectural interface, thereby forcing us to validate our strategic assumptions. Once we successfully pass this milestone, we might then generate a stream of new releases, according to the following sequence:

- Modify or delete a customer; modify or delete a product; modify an order; query a customer, order, and product.
- Integrate all similar supplier transactions, create a stocking order, create an invoice.
- Integrate remaining stocking transactions, create a report, create a shipment.
- Integrate remaining accounting transactions, create a receiving order.
- Integrate remaining shipping transactions.
- Complete remaining planning transactions.

For a 12–18 month development cycle, this probably means generating a reasonably stable release every 3 months or so, each building upon the functionality of the other. When we are done, we will have covered every transaction in the system.

As we discussed in Chapter 6, the key to success in this strategy is risk management, whereby for each release we identify the highest development risks and attack them directly. For client/sever applications such as this one, this means introducing capacity testing early in the evolutionary cycle (so that we identify any system bottlenecks early enough that we can do something about them). As our sequence of releases above suggests, this also means broadly selecting transactions for each release from across the functional elements of the system, so that we are not blindsided by unforeseen gaps in our analysis.

Application Generators

Domains such as the inventory-tracking system often include many different kinds of screen templates and hardcopy reports that must be generated. For large systems, these parts of the application are not technically difficult to write, just horribly tedious. This is precisely why application generators (or *4GLs*, for *fourth-generation languages*) are so popular for business enterprises. The use of 4GLs is not inconsistent with an object-oriented architecture. Indeed, the controlled use of 4GLs can eliminate writing a considerable amount of code.

Typically, we use 4GLs to automatically create screens and reports. Given the specification of a screen or report layout, a 4GL can generate the code necessary to produce the actual screen or report. We integrate this code with the remainder of our system by manually wrapping it in a very thin object-oriented layer. The products of the 4GL thus become class utilities that the rest of our application can build upon without knowing how they were created.

In this manner, we leverage off the benefits of the 4GL, yet still retain the illusion of a completely object-oriented architecture. The other advantage this strategy offers is that, as 4GLs become increasingly object-oriented and offer application programmatic interfaces (APIs) to object-oriented languages such as C++, the semantic gap across this particular seam in the system shrinks.

We can apply this same strategy to deal with all the various dialogs we might find in our client applications. Writing code for modal and modeless dialogs is tedious, because we have to deal with all sorts of detailed layout issues. Rather than writing raw code for dialogs,[*] a far better solution is to use a GUI builder that lets us "paint" our dialogs. As with a report application generator, we place a thin object-oriented skin over the products of our GUI builder, thereby giving us a clear separation of concerns.

---

[*] Writing object-oriented software may be fun, but it is far more important to focus on satisfying the requirements of the problem at hand. This means avoiding having to write new code whenever possible. Application generators and GUI builders are but two ways of doing this. Frameworks, such as we describe in Chapter 9, are another essential element along this same path.

10.4 Maintenance

A useful client/server system is rarely ever finished. This is not to say that we never get to the point where we have a stable system. Rather, the reality is that for applications that are central to a business, the software must adapt as the rules of the business change, otherwise our software becomes a liability rather than a competitive asset.

For the inventory-tracking system, we can envision several enhancements that changing business conditions may require us to address:

- Allow customers to electronically post their own orders and query the state of pending orders.

- Automatically generate personalized catalogs from our inventory database, tailored to target specific customer groups, or even individual customers.

- Completely automate all warehouse functions, thereby eliminating the human stockperson, as well as most receiving and shipping personnel.

Actually, the dominant risk in each of these particular changes is not technical, but social and political. By having a resilient object-oriented architecture, the development organization at least offers the company many degrees of freedom in being able to adapt nimbly to the changing marketplace.

Further Readings

More has been written about client/server computing than most mortals would care to read in a lifetime. Two particularly useful references are by Dewire [H 1992] and Berson [H 1992], who both offer a comprehensive and readable survey regarding a spectrum of client/server technologies. Bloom [H 1993] provides a short but lucid account of the basic concepts and issues of client/server architectures.

Downsizing is the not same thing as client/server computing, although downsizing a corporate management information system often involves the use of a client/server architecture. A study of the motivations for and risks surrounding downsizing may be found in Guengerich [H 1992].

A comprehensive treatment of relational database technology may be found in Date [E 1981, 1983; 1986]. Additionally, Date [E 1987] offers a description of the SQL standard. Various approaches to data analysis may be found in Veryard [B 1984], Hawryszkiewycz [E 1984], and Ross [F 1987].

Object-oriented databases represent the merging of conventional database technology and the object model. Reports of work in this field may be found in Cattell [E 1991], Atwood [E 1991], Davis et al. [H 1983], Kim and Lochovsky [E 1989], and Zdonik and Maier [E 1990].

The bibliography offers several references to various windowing systems and object-oriented user interfaces (see section K, "Tools and Environments"). Details about the Microsoft Windows API may be found in *Windows* [G 992]. A similar reference for Apple's MacApp may be found in *Macapp* [G 1992].

CHAPTER 11

Artificial Intelligence: Cryptanalysis

Sentient creatures exhibit a vastly complex set of behaviors that spring from the mind through mechanisms that we only poorly understand. For example, think about how you solve the problem of planning a route through a city to run a set of errands. Consider also how, when walking through a dimly lit room, you are able to recognize the boundaries of objects and avoid stumbling. Furthermore, think about how you can focus on one conversation at a party while dozens of people are talking simultaneously. None of these kinds of problems lends itself to a straightforward algorithmic solution. Optimal route planning is known to be an *np-complete* problem. Navigating through dark terrain involves deriving understanding from visual input that is (very literally) fuzzy and incomplete. Identifying a single speaker from dozens of sources requires that the listener distinguish meaningful data from noise and then filter out all unwanted conversation from the remaining cacophony.

Researchers in the field of artificial intelligence have pursued these and similar problems to improve our understanding of human cognitive processes. Activity in this field often involves the construction of intelligent systems that mimic certain aspects of human behavior. Erman, Lark, and Hayes-Roth point out that "intelligent systems differ from conventional systems by a number of attributes, not all of which are always present:

- They pursue goals which vary over time.
- They incorporate, use, and maintain knowledge.

- They exploit diverse, *ad hoc* subsystems embodying a variety of selected methods.
- They interact intelligently with users and other systems.
- They allocate their own resources and attention" [1].

Any one of these properties is sufficiently demanding to make the crafting of intelligent systems a very difficult task. When we consider that intelligent systems are being developed for a variety of domains that affect both life and property, such as for medical diagnosis or aircraft routing, the task becomes even more demanding because we must design these systems so that they are never actively dangerous: artificial intelligences rarely embody any kind of commonsense knowledge.

Although the field has at times been oversold by an overly enthusiastic press, the study of artificial intelligence has given us some very sound and practical ideas, among which we count approaches to knowledge representation and the evolution of common problem-solving architectures for intelligent systems, including rule-based expert systems and the blackboard model [2]. In this chapter, we turn to the design of an intelligent system that solves cryptograms using a blackboard framework in a manner that parallels the way a human would solve the same problem. As we will see, the use of object-oriented development is very well suited to this domain.

11.1 Analysis

Defining the Boundaries of the Problem

As outlined in the sidebar, our problem is one of cryptanalysis, the process of transforming ciphertext back to plaintext. In its most general form, deciphering cryptograms is an intractable problem that defies even the most sophisticated of techniques. For example, DES (the data encryption standard, a private-key encryption algorithm that uses multiple applications of substitution and transposition ciphers) appears to be free of any mathematical weaknesses and thus is safe against all currently known kinds of attack. Happily, our problem is much simpler, because we limit ourselves to single substitution ciphers.

As part of our analysis, let's walk through a scenario of solving a simple cryptogram. Spend the next few minutes solving the following problem, and as you proceed, record how you did it (no fair reading ahead!):

Q AZWS DSSC KAS DXZNN DASNN

As a hint, we note that the letter W represents the plaintext V.

Trying an exhaustive search is pretty much senseless. Assuming that the plaintext alphabet encompasses only the 26 uppercase English characters, there

Cryptanalysis Requirements

Cryptography "embraces methods for rendering data unintelligible to unauthorized parties" [3]. Using cryptographic algorithms, messages (plaintext) may be transformed into cryptograms (ciphertext) and back again.

One of the most basic kinds of cryptographic algorithms, employed since the time of the Romans, is called a *substitution cipher*. With this cipher, every letter of the plaintext alphabet is mapped to a different letter. For example, we might shift every letter to its successor: A becomes B, B becomes C, Z wraps around to become A, and so on. Thus, the plaintext

```
CLOS is an object-oriented programming language
```

may be enciphered to the cryptogram

```
DMPT jt bo pckfdu-psjfoufe qsphsbnnjoh mbohvbhf
```

Most often, the substitution of letters is jumbled. For example, A becomes G, B becomes J, and so on. As an example, consider the following cryptogram:

```
PDG TBCER CQ TCK AL S NGELCH QZBBR SBAJG
```

Hint: the letter C represents the plaintext letter O.

It is a vastly simplifying assumption to know that only a substitution cipher was employed to encode a plaintext message; nevertheless, deciphering the resulting cryptogram is not an algorithmically trivial task. Deciphering sometimes requires trial and error, wherein we make assumptions about a particular substitution and then evaluate their implications. For example, we may start with the one-and two-letter words in the cryptogram and hypothesize that they stand for common words such as I and a, or it, in, is, of, or, and on. By substituting the other occurrences of these ciphered letters, we may find hints for deciphering other words. For instance, if there is a three-letter word that starts with o, the word might reasonably be one, our, or off.

We can also use our knowledge of spelling and grammar to attack a substitution cipher. For example, an occurrence of double letters is not likely to represent the sequence qq. Similarly, we might try to expand a word ending with the letter g to the suffix ing. At a higher level of abstraction, we might assume that the sequence of words it is is more likely to occur than the sequence if is. Also, we might assume that the structure of a sentence typically includes a noun and a verb. Thus, if our analysis has identified a verb but no actor or agent, we might start a search for adjectives and nouns.

Sometimes we may have to backtrack. For example, we might have assumed that a certain two-letter word was or, but if the substitution for the letter r causes contradictions or blind alleys in other words, then we might have to try the word of or on instead, and consequently undo other assumptions we had based upon this earlier substitution.

> This leads us to the requirement of our problem: devise a system that, given a cryptogram, transforms it back to its original plaintext, assuming that only a simple substitution cipher was employed.

are 26! (approximately 4.03×10^{26}) possible combinations. Thus, we must try something other than a brute force attack. An alternate technique is to make an assumption based upon our knowledge of sentence, word, and letter structure, and then follow this assumption to its natural conclusions. Once we can go no further, we choose the next most promising assumption that builds upon the first one, and so on, as long as each succeeding assumption brings us closer to a solution. If we find that we are stuck, or we reach a conclusion that contradicts a previous one, we must backtrack and alter an earlier assumption.

Here is our solution, showing the results at each step:

1. According to the hint, we may directly substitute V for W.

   Q AZ̲V̲S DSSC KAS DXZNN DASNN

2. The first word is small, so it is probably either an A or an I; let's assume that it is an A.

   A̲ AZ̲V̲S DSSC KAS DXZNN DASNN

3. The third word needs a vowel, and it is likely to be the double letters. It is probably neither II nor UU, and it can't be AA because we have already used an A. Thus, we might try EE.

   A̲ AZ̲V̲E̲ DE̲E̲C KAE̲ DXZNN DAE̲NN

4. The fourth word is three letters long, and ends in an E; it is likely to be the word THE.

   A̲ H̲Z̲V̲E̲ DE̲E̲C T̲H̲E̲ DXI̲NN DH̲E̲NN

5. The second word needs a vowel, but only an I, O, or U (we've already used A). Only the I gives us a meaningful word.

   A̲ H̲I̲V̲E̲ DE̲E̲C T̲H̲E̲ DXI̲NN DH̲E̲NN

6. There are few four-letter words that have a double E, including DEER, BEER, and SEEN. Our knowledge of grammar suggests that the third word should be a verb, and so we select SEEN.

   A̲ H̲I̲V̲E̲ S̲E̲E̲N̲ T̲H̲E̲ S̲XI̲NN S̲H̲E̲NN

7. This sentence is not making any sense (hives cannot see), and so we probably made a bad assumption somewhere along the way. The problem seems to lie with the vowel in the second word, and so we might consider reversing our initial assumption.

I HAVE SEEN THE SXINN SHENN

8. Let's attack the last word. The double letters can't be SS (we've used an S, and besides, SHESS doesn't make any sense), but LL forms a meaningful word.

I HAVE SEEN THE SXINN SHELL

9. The final word is part of a noun phrase, and so is probably an adjective (STALL, for example, is rejected on this account). Searching for words that fit the pattern S?ALL yields SMALL.

I HAVE SEEN THE SMALL SHELL

Thus, we have reached a solution.

We may make the following three observations about this problem-solving process:

- We applied many different sources of knowledge, such as knowledge about grammar, spelling, and vowels.
- We recorded our assumptions in one central place and applied our sources of knowledge to these assumptions to reason about their consequences.
- We reasoned opportunistically. At times, we reasoned from general to specific rules (if the word is three letters long and ends in E, it is probably THE), and at other times, we reasoned from the specific to the general (?EE? might be DEER, BEER, or SEEN, but since the word must be a verb and not noun, only SEEN satisfies our hypothesis).

What we have described is a problem-solving approach known as a *blackboard model*. The blackboard model was first proposed by Newell in 1962, and later incorporated by Reddy and Erman into the Hearsay and Hearsay II projects, both of which dealt with the problems of speech recognition [4]. The blackboard model proved to be useful in this domain, and the framework was soon applied successfully to other domains, including signal interpretation, the modeling of three-dimensional molecular structures, image understanding, and planning [5]. Blackboard frameworks have proven to be particularly noteworthy with regard to the representation of declarative knowledge, and are space- and time-efficient when compared with alternate approaches [6].

A blackboard framework satisfies our definition for a framework, as described in Chapter 9. We can therefore codify its architecture in terms of a set of classes and mechanisms that describe how instances of those classes collaborate.

Architecture of the Blackboard Framework

Englemore and Morgan explain the blackboard model by analogy to the problem of a group of people solving a jigsaw puzzle:

> Imagine a room with a large blackboard and around it a group of people each holding over-size jigsaw pieces. We start with volunteers who put on the blackboard (assume it's sticky) their most 'promising' pieces. Each member of the group looks at his pieces and sees if any of them fit into the pieces already on the blackboard. Those with the appropriate pieces go up to the blackboard and update the evolving solution. The new updates cause other pieces to fall into place, and other people go to the blackboard to add their pieces. It does not matter whether one person holds more pieces than another. The whole puzzle can be solved in complete silence; that is, there need be no direct communication among the group. Each person is self-activating, knowing when his pieces will contribute to the solution. No *a priori* established order exists for people to go up to the blackboard. The apparent cooperative behavior is mediated by the state of the solution on the blackboard. If one watches the task being performed, the solution is built incrementally (one piece at a time) and opportunistically (as an opportunity for adding a piece arises), as opposed to starting, say, systematically from the left top corner and trying each piece [7].

As Figure 11-1 indicates, the blackboard framework consists of three elements: a blackboard, multiple knowledge sources, and a controller that mediates among these knowledge sources [8]. Notice how the following description parallels the principles of the object model. According to Nii, "the purpose of the blackboard is to hold computational and solution-state data needed by and produced by the knowledge sources. The blackboard consists of objects from the solution space. The objects on the blackboard are hierarchically organized into levels of analysis. The objects and their properties define the vocabulary of the solution space" [9].

As Englemore and Morgan explain, "The domain knowledge needed to solve a problem is partitioned into knowledge sources that are kept separate and independent. The objective of each knowledge source is to contribute information that will lead to a solution to the problem. A knowledge source takes a set of current information on the blackboard and updates it as encoded

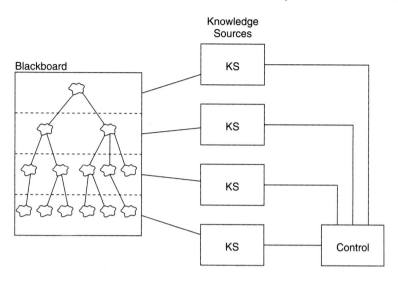

Figure 11-1
A Blackboard Framework

in its specialized knowledge. The knowledge sources are represented as procedures, sets of rules, or logic assertions" [10].

Knowledge sources, or KSs for short, are domain-specific. In speech-recognition systems, knowledge sources might include agents that can reason about phonemes, words, and sentences. In image-recognition systems, knowledge sources would include agents that know about simple picture elements, such as edges and regions of similar texture, as well as higher-level abstractions representing the objects of interest in each scene, such as houses, roads, fields, cars, and people.

Generally speaking, knowledge sources parallel the hierarchic structure of objects on the blackboard. Furthermore, each knowledge source uses objects at one level as its input and then generates and/or modifies objects at another level as its output. For instance, in a speech-recognition system, a knowledge source that embodies knowledge about words might look at a stream of phonemes (at a low level of abstraction) to form a new word (at a higher level of abstraction). Alternately, a knowledge source that embodies knowledge about sentence structure might hypothesize the need for a verb (at a high level of abstraction); by filtering a list of possible words (at a lower level of abstraction), this knowledge source can verify the hypothesis.

These two approaches to reasoning represent forward-chaining and backward-chaining, respectively. *Forward-chaining* involves reasoning from specific assertions to a general assertion, and *backward-chaining* starts with a hypothesis, then tries to verify the hypothesis from existing assertions. This is why we say that control in the blackboard model is opportunistic: depending upon the circumstances, a knowledge source might be selected for activation that uses either forward or backward chaining.

Knowledge sources usually embody two elements, namely, preconditions and actions. The preconditions of a knowledge source represent the state of the blackboard in which the knowledge source shows an interest. For example, a precondition for a knowledge source in an image-recognition system might be the discovery of a relatively linear region of picture elements (perhaps representing a road). Triggering a precondition causes the knowledge source to focus its attention on this part of the blackboard and then take action by processing its rules or procedural knowledge.

Under these circumstances, polling is unnecessary: when a knowledge source thinks it has something interesting to contribute, it notifies the blackboard controller. Figuratively speaking, it is as if each knowledge source raises its hand to indicate that it has something useful to do; then, from among eager knowledge sources, the controller calls on the one that looks the most promising.

Analysis of Knowledge Sources

Let's return to our specific problem, and consider the knowledge sources that can contribute to a solution. As is typical with most knowledge-engineering applications, the best strategy is to sit down with an expert in the domain and record the heuristics that this person applies to solve the problems in the domain. For our present problem, this might involve trying to solve a number of cryptograms and recording our thinking process along the way.

Our analysis suggests that thirteen knowledge sources are relevant; they appear with the knowledge they embody in the following list:

• Common prefixes	Common word beginnings such as re, anti, and un
• Common suffixes	Common word endings such as ly, ing, es, and ed
• Consonants	Nonvowel letters
• Direct substitution	Hints given as part of the problem statement
• Double letters	Common double letters, such as tt, ll, and ss
• Letter frequency	Probability of the appearance of each letter
• Legal strings	Legal and illegal combinations of letters, such as qu and zg, respectively
• Pattern matching	Words that match a specified pattern of letters
• Sentence structure	Grammar, including the meanings of noun and verb phrases
• Small words	Possible matches for one-, two-, three-, and four-letter words

- Solved   Whether or not the problem is solved, or if no further progress can be made
- Vowels   Nonconsonant letters
- Word structure   The location of vowels and the common structure of nouns, verbs, adjectives, adverbs, articles, conjunctives, and so on.

From an object-oriented perspective, each of these thirteen knowledge sources represents a candidate class in our architecture: each instance embodies some state (its knowledge), each exhibits certain class-specific behavior (a suffix knowledge source can react to words suspected of having a common ending), and each is uniquely identifiable (a small-word knowledge source exists independent of the pattern-matching knowledge source).

We may also arrange these knowledge sources in a hierarchy. Specifically, some knowledge sources operate upon sentences, others upon letters, still others on contiguous groups of letters, and the lowest-level ones on individual letters. Indeed, this hierarchy reflects the objects that may appear on the blackboard: sentences, words, strings of letters, and letters.

11.2 Design

Architecture of the Blackboard

We are now ready to design a solution to the cryptanalysis problem using the blackboard framework we have described. This is a classic example of reuse-in-the-large, in that we are able to reuse a proven architectural pattern as the foundation of our design. The structure of the blackboard framework suggests that among the highest-level objects in our system are a blackboard, several knowledge sources, and a controller. Our next task is to identify the domain-specific classes and objects that specialize these general abstractions.

Blackboard Objects The objects that appear on a blackboard exist in a structural hierarchy that parallels the different levels of abstraction of our knowledge sources. Thus, we have the following three classes:

- `Sentence`   A complete cryptogram
- `Word`   A single word in the cryptogram
- `CipherLetter`   A single letter of a word

Knowledge sources must also share knowledge about the assumptions each makes, so we include the following class of blackboard objects:

- `Assumption`   An assumption made by a knowledge source

Finally, it is important to know what plaintext and ciphertext letters in the alphabet have been used in assumptions made by the knowledge sources, so we include the following class:

- `Alphabet`   The plaintext alphabet, the ciphertext
                                                alphabet, and the mapping between the two

Is there anything in common among these five classes? We answer with a resounding yes: each one of these classes represents objects that may be placed on a blackboard, and that very property distinguishes them from, for example, knowledge sources and controllers. Thus, we invent the following class as the superclass of every object that may appear on a blackboard:

`class BlackboardObject ...`

Looking at this class from its outside view, we may define two applicable operations:

- `register`   Add the object to the blackboard
- `resign`   Remove the object from the blackboard

Why do we define `register` and `resign` as operations upon instances of `BlackboardObject`, instead of upon the blackboard itself? his situation is not unlike telling an object to draw itself in a window. The litmus test for deciding where to place these kinds of operations is whether or not the class itself has sufficient knowledge or responsibility to carry out the operation. In the case of `register` and `resign`, this is indeed the case: the blackboard object is the only abstraction with detailed knowledge of how to attach or remove itself from the blackboard (although it certainly does require collaboration with the blackboard object). In fact, it is an important responsibility of this abstraction that each blackboard object be self-aware it is attached to the blackboard, because only then can it begin to participate in opportunistically solving the problem on the blackboard.

Dependencies and Affirmations Individual sentences, words, and cipher-letters have another thing in common: each has certain knowledge sources that depend on it. A given knowledge source may express an interest in one or more of these objects, and therefore, a sentence, word, or cipher-letter must maintain a reference to each such knowledge source, so that when an assumption about the object changes, the appropriate knowledge sources can be notified that something interesting has happened. This mechanism is similar to the Smalltalk dependency mechanism that we mentioned in Chapter 4. To provide this mechanism, we introduce a simple mixin class:

```
class Dependent {
public:

  Dependent();
  Dependent(const Dependent&);
  virtual ~Dependent();

  ...

protected:

  UnboundedCollection<KnowledgeSource*> references;

};
```

We have leapt ahead to the implementation of this class, to show that it builds upon the foundation class library we describe in Chapter 9. Here, we see that the class `Dependent` has a single member object, that represents a collection of pointers to knowledge sources.[*]

We define the following operations for this class:

- `add`   Add a reference to the knowledge source
- `remove`   Remove a reference to the knowledge source
- `numberOfDependents`   Return the number of dependents
- `notify`   Broadcast an operation of each dependent

The operation `notify` has the semantics of a passive iterator, meaning that when we invoke it, we can supply an operation that we wish to perform upon every dependent in the collection.

Dependency is an independent property that can be "mixed in" with other classes. For example, a cipher-letter is a blackboard object as well as a dependent, so we can combine these two abstractions to achieve the desired behavior. Using mixins in this way increases the reusability and separation of concerns in our architecture.

Cipher-letters and alphabets have another property in common: instances of both of these classes may have assumptions made about them (and remember that an assertion is also a kind of `BlackboardObject`). For example, a certain knowledge source might assume that the ciphertext letter K represents the plaintext letter P. As we get closer to solving our problem, we might make the unchangeable assertion that G represents J. Thus, we include the following class:

```
class Affirmation...
```

_____

[*] In the architecture of the foundation classes from Chapter 9, we noted that unbounded structures require a storage manager. For simplicity, we omit this template argument in this and similar declarations in this chapter. Of course, a complete implementation would have to abide by the mechanisms of the foundation framework.

The responsibilities of this class are to maintain the assumptions or assertions about the associated object. We do not use `Affirmation` as a mixin class, but rather use it for aggregation. Letters *have* affirmations made about them, they are not *kinds of* affirmations

In our architecture, we will only make affirmations about individual letters as in cipher-letters and alphabets. As our earlier scenario implied, cipher-letters represent single letters about which statements might be made, and alphabets comprise many letters, each of which might have different statements made about them. Defining `Affirmation` as an independent class thus serves to capture the common behavior across these two disparate classes.

We define the following operations for instances of this class:

- `make`   Make a statement.
- `retract`   Retract a statement.
- `ciphertext`   Given a plaintext letter, return its ciphertext equivalent.
- `plaintext`   Given a ciphertext letter, return its plaintext equivalent.

Further analysis suggests that we should clearly distinguish between the two roles played by a statement: an assumption, which represents a temporary mapping between a ciphertext letter and its plaintext equivalent, and an assertion, which is a permanent mapping, meaning that the mapping is defined and therefore not changeable. During the solution of a cryptogram, knowledge sources will make many assumptions, and as we move closer to a final solution, these mappings eventually become assertions. To model these changing roles, we will refine the previously identified class `Assumption,` and introduce a new subclass named `Assertion` both of whose instances are managed by instances of the class `Affirmation` as well as placed on the blackboard. We begin by completing the signature of the operations `make` and `retract` to include an `Assumption` or `Assertion` argument, and then add the following selectors:

- `isPlainLetterAsserted`   A selector: is the plaintext letter defined?
- `isCipherLetterAsserted`   A selector: is the ciphertext letter defined?
- `plainLetterHasAssumption` A selector: is there an assumption about the plaintext letter?
- `cipherLetterHasAssumption` A selector: is there an assumption about the ciphertext letter?

Next, we define the class `Assumption`. Because this abstraction is largely a structural abstraction, we make some of its state unencapsulated:

```
class Assumption : public BlackboardObject {
public:

    ...

    BlackboardObject* target;
    KnowledgeSource* creator;
    String<char> reason;
    char plainLetter;
    char cipherLetter;

};
```

Notice that we reuse another class from the framework described in Chapter 9, the template class String.

Assumptions are kinds of blackboard objects because they represent state that is of general interest to all knowledge sources. The various member objects represent the following properties:

- target   The blackboard object about which the assumption was made
- creator   The knowledge source that created the assumption
- reason   The reason the knowledge source made the assumption
- plainLetter   The plaintext letter about which the assumption is being made
- cipherLetter   The assumed value of the plaintext letter

The need for each of these properties is largely derived from the very nature of an assumption: a particular knowledge source makes an assumption about a plaintext/ciphertext mapping, and does so for a certain reason (usually because some rule was triggered). The need for the first member, target, is less obvious. We include it because of the problem of backtracking. If we ever have to reverse an assumption, we must notify all blackboard objects for which the assumption was originally made, so that they in turn can alert the knowledge sources they depend upon (via the dependency mechanism) that their meaning has changed.

Next, we have the subclass named Assertion:

```
class Assertion : public Assumption ...
```

The classes assumption and assertion share the following operation, among others:

- isRetractable   A selector: is the mapping temporary?

All assumption objects answer true to the predicate isRetractable, whereas all assertion objects answer false. Additionally, once made, an assertion can neither be restated nor retracted.

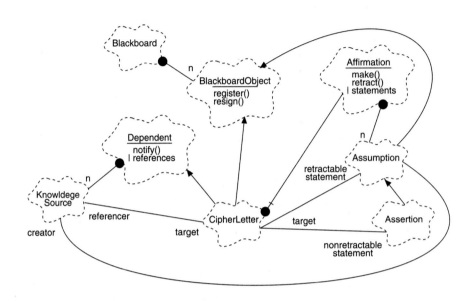

Figure 11-2
Dependency and Affirmation Classes

Figure 11-2 provides a class diagram that illustrates the collaboration of the dependency and affirmation classes. Pay particular attention to the roles each abstraction plays in the various associations. For example, a KnowledgeSource is the creator of an Assumption, and is also the referencer of a CipherLetter. Because a role represents a different view than an abstraction presents to the world, we would expect to see a different protocol between knowledge sources and assumptions than between knowledge sources and letters.

Design of the Blackboard Objects   Let's complete our design of the Sentence, Word, and CipherLetter classes, followed by the Alphabet class, by doing a little isolated class design. A sentence is quite simple: it is a blackboard object as well as a dependent, and it denotes a list of words that compose the sentence. Thus, we may write

```
class Sentence : public BlackboardObject,
                 virtual public Dependent {
public:
  ...
protected:

  List<Word*> words;

};
```

We make the superclass Dependent virtual, because we expect there may be other Sentence subclasses that try to inherit from Dependent as well. By marking this inheritance relationship virtual, we cause such subclasses to share a single Dependent superclass.

In addition to the operations register and resign defined by its superclass BlackboardObject, plus the four operations defined in Dependent, we add the following two sentence-specific operations:

- value   Return the current value of the sentence.
- isSolved   Return true if there is an assertion for all words in the sentence.

At the start of the problem, value returns a string representing the original cryptogram. Once isSolved evaluates as true, the operation value may be used to retrieve the plaintext solution. Accessing value before isSolved is true will yield partial solutions.

Just like the sentence class, a word is a kind of blackboard object as well as a kind of dependent. Furthermore, a word denotes a list of letters. To assist the knowledge sources that manipulate words, we include a reference from a word to its sentence, as well as from a word to the previous and next word in the sentence. Thus, we may write the following:

```
class Word : public BlackboardObject,
             virtual public Dependent {
public:

    ...

    Sentence& sentence() const;
    Word* previous() const;
    Word* next() const;

protected:

    List<CipherLetter*} letters;

};
```

As we did for the sentence operations, we define the following two operations for the class Word:

- value   Return the current value of the word.
- isSolved   Return true if there is an assertion for every letter in the word.

We may next define the class CipherLetter. An instance of this class is a kind of blackboard object and a kind of dependent. In addition to its inherited behaviors, each cipher-letter object has a value (such as the ciphertext letter H) together with a collection of assumptions and assertions regarding its corresponding plaintext letter. We can use the class `Affirmation` to collect these statements. Thus, we may write the following:

```
class CipherLetter : public BlackboardObject,
                     virtual public Dependent {
public:

  ...

  char value() const;
  int isSolved() const;...

protected:

  char letter;
  Affirmation affirmations;

};
```

Notice that we include the selectors `value` and `isSolved`, similar to our design of `Sentence` and `Word`. We must also eventually provide operations for the clients of `CipherLetter` to access its assumptions and assertions in a safe manner.

One comment about the member object `affirmations`: we expect this to be a collection of assumptions and assertions ordered according to their time of creation, with the most recent statement in this collection representing the current assumption or assertion. The reason we choose to keep a history of all assumptions is to permit knowledge sources to look at earlier assumptions that were rejected, so that they can learn from earlier mistakes. This decision influences our design decisions about the class `Affirmation`, to which we add the following operations:

- `mostRecent`   A selector: returns the most recent assumption or assertion
- `statementAt`   A selector: returns the *nth* statement

Now that we have refined its behavior, we can next make a reasonable implementation decision about the class `Affirmation`. Specifically, we can include the following protected member object:

```
UnboundedOrderedCollection<Assumption*> statements;
```

`UnboundedOrderedCollection` is another reusable class from the foundation class framework in Chapter 9.

Consider next the class named `Alphabet`. This class represents the entire plaintext and ciphertext alphabet, plus the mappings between the two. This information is important because each knowledge source can use it to determine which mappings have been made and which are yet to be done. For example, if we already have an assertion that the ciphertext letter C is really the letter M, then an alphabet object records this mapping so that no other knowledge source can apply the plaintext letter M. For efficiency, we need to query about the mapping both ways: given a ciphertext letter, return its plaintext mapping, and given a plaintext letter, return its ciphertext mapping. We may define the `Alphabet` class as follows:

```
class Alphabet : public BlackboardObject {
public:

  ...
  char plaintext(char) const;
  char ciphertext(char) const;
  int isBound(char) const;

};
```

Just as for the class `CipherLetter`, we also include a protected member object `affirmations`, and provide suitable operations to access its state.

Now we are ready to define the class `Blackboard`. This class has the simple responsibility of collecting instances of the class `BlackboardObject` and its subclasses. Thus we may write:

```
class Blackboard : public DynamicCollection<BlackboardObject*> ...
```

We have chosen to inherit from rather than contain an instance of the class `DynamicCollection`, because `Blackboard` passes our test for inheritance: a blackboard is indeed a kind of collection.

The `Blackboard` class provides operations such `add` and `remove`, which it inherits from the `Collection` class. Our design includes five operations specific to the blackboard.

• reset	Clean the blackboard.
• assertProblem	Place an initial problem on the blackboard.
• connect	Attach the knowledge source to the blackboard.
• isSolved	Return `true` if the sentence is solved.
• retrieveSolution	Return the solved plaintext sentence.

The second operation is needed to create a dependency between a blackboard and its knowledge sources.

In Figure 11-3, we summarize our design of the classes that collaborate with `Blackboard`. This diagram primarily shows inheritance relationships; for simplicity, it omits "using" relationships, such as that between an assumption and a blackboard object.

In this diagram, notice that we show the class `Blackboard` as both instantiating and inheriting from the template class `DynamicCollection`. This diagram also clearly shows why introducing the class `Dependent` as a mixin was a good design decision. Specifically, `Dependent` represents a behavior that encompasses only a partial set of `BlackboardObject` subclasses. We could have introduced `Dependent` as an intermediate superclass, but by making it a mixin rather than tying it to the `BlackboardObject` hierarchy, we increase its chances of being reused.

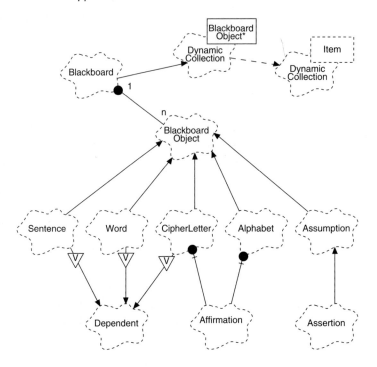

Figure 11-3
Blackboard Class Diagram

Design of the Knowledge Sources

In a previous section, we identified thirteen knowledge sources relevant to this problem. Just as we did for the blackboard objects, we may design a class structure encompassing these knowledge sources and thereby elevate all common characteristics to more abstract classes.

Design of Specialized Knowledge Sources Assume for the moment the existence of an abstract class called KnowledgeSource, whose purpose is much like that of the class BlackboardObject. Rather than treat each of the thirteen knowledge sources as a direct subclass of this more general class, it is useful to first perform a domain analysis and see if there are any clusters of knowledge sources. Indeed, there are such groups: some knowledge sources operate on whole sentences, others upon whole words, others upon contiguous strings of letters, and still others on individual letters. We may capture these design decisions by writing the following:

```
class SentenceKnowledgeSource : public KnowledgeSource ...
class WordKnowledgeSource : public KnowledgeSource ...
class LetterKnowledgeSource : public KnowledgeSource ...
```

For each of these abstract classes, we may provide specific subclasses. For example, the subclasses of the abstract class SentenceKnowledgeSource include

```
class SentenceStructureKnowledgeSource : public SentenceKnowledgeSource ...
class SolvedKnowledgeSource : public SentenceKnowledgeSource ...
```

Similarly, the subclasses of the intermediate class WordKnowledgeSource include

```
class WordStructureKnowledgeSource : public WordKnowledgeSource ...
class SmallWordKnowledgeSource : public WordKnowledgeSource ...
class PatternMatchingKnowledgeSource : public WordKnowledgeSource ...
```

The last class requires some explanation. Earlier, we said that the purpose of this class was to propose words that fit a certain pattern. We can use regular expression pattern-matching symbols similar to those used by UNIX's *grep* tool:

- Any item   ?
- Not item   ~
- Closure item   *
- Start group   {
- Stop group   }

With these symbols, we might give an instance of this class the pattern ?E~{ A E I O U}, thereby asking it to give us from its dictionary all the three-letter words starting with any letter, followed by an E, and ending with any letter except a vowel.

Pattern matching is a generally useful facility, so it is no surprise that scavenging for similar classes leads us to the pattern-matching classes we describe as part of our foundation library in Chapter 9. Thus, we may sketch out our pattern-matching knowledge source as follows, by borrowing from some existing classes:

```
class PatternMatchingKnowledgeSource : public WordKnowledgeSource {
public:

    ...

protected:

    static BoundedCollection<Word*> words;

    REPatternMatching patternMatcher;

};
```

All instances of this class share a dictionary of words, and each instance has its own regular expression pattern-matching agent.

The detailed behavior of this class is not important to us at this point in our design, so we will defer the invention of the remainder of its interface and implementation.

Continuing, we may declare the subclasses of the class `StringKnowledgeSource` as follows:

```
class CommonPrefixKnowledgeSource : public StringKnowledgeSource ...
class CommonSuffixKnowledgeSource : public StringKnowledgeSource ...
class DoubleLetterKnowledgeSource : public StringKnowledgeSource ...
class LegalStringKnowledgeSource : public StringKnowledgeSource ...
```

Lastly, we can introduce the subclasses of the abstract class `LetterKnowledgeSource`:

```
class DirectSubstitutionKnowledgeSource : public LetterKnowledgeSource ...
class VowelKnowledgeSource : public LetterKnowledgeSource ...
class ConsonantKnowledgeSource : public LetterKnowledgeSource ...
class LetterFrequencyKnowledgeSource : public LetterKnowledgeSource ...
```

Generalizing the Knowledge Sources Analysis suggests that there are only two primary operations that apply to all these specialized classes:

- reset   Restart the knowledge source.
- evaluate   Evaluate the state of the blackboard.

The reason for this simple interface is that knowledge sources are relatively autonomous entities: we point one to an interesting blackboard object, and then tell it to evaluate its rules according to the current global state of the blackboard. As part of the evaluation of its rules, a given knowledge source might do any one of several things:

- Propose an assumption about the substitution cipher.
- Discover a contradiction among previous assumptions, and cause the offending assumption to be retracted.
- Propose an assertion about the substitution cipher.
- Tell the controller that it has some interesting knowledge to contribute.

These are all general actions that are independent of the specific kind of knowledge source. To generalize even further, these actions represent the behavior of an inference engine. Simply stated, an *inference engine* is an object that, given a set of rules, evaluates those rules either to generate new rules (forward-chaining) or to prove some hypothesis (backward-chaining). Thus, we propose the following class:

```
class InferenceEngine {
public:

  InferenceEngine(DynamicSet<Rules*>);

  ...

};
```

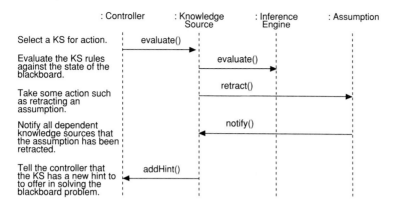

Figure 11-4
Scenario for Evaluating Knowledge Source Rules

The basic responsibility of the constructor is to create an instance of this class and populate it with a set of rules, which it then uses for evaluation.

In fact this class has only one critical operation that it makes visible to knowledge sources:

- evaluate   Evaluate the rules of the inference engine

This then is how knowledge sources collaborate: each specialized knowledge source defines its own knowledge-specific rules, and delegates responsibility for evaluating these rules to the class InferenceEngine. More precisely, we may say that the operation KnowledgeSource::evaluate ultimately invokes the operation InferenceEngine::evaluate, the results of which are used to carry out any of the four actions we discussed earlier. In Figure 11-4, we illustrate a common scenario of this collaboration.

What exactly is a rule? Using a Lisp-like format, we might compose the following rule for the common suffix knowledge source:

```
((* I ? ?)
  (* I N G)
  (* I E S)
  (* I E D))
```

This rule means that, given a string of letters matching the regular expression pattern *I?? (the antecedent), the candidate suffixes include ING, IES, and IED (the consequents). In C++, we might define a class that represents a rule as follows:

```
class Rule {
public:

  ...

  int bind(String<char>& antecedent, String<char>& consequent);
  int remove(String<char>& antecedent);
  int remove(String<char>& antecedent, String<char>& consequent);

  int hasConflict(const String<char>& antecedent) const;

protected:

  String<char> antecedent;
  List<String<char> > consequents;

};
```

The intended semantics of these operations follow their names. Again, we reuse some of the classes described in Chapter 9.

In terms of its class structure, we may thus say that a knowledge source is a kind of inference engine. Additionally, each knowledge source must have some association with a blackboard object, for that is where it finds the objects upon which it operates. Finally, each knowledge source must have an association to a controller, with which it collaborates by sending hints of solutions; in turn, the controller might trigger the knowledge source from time to time.

We may express these design decisions as follows:

```
class KnowledgeSource : public InferenceEngine,
                        public Dependent {
public:

  KnowledgeSource(Blackboard*, Controller*);

  ...

  void reset();
  void evaluate();

protected:

  Blackboard* blackboard;
  Controller* controller;
  UnboundedOrderedCollection<Assumption*> pastAssumptions;

};
```

We also introduce the protected object pastAssumptions, so that the knowledge source can keep track of all the assumptions and assertions it has ever made, in order to learn from its mistakes.

Instances of the class Blackboard serve as a repository of blackboard objects. For a similar reason, we need a KnowledgeSources class, denoting the entire collection of knowledge sources for a particular problem. Thus, we may write

```
class KnowledgeSources : public DynamicCollection<KnowledgeSource*> ...
```

One of the responsibilities of this class is that when we create an instance of KnowledgeSources, we also create the thirteen individual knowledge source objects. We may perform three operations upon instances of this class:

- restart   Restart the knowledge sources.
- startKnowledgeSource   Give a specific knowledge source its initial conditions.
- connect   Attach the knowledge source to the blackboard or to the controller.

Figure 11-5 provides the class structure of the KnowledgeSource classes, according to these design decisions.

Design of the Controller

Consider for a moment how the controller and individual knowledge sources interact. At each stage in the solution of a cryptogram, a particular knowledge source might discover that it has a useful contribution to make, and so gives a hint to the controller. Conversely, the knowledge source might decide that its earlier hint no longer applies, and so may remove the hint. Once all knowledge sources have been given a chance, the controller selects the most promising hint and activates the appropriate knowledge source by invoking its evaluate operation.

How does the controller decide which knowledge source to activate? We may devise a few suitable rules:

- An assertion has a higher priority than an assumption.
- The solver knowledge source provides the most useful hints.
- The pattern-matcher knowledge source provides higher-priority hints than the sentence-structure knowledge source.

A controller thus acts an agent responsible for mediating among the various knowledge sources that operate upon a blackboard.

The controller must have an association to its knowledge sources, which it can access through the appropriately-named class KnowledgeSources. Additionally, the controller must have as one of its properties a collection of hints, ordered according to its priority. In this manner, the controller can easily select for activation the knowledge source with the most interesting hint to offer.

Engaging in a little more isolated class design, we offer the following operations for the Controller class:

- reset   Restart the controller.
- addHint   Add a knowledge source hint.

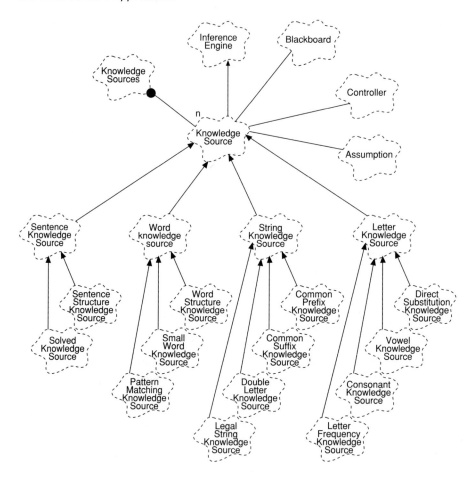

Figure 11-5
Knowledge Sources Class Diagram

- removeHint   Remove a knowledge source hint.
- processNextHint   Evaluate the next highest priority hint.
- isSolved   A selector: return true if the problem is solved.
- unableToProceed   A selector: return true if the knowledge.
                      sources are stuck.
- connect   Attach the controller to the knowledge source.

We may capture these decisions in the following declaration:

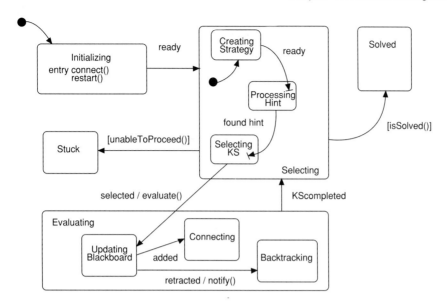

Figure 11-6
Controller Finite State Machine

```
class Controller {
public:

    ...
    void reset();
    void connect(KnowledgeSource&);
    void addHint(KnowledgeSource&);
    void removeHint(KnowledgeSource&);
    void processNextHint();

    int isSolved() const;
    int unableToProceed() const;

};
```

The controller is in a sense driven by the hints it receives from various knowledge sources. As such, finite state machines are well suited for capturing the dynamic behavior of this class.

For example, consider the state transition diagram shown in Figure 11-6. Here we see that a controller may be in one of five major states: Initializing, Selecting, Evaluating, Stuck, and Solved. The controller's most interesting activity occurs between the Selecting and Evaluating states. While selecting, the controller naturally transitions from the state CreatingStrategy to ProcessingHint to and eventually to SelectingKS. If a knowledge source is in fact selected, then the controller transitions to the Evaluating state, wherein it first is in UpdatingBlackboard. It transitions to Connecting if objects are added, and to Backtracking if assumptions are retracted, at which time it also notifies all dependents.

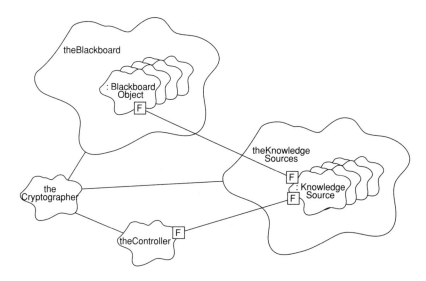

Figure 11-7
Cryptanalysis Object Diagram

The controller unconditionally transitions to Stuck if it cannot proceed, and to Solved if it finds a solved blackboard problem.

11.3 Evolution

Integrating the Blackboard Framework

Now that we have defined the key abstractions for our domain, we may continue by putting them together to form a complete application. We will proceed by implementing and testing a vertical slice through the architecture, and then by completing the system one mechanism at a time.

Integrating the Topmost Objects Figure 11-7 is an object diagram that captures our design of the topmost object in the system, paralleling the structure of the generic blackboard framework in Figure 11-1. In Figure 11-7, we show the physical containment of blackboard objects by the collection theBlackboard and knowledge sources by the collection theKnowledgeSources, using a shorthand style identical to that for showing nested classes.

In this diagram, we introduce an instance of a new class that we call Cryptographer. The intent of this class is to serve as an aggregate encompassing the blackboard, the knowledge sources, and the controller. In this manner, our application might provide several instances of this class, and thus have several blackboards running simultaneously.

We define two primary operations for this class:

- reset   Restart the blackboard.
- decipher   Solve the given cryptogram.

The behavior we require as part of this class's constructor is to create the dependencies between the blackboard and its knowledge sources, as well as between the knowledge sources and the controller. The reset method is similar, in that it simply resets these connections and returns the blackboard, the knowledge sources, and the controller back to a stable initial state.

Although we will not show its details here, the signature of the operation decipher includes a string, through which we provide the ciphertext to be solved. In this manner, the root of our main program becomes embarrassingly simple, as is common in well-designed object-oriented systems:

```
char* solveProblem(char* ciphertext)
{
  Cryptographer theCryptographer;
  return theCryptographer.decipher(ciphertext);
}
```

The implementation of the decipher operation is, not surprisingly, slightly more complicated. Basically, we must first invoke the operation assertProblem to set up the problem on the blackboard. Next, we must start the knowledge sources by bringing their attention to this new problem. Finally, we must loop, telling the controller to process the next hint at each new pass, either until the problem is solved or until all the knowledge sources are unable to proceed. We could use an interaction diagram or object diagram to show this flow of control, although C++ code fragments work equally well for so simple an algorithm:

```
theBlackboard.assertProblem();
theKnowledgeSources.reset();
while (!theController.isSolved() || theController.unableToProceed())
  theController.processNextHint();
if (theBlackboard.isSolved())
  return theBlackboard.retrieveSolution();
```

As part of our evolution, we would be best advised to complete enough of the relevant architectural interfaces so that we could complete this algorithm and execute it. Although at this point it would have minimal functionality, its implementation as a vertical slice through the architecture would force us to validate certain key architectural decisions.

Continuing, let's look at two of the key operations used in decipher, namely, assertProblem and retrieveSolution. The assertProblem operation is particularly interesting, because it must generate an entire set of blackboard objects. In the form of a simple script, our algorithm is as follows:

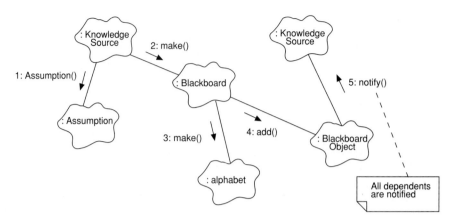

Figure 11-8
Assumption Mechanism

```
trim all leading and trailing blanks from the string
return if the resulting string is empty
create a sentence object
add the sentence to the blackboard
create a word object (this will be the leftmost word in the sentence)
add the word to the blackboard
add the word to the sentence
for each character in the string, from left to right
  if the character is a space
    make the current word the previous word
      create a word object
      add the word to the blackboard
      add the word to the sentence
  else
      create a cipher-letter object
      add the letter to the blackboard
      add the letter to the word
```

As we described in Chapter 6, the purpose of design is simply to provide a blueprint for implementation. This script supplies a sufficiently detailed algorithm, so we need not show its complete implementation in C++.

The operation `retrieveSolution` is far simpler; we simply return the value of the sentence on the blackboard: Calling `retrieveSolution` before `isSolved` evaluates true will yield partial solutions.

Implementing the Assumption Mechanism At this point, we have implemented the mechanisms that allow us to set and retrieve values for blackboard objects. The next major function point involves the mechanism for making assumptions about blackboard objects. This is a particularly significant issue, because assumptions are dynamic (meaning that they are routinely created and destroyed during the process of forming a solution) and their creation or retraction triggers controller events.

Figure 11-8 illustrates the primary scenario of when a knowledge source states an assumption. As this diagram shows, once the knowledge source creates an assumption, it notifies the blackboard, which in turn makes the assumption for its alphabet and then for each blackboard object to which the assumption applies. Using the dependency mechanism, the affected blackboard object in turn might notify its dependent knowledge sources.

In its most naive implementation, retracting an assumption simply undoes the work of this mechanism. For example, to retract an assumption about a cipher letter, we just pop its collection of assumptions, up to and including the assumption we are retracting. In this manner, the given assumption and all assumptions that built upon it are undone.

A more sophisticated mechanism is possible. For example, suppose that we made an assumption that a certain one–letter word is really just the letter I (assuming we need a vowel). We might make a later assumption that a certain double-letter word is NN (assuming we need a consonant). If we then find we must retract the first assumption, we probably don't have to retract the second one. This approach requires us to add a new behavior to the class Assumption, so that it can keep track of what assumptions are dependent upon others. We can reasonably defer this enhancement until much later in the evolution of this system, because adding this behavior has no architectural impact.

Adding New Knowledge Sources

Now that we have the key abstractions of the blackboard framework in place, and once the mechanisms for stating and retracting assumptions are working, our next step is to implement the InferenceEngine class, since all knowledge sources depend upon it. As we mentioned earlier, this class has only one really interesting operation, namely, evaluateRules. We will not show its details here, because this particular method reveals no new important design issues.

Once we are confident that our inference engine works properly, we may incrementally add each knowledge source. We emphasize the use of an incremental process for two reasons:

- For a given knowledge source, it is not clear what rules are really important until we apply them to real problems.
- Debugging the knowledge base is far easier if we implement and test smaller related sets of rules, rather than trying to test them all at once.

Fundamentally, implementing each knowledge source is largely a problem of knowledge engineering. For a given knowledge source, we must confer with an expert (perhaps a cryptologist) to decide what rules are meaningful. As we test each knowledge source, our analysis may reveal that certain rules are useless, others are either too specific or too general, and perhaps some are missing. We may then choose to alter the rules of a given knowledge source or even add new sources of knowledge.

As we implement each knowledge source, we may discover the existence of common rules as well as common behavior. For example, we might notice that the `WordStructureKnowledgeSource` and the `SentenceStructureKnowledgeSource` share a common behavior, in that both must know how to evaluate rules regarding the legal ordering of certain constructs. The former knowledge source is interested in the arrangement of letters; the latter is interested in the arrangement of words. In either case, the processing is the same; thus it is reasonable for us to alter the knowledge source class structure by developing a new mixin class, called `StructureKnowledgeSource`, in which we place this common behavior.

This new knowledge source class hierarchy highlights the fact that evaluating a set of rules is dependent upon both the kind of knowledge source as well as the kind of blackboard object. For example, given a specific knowledge source, it might use forward-chaining on one kind of blackboard object, and backward-chaining on another. Furthermore, given a specific blackboard object, how it is evaluated will depend upon which knowledge source is applied.

11.4 Maintenance

Adding New Functionality

In this section, we consider an improvement to the functionality of the cryptanalysis system and observe how our design weathers the change.

In any intelligent system, it is important to know what the final answer is to a problem, but it is often equally important to know how the system arrived at this solution. Thus, we desire our application to be introspective: it should keep track of when knowledge sources were activated, what assumptions were made and why, and so on, so that we can later question it, for example, about why it made an assumption, how it arrived at another assumption, and when a particular knowledge source was activated.

To add this new functionality, we need to do two things. First, we must devise a mechanism for keeping track of the work that the controller and each knowledge source perform, and second, we must modify the appropriate operations so that they record this information. Basically, the design calls for the knowledge sources and the controller to register what they did in some central repository.

Let's start by inventing the classes needed to support this mechanism. First, we might define the class `Action`, which serves to record what a particular knowledge source or controller did:

```
class Action {
public:

    Action(KnowledgeSource* who, BlackboardObject* what, char* why);
    Action(Controller* who, KnowledgeSource* what, char* why);

    ...

};
```

For example, if the controller selected a particular knowledge source for activation, it would create an instance of this class, set the `who` argument to itself, set the `what` argument to the knowledge source, and set the `why` argument to some explanation (perhaps including the current priority of the hint).

The first part of our task is done, and the second part is almost as easy. Consider for a moment where important events take place in our application. As it turns out, there are five primary kinds of operations that are affected:

- Methods that state an assumption
- Methods that retract an assumption
- Methods that activate a knowledge source
- Methods that cause rules to be evaluated
- Methods that register hints from a knowledge source

Actually, these events are largely constrained to two places in the architecture: as part of the controller's finite state machine, and as part of the assumption mechanism. Our maintenance task, therefore, involves touching all the methods that play a role in these two places, a task which is tedious but by no means rocket science. Indeed, the most important discovery is that adding this new behavior requires no significant architectural change.

To complete our work here, we must also implement a class that can answer who, what, when, and why questions from the user. The design of such an object is not terribly difficult, because all the information it needs to know may be found as the state of instances of the class `actions`.

Changing the Requirements

Once we have a stable implementation in place, many new requirements can be incorporated with minimal change to our design. Let's consider three kinds of new requirements:

- The ability to decipher languages other than English
- The ability to decipher using transposition ciphers as well as single-substitution ciphers
- The ability to learn from experience

The first change is fairly easy, because the fact that our application uses English is largely immaterial to our design. Assuming the same character set is used, it is mainly a matter of changing the rules associated with each knowledge source. Actually, changing the character set is not that difficult either, because even the `alphabet` class is not dependent upon what characters it manipulates.

The second change is much harder, but it is still possible in the context of the blackboard framework. Basically, our approach is to add new sources of knowledge that embody information about transposition ciphers. Again, this change does not alter any existing key abstraction or mechanism in our design; rather, it involves the addition of new classes that use existing facilities, such as the `InferenceEngine` class and the assumption mechanism.

The third change is the hardest of all, mainly because machine learning is on the fringes of our knowledge in artificial intelligence. As one approach, when the controller discovers it can no longer proceed, it might ask the user for a hint. By recording this hint, along with the actions that led up to the system being stuck, the blackboard application can avoid a similar problem in the future. We can incorporate this simplistic learning mechanism without vastly altering any of our existing classes; as with all the other changes, this one can build on existing facilities.

Further Readings

In the context of architectural patterns, Shaw [A 1991] discusses blackboard frameworks as well as other kinds of application frameworks.

Englemore and Morgan [C 1988] furnish a comprehensive treatment of blackboard systems, including their evolution, theory, design, and application. Among other topics, there are descriptions of two object-oriented blackboard systems, BB1 from Stanford, and BLOB, developed for the British Ministry of Defense. Other useful sources of information regarding blackboard systems may be found in Hayes-Roth [J 1985] and Nii [J 1986].

Detailed discussions concerning forward- and backward-chaining in rule-based systems may be found in Barr and Feigenbaum [J 1981]; Brachman and Levesque [J 1985]; Hayes-Roth, Waterman, and Lenat [J 1983]; and Winston and Horn [G 1989].

Meyer and Matyas [I 1982] cover the strengths and weaknesses of various kinds of ciphers, along with algorithmic approaches to breaking them.

CHAPTER 12

Command and Control: Traffic Management

The economics of software development have progressed to the point where it is now feasible to automate many more kinds of applications than ever before, ranging from embedded microcomputers that control automobile engines to tools that eliminate much of the drudgery associated with producing an animated film, to systems that manage the distribution of interactive video services to millions of consumers. The distinguishing characteristic of all these larger systems is that they are extremely complex. Building systems so that their implementation is small is certainly an honorable task, but reality tells us that certain large problems demand large implementations. For some massive applications, it is not unusual to find software development organizations that employ several hundred programmers who must collaborate to produce a million or more lines of code against a set of requirements that are guaranteed to be unstable during development. Such projects rarely involve the development of single programs; they more often encompass multiple, cooperative programs that must execute across a distributed target system consisting of many computers connected to one another in a variety of ways. To reduce development risk, such projects usually involve a central organization that is responsible for systems architecture and integration; the remaining work is subcontracted to other companies. Thus, the development team as a whole never assembles as one; it is typically distributed over space and – because of the personnel turnover common in large projects – over time.

Developers who are content with writing small, stand-alone, single-user, window-based tools may find the problems associated with building massive applications staggering – so much so that they view it as folly even to try. However, the actuality of the business and scientific world is such that complex software systems must be built. Indeed, in some cases, it is folly not to try. Imagine using a manual system to control air traffic around a major metropolitan center or to manage the life-support system of a manned spacecraft or the accounting activities of a multinational bank. Successfully automating such systems not only addresses the very real problems at hand, but also leads to a number of tangible and intangible benefits, such as lower operational costs, greater safety, and increased functionality. Of course, the operative word here is *successfully*. Building complex systems is plain hard work, and requires the application of the best engineering practices we know, along with the creative insight of a few great designers.

This chapter tackles such a problem, to demonstrate that the notation and process of object-oriented development scale up to programming-in-the-colossal.

12.1 Analysis

Defining the Boundaries of the Problem

To most people living in the United States, trains are an artifact of an era long past; in Europe and in many parts of the Orient, the situation is entirely the opposite. Unlike the United States, for example, Europe has few national and international highways, and gasoline and automobile prices are comparatively very high. Thus, trains are an essential part of the continent's transportation network; tens of thousands of kilometers of track carry people and goods daily, both within cities and across national borders. In all fairness, trains do still provide an important and economical means of transporting goods within the United States. Additionally, as major metropolitan centers grow more crowded, light rail transport is increasingly viewed as an attractive option to easing congestion and addressing the problems of pollution from internal combustion engines.

Still, railroads are a business and consequently must be profitable. Railroad companies must delicately balance the demands of frugality and safety and the pressures to increase traffic against efficient and predictable train scheduling. These conflicting needs suggest an automated solution to train traffic management, including computerized train routing and monitoring of all elements of the train system.

Such automated and semiautomated train systems exist today in Sweden, Great Britain, West Germany, France, and Japan [1]. A similar system, called the Advanced Train Control System, has been under development in Canada and the United States, with participation by Amtrak, Burlington, the Canadian National Railway Company, CP Rail, CSX Transportation, the Norfolk and

Western Railway Company, the Southern Railway Company, and Union Pacific. The motivation for each of these systems is largely economic and social: lower operating costs and more efficient utilization of resources are the goals, with improved safety as an integral by-product.

The sidebar provides the basic requirements for a train traffic management system. Obviously, this is a highly simplified statement of requirements. In practice, detailed requirements for an application as large as this come about only after the viability of an automated solution is demonstrated, and then only after many hundreds of person/months of analysis involving the participation of numerous domain experts and the eventual users and clients of the system. Ultimately, the requirements for a large system may encompass thousands of pages of documentation, specifying not only the general behavior of the system, but intricate details such as the screen layouts to be used for human/machine interaction.

Even from these highly elided system requirements, we can make two observations about the process of developing a traffic management system:

- The architecture must be allowed to evolve over time.
- The implementation must rely upon existing standards to the largest extent practical.

Our experience with developing large systems has been that an initial statement of requirements is never complete, often vague, and always self-contradictory. For these reasons, we must consciously concern ourselves with the management of uncertainty during development, and therefore we strongly suggest that the development of such a system be deliberately allowed to evolve over time in an incremental and iterative fashion. As we pointed out in Chapter 7, the very process of development gives both users and developers better insight into what requirements are really important – far better than any paper exercise in writing requirements documents in the absence of an existing implementation or prototype. Also, since developing the software for a large system may take several years, software requirements must be allowed to change to take advantage of the rapidly changing hardware technology.[*] It is undeniably futile to craft an elegant software architecture targeted to a hardware technology that is guaranteed to be obsolete by the time the system is fielded. This is why we suggest that, whatever mechanisms we craft as part of our software architecture, we should rely upon existing standards for communications, graphics, networking, and sensors. For truly novel systems, it

---

[*] In fact, for many such systems of this complexity, it is common to have to deal with many different kinds of computers. Having a well-thought out and stable architecture mitigates much of the risk of changing hardware in the middle of development, an event that happens all too often in the face of the rapidly changing hardware business. Hardware products come and go, and therefore it is important to manage the hardware/software boundary of a system so that new products can be introduced that reduce the system's cost or improve its performance, while at the same time preserving the integrity of the system's architecture.

Traffic Management System Requirements

The traffic management system has two primary functions: train routing and train-systems monitoring. Related functions include traffic planning, train-location tracking, traffic monitoring, collision avoidance, failure prediction, and maintenance logging. Figure 12-1 provides a block diagram for the major elements of the traffic management system [2].

The locomotive analysis and reporting system includes several discrete and analog sensors for monitoring elements such as oil temperature, oil pressure, fuel quantity, alternator volts and amperes, throttle setting, engine RPM, water temperature, and drawbar force. Sensor values are presented to the train engineer via the on-board display system and to dispatchers and maintenance personnel elsewhere on the network. Warning or alarm conditions are registered whenever certain sensor values fall outside of normal operating range. A log of sensor values is maintained to support maintenance and fuel management.

The energy management system advises the train engineer in real time as to the most efficient throttle and brake settings. Inputs to this system include track profile and grade, speed limits, schedules, train load, and power available, from which the system can determine fuel-efficient throttle and brake settings that are consistent with the desired schedule and safety concerns. Suggested throttle and brake settings, track profile and grade, and train position and speed are made available for display on the on-board display system.

The on-board display system provides the human/machine interface for the train engineer. Information from the locomotive analysis and reporting system, the energy management system, and the data management unit are made available for display. Soft keys exist to permit the engineer to select different displays.

The data management unit serves as the communications gateway between all on-board systems and the rest of the network, to which all trains, dispatchers, and other users are connected.

Train-location tracking is achieved via two devices on the network: location transponders and the Navstar global positioning system (GPS). The locomotive analysis and reporting system can determine the general location of a train via dead reckoning, simply by counting wheel revolutions. This information is augmented by information from location transponders, which are placed every kilometer along a track and at critical track junctions. These transponders relay their identity to passing trains via their data management units, from which a more exact train location may be determined. Trains may also be equipped with GPS receivers, from which train location may be determined to within 1 meter.

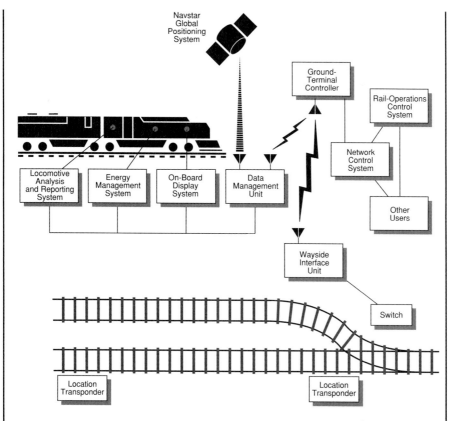

Figure 12-1
Traffic Management System

A wayside interface unit is placed wherever there is some controllable device (such as a switch) or a sensor (such as an infrared sensor for detecting overheated wheel bearings). Each wayside interface unit may receive commands from a local ground-terminal controller (for example, to turn a signal on or off). Devices may be overridden by local manual control. Each unit can also report its current setting. A ground-terminal control serves to relay information to and from passing trains and to and from wayside interface units. Ground-terminal controllers are placed along a track, spaced close enough so that every train is always within range of at least one terminal.

Every ground-terminal controller relays its information to a common network control system. Connections between the network-control system and each ground-terminal controller may be made via microwave link, landlines, or fiber optics, depending upon the remoteness of each ground-terminal controller. The network control system monitors the health of the entire network and can automatically route information in alternate ways in the event of equipment failure.

The network control system is ultimately connected to one or more dispatch centers, which comprise the rail-operations control system and other users. At the rail-operations control system, dispatchers can establish train routes and track the progress of individual trains. Individual dispatchers control different territories; each dispatcher's control console may be set up to control one or more territories. Train routes include instructions for automatically switching trains from track to track, setting speed restrictions, setting out or picking up cars, and allowing or denying train clearance to a specific track section. Dispatchers may note the location of track work along train routes for display to train engineers. Trains may be stopped from the rail-operations control system (manually by dispatchers or automatically) when hazardous conditions are detected (such as a runaway train, track failure, or a potential collision condition). Dispatchers can also call up any information available to individual train engineers, as well as send movement authority, wayside device settings, and plan revisions.

Track layouts and wayside equipment may change over time. The numbers of trains and their routes may change daily. The system must be designed to permit incorporation of new sensor, network, and processor technology.

is sometimes necessary to pioneer new hardware or software technology. This adds risk to a large project, however, which already involves a customarily high risk. Software development clearly remains the technology of highest risk in the successful deployment of any large automated application, and our goal is to limit this risk to a manageable level, not to increase it.

Obviously, we cannot carry out a complete analysis or design of this problem in a single chapter, much less a single book. Since our intent here is to explore how our notation and process scale up, we will focus upon the problem of building a resilient architecture for this domain.

System Requirements Versus Software Requirements

Large projects such as this one are usually organized around some small, centrally located team responsible for establishing the overall system architecture, with the actual development work subcontracted out to other companies or different teams within the same company. Even during analysis, system architects usually have in mind some conceptual model that divides the hardware and software elements of the implementation. One may argue that this is design, not analysis, but we counter by saying that one must start constraining the design space at some point. Indeed, it is difficult to ascertain if the block diagram in Figure 12-1 represents system requirements or a system design. Regardless of this issue, the block diagram clearly suggests that the system architecture at this stage of development is principally object-oriented. For example, it shows complex objects such as the energy management system and the rail-operations control system, each of which performs a major function in the system. This is just as we discussed in Chapter 4: in large systems, the

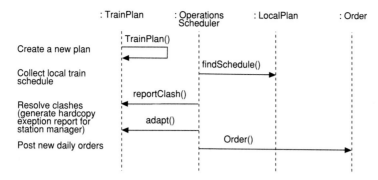

Figure 12-2
Scenario for Processing Daily Train Orders

objects at the highest levels of abstraction tend to be clustered along the lines of major system functions. How we identify and refine these objects during analysis is little different than how we do so during design.

Once we have a straw-man architecture at the level of a block diagram like the one in Figure 12-1, we can begin our analysis by working with domain experts to articulate the primary scenarios that cover the system's desired behavior, just as we described in Chapter 6. For more detail, we might use interaction diagrams, object diagrams, simple scripts, or prototypes to illustrate the expected behavior of the system. For example, in Figure 12-2, we provide an interaction diagram that captures one simple scenario for processing a daily train order. At this level of analysis, it is sufficient for us to capture only the major events and interactions that must occur to carry out each behavior. Details such as operation signatures and the representation of associations are tactical issues that should be deferred until later phases of design.

For a system of this magnitude, it would not be unusual for us to identify a few hundred primary scenarios.[*] As we also suggested in Chapter 6, the 80% rule applies here: it is sufficient for us to capture 80% of a system's scenarios before we move on to architectural design. Trying to "finish" analysis before proceeding is both futile and misleading.

Eventually, we must translate these system requirements into requirements for the hardware and software segments of the system, so that different organizations, each with different skills, can proceed in parallel to attack their particular part of the problem (but always with some central group promoting and preserving the system's architectural vision). Making these hardware and software trade-offs is a difficult task, particularly if the hardware and software organizations are loosely coupled, and especially if they are parts of entirely different companies. Sometimes it is intuitively obvious that certain hardware

---

[*] We have encountered software projects whose products of analysis alone consumed more than 8,000 pages of documentation, a sign of overzealous analysts. Projects that start off in this manner are rarely successful.

should be employed. For example, one might use off-the-shelf terminals or workstations for both the on-board display system and for the displays in the rail-operations control centers. Similarly, it may be obvious, for example, that software is the right implementation vehicle for describing train schedules. The decisions about which platform to use for everything else, either a hardware or software implementation, depends as much on the personal preferences of the system architects as on anything else. One might throw special hardware at the problem where performance needs are critical, or use software where flexibility is more important.

For the purposes of our problem, we assume that an initial hardware architecture has been chosen by the system architects. This choice need not be considered irreversible, but at least it gives us a starting point in terms of where to allocate software requirements. As we proceed with our analysis and then design, we need the freedom to trade off hardware and software: we might later decide that additional hardware is needed to satisfy some requirement, or that certain functions can be performed better through software than hardware.

Figure 12-3 illustrates the target hardware for the traffic management system, using our notation for process diagrams. This process architecture parallels the block diagram of the system in Figure 12-1. Specifically, there is one computer on board each train, encompassing the locomotive analysis and reporting system, the energy management system, the on-board display system, and the data management unit. We expect that some of the on-board devices, such as the display, are intelligent, but we assume that these devices are not necessarily programmable. Continuing, each location transponder is connected to a transmitter, through which messages may be sent to passing trains; no computer is associated with a location transponder. On the other hand, each collection of wayside devices (each of which encompasses a wayside interface unit and its switches) is controlled by a computer that may communicate via its transmitter and receiver with a passing train or a ground-terminal controller. Each ground-terminal controller ultimately connects to a local area network, one for each dispatch center (encompassing the rail-operations control system). Because of the need for uninterrupted service, we have chosen to place two computers at each dispatch center: a primary computer and a backup computer that we expect will be brought on-line whenever the primary computer fails. During idle periods, the backup computer can be used to service the computational needs of other, lower priority users

When operational, the traffic management system may involve hundreds of computers, including one for each train, one for each wayside interface unit, and two at each dispatch center. The process diagram only shows the presence of a few of these computers, since the configurations of similar computers are completely redundant.

As we discussed in Chapters 6 and 7, the key to maintaining sanity during the development of any complex project is to engineer sound and explicit interfaces among the key parts of the system. This is particularly important when defining hardware and software interfaces. At the start, interfaces can be loosely defined, but they must quickly be formalized so that different parts of

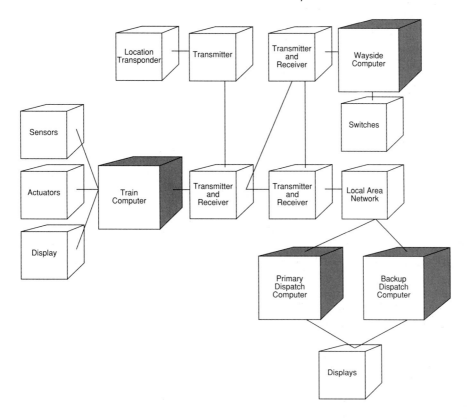

Figure 12-3
Traffic Management System Process Diagram

the system can be developed, tested, and released in parallel. Well-defined interfaces also make it far easier to make hardware/software trade-offs as opportunities arise, without disrupting already completed parts of the system. Furthermore, we cannot expect all of the developers in a large development organization to be programming athletes. We must therefore leave the specification of these key abstractions and mechanisms to our best architects.

Key Abstractions and Mechanisms

A study of the requirements for the traffic management system suggests that we really have four different subproblems to solve:

- Networking
- Database
- Human/machine interface
- Real-time analog device control

How did we come to identify these problems as those involving the greatest development risk?

The thread that ties this system together is a distributed communications network. Messages pass by radio from transponders to trains, between trains and ground-terminal controllers, between trains and wayside interface units, and between ground-terminal controllers and wayside interface units. Messages must also pass between dispatch centers and individual ground-terminal controllers. The safe operation of this entire system depends upon the timely and reliable transmission and reception of messages.

Additionally, this system must keep track of the current locations and planned routes of many different trains simultaneously. We must keep this information current and self-consistent, even in the presence of concurrent updates and queries from around the network. This is basically a distributed database problem.

The engineering of the human/machine interfaces poses a different set of problems. Specifically, the users of this system are principally train engineers and dispatchers, none of whom are necessarily skilled in using computers. The user interface of an operating system such as UNIX or Windows might be marginally acceptable to a professional software engineer, but it is often regarded as user-hostile by end users of applications such as the traffic management system. All forms of user interaction must therefore be carefully engineered to suit this domain-specific group of users.

Lastly, the traffic management system must interact with a variety of sensors and actuators. No matter what the device, the problems of sensing and controlling the environment are similar, and so should be dealt with in a consistent manner by the system.

Each of these four subproblems involves largely independent issues. Our system architects need to identify the key abstractions and mechanisms involved in each, so that we can assign experts in each domain to tackle their particular subproblem in parallel with the others. Note that this is not a problem of analysis or design: our analysis of each problem will impact our architecture, and our designs will uncover new aspects of the problem that require further analysis. Development is thus unavoidably iterative and incremental.

If we do a brief domain analysis across these four problem areas, we find that there are three common high-level key abstractions:

- Trains   Including locomotives and cars
- Tracks   Encompassing profile, grade, and wayside
                  devices
- Plans   Including schedules, orders, clearances,
                  authority, and crew assignments

Every train has a current location on the tracks, and each train has exactly one active plan. Similarly, the number of trains at each point on the tracks may be zero or one; for each plan, there is exactly one train, involving many points on the tracks.

Continuing, we may devise a key mechanism for each of these four nearly-independent subproblems:

- Message passing
- Train-schedule planning
- Displaying
- Sensor data acquisition

These four mechanisms form the soul of our system. They represent approaches to what we have identified as the areas of highest development risk. It is therefore essential that we deploy our best system architects here to experiment with alternative approaches and eventually settle upon a framework from which more junior developers may compose the rest of the system.

12.2 Design

As we discussed in Chapter 6, architectural design involves the establishment of the central class structure of the system, plus a specification of the common collaborations that animate these classes. Focusing upon these mechanisms early directly attacks the elements of highest risk in the system, and serves to concretely capture the vision of the system's architects. Ultimately, the products of this phase serve as the framework of classes and collaborations upon which the other functional elements of the final system build.

In this section, we will examine the semantics of each of this system's four key mechanisms.

Message Passing

By *message*, we do not mean to imply method invocation, as in an object-oriented programming language; rather, we are referring to a concept in the vocabulary of the problem domain, at a much higher level of abstraction. For example, typical messages in the traffic management system include signals to activate wayside devices, indications of trains passing specific locations, and orders from dispatchers to train engineers. In general, these kinds of messages are passed at two different levels within the traffic management system:

- Between computers and devices
- Among computers

Our interest is in the second level of message passing. Because our problem involves a geographically distributed communications network, we must consider issues such as noise, equipment failure, and security.

We can make a first cut at identifying these messages by examining each pair of communicating computers, as shown in our process diagram in Figure 12-3. For each pair, we must ask three questions: (1) What information does each computer manage? (2) What information should be passed from one computer to the other? (3) At what level of abstraction should this information be? There is no empirical solution for these questions. Rather, we must use an iterative approach until we are satisfied that the right messages have been defined and that there are no communications bottlenecks in the system (perhaps because of too many messages over one path, or messages being too large or too small).

It is absolutely critical at this level of design to focus upon the substance, not the form, of these messages. Too often, we have seen system architects start off by selecting a bit-level representation for messages. The real problem with prematurely choosing such a low-level representation is that it is guaranteed to change and thus disrupt every client that depends upon a particular representation. Furthermore, at this point in the design process, we cannot know enough about how these messages will be used to make intelligent decisions about time- and space-efficient representations.

By focusing upon the substance of these messages, we mean to urge a focus upon the outside view of each class of messages. In other words, we must decide upon the roles and responsibilities of each message, and what operations we can meaningfully perform upon each message.

The class diagram in Figure 12-4 captures our design decisions regarding some of the most important messages in the traffic management system. Note that all messages are ultimately instances of a generalized abstract class named Message, which encompasses the behavior common to all messages. Three lower-level classes represent the major categories of messages, namely, train status messages, train plan messages, and wayside device messages. Each of these classes is further specialized. Indeed, our final design might include dozens of such specialized classes, at which time the existence of these intermediate classes becomes even more important; without them, we would end up with many unrelated – and therefore difficult to maintain – modules representing each distinct specialized class. As our design unfolds, we are likely to discover other important groupings of messages and so invent other intermediate classes. Fortunately, reorganizing our class lattice in this manner tends to have minimal semantic impact upon the clients that ultimately use the leaf classes.

As part of architectural design, we would be wise to stabilize the interface of the key message classes early. We might start with a domain analysis of the more interesting leaf classes in this hierarchy, in order to formulate the roles and responsibilities of all such classes, which we could then capture concretely in C++ class declarations. We begin with the invention of two typedefs:

```
// Number denoting a unique packet number
typedef unsigned int PacketId;

// Number denoting a unique network id
typedef unsigned int NodeId;
```

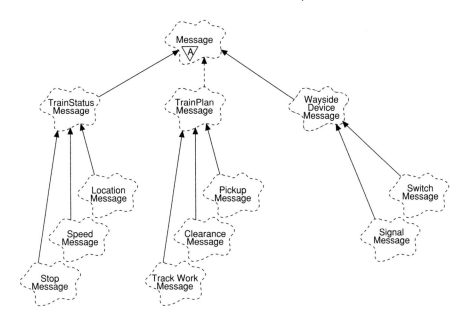

Figure 12-4
Message Class Diagram

We follow this with the declaration of the abstract base class `Message`:

```
class Message {
public:

    Message();
    Message(NodeId sender);
    Message(const Message&);
    virtual ~Message();

    virtual Message& operator=(const Message&);
    virtual Boolean operator==(const Message&);
    Boolean operator!=(const Message&);

    PacketId id() const;
    Time timeStamp() const;
    NodeId sender() const;
    virtual Boolean isIntact() const = 0;

};
```

The responsibilities of this class include managing a unique message id, time stamp, and sender id, as well as ensuring message integrity (namely, knowing whether or not a message is a syntactically or semantically legal message in the system). This latter behavior is what makes messages more than just simple records of data. As usual, messages are also responsible for knowing how to copy, assign, and test (for equality) themselves.

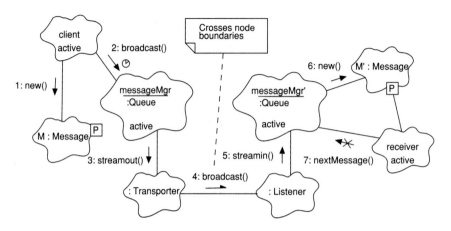

Figure 12-5
Message Passing

Once we have designed the interface of the more important messages, we can write programs that build upon these classes to simulate the creation and reception of streams of messages. We can use these programs as a temporary scaffolding to test different parts of the system during development and before the pieces with which they interface are completed.

The class diagram in Figure 12-4 is unquestionably incomplete. In practice, we find that we can identify the most important messages first and let all others evolve as we uncover the less common forms of communication. Using an object-oriented architecture allows us to add these messages incrementally without disrupting the existing design of the system, because such changes are generally upwardly compatible.

Once we are satisfied with this class structure, we can begin to design the message passing mechanism itself. Here we have two competing goals: to devise a mechanism that provides for the reliable delivery of messages, and that does so at a high enough level of abstraction so that clients need not worry about how message delivery takes place. Such a message passing mechanism allows its clients to make simplifying assumptions about how messages are sent and received.

Figure 12-5 provides a scenario that captures our design of the message passing mechanism. As this diagram indicates, to send a message, a client first creates a new message M, and then broadcasts it to its node's message manager, whose responsibility is to queue the message for eventual transmission. Notice that our design allows the client to time out if the message manager cannot carry out the broadcast in a timely fashion. Notice also that the message manager receives the message to be broadcast as a parameter and then uses the services of a Transporter object to reduce the message to its canonical form and broadcast it across the network.

As this diagram suggests, we choose to make this an asynchronous operation because we don't want to make the client wait for the message to be sent across a radio link, which requires time for encoding, decoding, and perhaps retransmission because of noise. Eventually, some Listener object on the other side of the network receives this message, and presents it in a canonical form to its node's message manager, which in turn creates a parallel message and queues it. A receiver can block at the head of the message manager's queue, waiting for the next message to arrive, which is delivered as a parameter to the operation nextMessage, a synchronous operation.

Our design of the message manager places it at the application layer in the ISO OSI model for networks [4]. This allows all message-sending clients and message-receiving clients to operate at the highest level of abstraction, namely, in terms of application-specific messages.

We expect the final implementation of this mechanism to be a bit more complex. For example, we might want to add behaviors for encryption and decryption and introduce codes to detect and correct errors, so as to ensure reliable communication in the presence of noise or equipment failures.

Train-Schedule Planning

As we noted earlier, the concept of a train plan is central to the operation of the traffic management system. Each train has exactly one active plan, and each plan is assigned to exactly one train and may involve many different orders and locations on the track.

Our first step is to decide exactly what parts constitute a train plan. To do so, we need to consider all the potential clients of a plan and how we expect each of them to use that plan. For example, some clients might be allowed to create plans, others might be allowed to modify plans, and still others might be allowed only to read plans. In this sense, a train plan acts as a repository for all the pertinent information associated with the route of one particular train and the actions that take place along the way, such as picking up or setting out cars.

Figure 12-6 captures our strategic decisions regarding the structure of the TrainPlan class. As in Chapter 10, we use a class diagram to show the parts that compose a train plan (much as a traditional entity-relationship diagram would do). Thus, we see that each train plan has exactly one crew and may have many general orders and many actions. We expect these actions to be time-ordered, with each action composed of information such as time, a location, speed, authority, and orders. For example, a specific train plan might consist of the following actions:

Time	Location	Speed	Authority	Orders
0800	Pueblo	As posted	See yardmaster	Depart yard
1100	Colorado Springs	40 MPH		Set out 30 cars
1300	Denver	45 MPH		Set out 20 cars
1600	Pueblo	As posted		Return to yard

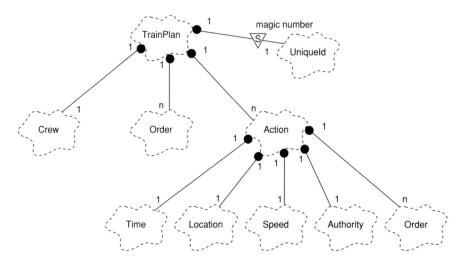

Figure 12-6
TrainPlan Class Diagram

As this diagram indicates, the class `TrainPlan` has one static member object, of the type `UniqueId`, whose purpose is to provide a so-called *magic number* for uniquely identifying each `TrainPlan` instance.

As we did for the `Message` class and its subclasses, we can design the most important elements of a train plan early in the development process; its details will evolve over time, as we actually apply plans to various kinds of clients.

The fact that we may have a plethora of active and inactive train plans at any one time confronts us with the database problem we spoke of earlier. The class diagram in Figure 12-6 can serve as an outline for the logical schema of this database. The next question we might therefore ask is simply, Where are train plans kept?

In a more perfect world, with no communication noise or delays and infinite computing resources, our solution would be to place all train plans in a single, centralized database. This approach would yield exactly one instance of each train plan. However, the real world is much more perverse, and so this solution is not practical. We must expect communication delays, and we don't have unlimited processor cycles. Thus, having to access a plan located in the dispatch center from a train would not at all satisfy our real-time and near-real-time requirements However, we can create the illusion of a single, centralized database in our software. Basically, our solution is to have a database of train plans located on the computers at the dispatch center, with copies of individual plans distributed as needed at sites around the network. For efficiency, then, each train computer could retain a copy of its current plan. Thus, on-board software could query this plan with negligible delay. If the plan

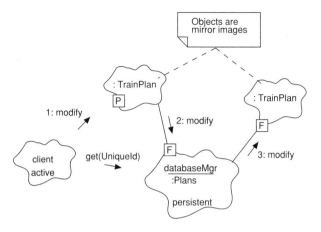

Figure 12-7
Train-Schedule Planning

changed, either as a result of dispatcher action or (less likely) by the decision of the train engineer, our software would have to ensure that all copies of that plan were updated in a timely fashion.

The way this scenario plays out is a function of our train-schedule planning mechanism, shown in Figure 12-7. The primary version of each train plan resides in a centralized database at a dispatch center, with zero or more mirror-image copies scattered about the network. Whenever some client requests a copy of a particular train plan (via the operation get, invoked with a value of UniqueId as an argument), the state of this primary version is cloned and delivered to the client as a parameter. The location of the copy in the network is recorded in the database, and the copy of the plan retains a link back to the database. Now, suppose that a client on a train needed to make a change to a particular plan, perhaps as a result of some action by the train engineer. Ultimately, this client would invoke operations upon its copy of the train plan and so modify its state. These operations would also send messages to the centralized database, to modify the state of the primary version of the plan in the same way. Since we record the location in the network of each copy of a train plan, we can also broadcast messages to the centralized repository that force a corresponding update to the state of all remaining copies. To ensure that changes are made consistently across the network, we could employ a record-locking mechanism, so that train-plan changes would not be committed until all copies and the primary version were updated.

This mechanism applies equally well if some client at the dispatch center initiates the change, perhaps as a result of some dispatcher action. First, the primary version of the plan would be updated, and then changes to all copies would be broadcast throughout the network, using the same mechanism. In either case, how exactly do we broadcast these changes? The answer is that we use the message passing mechanism devised earlier. Specifically, we would need to add to our design some new train-plan messages and then build our train-plan mechanism upon this lower-level message passing mechanism.

Using commercial, off-the-shelf database management systems on the dispatch computers allows us to address any requirements for database backup, recovery, audit trails, and security.

Displaying

Using off-the-shelf technology for our database needs helps us to focus upon the domain-specific parts of our problem. We can achieve similar leverage for our display needs by using standard graphics facilities, such as Microsoft Windows, or X Windows. Using off-the-shelf graphics software effectively raises the level of abstraction in our system, so that developers never need to worry about manipulating the visual representation of displayable objects at the pixel level. Still, it is important to encapsulate our design decisions regarding how various objects are represented visually.

For example, consider displaying the profile and grade of a specific section of track. Our requirements dictate that such a display may appear in two different places: at a dispatch center and on board a train (with the display focusing only upon the track that lies ahead of the train). Assuming that we have some class whose instances represent sections of track, we might take two approaches to representing the state of such objects visually. First, we might have some display-manager object that builds a visual representation by querying the state of the object to be displayed. Alternately, we could eliminate this external object and have each displayable object encapsulate the knowledge of how to display itself. We prefer this second approach, because it is simpler and more in the spirit of the object model.

There is a potential disadvantage to this approach, however. Ultimately, we might have many different kinds of displayable objects, each implemented by different groups of developers. If we let the implementation of each displayable object proceed independently, we are likely to end up with redundant code, different implementation styles, and a generally unmaintainable mess. A far better solution is to do a domain analysis of all the kinds of displayable objects, determine what visual elements they have in common, and devise an intermediate set of class utilities that provide display routines for these common picture elements. These class utilities in turn can build upon lower level, off-the-shelf graphics packages.

Figure 12-8 illustrates this design, showing that the implementation of all displayable objects shares common class utilities. These utilities in turn build upon lower-level Windows interfaces, which are hidden from all of the higher-level classes. Pragmatically, interfaces such as the Windows API cannot easily be expressed in a single class or a class utility. Therefore, our diagram is a bit of a simplification: it is more likely that our implementation will require a set of peer class utilities for the Windows API as well as for the train display utilities.

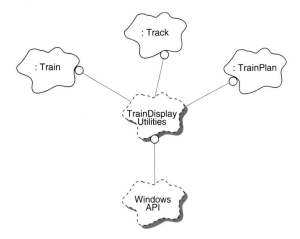

Figure 12-8
Displaying

The principle advantage of this approach is that it limits the impact of any lower-level changes resulting from hardware/software trade-offs. For example, if we find that we need to replace our display hardware with more or less powerful devices, then we need only reimplement the routines in the class `TrainDisplayUtilities`. Without this collection of routines, low-level changes would require us to modify the implementation of every displayable object.

Sensor Data Acquisition

As our requirements suggest, the traffic management system includes many different kinds of sensors. For example, sensors on each train monitor the oil temperature, fuel quantity, throttle setting, water temperature, drawbar load, and so on. Similarly, active sensors in some of the wayside devices report among other things the current positions of switches and signals. The kinds of values returned by the various sensors are all different, but the processing of different sensor data is all very much the same. For example, assuming that our computers use memory-mapped I/O, each sensor value is ultimately read as a set of bits from a specific place in memory and then converted to some sensor-specific value. Furthermore, most sensors must be sampled periodically. If a value is within a certain range, then nothing special happens other than notifying some client of the new value. If this value exceeds certain preset limits, then a different client might be warned. Finally, if this value goes far beyond its limits, then we might need to sound some sort of alarm, and notify yet another client to take drastic action (for example, when locomotive oil pressure drops to dangerous levels).

Replicating this behavior for every kind of sensor is not only tedious and error-prone, it also usually results in redundant code. Unless we exploit this commonality, different developers will end up inventing multiple solutions to the same problem, leading to the proliferation of slightly different sensor mechanisms and, in turn, a system that is more difficult to maintain. It is highly desirable, therefore, to do a domain analysis of all periodic, nondiscrete sensors, so that we might invent a common sensor mechanism for all kinds of sensors.

We have encountered this problem before, introduced in Chapter 8 as part of the architecture of the weather monitoring system. There we found an architecture that encompassed a hierarchy of sensor classes, and a frame-based mechanism that periodically acquired data from these sensors. Rather than reinventing this architecture, it makes sense for us to plagiarize the architecture from this earlier chapter, and apply it to our traffic management system.

This is an example of cross-domain reuse of patterns.

12.3 Evolution

Module Architecture

As we have discussed, the module is a necessary but insufficient means of decomposition; and thus, for a problem of the size of the traffic management system, we must focus upon a subsystem-level decomposition. Two important factors suggest that an early activity of evolution should include devising the module architecture of the traffic management system, representing its physical software structure.

The software design for very large systems must often commence before the target hardware is completed. Software design frequently takes far longer than hardware design, and in any case, trade-offs must be made against each along the way. This implies that hardware dependencies in the software must be isolated to the greatest extent possible, so that software design can proceed in the absence of a stable target environment. It also implies that the software must be designed with the idea of replaceable subsystems in mind. In a command and control system such as the traffic management system, we might wish to take advantage of new hardware technology that has matured during the development of the system's software.

We must also have an early and intelligent physical decomposition of the system's software, so that subcontractors working on different parts of the system (perhaps even using different programming languages) can work in parallel. As we explained in Chapter 7, there are often many nontechnical reasons that drive the physical decomposition of a large system. Perhaps the most important of these concerns the assignment of work to independent teams of developers. Subcontractor relationships are usually established early in the life of a complex system, often before there is enough information to make sound technical decisions regarding proper subsystem decomposition.

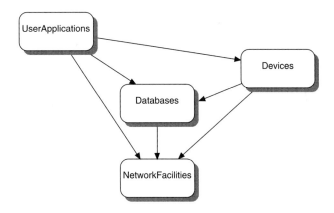

Figure 12-9
Traffic Management System Top-Level Module Diagram

We recommend that system architects be given the opportunity to experiment with alternative subsystem decompositions, so that we can have a fairly high level of confidence that our global physical design decisions are sound. This may involve prototyping on a very large scale (but with all subsystem implementations stubbed out) and simulations of processor loading, message traffic, and external events. These prototypes and simulations can then be carried on through the maturation of this system, as vehicles for regression testing.

How do we select a suitable subsystem decomposition? As we suggested in Chapter 4, the highest-level objects are often clustered around functional lines. Again, this is not orthogonal to the object model, because by the term *functional*, we do not mean algorithmic abstractions, embodying simple input/output mappings. We are speaking of system function points that represent outwardly visible and testable behaviors, resulting from the cooperative action of logical collections of objects. Thus, the highest-level abstractions and mechanisms that we first identify are good candidates around which to organize our subsystems. We may assert the existence of such subsystems first, and then evolve their interfaces over time.

The module diagram in Figure 12-9 represents our design decisions regarding the top-level module architecture of the traffic management system. Here we see a highly layered architecture, with each level encompassing the functions of the four subproblems we identified earlier, namely, networking, database, real-time analog device control, and the human/machine interface.

Subsystem Specification

If we focus upon the outside view of any of these subsystems, we find that it has all the characteristics of an object. It has a unique, albeit static, identity; it embodies a significant amount of state and it exhibits very complex behavior.

Subsystems serve as the repositories of other classes, class utilities, and objects; thus, they are best characterized by the resources they export. Practically, with the use of C++, these subsystems are captured as directories, denoting logical collections of modules and nested subsystems.

The module diagram in Figure 12-9 is useful but incomplete, because each subsystem in this diagram is far too large to be developed by a small team of developers. We must zoom inside each of the top-level subsystems, and further decompose them into their nested modules and subsystems.

For example, consider the subsystem NetworkFacilities. We choose to decompose this subsystem into two other subsystems, one private (which we name RadioCommunication) and one public (which we name Messages). The private subsystem hides the details of software control of the physical radio devices, while the exported subsystem provides the functionality of the message passing mechanism we designed earlier.

The subsystem named Databases builds upon the resources of the subsystem NetworkFacilities and serves to implement the train-plan mechanism we created earlier. We choose to further decompose this subsystem into two exported subsystems, representing the major database elements in the system. We name these nested subsystems TrainPlanDatabase and TrackDatabase, respectively. We also expect to have one private subsystem, DatabaseManager, whose purpose is to provide all the services common to the two domain-specific databases.

The Devices subsystem also decomposes naturally into several smaller subsystems. We choose to group the software related to all wayside devices into one subsystem and the software associated with all on-board locomotive actuators and sensors into another. These two subsystems are available to clients of the Devices subsystem, and both are built upon the resources of the TrainPlanDatabase and Messages. Thus, we have designed the Devices subsystem to implement the sensor mechanism we described earlier.

Finally, we choose to decompose the top-level UserApplications subsystem into several smaller ones, including the subsystems EngineerApplications and DispatcherApplications, to reflect the different roles of the two main users of the traffic management system. The subsystem EngineerApplications includes resources that provide all the train-engineer/machine interaction specified in the requirements, including the functionality of the locomotive analysis and reporting system and the energy management system. We include the subsystem DispatcherApplications to encompass the software that provides the functionality of all dispatcher/machine interactions. Both EngineerApplications and DispatcherApplications share common private resources, as exported from the subsystem Displays, which embodies the display mechanism we described earlier.

This design leaves us with four top-level subsystems, encompassing several smaller ones, to which we have allocated all of the key abstractions and mechanisms we invented earlier. Equally important, as we discussed in Chapter 7, these lower-level subsystems form the units for work assignments as well as the units for configuration management and version control. As we also suggested, each subsystem should be owned by one person, yet may be implemented by many more. The subsystem owner directs the detailed design and implementation of the subsystem and manages its interface relative to other subsystems at the same level of abstraction. Thus, the management of a very large development project is made possible by taking a very complex problem and decomposing it into several smaller ones.

As we discussed in Chapter 7, this strategy also makes it possible to have several different simultaneous views of the system under development. A set of compatible versions of each subsystem forms a release, and we may have many such releases: one for each developer, one for our quality-assurance team, and perhaps one for early customer use. Individual developers can create their own stable release into which they integrate new versions of the software for which they are responsible, before releasing it to the rest of the team. In this manner, we have a platform for continuous integration of new code.

The key to making this work is the careful engineering of subsystem interfaces. Once engineered, these interfaces must be rigorously guarded. How do we determine the outside view of each subsystem? We do so by looking at each subsystem as an object. Thus, we ask the same questions we did in Chapter 4 for much more primitive objects: What state does this object embody, what operations can clients meaningfully perform upon it, and what operations does it require of other objects?

For example, consider the subsystem `TrainPlanDatabase`. It builds upon three other subsystems (`Messages`, `TrainDatabase`, and `TrackDatabase`) and has several important clients, namely, the four subsystems `WaysideDevices`, `LocomotiveDevices`, `EngineerApplications`, and `DispatcherApplications`. The `TrainPlanDatabase` embodies a relatively straightforward state, specifically, the state of all train plans. Of course, the twist is that this subsystem must support the behavior of the distributed train-plan mechanisms. Thus, from the outside, clients see a monolithic database, but from the inside, we know that this database is really distributed and must therefore be constructed on top of the message passing mechanism found in the subsystem `Messages`.

What services does the `TrainPlanDatabase` provide? All the usual database operations seem to apply: adding records, deleting records, modifying records, and querying records. As we did for our database problem in Chapter 10, we would eventually capture all of these design decisions that make up this subsystem in the form of C++ classes that provide the declarations of all these operations.

At this stage in the design, we would continue the design process for each subsystem. Again, we expect that these interfaces will not be exactly right at first; we must allow them to evolve over time. Happily, as for smaller objects, our experience suggests that most of the changes we will need to make to these interfaces will be upwardly compatible, assuming that we did a good job up front in characterizing the behavior of each subsystem in an object-oriented manner.

12.4 Maintenance

Adding New Functionality

Old software never dies, it just gets maintained or preserved, especially for systems as large as this one. This is the reason we still find software in production use that was developed over twenty years ago (which is absolutely ancient in software years). As more users apply the traffic management system, and as we adapt this design to new implementations, clients will discover new, unanticipated uses for existing mechanisms, creating pressure to add new functionality to the system.

Let's consider a significant addition to our requirements, namely, payroll processing. Specifically, suppose that our analysis shows that train-company payroll is currently being supported by a piece of hardware that is no longer being manufactured and that we are at great risk of losing our payroll processing capability because a single serious hardware failure would put our accounting system out of action forever. For this reason, we might choose to integrate payroll processing with the traffic management system. At first, it is not difficult to conceive how these two seemingly unrelated problems could coexist; we could simply view them as separate applications, with payroll processing running as a background activity.

Further examination shows that there is actually tremendous value to be gained from integrating payroll processing. You may recall from our earlier discussion that, among other things, train plans contain information about crew assignments. Thus, it is possible for us to track actual versus planned crew assignments, and from this we can calculate hours worked, amount of overtime, and so on. By getting this information directly, our payroll calculations will be more precise and certainly more timely.

What does adding this functionality do to our existing design? Very little. Our approach would be to add one more subsystem inside the `UserApplications` subsystem, representing the functionality of payroll processing. At this location in the architecture, such a subsystem would have visibility to all the important mechanisms upon which it could build. This is indeed quite common in well-structured object-oriented systems: a significant addition in the requirements for the system can be dealt with fairly easily by building new applications upon existing mechanisms.

Let's consider an even more radical change. Suppose we wanted to introduce expert system technology into our system by building a dispatcher's assistant that could advise about traffic routing and emergency responses. How would this new requirement affect our architecture?

Again, the answer is very little. Our solution would be to add a new subsystem between the subsystems `TrainPlanDatabase` and `DispatcherApplications`, because the knowledge base embodied by this expert system parallels the contents of the `TrainPlanDatabase`; furthermore, the subsystem `DispatcherApplications` is the sole client of this expert system. We would need to invent some new mechanisms to establish the manner in which advice is presented to the ultimate user. For example, we might use a blackboard architecture, as we did in Chapter 11.

Changing the Target Hardware

As we mentioned earlier, hardware technology is still moving at a faster pace than our ability to generate software. Furthermore, it is likely that a number of political and historical reasons will have caused us to make certain hardware and software choices early in the development process that we may later regret.[*] For this reason, the target hardware for large systems becomes obsolete far earlier than does its software. For example, after several years of operational use, we might decide it was necessary to replace the displays on each train and at each dispatch center. How might this affect our existing architecture? If we have kept our subsystem interfaces at a high level of abstraction during the evolution of our system, this hardware change would affect our software in only minimal ways. Since we chose to encapsulate all design decisions regarding specific displays, no other subsystem was ever written to depend upon the specific characteristics of a given workstation; the system encapsulates all such hardware secrets. This means that the behavior of workstations was hidden in the subsystem named Displays. Thus, this subsystem acts as an abstraction firewall, which shields all other clients from the intricacies of our particular display technology.

In a similar fashion, a radical change in telecommunications standards would affect our implementation, but only in limited ways. Specifically, our design ensures that only the subsystem named Messages knows about network communications. Thus, even a fundamental change in networking would never affect any higher-level client; the subsystem Messages shields them from the perversity of the real world.

None of the changes we have introduced rends the fabric of our existing architecture. This is indeed the ultimate mark of a well-designed, object-oriented system.

Further Readings

The requirements for the traffic management system are based upon those for the Advanced Train Control System, as described by Murphy [C 1988].

---

[*] For example, our project might have chosen a particular hardware or software product from a third-party vendor, only to later find out that the product didn't live up to its promises. Even worse, we might find that the only supplier of a critical product went out of business. In such cases, the project manager usually has one of two choices: (1) run screaming into the night, or (2) choose another product, and hope that the system's architecture is resilient enough to accommodate the change. The use of object-oriented analysis and design helps us to achieve (2), although it is sometimes still very satisfying to carry out (1).

Message translation and verification occur in virtually all command and control systems. Plinta, Lee, and Rissman [C 1989] provide an excellent discourse on the issues, and offer the design of a mechanism for passing messages in a type-safe way across processors in a distributed system.

For books are only partly from the minds and the guts of their authors. A large part of them comes from somewhere else, and we the authors sit at our typewriters waiting for books to happen.

GUY LEFRANCOIS
Of Children

Object-oriented development is a proven technology. Our method has been used to successfully build and deliver a multitude of complex systems in a variety of problem domains.

Still, the demand for complex software continues to rise at a staggering rate. The ever-growing capabilities of our hardware and an increasing social awareness of the utility of computers create tremendous pressure to automate more and more applications of even greater complexity. The fundamental value of object-oriented development, with its well-defined notation and process, is that it releases the human spirit so that it can focus its creative energies upon the truly demanding parts in the crafting of a complex system.

Object-Oriented Programming Languages

The use of object-oriented technology is not restricted to any particular language; rather, it is applicable to a wide spectrum of object-based and object-oriented programming languages. As important as analysis and design are, however, we cannot ignore the details of coding, for ultimately our software architectures must be expressed in some programming language. Indeed, as Wulf has suggested, a programming language serves three purposes:

- It is a design tool
- It is a vehicle for human consumption
- It is a vehicle for instructing a computer [1]

This appendix is for the reader who may not be familiar with certain of the object-oriented programming languages we mention in this book. Herein we provide a summary description of a number of the more important languages, together with a common example that provides a basis for comparing the syntax, semantics, and idioms of two of the more interesting object-oriented programming languages, namely C++ and Smalltalk.

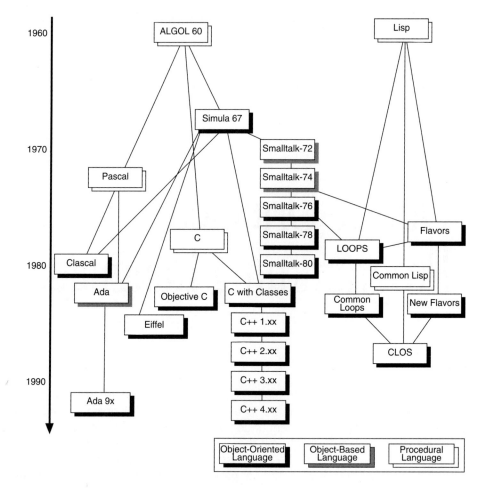

Figure A-1
A Genealogy of Object-Based and Object-Oriented Programming Languages

A.1 Concepts

Currently, there are over 2,000 different high-order programming languages. We see so many different languages because each was shaped by the particular requirements of its perceived problem domain. Furthermore, the existence of each new language enabled developers to move on to more and more complex problems. With each previously unexplored application, language designers learned new lessons that changed their basic assumptions about what was important in a language and what was not. This evolution of languages was also heavily influenced by progress in the theory of computing, which has led to a formal understanding of the semantics of statements, modules, abstract data types, and processes.

As we discussed in Chapter 2, programming languages may be grouped into four generations, according to whether they support mathematic, algorithmic, data, or object-oriented abstractions. The most recent advances in programming languages have been due to the influence of the object model. By our count, there are currently over 100 different object-based and object-oriented programming languages today. As we also discussed in Chapter 2, a language is considered object-based if it directly supports data abstraction and classes. An object-oriented language is one that is object-based, but also provides support for inheritance and polymorphism.

The common ancestor of almost every contemporary object-based and object-oriented programming language is Simula, developed in the 1960s by Dahl, Myhrhaug, and Nygard [2]. Simula built upon the ideas of ALGOL, but added the concepts of encapsulation and inheritance. Perhaps even more important, Simula – as a language for describing systems and for developing simulations – introduced the discipline of writing programs that mirror the vocabulary of their problem domain.

Figure A-1 is derived from Schmucker [3] and shows the genealogy of the most influential and widely used object-based and object-oriented programming languages. In the next several sections, we examine several of these languages relative to the support they offer to the elements of the object model.

A.2 Smalltalk

Background

Smalltalk was created by the members of the Xerox Palo Alto Research Center Learning Research Group as the software element of the Dynabook, a visionary project of Alan Kay. Simula was its primary influence, although Smalltalk also took some ideas from the language FLEX and the work of Seymore Papert and Wallace Feurzeig. Smalltalk represents both a language and a software development environment. It is a pure object-oriented programming language, in that everything is viewed as an object even integers are classes. Next to Simula, Smalltalk is perhaps the most important object-oriented programming language, because its concepts have influenced not only the design of almost every subsequent object-oriented programming language, but also the look and feel of graphic user interfaces such as the Macintosh user interface, Windows, and Motif, all of which are now largely taken for granted.

Smalltalk evolved over almost a decade of work, and was the product of synergistic group activity. Dan Ingalls was the lead architect during most of Smalltalk's development, but there were also seminal contributions by Peter Deutsch, Glenn Krasner, and Kim McCall. In parallel, the elements of the Smalltalk environment were developed by James Althoff, Robert Flegal, Ted Kaehler, Diana Merry, and Steve Putz. Among other important roles that they played, Adele Goldberg and David Robson served as chroniclers of the Smalltalk project.

Abstraction	Instance variables	Yes
	Instance methods	Yes
	Class variables	Yes
	Class methods	Yes
Encapsulation	Of variables	Private
	Of methods	Public
Modularity	Kinds of modules	None
Hierarchy	Inheritance	Single
	Generic units	No
	Metaclasses	Yes
Typing	Strongly typed	No
	Polymorphism	Yes (single)
Concurrency	Multitasking	Indirectly (by classes)
Persistence	Persistent objects	No

Table A-1
Smalltalk

There are five identifiable releases of Smalltalk, indicated by their year of release: Smalltalk-72, -74, -76, -78, and the most current incarnation, Smalltalk-80. Smalltalk-72 and -74 did not provide support for inheritance, but they did lay much of the conceptual foundation of the language, including the ideas of message passing and polymorphism. Later releases of the language turned classes into first-class citizens, thus completing the view that everything in the environment could be treated as an object. Smalltalk-80 has been ported to a variety of machine architectures.

There is also an important dialect of Smalltalk provided by Digitalk, Smalltalk/V, that is very similar to Smalltalk-80 and is available on the IBM PC (Windows and OS/2) and Macintosh. Except for the user interface classes, the class libraries are quite similar to each other. Also like Smalltalk-80, there is a development environment and development tools that are similar in capability, but different in structure and function [4].

Overview

Ingalls states that "the purpose of the Smalltalk project is to support children of all ages in the world of information. The challenge is to identify and harness metaphors of sufficient simplicity and power to allow a single person to have access to, and creative control over, information which ranges from number and text through sounds and images" [5]. To this end, Smalltalk is built around two simple concepts: everything is treated as an object, and objects communicate by passing messages.

Table A-1 summarizes Smalltalk's features, relative to the seven elements of the object model. Although the table does not indicate it, multiple inheritance is possible by the redefinition of certain primitive methods [6].

Example

Consider the problem in which we have a heterogeneous list of shapes, in which each particular shape object might be a circle, a rectangle, or a solid rectangle (this is similar to the problem we introduced in Chapter 3). Smalltalk has an extensive class library that already contains classes for circles and rectangles, and so our solution in this language would be almost trivial; this demonstrates the importance of reuse. However, for the sake of comparison, lets assume that we only have primitive classes for drawing lines and arcs. Therefore, we might define the class AShape as follows:

```
Object subclass: #AShape
    instanceVariableNames: 'theCenter'
    classVariableNames: ''
    poolDictionaries: ''
    category: 'Appendix'

initialize
    "Initialize the shape"

    theCenter := Point new

setCenter: aPoint
    "Set the center of the shape"

    theCenter := aPoint

center
    "Return the center of the shape"

    ^theCenter

draw
    "Draw the shape"

    self subclassResponsibility
```

We may next define the subclass ACircle as follows:

```
AShape subclass: #ACircle
    instanceVariableNames: 'theRadius'
    classVariableNames: ''
    poolDictionaries: ''
    category: 'Appendix'

setRadius: anInteger
    "Set the radius of the circle"

    theRadius := anInteger

radius
    "Return the radius of the circle"

    ^theRadius
```

draw
    "Draw the circle"

```
| anArc index |
anArc := Arc new.
index := 1.
[index <= 4]
    whileTrue:
        [anArc
            center: theCenter
            radius: theRadius
            quadrant: index.
            anArc display.
            index := index + 1]
```

Continuing, the subclass `ARectangle` may be defined as follows:

```
AShape subclass: #ARectangle
    instanceVariableNames: ´theHeight theWidth´
    classVariableNames: ´´
    poolDictionaries: ´´
    category: ´Appendix´
```

draw
    "Draw the rectangle"

```
| aLine upperLeftCorner |
aLine := Line new.
upperLeftCorner := theCenter x - (theWidth / 2) @ (theCenter y - (theHeight / 2)).
aLine beginPoint: upperLeftCorner.
aLine endPoint: upperLeftCorner x + theWidth @ upperLeftCorner y.
aLine display.
aLine beginPoint: aLine endPoint.
aLine endPoint: upperLeftCorner x + theWidth @ (upperLeftCorner y + theHeight).
aLine display.
aLine beginPoint: aLine endPoint.
aLine endPoint: upperLeftCorner x @ (upperLeftCorner y + theHeight).
aLine display.
aLine beginPoint: aLine endPoint.
aLine endPoint: upperLeftCorner.
aLine display
```

setHeight: anInteger
    "Set the height of the rectangle"

    theHeight := anInteger

setWidth: anInteger
    "Set the width of the rectangle"

    theWidth := anInteger

height
    "Return the height of the rectangle"

    ^theHeight

width
>   "Return the width of the rectangle"

>   ^theWidth

Lastly, the subclass ASolidRectangle may be defined as:

ARectangle subclass: #ASolidRectangle
>   instanceVariableNames: ´´
>   classVariableNames: ´´
>   poolDictionaries: ´´
>   category: ´Appendix´

draw
>   "Draw the solid rectangle"

```
| upperLeftCorner lowerRightCorner |
super draw.
upperLeftCorner  := theCenter x - (theWidth quo: 2) + 1 @
                    (theCenter y - (theHeight quo: 2) + 1).
lowerRightCorner := upperLeftCorner x + theWidth - 1 @
                    (upperLeftCorner y + theHeight - 1).
Display
    fill: (upperLeftCorner corner: lowerRightCorner)
    mask: Form gray
```

References

The primary references for Smalltalk are *Smalltalk-80: The Language*, by Goldberg and Robson [7]; *Smalltalk-80: The Interactive Programming Environment*, by Goldberg [8]; and *Smalltalk-80: Bits of History, Words of Advice*, by Krasner [9]. LaLonde and Pugh [10] explore Smalltalk-80 in great depth, including both the class libraries and application development.

A.3 Object Pascal

Background

Object Pascal was created by developers from Apple Computer (some of whom were involved in the development of Smalltalk), in conjunction with Niklaus Wirth, the designer of Pascal. Object Pascal's immediate ancestor is Clascal, an object-oriented version of Pascal for the Lisa. Object Pascal was made publicly available in 1986 and is the first object-oriented programming language supported by the Macintosh Programmer's Workshop (MPW), the development environment for Apple's family of Macintosh computers. The class library for MPW, called MacApp, provides the framework for constructing applications that conform to the Macintosh user interface guidelines.

Abstraction	Instance variables	Yes
	Instance methods	Yes
	Class variables	No
	Class methods	No
Encapsulation	Of variables	Public
	Of methods	Public
Modularity	Kinds of modules	Unit
Hierarchy	Inheritance	Single
	Generic units	No
	Metaclasses	No
Typing	Strongly typed	Yes
	Polymorphism	Yes (single)
Concurrency	Multitasking	No
Persistence	Persistent objects	No

Table A-2
Object Pascal

Overview

As Schmucker states, "Object Pascal is a 'bare bones' object-oriented language. It makes no provision for class methods, class variables, multiple inheritance, or metaclasses. These concepts were specifically excluded in an attempt to streamline the learning curve encountered by most novice object-oriented programmers" [11].

We summarize the features of Object Pascal in Table A-2, relative to the seven elements of the object model.

References

The primary reference for Object Pascal is the *MPW Object Pascal Reference* from Apple [12].

A.4 C++

Background

C++ was designed by Bjarne Stroustrup of AT&T Bell Laboratories. The immediate ancestor of C++ is a language called C with Classes, also developed by Stroustrup in 1980. In turn, C with Classes was heavily influenced by the languages C and Simula. C++ is largely a superset of C. However, in one sense, C++ is simply a better C, in that it provides type checking, overloaded functions, and many other improvements. Most importantly, however, C++ adds object-oriented programming features to C.

Abstraction	Instance variables	Yes
	Instance methods	Yes
	Class variables	Yes
	Class methods	Yes
Encapsulation	Of variables	Public, protected, private
	Of methods	Public, protected, private
Modularity	Kinds of modules	File
Hierarchy	Inheritance	Multiple
	Generic units	Yes
	Metaclasses	No
Typing	Strongly typed	Yes
	Polymorphism	Yes (single)
Concurrency	Multitasking	Indirectly (by class)
Persistence	Persistent objects	No

Table A-3
C++

There have been several major releases of the C++ language. Version 1.0 and its minor releases added basic object-oriented programming features to C, such as single inheritance and polymorphism, plus type checking and overloading. Version 2.0, released in 1989, improved upon the previous versions in a variety of ways (such as the introduction of multiple inheritance), based upon extensive experience with the language by a relatively large user community. Version 3.0, released in 199 introduced, templates (parameterized classes) and exception handling. The ANSI X3J16 C++ committee has recently adopted proposals for namespace control (consistent with our notion of class categories) and run-time type identification.

Early translator technology for C++ involved the use of a preprocessor for C, called *cfront*. Because this translator emitted C code as an intermediate representation, it was possible to port C++ to virtually every UNIX architecture quite quickly. Now, C++ translators and native compilers are available commercially for almost every kind of instruction-set architecture.

Overview

Stroustrup states that "C++ was primarily designed so that the author and his friends would not have to program in assembler, C, or various modern high-order languages. Its main purpose is to make writing good programs easier and more pleasant for the individual programmer. There never was a C++ paper design; design, documentation, and implementation went on simultaneously" [13]. C++ corrects many of the deficiencies of C, and adds to the language support for classes, type checking, overloading, free store management, constant types, references, inline functions, derived classes, and virtual functions [14].

We summarize the features of C++ in Table A-3 on page 481, relative to the seven elements of the object model.

Example

Again we reimplement the shape problem. The common style in C++ is to place the outside view of each class in header files. Thus, we may write:

```cpp
struct Point {
  int x;
  int y;
};

class Shape {
public:
  Shape();
  void setCenter(Point p);
  virtual void draw() = 0;
  Point center() const;
private:
  Point theCenter;
};

class Circle : public Shape {
public:
  Circle();
  void setRadius(int r);
  virtual void draw();
  int radius() const;
private:
  int theRadius;
};

class Rectangle : public Shape {
public:
  Rectangle();
  void setHeight(int h);
  void setWidth(int w);
  virtual void Draw();
  int height() const;
  int width() const;
private:
  int theHeight;
  int theWidth;
};

class SolidRectangle : public Rectangle {
public:
  virtual void draw ();
};
```

The definition of C++ does not include a class library. For our purposes, we assume the existence of a programmatic interface to X Windows, and the global objects Display, Window, and GraphicsContext (which are needed by Xlib). Thus, we may complete the methods above in a separate file, as follows:

```
Shape::Shape()
{
  theCenter.x = 0;
  theCenter.y = 0;
};

void Shape::setCenter(Point p)
{
  theCenter = p;
};

Point Shape::center() const
{
  return theCenter;
};

Circle::Circle() : theRadius(0) {}

void Circle::setRadius(int r)
{
  theRadius = r;
};

void Circle::draw()
{
  int X = (center().x - theRadius);
  int Y = (center().y - theRadius);
  XDrawArc(Display, Window, GraphicsContext, X, Y,
           (theRadius * 2), (theRadius * 2), 0, (360 * 64));
};

int Circle::radius () const
{
  return theRadius;
};

Rectangle::Rectangle() : theHeight(0), theWidth(0) {}

void Rectangle::setHeight (int h)
{
  theHeight = h;
};

void Rectangle::setWidth (int w)
{
    theWidth = w;
};

void Rectangle::draw()
{
  int X = (center().x - (theWidth / 2));
  int Y = (center().y - (theHeight / 2));
  XDrawRectangle(Display, Window, GraphicsContext, X, Y,
                 theWidth, theHeight);
};

int Rectangle::height() const
{
  return theHeight;
};
```

```
int Rectangle::width() const
{
  return theWidth;
};

void SolidRectangle::draw()
{
  Rectangle::draw();
  int X = (center().x - (width() / 2));
  int Y = (center().y - (height() / 2));
  gc oldGraphicsContext = GraphicsContext;
  XSetForeground(Display, GraphicsContext, Gray);
  XDrawFilled(Display, Window, GraphicsContext, X, Y, width(), height());
    GraphicsContext = oldGraphicsContext;
};
```

References

The primary reference for C++ is the *Annotated C++ Reference Manual* by Ellis and Stroustrup [15]. Stroustrup [16] provides in-depth coverage of the language and its use in the context of object-oriented design.

A.5 Common Lisp Object System

Background

There are literally dozens of dialects of Lisp, including MacLisp, Standard Lisp, SpiceLisp, S-1 Lisp, Nil, ZetaLisp, InterLisp, and Scheme. Starting in the early 1980's, a plethora of new dialects of Lisp emerged that supported object-oriented programming, many of which were invented to support ongoing research in knowledge representation. Spurred by the success in standardizing Common Lisp, a similar effort was undertaken in 1986 to standardize these object-oriented dialects.

The idea of standardization was put forth at the summer 1986 ACM Lisp and Functional Programming Conference, resulting in the formation of a special subcommittee as part of the X3J13 ANSI committee (for the standardization of Common Lisp). Because this new dialect was conceived to be a proper superset of Common Lisp, it was called the Common Lisp Object System, or CLOS for short. Daniel Bobrow chaired the committee, whose members included Sonya Keene, Linda DeMichiel, Patrick Dussud, Richard Gabriel, James Kempf, Gregor Kicazles, and David Moon.

The design of CLOS was heavily influenced by the languages New Flavors and CommonLoops. After about two years of work, the complete specification of CLOS was published in late 1988.

Abstraction	Instance variables	Yes
	Instance methods	Yes
	Class variables	Yes
	Class methods	Yes
Encapsulation	Of variables	Reader, writer, accessor
	Of methods	Public
Modularity	Kinds of modules	Package
Hierarchy	Inheritance	Multiple
	Generic units	No
	Metaclasses	Yes
Typing	Strongly typed	Optional
	Polymorphism	Yes (multiple)
Concurrency	Multitasking	Yes
Persistence	Persistent objects	No

Table A-4
CLOS

Overview

Keene reports that there were three design goals for CLOS:

- CLOS should be a standard language extension that includes the most useful aspects of the existing object-oriented paradigms.
- The CLOS programmer interface should be powerful and flexible enough for developing most application programs.
- CLOS itself should be designed as an extensible protocol, to allow for customization of its behavior and to encourage further research in object-oriented programming [17].

We summarize the features of CLOS in Table A-4, relative to the seven elements of the object model. Although CLOS does not support persistent objects directly, there are straightforward extensions using the metaobject protocol to add persistency [18].

References

The primary reference for CLOS is the *Common Lisp Object System Specification* [19].

A.6 Ada

Background

The United States Department of Defense (DoD) is perhaps the largest user of computers in the world. By the mid-1970s, software development for its systems had reached crisis proportions: projects were often late, over budget, and they often failed to meet their stated requirements. It was evident that the problems would only worsen as software development costs continued to rise and the demand for software increased at an exponential rate. To help resolve these problems, which were further compounded by the proliferation of hundreds of different languages, the DoD sponsored the development of a single, common, high-order programming language. In a sense, Ada represents one of the first engineered production-quality languages. A set of requirements was developed starting in 1975 and culminated in the Steelman document, which was released in 1978. An international request for proposal (RFP) was then issued, inviting companies to design a language based upon these requirements. The RFP drew seventeen responses. This number was reduced to four, then two, and then one by an extensive design and evaluation period involving hundreds of computer scientists throughout the world.

The winning design was originally called the Green language (so called because of its color code during the competition), and was then renamed Ada, in honor of Ada Augusta, Countess of Lovelace, who was noted for her early observations on the potential power of the computer. The primary author of this language was Jean Ichbiah of France. Other members of the design team included Bernd Krieg-Brueckner, Brian Wichmann, Henry Ledgard, Jean-Claude Heliard, Jean-Loup Gailly, Jean-Raymond Abrial, John Barnes, Mike Woodger, Olivier Roubine, S. A. Schuman, and S. C. Vestal.

The immediate ancestors of Ada are Pascal and its derivatives, including Euclid, Lis, Mesa, Modula, and Sue. A number of concepts from ALGOL 68, Simula, CLU, and Alphard were also incorporated. The ANSI standard for Ada was finally released in 1983. Translators for Ada were slow in coming, but today there are translators for almost every major family of instruction-set architectures. Although Ada was originally sponsored by the DoD, it has found an important worldwide role in government and commercial software projects, and is usually the language of choice for large-scale software projects, such as the United States and Canadian air traffic control systems. Since ANSI standards must be reviewed every five years, a project called Ada 9x has been established to update this standard. Through Ada9x, the original language definition has changed in a number of small ways, involving clarifications, the filling of gaps, and the correction of errors. In its current definition, Ada is object-based, not object-oriented. However, Ada9x adds object-oriented programming extensions to the original language definition.

Abstraction	Instance variables	Yes
	Instance methods	Yes
	Class variables	No
	Class methods	No
Encapsulation	Of variables	Public, private
	Of methods	Public, private
Modularity	Kinds of modules	Package
Hierarchy	Inheritance	No (part of Ada9x)
	Generic units	Yes
	Metaclasses	No
Typing	Strongly typed	Yes
	Polymorphism	No (part of Ada9x)
Concurrency	Multitasking	Yes
Persistence	Persistent objects	No

Table A-5
Ada

Overview

According to its designers, Ada was designed with three concerns in mind:

- Program reliability and maintenance
- Programming as a human activity
- Efficiency [20]

We summarize the features of Ada in Table A-5, relative to the seven elements of the object model.

References

The primary reference for Ada's syntax and semantics is the *Reference Manual for the Ada Programming Language* [21].

A.7 Eiffel

Background

Eiffel was created by Bertrand Meyer not only as an object-oriented programming language, but also as a software engineering tool. While Eiffel is influenced by Simula, it was designed from the beginning to be an independent object-oriented language and development environment.

Abstraction	Instance variables	Yes
	Instance methods	Yes
	Class variables	No
	Class methods	No
Encapsulation	Of variables	Private
	Of methods	Public, private
Modularity	Kinds of modules	Unit
Hierarchy	Inheritance	Multiple
	Generic units	Yes
	Metaclasses	No
Typing	Strongly typed	Yes
	Polymorphism	Yes
Concurrency	Multitasking	No
Persistence	Persistent objects	No

Table A-6
Eiffel

The language supports dynamic binding and static typing, providing for flexibility in the design of a class interface, but taking advantage of the type safety that static typing provides. There are several significant features that give support for more rigorous software engineering, including parameterized classes, assertions, and exceptions. Meyer contends that generic classes complement the inheritance relationship by allowing for horizontal genericity: new classes at the same level of abstraction in an inheritance hierarchy may be created based on type parameters, rather than duplicating behaviors in sibling subclasses.

Preconditions and postconditions, both integral parts of the language, implement assertions upon entering and leaving a method, respectively. If a precondition fails upon entering a method, or if a postcondition fails when leaving, an exception is raised. A mechanism exists in the language to handle the exception through the use of the rescue clause and retry instruction.

Overview

Eiffel stresses the concepts of good software engineering: good class specification, strong typing, and facilities of taking advantage of reuse through both inheritance and generic classes. The formal treatment of exceptions allows rigorous specification of class interfaces in the implementation.

Eiffel also provides a full development environment including a syntax-directed editor, documentation generation, class libraries, and a browser. In addition, code management and build management facilities are supported.

Eiffel's features relative to our object model are summarized in Table A-6.

ABCL/1	Concurrent Smalltalk	Lore	Plasma II
ABE	CSSA	Mace	POOL-T
Acore	CST	MELD	PROCOL
Act/1	Director	Mjolner	Quick Pascal
Act/2	Distributed Smalltalk	ModPascal	Quicktalk
Act/3	Eiffel	Neon	ROSS
Actor	Emerald	New Flavors	SAST
Actors	ExperCommonLisp	NIL	SCOOP
Actra	Extended Smalltalk	O-CPU	SCOOPS
Ada	Felix Pascal	OakLisp	Self
Argus	Flavors	Oberon	Simula
ART	FOOPlog	Object Assembler	SINA
Berkeley Smalltalk	FOOPS	Object Cobol	Smalltalk
Beta	FRL	Object Lisp	Smalltalk AT
Blaze	Galileo	Object Logo	Smalltalk V
Brouhaha	Garp	Object Oberon	Smallworld
C with Classes	GLISP	Object Pascal	SPOOL
C++	Gypsy	Objective-C	SR
C_talk	Hybrid	ObjVLisp	SRL
Cantor	Inheritance	OOPC	STROBE
Clascal	InnovAda	OOPS+	T
Classic Ada	Intermission	OPAL	Trellis/Owl
CLOS	Jasmine	Orbit	Turbo Pascal 5.x
Cluster 86	KL-One	Orient84/K	Uniform
Common Loops	KRL	OTM	UNITS
Common Objects	KRS	PCOL	Vulcan
Common ORBIT	Little Smalltalk	PIE	XLISP
Concurrent Prolog	LOOPS	PL/LL	Zoom/VM

Figure A-2
Object-Based and Object-Oriented Programming Languages

References

The best treatment of the Eiffel language is found in Meyer's book, *Object-Oriented Software Construction* [22].

A.8 Other Object-Oriented Programming Languages

Figure A-2 provides the names of many other important or influential object-based and object-oriented programming languages; the Classified Bibliography offers references to sources of information for most of them.

Saunders [23] provides a survey of over 80 different object-based and object-oriented programming languages. He suggests that object-oriented programming languages may be grouped into seven categories [24]:

- Actor — Languages supporting delegation
- Concurrent — Object-oriented languages emphasizing concurrency
- Distributed — Object-oriented languages emphasizing distributed objects
- Frame-based — Languages supporting frame theory
- Hybrid — Object-oriented extensions to traditional languages
- Smalltalk-based — Smalltalk and its dialects

- Ideological   Application of object-oriented features to
                           other domains
- Miscellaneous   Object-oriented languages that do not fit any
                           other category

Preface

Mills, H. 1985. *DPMA and Human Productivity*. Houston, TX: Data Processing Management Association.

The First Section: Concepts

Wagner, J. 1986. *The Search for Signs of Intelligent Life in the Universe*. New York, NY: Harper and Row, p. 202. By permission of ICM, Inc.

Chapter 1: Complexity

[1]   Brooks, F. April 1987. No Silver Bullet: Essence and Accidents of Software Engineering. *IEEE Computer* vol. 20(4), p. 12.

[2]   Peters, L. 1981. *Software Design*. New York, NY: Yourdon Press, p. 22.

[3]   Brooks. No Silver Bullet, p. 11.

[4]   Parnas, D. July 1985. *Software Aspects of Strategic Defense Systems*. Victoria, Canada: University of Victoria, Report DCS-47-IR.

[5]   Peter, L. 1986. *The Peter Pyramid*. New York, NY: William Morrow, p. 153.

[6]   Waldrop, M. 1992. *Complexity: The Emerging Science at the Edge of Order and Chaos*. New York, NY: Simon and Schuster.

[7]   Courtois, P. June 1985. On Time and Space Decomposition of Complex Structures. *Communications of the ACM* vol. 28(6), p. 596.

[8]   Simon, H. 1982. *The Sciences of the Artificial*. Cambridge, MA: The MIT Press, p.218.

[9]   Rechtin, E. October 1992. The Art of Systems Architecting. *IEEE Spectrum*, vol. 29(10), p. 66.

[10]   Simon. *Sciences*, p. 217.

[11]   Ibid., p. 221.

[12]   Ibid., p. 209.

[13]   Gall, J. 1986. *Systemantics: How Systems Really Work and How They Fail*. Second Edition. Ann Arbor, MI: The General Systemantics Press, p. 65.

[14]   Miller, G. March 1956. The Magical Number Seven, Plus or Minus Two: Some Limits on Our Capacity for Processing Information. *The Psychological Review* vol. 63(2), p. 86.

[15]   Simon. *Sciences*, p. 81.

[16]   Dijkstra, E. 1979. Programming Considered as a Human Activity. *Classics in Software Engineering*. New York, NY: Yourdon Press, p.5.

[17]   Parnas, D. December 1985. Software Aspects of Strategic Defense Systems. *Communications of the ACM* vol. 28(12), p. 1328.

[18]   Tsai, J. and Ridge, J. November 1988. Intelligent Support for Specifications Transformation. *IEEE Software* vol. 5(6), p. 34.

[19]   Stein, J. March 1988. Object-Oriented Programming and Database Design. *Dr. Dobb's Journal of Software Tools for the Professional Programmer*, No. 137, p.18.

[20]   Peters. *Software Design*.

[21]   Yau, S. and Tsai, J. June 1986. A Survey of Software Design Techniques. *IEEE Transactions on Software Engineering* vol. SE-12(6).

[22]   Teledyne Brown Engineering. *Software Methodology Catalog*, Report MC87-COMM/ADP-0036. October 1987. Tinton Falls, NJ.

[23]   Sommerville, I. 1985. *Software Engineering*. Second Edition. Workingham, England: Addison-Wesley, p. 68.

[24]   Yourdon, E. and Constantine, L. 1979. *Structured Design*. Englewood Cliffs, NJ: Prentice-Hall.

[25]   Myers, G. 1978. *Composite/Structured Design*. New York, NY: Van Nostrand Reinhold.

[26]   Page-Jones, M. 1988. *The Practical Guide to Structured Systems Design*. Englewood Cliffs, NJ: Yourdon Press.

[27]   Wirth, N. January 1983. Program Development by Stepwise Refinement. *Communications of the ACM* vol. 26(1).

[28]   Wirth, N. 1986. *Algorithms and Data Structures*. Englewood Cliffs, NJ: Prentice-Hall.

[29]   Dahl, O., Dijkstra, E., and Hoare, C. A. R. 1972. *Structured Programming*. London, England: Academic Press.

[30] Mills, H., Linger, R., and Hevner, A. 1986. *Principles of Information System Design and Analysis*. Orlando, FL: Academic Press.

[31] Jackson, M. 1975. *Principles of Program Design*. Orlando, FL: Academic Press.

[32] Jackson, M. 1983. *System Development*. Englewood Cliffs, NJ: Prentice-Hall.

[33] Orr, K. 1971. *Structured Systems Development*. New York, NY: Yourdon Press.

[34] Langdon, G. 1982. *Computer Design*. San Jose, CA: Computeach Press, p. 6.

[20] Miller. Magical Number, p.95.

[36] Shaw, M. 1981. *ALPHARD: Form and Content*. New York, NY: Springer-Verlag, p. 6.

[37] Goldberg, A. 1984. *Smalltalk-80: The Interactive Programming Environment*. Reading, MA: Addison-Wesley, p. 80.

[38] Petroski, H. 1985. *To Engineer Is Human*. St Martin's Press: New York, p. 40.

[39] Dijkstra, E. January 1993. *American Programmer* vol. 6(1).

[40] Mostow, J. Spring 1985. Toward Better Models of the Design Process. *AI Magazine* vol. 6(1), p. 44.

[41] Stroustrup, B. 1991. *The C+ Programming Language*, Second Edition. Reading, MA: Addison-Wesley, p. 366.

[42] Eastman, N. 1984. Software Engineering and Technology. *Technical Directions* vol. 10(1): Bethesda, MD: IBM Federal Systems Division, p. 5.

[43] Brooks. No Silver Bullet, p. 10.

Chapter 2: The Object Model

[1] Rentsch, T. September 1982. Object-Oriented Programming. *SIGPLAN Notices* vol. 17(12), p. 51.

[2] Wegner, P. June 1981. *The Ada Programming Language and Environment*. Unpublished draft.

[3] Abbott, R. August 1987. Knowledge Abstraction. *Communications of the ACM* vol. 30(8), p. 664.

[4] Ibid., p. 664.

[5] Shankar, K. 1984. Data Design: Types, Structures, and Abstractions. *Handbook of Software Engineering*. New York, NY: Van Nostrand Reinhold, p. 253.

[6] *Macintosh MacApp 1.1.1 Programmer's Reference*. 1986. Cupertino, CA: Apple Computer, p. 2.

[7] Bhaskar, K. October 1983. How Object-Oriented Is Your System? *SIGPLAN Notices* vol. 18(10), p. 8.

[8] Stefik, M. and Bobrow, D. Winter 1986. Object-Oriented Programming: Themes and Variations, *AI Magazine* vol. 6(4), p. 41.

[9] Yonezawa, A. and Tokoro, M. 1987. Object-Oriented Concurrent Programming: An Introduction, in *Object-Oriented Concurrent Programming*. Cambridge, MA: The MIT Press, p. 2.

[10] Levy, H. 1984. *Capability-Based Computer Systems*. Bedford, MA: Digital Press, p. 13.

[11] Ramamoorthy, C. and Sheu, P. Fall 1988. Object-Oriented Systems. *IEEE Expert* vol. 3(3), p. 14.

[12] Myers, G. 1982. *Advances in Computer Architecture.* Second Edition. New York, NY: John Wiley and Sons, p. 58.

[13] Levy. *Capability-Based Computer.*

[14] Kavi, K. and Chen, D. 1987. Architectural Support for Object-Oriented Languages. *Proceedings of the Thirty-second IEEE Computer Society International Conference.* IEEE.

[15] *iAPX 432 Object Primer.* 1981. Santa Clara, CA: Intel Corporation.

[16] Dally, W. J. and Kajiya, J. T. March 1985. An Object-Oriented Architecture. *SIGARCH Newsletter* vol. 13(3).

[17] Dahlby, S., Henry, G., Reynolds, D., and Taylor, P. 1982. The IBM System/38: A High Level Machine, in *Computer Structures: Principles and Examples.* New York, NY: McGraw-Hill.

[18] Dijkstra, E. May 1968. The Structure of the "THE" Multiprogramming System. *Communications of the ACM* vol. 11(5).

[19] Pashtan, A. 1982. Object-Oriented Operating Systems: An Emerging Design Methodology. *Proceedings of the ACM '82 Conference.* ACM.

[20] Parnas, D. 1979. On the Criteria to Be Used in Decomposing Systems into Modules, in *Classics in Software Engineering.* New York, NY: Yourdon Press.

[21] Liskov, B. and Zilles, S. 1977. An Introduction to Formal Specifications of Data Abstractions. *Current Trends in Programming Methodology: Software Specification and Design* vol. 1. Englewood Cliffs, NJ: Prentice-Hall.

[22] Guttag, J. 1980. Abstract Data Types and the Development of Data Structures, in *Programming Language Design.* New York, NY: Computer Society Press.

[23] Shaw. Abstraction Techniques.

[24] Nygaard, K. and Dahl, O-J. 1981. The Development of the Simula Languages, in *History of Programming Languages.* New York, NY: Academic Press, p. 460.

[25] Atkinson, M. and Buneman, P. June 1987. Types and Persistence in Database Programming Languages. *ACM Computing Surveys* vol. 19(2), p. 105.

[26] Rumbaugh, J. April 1988. Relational Database Design Using an Object-Oriented Methodology. *Communications of the ACM* vol. 31(4), p. 415.

[27] Chen, P. March 1976. The Entity-Relationship Model – Toward a Unified View of Data. *ACM Transactions on Database Systems* vol. 1(1).

[28] Barr, A. and Feigenbaum, E. 1981. *The Handbook of Artificial Intelligence.* Vol. 1. Los Altos, CA: William Kaufmann, p. 216.

[29] Stillings, N., Feinstein, M., Garfield, J., Rissland, E., Rosenbaum, D., Weisler, S, Baker-Ward, L. 1987. *Cognitive Science: An Introduction.* Cambridge, MA: The MIT Press, p. 305.

[30] Rand, Ayn. 1979. *Introduction to Objectivist Epistemology.* New York, NY: New American Library.

[31] Minsky, M. 1986. *The Society of Mind.* New York, NY: Simon and Schuster.

[32] Jones, A. 1979. The Object Model: A Conceptual Tool for Structuring Software. *Operating Systems.* New York, NY: Springer-Verlag, p. 8.

[33] Stroustrup, B. May 1988. What Is Object-Oriented Programming? *IEEE Software* vol. 5(3), p. 10.

[34] Cardelli, L. and Wegner, P. On Understanding Types, Data Abstraction, and Polymorphism. December 1985. *ACM Computing Surveys* vol. 17(4), p. 481.

[35] DeMarco, T. 1979. *Structured Analysis and System Specification.* Englewood Cliffs, NJ: Prentice-Hall.

[36] Yourdon, E. 1989. *Modern Structured Analysis.* Englewood Cliffs, NJ: Prentice-Hall.

[37] Gane, C. and Sarson, T. 1979. *Structured Systems Analysis.* Englewood Cliffs, NJ: Prentice-Hall.

[38] Ward, P. and Mellor, S. 1985. *Structured Development for Real-Time Systems* Englewood Cliffs, NJ: Yourdon Press.

[39] Hatley, D. and Pirbhai, I. 1988. *Strategies for Real-Time System Specification.* New York, NY: Dorset House.

[40] Jenkins, M. and Glasgow, J. January 1986. Programming Styles in Nial. *IEEE Software* vol. 3(1), p. 48.

[41] Bobrow, D. and Stefik, M. February 1986. Perspectives on Artificial Intelligence Programming. *Science* vol. 231, p. 951.

[42] Dahl, O., Dijkstra, E., and Hoare, C. A. R. 1972. *Structured Programming.* London, England: Academic Press, p. 83.

[43] Shaw, M. October 1984. Abstraction Techniques in Modern Programming Languages. *IEEE Software* vol. 1(4), p. 10.

[44] Berzins, V., Gray, M., and Naumann, D. May 1986. Abstraction-Based Software Development. *Communications of the ACM* vol. 29(5), p. 403.

[45] Abelson, H. and Sussman, G. 1985. *Structure and Interpretation of Computer Programs.* Cambridge, MA: The MIT Press, p. 126.

[46] Ibid., p. 132.

[47] Seidewitz, E. and Stark, M. 1986. Towards a General Object-Oriented Software Development Methodology. *Proceedings of the First International Conference on Ada Programming Language Applications for the NASA Space Station.* NASA Lyndon B. Johnson Space Center, TX: NASA, p. D.4.6.4.

[48] Meyer, B. 1988. *Object-Oriented Software Construction.* New York, NY: Prentice Hall.

[49] Wirfs-Brock, R. and Wilkerson, B. October 1989. Object-Oriented Design: A Responsibility-Driven Approach. *SIGPLAN Notices* vol. 24(10).

[50] Ingalls, D. The Smalltalk-76 Programming System Design and Implementation. *Proceedings of the Fifth Annual ACM Symposium on Principles of Programming Languages.* ACM, p. 9.

[51] Gannon, J., Hamlet, R., and Mills, H. July 1987. Theory of Modules. *IEEE Transactions on Software Engineering* vol. SE-13(7), p. 820.

[52] Date, C. 1986. *Relational Database: Selected Writings.* Reading, MA: Addison-Wesley, p. 180.

[53] Liskov, B. May 1988. Data Abstraction and Hierarchy. *SIGPLAN Notices* vol. 23(5), p. 19.

[54] Britton, K. and Parnas, D. December 8, 1981. *A-7E Software Module Guide.* Washington, D.C. Naval Research Laboratory, Report 4702, p. 24.

[55] Gabriel, R. 1990. Private communication.

[56] Stroustrup, B. 1988. Private communication.

[57] Myers, G. 1978. *Composite/Structured Design.* New York, NY: Van Nostrand Reinhold, p. 21.

[58] Liskov, B. 1980. A Design Methodology for Reliable Software Systems, in *Tutorial on Software Design Techniques.* Third Edition. New York, NY: IEEE Computer Society, p. 66.

[59] Zelkowitz, M. June 1978. Perspectives on Software Engineering. *ACM Computing Surveys* vol. 10(2), p. 20.

[60] Parnas, D., Clements, P., and Weiss, D. March 1985. The Modular Structure of Complex Systems. *IEEE Transactions on Software Engineering* vol. SE-11(3), p. 260.

[61] Britton and Parnas. *A-7E Software*, p. 2.

[62] Parnas, D., Clements, P., and Weiss, D. 1983. Enhancing Reusability with Information Hiding. *Proceedings of the Workshop on Reusability in Programming,* Stratford, CT: ITT Programming, p. 241.

[63] Meyer,, *Object-Oriented Software Construction*, p. 47.

[64] Cox, B. 1986. *Object-Oriented Programming: An Evolutionary Approach.* Reading, MA: Addison-Wesley, p. 69.

[65] Danforth, S. and Tomlinson, C. March 1988. Type Theories and Object-Oriented Programming. *ACM Computing Surveys* vol. 20(1), p. 34.

[66] Liskov. 1988, p. 23.

[67   As quoted in Liskov. 1980, p. 67.

[68] Zilles, S. 1984. Types, Algebras, and Modeling, in *On Conceptual Modeling: Perspectives from Artificial Intelligence, Databases, and Programming Languages.* New York, NY: Springer-Verlag, p. 442.

[69] Borning, A. and Ingalls, D. 1982. A Type Declaration and Inference System for Smalltalk. Palo Alto, CA: Xerox Palo Alto Research Center, p. 134.

[70] Wegner, P. October 1987. Dimensions of Object-Based Language Design. *SIGPLAN Notices* vol. 22(12), p. 171.

[71] Stroustrup, B. 1992. Private communication.

[72] Tesler, L. August 1981. The Smalltalk Environment. *Byte* vol. 6(8), p. 142.

[73] Borning and Ingalls. Type Declaration, p. 133.

[74] Thomas, D. March 1989. What's in an Object? *Byte* vol. 14(3), p. 232.

[75] Lim, J. and Johnson, R. April 1989. The Heart of Object-Oriented Concurrent Programming. *SIGPLAN Notices* vol. 24(4), p. 165.

[76] Ibid., p. 165.

[77   Black, A., Hutchinson, N., Jul, E., Levy, H., and Carter, L. July 1986. *Distribution and Abstract Types in Emerald.* Report 86-02-04. Seattle, WA: University of Washington, p. 3.

[78] Proceedings of the ACM SIGPLAN Workshop on Object-Based Concurrent Programming. April 1989. *SIGPLAN Notices* vol. 24(4), p. 1.

[79] Atkinson, M., Bailey, P., Chisholm, K., Cockshott, P., and Morrison, R. 1983. An Approach to Persistent Programming. *The Computer Journal* vol. 26(4), p. 360.

[80] Khoshafian, S. and Copeland, G. November 1986. Object Identity. *SIGPLAN Notices* vol. 21(11), p. 409.

[81] *Vbase Technical Overview*. September 1987. Billerica, MA: Ontologic, p. 4.

[82] Stroustrup, B. November 1987. Possible Directions for C++. *Proceedings of the USENIX C++ Workshop*. Santa Fe, NM, p. 14.

[83] Meyer. *Object-Oriented Software Construction*, p. 30-31.

[84] Robson, D. August 1981. Object-Oriented Software Systems. *Byte* vol. 6(8), p. 74.

Chapter 3: Classes and Objects

[1] Lefrancois, G. 1977. *Of Children: An Introduction to Child Development*. Second Edition. Belmont, CA: Wadsworth, p. 244–246.

[2] Nygaard, K. and Dahl, O-J. 1981. The Development of the Simula Languages, in *History of Programming Languages*. New York, NY: Academic Press, p. 462.

[3] Halbert, D. and O'Brien, P. September 1988. Using Types and Inheritance in Object-Oriented Programming. *IEEE Software* vol. 4(5), p. 73.

[4] Smith, M. and Tockey, S. 1988. *An Integrated Approach to Software Requirements Definition Using Objects*. Seattle, WA: Boeing Commercial Airplane Support Division, p. 132.

[5] Cox, B. 1986. *Object-Oriented Programming: An Evolutionary Approach*. Reading, MA: Addison-Wesley, p. 29.

[6] MacLennan, B. December 1982. Values and Objects in Programming Languages. *SIGPLAN Notices* vol. 17(12), p. 78.

[7] Lippman, S. 1989. *C++ Primer*. Reading, MA: Addison-Wesley, p. 185.

[8] Adams, S. 1993. Private communication.

[9] Wirfs-Brock, R., Wilkerson, B., and Wiener, L. 1990. *Designing Object-Oriented Software*. Englewood Cliffs, New Jersey: Prentice Hall, p. 61.

[10] Rubin, K. 1993. Private communication.

[11] *Macintosh MacApp 1.1.1 Programmer's Reference*. 1986. Cupertino, CA: Apple Computer, p. 4.

[12] Khoshafian, S. and Copeland, G. November 1986. Object Identity. *SIGPLAN Notices* vol. 21(11), p. 406.

[13] Ingalls, D. 1981. Design Principles behind Smalltalk. *Byte* vol. 6(8), p. 290.

[14] Gall, J. 1986. *Systemantics: How Systems Really Work and How They Fail*. Second Edition. Ann Arbor, MI: The General Systemantics Press, p. 158.

[15] Seidewitz, E. and Stark, M. 1986. Towards a General Object-Oriented Software Development Methodology. *Proceedings of the First International Conference on Ada Programming Language Applications for the NASA Space Station*. NASA Lyndon B. Johnson Space Center, TX: NASA, p. D.4.6.4.

[16] Rumbaugh, J., Blaha, M., Premerlani, W., Eddy, F., and Lorensen, W. 1991. *Object-Oriented Modeling and Design*. Englewood Cliffs, New Jersey: Prentice-Hall, p. 459.

[17] *Webster's Third New International Dictionary of the English Language,* unabridged. 1986. Chicago, Illinois: Merriam-Webster.

[18] Stroustrup, B. 1991. *The C+ Programming Language*, Second Edition. Reading, MA: Addison-Wesley, p. 422.

[19] Meyer, B. 1987. *Programming as Contracting*. Report TR-EI-12/CO. Goleta, CA: Interactive Software Engineering.

[20] Snyder, A. November 1986. Encapsulation and Inheritance in Object-Oriented Programming Languages. *SIGPLAN Notices* vol. 21(11).

[21] LaLonde, W. April 1989. Designing Families of Data Types Using Exemplars. *ACM Transactions on Programming Languages and Systems* vol. 11(2), p. 214.

[22] Rumbaugh, J. April 1988. Relational Database Design Using an Object-Oriented Methodology. *Communications of the ACM* vol. 31(4), p. 417.

[23] Lieberman, H. November 1986. Using Prototypical Objects to Implement Shared Behavior in Object-Oriented Systems. *SIGPLAN Notices* vol. 21(11).

[24] Rumbaugh, 1991. p. 312.

[25] Brachman, R. October 1983. What IS-A Is and Isn't: An Analysis of Taxonomic Links in Semantic Networks. *IEEE Computer* vol. 16(10), p. 30.

[26] Micallef, J. April/May 1988. Encapsulation, Reusability, and Extensibility in Object-Oriented Programming Languages. *Journal of Object-Oriented Programming* vol. 1(1), p. 15.

[27] Snyder. Encapsulation, p. 39.

[28] Cardelli, L. and Wegner, P. On Understanding Types, Data Abstraction, and Polymorphism. December 1985. *ACM Computing Surveys* vol. 17(4), p. 475.

[29] As quoted in Harland, D., Szyplewski, M., and Wainwright, J. October 1985. An Alternative View of Polymorphism. *SIGPLAN Notices* vol. 20(10).

[30] Kaplan, S. and Johnson, R. July 21, 1986. *Designing and Implementing for Reuse*. Urbana, IL: University of Illinois, Department of Computer Science, p. 8.

[31] Deutsch, P. 1983. Efficient Implementation of the Smalltalk-80 System, in *Proceedings of the 11th Annual ACM Symposium on the Principles of Programming Languages*, p. 300.

[32] Ibid., p. 299.

[33] Duff, C. August 1986. Designing an Efficient Language. *Byte* vol. 11(8), p. 216.

[34] Stroustrup, B. 1988. Private communication.

[35] Stroustrup, B. November 1987. Possible Directions for C++. *Proceedings of the USENIX C++ Workshop*. Santa Fe, New Mexico, p. 8.

[36] Keene, S. 1989. *Object-Oriented Programming in Common Lisp*. Reading, MA: Addison-Wesley, p. 44.

[37] Winston, P. and Horn, B. 1989. *Lisp*. Third Edition. Reading, MA: Addison-Wesley, p. 510.

[38] Micallef, J. April/May 1988. Encapsulation, Reusability, and Extensibility in Object-Oriented Programming Languages. *Journal of Object-Oriented Programming* vol. 1(1), p. 25.

[39] Snyder. Encapsulation, p. 41.

[40] Vlissides, J. and Linton, M. 1988. Applying Object-Oriented Design to Structured Graphics. *Proceedings of USENIX C++ Conference.* Berkeley, CA: USENIX Association, p. 93.

[41] Meyer, B. 1988. *Object-Oriented Software Construction.* New York, NY: Prentice Hall, p. 274.

[42] Keene. *Object-Oriented Programming,* p. 118.

[43] Snyder. Encapsulation, p. 43.

[44] Hendler, J. October 1986. Enhancement for Multiple Inheritance. *SIGPLAN Notices* vol. 21(10), p. 100.

[45] Stroustrup, 1987, p. 3.

[46] Stroustrup, B. 1988. Parameterized Types for C++. *Proceedings of USENIX C++ Conference.* Berkeley, CA: USENIX Association, p. 1.

[47] Meyer, B. November 1986. Genericity versus Inheritance. *SIGPLAN Notices* vol. 21(11), p. 402.

[48] Stroustrup. 1988, p. 4.

[49] Robson, D. August 1981. Object-Oriented Software Systems. *Byte* vol. 6(8), p. 86.

[50] Goldberg, A. and Robson, D. 1983. *Smalltalk-80: The Language and Its Implementation.* Reading, MA: Addison-Wesley, p. 287.

[51] Ingalls, D. August 1981. Design Principles behind Smalltalk. *Byte* vol. 6(8), p. 286.

[52] Stevens, W., Myers, G., and Constantine, L. 1979. Structured Design, in *Classics in Software Engineering.* New York, NY: Yourdon Press, p. 209.

[53] Page-Jones, M. 1988. *The Practical Guide to Structured Systems Design.* Englewood Cliffs, NJ: Yourdon Press, p. 59.

[54] Meyer. 1987, p. 4.

[55] Halbert, D. and O'Brien, P. September 1988. Using Types and Inheritance in Object-Oriented Programming. *IEEE Software* vol. 4(5), p. 74.

[56] Sakkinen, M. December 1988. Comments on "the Law of Demeter" and C++. *SIGPLAN Notices* vol. 23(12), p. 38.

[57] Lea, D. August 12, 1988. *User's Guide to GNU C++ Library.* Cambridge, MA: Free Software Foundation, p. 12

[58] Ibid.

[59] Meyer. 1988, p. 332.

[60] Wirth, N. 1986. *Algorithms and Data Structures.* Englewood Cliffs, NJ: Prentice-Hall, p. 37.

[61] Keene. *Object-Oriented Programming,* p. 68.

[62] Parnas, D., Clements, P., and Weiss, D. 1989. Enhancing Reusability with Information Hiding. *Software Reusability.* New York, NY: ACM Press, p. 143.

Chapter 4: Classification

[1]   As quoted in Swaine, M. June 1988. Programming Paradigms. *Dr. Dobb's Journal of Software Tools*, No. 140, p. 110.

[2]   Michalski, R. and Stepp, R. 1983. Learning from Observation: Conceptual Clustering, in *Machine Learning: An Artificial Intelligence Approach*. Palo Alto, CA: Tioga, p. 332.

[3]   Alexander, C. 1979. *The Timeless Way of Building*. New York, NY: Oxford University Press, p. 203.

[4]   Darwin, C. 1984. *The Origin of Species. Vol. 49 of Great Books of the Western World*. Chicago, IL: Encyclopedia Britannica, p. 207.

[5]   *The New Encyclopedia Britannica*. 1985. Chicago, IL: Encyclopedia Britannica. vol. 3, p. 356.

[6]   Gould, S. June 1992. We Are All Monkey's Uncles. *Natural History*.

[7]   May, R. September 16, 1988. How Many Species Are There on Earth? *Science* vol. 241, p. 1441.

[8]   As quoted in Lewin, R. November 4, 1988. Family Relationships Are a Biological Conundrum. *Science* vol. 242, p. 671.

[9]   *The New Encyclopedia Britannica* vol. 3, p. 156.

[10]   Descartes, R. 1984. Rules for the Direction of the Mind. Vol. 31 of Great Books of the Western World. Chicago, IL: Encyclopedia Britannica, p. 32.

[11]   Shaw, M. May 1989. Larger Scale Systems Require Higher-Level Abstractions. *SIGSOFT Engineering Notes* vol. 14(3), p. 143.

[12]   Goldstein, T. May 1989. The Object-Oriented Programmer. *The C++ Report* vol. 1(5).

[13]   Coombs, C., Raiffa, H., and Thrall, R. 1954. Some Views on Mathematical Models and Measurement Theory. *Psychological Review* vol. 61(2), p. 132.

[14]   Flood, R. and Carson, E. 1988. *Dealing with Complexity*. New York, NY: Plenum Press, p. 8.

[15]   Birtwistle, G., Dahl, O-J., Myhrhaug, B., and Nygard, K. 1979. *Simula begin*. Lund, Sweden: Studentlitteratur, p. 23.

[16]   Heinlein, R. 1966. *The Moon Is a Harsh Mistress*. New York, NY: The Berkeley Publishing Group, p. 11.

[17]   Sowa, J. 1984. *Conceptual Structures: Information Processing in Mind and Machine*. Reading, MA: Addison-Wesley, p. 16.

[18]   Lakoff, G. 1987. *Women, Fire, and Dangerous Things: What Categories Reveal About the Mind*. Chicago, IL: The University of Chicago Press, p. 161.

[19]   Stepp, R. and Michalski, R. February 1986. Conceptual Clustering of Structured Objects: A Goal-Oriented Approach. *Artificial Intelligence* vol. 28(1), p. 53.

[20]   Wegner, P. 1987. The Object-Oriented Classification Paradigm, in *Research Directions in Object-Oriented Programming*. Cambridge, MA: The MIT Press, p. 480.

[21]   Aquinas, T. 1984. *Summa Theologica. Vol. 19 of Great Books of the Western World*. Chicago, IL: Encyclopedia Britannica, p. 71.

[22] Maier, H. 1969. *Three Theories of Child Development: The Contributions of Erik H. Erickson, Jean Piaget, and Robert R. Sears, and Their Applications.* New York, NY: Harper and Row, p. 111.

[23] Lakoff. *Women, Fire,* p. 32.

[24] Minsky, M. 1986. *The Society of Mind.* New York, NY: Simon and Schuster, p. 199.

[25] *The Great Ideas: A Syntopicon of Great Books of the Western World.* 1984. *Vol. 1 of Great Books of the Western World.* Chicago, IL: Encyclopedia Britannica, p. 293.

[26] Kosko, B. 1992. *Neural Networks and Fuzzy Systems.* Englewood Cliffs, NJ: Prentice-Hall, p. xx.

[27] Stepp, p. 44.

[28] Lakoff. *Women, Fire, and Dangerous Things,* p. 7.

[29] Ibid., p. 16.

[30] Lakoff, G. and Johnson, M. 1980. *Metaphors We Live By.* Chicago, IL: The University of Chicago Press, p. 122.

[31 Meyer, B. 1988. Private communication.

[32] Shlaer, S. and Mellor, S. 1988. *Object-Oriented Systems Analysis: Modeling the World in Data.* Englewood Cliffs, NJ: Yourdon Press, p. 15.

[33] Ross, R. 1987. *Entity Modeling: Techniques and Application.* Boston, MA: Database Research Group, p. 9.

[34] Coad, P. and Yourdon, E. 1990. *Object-Oriented Analysis.* Englewood Cliffs, NJ: Prentice-Hall, p. 62.

[35] Shlaer, S. and Mellor, S. 1992. *Object Lifecycles: Modeling the World in States.* Englewood Cliffs, New Jersey: Yourdon Press.

[36] Wirfs-Brock, R., Wilkerson, B., and Wiener, L. 1990. *Designing Object-Oriented Software.* Englewood Cliffs, New Jersey: Prentice Hall, p. 61.

[37] Rubin, K. and Goldberg, A. September 1992. Object Behavior Analysis. *Communications of the ACM,* vol. 35(9), p. 48.

[38] Dreger, B. 1989. *Function Point Analysis.* Englewood Cliffs, NJ: Prentice Hall, p. 4.

[39] Arango, G. May 1989. Domain Analysis: From Art Form to Engineering Discipline. *SIGSOFT Engineering Notes* vol. 14(3), p. 153.

[40] Moore, J. and Bailin, S. 1988. *Position Paper on Domain Analysis.* Laurel, MD: CTA, p. 2.

[41] Jacobson, I., Christerson, M., Jonsson, P., and Overgaard, G. 1992. *Object-Oriented Software Engineering.* Workingham, England: Addison-Wesley, p. viii.

[42] Zahniseer, R. July/August 1990. Building Software In Groups. *American Programmer,* vol. 3(7-8).

[43] Goldstein, N. and Alger, J. 1992. *Developing Object-Oriented Software for the Macintosh.* Reading, Massachusetts: Addison-Wesley, p. 161.

[44] Beck, K. and Cunningham, W. October 1989. A Laboratory for Teaching Object-Oriented Thinking. *SIGPLAN Notices* vol. 24(10).

[45] Abbott, R. November 1983. Program Design by Informal English Descriptions. *Communications of the ACM* vol. 26(11).

[46] Saeki, M., Horai, H., and Enomoto, H. May 1989. Software Development Process from Natural Language Specification. *Proceedings of the 11th International Conference on Software Engineering.* New York, NY: Computer Society Press of the IEEE.

[47] McMenamin, S. and Palmer, J. 1984. *Essential Systems Analysis.* New York, NY: Yourdon Press, p. 267.

[48] Ward, P. and Mellor, S. 1985. *Structured Development for Real-time Systems.* Englewood Cliffs, NJ: Yourdon Press.

[49] Seidewitz, E. and Stark, M. August 1986. *General Object-Oriented Software Development,* Report SEL-86-002. Greenbelt, MD: NASA Goddard Space Flight Center, p. 5-2.

[50] Seidewitz, E. 1990. Private communication.

[51] Goldberg, A. 1984. *Smalltalk-80: The Interactive Programming Environment.* Reading, MA: Addison-Wesley, p. 77.

[52] Thomas, D. May/June 1989. In Search of an Object-Oriented Development Process. *Journal of Object-Oriented Programming* vol. 2(1), p. 61.

[53] Stroustrup, B. 1986. *The C++ Programming Language.* Reading, MA: Addison-Wesley, p. 7.

[54] Halbert, D. and O'Brien, P. September 1988. Using Types and Inheritance in Object-Oriented Programming. *IEEE Software* vol. 4(5), p. 75.

[55] Stefik, M. and Bobrow, D. Winter 1986. Object-Oriented Programming: Themes and Variations, *AI Magazine* vol. 6(4), p. 60.

[56] Stroustrup, B. 1991. *The C+ Programming Language,* Second Edition. Reading, Massachusetts: Addison-Wesley, p. 377.

[57] Stefik and Bobrow. Object-Oriented Programming, p. 58.

[58] Lins, C. 1989. A First Look at Literate Programming. *Structured Programming.*

[59] Gabriel, R. 1990. Private communication.

[60] Coplien, J. 1992. *Advanced C++ Programming Styles and Idioms.* Reading, Massachusetts: Addison-Wesley.

[61] Adams, S. July 1986. MetaMethods: The MVC Paradigm, in *HOOPLA: Hooray for Object-Oriented Programming Languages.* Everette, WA: Object-Oriented Programming for Smalltalk Applications Developers Association vol. 1(4), p. 6.

[62] Russo, V., Johnston, G., and Campbell, R. September 1988. Process Management and Exception Handling in Multiprocessor Operating Systems Using Object-Oriented Design Techniques. *SIGPLAN Notices* vol. 23(11), p. 249.

[63] Englemore, R. and Morgan, T. 1988. *Blackboard Systems.* Wokingham, England: Addison-Wesley, p. v.

[64] Coad, P. September 1992. Object-Oriented Patterns. *Communications of the ACM,* vol. 35(9)

The Second Section: The Method

Petroski, H. 1985. *To Engineer is Human.* New York, NY: St Martin's Press, p. 73.

Chapter 5: The Notation

[1]   Shear, D. December 8, 1988. CASE Shows Promise, but Confusion Still Exists. *EDN* vol. 33(25), p. 168.

[2]   Whitehead, A. 1958. *An Introduction to Mathematics.* New York, NY: Oxford University Press.

[3]   Defense Science Board. *Report of the Defense Science Board Task Force on Military Software.* September 1987. Washington, D.C.: Office of the Undersecretary of Defense for Acquisition, p. 8.

[4]   Kleyn, M. and Gingrich, P. September 1988. GraphTrace – Understanding Object-Oriented Systems Using Concurrently Animated Views. *SIGPLAN Notices* vol. 23(11), p. 192.

[5]   Weinberg, G. 1988. *Rethinking Systems Analysis and Design.* New York, NY: Dorset House, p. 157.

[6]   Intel. 1981. *iAPX 432 Object Primer.* Santa Clara, CA.

[7]   Rumbaugh, J., Blaha, M., Premerlani, W., Eddy, F., and Lorensen, W. 1991. *Object-Oriented Modeling and Design.* Englewood Cliffs, New Jersey: Prentice-Hall.

[8]   Stroustrup, B. 1991. *The C+ Programming Language*, Second Edition. Reading, Massachusetts: Addison-Wesley Publishing Company.

[9]   Kiczales, G., Rivieres, J., and Bobrow, D. 1991. *The Art of the Metaobject Protocol.* Cambridge, Massachusetts: The MIT Press.

[10]   Gamma, E., Helm, R., Johnson, R., Vlissides, J. 1993. A Catalog of Object-Oriented Design Patterns. Cupertino, California: Taligent

[11]   Harel, D. 1987. Statecharts: A Visual Formalism for Complex Systems. *Science of Computer Programming* vol. 8.

[12]   Rumbaugh, *Object-Oriented Modeling and Design*

[13]   Bear, S., Allen, P., Coleman, D., and Hayes, F. Graphical Specification of Object-Oriented Systems. *Object-Oriented Programming Systems, Languages, and Applications.* Ottawa, Canada: OOPSLA'90.

[14]   Rumbaugh, *Object-Oriented Modeling and Design*

[15]   Jacobson, I., Christerson, M., Jonsson, P., and Overgaard, G. 1992. *Object-Oriented Software Engineering.* Workingham, England: Addison-Wesley Publishing Company.

Chapter 6: The Process

[1]   Brooks, F. 1975. *The Mythical Man-Month.* Reading, MA: Addison-Wesley, p. 42.

[2]   Stroustrup, B. 1991. *The C+ Programming Language*, Second Edition. Reading, MA: Addison-Wesley.

[3]   Maccoby, M. December 1991. The Innovative Mind at Work. *IEEE Spectrum*, vol. 28(12).

[4]   Lammers, S. 1986. *Programmers at Work.* Redmond, WA: Microsoft Press.

[5]   Druke, M. 1989. Private communication.

[6]   Jones, C. September 1984. Reusability in Programming: A Survey of the State of the Art. *IEEE Transactions on Software Engineering*. vol. SE-10(5).

[7]   Humphrey, W. 1989. *Managing the Software Process*. Reading, MA: Addison-Wesley, p. 5.

[8]   Curtis, B. May 17, 1989. . . . *But You Have to Understand, This Isn't the Way We Develop Software at Our Company*. MCC Technical Report Number STP-203-89. Austin, TX: Microelectronics and Computer Technology Corporation, p. x.

[9]   Parnas, D. and Clements, P. 1986. A Rational Design Process: How and Why to Fake It. *IEEE Transactions on Software Engineering* vol. SE-12(2).

[10] Boehm, B. August 1986. A Spiral Model of Software Development and Enhancement. *Software Engineering Notes vol.* 11(4), p. 22.

[11] Stroustrup, B. 1991. *The C+ Programming Language*, Second Edition. Reading, MA: Addison-Wesley, p. 362.

[12] Brownsword, L. 1989. Private communication.

[13] Stroustrup, p. 373.

[14] Vonk, R. 1990. *Prototyping*. Englewood Cliffs, NJ: Prentice-Hall, p. 31.

[15] Gilb, T. 1988. *Principles of Software Engineering Management*. Reading, Massachusetts Addison-Wesley, p. 92.

[16] Mellor, S., Hecht, A., Tryon, D., and Hywari, W. September 1988. Object-Oriented Analysis: Theory and Practice, Course Notes, in *Object-Oriented Programming Systems, Languages, and Applications*. San Diego, CA: OOPSLA'88, p. 1.3.

[17] Symons, C. 1988. Function Point Analysis: Difficulties and Improvements. *IEEE Transactions on Software Engineering* vol.(14)1.

[18] Dreger, B. 1989. *Function Point Analysis*. Englewood Cliffs, New Jersey: Prentice Hall, p. 5.

[19] deChampeaux, D., Balzer, B., Bulman, D., Culver-Lozo, K., Jacobson, I., Mellor, S. *The Object-Oriented Software Development Process*. Vancouver, Canada: OOPSLA'92.

[20] Davis, A. 1990. *Software Requirements: Analysis and Specification*. Englewood Cliffs, New Jersey: Prentice-Hall.

[21] Rubin, K. 1993. Private communication.

[22] Jacobson, I., Christerson, M., Jonsson, P., and Overgaard, G. 1992. *Object-Oriented Software Engineering*. Workingham, England: Addison-Wesley Publishing Company.

[23] Rubin, K. and Goldberg, A. September 1992. *Object Behavior Analysis*. Communications of the ACM vol. 35(9).

[24] Andert, G. 1992. Private communication.

[25] Page-Jones, M. 1988. *The Practical Guide to Structured Systems Design*. Englewood Cliffs, NJ: Yourdon Press. pp. 261–265.

[26] Stefik, M. and Bobrow, D. Winter 1986. Object-Oriented Programming: Themes and Variations, *AI Magazine* vol. 6(4), p. 41.

[27] Meyer, B. 1988. *Object-Oriented Software Construction*. New York, NY: Prentice Hall, p. 340.

[28] Andert, G. 1993. Private communication.

[29] Walsh, J. *Preliminary Defect Data from the Iterative Development of a Large C++ Program*. Vancouver, Canada: OOPSLA'92.

[30] Chmura, L, Norcio, A., and Wicinski, T. July 1990. Evaluating Software Design Processes by Analyzing Change Date Over Time. *IEEE Transactions on Software Engineering* vol. 16(7).

[31] As quoted in Sommerville, I. 1989. *Software Engineering*. Third Edition. Wokingham, England: Addison-Wesley, p. 546.

Chapter 7: Pragmatics

[1] Dijkstra, E. May 1968. The Structure of the "THE" Multiprogramming System. *Communications of the ACM* vol. 11(5), p. 341.

[2] Kishida, K., Teramoto, M., Torri, K., and Urano, Y. September 1988. Quality Assurance Technology in Japan. *IEEE Software* vol. 4(5), p. 13.

[3] Hawryszkiewycz, I. 1984. *Database Analysis and Design*. Chicago, IL: Science Research Associates, p. 115.

[4] van Genuchten, M. June 1991. Why is Software Late? An Empirical Study of Reasons for Delay in Software Development. *IEEE Transactions on Software Engineering* vol. 17(6), p. 589.

[5] Gilb, T. 1988. *Principles of Software Engineering Management*. Reading, Massachusetts Addison-Wesley Publishing Company, p. 73.

[6] As quoted in Zelkowitz, M. June 1978. Perspectives on Software Engineering. *ACM Computing Surveys* vol. 10(2), p. 204.

[7] Showalter, J. 1989. Private communication.

[8] Davis, A., Bersoff, E., and Comer, E. October 1988. A Strategy for Comparing Alternative Software Development Life Cycle Models. *IEEE Transactions on Software Engineering* vol. 14(10), p. 1456.

[9] Goldberg, A. 1993. Private communication.

[10] Schulmeyer, G. and McManus, J. 1992. *Handbook of Software Quality Assurance, Second Edition*. New York, New York: Van Nostrand Reinhold, p. 5.

[11] Schulmeyer, p. 7.

[12] Schulmeyer, p. 184.

[13] Schulmeyer, p. 169.

[14] Walsh, J. *Preliminary Defect Data from the Iterative Development of a Large C++ Program*. Vancouver, Canada: OOPSLA'92.

[15] Chidamber, S. and Kemerer, C. 1993. *A Metrics Suite for Object-Oriented Design*. Cambridge, Massachusetts: MIT Sloan School of Management.

[16] Lang, K. and Peralmutter, B. November 1986. Oaklisp: an Object-Oriented Scheme with First-Class Types. *SIGPLAN Notices* vol. 21(11), p. 34.

[17] Meyrowitz, N. November 1986. Intermedia: The Architecture and Construction of an Object-Oriented Hypermedia System and Applications Framework. *SIGPLAN Notices* vol. 21(11), p. 200.

[18] Kempf, R. October 1987. Teaching Object-Oriented Programming with the KEE System. *SIGPLAN Notices* vol. 22(12), p. 11.

[19] Schmucker, K. 1986. *Object-Oriented Programming for the Macintosh*. Hasbrouk Heights, NJ: Hayden, p. 11.

[20] Taylor, D. 1992. *Object-Oriented Information Systems*. New York, New York John Wiley and Sons.

[21] Pinson, L. and Wiener, R. 1990. *Applications of Object-Oriented Programming*. Reading, Massachusetts: Addison-Wesley Publishing Company.

[22] Simonian, R. and Crone, M. November/December 1988. InnovAda: True Object-Oriented Programming in Ada. *Journal of Object-Oriented Programming* vol. 1(4), p. 19.

[23] Pascoe, G. August 1986. Elements of Object-Oriented Programming. *Byte* vol. 11(8), p. 144.

[24] Russo, V. and Kaplan, S. 1988. A C++ Interpreter for Scheme. *Proceedings of USENIX C++ Conference*. Berkeley, CA: USENIX Association, p. 106.

The Third Section: Applications

Minsky, M. April 1970. Form and Content in Computer Science. *Journal of the Association for Computing Machinery* vol. 17(2), p. 197.

Chapter 9: Frameworks: Foundation Class Library

[1]   *C++ Booch Components Class Catalog*. 1992. Santa Clara, CA: Rational.

[2]   Knuth, D. 1973. *The Art of Computer Programming*, Vol. 1-3. Reading, MA: Addison-Wesley.

[3]   Aho, A., Hopcroft, J. and Ullman, J. 1974. *The Design and Analysis of Computer Programs*. Reading, MA: Addison-Wesley.

[4]   Kernighan, B. and Plauger, P. 1981. *Software Tools in Pascal*. Reading, MA: Addison-Wesley.

[5]   Sedgewick, R. 1983. *Algorithms*. Reading, MA: Addison-Wesley.

[6]   Stubbs, D. and Webre, N. 1985. *Data Structures with Abstract Data Types and Pascal*. Monterey, CA: Brooks/Cole.

[7]   Tenenbaum, A. and Augenstein, M. 1981. *Data Structures Using Pascal*. Englewood Cliffs, NJ: Prentice-Hall.

[8]   Wirth, N. 1986. *Algorithms and Data Structures*, Second Edition. Englewood Cliffs, NJ: Prentice-Hall.

[9]   Wirfs-Brock, R. October 1991. Object-Oriented Frameworks. *American Programmer* vol. 4(10), p. 27.

[10] Stroustrup, Bjarne. 1991. *The C++ Programming Language, Second Edition*. Reading, Massachusetts: Addison-Wesley, p. 429

[11] Coggins, J. September 1990. *Design and Management of C+ Libraries*. Chapel Hill, North Carolina: University of North Carolina, p. 1.

[12] Ellis, M. and Stroustrup, B. 1990. *The Annotated C++ Reference Manual. Reading*, Massachusetts: Addison-Wesley, p. 155.

[13] Ellis and Stroustrup, p. 297.

[14] Ellis and Stroustrup, p. 90.

[15] Wirfs-Brock, 1993. Private communication.

[16] Jacobson, I., Christerson, M., Jonsson, P., and Overgaard, G. 1992. *Object-Oriented Software Engineering*. Workingham, England: Addison-Wesley Publishing Company, p. 184.

Chapter 10: Client//Server Computing: Inventory Tracking

[1] Mimno, P., April 1993. Client-Server Computing. *American Programmer*, Arlington MA: Cutter Information Corporation, p. 19.

[2] Mimno, p. 21.

[3] Berson, A. 1992. *Client/Server Architecture*. New York, NY: McGraw-Hill, p. 34.

[4] Berson, p. 37.

[5] Berson, p. 12.

[6] Berson, p. 13.

[7] Date, C. 1981. *An Introduction to Database Systems*. Vol. 1. Reading, MA: Addison-Wesley, p. 4.

[8] Date. *An Introduction*, p. 10.

[9] Hawryszkiewycz, I. 1984. *Database Analysis and Design*. Chicago, IL: Science Research Associates, p. 425.

[10] Wiorkowski, G. and Kull, D. 1988. *DB2 Design and Development Guide*. Reading, MA: Addison-Wesley, p. 29.

[11] Date. *An Introduction*, p. 63.

[12] Wiorkowski and Kull. *DB2 Design*, p. 2.

[13] Date. *An Introduction*. p. 238.

[14] Wiorkowski and Kull. *DB2 Design*. p. 15.

[15] Date, C. 1986. *Relational Database: Selected Writings*. Reading, MA: Addison-Wesley, p. 461.

[16] Rumbaugh, J. July/August 1992. Onward to OOPSLA. Journal of Object-Oriented Programming, vol. 5(4).

[17] Rumbaugh, J., Blaha, M., Premerlani, W., Eddy, F., and Lorensen, W. 1991. *Object-Oriented Modeling and Design*. Englewood Cliffs, New Jersey: Prentice-Hall, p. 386.

[18] Ibid.

[19] Date. *An Introduction*. p. 237.

[20] Berson, p. 39.

[21] Berson, p. 441.

[22] Date, C. 1987. *The Guide to the SQL Standard.* Reading, MA: Addison-Wesley, p. 32.

[23] Berson, p. 244.

[24] Berson, p. 61.

[25] Ibid.

Chapter 11: Artificial Intelligence: Cryptanalysis

[1] Erman, L., Lark, J., and Hayes-Roth, F. December 1988. ABE: An Environment for Engineering Intelligent Systems. *IEEE Transactions on Software Engineering* vol. 14(12), p. 1758.

[2] Shaw, M. 1991. *Heterogeneous Design Idioms for Software Architecture.* Pittsburgh, Pennsylvania: Carnegie Mellon University.

[3] Meyer, C. and Matyas. 1982. *Cryptography.* New York, NY: John Wiley and Sons, p. 1.

[4] Nii, P. Summer 1986. Blackboard Systems: The Blackboard Model of Problem Solving and the Evolution of Blackboard Architectures. *AI Magazine* vol. 7(2), p. 46.

[5] Englemore, R. and Morgan, T. 1988. *Blackboard Systems.* Wokingham, England: Addison-Wesley, p. 16.

[6] Ibid., p. 19.

[7] Ibid., p. 6.

[8] Ibid., p. 12.

[9] Nii. Blackboard Systems, p. 43.

[10] Englemore and Morgan. *Blackboard Systems,* p. 11.

Chapter 12: Command and Control: Traffic Management

[1] Murphy, E. December 1988. All Aboard for Solid State. *IEEE Spectrum* vol. 25(13), p. 42.

[2] *Rockwell Advanced Railroad Electronic Systems.* 1989. Cedar Rapids, IA: Rockwell International.

[3] Tanenbaum, A. 1981. *Computer Networks.* Englewood Cliffs, NJ: Prentice-Hall.

Afterword

Lefrancois, G. 1977. *Of Children: An Introduction to Child Development, Second Edition.* Belmont, CA: Wadsworth, p. 371.

Appendix

[1]   Wulf, W. January 1980. Trends in the Design and Implementation of Programming Languages. *IEEE Computer* vol. 13(1), p. 15.

[2]   Birtwistle, G., Dahl, O-J., Myhrhaug, B., and Nygard, K. 1979. *Simula begin*. Lund, Sweden: Studentlitteratur.

[3]   Schmucker, K. 1986. *Object-Oriented Programming for the Macintosh*. Hasbrouk Heights, NJ: Hayden, p. 346.

[4]   LaLonde, W. and Pugh, J. 1990. *Inside Smalltalk, Volumes 1 and 2.* Englewood Cliffs, New Jersey: Prentice Hall.

[5]   Ingalls, D. The Smalltalk-76 Programming System Design and Implementation. *Proceedings of the Fifth Annual ACM Symposium on Principles of Programming Languages*, ACM, p. 9.

[6]   Borning, A. and Ingalls, D. 1982. Multiple Inheritance in Smalltalk-80. *Proceedings of the National Conference on Artificial Intelligence*. Menlo Park, CA: AAAI.

[7]   Goldberg, A. and Robson, D. 1989. *Smalltalk-80: The Language*. Reading, MA: Addison-Wesley.

[8]   Goldberg, A. 1984. *Smalltalk-80: The Interactive Programming Environment*. Reading, MA: Addison-Wesley.

[9]   Krasner, G. 1983. *Smalltalk-80: Bits of History, Words of Advice*. Reading, MA: Addison-Wesley.

[10] LaLonde, 1990.

[11] Schmucker, K. August 1986. Object-Oriented Languages for the Macintosh. *Byte* vol. 11(8), p. 179.

[12] *Macintosh Programmer's Workshop Pascal 3.0 Reference*. 1989. Cupertino, CA: Apple Computer.

[13] Stroustrup, B. 1986. *The C++ Programming Language, Second Edition*. Reading, MA: Addison-Wesley, p. 4.

[14] Gorlen, K. 1989. An Introduction to C++, in *UNIX System V AT&T C++ Language System, Release 2.0 Selected Readings*. Murray Hill, NJ: AT&T Bell Laboratories, p. 2-1.

[15] Ellis, M. and Stroustrup, B. 1990. *The Annotated C++ Reference Manual. Reading*, Massachusetts: Addison-Wesley Publishing Company.

[16] Stroustrup, B. 1991. *The C+ Programming Language*, Second Edition. Reading, MA: Addison-Wesley.

[17] Keene, S. 1989. *Object-Oriented Programming in Common Lisp*. Reading, MA: Addison-Wesley, p. 215.

[18] Bobrow, D. 1990. Private communication.

[19] Bobrow, D., DeMichiel, L., Gabriel, R., Keene, S., Kiczales, G., and Moon, D. September 1988. Common Lisp Object System Specification X3J13 Document 88-002R. *SIGPLAN Notices* vol. 23.

[20] *Reference Manual for the Ada Programming Language*. February 1983. Washington, D.C.: Department of Defense, Ada Joint Program Office, p. 1-3.

[21] Ibid.

[22] Meyer, B. 1988. *Object-Oriented Software Construction.* New York, NY: Prentice Hall.

[23] Saunders, J. March/April 1989. A Survey of Object-Oriented Programming Languages. *Journal of Object-Oriented Programming* vol. 1(6).

[24] Ibid., p. 6.

abstract class A class that has no instances. An abstract class is written with the expectation that its concrete subclasses will add to its structure and behavior, typically by implementing its abstract operations.

abstract operation An operation that is declared but not implemented by an abstract class. In C++, an abstract operation is declared as a pure virtual member function.

abstraction The essential characteristics of an object that distinguish it from all other kinds of objects and thus provide crisply-defined conceptual boundaries relative to the perspective of the viewer; the process of focusing upon the essential characteristics of an object. Abstraction is one of the fundamental elements of the object model.

access control The mechanism for control of access to the structure or behavior of a class. Public items are accessible by all; protected items are accessible only by the subclasses, implementation, and friends of the class containing the item; private items are accessible only by the implementation and friends of the class containing the item; implementation items are accessible only by the implementation of the class containing the item.

action An operation that, for all practical purposes, takes zero time. An action may denote the invocation of a method, the triggering of another event, or the starting or stopping of an activity.

active object An object that encompasses its own thread of control.

activity An operation that takes some time to complete.

actor An object that can operate upon other objects but is never operated upon by other objects. In some contexts, the terms *active object* and *actor* are interchangeable.

agent An object that can both operate upon other objects and be operated upon by other objects. An agent is usually created to do some work on behalf of an actor or another agent.

aggregate object An object composed of one or more other objects, each of which is considered a part of the aggregate object.

algorithmic decomposition The process of breaking a system into parts, each of which represents some small step in a larger process. The application of structured design methods leads to an algorithmic decomposition, whose focus is upon the flow of control within a system.

architecture The logical and physical structure of a system, forged by all the strategic and tactical design decisions applied during development.

assertion The Boolean expression of some condition whose truth must be preserved.

association A relationship denoting a semantic connection between two classes.

attribute A part of an aggregate object.

base class The most generalized class in a class structure. Most applications have many such root classes. Some languages define a primitive base class, which serves as the ultimate superclass of all classes.

behavior How an object acts and reacts, in terms of its state changes and message passing; the outwardly visible and testable activity of an object.

blocking object A passive object whose semantics are guaranteed in the presence of multiple threads of control. Invoking an operation of a blocking object blocks the client for the duration of the operation.

cardinality The number of instances that a class may have; the number of instances that participate in a class relationship.

class A set of objects that share a common structure and a common behavior. The terms *class* and *type* are usually (but not always) interchangeable; a class is a slightly different concept than a type, in that it emphasizes the classification of structure and behavior.

class category A logical collection of classes, some of which are visible to other class categories, and others of which are hidden. The classes in a class category collaborate to provide a set of services.

class diagram Part of the notation of object-oriented design, used to show the existence of classes and their relationships in the logical design of a system. A class diagram may represent all or part of the class structure of a system.

class operation An operation, such as a constructor or destructor, directed at a class rather than an object.

class structure A graph whose vertices represent classes and whose arcs represent relationships among these classes. The class structure of a system is represented by a set of class diagrams.

class utility A collection of free subprograms or, in C++, a class that only provides static members and/or static member functions.

class variable Part of the state of a class. Collectively, the class variables of a class constitute its structure. A class variable is shared by all instances of the same class. In C++, a class variable is declared as a static member.

client An object that uses the services of another object, either by operating upon it or by referencing its state.

collaboration The process whereby several objects cooperate to provide some higher-level behavior.

concrete class A class whose implementation is complete and thus may have instances.

concurrency The property that distinguishes an active object from one that is not active.

concurrent object An active object whose semantics are guaranteed in the presence of multiple threads of control.

constraint The expression of some semantic condition that must be preserved.

constructor An operation that creates an object and/or initializes its state.

container class A class whose instances are collections of other objects. Container classes may denote homogeneous collections (all of the objects in the collection are of the same class) or heterogeneous collections (each of the objects in the collection may be of a different class, although all must generally share a common superclass). Container classes are most often defined as parameterized classes, with some parameter designating the class of the contained objects.

CRC cards Class/Responsibilities/Collaborators; a simple tool for brainstorming about the key abstractions and mechanisms in a system.

data dictionary A comprehensive repository enumerating all the classes in a system.

delegation The act of one object forwarding an operation to another object, to be performed on behalf of the first object.

destructor An operation that frees the state of an object and/or destroys the object itself.

device A piece of hardware that has no computational resources.

dynamic binding Binding denotes the association of a name (such as a variable declaration) with a class; dynamic binding is a binding in which the name/class association is not made until the object designated by the name is created at execution time.

encapsulation The process of compartmentalizing the elements of an abstraction that constitute its structure and behavior; encapsulation serves to separate the contractual interface of an abstraction and its implementation.

event Some occurrence that may cause the state of a system to change.

exception An indication that some invariant has not or cannot be satisfied. In C++, we throw an exception to abandon processing and alert some other object of the problem, which in turn may catch the exception and handle the problem.

field A repository for part of the state of an object; collectively, the fields of an object constitute its structure. The terms *field*, *instance variable*, *member object*, and *slot* are interchangeable.

forward-engineering The production of executable code from a logical or physical model.

free subprogram A procedure or function that serves as a nonprimitive operation upon an object or objects of the same or different classes. A free subprogram is any subprogram that is not a method of an object.

framework A collection of classes that provide a set of services for a particular domain; a framework thus exports a number of individual classes and mechanisms that clients can use or adapt.

friend A class or operation whose implementation may reference the private parts of another class, who alone can extend the offer of friendship.

function An input/output mapping resulting from some object's behavior.

function point In the context of a requirements analysis, a single, outwardly visible and testable activity.

generic class A class that serves as a template for other classes, in which the template may be parameterized by other classes, objects, and/or operations. A generic class must be instantiated (its parameters filled in) before objects can be created. Generic classes are typically used as container classes. The terms *generic class* and *parameterized class* are interchangeable.

generic function An operation upon an object. A generic function of a class may be redefined in subclasses; thus, for a given object, it is implemented through a set of methods declared in various classes related via their inheritance hierarchy. The terms *generic function* and *virtual function* are usually interchangeable.

guard A Boolean expression applied to an event; if true, the expression permits the event to cause the state of the system to change.

hierarchy A ranking or ordering of abstractions. The two most common hierarchies in a complex system include its class structure (including "kind of" hierarchies) and its object structure (including "part of" and collaboration hierarchies); hierarchies may also be found in the module and process architectures of a complex system.

identity The nature of an object that distinguishes it from all other objects.

idiom An expression peculiar to a certain programming language or application culture, representing a generally accepted convention for use of the language.

implementation The inside view of a class, object, or module, including the secrets of its behavior.

information hiding The process of hiding all the secrets of an object that do not contribute to its essential characteristics; typically, the structure of an object is hidden, as well as the implementation of its methods.

inheritance A relationship among classes, wherein one class shares the structure or behavior defined in one (single inheritance) or more (multiple inheritance) other classes. Inheritance defines an "is-a" hierarchy among classes in which a subclass inherits from one or more generalized superclasses; a subclass typically specializes its superclasses by augmenting or redefining existing structure and behavior.

instance Something you can do things to. An instance has state, behavior, and identity. The structure and behavior of similar instances are defined in their common class. The terms *instance* and *object* are interchangeable.

instance variable A repository for part of the state of an object. Collectively, the instance variables of an object constitute its structure. The terms *field, instance variable, member object,* and *slot* are interchangeable.

instantiation The process of filling in the template of a generic or parameterized class to produce a class from which one can create instances.

interaction diagram Part of the notation of object-oriented design, used to show the execution of a scenario in the context of an object diagram.

interface The outside view of a class, object, or module, which emphasizes its abstraction while hiding its structure and the secrets of its behavior.

invariant The Boolean expression of some condition whose truth must be preserved.

iterator An operation that permits the parts of an object to be visited.

key An attribute whose value uniquely identifies a single target object.

key abstraction A class or object that forms part of the vocabulary of the problem domain.

layer The collection of class categories or subsystems at the same level of abstraction.

level of abstraction The relative ranking of abstractions in a class structure, object structure, module architecture, or process architecture. In terms of its "part of" hierarchy, a given abstraction is at a higher level of abstraction than others if it builds upon the others; in terms of their "kind of" hierarchy, high-level abstractions are generalized, and low-level abstractions are specialized.

link Between two objects, one instance of an association.

mechanism A structure whereby objects collaborate to provide some behavior that satisfies a requirement of the problem.

member function An operation upon an object, defined as part of the declaration of a class; all member functions are operations, but not all operations are member functions. The terms *member function* and *method* are usually interchangeable. In some languages, a member function stands alone and may be redefined in a subclass; in other languages, a member function may not be redefined, but serves as part of the implementation of a generic function or virtual function, both of which may be redefined in a subclass.

member object A repository for part of the state of an object; collectively, the member objects of an object constitute its structure. The terms *field*, *instance variable*, *member object*, and *slot* are interchangeable.

message An operation that one object performs upon another. The terms *message*, *method*, and *operation* are usually interchangeable.

metaclass The class of a class; a class whose instances are themselves classes.

method An operation upon an object, defined as part of the declaration of a class; all methods are operations, but not all operations are methods. The terms *message, method*, and *operation* are usually interchangeable. In some languages, a method stands alone and may be redefined in a subclass; in other languages, a method may not be redefined, but serves as part of the implementation of a generic function or a virtual function, both of which may be redefined in a subclass.

mixin A class that embodies a single, focused behavior, used to augment the behavior of some other class via inheritance; the behavior of a mixin is usually orthogonal to the behavior of the classes with which it is combined.

modifier An operation that alters the state of an object.

modularity The property of a system that has been decomposed into a set of cohesive and loosely coupled modules.

module A unit of code that serves as a building block for the physical structure of a system; a program unit that contains declarations, expressed in the vocabulary of a particular programming language, that form the physical realization of some or all of the classes and objects in the logical design of the system. A module typically has two parts: its interface and its implementation.

module architecture A graph whose vertices represent modules and whose arcs represent relationships among these modules. The module architecture of a system is represented by a set of module diagrams.

module diagram Part of the notation of object-oriented design, used to show the allocation of classes and objects to modules in the physical design of a system. A module diagram may represent all or part of the module architecture of a system.

monomorphism A concept in type theory, according to which a name (such as a variable declaration) may only denote objects of the same class.

object Something you can do things to. An object has state, behavior, and identity; the structure and behavior of similar objects are defined in their common class. The terms *instance* and *object* are interchangeable.

object diagram Part of the notation of object-oriented design, used to show the existence of objects and their relationships in the logical design of a system. An object diagram may represent all or part of the object structure of a system, and primarily illustrates the semantics of mechanisms in the logical design. A single object diagram represents a snapshot in time of an otherwise transitory event or configuration of objects.

object model The collection of principles that form the foundation of object-oriented design; a software engineering paradigm emphasizing the principles of abstraction, encapsulation, modularity, hierarchy, typing, concurrency, and persistence.

object structure A graph whose vertices represent objects and whose arcs represent relationships among those objects. The object structure of a system is represented by a set of object diagrams.

object-based programming A method of programming in which programs are organized as cooperative collections of objects, each of which represents an instance of some type, and whose types are all members of a hierarchy of types united via other than inheritance relationships. In such programs, types are generally viewed as static, whereas objects typically have a much more dynamic nature, somewhat constrained by the existence of static binding and monomorphism.

object-oriented analysis A method of analysis in which requirements are examined from the perspective of the classes and objects found in the vocabulary of the problem domain.

object-oriented decomposition The process of breaking a system into parts, each of which represents some class or object from the problem domain. The application of object-oriented design methods leads to an object-oriented decomposition, in which we view the world as a collection of objects that cooperate with one another to achieve some desired functionality.

object-oriented design A method of design encompassing the process of object-oriented decomposition and a notation for depicting both logical and physical as well as static and dynamic models of the system under design; specifically, this notation includes class diagrams, object diagrams, module diagrams, and process diagrams.

object-oriented programming A method of implementation in which programs are organized as cooperative collections of objects, each of which represents an instance of some class, and whose classes are all members of a hierarchy of classes united via inheritance relationships. In such programs, classes are generally viewed as static, whereas objects typically have a much more dynamic nature, which is encouraged by the existence of dynamic binding and polymorphism.

operation Some work that one object performs upon another in order to elicit a reaction. All of the operations upon a specific object may be found in free subprograms and member functions or methods. The terms *message, method,* and *operation* are usually interchangeable.

parameterized class A class that serves as a template for other classes, in which the template may be parameterized by other classes, objects, and/or operations. A parameterized class must be instantiated (its parameters filled in) before instances can be created. Parameterized classes are typically used as container classes; the terms *generic class* and *parameterized class* are interchangeable.

partition The class categories or subsystems that form a part of a given level of abstraction.

passive object An object that does not encompass its own thread of control.

persistence The property of an object by which its existence transcends time (i.e., the object continues to exist after its creator ceases to exist) and/or space (i.e., the object's location moves from the address space in which it was created).

polymorphism A concept in type theory, according to which a name (such as a variable declaration) may denote objects of many different classes that are related by some common superclass; thus, any object denoted by this name is able to respond to some common set of operations in different ways.

postcondition An invariant satisfied by an operation.

precondition An invariant assumed by an operation.

private A declaration that forms part of the interface of a class, object, or module; what is declared as private is not visible to any other classes, objects, or modules.

process The activation of a single thread of control.

process architecture A graph whose vertices represent processors and devices and whose arcs represent connections among these processors and devices. The process architecture of a system is represented by a set of process diagrams.

process diagram Part of the notation of object-oriented design, used to show the allocation of processes to processors in the physical design of a system. A process diagram may represent all or part of the process architecture of a system.

processor A piece of hardware that has computational resources.

protected A declaration that forms part of the interface of a class, object, or module, but that is not visible to any other classes, objects, or modules except those that represent subclasses.

protocol The ways in which an object may act and react, constituting the entire static and dynamic outside view of the object; the protocol of an object defines the envelope of the object's allowable behavior.

public A declaration that forms part of the interface of a class, object, or module, and that is visible to all other classes, objects, and modules that have visibility to it.

reactive system An event-driven system; the behavior of a reactive system is not a simple input/output mapping.

real-time system A system whose essential processes must meet certain critical time deadlines. A hard-real-time system must be deterministic; missing a deadline may lead to catastrophic results.

responsibility Some behavior for which an object is held accountable; a responsibility denotes the obligation of an object to provide a certain behavior.

reverse-engineering The production of a logical or physical model from executable code.

role The purpose or capacity wherein one class or object participates in a relationship with another; the role of an object denotes the selection of a set of behaviors that are well-defined at a single point in time; a role is the face an object presents to the world at a given moment.

round-trip gestalt design A style of design that emphasizes the incremental and iterative development of a system, through the refinement of different yet consistent logical and physical views of the system as a whole; the process of object-oriented design is guided by the concepts of round-trip gestalt design; round-trip gestalt design is a recognition of the fact that the big picture of a design affects its details, and that the details often affect the big picture.

scenario An outline of events that elicits some system behavior.

selector An operation that accesses the state of an object but does not alter that state.

sequential object A passive object whose semantics are guaranteed only in the presence of a single thread of control.

server An object that never operates upon other objects, but is only operated upon by other objects; an object that provides certain services.

service The behavior provided by a given part of a system.

signature The complete profile of an operation's formal arguments and return type.

slot A repository for part of the state of an object; collectively, the slots of an object constitute its structure. The terms *field*, *instance variable*, *member object*, and *slot* are interchangeable.

space complexity The relative or absolute time in which some operation completes.

state The cumulative results of the behavior of an object; one of the possible conditions in which an object may exist, characterized by definite quantities that are distinct from other quantities; at any given point in time, the state of an object encompasses all of the (usually static) properties of the object plus the current (usually dynamic) values of each of these properties.

state transition diagram Part of the notation of object-oriented design, used to show the state space of a given class, the events that cause a transition from one state to another, and the actions that result from a state change.

state space An enumeration of all the possible states of an object. The state space of an object encompasses an indefinite yet finite number of possible (although not always desirable nor expected) states.

static binding Binding denotes the association of a name (such as a variable declaration) with a class; static binding is a binding in which the name/class association is made when the name is declared (at compile time) but before the creation of the object that the name designates.

strategic design decision A design decision that has sweeping architectural implications.

strongly typed A characteristic of a programming language, according to which all expressions are guaranteed to be type-consistent.

structure The concrete representation of the state of an object. An object does not share its state with any other object, although all objects of the same class do share the same representation of their state.

structured design A method of design encompassing the process of algorithmic decomposition.

subclass A class that inherits from one or more classes (which are called its immediate *superclasses*).

subsystem A collection of modules, some of which are visible to other subsystems and others of which are hidden.

superclass The class from which another class inherits (which is called its immediate *subclass*).

synchronization The concurrency semantics of an operation. An operation may be simple (only one thread of control is involved), synchronous (two processes rendezvous), balking (one process may rendezvous with another only if the second process is already waiting), timeout (one process may rendezvous with another, but will wait for the second process only for a specified amount of time), or asynchronous (the two processes operate independently).

tactical design decision A design decision that has local architectural implications.

thread of control A single process. The start of a thread of control is the root from which independent dynamic action within a system occurs; a given system may have many simultaneous threads of control, some of which may dynamically come into existence and then cease to exist. Systems executing across multiple CPUs allow for truly concurrent threads of control, whereas systems running on a single CPU can only achieve the illusion of concurrent threads of control.

time complexity The relative or absolute space consumed by an object.

transformational system An system whose behavior is an input/output mapping.

transition The passing from one state to another state.

type The definition of the domain of allowable values that an object may possess and the set of operations that may be performed upon the object. The terms *class* and *type* are usually (but not always) interchangeable; a type is a slightly different concept than a class, in that it emphasizes the importance of conformance to a common protocol.

typing The enforcement of the class of an object, which prevents objects of different types from being interchanged or, at the most, allows them to be interchanged only in very restricted ways.

use To reference the outside view of an abstraction.

virtual function An operation upon an object. A virtual function may be redefined by subclasses; thus, for a given object, it is implemented through a set of methods declared in various classes that are related via their inheritance hierarchy. The terms *generic function* and *virtual function* are usually interchangeable.

visibility The ability of one abstraction to see another and thus reference resources in its outside view. Abstractions are visible to one another only where their scopes overlap. Export control may further restrict access to visible abstractions.

This classified bibliography is divided into eleven sections, labeled from A to K. References at the ends of chapters to items appearing in the bibliography take the form [<label> <year>]. For example, Brooks [H 1975] refers to his 1975 book, *The Mythical Man-Month,* in section H (Software Engineering) of the bibliography.

A. Classification

Allen, T. and Starr, T. 1982. *Hierarchy: Perspectives for Ecological Complexity.* Chicago, Illinois: The University of Chicago Press.

Aquinas, T. *Summa Theologica.* Vol. 19 of Great Books of the Western World. Chicago, IL: Encyclopedia Britannica.

Aristotle. *Categories.* Vol. 8 of Great Books of the Western World. Chicago, IL: Encyclopedia Britannica.

Bateson, G. 1979. *Mind and Nature: A Necessary Unity.* New York, New York Bantam Books.

Brachman, R., McGuinness, D., Patel-Schneider, P., and Resnick, L. *Living with Classic. Principles of Semantic Networks.* San Mateo, California: Morgan Kaufman Publishers.

Bulman, D. January 1991. Refining Candidate Objects. *Computer Language* vol. 8(1).

Cant, S., Jeffery, D. and Henderson-Sellers, B. October 1991. *A Conceptual Model of Cognitive Complexity of Elements of the Programming Process.* New South Wales, Australia University of New South Wales.

Classification Society of North America. *Journal of Classification.* New York, NY: Springer-Verlag.

Coad, P. September 1992. Object-Oriented Patterns. *Communications of the ACM* vol. 35(9).

Coad, P. 1993. *The Object Game.* Austin, TX: Object International.

Coombs, C., Raiffa, H., and Thrall, R. 1954. Some Views on Mathematical Models and Measurement Theory. *Psychological Review* vol. 61(2).

Courtois, P. June 1985. On Time and Space Decomposition of Complex Structures. *Communications of the ACM* vol. 28(6).

Cunningham, W. and Beck, K. July/August 1989. Constructing Abstractions for Object-Oriented Abstractions. *Journal of Object-Oriented Programming* vol. 2(2).

Darwin, C. *The Origin of Species.* Vol. 49 of Great Books of the Western World. Chicago, IL: Encyclopedia Britannica.

Descartes, R. *Rules for the Direction of the Mind.* Vol. 31 of Great Books of the Western World. Chicago, IL: Encyclopedia Britannica.

Flood, R. and Carson, E. 1988. *Dealing with Complexity.* New York, NY: Plenum Press.

Gould, S. June 1992. We Are All Monkey's Uncles. *Natural History.*

Johnson, R. *Documenting Frameworks using Patterns.* Vancouver, Canada: OOPSLA'92.

Lakoff, G. 1987. Women, *Fire, and Dangerous Things: What Categories Reveal About the Mind.* Chicago, IL: The University of Chicago Press.

Lefrancois, G. 1977. *Of Children: An Introduction to Child Development.* Second edition. Belmont, CA: Wadsworth.

Lewin, R. 4 November 1988. Family Relationships Are a Biological Conundrum. *Science* vol. 242.

Maccoby, M. December 1991. The Innovative Mind at Work. *IEEE Spectrum* vol. 28(12).

Maier, H. 1969. *Three Theories of Child Development: The Contributions of Erik H. Erickson, Jean Piaget, and Robert R. Sears, and Their Applications.* New York, NY: Harper and Row.

May, R. 16 September 1988. How Many Species Are There on Earth? *Science* vol. 241.

Michalski, R. and Stepp, R. 1983. *Learning from Observation: Conceptual Clustering, in Machine Learning: An Artificial Intelligence Approach.* ed. R. Michalski, J. Carbonell, and T. Mitchell. Palo Alto, CA: Tioga.

Miller, G. March 1956. The Magical Number Seven, Plus or Minus Two: Some Limits on Our Capacity for Processing Information. *The Psychological Review* vol. 63(2).

Minsky, M. 1986. *The Society of Mind.* New York, NY: Simon and Schuster.

—— April 1970. Form and Content in Computer Science. *Journal of the ACM* vol. 17(2).

Moldovan, D. and Wu, C. December 1988. A Hierarchical Knowledge-Based System for Airplane Classification. *IEEE Transactions on Software Engineering* vol. 14(12).

Newell, A. 1990. *Unified Theories of Cognition.* Cambridge, Massachusetts: Harvard University Press.

Newell, A. and Simon, H. 1972. *Human Problem Solving*. Englewood Cliffs, New Jersey: Prentice-Hall.

Papert, S. 1980. *Mindstorms: Children, Computers, and Powerful Ideas*. New York, NY: Basic Books.

Plato. *Statesman*. Vol. 7 of Great Books of the Western World. Chicago, IL: Encyclopedia Britannica.

Prieto-Diaz, R. and Arango, G. 1991. *Domain Analysis and Software Systems Modeling*. Las Alamitos, California: Computer Society Press of the IEEE.

Shaw, M. 1989. Larger Scale Systems Require Higher-Level Abstractions. *Proceedings of the Fifth International Workshop on Software Specification and Design*. IEEE Computer Society.

—— 1990. Elements of a Design Language for Software Architecture. Pittsburgh, PA: Carnegie Mellon University.

—— 1991. *Heterogeneous Design Idioms for Software Architecture*. Pittsburgh, Pennsylvania: Carnegie Mellon University.

Siegler, R. and Richards, D. 1982. The Development of Intelligence, in *Handbook of Human Intelligence*. ed. R. Sternberg. Cambridge, London: Cambridge University Press.

Simon, H. 1962. The Architecture of Complexity. *Proceedings of the American Philosophical Society*. vol. 106.

—— 1982. *The Sciences of the Artificial*. Cambridge, MA: The MIT Press.

Sowa, J. 1984. *Conceptual Structures: Information Processing in Mind and Machine*. Reading, MA: Addison-Wesley.

—— 1991. *Principles of Semantic Networks*. San Mateo, California: Morgan Kaufman Publishers.

Stepp, R. and Michalski, R. 1986. Conceptual Clustering of Structured Objects: A Goal-Oriented Approach. *Artificial Intelligence* vol. 28(1).

Stevens, S. June 1946. On the Theory of Scales of Measurement, *Science* vol. 103(2684).

Stillings, N., Feinstein, M., Garfield, J., Rissland, E., Rosenbaum, D., Weisler, S. and Baker-Ward, L. 1987. *Cognitive Science: An Introduction*. Cambridge, MA: The MIT Press.

Waldrop, M. 1992. *Complexity: The Emerging Science at the Edge of Order and Chaos*. New York, New York: Simon and Schuster.

B. Object-Oriented Analysis

Arango, G. May 1989. Domain Analysis: From Art Form to Engineering Discipline. *SIGSOFT Engineering Notes* vol. 14(3).

Bailin, S. 1988. *Remarks on Object-Oriented Requirements Specification*. Laurel, MD: Computer Technology Associates.

Bailin, S. and Moore, J. 1987. *An Object-Oriented Specification Method for Ada*. Laurel, MD: Computer Technology Associates.

Barbier, F. May 1992. Object-Oriented Analysis of Systems through their Dynamical Aspects. *Journal of Object-Oriented Programming* vol. 5(2).

Borgida, A., Mylogoulos, J., and Wong, H. 1984. Generalization/Specialization as a Basis for Software Specification, in *On Conceptual Modeling: Perspectives from Artificial Intelligence, Databases, and Programming Languages*. ed. M. Brodie, J. Mylopoulos, and J. Schmidt. New York, NY: Springer-Verlag.

Cernosek, G., Monterio, E., and Pribyl, W. 1987. *An Entity-Relationship Approach to Software Requirements Analysis for Object-Based Development.* Houston, TX: McDonnell Douglas Astronautics.

Coad, P. Summer 1989. OOA: Object-Oriented Analysis. *American Programmer* vol. 2(7-8).

—— April 1990. *New Advances in Object-Oriented Analysis.* Austin, Texas: Object International.

Coad, P. and Yourdon, E. 1991. *Object-Oriented Analysis*, Second Edition. Englewood Cliffs, New Jersey: Yourdon Press.

Dahl, O-J. 1987. Object-Oriented Specifications, in *Research Directions in Object-Oriented Programming*. ed. B. Schriver and P. Wegner. Cambridge, MA: The MIT Press.

deChampeaux, D. April 1991. *A Comparative Study of Object-Oriented Analysis Methods*. Palo Alto, California: Hewlett-Packard Laboratories.

—— April 1991. *Object-Oriented Analysis and Top-Down Software Development*. Palo Alto, California: Hewlett Packard Laboratories.

DeMarco, T. 1979. *Structured Analysis and System Specification*. Englewood Cliffs, NJ: Prentice-Hall.

Embley, D., Kurtz, B., and Woodfield, S. 1992. *Object-Oriented Systems Analysis: A Model-Driven Approach*. Englewood Cliffs, New Jersey: Yourdon Press.

EVB Software Engineering. 1989. *Object-Oriented Requirements Analysis*. Frederick, MD.

Gane, C. and Sarson, T. 1979. *Structured Systems Analysis*. Englewood Cliffs, NJ: Prentice-Hall.

Hatley, D. and Pirbhai, I. 1988. *Strategies for Real-Time System Specification*. New York, NY: Dorset House.

Ho, D. and Parry, T. July 1991. *The Hewlett-Packard Method of Object-Oriented Analysis*. Palo Alto, California: Hewlett-Packard laboratories.

Iscoe, N. 1988. *Domain Models for Program Specification and Generation*. Austin, TX: University of Texas.

Iscoe, N., Browne, J., and Werth, J. 1989. *Modeling Domain Knowledge: An Object-Oriented Approach to Program Specification and Generation*. Austin, TX: The University of Texas.

Lang, N. January 1993. *Shlaer-Mellor Object-Oriented Analysis Rules*. Software Engineering Notes vol. 18(1).

Marca, D. and McGowan, C. 1988. *SADT™: Structured Analysis and Design Technique*. New York, NY: McGraw-Hill.

Martin, J. and Odell, J. 1992. *Object-Oriented Analysis and Design*. Englewood Cliffs, New Jersey: Prentice Hall.

McMenamin, S. and Palmer, J. 1984. *Essential Systems Analysis*. New York, NY: Yourdon Press.

Mellor, S., Hecht, A., Tryon, D., and Hywari, W. September 1988. *Object-Oriented Analysis: Theory and Practice, Course Notes*. San Diego, CA: OOPSLA'88.

Moore, J. and Bailin, S. 1988. *Position Paper on Domain Analysis*. Laurel, MD: Computer Technology Associates.

Page-Jones, M. and Weiss, S. Summer 1989. Synthesis: An Object-Oriented Analysis and Design Method. *American Programmer* vol. 2(7-8).

Rubin, K. and Goldberg, A. September 1992. *Object Behavior Analysis*. Communications of the ACM vol. 35(9).

Saeki, M., Horai, H., and Enomoto, H. May 1989. Software Development Process from Natural Language Specification. *Proceedings of the 11th International Conference on Software Engineering*. New York, NY: Computer Society Press of the IEEE.

Shemer, I. June 1987. Systems Analysis: A Systemic Analysis of a Conceptual Model. *Communications of the ACM* vol. 30(6).

Shlaer, S. and Mellor, S. 1988. *Object-Oriented Systems Analysis: Modeling the World in Data*. Englewood Cliffs, New Jersey: Yourdon Press.

—— July 1989. An Object-Oriented Approach to Domain Analysis. *Software Engineering Notes* vol. 14(5).

—— Summer 1989. Understanding Object-Oriented Analysis. *American Programmer* vol. 2(7-8).

—— 1992. *Object Lifecycles: Modeling the World in States*. Englewood Cliffs, New Jersey: Yourdon Press.

Stoecklin, S., Adams, E., and Smith, S. 1987. *Object-Oriented Analysis*. Tallahassee, FL: East Tennessee State University.

Sully, P. Summer 1989. Structured Analysis: Scaffolding for Object-Oriented Development. *American Programmer* vol. 2(7-8).

Tsai, J. and Ridge, J. November 1988. Intelligent Support for Specifications Transformation. *IEEE Software* vol. 5(6).

Veryard, R. 1984. *Pragmatic Data Analysis*. Oxford, England: Blackwell Scientific Publications.

Ward, P. March 1989. How to Integrate Object Orientation with Structured Analysis and Design. *IEEE Software* vol. 6(2).

Weinberg, G. 1988. *Rethinking Systems Analysis and Design*. New York, NY: Dorset House.

C. Object-Oriented Applications

Abdali, K., Cherry, G., and Soiffer, N. November 1986. A Smalltalk System for Algebraic Manipulation. *SIGPLAN Notices* vol. 21(11).

Abdel-Hamid, T. and Madnick, S. December 1989. Lessons Learned from Modeling the Dynamics of Software Development. *Communications of the ACM* vol. 32(12).

Almes, G. and Holman, C. September 1987. Edmas: An Object-Oriented, Locally Distributed Mail System. *IEEE Transactions on Software Engineering* vol. SE-13(9).

Anderson, D. November 1986. Experience with Flamingo: A Distributed, Object-Oriented User Interface System. *SIGPLAN Notices* vol. 21(11).

Archer, J. and Devlin, M. 1987. *Rational's Experience Using Ada for Very Large Systems.* Mountain View, CA: Rational.

Bagrodia, R., Chandy, M., and Misra, J. June 1987. A Message-Based Approach to Discrete-Event Simulation. *IEEE Transactions on Software Engineering* vol. SE-13(6).

Barry, B. October 1989. Prototyping a Real-Time Embedded System in Smalltalk. *SIGPLAN Notices* vol. 24(10).

Barry, B., Altoft, J., Thomas, D., and Wilson, M. October 1987. Using Objects to Design and Build Radar ESM Systems. *SIGPLAN Notices* vol. 22(12).

Basili, V., Caldiera, G., and Cantone, G. January 1992. A Reference Architecture for the Component Factory. *ACM Transactions on Software Engineering and Methodology* vol. 1(1).

Batory, D. and O'Malley, S. October 1992. The Design and Implementation of Hierarchical Software Systems with Reusable Components. *ACM Transactions on Software Engineering and Methodology* vol. 1(4).

Bezivin, J. October 1987. Some Experiments in Object-Oriented Simulation. *SIGPLAN Notices* vol. 22(12).

Bhaskar, K. and Peckol, J. November 1986. Virtual Instruments: Object-Oriented Program Synthesis. *SIGPLAN Notices* vol. 21(11).

Bihair, T. and Gopinath, P. December 1992. Object-Oriented Real-Time Systems: Concepts and Examples. *IEEE Computer* vol. 25(12).

Bjornerstedt, A. and Britts, S. September 1988. AVANCE: An Object Management System. *SIGPLAN Notices* vol. 23(11).

Bobrow, D. and Stefik, M. February 1986. Perspectives on Artificial Intelligence Programming. *Science* vol. 231.

Boltuck-Pasquier, J., Grossman, E., and Collaud, G. August 1988. Prototyping an Interactive Electronic Book System Using an Object-Oriented Approach. *Proceedings of ECOOP'88: European Conference on Object-Oriented Programming.* New York, NY: Springer-Verlag.

Bonar, J., Cunningham R., and Schultz, J. November 1986. An Object-Oriented Architecture of Intelligent Tutoring Systems. *SIGPLAN Notices* vol. 21(11).

Booch, G. 1987. *Software Components with Ada: Structures, Tools, and Subsystems.* Menlo Park, CA: Benjamin/Cummings.

Borning, A. October 1981. The Programming Language Aspects of ThingLab, a Constraint-Oriented Simulation Laboratory. *ACM Transactions on Programming Languages and Systems* vol. 3(4).

Bowman, W. and Flegal, B. August 1981. ToolBox: A Smalltalk Illustration System. *Byte* vol. 6(8).

Britcher, R. and Craig, J. May 1986. Using Modern Design Practices to Upgrade Aging Software Systems. *IEEE Software* vol. 3(3).

Britton, K. and Parnas, D. December 8, 1981. *A-7E Software Module Guide*, Report 4702. Washington, D.C.: Naval Research Laboratory.

Brooks, R. 1987. *A Hardware Retargetable Distributed Layered Architecture for Mobile Robot Control.* Cambridge, Massachusetts MIT Artificial Intelligence Laboratory.

Brooks, R. and Flynn, A. June 1989. *Fast, Cheap, and Out of Control A Robot Invasion of the Solar System.* Cambridge, Massachusetts: MIT Artificial Intelligence Laboratory.

Bruck, D. 1988. Modeling of Control Systems with C++ and PHIGS. *Proceedings of USENIX C++ Conference.* Berkeley, CA: USENIX Association.

Budd, T. January 1989. The Design of an Object-Oriented Command Interpreter. *Software – Practice and Experience* vol. 19(1).

C++ Booch Components Class Catalog. 1992. Santa Clara, CA: Rational.

Call, L., Cohrs, D., and Miller, B. October 1987. CLAM – an Open System for Graphical User Interfaces. *SIGPLAN Notices* vol. 22(12).

Campbell, R., Islam, N., and Madany, P. 1992. The Design of an *Object-Oriented Operating System: A Case Study of Choices.* Vancouver, Canada: OOPSLA'92.

Caplinger, M. October 1987. An Information System Based on Distributed Objects. *SIGPLAN Notices* vol. 22(12).

Cargill, T. November 1986. Pi: A Case Study in Object-Oriented Programming. *SIGPLAN Notices* vol. 21(11).

Carroll, M. September 1990. *Building Reusable C++ Components.* Murray Hills, New Jersey: AT&T Bell Laboratories.

Cmelik, R. and Genani, N. May 1988. Dimensional Analysis with C++. *IEEE Software* vol. 5(3).

Coggins, J. September 1990. *Design and Management of C+ Libraries.* Chapel Hill, North Carolina: University of North Carolina.

Cointe, P., Briot, J., and Serpette, B. 1987. The Formes System: A Musical Application of Object-Oriented Concurrent Programming, in *Object-Oriented Concurrent Programming.* ed. Yonezawa and M. Tokoro. Cambridge, MA: The MIT Press.

Collins, D. 1990. *What is an Object-Oriented User Interface?* Thornwood, New York: IBM Systems Research Education Center.

Comeau, G. March 1991. C++ In the Real World Interviews with C++ Application Developers. *The C++ Report* vol. 3(3).

Coplien, J. September 1991. Experience with CRC Cards in AT&T. *The C++ Report* vol. 3(8).

Coutaz, J. September 1985. Abstractions for User Interface Design. *IEEE Computer* vol. 18(9).

Custer, H. 1993. *Inside Windows NT.* Redmond, Washington: Microsoft Press.

Dasgupta, P. November 1986. A Probe-Based Monitoring Scheme for an Object-Oriented Operating System. *SIGPLAN Notices* vol. 21(11).

Davidson, C. and Moseley, R. 1987. *An Object-Oriented Real-Time Knowledge-Based System.* Albuquerque, NM: Applied Methods.

Davis, J. and Morgan, T. January 1993. Object-Oriented Development at Brooklyn Union Gas. *IEEE Software* vol. 10(1).

deChampeaux, D., Anderson, A., Lerman, D., Gasperina, M., Feldhousen, E., Glei, M, Fulton, F., Groh, C., Houston, D, Monroe, C., Raj, Rommel, and Shultheis, D. October 1991. *Case Study of Object-Oriented Software Development.* Palo Alto, California Hewlett-Packard Laboratories.

Dietrich, W., Nackman, L., and Gracer, F. October 1989. Saving a Legacy with Objects. *SIGPLAN Notices* vol. 24(10).

Dijkstra, E. May 1968. The Structure of the "THE" Multiprogramming System. *Communications of the ACM* vol. 11(5).

Durand, G., Benkiran, A., Durel, C., Nga, H., and Tag, M. 9 March 1988. *Distributed Mail Service in CSE System.* Paris, France: Synergie Informatique et Development.

Englemore, R. and Morgan, T. 1988. *Blackboard Systems.* Wokingham, England: Addison-Wesley.

Epstein, D. and LaLonde, W. September 1988. A Smalltalk Window System Based on Constraints. *SIGPLAN Notices* vol. 23(11).

Ewing, J. November 1986. An Object-Oriented Operating System Interface. *SIGPLAN Notices* vol. 21(11).

Fenton, J. and Beck, K. October 1989. Playground: An Object-Oriented Simulation System with Agent Rules for Children of All Ages. *SIGPLAN Notices* vol. 24(10).

Fischer, G. 1987. *An Object-Oriented Construction and Tool Kit for Human-Computer Communication.* Boulder, CO: University of Colorado Department of Computer Science and Institute of Cognitive Science.

Foley, J. and van Dam, A. 1982. *Fundamentals of Interactive Computer Graphics.* Reading, MA: Addison-Wesley.

Frankowski, E. 20 March 1986. *Advantages of the Object Paradigm for Prototyping.* Golden Valley, MN: Honeywell.

Freburger, K. October 1987. RAPID: Prototyping Control Panel Interfaces. *SIGPLAN Notices* vol. 22(12).

Freitas, M., Moreira, A., and Guerreiro, P. July/August 1990. Object-Oriented Requirements Analysis in an Ada Project. *Ada Letters* vol. X(6).

Funk, D. 1986. Applying Ada to Beech Starship Avionics. *Proceedings of the First International Conference on Ada Programming Language Applications for the NASA Space Station.* Houston, TX: NASA Lyndon B. Johnson Space Center.

Garrett, N. and Smith, K. November 1986. Building a Timeline Editor from Prefab Parts: The Architecture of an Object-Oriented Application. *SIGPLAN Notices* vol. 21(11).

Goldberg, A. 1978. *Smalltalk in the Classroom.* Palo Alto, CA: Xerox Palo Alto Research Center.

Goldberg, A. and Rubin, K. October 1990. Taming Object-Oriented Technology. *Computer Language* vol. 7(10).

Goldstein, N. and Alger, J. 1992. *Developing Object-Oriented Software for the Macintosh.* Reading, Massachusetts: Addison-Wesley Publishing Company.

Gorlen, K. December 1987. An Object-Oriented Class Library for C++ Programs. *Software – Practice and Experience* vol. 17(12).

Gray, L. 1987. *Transferring Object-Oriented Design Techniques into Use: AWIS Experience.* Fairfax, VA: TRW Federal Systems Group.

Grimshaw, A. and Liu, J. October 1987. Mentat: An Object-Oriented Macro Data Flow System. *SIGPLAN Notices* vol. 22(12).

Grossman, M. and Ege, R. October 1987. Logical Composition of Object-Oriented Interfaces. *SIGPLAN Notices* vol. 22(12).

Gutfreund, S. October 1987. ManiplIcons in ThinkerToy. *SIGPLAN Notices* vol. 22(12).

Gwinn, J. February 1992. Object-Oriented Programs in Realtime. *SIGPLAN Notices* vol. 27(2).

Harrison, W., Shilling, J., and Sweeney, P. October 1989. Good News, Bad News: Experience Building a Software Development Environment Using the Object-Oriented Paradigm. *SIGPLAN Notices* vol. 24(10).

Hekmatpour, A., Orailoglu, A., and Chau, P. April 1991. Hierarchical Modeling of the VLSI Design Process. *IEEE Expert* vol. 6(2).

Hollowell, G. November 1991. Leading the U.S. Semiconductor Manufacturing Industry Toward an Object-Oriented Technology Standard. *Hotline on Object-Oriented Technology* vol. 3(1).

Ingalls, D., Wallace, S., Chow, Y., Ludolph, F., and Doyle, K. September 1988. Fabrik: A Visual Programming Environment. *SIGPLAN Notices* vol. 23(11).

Jacky, J. and Kalet, I. November 1986. An Object-Oriented Approach to a Large Scientific Application. *SIGPLAN Notices* vol. 21(11).

Jacobson, I. January 1993. Iş Object Technology Software's Industrial Platform? *IEEE Software* vol. 10(1).

Jerrell, M. October 1989. Function Minimization and Automatic Differentiation using C++. *SIGPLAN Notices* vol. 24(10).

Johnson, R. and Foote, B. June/July 1988. Designing Reusable Classes. *Journal of Object-Oriented Programming* vol. 1(2).

Jones, M. and Rashid, R. November 1986. Mach and Matchmaker: Kernel and Language Support for Object-Oriented Distributed Systems. *SIGPLAN Notices* vol. 21(11).

Jurgen, R. May 1991. Smart Cars and Highways Go Global. *IEEE Spectrum* vol. 28(5).

Kamath, Y. and Smith, J. November/December 1992. Experiences in C++ and O-O Design. *Journal of Object-Oriented Programming* vol. 5(7).

Kay, A. and Goldberg, A. March 1977. Personal Dynamic Media. *IEEE Computer.*

Kerr, R. and Percival, D. October 1987. Use of Object-Oriented Programming in a Time Series Analysis System. *SIGPLAN Notices* vol. 22(12).

Kiyooka, G. December 1992. Object-Oriented DLLs. *Byte* vol. 17(14).

Kozaczynski, W. and Kuntzmann-Combelles, A. January 1993. What it Takes to Make O-O Work. *IEEE Software* vol. 10(1).

Krueger, C. June 1992. Software Reuse. *ACM Computing Surveys* vol.. 24(2).

Kuhl, F. 1988. *Object-Oriented Design for a Workstation for Air Traffic Control.* McLean, VA: The MITRE Corporation.

LaPolla, M. 1988. *On the Classification of Object-Oriented Design: The Object-Oriented Design of the AirLand Battle Management Menu System.* Austin, TX: Lockheed Software Technology Center.

Lea, D. 12 August 1988. *User's Guide to GNU C++ Library.* Cambridge, MA: Free Software Foundation.

—— 1988. The GNU C++ Library. *Proceedings of USENIX C++ Conference.* Berkeley, CA: USENIX Association.

Leathers, B. July 1990. Cognos and Eiffel A Cautionary Tale. *Hotline on Object-Oriented Technology* vol. 1(9).

Ledbetter, L. and Cox, B. June 1985. Software-ICs. *Byte* vol. 10(6).

Lee, K. and Rissman, M. February 1989. *An Object-Oriented Solution Example: A Flight Simulator Electrical System.* Pittsburgh, PA: Software Engineering Institute.

Lee, K., Rissman, M., D'Ippolito, R., Plinta, C., and Van Scoy, R. December 1987. *An OOD Paradigm for Flight Simulators*, Report CMU/SEI-87-TR-43. Pittsburgh, PA: Software Engineering Institute.

Levy, P. 1987. *Implementing Systems Software in Ada.* Mountain View, CA: Rational.

Lewis, J., Henry, S., Kafura, D., and Shulman, R. July/August 1992. On the Relationship Between the Object-Oriented Paradigm and Software Reuse: An Empirical Investigation. *Journal of Object-Oriented Programming* vol. 5(4).

Linton, M., Vlissides, J., and Calder, P. February 1989. Composing User Interfaces with InterViews. *IEEE Computer.* vol. 22(2).

Liu, L. and Horowitz, E. February 1989. Object Database Support for a Software Project Management Environment. *SIGPLAN Notices* vol. 24(2).

Locke, D. and Goodenough, J. 1988. *A Practical Application of the Ceiling Protocol in a Real-Time System*, Report CMU/SEI-88-SR-3. Pittsburgh, PA: Software Engineering Institute.

Love, T. 1993. *Object Lessons.* New York, New York: SIGS Publications.

Lu, Cary. December 1992. Objects For End Users. *Byte* vol. 17(14).

Madany, P., Leyens, D., Russo, V., and Campbell, R. 1988. A C++ Class Hierarchy for Building UNIX-like File Systems. *Proceedings of USENIX C++ Conference.* Berkeley, CA: USENIX Association.

Madduri, H., Raeuchle, T., and Silverman, J. 1987. *Object-Oriented Programming for Fault-Tolerant Distributed Systems.* Golden Valley, MN: Honeywell Computer Science Center.

Maloney, J., Borning, A., and Freeman-Benson, B. October 1989. Constraint Technology for User Interface Construction in ThingLab II. *SIGPLAN Notices* vol. 24(10).

McDonald, J. October 1989. Object-Oriented Programming for Linear Algebra. *SIGPLAN Notices* vol. 24(10).

Mentor's Lessons in the School of Hard Knocks. January 25, 1993. *Business Week.*

Meyrowitz, N. November 1986. Intermedia: The Architecture and Construction of an Object-Oriented Hypermedia System and Applications Framework. *SIGPLAN Notices* vol. 21(11).

Miller, M., Cunningham, H., Lee, C., and Vegdahl, S. November 1986. The Application Accelerator Illustration System. *SIGPLAN Notices* vol. 21(11).

Mohan, L. and Kashyap, R. May 1988. An Object-Oriented Knowledge Representation for Spatial Information. *IEEE Transactions on Software Engineering* vol. 14(5).

Morgan, T. and Davis, J. March 1991. Large-Scale Object Systems Development. *Hotline on Object-Oriented Technology* vol. 2(5).

Mraz, R. December 1986. *Performance Evaluation of Parallel Branch and Bound Search with the Intel iPSE Hypercube Computer.* Wright-Patterson Air Force Base, Ohio: Air Force Institute of Technology.

Muller, H., Rose, J., Kempf, J., and Stansbury, T. October 1989. The Use of Multimethods and Method Combination in a CLOS-Based Window Interface. *SIGPLAN Notices* vol. 24(10).

Murphy, E. December 1988. All Aboard for Solid State. *IEEE Spectrum* vol. 25(13).

Nerson, J. September 1992. Applying Object-Oriented Analysis and Design. *Communications of the ACM* vol. 35(9).

NeXT Embraces a New Way of Programming. 25 November 1988. *Science* vol. 242.

Orden, E. 1987. Application Talk. *HOOPLA: Hooray for Object-Oriented Programming Languages* vol. 1(1). Everette, WA: Object-Oriented Programming for Smalltalk Application Developers Association.

Orfali, R. and Harkey, D. 1992. *Client/Server Programming with OS/2*. New York, New York: Van Nostrand Reinhold.

Oshima, M. and Shirai, Y. July 1983. Object Recognition Using Three-Dimensional Information. *IEEE Transactions on Pattern Analysis and Machine Intelligence* vol. 5(4).

Page, T., Berson, S., Cheng, W., and Muntz, R. October 1989. An Object-Oriented Modeling Environment. *SIGPLAN Notices* vol. 24(10).

Pashtan, A. 1982. Object-Oriented Operating Systems: An Emerging Design Methodology. *Proceedings of the ACM '82 Conference.* New York, NY: Association of Computing Machinery.

Piersol, K. November 1986. Object-Oriented Spreadsheets: The Analytic Spreadsheet Package. *SIGPLAN Notices* vol. 21(11).

Pinson, L. and Wiener, R. 1990. *Applications of Object-Oriented Programming*. Reading, Massachusetts: Addison-Wesley Publishing Company.

Pittman, M. January 1993. Lessons Learned in Managing Object-Oriented Development. *IEEE Software* vol. 10(1).

Plinta, C., Lee, K., and Rissman, M. 29 March 1989. A Model Solution for C3I: Message Translation and Validation. Pittsburgh, PA: Software Engineering Institute.

Pope, S. April/May 1988. Building Smalltalk-80-based Computer Music Tools. *Journal of Object-Oriented Programming* vol. 1(1).

Raghavan, R. 1990. *Taming Windows 3.0 and DOS Using C++*. Lake Oswego, Oregon: Wyatt Software.

Rockwell International. 1989. *Rockwell Advanced Railroad Electronic Systems.* Cedar Rapids, IA.

Rombach, D. March 1990. Design Measurement: Some Lessons Learned. *IEEE Software* vol. 7(2).

Rubin, K., Jones, P., Mitchell, C., and Goldstein, T. September 1988. A Smalltalk Implementation of an Intelligent Operator's Associate. *SIGPLAN Notices* vol. 23(11).

Rubin, R., Walker, J., and Golin, E. October 1990. Early Experience with the Visual Programmer's WorkBench. *IEEE Transactions on Software Engineering* vol. 16(10).

Ruspini, E. and Fraley, R. 1983. ID: An Intelligent Information Dictionary System, in *Entity-Relationship Approach to Software Engineering.* ed. C. Davis et al. Amsterdam, The Netherlands: Elsevier Science.

Russo, V., Johnston, G., and Campbell, R. September 1988. Process Management and Exception Handling in Multiprocessor Operating Systems Using Object-Oriented Design Techniques. *SIGPLAN Notices* vol. 23(11).

Sampson, J. and Womble, B. 1988. *SEND: Simulation Environment for Network Design*. Dallas, TX: Southern Methodist University.

Santori, M. August 1990. An Instrument that Isn't Really. *IEEE Spectrum* vol. 27(8).

Scaletti, C. and Johnson, R. September 1988. An Interactive Environment for Object-Oriented Music Composition and Sound Synthesis. *SIGPLAN Notices* vol. 23(11).

Schindler, J. and Joy, S. February 1992. *An Introduction to Object Technology at Liberty Mutual.* Liberty Mutual Information Systems Research and Development.

Schoen, E., Smith, R., and Buchanan, B. December 1988. Design of Knowledge-Based Systems with a Knowledge-Based Assistant. *IEEE Transactions on Software Engineering* vol. 14(12).

Schulert, A. and Erf, K. 1988. Open Dialogue: Using an Extensible Retained Object Workspace to Support a UIMS. *Proceedings of USENIX C++ Conference.* Berkeley, CA: USENIX Association.

Scott, R., Reddy, P., Edwards, R., and Campbell, D. 1988. GPIO: Extensible Objects for Electronic Design. *Proceedings of USENIX C++ Conference.* Berkeley, CA: USENIX Association.

Smith, R., Barth, P., and Young, R. 1987. A Substrate for Object-Oriented Interface Design. *Research Directions in Object-Oriented Programming.* Cambridge, MA: The MIT Press.

Smith, R., Dinitz, R., and Barth, P. November 1986. Impulse-86: A Substrate for Object-Oriented Interface Design. *SIGPLAN Notices* vol. 21(11).

Sneed, H. and Gawron, W. 1983. The Use of the Entity/Relationship Model as a Schema for Organizing the Data Processing Activities at the Bavarian Motor Works, in *Entity-Relationship Approach to Software Engineering.* ed. C. Davis et al. Amsterdam, The Netherlands: Elsevier Science.

Snodgrass, R. 1987. An Object-Oriented Command Language, in *Object-Oriented Computing: Implementations* vol. 2. ed. G. Peterson. New York, NY: Computer Society Press of the IEEE.

Software Made Simple. September 30, 1991. *Business Week.*

Sridhar, S. September 1988. Configuring Stand-Alone Smalltalk-80 Applications. *SIGPLAN Notices* vol. 23(11).

Stadel, M. January 1991. Object-Oriented Programming Techniques to Replace Software Components on the Fly in a Running Program. *SIGPLAN Notices* vol. 26(1).

Stevens, A. 1992. *C++ Database Development.* New York, New York: MIS Press.

Stokes, R. 1988. Prototyping Database Applications with a Hybrid of C++ and 4GL. *Proceedings of USENIX C++ Conference.* Berkeley, CA: USENIX Association.

Szcur, M. and Miller, P. September 1988. Transportable Applications Environment(TAE) PLUS: Experiences in "Objectively Modernizing a User Interface Environment. *SIGPLAN Notices* vol. 23(11).

Szekely, P. and Myers, B. September 1988. A User Interface Toolkit Based on Graphical Objects and Constraints. *SIGPLAN Notices* vol. 23(11).

Tanner, J. 1 April 1986. *Fault Tree Analysis in an Object-Oriented Environment.* Mountain View, CA: IntelliCorp.

Taylor, D. 1992. *Object-Oriented Information Systems.* New York, New York John Wiley and Sons.

Temte, M. November/December 1984. Object-Oriented Design and Ballistics Software. *Ada Letters* vol. 4(3).

Tripathi, A. and Aksit, M. November/December 1988. Communication, Scheduling, and Resource Management in SINA. *Journal of Object-Oriented Programming* vol. 1(4).

Tripathi, A., Ghonami, A., and Schmitz, T. 1987. Object Management in the NEXUS Distributed Operating System. *Proceedings of the Thirty-second IEEE Computer Society International Conference.* New York, NY: Computer Society Press of the IEEE.

Ursprung, P. and Zehnder, C. 1983. HIQUEL: An Interactive Query Language to Define and Use Hierarchies, in *Entity-relationship Approach to Software Engineering.* ed. C. Davis et al. Amsterdam, The Netherlands: Elsevier Science.

van der Meulen, P. October 1987. INSIST: Interactive Simulation in Smalltalk. *SIGPLAN Notices* vol. 22(12).

Vernon, V. September/October 1989. The Forest for the Trees. *Programmer's Journal* vol. 7(5).

Vilot, M. Fall 1990. Using Object-Oriented Design and C++. *The C++ Journal* vol. 1(1).

Vines, D. and King, T. 1987. *Experiences in Building a Prototype Object-Oriented Framework in Ada.* Minneapolis, MN: Honeywell.

Vlissides, J. and Linton, M. 1988. Applying Object-Oriented Design to Structured Graphics. *Proceedings of USENIX C++ Conference.* Berkeley, CA: USENIX Association.

Volz, R. Mudge, T., and Gal, D. 1987. Using Ada as a Programming Language for Robot-Based Manufacturing Cells, in *Object-Oriented Computing: Concepts* vol. 1. ed. G. Peterson. New York, NY: Computer Society Press of the IEEE.

Walther, S. and Peskin, R. October 1989. Strategies for Scientific Prototyping in Smalltalk. *SIGPLAN Notices* vol. 24(10).

Wasserman, A. and Pircher, P. January 1991. Object-Oriented Structured Design and C++. *Computer Language* vol. 8(1).

Weinand, A., Gamma, E., and Marty, R. September 1988. ET++ – An Object-Oriented Application Framework in C++. *SIGPLAN Notices* vol. 23(11).

Welch, B. July/August 1991. Securities Objects - The Complexity. *Object Magazine* vol. 1(2).

White, S. October 1986. Panel Problem: Software Controller for an Oil Hot Water Heating System. *Proceedings of COMPSAC.* New York, NY: Computer Society Press of the IEEE.

Wirfs-Brock, R. September 1988. An Integrated Color Smalltalk-80 System. *SIGPLAN Notices* vol. 23(11).

—— October 1991. Object-Oriented Frameworks. *American Programmer* vol. 4(10).

WOSA Extensions for Financial Services. December 1992. Banking Systems Vendor Council.

Wu, P. January 1992. An Object-Oriented Specification for a Compiler. *SIGPLAN Notices* vol. 27(1).

Yoshida, N. and Hino, K. September 1988. An Object-Oriented Framework of Pattern Recognition. *SIGPLAN Notices* vol. 23(11).

Yoshida, T. and Tokoro, M. 31 March 1986. *Distributed Queueing Network Simulation: An Application of a Concurrent Object-Oriented Language.* Yokohama, Japan: Keio University.

Young, R. October 1987. An Object-Oriented Framework for Interactive Data Graphics. *SIGPLAN Notices* vol. 22(12).

D. Object-Oriented Architectures

Athas, W. and Seitz, C. August 1988. Multicomputers: Message-Passing Concurrent Computers. *IEEE Computer* vol. 21(8).

Dahlby, S., Henry, G., Reynolds, D., and Taylor, P. 1982. The IBM System/38: A High Level Machine, in *Computer Structures: Principles and Examples.* ed. G. Bell and A. Newell. New York, NY: McGraw-Hill.

Dally, W. and Kajiya, J. March 1985. An Object-Oriented Architecture. *SIGARCH Newsletter* vol. 13(3).

Fabry, R. 1987. Capability-Based Addressing, in *Object-Oriented Computing: Implementations* vol. 2. ed. G. Peterson. New York, NY: Computer Society Press of the IEEE.

Flynn, M. October 1980. Directions and Issues in Architecture and Language. *IEEE Computer* vol. 13(10).

Harland, D. and Beloff, B. December 1986. Microcoding an Object-Oriented Instruction Set. *Computer Architecture News* vol. 14(5).

Hillis, D. 1985. *The Connection Machine.* Cambridge, Massachusetts: The MIT Press.

Iliffe, J. 1982. *Advanced Computer Design.* London, England: Prentice/Hall International.

Intel. 1981. *iAPX 432 Object Primer.* Santa Clara, CA.

Ishikawa, Y. and Tokoro, M. March 1984. The Design of an Object-Oriented Architecture. *SIGARCH Newsletter* vol. 12(3).

Kavi, K. and Chen, D. 1987. Architectural Support for Object-Oriented Languages. *Proceedings of the Thirty-second IEEE Computer Society International Conference.* New York, NY: Computer Society Press of the IEEE.

Lahtinen, P. September/October 1982. A Machine Architecture for Ada. *Ada Letters* vol. 2(2).

Lampson, B. and Pier, K. January 1981. A Processor for a High-Performance Personal Computer, in *The Dorado: A High Performance Personal Computer,* Report CSL-81-1. Palo Alto, CA: Xerox Palo Alto Research Center.

Langdon, G. 1982. *Computer Design.* San Jose, CA: Computeach Press.

Levy, H. 1984. *Capability-Based Computer Systems.* Bedford, MA: Digital Press.

Lewis, D., Galloway, D., Francis, R., and Thomson, B. November 1986. Swamp: A Fast Processor for Smalltalk-80. *SIGPLAN Notices* vol. 21(11).

Mashburn, H. 1982. The C.mmp/Hydra Project: An Architectural Overview, in *Computer Structures: Principles and Examples.* ed. G. Bell and A. Newell. New York, NY: McGraw-Hill.

Myers, G. 1982. *Advances in Computer Architecture,* Second Edition. New York, NY: John Wiley and Sons.

Rattner, J. 1982. Hardware/Software Cooperation in the iAPX-432. *Proceedings of the Symposium on Architectural Support for Programming Languages and Operating Systems.* New York, NY: Association of Computing Machinery.

Rose, J. September 1988. Fast Dispatch Mechanisms for Stock Hardware. *SIGPLAN Notices* vol. 23(11).

Samples, D., Ungar, D., and Hilfinger, P. November 1986. SOAR: Smalltalk Without Bytecodes. *SIGPLAN Notices* vol. 21(11).

Soltis, R. and Hoffman, R. 1987. Design Considerations for the IBM System/38, in *Object-Oriented Computing: Implementations* vol. 2. ed. G. Peterson. New York, NY: Computer Society Press of the IEEE.

Thacker, C., McCreight, E., Lampson, B., Sproull, R., and Boggs, D. August 1979. *Alto: A Personal Computer,* Report CSL-79-11. Palo Alto, CA: Xerox Palo Alto Research Center.

Ungar, D. 1987. *The Design and Evaluation of a High-Performance Smalltalk System.* Cambridge, MA: The MIT Press.

Ungar, D. and Patterson, D. January 1987. What Price Smalltalk? *IEEE Computer* vol. 20(1).

Ungar, D., Blau, R., Foley, P., Samples, D., and Patterson, D. March 1984. Architecture of SOAR: Smalltalk on a RISC. *SIGARCH Newsletter* vol. 12(3).

Wah, B. and Li, G. April 1986. Survey on Special Purpose Computer Architectures for AI. *SIGART Newsletter,* no. 96.

Wulf, W. January 1980. Trends in the Design and Implementation of Programming Languages. *IEEE Computer* vol. 13(1).

Wulf, W., Levin, R., and Harbison, S. 1981. *HYDRA/C.mmp: An Experimental Computer System.* New York, NY: McGraw-Hill.

E. Object-Oriented Databases

Alford, M. 1983. Derivation of Element-Relation-Attribute Database Requirements by Decomposition of System Functions, in *Entity-Relationship Approach to Software Engineering.* ed. C. Davis et al. Amsterdam, The Netherlands: Elsevier Science.

Andleigh, P. and Gretzinger, M. 1992. *Distributed Object-Oriented Data-Systems Design.* Englewood Cliffs, New Jersey: Prentice-Hall.

Atkinson, M., Bailey, P., Chisholm, K., Cockshott, P., and Morrison, R. 1983. An Approach to Persistent Programming. *The Computer Journal* vol. 26(4).

Atkinson, M. and Buneman, P. June 1987. Types and Persistence in Database Programming Languages. *ACM Computing Surveys* vol. 19(2).

Atkinson, M. and Morrison, R. October 1985. Procedures as Persistent Data Objects. *ACM Transactions on Programming Languages and Systems* vol. 7(4).

Atwood, T. February 1991. Object-Oriented Databases. *IEEE Spectrum* vol. 28(2).

Bachman, C. 1983. The Structuring Capabilities of the Molecular Data Model, in *Entity-Relationship Approach to Software Engineering.* ed. C. Davis et al. Amsterdam, The Netherlands: Elsevier Science.

Batini, C. and Lenzerini, M. 1983. A Methodology for Data Schema Integration in the Entity-Relationship Model, in *Entity-Relationship Approach to Software Engineering* ed. C. Davis et al. Amsterdam, The Netherlands: Elsevier Science.

Beech, D. 1987. Groundwork for an Object Database Model, in *Research Directions in Object-Oriented Programming*. ed. B. Schriver and P. Wegner. Cambridge, MA: The MIT Press.

—— September 1988. Intensional Concepts in an Object Database Model. *SIGPLAN Notices* vol. 23(11).

Bertino, E. 1983. Distributed Database Design Using the Entity-Relationship Model, in *Entity-Relationship Approach to Software Engineering*. ed. C. Davis et al. Amsterdam, The Netherlands: Elsevier Science.

Blackwell, P., Jajodia, S., and Ng, P. 1983. A View of Database Management Systems as Abstract Data Types, in *Entity-Relationship Approach to Software Engineering* ed. C. Davis et al. Amsterdam, The Netherlands: Elsevier Science.

Bloom, T. October 1987. Issues in the Design of Object-Oriented Database Programming Languages. *SIGPLAN Notices* vol. 22(12).

Bobrow, D., Fogelsong, D., and Miller, M. 1987. Definition Groups: Making Sources into First-class Objects, in *Research Directions in Object-Oriented Programming*. ed. B. Schriver and P. Wegner. Cambridge, MA: The MIT Press.

Brathwaite, K. 1983. An Implementation of A Data Dictionary to Support Databases Designed Using the Entity-Relationship(E-R) Approach, in *Entity-Relationship Approach to Software Engineering*. ed. C. Davis et al. Amsterdam, The Netherlands: Elsevier Science.

Breazeal, J., Blattner, M., and Burton, H. 28 March 1986. *Data Standardization Through the Use of Data Abstraction*. Livermore, CA: Lawrence Livermore National Laboratory.

Brodie, M. 1984. On the Development of Data Models, in *On Conceptual Modeling: Perspectives from Artificial Intelligence, Databases, and Programming Languages*. ed. M. Brodie, J. Mylopoulos, and J. Schmidt. New York, NY: Springer-Verlag.

Brodie, M. and Ridjanovic, D. 1984. On the Design and Specification of Database Transactions. *On Conceptual Modeling: Perspectives from Artificial Intelligence, Databases, and Programming Languages*. ed. M. Brodie, J. Mylopoulos, and J. Schmidt. New York, NY: Springer-Verlag.

Butterworth, P., Otis, A. and Stein, J. October 1991. The GemStone Object Database Management System. *Communications of the ACM* vol. 34(10).

Carlson, C. and Arora, A. 1983. UPM: A Formal Tool for Expressing Database Update Semantics, in *Entity-Relationship Approach to Software Engineering* ed. C. Davis et al. Amsterdam, The Netherlands: Elsevier Science.

Casanova, M. 1983. Designing Entity-Relationship Schemes for Conventional Information Systems, in *Entity-Relationship Approach to Software Engineering* ed. C. Davis et al. Amsterdam, The Netherlands: Elsevier Science.

Cattell, R. 1991. *Object Data Management*. Reading, Massachusetts: Addison-Wesley Publishing Company.

—— R. May 1983. *Design and Implementation of a Relationship-Entity-Datum Data Model*, Report CSL-83-4. Palo Alto, CA: Xerox Palo Alto Research Center.

Chen, P. 1983. ER – A Historical Perspective and Future Directions, in *Entity-Relationship Approach to Software Engineering*. ed. C. Davis et al. Amsterdam, The Netherlands: Elsevier Science.

—— March 1976. The Entity-Relationship Model – Toward a Unified View of Data. *ACM Transactions on Database Systems* vol. 1(1).

Claybrook, B., Claybrook, A., and Williams, J. January 1985. Defining Database Views as Data Abstractions. *IEEE Transactions on Software Engineering* vol. SE-11(1).

D'Cunha, A. and Radhakrishnan, T. 1983. Applications of E-R Concepts to Data Administration, *Entity-Relationship Approach to Software Engineering.* ed. C. Davis et al. Amsterdam, The Netherlands: Elsevier Science.

Date, C. 1981, 1983. *An Introduction to Database Systems.* Reading, MA: Addison-Wesley.

—— 1986. *Relational Database: Selected Writings.* Reading, MA: Addison-Wesley.

—— 1987. *The Guide to the SQL Standard.* Reading, MA: Addison-Wesley.

Duhl, J. and Damon, C. September 1988. A Performance Comparison of Object and Relational Databases Using the Sun Benchmark. *SIGPLAN Notices* vol. 23(11).

Harland, D. and Beloff, B. April 1987. OBJEKT – A Persistent Object Store with an Integrated Garbage Collector. *SIGPLAN Notices* vol. 22(4).

Hawryszkiewycz, I. 1984. *Database Analysis and Design.* Chicago, IL: Science Research Associates.

Higa, K., Morrison, M., Morrison, J. and Sheng, O. June 1992. An Object-Oriented Methodology for Knowledge Base/Database Coupling. *Communications of the ACM* vol. 35(6).

Hull, R. and King, R. September 1987. Semantic Database Modeling: Survey, Applications, and Research Issues. *ACM Computing Surveys* vol. 19(3).

Jajodia, S., Ng, P., and Springsteel, F. 1983. On Universal and Representative Instances for Inconsistent Databases, in *Entity-Relationship Approach to Software Engineering.* ed. C. Davis et al. Amsterdam, The Netherlands: Elsevier Science.

Ketabchi, M. and Berzins, V. January 1988. Mathematical Model of Composite Objects and Its Application for Organizing Engineering Databases. *IEEE Transactions on Software Engineering* vol. 14(1).

Ketabchi, M. and Wiens, R. 1987. Implementation of Persistent Multi-User Object-Oriented Systems. *Proceedings of the Thirty-second IEEE Computer Society International Conference.* New York, NY: Computer Society Press of the IEEE.

Khoshafian, S., and Abnous, R. 1990. *Object-Orientation: Concepts, Languages, Databases, User Interfaces.* New York, New York: John Wiley and Sons.

Kim, W. and Lochovsky, K. 1989. *Object-Oriented Concepts, Databases, and Applications.* Reading, MA: Addison-Wesley.

Kim, W., Ballou, N., Chou, H., Garze, J., Woelk, D. and Banerjee, J. September 1988. Integrating an Object-Oriented Programming System with a Database System. *SIGPLAN Notices* vol. 23(11).

Kim, W., Banerjee, J., Chou, H., Garza, J., and Woelk, D. October 1987. Composite Object Support in an Object-Oriented Database System. *SIGPLAN Notices* vol. 22(12).

Kung, C. Object Subclass Hierarchy in SQL: A Simple Approach. Communications of the ACM vol. 33(7).

Laenens, E. and Vermeir, D. August 1988. An Overview of OOPS+, An Object-Oriented Database Programming Language. *Proceedings of ECOOP'88: European Conference on Object-Oriented Programming.* New York, NY: Springer-Verlag.

Lamb, C., Landis, G., Orenstein, J., and Weinreb, D. October 1991. The ObjectStore Database System. *Communications of the ACM* vol. 34(10).

Larson, J. and Dwyer, P. 1983. Defining External Schemas for an Entity-Relationship Database, in *Entity-Relationship Approach to Software Engineering.* ed. C. Davis et al. Amsterdam, The Netherlands: Elsevier Science.

Maier, D. and Stein, J. 1987. Development and Implementation of an Object-Oriented DBMS, in *Research Directions in Object-Oriented Programming.* ed. B. Schriver and P. Wegner. Cambridge, MA: The MIT Press.

Margrave, G., Lusk, E., and Overbeek, R. 1983. Tools for the Creation of IMS Database Designs from Entity-Relationship Diagrams, in *Entity-Relationship Approach to Software Engineering.* ed. C. Davis et al. Amsterdam, The Netherlands: Elsevier Science.

Mark, L. and Poussopoulos, N. 1983. Integration of Data, Schema, and Meta-schema in the Context of Self-documenting Data Models, in *Entity-Relationship Approach to Software Engineering.* ed. C. Davis et al. Amsterdam, The Netherlands: Elsevier Science.

Markowitz, V. and Makowsky, J. August 1990. Identifying Extended Entity-Relationship Object Structures in Relational Schemas. *IEEE Transactions on Software Engineering* vol. 16(8).

Marti, R. 1983. Integrating Database and Program Descriptions using an ER Data Dictionary, in *Entity-Relationship Approach to Software Engineering.* ed. C. Davis et al. Amsterdam, The Netherlands: Elsevier Science.

Merrow, T. and Laursen, J. October 1987. A Pragmatic System for Shared Persistent Objects. *SIGPLAN Notices* vol. 22(12).

Mitchell, J. and Wegbreit, B. 1977. Schemes: A High-Level Data Structuring Concept, in *Current Trends in Programming Methodology: Data Structuring* vol. 4. ed. R. Yeh. Englewood Cliffs, NJ: Prentice-Hall.

Morrison, R., Atkinson, M., Brown, A., and Dearle, A. April 1988. Bindings in Persistent Programming Languages. *SIGPLAN Notices* vol. 23(4).

Moss, E., Herlihy, M., and Zdonik, S. September 1988. *Object-Oriented Databases, Course Notes.* San Diego, CA: OOPSLA'88.

Moss, J. August 1992. Working with Persistent Objects To Swizzle or Not to Swizzle. *IEEE Transactions on Software Engineering* vol. 18(8).

Nastos, M. January 1988. Databases, Etc. *HOOPLA: Hooray for Object-Oriented Programming Languages* vol. 1(2). Everette, WA: Object Oriented Programming for Smalltalk Application Developers Association.

Navathe, S. and Cheng, A. 1983. A Methodology for Database Schema Mapping from Extended Entity Relationship Models into the Hierarchical Model, in *Entity-Relationship Approach to Software Engineering.* ed. C. Davis et al. Amsterdam, The Netherlands: Elsevier Science.

Ontologic. 1987. *Vbase Technical Overview.* Billerica, MA.

Oracle. 1989. *Oracle for Macintosh: References, Version 1.1.* Belmont, CA.

Penny, J. and Stein, J. October 1987. Class Modification in the GemStone Object-Oriented DBMS. *SIGPLAN Notices* vol. 22(12).

Peterson, R. 1987. Object-Oriented Database Design, in *Object-Oriented Computing: Implementations* vol. 2. ed. G. Peterson. New York, NY: Computer Society Press of the IEEE.

Premerlani, W., Blaha, M., Rumbaugh, J., and Varwig, T. November 1990. An Object-Oriented Relational Database. *Communications of the ACM* vol. 33(11).

Sakai, H. 1983. Entity-Relationship Approach to Logical Database Design, in *Entity-Relationship Approach to Software Engineering*. ed. C. Davis et al. Amsterdam, The Netherlands: Elsevier Science.

Skarra, A. and Zdonik, S. 1987. Type Evolution in an Object-Oriented Database, in *Research Directions in Object-Oriented Programming*. ed. B. Schriver and P. Wegner. Cambridge, MA: The MIT Press.

Skarra, A. and Zdonik, S. November 1986. The Management of Changing Types in an Object-Oriented Database. *SIGPLAN Notices* vol. 21(11).

Smith, D. and Smith, J. 1980. Conceptual Database Design, in *Tutorial on Software Design Techniques*, Third Edition. ed. P. Freeman and A. Wasserman. New York, NY: Computer Society Press of the IEEE.

Smith, J. and Smith, D. Database Abstractions: Aggregation and Generalization. *ACM Transactions on Database Systems* vol. 2(2).

Smith, K. and Zdonik, S. October 1987. Intermedia: A Case Study of the Differences Between Relational and Object-Oriented Database Systems. *SIGPLAN Notices* vol. 22(12).

Stein, J. March 1988 Object-Oriented Programming and Database Design. *Dr. Dobb's Journal* vol. 13(3).

—— March 1988. Object-Oriented Programming and Database Design. *Dr. Dobb's Journal of Software Tools for the Professional Programmer*, no. 137.

Teorey, T., Yang, D., and Fry, J. June 1986. A Logical Design Methodology for Relational Databases Using the Extended Entity-Relationship Model. *ACM Computing Surveys* vol. 18(2).

Thuraisingham, M. October 1989. Mandatory Security in Object-Oriented Database Systems. *SIGPLAN Notices* vol. 24(10).

Veloso, P. and Furtado, A. 1983. View Constructs for the Specification and Design of External Schemas, in *Entity-Relationship Approach to Software Engineering*. ed. C. Davis et al. Amsterdam, The Netherlands: Elsevier Science.

Wiebe, D. November 1986. A Distributed Repository for Immutable Persistent Objects. *SIGPLAN Notices* vol. 21(11).

Wiederhold, G. December 1986. Views, Objects, and Databases. *IEEE Computer* vol. 19(12).

Wile, D. and Allard, D. May 1982. Worlds: an Organizing Structure for Object-bases. *SIGPLAN Notices* vol. 19(5).

Zdonik, S. and Maier, D. 1990. *Readings in Object-Oriented Database Systems*. San Mateo, CA: Morgan Kaufmann.

Zhang, Z. and Mendelzon, A. 1983. A Graphical Query Language for Entity-Relationship Databases, in *Entity-Relationship Approach to Software Engineering*. ed. C. Davis et al. Amsterdam, The Netherlands: Elsevier Science.

F. Object-Oriented Design

Abbott, R. August 1987. Knowledge Abstraction. *Communications of the ACM* vol. 30(8).

—— November 1983. Program Design by Informal English Descriptions. *Communications of the ACM* vol. 26(11).

Ackroyd, M. and Daum, D. 1991. Graphical Notation for Object-Oriented Design and Programming. *Journal of Object-Oriented Programming* vol. 3(5).

Alabios, B. September 1988. Transformation of Data Flow Analysis Models to Object-Oriented Design. *SIGPLAN Notices* vol. 23(11).

Arnold, P, Bodoff, S., Coleman, D., Gilchrist, H., and Hayes, F. June 1991. *An Evaluation of Five Object-Oriented Development Methods*. Bristol, England: Hewlett-Packard Laboratories.

Bear, S., Allen, P., Coleman, D., and Hayes, F. Graphical Specification of Object-Oriented Systems. *Object-Oriented Programming Systems, Languages, and Applications*. Ottawa, Canada: OOPSLA'90.

Beck, K. and Cunningham, W. October 1989. A Laboratory for Teaching Object-Oriented Thinking. *SIGPLAN Notices* vol. 24(10).

Berard, E. 1986. *An Object-Oriented Design Handbook*. Rockville, MD: EVB Software Engineering.

Berzins, V., Gray, M., and Naumann, D. May 1986. Abstraction-Based Software Development. *Communications of the ACM* vol. 29(5).

Blaha, M. April 1988. Relational Database Design Using an Object-Oriented Methodology. *Communications of the ACM* vol. 31(4).

Booch, G. September 1981. Describing Software Design in Ada. *SIGPLAN Notices* vol. 16(9).

—— March/April 1982. Object-Oriented Design. *Ada Letters* vol. 1(3).

—— February 1986. Object-Oriented Development. *IEEE Transactions on Software Engineering* vol. 12(2).

—— 1987. *On the Concepts of Object-Oriented Design*. Denver, CO: Rational.

—— Summer 1989. What Is and What Isn't Object-Oriented Design. *American Programmer* vol. 2(7-8).

Booch, G. and Vilot, M. Object-Oriented Design. *The C++ Report*.

Booch, G., Jacobson, I., and Kerth, N. September 1988. *Specification and Design Methodologies in Support of Object-Oriented Programming, Course Notes*. San Diego, CA: OOPSLA'88.

Bowles, A. November/December 1991. Evolution Vs Revolution: Should Structured Methods Be Objectified? *Object Magazine* vol. 1(4).

Boyd, S. July/August 1987. Object-Oriented Design and PAMELA™. *Ada Letters* vol. 7(4).

Bril, R., deBunje, T., and Ouvry, A. October 1991. *Development of SCORE: Towards the Industrialization of an Object-Oriented Method using the Formal Design Language COLD-1 as Notation*. Eindhoven, The Netherlands: Philips Research Laboratories.

Brookman, D. November/December 1991. SA/SD versus OOD. *Ada Letters* vol. XI(9).

Bruno, G. and Balsamo, A. November 1986. Petri Net-Based Object-Oriented Modeling of Distributed Systems. *SIGPLAN Notices* vol. 21(11).

Buhr, R. 1984. *System Design with Ada.* Englewood Cliffs, NJ: Prentice-Hall.

—— 22 August 1988. *Machine Charts for Visual Prototyping in System Design.* SCE Report 88-2. Ottawa, Canada: Carleton University.

—— 14 September 1988. *Visual Prototyping in System Design.* SCE Report 88-14. Ottawa, Canada: Carleton University.

—— 1989. *System Design with Machine Charts: A CAD Approach with Ada Examples.* Englewood Cliffs, NJ: Prentice-Hall.

Buhr, R., Karam, G., Hayes, C., and Woodside, M. March 1989. Software CAD: A Revolutionay Approach. *IEEE Transactions on Software Engineering* vol. 15(3).

Bulman, D. August 1989. An Object-Based Development Model. *Computer Language* vol. 6(8).

Cherry, G. 1987. *PAMELA 2: An Ada-Based Object-Oriented Design Method.* Reston, VA: Thought**Tools.

—— 1990. *Software Construction by Object-Oriented Pictures.* Canandaigua, NY: Thought**Tools.

Clark, R. June 1987. Designing Concurrent Objects. *Ada Letters vol.* 7(6).

Coad, P. September 1991. OOD Criteria. *Journal of Object-Oriented Programming* vol.(5).

Coleman, D., Hayes, F., and Bear, S. December 1990. *Introducing Objectcharts or How to Use Statecharts in Object-Oriented Design.* Bristol, England: Hewlett-Packard Laboratories.

Comer, E. July 1989. *Ada Box Structure Methodology Handbook.* Melbourne, FL: Software Productivity Solutions.

Constantine, L. Summer 1989. Object-Oriented and Structured Methods: Towards Integration. *American Programmer vol.* 2(7-8).

CRI, CISI Ingenierie, and Matra. 20 June 1987. *HOOD: Hierarchical Object-Oriented Design.* Paris, France.

Cribbs, J., Moon, S., and Roe, C. 1992. *An Evaluation of Object-Oriented Analysis and Design Methodologies.* Raleigh, North Carolina: Alcatel Network Systems.

Cunningham, W. and Beck, K. November 1986. A Diagram for Object-Oriented Programs. *SIGPLAN Notices* vol. 21(11).

Davis, N., Irving, M., and Lee, J. *The Evolution of Object-Oriented Design from Concept to Method.* 1988. Surrey, United Kingdom: Logica Space and Defence Systems Limited.

Dean, H. May 1991. Object-Oriented Design Using Message Flow Decomposition, *Journal of Object-Oriented Programming* vol. 4(2).

deChampeaux, D., Balzer, B., Bulman, D., Culver-Lozo, K., Jacobson, I., Mellor, S. *The Object-Oriented Software Development Process.* Vancouver, Canada: OOPSLA'92.

deChampeaux, D., Lea, D., and Faure, P. *The Process of Object-Oriented Design.* Vancouver, Canada: OOPSLA'92.

Edwards, J. and Henderson-Sellers, B. November 1991. *A Graphical Notation for Object-Oriented Analysis and Design.* New South Wales, Australia University of New South Wales.

Felsinger, R. 1987a. *Integrating Object-Oriented Design, Structured Analysis/Structured Design, and Ada for Real-time Systems.* Mt. Pleasant, SC.

—— 1987b. *Object-Oriented Design, Course Notes*. Torrance, CA: Data Processing Management Association.

Fichman, R. and Kemerer, C. October 1992. Object-Oriented and Conventional Analysis and Design Methodologies. *IEEE Computer* vol. 25(10).

Firesmith, D. May 6, 1986. *Object-Oriented Development*. Fort Wayne, Indiana: Magnavox Electronic Systems Co.

—— 1993. *Object-Oriented Requirements Analysis and Logical Design*. New York, New York: John Wiley and Sons.

Fowler, M. 1992. *A Comparison of Object-Oriented Analysis and Design Methods*. Vancouver, Canada: OOPSLA '92.

Gamma, E., Helm, R., Johnson, R., Vlissides, J. 1993. A Catalog of Object-Oriented Design Patterns. Cupertino, California: Taligent

Gane, C. Summer 1989. Object-Oriented Data/Process Modeling. *American Programmer* vol. 2(7-8).

Giddings, R. May 1984. Accommodating Uncertainty in Software Design. *Communications of the ACM* vol. 27(5).

Gomaa, H. September 1984. A Software Design Method for Real-Time Systems. *Communications of the ACM* vol. 27(9).

Gossain, S. and Anderson, B. *An Iterative Design Model for Reusable Objects*. Ottawa, Canada: OOPSLA'90.

Gouda, M., Han, Y., Jensen, E., Johnson, W., and Kain, R. November 1977. Towards a Methodology of Distributed Computer System Design. *Sixth Texas Conference on Computing Systems*. New York, NY: Association of Computing Machinery.

Graham, I. 1991. *Object-Oriented Methods*. Workingham, England: Addison-Wesley Publishing Company.

Grosch, J. December 1983. Type Derivation Graphs – A Way to Visualize the Type Building Possibilities of Programming Languages. *SIGPLAN Notices* vol. 18(12).

Harel, D. 1987. Statecharts: A Visual Formalism for Complex Systems. *Science of Computer Programming* vol. 8.

—— May 1988. On Visual Formalisms. *Communications of the ACM* vol. 31(5).

Henderson-Sellers, B. 1992. *A Book of Object-Oriented Knowledge*. Englewood Cliffs, New Jersey: Prentice Hall.

Inwood, C. 1992. Analysis versus Design: Is there a Difference? *The C++ Journal vol. 2(1)*.

Jackson, M. Summer 1989. Object-Oriented Software. *American Programmer* vol. 2(7-8).

Jacobson, I. August 1985. *Concepts for Modeling Large Real-Time Systems*. Academic dissertation. Stockholm, Sweden: Royal Institute of Technology, Department of Computer Science.

—— October 1987. Object-Oriented Development in an Industrial Environment. *SIGPLAN Notices* vol. 22(12).

Jacobson, I., Christerson, M., Jonsson, P., and Overgaard, G. 1992. *Object-Oriented Software Engineering*. Workingham, England: Addison-Wesley Publishing Company.

Jamsa, K. January 1984. Object-Oriented Design vs. Structured Design – A Student's Perspective. *Software Engineering Notes vol.* 9(1).

Johnson, R. and Russo, V. May 1991. *Reusing Object-Oriented Designs*. Urbana, Illinois: University of Illinois.

Jones, A. 1979. The Object Model: A Conceptual Tool for Structuring Software, in *Operating Systems*. ed. R. Bayer et. al. New York, NY: Springer-Verlag.

Kadie, C. 1986. *Refinement Through Classes: A Development Methodology for Object-Oriented Languages*. Urbana, IL: University of Illinois.

Kaplan, S. and Johnson, R. 21 July 1986. *Designing and Implementing for Reuse*. Urbana, IL: University of Illinois, Department of Computer Science.

Kay, A. August 1969. *The Reactive Engine*. Salt Lake City, Utah: The University of Utah, Department of Computer Science.

Kelly, J. 1986 A Comparison of Four Design Methods for Real-Time Systems. *Proceedings of the Ninth International Conference on Software Engineering*. New York, NY: Computer Society Press of the IEEE.

Kent, W. 1983. Fact-Based Data Analysis and Design, in *Entity-Relationship Approach to Software Engineering*. ed. C. Davis et al. Amsterdam, The Netherlands: Elsevier Science.

Kim, J. and Lerch, J. 1992. *Towards a Model of Cognitive Process in Logical Design: Comparing Object-Oriented and Traditional Functional Decomposition Software Methodologies*. Pittsburgh, Pennsylvania: Carnegie Mellon University.

Ladden, R. July 1988. A Survey of Issues to Be Considered in the Development of an Object-Oriented Development Methodology for Ada. *Software Engineering Notes* vol. 13(3).

Lieberherr, K. and Riel, A. October 1989. Contributions to Teaching Object-Oriented Design and Programming. *SIGPLAN Notices* vol. 24(10).

Liskov, B. 1980. A Design Methodology for Reliable Software Systems, in *Tutorial on Software Design Techniques*. Third Edition. ed. P. Freeman and A. Wasserman. New York, NY: Computer Society Press of the IEEE.

Lorenz, M. 1993. *Object-Oriented Software Development*. Englewood Cliffs, New Jersey: Prentice-Hall.

Mannino, P. April 1987. A Presentation and Comparison of Four Information System Development Methodologies. *Software Engineering Notes* vol. 12(2).

Martin, B. 1993. *Designing Object-Oriented C++ Applications Using the Booch Method*. Englewood Cliffs, New Jersey: Prentice-Hall.

Masiero, P. and Germano, F. July 1988. JSD As an Object-Oriented Design Method. *Software Engineering Notes* vol. 13(3).

Meyer, B. 1988. *Object-Oriented Software Construction*. New York, NY: Prentice Hall.

Meyer, B. March 1987. Reusability: The Case for Object-Oriented Design. *IEEE Software* vol. 4(2).

—— 1989. From Structured Programming to Object-Oriented Design: The Road to Eiffel. *Structured Programming* vol. 10(1).

Mills, H. June 1988. Stepwise Refinement and Verification in Box-Structured Systems. *IEEE Computer* vol. 21(6).

Mills, H., Linger, R., and Hevner, A. 1986. *Principles of Information System Design and Analysis.* Orlando, FL: Academic Press.

Minkowitz, C. and Henderson, P. March 1987. *Object-Oriented Programming of Discrete Event Simulation Using Petri Nets.* Stirling, Scotland: University of Stirling.

Monarchi, D. and Puhr, G. September 1992. A Research Typology for Object-Oriented Analysis and Design. *Communications of the ACM* vol. 35(9).

Mostow, J. Spring 1985. Toward Better Models of the Design Process. *AI Magazine* vol. 6(1).

Moulin, B. 1983. The Use of EPAS/IPSO Approach for Integrating Entity Relationship Concepts and Software Engineering Techniques, in *Entity-Relationship Approach to Software Engineering.* ed. C. Davis et al. Amsterdam, The Netherlands: Elsevier Science.

Mullin, M. 1989. *Object-Oriented Program Design with Examples in C++.* Reading, MA: Addison-Wesley.

Nielsen, K. and Shumate, K. August 1987. Designing Large Real-Time Systems with Ada. *Communications of the ACM* vol. 30(8).

Nielsen, K. March 1988. *An Object-Oriented Design Methodology for Real-Time Systems in Ada.* San Diego, CA: Hughes Aircraft Company.

Nies, S. 1986. The Ada Object-Oriented Approach. *Proceedings of the First International Conference on Ada Programming Language Applications for the NASA Space Station.* Houston, TX: NASA Lyndon B. Johnson Space Center.

Ossher, H. 1987. A Mechanism for Specifying the Structure of Large, Layered, Systems, in *Research Directions in Object-Oriented Programming.* ed. B. Schriver and P. Wegner. Cambridge, MA: The MIT Press.

Page-Jones, M., Constantine, L., and Weiss, S. October 1990. Modeling Object-Oriented Systems: The Uniform Object Notation. *Computer Language* vol. 7(10).

Parnas, D. 1979. On the Criteria to be Used in Decomposing Systems into Modules. *Classics in Software Engineering,* ed. E. Yourdon. New York, NY: Yourdon Press.

Parnas, D., Clements, P., and Weiss, D. March 1985. The Modular Structure of Complex Systems. *IEEE Transactions on Software Engineering* vol. SE-11(3).

Pasik, A. and Schor, M. January 1984. Object-Centered Representation and Reasoning. *SIGART Newsletter,* no. 87.

Rajlich, V. and Silva, J. 1987. *Two Object-Oriented Decomposition Methods.* Detroit, Michigan: Wayne State University.

Ramamoorthy, C. and Sheu, P. Fall 1988. Object-Oriented Systems. *IEEE Expert* vol. 3(3).

Reenskaug, T. August 1981. User-Oriented Descriptions of Smalltalk Systems. *Byte* vol. 6(8).

Reiss, S. 1987. An Object-Oriented Framework for Conceptual Programming, in *Research Directions in Object-Oriented Programming.* ed. B. Schriver and P. Wegner. Cambridge, MA: The MIT Press.

Richter, C. August 1986. An Assessment of Structured Analysis and Structured Design. *Software Engineering Notes* vol. 11(4).

Rine, D. October 1987. A Common Error in the Object Structure of Object-Oriented Methods. *Software Engineering Notes* vol. 12(4).

Rosenberg, D. and Jennett, P. July 1992. Object-Oriented Analysis and Design Methods. *Frameworks* vol. 6(4).

Ross, R. 1987. *Entity Modeling: Techniques and Application.* Boston, MA: Database Research Group.

Rosson, M. and Gold, E. October 1989. Problem-Solution Mapping in Object-Oriented Design. *SIGPLAN Notices* vol. 24(10).

Rumbaugh, J., Blaha, M., Premerlani, W., Eddy, F., and Lorensen, W. 1991. *Object-Oriented Modeling and Design.* Englewood Cliffs, New Jersey: Prentice-Hall.

Sahraoui, A. 1987. *Towards a Design Approach Methodology Combining OOP and Petri Nets for Software Production.* Toulouse, France: Laboratoire d'Automatique et d'analyses des systemes du C.N.R.S.

Sakai, H. 1983. A Method for Entity-Relationship Behavior Modeling, in *Entity-Relationship Approach to Software Engineering.* ed. C. Davis et al. Amsterdam, The Netherlands: Elsevier Science.

Seidewitz, E. May 1985. *Object Diagrams.* Greenbelt, MD: NASA Goddard Space Flight Center.

Seidewitz, E. and Stark, M. 1986. Towards a General Object-Oriented Software Development Methodology. *Proceedings of the First International Conference on Ada Programming Language Applications for the NASA Space Station.* Houston, TX: NASA Lyndon B. Johnson Space Center.

—— August 1986. *General Object-Oriented Software Development,* Report SEL-86-002. Greenbelt, MD: NASA Goddard Space Flight Center.

—— July/August 1987. Towards a General Object-Oriented Design Methodology. *Ada Letters* vol. 7(4).

—— 1988. *An Introduction to General Object-Oriented Software Development.* Rockville, MD: Millennium Systems.

Shilling, J. and Sweeney, P. October 1989. Three Steps to Views: Extending the Object-Oriented Paradigm. *SIGPLAN Notices* vol. 24(10).

Shlaer, S., Mellor, S., and Hywari, W. 1990. *OODLE: A Language-Independent Notation for Object-Oriented Design.* Berkeley, California: Project Technology, California.

Shumate, K. 1987. *Layered Virtual Machine/Object-Oriented Design.* San Diego, CA: Hughes Aircraft Company.

Smith, M. and Tockey, S. 1988. *An Integrated Approach to Software Requirements Definition Using Objects.* Seattle, WA: Boeing Commercial Airplane Support Division.

Solsi, S. and Jones, E. March/April 1991. Simple Yet Complete Heuristics for Transforming Data Flow Diagrams into Booch Style Diagrams. *Ada Letters* vol. XI(2).

Song, X. May 1992. *Comparing Software Design Methodologies Through Process Modeling.* Irvine, California: University of California.

Stark, M. April 1986. *Abstraction Analysis: From Structured Analysis to Object-Oriented Design.* Greenbelt, MD: NASA Goddard Space Flight Center.

Strom, R. October 1986. A Comparison of the Object-Oriented and Process Paradigms. *SIGPLAN Notices* vol. 21(10).

Teledyne Brown Engineering. October 1987. *Software Methodology Catalog*, Report MC87-COMM/ADP-0036. Tinton Falls, NJ.

The Fusion Object-Oriented Analysis and Design Method. May 1992. Bristol, England: Hewlett Packard Laboratories.

Thomas, D. May/June 1989. In Search of an Object-Oriented Development Process. *Journal of Object-Oriented Programming* vol. 2(1).

Wahl, S. 13 December 1988. Introduction to Object-Oriented Software. *C++ Tutorial Program of the USENIX Conference*. Denver, CO: USENIX Association.

Walters, N. July/August 1991. An Ada Object-Based Analysis and Design Approach. *Ada Letters* vol. XI(5).

Wasserman, T., Pircher, P., and Muller, R. December 1988. *An Object-Oriented Structured Design Method for Code Generation*. San Francisco, CA: Interactive Development Environments.

—— Summer 1989. Concepts of Object-Oriented Structured Design. *American Programmer* vol. 2(7-8).

—— March 1990. The Object-Oriented Structured Design Notation for Software Design Representation. *IEEE Computer* vol. 23(3).

Webster, D. December 1988. Mapping the Design Information Representation Terrain. *IEEE Spectrum* vol. 21(12).

Williams, L. 1986. *The Object Model in Software Engineering*. Boulder, CO: Software Engineering Research.

Wirfs-Brock, R. and Wilkerson, B. October 1989. Object-Oriented Design: A Responsibility-Driven Approach. *SIGPLAN Notices* vol. 24(10).

Wirfs-Brock, R., Wilkerson, B., and Wiener, L. 1990. *Designing Object-Oriented Software*. Englewood Cliffs, New Jersey: Prentice Hall.

Xong, X. and Osterweil, L. June 1992. *A Detailed Objective Comparison and Integration of Two Object-Oriented Design Methodologies*. Irvine, California: University of California.

Yau, S. and Tsai, J. June 1986. A Survey of Software Design Techniques. *IEEE Transactions on Software Engineering* vol. SE-12(6).

Zachman, J. 1987. A Framework for Information Systems Architecture. *IBM Systems Journal* vol. 26(3).

Zimmerman, R. 1983. Phases, Methods, and Tools – A Triad of System Development, in *Entity-Relationship Approach to Software Engineering*. ed. C. Davis et al. Amsterdam, The Netherlands: Elsevier Science.

G. Object-Oriented Programming

Ada and C++: Business Case Analysis. July 1991. Washington, D.C.: Deputy Assistant Secretary of the Air Force.

Adams, S. July 1986. MetaMethods: The MVC Paradigm. *HOOPLA: Hooray for Object-Oriented Programming Languages* vol. 1(4). Everette, WA: Object-Oriented Programming for Smalltalk Applications Developers Association.

Agha, G. October 1986. An Overview of Actor Languages. *SIGPLAN Notices* vol. 21(10).

—— 1988. *Actors: A Model of Concurrent Computation in Distributed Systems.* Cambridge, MA: The MIT Press.

Agha, G. and Hewitt, C. 1987. Actors: A Conceptual Foundation for Concurrent Object-Oriented Programming, in *Research Directions in Object-Oriented Programming.* ed. B. Schriver and P. Wegner. Cambridge, MA: The MIT Press.

Aksit, M. and Tripathi, A. September 1988. Data Abstraction Mechanisms in Sina/st. *SIGPLAN Notices* vol. 23(11).

Albano, A. June 1983. Type Hierarchies and Semantic Data Models. *SIGPLAN Notices* vol. 18(6).

Almes, G., Black, A., Lazowska, E., and Noe, J. January 1985. The Eden System: A Technical Review. *IEEE Transactions on Software Engineering* vol. SE-11(1).

Alpert, S., Woyak, S., Shrobe, H. and Arowood, L. December 1990. Object-Oriented Programming in AI. *IEEE Expert* vol. 5(6).

Althoff, J. August 1981. Building Data Structures in the Smalltalk-80 System. *Byte* vol. 6(8).

Ambler, A. 1980. Gypsy: A Language for Specification and Implementation of Verifiable Programs, in *Programming Language Design.* ed. A. Wasserman. New York, NY: Computer Society Press.

America, P. 1987. POOL-T: A Parallel Object-Oriented Language, in *Object-Oriented Concurrent Programming.* ed. Yonezawa and M. Tokoro. Cambridge, MA: The MIT Press.

Apple Computer. 1989. *MacApp: The Expandable Macintosh Application,* version 2.0B9. Cupertino, CA.

—— *Macintosh Programmer's Workshop Pascal 3.0 Reference.* Cupertino, CA.

AT&T Bell Laboratories. 1989. *UNIX System V ATT C++ Language System, Release 2.0 Library Manual.* Murray Hill, NJ.

—— *UNIX System V ATT C++ Language System, Release 2.0 Product Reference Manual.* Murray Hill, NJ.

—— *UNIX System V ATT C++ Language System, Release 2.0 Release Notes.* Murray Hill, NJ.

—— *UNIX System V ATT C++ Language System, Release 2.0 Selected Readings.* Murray Hill, NJ.

Attardi, G. 1987. Concurrent Strategy Execution in Omega, in *Object-Oriented Concurrent Programming.* ed. Yonezawa and M. Tokoro. Cambridge, MA: The MIT Press.

Bach, I. November/December 1982. On the Type Concept of Ada. *Ada Letters* vol. II(3).

Badrinath, B. and Ramamritham, K. May 1988. Synchronizing Transactions on Objects. *IEEE Transactions on Computers* vol. 37(5).

Ballard, M., Maier, D., and Wirfs-Brock, A. November 1986. QUICKTALK: A Smalltalk-80 Dialect for Defining Primitive Methods. *SIGPLAN Notices* vol. 21(11).

Beaudet, P. and Jenkins, M. June 1988. Simulating the Object-Oriented Paradigm in Nial. *SIGPLAN Notices* vol. 23(6).

Bennett, J. October 1987. The Design and Implementation of Distributed Smalltalk. *SIGPLAN Notices* vol. 22(12).

Bergin, J. and Greenfield, S. March 1988. What Does Modula-2 Need to Fully Support Object-Oriented Programming? *SIGPLAN Notices* vol. 23(3).

Bhaskar, K. October 1983. How Object-Oriented Is Your System? *SIGPLAN Notices* vol. 18(10).

Birman, K., Joseph, T., Raeuchle, T., and Abbadi, A. June 1985. Implementing Fault-tolerant Distributed Objects. *IEEE Transactions on Software Engineering* vol. SE-11(6).

Birtwistle, G., Dahl, O-J., Myhrhaug, B., and Nygard, K. 1979. *Simula begin.* Lund, Sweden: Studentlitteratur.

Black, A., Hutchinson, N., Jul, E., and Levy, H. November 1986. Object Structure in the Emerald System. *SIGPLAN Notices* vol. 21(11).

Black, A., Hutchinson, N., Jul, E., Levy, H., and Carter, L. July 1986. *Distribution and Abstract Types in Emerald.* Report 86-02-04. Seattle, WA: University of Washington.

Blaschek, G. 1989. Implementation of Objects in Modula-2. *Structured Programming* vol. 10(3).

Blaschek, G., Pomberger, G., and Stritzinger, A. 1989. A Comparison of Object-Oriented Programming Languages. *Structured Programming* vol. 10(4).

Block, F. and Chan, N. October 1989. An Extended Frame Language. *SIGPLAN Notices* vol. 24(10).

Bobrow, D. November 1984. *If Prolog Is the Answer, What Is the Question?* Palo Alto, California. Xerox Palo Alto Research Center.

—— 1985. An Overview of KRL, a Knowledge Representation Language, in *Readings in Knowledge Representation.* ed. R. Brachman and H. Levesque. Los Altos, CA: Morgan Kaufmann.

Bobrow, D., DeMichiel, L., Gabriel, R., Keene, S., Kiczales, G., and Moon, D. September 1988. Common Lisp Object System Specification X3J13 Document 88-002R. *SIGPLAN Notices* vol. 23.

Bobrow, D., Kahn, K., Kiczales, G., Masinter, L., Stefik, M., and Zdybel, F. August 1985. *COMMONLOOPS: Merging Common Lisp and Object-Oriented Programming,* Report ISL-85-8. Palo Alto, CA: Xerox Palo Alto Research Center, Intelligent Systems Laboratory.

Borgida, A. January 1985. Features of Languages for the Development of Information Systems at the Conceptual Level. *IEEE Software* vol. 2(1).

—— October 1986. Exceptions in Object-Oriented Languages. *SIGPLAN Notices* vol. 21(10).

Borning, A. and Ingalls, D. 1982a. A Type Declaration and Inference System for Smalltalk. Palo Alto, CA: Xerox Palo Alto Research Center.

—— 1982b. Multiple Inheritance in Smalltalk-80. *Proceedings of the National Conference on Artificial Intelligence.* Menlo Park, CA: AAAI.

Bos, J. September 1987. PCOL – A Protocol-Constrained Object Language. *SIGPLAN Notices* vol. 22(9).

Briot, J. and Cointe, P. October 1989. Programming with Explicit Metaclasses in Smalltalk. *SIGPLAN Notices* vol. 24(10).

Buzzard, G. and Mudge, T. 1987. Object-Based Computing and the Ada Programming Language, in *Object-Oriented Computing: Concepts* vol. 1. ed. G. Peterson. New York, NY: Computer Society Press of the IEEE.

Canning, P., Cook, W., Hill, W., and Olthoff, W. October 1989. Interfaces for Strongly-Typed Object-Oriented Programming. *SIGPLAN Notices* vol. 24(10).

Caudill, P. and Wirfs-Brock, A. November 1986. A Third Generation Smalltalk-80 Implementation. *SIGPLAN Notices* vol. 21(11).

Chambers, C., Ungar, D., and Lee, E. October 1989. An Efficient Implementation of Self, a Dynamically-Typed Object-Oriented Language Based on Prototypes. *SIGPLAN Notices* vol. 24(10).

Chang, S. 1990. *Visual Languages and Visual Programming.* New York, New York: Plenum Press.

Chin, R. and Chanson, S. March 1991. Distributed Object-based Programming Systems. *ACM Computing Surveys* vol. 23(1).

Clark, K. December 1988. PARLOG and Its Application. *IEEE Transactions on Software Engineering* vol. 14(12).

Cleaveland, C. 1980. Programming Languages Considered as Abstract Data Types. *Communications of the ACM.*

Coad, P. and Nicola, J. 1993. *Object-Oriented Programming.* Englewood Cliffs, New Jersey: Yourdon Press.

Cointe, P. October 1987. Metaclasses Are First Class: the ObjVlisp Model. *SIGPLAN Notices* vol. 22(12).

Connor, R., Dearle, A., Morrison, R., and Brown, A. October 1989. An Object Addressing Mechanism for Statically Typed Languages with Multiple Inheritance. *SIGPLAN Notices* vol. 24(10).

Conroy, T. and Pelegri-Llopart, E. 1983. An Assessment of Method-lookup Caches for Smalltalk-80 Implementations, in *Smalltalk-80: Bits of History, Words of Advice.* ed. G. Krasner. Reading, MA: Addison-Wesley.

Coplien, J. 1992. *Advanced C++ Programming Styles and Idioms.* Reading, Massachusetts: Addison-Wesley Publishing Company.

Corradi, A. and Leonardi, L. December 1988. The Role of Opaque Types in Building Abstractions. *SIGPLAN Notices* vol. 23(12).

Cox, B. 1986. *Object-Oriented Programming: An Evolutionary Approach.* Reading, MA: Addison-Wesley.

Cox, B. January 1983. The Object-Oriented Pre-compiler. *SIGPLAN Notices* vol. 18(1).

—— January 1984. Message/Object Programming: An Evolutionary Change in Programming Technology. *IEEE Software* vol. 1(1).

—— February/March 1984. Object-Oriented Programming: A Power Tool for Software Craftsmen. *Unix Review.*

—— October/November 1983. Object-Oriented Programming in C. *Unix Review.*

Cox, B. and Hunt, B. August 1986. Objects, Icons, and Software-ICs. *Byte* vol. 11(8).

Cox, P. and Pietrzykowski, T. March 1989. *Prograph: A Pictorial View of Object-Oriented Programming.* Nova Scotia, Canada: Technical University of Nova Scotia.

deJong, P. October 1986. Compilation into Actors. *SIGPLAN Notices* vol. 21(10).

Deutsch, P. August 1981. Building Control Structures in the Smalltalk-80 System. *Byte* vol. 6(8).

—— 1983. Efficient Implementation of the Smalltalk-80 System. *Proceedings of the 11th Annual ACM Symposium on the Principles of Programming Languages.* New York, NY: Association of Computing Machinery.

Dewhurst, S. and Stark, K. 1989. *Programming in C++.* Englewood Cliffs, NJ: Prentice Hall.

Diederich, J. and Milton, J. May 1987. Experimental Prototyping in Smalltalk. *IEEE Software* vol. 4(3).

Dixon, R., McKee, T., Schweizer, P., and Vaughn, M. October 1989. A Fast Method Dispatcher for Compiled Languages with Multiple Inheritance. *SIGPLAN Notices* vol. 24(10).

Dony, C. August 1988. An Object-Oriented Exception Handling System for an Object-Oriented Language. *Proceedings of ECOOP'88: European Conference on Object-Oriented Programming.* New York, NY: Springer-Verlag.

Duff, C. August 1986. Designing an Efficient Language. *Byte* vol. 11(8).

Dussud, P. October 1989. TICLOS: An Implementation of CLOS for the Explorer Family. *SIGPLAN Notices* vol. 24(10).

Eccles, J. 1988. Porting from Common Lisp with Flavors to C++. *Proceedings of USENIX C++ Conference.* Berkeley, CA: USENIX Association.

Edelson, D. September 1987. How Objective Mechanisms Facilitate the Development of Large Software Systems in Three Programming Languages. *SIGPLAN Notices* vol. 22(9).

Ellis, M. and Stroustrup, B. 1990. *The Annotated C++ Reference Manual. Reading,* Massachusetts: Addison-Wesley Publishing Company.

Endres, T. May 1985. Clascal – An Object-Oriented Pascal. *Computer Language* vol. 2(5).

Entsminger, G. 1990. *The Tao of Objects.* Redwood City, California: M & T Books.

Filman, R. October 1987. Retrofitting Objects. *SIGPLAN Notices* vol. 22(12).

Finzer, W. and Gould, L. June 1984. Programming by Rehearsal. *Byte* vol. 9(6).

Foote, B. and Johnson, R. October 1989. Reflective Facilities in Smalltalk-80. *SIGPLAN Notices* vol. 24(10).

Freeman-Benson, B. October 1989. A Module Mechanism for Constraints in Smalltalk. *SIGPLAN Notices* vol. 24(10).

Fukunaga, K. and Jirose, S. November 1986. An Experience with a Prolog-Based Object-Oriented Language. *SIGPLAN Notices* vol. 21(11).

Gabriel, R., White, J., and Bobrow, D. September 1991. CLOS Integrating Object-Oriented and Functional Programming. *Communications of the ACM* vol. 34(9).

Goldberg, A. August 1981. Introducing the Smalltalk-80 System. *Byte* vol. 6(8).

Goldberg, A. September 1988. Programmer as Reader. *IEEE Software* vol. 4(5).

Goldberg, A. and Kay, A. March 1976. *Smalltalk-72 Instruction Manual.* Palo Alto, CA: Xerox Palo Alto Research Center.

—— A. 1977. *Methods for Teaching the Programming Language Smalltalk,* Report SSL 77-2. Palo Alto, CA: Xerox Palo Alto Research Center.

Goldberg, A. and Pope, S. Summer 1989. Object-Oriented Programming Is Not Enough. *American Programmer* vol. 2(7-8).

Goldberg, A. and Robson, D. 1983. *Smalltalk-80: The Language and Its Implementation.* Reading, MA: Addison-Wesley.

—— 1989. *Smalltalk-80: The Language.* Reading, MA: Addison-Wesley.

Goldberg, A. and Ross, J. August 1981. Is the Smalltalk-80 System for Children? *Byte* vol. 6(8).

Goldstein, T. May 1989. The Object-Oriented Programmer. *The C++ Report* vol. 1(5).

Gonsalves, G. and Silvestri, A. December 1986. Programming in Smalltalk-80: Observations and Remarks from the Newly Initiated. *SIGPLAN Notices* vol. 21(12).

Gorlen, K. 1989. An Introduction to C++, in *UNIX System V ATT C++ Language System, Release 2.0 Selected Readings.* 1989. Murray Hill, NJ: ATT Bell Laboratories.

Gorlen, K., Orlow, S., and Plexico, P. 1990. *Data Abstraction and Object-Oriented Programming in C++.* New York, New York: John Wiley and Sons.

Gougen, J. and Meseguer, J. 1987. Unifying Functional, Object-Oriented, and Relational Programming with Logical Semantics, in *Research Directions in Object-Oriented Programming.* ed. B. Schriver and P. Wegner. Cambridge, MA: The MIT Press.

Graube, N. August 1988. Reflexive Architecture: From ObjVLisp to CLOS. *Proceedings of ECOOP'88: European Conference on Object-Oriented Programming.* New York, NY: Springer-Verlag.

Grogono, P. November 1989. Polymorphism and Type Checking in Object-Oriented Languages. *SIGPLAN Notices* vol. 24(11).

—— 1991. Issues in the Design of an Object-Oriented Programming Language. *Structured Programming* vol. 12(1).

Hagmann, R. 1983. Preferred Classes: A Proposal for Faster Smalltalk-80 Execution, in *Smalltalk-80: Bits of History, Words of Advice.* ed. G. Krasner. Reading, MA: Addison-Wesley.

Hailpern, B. and Nguyen, V. 1987. A Model for Object-Based Inheritance, in *Research Directions in Object-Oriented Programming.* ed. B. Schriver and P. Wegner. Cambridge, MA: The MIT Press.

Halbert, D. and O'Brien, P. September 1988. Using Types and Inheritance in Object-Oriented Programming. *IEEE Software* vol. 4(5).

Halstead, R. 1987. Object Management on Distributed Systems, in *Object-Oriented Computing: Implementations* vol. 2. ed. G. Peterson. New York, NY: Computer Society Press of the IEEE.

Harland, D., Szyplewski, M., and Wainwright, J. October 1985. An Alternative View of Polymorphism. *SIGPLAN Notices* vol. 20(10).

Hendler, J. October 1986. Enhancement for Multiple Inheritance. *SIGPLAN Notices* vol. 21(10).

Hines, T. and Unger, E. 1986. *Conceptual Object-Oriented Programming.* Manhattan, Kansas: Kansas State University.

Ingalls, D. The Smalltalk-76 Programming System Design and Implementation. *Proceedings of the Fifth Annual ACM Symposium on Principles of Programming Languages,* New York, NY: Association of Computing Machinery.

—— August 1981a. Design Principles Behind Smalltalk. *Byte* vol. 6(8).

—— August 1981b. The Smalltalk Graphics Kernel. *Byte* vol. 6(8).

—— 1983. The Evolution of the Smalltalk Virtual Machine, in *Smalltalk-80: Bits of History, Words of Advice*. ed. G. Krasner. Reading, MA: Addison-Wesley.

—— November 1986. A Simple Technique for Handling Multiple Polymorphism. *SIGPLAN Notices* vol. 21(11).

Ishikawa, Y. and Tokoro, M. 1987. Orient84/K: An Object-Oriented Concurrent Programming Language for Knowledge Representation, in *Object-Oriented Concurrent Programming*. ed. Yonezawa and M. Tokoro. Cambridge, MA: The MIT Press.

Jackson, M. May 1988. Objects and Other Subjects. *SIGPLAN Notices* vol. 23(5).

Jacky, J. and Kalet, I. September 1987. An Object-Oriented Programming Discipline for Standard Pascal. *Communications of the ACM* vol. 30(9).

Jacobson, I. November 1986. Language Support for Changeable, Large, Real-Time Systems. *SIGPLAN Notices* vol. 21(11).

Jeffery, D. February 1989. Object-Oriented Programming in ANSI C. *Computer Language*.

Jenkins, M. and Glasgow, J. January 1986. Programming Styles in Nial. *IEEE Software* vol. 3(1).

Johnson, R. November 1986. Type-Checking Smalltalk. *SIGPLAN Notices* vol. 21(11).

Johnson, R., Graver, J., and Zurawski, L. September 1988. TS: An Optimizing Compiler for Smalltalk. *SIGPLAN Notices* vol. 23(11).

Kaehler, T. and Patterson, D. 1986. *A Taste of Smalltalk*. New York, NY: W. W. Norton.

—— August 1986. A Small Taste of Smalltalk. *Byte* vol. 11(8).

Kaehler, T. November 1986. Virtual Memory on a Narrow Machine for an Object-Oriented Language. *SIGPLAN Notices* vol. 21(11).

Kahn, K., Tribble, E., Miller, M., and Bobrow, D. 1987. Vulcan: Logical Concurrent Objects, in *Research Directions in Object-Oriented Programming*. ed. B. Schriver and P. Wegner. Cambridge, MA: The MIT Press.

—— November 1986. Objects in Concurrent Logic Programming Languages. *SIGPLAN Notices* vol. 21(11).

Kaiser, G. and Garlan, D. October 1987. MELDing Data Flow and Object-Oriented Programming. *SIGPLAN Notices* vol. 22(12).

Kalme, C. 27 March 1986. *Object-Oriented Programming: A Rule-Based Perspective*. Los Angeles, CA: Inference Corporation.

Kay, A. *New Directions for Novice Programming in the 1980s*. Palo Alto, CA: Xerox Palo Alto Research Center.

Keene, S. 1989. *Object-Oriented Programming in Common Lisp*. Reading, MA: Addison-Wesley.

Kelly, K., Rischer, R., Pleasant, M., Steiner, D., McGrew, C., Rowe, J., and Rubin, M. 30 March 1986. *Textual Representations of Object-Oriented Programs for Future Programmers*. Palo Alto, CA: Xerox AI Systems.

Kempf, R. October 1987. Teaching Object-Oriented Programming with the KEE System. *SIGPLAN Notices* vol. 22(12).

Kempf, J., Harris, W., D'Souza, R., and Snyder, A. October 1987. Experience with CommonLoops. *SIGPLAN Notices* vol. 22(12).

Khoshafian, S. and Copeland, G. November 1986. Object Identity. *SIGPLAN Notices* vol. 21(11).

Kiczales, G., Rivieres, J., and Bobrow, D. 1991. *The Art of the Metaobject Protocol.* Cambridge, Massachusetts: The MIT Press.

Kilian, M. April 1987. *An Overview of the Trellis/Owl Compiler.* Hudson, MA: Digital Equipment Corporation.

Kimminau, D. and Seagren, M. 1987. *Comparison of Two Prototype Developments Using Object-Based Programming.* Naperville, IL: AT&T Bell Laboratories.

Knowledge Systems Corporation. 1987. *PluggableGauges Version 1.0 User Manual.* Cary, NC.

Knudsen, J. and Madsen, O. August 1988. Teaching Object-Oriented Programming Is More than Teaching Object-Oriented Programming Languages. *Proceedings of ECOOP'88: European Conference on Object-Oriented Programming.* New York, NY: Springer-Verlag.

Knudsen, J. August 1988. Name Collision in Multiple Classification Hierarchies. *Proceedings of ECOOP'88: European Conference on Object-Oriented Programming.* New York, NY: Springer-Verlag.

Korson, T. and McGregor, J. September 1990. Understanding Object-Oriented: A Unifying Paradigm. *Communications of the ACM* vol. 33(9).

Koshmann, T. and Evens, M. July 1988. Bridging the Gap Between Object-Oriented and Logic Programming. *IEEE Software* vol. 5(4).

Koskimies, K. and Paakki, J. July 1987. TOOLS: A Unifying Approach to Object-Oriented Language Interpretation. *SIGPLAN Notices* vol. 22(7).

Krasner, G. August 1981. The Smalltalk-80 Virtual Machine. *Byte* vol. 6(8).

—— ed. 1983. *Smalltalk-80: Bits of History, Words of Advice.* Reading, MA: Addison-Wesley.

Krasner, G. and Pope, S. August/September 1988. A Cookbook for Using the Model-View-Controller User Interface Paradigm in Smalltalk-80. *Journal of Object-Oriented Programming* vol. 1(3).

Kristensen, B., Madsen, O., Moller-Pedersen, B., and Nygaard, K. 1987. The BETA Programming Language, in *Research Directions in Object-Oriented Programming.* ed. B. Schriver and P. Wegner. Cambridge, MA: The MIT Press.

LaLonde, W. April 1989. Designing Families of Data Types Using Exemplars. *ACM Transactions on Programming Languages and Systems* vol. 11(2).

LaLonde, W., Thomas, D., and Pugh, J. November 1986. An Examplar Based Smalltalk. *SIGPLAN Notices* vol. 21(11).

LaLonde, W. and Pugh, J. 1990. *Inside Smalltalk, Volumes 1 and 2.* Englewood Cliffs, New Jersey: Prentice Hall.

Lang, K. and Peralmutter, B. November 1986. Oaklisp: an Object-Oriented Scheme with First Class Types. *SIGPLAN Notices* vol. 21(11).

Laursen, J. and Atkinson, R. October 1987. Opus: A Smalltalk Production System. *SIGPLAN Notices* vol. 22(12).

Lieberherr, K. and Holland, I. March 1989. Formulations and Benefits of the Law of Demeter. *SIGPLAN Notices* vol. 24(3).

—— September 1989. Assuring Good Style for Object-Oriented Programs. *IEEE Software* vol. 6(5).

Lieberherr, K., Holland, I., Lee, G., and Riel, A. June 1988. An Objective Sense of Style. *IEEE Computer* vol. 21(6).

Lieberman, H. November 1986. Using Prototypical Objects to Implement Shared Behavior in Object-Oriented Systems. *SIGPLAN Notices* vol. 21(11).

—— 1987. Concurrent Object-Oriented Programming in Act 1, in *Object-Oriented Concurrent Programming*. ed. Yonezawa and M. Tokoro. Cambridge, MA: The MIT Press.

Lieberman, H., Stein, L., and Ungar, D. May 1988. Of Types and Prototypes: The Treaty of Orlando. *SIGPLAN Notices* vol. 23(5).

Lim, J. and Johnson, R. April 1989. The Heart of Object-Oriented Concurrent Programming. *SIGPLAN Notices* vol. 24(4).

Linowes, J. August 1988. It's an Attitude. *Byte* vol. 13(8).

Lippman, S. 1991. *C++ Primer,* Second Edition. Reading, Massachusetts: Addison-Wesley Publishing Company.

Liskov, B., Atkinson, R., Bloom, T., Moss, E., Schaffert, C., Scheifler, R., and Snyder, R. 1981. *CLU Reference Manual*. New York, NY: Springer-Verlag.

Liskov, B., Snyder, A., Atkinson, R., and Schaffert, C. 1980. Abstraction Mechanisms in CLU, in *Programming Language Design*. ed. A. Wasserman. New York, NY: Computer Society Press.

Liu, C. March 1991. On the Object-Orientedness of C++. *SIGPLAN Notices* vol. 26(3).

Lujun, S. and Zhongxiu. August 1987. An Object-Oriented Programming Language for Developing Distributed Software. *SIGPLAN Notices* vol. 22(8).

MacLennan, B. 1987. Values and Objects in Programming Languages,, in *Object-Oriented Computing: Concepts vol.* 1. ed. G. Peterson. New York, NY: Computer Society Press of the IEEE.

Madsen, O. 1987. Block Structure and Object-Oriented Languages, in *Research Directions in Object-Oriented Programming*. ed. B. Schriver and P. Wegner. Cambridge, MA: The MIT Press.

Madsen, O. and Moller-Pedersen, B. August 1988. What Object-Oriented Programming May Be – And What It Does Not Have To Be. *Proceedings of ECOOP'88: European Conference on Object-Oriented Programming*. New York, NY: Springer-Verlag.

Madsen, O. and Moller-Pedersen, B. October 1989. Virtual Classes: A Powerful Mechanism in Object-Oriented Programming. *SIGPLAN Notices* vol. 24(10).

Manci, D. 1990. *Use of Metrics to Evaluate C++*. Liberty Corner, New Jersey: AT&T Bell Laboratories.

Mannino, M., Choi, I., and Batory, D. November 1990. The Object-Oriented Functional Data Language. *IEEE Transactions on Software Engineering* vol. 16(11).

Marcus, R. November 1985. Generalized Inheritance. *SIGPLAN Notices* vol. 20(11).

Markowitz, V. and Raz, Y. 1983. Eroll: An Entity-Relationship, Role-Oriented Query Language, in *Entity-Relationship Approach to Software Engineering*. ed. C. Davis et al. Amsterdam, The Netherlands: Elsevier Science.

Masini, G., Napoli, A., Colnet, D., Leonard, D., and Tompre, K. 1991. *Object-Oriented Languages*. London, England: Academic Press.

Mellender, F. October 1988. An Integration of Logic and Object-Oriented Programming. *SIGPLAN Notices* vol. 23(10).

Methfessel, R. April 1987. Implementing an Access and Object-Oriented Paradigm in a Language That Supports Neither. *SIGPLAN Notices* vol. 22(4).

Meyer, B. November 1986. Genericity versus Inheritance. *SIGPLAN Notices* vol. 21(11).

—— February 1987. Eiffel: Programming for Reusability and Extendability. *SIGPLAN Notices* vol. 22(2).

—— November/December 1988. Harnessing Multiple Inheritance. *Journal of Object-Oriented Programming* vol. 1(4).

Micallef, J. April/May 1988. Encapsulation, Reusability, and Extensibility in Object-Oriented Programming Languages. *Journal of Object-Oriented Programming* vol. 1(1).

Microsoft C++ Tutorial. 1992. Redmond, Washington: Microsoft Corporation.

Microsoft Windows Guide to Programming. 1992. Redmond, Washington: Microsoft Corporation.

Minsky, N. and Rozenshtein, D. October 1987. A Law-Based Approach to Object-Oriented Programming. *SIGPLAN Notices* vol. 22(12).

—— October 1989. Controllable Delegation: An Exercise in Law-Governed Systems. *SIGPLAN Notices* vol. 24(10).

Miranda, E. October 1987. BrouHaHa – A Portable Smalltalk Interpreter. *SIGPLAN Notices* vol. 22(12).

Mittal, S., Bobrow, D., and Kahn, K. November 1986. Virtual Copies: At the Boundary Between Classes and Instances. *SIGPLAN Notices* vol. 21(11).

Moon, D. November 1986. Object-Oriented Programming with Flavors. *SIGPLAN Notices* vol. 21(11).

Morrison, R., Dearle, A., Connor, R., and Brown, A. July 1991. An Ad Hoc Approach to the Implementation of Polymorphism. *ACM Transactions on Programming Languages and Systems* vol. 13(3).

Mossenbock, H. and Templ, J. 1989. Object Oberon – A Modest Object-Oriented Language. *Structured Programming* vol. 10(4).

Mudge, T. March 1985. Object-Based Computing and the Ada Language. *IEEE Computer* vol. 18(3).

Murray, R. 1990. *C++ Tactics.* Liberty Corner, New Jersey: AT&T Bell Laboratories.

Nelson, M. October 1991. Concurrency and Object-Oriented Programming. *SIGPLAN Notices* vol. 26(10).

Nierstrasz, O. October 1987. Active Objects in Hybrid. *SIGPLAN Notices* vol. 22(12).

Novak, G. June 1983. Data Abstraction in GLISP. *SIGPLAN Notices* vol. 18(6).

—— Fall 1983. GLISP: A Lisp-Based Programming System with Data Abstraction. *AI Magazine* vol. 4(3).

Nygaard, K. October 1986. Basic Concepts in Object-Oriented Programming. *SIGPLAN Notices* vol. 21(10).

Nygaard, K. and Dahl, O-J. 1981. The Development of the Simula Languages, in *History of Programming Languages.* ed. R. Wexelblat. New York, NY: Academic Press.

O'Brien, P. 15 November 1985. *Trellis Object-Based Environment: Language Tutorial.* Hudson, MA: Digital Equipment Corporation.

O'Grady, F. July/August 1990. Is There Life After COBOL?. *American Programmer* vol. 3(7-8).

Object-Oriented Programming Workshop. October 1986. *SIGPLAN Notices* vol. 21(10).

Olthoff, W. 1986. *Augmentation of Object-Oriented Programming by Concepts of Abstract Data Type Theory: The ModPascal Experience.* Kaiserslautern, West Germany: University of Kaiserslautern.

Osterbye, K. June/July 1988. Active Objects: An Access-Oriented Framework for Object-Oriented Languages. *Journal of Object-Oriented Programming* vol. 1(2).

Paepcke, A. October 1989. PCLOS: A Critical Review. *SIGPLAN Notices* vol. 24(10).

Parc Place Systems. 1988. *The Smalltalk-80 Programming System Version VI 2.3.* Palo Alto, CA.

Pascoe, G. August 1986. Elements of Object-Oriented Programming. *Byte* vol. 11(8).

—— November 1986. Encapsulators: A New Software Paradigm in Smalltalk-80. *SIGPLAN Notices* vol. 21(11).

Perez, E. September/October 1988. Simulating Inheritance with Ada. *Ada Letters* vol. 8(7).

Peterson, G. ed. 1987. *Object-Oriented Computing Concepts.* New York, NY: Computer Society Press of the IEEE.

Pinson, L. and Wiener, R. 1988. *An Introduction to Object-Oriented Programming and Smalltalk.* Reading, MA: Addison-Wesley.

Pohl, I. 1989. *C++ for C Programmers.* Redwood City, CA: Benjamin/Cummings.

Pokkunuri, B. November 1989. Object-Oriented Programming. *SIGPLAN Notices* vol. 24(11).

Ponder, C. and Bush, B. June 1992. Polymorphism Considered Harmful. *SIGPLAN Notices* vol. 27(6).

Pountain, D. August 1986. Object-Oriented FORTH. *Byte* vol. 11(8).

Proceedings of ECOOP'88: European Conference on Object-Oriented Programming. August 1988. New York, NY: Springer-Verlag.

Proceedings of OOPSLA'86: Object-Oriented Programming Systems, Languages, and Applications. November 1986. *SIGPLAN Notices* vol. 21(11).

Proceedings of OOPSLA'87: Object-Oriented Programming Systems, Languages, and Applications. October 1987. *SIGPLAN Notices* vol. 22(12).

Proceedings of OOPSLA'88: Object-Oriented Programming Systems, Languages, and Applications. September 1988. *SIGPLAN Notices* vol. 23(11).

Proceedings of OOPSLA'89: Object-Oriented Programming Systems, Languages, and Applications. October 1989. *SIGPLAN Notices* vol. 24(10).

Proceedings of OOPSLA'90. Object-Oriented Programming Systems, Languages, and Applications. October 1990. SIGPLAN Notices vol. 25(10).

Proceedings of OOPSLA'91. Object-Oriented Programming Systems, Languages, and Applications. November 1991. SIGPLAN Notices vol. 26(11).

Proceedings of OOPSLA'92. Object-Oriented Programming Systems, Languages, and Applications. October 1992. SIGPLAN Notices vol. 27(10).

Proceedings of the ACM SIGPLAN Workshop on Object-Based Concurrent Programming. April 1989. *SIGPLAN Notices* vol. 24(4).

Proceedings of the USENIX Association C++ Workshop. November 1987. Berkeley, CA: USENIX Association.

Proceedings of the Workshop on Data Abstraction, Databases, and Conceptual Modeling. 1980. *SIGPLAN Notices* vol. 16(1).

Pugh, J. March 1984. Actors – The Stage is Set. *SIGPLAN Notices* vol. 19(3).

Rathke, C. 1986. *ObjTalk: Repräsentation von Wissen in einer objektorientierten Sprache* Stuttgart, West Germany: Institut für Informatik der Universität Stuttgart.

Rentsch, T. September 1982. Object-Oriented Programming. *SIGPLAN Notices* vol. 17(12).

Rettig, M., Morgan, T., Jacobs, J., and Wimberly, D. January 1989. Object-Oriented Programming in AI. *AI Expert.*

Robson, D. August 1981. Object-Oriented Software Systems. *Byte* vol. 6(8).

Rumbaugh, J. October 1987. Relations as Semantic Constructs in an Object-Oriented Language. *SIGPLAN Notices* vol. 22(12).

Russo, V. and Kaplan, S. 1988. A C++ Interpreter for Scheme. *Proceedings of USENIX C++ Conference.* Berkeley, CA: USENIX Association.

Sakkinen, M. August 1988. On the Darker Side of C++. *Proceedings of ECOOP'88: European Conference on Object-Oriented Programming* New York, NY: Springer-Verlag.

—— December 1988. Comments on "the Law of Demeter" and C++. *SIGPLAN Notices* vol. 23(12).

Saltzer, J. 1979. Naming and Binding of Objects, in *Operating Systems.* ed. R. Bayer et. al. New York, NY: Springer-Verlag.

Sandberg, D. November 1986. An Alternative To Subclassing. *SIGPLAN Notices* vol. 21(11).

—— October 1988. Smalltalk and Exploratory Programming. *SIGPLAN Notices* vol. 23(10).

Saunders, J. March/April 1989. A Survey of Object-Oriented Programming Languages. *Journal of Object-Oriented Programming* vol. 1(6).

Schaffert, C., Cooper, T. and Wilpolt, C. November 25, 1985. *Trellis Object-Based Environment: Language Reference Manual.* Hudson, MA: Digital Equipment Corporation.

Schaffert, C., Cooper, T., Bullis, B., Kilian, M., and Wilpolt, C. November 1986. An Introduction to Trellis/Owl. *SIGPLAN Notices* vol. 21(11).

Schmucker, K. 1986a. MacApp: An Application Framework. *Byte* vol. 11(8).

—— 1986b. Object-Oriented Languages for the Macintosh. *Byte* vol. 11(8).

—— 1986c. *Object-Oriented Programming for the Macintosh.* Hasbrouk Heights, NJ: Hayden.

Schriver, B. and Wegner, P. eds. 1987. *Research Directions in Object-Oriented Programming.* Cambridge, MA: The MIT Press.

Seidewitz, E. March/April 1992. Object-Oriented Programming with Mixins in Ada. *Ada Letters* vol. XII(2).

—— October 1987. Object-Oriented Programming in Smalltalk and Ada. *SIGPLAN Notices* vol. 22(12).

Shafer, D. 1988. *Hyper Talk Programming.* Indianapolis, IN: Hayden.

Shah, A., Rumbaugh, J., Hamel, J., and Borsari, R. October 1989. DSM: An Object-Relationship Modeling Language. *SIGPLAN Notices* vol. 24(10).

Shammas, N. October 1988. Smalltalk a la C. *Byte* vol. 13(10).

Shan, Y. October 1989. An Event-Driven Model-View-Controller Framework for Smalltalk. *SIGPLAN Notices* vol. 24(10).

Shapiro, J. 1991. *A C++ Toolkit.* Englewood Cliffs, New Jersey Prentice-Hall.

Shaw, M. 1981. *ALPHARD: Form and Content.* New York, NY: Springer-Verlag.

Shibayama, E. September 1988. How to Invent Distributed Implementation Schemes of an Object-Based Concurrent Language – A Transformational Approach. *SIGPLAN Notices* vol. 23(11).

Shibayama, E. and Yonezawa, A. 1987. Distributed Computing in ABCL/1, in *Object-Oriented Concurrent Programming.* ed. Yonezawa and M. Tokoro. Cambridge, MA: The MIT Press.

Shopiro, J. 13 December 1988. Programming Techniques with C++. *C++ Tutorial Program of the USENIX Conference.* Denver, CO: USENIX Association.

—— December 1989. An Example of Multiple Inheritance in C++: A Model of the Iostream Library. *SIGPLAN Notices* vol. 24(12).

Simonian, R. and Crone, M. November/December 1988. InnovAda: True Object-Oriented Programming in Ada. *Journal of Object-Oriented Programming* vol. 1(4).

Snyder, A. February 1985. *Object-Oriented Programming for Common Lisp.* Report ATC-85-1. Palo Alto, CA: Hewlett-Packard.

—— November 1986. Encapsulation and Inheritance in Object-Oriented Programming Languages. *SIGPLAN Notices* vol. 21(11).

—— 1987. Inheritance and the Development of Encapsulated Software Components, in *Research Directions in Object-Oriented Programming.* ed. B. Schriver and P. Wegner. Cambridge, MA: The MIT Press.

—— January 1993. The Essence of Objects: Concepts and Terms. *IEEE Software* vol. 10(1).

Software Productivity Solutions. 1988. *Classical-Ada User Manual.* Melbourne, FL.

Stankovic, J. April 1982. Software Communication Mechanisms: Procedure Calls Versus Messages. *IEEE Computer* vol. 15(4).

Stefik, M. and Bobrow, D. Winter 1986. Object-Oriented Programming: Themes and Variations, *AI Magazine* vol. 6(4).

Stefik, M., Bobrow, D., Mittal, S., and Conway, L. Fall 1983, Knowledge Programming in Loops. *AI Magazine* vol. 4(3).

Stein, L. October 1987. Delegation Is Inheritance. *SIGPLAN Notices* vol. 22(12).

Stroustrup, B. January 1982. Classes: An Abstract Data Type Facility for the C Language. *SIGPLAN Notices* vol. 17(1).

—— October 1986. An Overview of C++. *SIGPLAN Notices* vol. 21(10).

—— 1987. The Evolution of C++. *Proceedings of the USENIX C++ Workshop.* Santa Fe, NM: USENIX Association.

—— November 1987. Possible Directions for C++. *Proceedings of the USENIX C++ Workshop.* Santa Fe, NM: USENIX Association.

—— 1988. Parameterized Types for C++. *Proceedings of USENIX C++ Conference.* Berkeley, CA: USENIX Association.

—— May 1988. What Is Object-Oriented Programming? *IEEE Software vol.* 5(3).

—— August 1988. A Better C? *Byte* vol. 13(8).

—— 1991. *The C+ Programming Language,* Second Edition. Reading, Massachusetts: Addison-Wesley Publishing Company.

Suzuki, N. 1981. Inferring Types in Smalltalk, *Proceedings of the Eighth Annual Symposium of ACM Principles of Programming Languages.* New York, NY: Association of Computing Machinery.

Suzuki, N. and Terada, M. 1983. Creating Efficient Systems for Object-Oriented Languages. *Proceedings of the 11th Annual ACM Symposium on the Principles of Programming Languages.* New York, NY: Association of Computing Machinery.

Symposium on Actor Languages. October 1980. *Creative Computing.*

Tektronix. 1988. Modular Smalltalk.

Tesler, L. August 1986. Programming Experiences. *Byte* vol. 11(8).

The Smalltalk-80 System. August 1981. *Byte* vol. 6(8).

Thomas, D. March 1989. What's in an Object? *Byte* vol. 14(3).

Tieman, M. 1 May 1988. *User's Guide to GNU C++.* Cambridge, MA: Free Software Foundation.

Tokoro, M. and Ishikawa, Y. October 1986. Concurrent Programming in Orient84/K: An Object-Oriented Knowledge Representation Language. *SIGPLAN Notices* vol. 21(10).

Touati, H. May 1987. Is Ada an Object-Oriented Programming Language? *SIGPLAN Notices* vol. 22(5).

Touretzky, D. 1986. *The Mathematics of Inheritance Systems.* Los Altos, California: Morgan Kaufman Publishers.

Tripathi, A. and Berge, E. An Implementation of the Object-Oriented Concurrent Programming Language SINA. *Software – Practice and Experience* vol. 19(3).

U. S. Department of Defense. February 1983. *Reference Manual for the Ada Programming Language.* Washington, D.C.: Ada Joint Program Office.

Ungar, D. September 1988. Are Classes Obsolete? *SIGPLAN Notices* vol. 23(11).

Ungar, D. and Smith, R. October 1987. Self: The Power of Simplicity. *SIGPLAN Notices* vol. 22(12).

van den Bos, J. and Laffra, C. October 1989. PROCOL: A Parallel Object Language with Protocols. *SIGPLAN Notices* vol. 24(10).

Vaucher, J., Lapalme, G., and Malenfant, J. August 1988. SCOOP: Structured Concurrent Object-Oriented Prolog. *Proceedings of ECOOP'88: European Conference on Object-Oriented Programming.* New York, NY: Springer-Verlag.

Warren, S. and Abbe, D. May 1980. Presenting Rosetta Smalltalk. *Datamation.*

Watanabe, T. and Yonezawa, A. September 1988. Reflection in an Object-Oriented Concurrent Language. *SIGPLAN Notices* vol. 23(11).

Wegner, P. October 1987. Dimensions of Object-Based Language Design. *SIGPLAN Notices* vol. 22(12).

—— January 1988. Workshop on Object-Oriented Programming at ECOOP 1987. *SIGPLAN Notices* vol. 23(1).

—— August 1990. Concepts and Paradigms of Object-Oriented Programming. *OOPS Messenger* vol. 1(1).

—— October 1992. Dimensions of Object-Oriented Modeling. *IEEE Computer* vol. 25(10).

Wiener, R. June 1987. Object-Oriented Programming in C++ – A Case Study. *SIGPLAN Notices* vol. 22(6).

Williams, G. Summer 1989. Designing the Future: The Power of Object-Oriented Programming. *American Programmer* vol. 2(7-8).

Wilson, R. 1 November 1987. Object-Oriented Languages Reorient Programming Techniques. *Computer Design* vol. 26(20).

Winblad, A., Edwards, S., and King, D. 1990. *Object-Oriented Software*. Reading, Massachusetts: Addison-Wesley Publishing Company.

Winston, P. and Horn, B. 1989. *Lisp*. Third Edition. Reading, MA: Addison-Wesley.

Wirfs-Brock, R. and Wilkerson, B. September 1988. An Overview of Modular Smalltalk. *SIGPLAN Notices* vol. 23(11).

Wirth, N. June 1987. Extensions of Record Types. *SIGCSE Bulletin* vol. 19(2).

—— July 1988a. From Modula to Oberon. *Software – Practice and Experience* vol. 18(7).

—— July 1988b. The Programming Language Oberon. *Software – Practice and Experience* vol. 18(7).

Wolf, W. September 1989. A Practical Comparison of Two Object-Oriented Languages. *IEEE Software* vol. 6(5).

Yokote, Y. and Tokoro, M. November 1986. The Design and Implementation of Concurrent Smalltalk. *SIGPLAN Notices* vol. 21(11).

—— October 1987. Experience and Evolution of Concurrent Smalltalk. *SIGPLAN Notices* vol. 22(12).

Yonezawa, A. and Tokoro, M. eds. 1987. *Object-Oriented Concurrent Programming*. Cambridge, MA: The MIT Press.

Yonezawa, A., Briot, J., and Shibayama, E. November 1986. Object-Oriented Concurrent Programming in ABCL/1. *SIGPLAN Notices* vol. 21(11).

Yonezawa, A., Shibayama, E., Takada, T., and Honda, Y. 1987. Modeling and Programming in an Object-Oriented Concurrent Language ABCL/1, in *Object-Oriented Concurrent Programming*. ed. Yonezawa and M. Tokoro. Cambridge, MA: The MIT Press.

Yourdon, E. February 1990. Object-Oriented COBOL. *American Programmer* vol. 3(2).

—— January 1992. Modeling Magic. *American Programmer* vol. 5(1).

Zave, P. September 1989. A Compositional Approach to Multiparadigm Programming. *IEEE Software* vol. 6(5).

H. Software Engineering

Abdel-Hamid, T. and Madnick, S. 1991. *Software Project Dynamics*. Englewood Cliffs, New Jersey Prentice-Hall.

Abelson, H. and Sussman, G. 1985. *Structure and Interpretation of Computer Programs*. Cambridge, MA: The MIT Press.

Andrews, D. and Leventhal, N. 1993. *FUSION: Integrating IE, CASE, and JAD: A Handbook for Reengineering the Systems Organization*. Englewood Cliffs, New Jersey: Yourdon Press.

Appleton, D. 15 January 1986. Very Large Projects. *Datamation.*

Aron, J. 1974a. *The Program Development Process: The Individual Programmer*. Vol. 1. Reading, MA: Addison-Wesley.

—— 1974b. *The Program Development Process: The Programming Team.* Vol. 2. Reading, MA: Addison-Wesley.

Babich, W. 1986. *Software Configuration Management*. Reading, Massachusetts: Addison-Wesley Publishing Company.

Ben-Ari, M. 1982. *Principles of Concurrent Programming*. Englewood Cliffs, NJ: Prentice-Hall.

Berard, E. 1993. *Essays on Object-Oriented Software Engineering*. Englewood Cliffs, New Jersey: Prentice-Hall.

Berson, A. 1992. Client/Server Architecture. New York, NY: McGraw-Hill.

Berzins, V. and Luqi. 1991 *Software Engineering with Abstractions*. Reading, Massachusetts: Addison-Wesley Publishing Company.

Biggerstaff, T. and Perlis, A. 1989. *Software Reusability*. New York, New York: ACM Press.

Bisant, D., and Lyle, J. October 1989. A Two-Person Inspection Method to Improve Programming Productivity. *IEEE Transactions on Software Engineering* vol. 15(10).

Bischofberger, W. and Keller, R. 1989 Enhancing the Software Life Cycle by Prototyping. *Structured Programming*.

Bloom, P. April 1993. Trends in Client-Server/Cooperative Processing Application Development Tools. *American Programmer,* Arlington MA: Cutter Information Corporation.

Boar, B. 1984. *Application Prototyping*. New York, New York: John Wiley and Sons.

Boehm, B. August 1986. A Spiral Model of Software Development and Enhancement. *Software Engineering Notes* vol. 11(4).

—— September 1992. Risk Control. *American Programmer* vol. 5(7).

Boehm, B. and Papaccio, P. 1988. Understanding and Controlling Software Costs. *IEEE Transactions on Software Engineering* vol. 4(10).

Boehm-Davis, D. and Ross, L. October 1984. *Approaches to Structuring the Software Development Process*, Report GEC/DIS/TR-84-B1V-1. Arlington, VA: General Electric.

Booch, G. 1986. *Software Engineering with Ada*. Menlo Park, CA: Benjamin/Cummings.

Brooks, F. 1975. *The Mythical Man-Month*. Reading, MA: Addison-Wesley.

—— April 1987. No Silver Bullet: Essence and Accidents of Software Engineering. *IEEE Computer* vol. 20(4).

Charette, R. 1989. *Software Engineering Risk Analysis and Management*. New York, New York: McGraw-Hill Book Company.

Chidamber, S. and Kemerer, C. *Towards a Metrics Suite for Object-Oriented Design*. Phoenix, Arizona: OOPSLA'91.

—— 1993. *A Metrics Suite for Object-Oriented Design*. Cambridge, Massachusetts: MIT Sloan School of Management.

Chmura, L, Norcio, A., and Wicinski, T. July 1990. Evaluating Software Design Processes by Analyzing Change Date Over Time. *IEEE Transactions on Software Engineering* vol. 16(7).

Cox, B. November 1990. Planning the Software Industrial Revolution. *IEEE Software* vol. 7(6).

Curtis, B. 17 May 1989. . . . *.But You Have To Understand, This Isn't The Way We Develop Software At Our Company.* MCC Technical Report Number STP-203-89. Austin, TX: Microelectronics and Computer Technology Corporation.

Curtis, B., Kellner, M., and Over, J. September 1992. Process Modeling, *Communications of the ACM* vol. 35(9).

Dahl, O., Dijkstra, E., and Hoare, C. A. R. 1972. *Structured Programming.* London, England: Academic Press.

Davis, A. 1990. *Software Requirements: Analysis and Specification.* Englewood Cliffs, New Jersey: Prentice-Hall.

Davis, A., Bersoff, E., and Comer, E. October 1988. A Strategy for Comparing Alternative Software Development Life Cycle Models. *IEEE Transactions on Software Engineering* vol. 14(10).

Davis, C., Jajodia, S., Ng, P., and Yeh, R. eds. 1983. *Entity-Relationship Approach to Software Engineering.* Amsterdam, The Netherlands: Elsevier Science.

DeMarco, T. and Lister, T. 1987. *Peopleware.* New York, NY: Dorset House.

DeRemer, F. and Kron, H. 1980. Programming-in-the-Large versus Programming-in-the-Small. *Tutorial on Software Design Techniques.* Third Edition. ed. P. Freeman and A. Wasserman. New York, NY: Computer Society Press of the IEEE.

Dewire, D. 1992. *Client/Server Computing.* New York, NY: McGraw-Hill.

Dijkstra, E. 1979. Programming Considered as a Human Activity, in *Classics in Software Engineering.* ed. E. Yourdon. New York, NY: Yourdon Press.

—— 1982. *Selected Writings on Computing: A Personal Perspective.* New York, NY: Springer-Verlag.

Dowson, M. August 1986. The Structure of the Software Process. *Software Engineering Notes vol.* 11(4).

Dowson, M., Nejmeh, B., and Riddle, W. February 1990. *Software Engineering Practices in Europe, Japan, and the U.S.* Boulder, Colorado Software Design and Analysis,.

Dreger, B. 1989. *Function Point Analysis.* Englewood Cliffs, New Jersey: Prentice Hall.

Eastman, N. 1984. Software Engineering and Technology. *Technical Directions* vol. 10(1). Bethesda, MD: IBM Federal Systems Division.

Fagan, M. June 1976. *Design and Code Inspections and Process Control in the Development of Programs.* IBM-TR-00.73.

Foster, C. 1981. *Real-Time Programming.* Reading, MA: Addison-Wesley.

Freedman, D. February 1992. The Devil Is in the Details Everything Important Must be Reviewed. *American Programmer* vol. 5(2).

Freeman, P. 1975. *Software Systems Principles.* Chicago, IL: Science Research Associates.

Freeman, P. and Wasserman, A. eds. 1983. *Tutorial on Software Design Techniques.* Fourth Edition. New York, NY: Computer Society Press of the IEEE.

Gehani, N. and McGettrick, A. 1986. *Software Specification Techniques.* Reading, Massachusetts: Addison-Wesley Publishing Company.

Gilb, T. 1988. *Principles of Software Engineering Management.* Reading, Massachusetts Addison-Wesley Publishing Company.

Glass, R. 1982. *Modern Programming Practices: A Report from Industry.* Englewood Cliffs, NJ: Prentice-Hall.

—— 1983. *Real-Time Software.* Englewood Cliffs, NJ: Prentice-Hall.

—— 1991. *Software Conflict.* Englewood Cliffs, New Jersey: Yourdon Press.

Goldberg, A. and Rubin, K. 1992. *Tutorial on Object-Oriented Project Management.* Vancouver, Canada: OOPSLA '92.

Guengerich, S. 1992. *Downsizing Information Systems.* Carmel, Indiana: Sams.

Guindon, R., Krasner, H., and Curtis, B. 1987. *Breakdowns and Processes During the Early Activities of Software Design by Professionals. Empirical Studies of Programmers, Second Workshop.* Norwood, New Jersey: Ablex Publishing Company.

Guttman, M. and Matthews, J. November/December 1992. Managing a Large Project. *Object Magazine* vol. 2(4).

Hansen, P. 1977. *The Architecture of Concurrent Programs.* Englewood Cliffs, NJ: Prentice-Hall.

Henderson-Sellers, B. and Edwards, J. September 1990. The Object-Oriented Systems Lifecycle. *Communications of the ACM* vol. 33(9).

Hoare, C. April 1984. Programming: Sorcery or Science? *IEEE Software* vol. 1(2).

Holt, R., Lazowska, E., Graham, G., and Scott, M. 1978. *Structured Concurrent Programming.* Reading, MA: Addison-Wesley.

Humphrey, W. 1988. Characterizing the Software Development Process: A Maturity Framework. *IEEE Software* vol. 5(2).

—— 1989. *Managing the Software Process.* Reading, MA: Addison-Wesley.

Jackson, M. 1975. *Principles of Program Design.* Orlando, FL: Academic Press.

—— 1983. *System Development.* Englewood Cliffs, NJ: Prentice-Hall.

Jensen, R. and Tonies, C. 1979. *Software Engineering.* Englewood Cliffs, NJ: Prentice-Hall.

Jones, C. September 1984. Reusability in Programming: A Survey of the State of the Art. *IEEE Transactions on Software Engineering.* vol. SE-10(5).

—— September 1992. Risky Business: The Most Common Software Risks. *American Programmer* vol. 5(7).

Karam, G. and Casselman, R. February 1993. A Cataloging Framework for Software Development Methods. *IEEE Computer.*

Kishida, K., Teramoto, M., Torri, K., and Urano, Y. September 1988. Quality Assurance Technology in Japan. *IEEE Software* vol. 4(5).

Lammers, S. 1986. *Programmers at Work.* Redmond, WA: Microsoft Press.

Laranjeira, L. May 1990. Software Size Estimation of Object-Oriented Systems. *IEEE Transactions on Software Engineering* vol. 16(5).

Ledgard, H. Summer 1985. Programmers: The Amateur vs. the Professional. *Abacus* vol. 2(4).

Lejter, M., Myers, S., and Reiss, S. December 1992. Support for Maintaining Object-Oriented Programs. *IEEE Transactions on Software Engineering* vol. 18(12).

Linger, R. and Mills, H. 1977. On the Development of Large Reliable Programs, in *Current Trends in Programming Methodology: Software Specification and Design* vol. 1. ed. R. Yeh. Englewood Cliffs, NJ: Prentice-Hall.

Linger, R., Mills, H., and Witt, B. 1979. *Structured Programming: Theory and Practice.* Reading, MA: Addison-Wesley.

Liskov, B. and Guttag, J. 1986. *Abstraction and Specification in Program Development.* Cambridge, MA: The MIT Press.

Lorin, H. 1972. *Parallelism in Hardware and Software.* Englewood Cliffs, NJ: Prentice-Hall.

Luqi, August 1990. A Graph Model for Software Evolution. *IEEE Transactions on Software Engineering* vol. 16(8).

—— May 1909. Software Evolution Through Rapid Prototyping. *IEEE Computer* vol. 22(5).

Martin, J. and McClure, C. 1988. *Structured Techniques: The Basis for CASE.* Englewood Cliffs, NJ: Prentice-Hall.

Mascot, Version 3.1, The Official Handbook of. June 1987. London, England: Crown Copyright.

Matsubara, T. July/August 1990. Bringing up Software Designers. *American Programmer* vol. 3(7-8).

McCabe, T. and Butler, C. December 1989. Design Complexity Measurement and Testing. *Communications of the ACM* vol. 32(12).

Mellichamp, D. 1983. *Real-Time Computing.* New York, NY: Van Nostrand Reinhold.

Mills, H. November 1986. Structured Programming: Retrospect and Prospect. *IEEE Software* vol. 3(6).

Mills, J. July 1985. A Pragmatic View of the System Architect. *Communications of the ACM* vol. 28(7).

Mimno, P., April 1993. Cilent-Server Computing. *American Programmer,* Arlington MA: Cutter Information Corporation.

Mullin, M. 1990. *Rapid Prototyping for Object-Oriented Systems.* Reading, Massachusetts Addison-Wesley Publishing Company.

Munck, R. 1985. Toward Large Software Systems That Work. *Proceedings of the AIAA/ACM/NASA/IEEE Computers in Aerospace V Conference.* Menlo Park, CA: AIAA.

Myers, G. 1978. *Composite/Structured Design.* New York, NY: Van Nostrand Reinhold.

Newport, J. 28 April 1986. A Growing Gap in Software. *Fortune.*

Ng, P. and Yeh, R. 1990. *Modern Software Engineering.* New York, New York: Van Nostrand Reinhold.

Office of the Under Secretary of Defense for Acquisition. September 1987. *Report of the Defense Science Board Task Force on Military Software.* Washington, D.C.

Oman, P. and Lewis, T. 1990. *Milestones in Software Evolution.* Los Alamitos, California: Computer Society Press of the IEEE.

Orr, K. 1971. *Structured Systems Development.* New York, NY: Yourdon Press.

Page-Jones, M. 1988. *The Practical Guide to Structured Systems Design*. Englewood Cliffs, NJ: Yourdon Press.

Parnas, D. December 1985. Software Aspects of Strategic Defense Systems. *Communications of the ACM* vol. 28(12).

—— July 1985a. Why Conventional Software Development Does Not Produce Reliable Programs. *Software Aspects of Strategic Defense Systems*, Report DCS-47-IR. Victoria, Canada: University of Victoria.

—— July 1985b. Why Software is Unreliable. *Software Aspects of Strategic Defense Systems*, Report DCS-47-IR. Victoria, Canada: University of Victoria.

Parnas, D. and Clements, P. 1986. A Rational Design Process: How and Why to Fake It. *IEEE Transactions on Software Engineering* vol. SE-12(2).

Peters, L. 1981. *Software Design*. New York, NY: Yourdon Press.

Pressman, R. 1988. *Making Software Happen*. Englewood Cliffs, New Jersey: Prentice Hall.

—— 1992. *Software Engineering: A Practitioner's Approach*, Third Edition. New York, New York: McGraw-Hill Book Company.

Rakos, J. 1990. *Software Project Management for Small to Medium Sized Projects*. Englewood Cliffs, New Jersey: Prentice-Hall.

Ramamoorthy, C., Garg, V. and Prakask, A. July 1986. Programming in the Large. *IEEE Transactions on Software Engineering* vol. SE-12(7).

Rechtin, E. October 1992. The Art of Systems Architecting. *IEEE Spectrum* vol. 29(10).

Rettig, M. October 1990. Software Teams. *Communications of the ACM* vol. 33(10).

Ross, D., Goodenough, J., and Irvine, C. 1980. Software Engineering: Process, Principles, and Goals. *Tutorial on Software Design Techniques*. Third Edition. ed. P. Freeman and A. Wasserman. New York, NY: Computer Society Press of the IEEE.

Rubinstein, R. and Hersh, H. 1984. *The Human Factor*. Burlington, Massachusetts Digital Press.

Schulmeyer, G. and McManus, J. 1992. *Handbook of Software Quality Assurance,* Second Edition. New York, New York: Van Nostrand Reinhold.

Shaw, M. November 1990. Prospects for an Engineering Discipline of Software. *IEEE Software* vol. 7(6).

Smith, M. and Robson, D. June 1992. A Framework for Testing Object-Oriented Programs. *Journal of Object-Oriented Programming* vol. 5(3).

Software Process Workshop. May 1988. *SIGSOFT Software Engineering Notes* vol. 14(4).

Sommerville, I. 1989. *Software Engineering*. Third Edition. Wokingham, England: Addison-Wesley.

Song, X., and Osterweil, L. 1993. *Executing an Iterative Design Process*. Irvine, California: University of California.

Spector, A. and Gifford, D. April 1986. Computer Science Perspective of Bridge Design. *Communications of the ACM* vol. 29(4).

Stevens, W. Myers, G., and Constantine, L. 1979. Structured Design, in *Classics in Software Engineering*. ed. E. Yourdon. New York, NY: Yourdon Press.

Symons, C. 1988. Function Point Analysis: Difficulties and Improvements. *IEEE Transactions on Software Engineering* vol.(14)1.

Taylor, D. 1990. *Object-Oriented Technology A Manager's Guide*. Alameda, California: Servio Corporation.

The Software Trap: Automate – Or Else. 9 May 1988. *Business Week*.

Thomsett R. July/August 1990. Effective Project Teams. *American Programmer* vol. 3(7-8).

—— June 1991. Managing Superlarge Projects: A Contingency Approach. *American Programmer* vol. 4(6).

U. S. Department of Defense. 30 July 1982. *Report of the DoD Joint Service Task Force on Software Problems*. Washington, D.C.

van Genuchten, M. June 1991. Why is Software Late? An Empirical Study of Reasons for Delay in Software Development. *IEEE Transactions on Software Engineering* vol. 17(6).

Vick, C. and Ramamoorthy, C. 1984. *Software Engineering*. New York, NY: Van Nostrand Reinhold.

Vonk, R. 1990. *Prototyping*. Englewood Cliffs, NJ: Prentice-Hall.

Walsh, J. *Preliminary Defect Data from the Iterative Development of a Large C++ Program*. Vancouver, Canada: OOPSLA'92.

—— January 1993. *Software Quality in an Iterative Object-Oriented Development Paradigm*. Santa Clara, California: Rational.

Ward, M. 1990. *Software that Works*. San Diego, California: Academic Press.

Ward, P. and Mellor, S. 1985. *Structured Development for Real-Time Systems: Introduction and Tools*. Englewood Cliffs, NJ: Yourdon Press.

Wegner, P. 1980. *Research Directions in Software Technology*. Cambridge, MA: The MIT Press.

—— July 1984. Capital-intensive Software Technology. *IEEE Software* vol. 1(3).

Weinberg, G. 1988. *Understanding the Professional Programmer*. New York, New York: Dorset House Publishing.

Weinberg, G. and Freedman, D. 1990. *Handbook of Walkthroughs, Inspections, and Technical Reviews*. New York, New York Dorset House.

Whitten, N. 1990. *Managing Software Development Projects*. New York, New York: John Wiley and Sons.

Wilde, N. and Huitt, R. December 1992. Maintenance Support for Object-Oriented Programs. *IEEE Transactions on Software Engineering* vol. 18(12).

Wilde, N., Matthews, P., and Huitt, R. January 1993. Maintaining Object-Oriented Software. *IEEE Software* vol. 10(1).

Wirth, N. 1986. *Algorithms and Data Structures*. Englewood Cliffs, NJ: Prentice-Hall.

Workshop on Software Configuration Management. November 1989. *SIGSOFT Software Engineering Notes* vol. 17(7).

Yamaura, T. January 1992. Standing Naked in the Snow. *American Programmer* vol. 5(1).

Yeh, R. ed. 1977. *Current Trends in Programming Methodology: Software Specification and Design*. Englewood Cliffs, NJ: Prentice-Hall.

Yourdon, E. 1975. *Techniques of Program Structure and Design*. Englewood Cliffs, NJ: Prentice-Hall.

—— 1979. ed. *Classics in Software Engineering*. New York, NY: Yourdon Press.

—— 1989a. *Modern Structured Analysis*. Englewood Cliffs, NJ: Prentice-Hall.

—— 1989b. *Structured Walkthroughs*. Englewood Cliffs, NJ: Prentice-Hall.

—— August 1989c. The Year of the Object. *Computer Language* vol. 6(8).

—— Summer 1989d. Object-Oriented Observations. *American Programmer* vol. 2(7-8).

Yourdon, E. and Constantine, L. 1979. *Structured Design*. Englewood Cliffs, NJ: Prentice-Hall.

Zahniseer, R. July/August 1990. Building Software In Groups. American Programmer vol. 3(7-8).

Zave, P. February 1984. The Operational versus the Conventional Approach to Software Development. *Communications of the ACM* vol. 27(2).

Zelkowitz, M. June 1978. Perspectives on Software Engineering. *ACM Computing Surveys* vol. 10(2).

I. Special References

Alexander, C. 1979. *The Timeless Way of Building*. New York, New York: Oxford University Press.

DeGrace, P. and Stahl, L. 1990. *Wicked Problems, Righteous Solutions*. Englewood Cliffs, New Jersey: Yourdon Press.

Fukuyama, F. 1992. *The End of History and the Last Man*. New York, New York: The Free Press.

Gall, J. 1986. *Systemantics: How Systems Really Work and How They Fail*. Second Edition. Ann Arbor, MI: The General Systemantics Press.

Gleick, J. 1987. *Chaos*. New York, NY: Penguin Books.

Heckbert, P. 1988. Ray Tracing Jell-O Brand Gelatin. *Communications of the ACM* vol. 31(2).

Heinlein, R. 1966. *The Moon Is a Harsh Mistress*. New York, NY: The Berkeley Publishing Group.

Hofstadter, D. 1979. *Gödel, Escher, Bach: An Eternal Golden Braid*. New York, NY: Vintage Books.

Inside Macintosh Volumes 1-5. 1988. Reading, MA: Addison-Wesley.

Kawasaki, G. 1990. *The Macintosh Way*. Glenview, Illinois Scott, Foresman and Company.

Lakoff, G. and Johnson, M. 1980. *Metaphors We Live By*. Chicago, Illinois: The University of Chicago Press.

Lammers, S. 1986. *Programmers at Work*. Bellevue, Washington, Microsoft Press.

Meyer, C. and Matyas. 1982. *Cryptography*. New York, NY: John Wiley and Sons.

Parker, T. 1983. *Rules of Thumb*. Boston, Massachusetts: Houghton Mifflin Company.

Peter, L. 1986. *The Peter Pyramid*. New York, NY: William Morrow.

Petroski, H. 1985. *To Engineer Is Human*. New York, NY: St. Martin's Press.

Rand, Ayn. 1979. *Introduction to Objectivist Epistemology.* New York, NY: New American Library.

Reti, L. 1988. *The Unknown Leonard.* New York, New York: Abradale Press.

Sears, F., Zemansky, M., and Young., H. 1987. *University Physics.* Seventh edition. Reading, MA: Addison-Wesley.

vonOech, R.1990. *A Whack on the Side of the Head.* New York, New York: Warner Books, Incorporated.

Wagner, J. 1986. *The Search for Signs of Intelligent Life in the Universe.* New York, NY: Harper and Row.

Whitehead, A. 1958. *An Introduction to Mathematics.* New York, NY: Oxford University Press.

J. Theory

Aho, A., Hopcroft, J., and Ullman, J. 1974. *The Design and Analysis of Computer Programs.* Reading, MA: Addison-Wesley.

Almarode, J. October 1989. Rule-Based Delegation for Prototypes. *SIGPLAN Notices* vol. 24(10).

Appelbe, W. and Ravn, A. April 1984. Encapsulation Constructs in Systems Programming Languages. *ACM Transactions on Programming Languages and Systems* vol. 6(2).

Averill, E. April 1982. Theory of Design and Its Relationship to Capacity Measurement. *Proceedings of the Fourth Annual International Conference on Computer Capacity Management* . San Francisco, CA: Association of Computing Machinery.

Barr, A. and Feigenbaum, E. 1981. *The Handbook of Artificial Intelligence.* Los Altos, CA: William Kaufmann.

Bastani, F. and Iyengar, S. March 1987. The Effect of Data Structures on the Logical Complexity of Programs. *Communications of the ACM* vol. 30(3).

Bastani, F., Hilal, W., and Sitharama, S. October 1987. Efficient Abstract Data Type Components for Distributed and Parallel Systems. *IEEE Computer* vol. 20(10).

Belkhouche, B. and Urban, J. May 1986. Direct Implementation of Abstract Data Types from Abstract Specifications. *IEEE Transactions on Software Engineering* vol. SE-12(5).

Bensley, E., Brando, T., and Prelle, M. September 1988. An Execution Model for Distributed Object-Oriented Computation. *SIGPLAN Notices* vol. 23(11).

Berztiss, A. 1980. Data Abstraction, Controlled Iteration, and Communicating Processes. *Communications of the ACM.*

Bishop, J. 1986. *Data Abstraction in Programming Languages.* Wokingham, England: Addison-Wesley.

Boehm, H., Demers, A., and Donahue, J. October 1980. *An Informal Description of Russell.* Technical Report TR 80-430. Ithaca, NY: Cornell University.

Borning, A., Duisberg, R., Freeman-Benson, B., Kramer, A., and Woolf, M. October 1987. Constraint Hierarchies. *SIGPLAN Notices* vol. 22(12).

Boute, R. January 1988. Systems Semantics: Principles, Applications, and Implementation. *ACM Transactions on Programming Languages and Systems* vol. 10.(1).

Brachman, R. October 1983. What Is-a Is and Isn't: An Analysis of Taxonomic Links in Semantic Networks. *IEEE Computer* vol. 16(10).

Brachman, R. and Levesque, H. eds. 1985. *Readings in Knowledge Representation.* Los Altos, CA: Morgan Kaufmann.

Brooks, R. April 1987. *Intelligence without Representation.* Cambridge, Massachusetts MIT Artificial Intelligence Laboratory.

Bruce, K. and Wegner, P. October 1986. An Algebraic Model of Subtypes in Object-Oriented Languages. *SIGPLAN Notices* vol. 21(10).

Card, S., Moran, T., and Newell, A. 1983. *The Psychology of Human-Computer Interaction.* Hillsdale, New Jersey: Lawrence Erlbaum Associates.

Cardelli, L. and Wegner, P. December 1985. On Understanding Types, Data Abstraction, and Polymorphism. *ACM Computing Surveys* vol. 17(4).

Claybrook, B. and Wyckof, M. 1980. Module: an Encapsulation Mechanism for Specifying and Implementing Abstract Data Types. *Communications of the ACM.*

Cline, A. and Rich, E. December 1983. *Building and Evaluating Abstract Data Types,* Report TR-83-26. Austin, TX: University of Texas, Department of Computer Sciences.

Cohen, A. January 1984. Data Abstraction, Data Encapsulation, and Object-Oriented Programming. *SIGPLAN Notices* vol. 19(1).

Cohen, N. November/December 1985. Tasks as Abstraction Mechanisms. *Ada Letters* vol. 5(3-6).

Cohen, P. and Loiselle, C. August 1988. Beyond ISA: Structures for Plausible Inference in Semantic Nets. *Proceedings of the Seventh National Conference on Artificial Intelligence.* Saint Paul, MN: American Association for Artificial Intelligence.

Collins, W. 1992. *Data Structures: An Object-Oriented Approach.* Reading, Massachusetts Addison-Wesley Publishing Company.

Cook, W. and Palsberg, J. October 1989. A Denotational Semantics of Inheritance and Its Correctness. *SIGPLAN Notices* vol. 24(10).

Courtois, P., Heymans, F., and Parnas, D. October 1971, Concurrent Control with "Readers" and "Writers." *Communications of the ACM* vol. 14(10).

Danforth, S. and Tomlinson, C. March 1988. Type Theories and Object-Oriented Programming. *ACM Computing Surveys* vol. 20(1).

Demers, A., Donahue, J., and Skinner, G. Data Types as Values: Polymorphism, Type-Checking, Encapsulation. *Proceedings of the Fifth Annual ACM Symposium on Principles of Programming Languages.* New York, NY: Association of Computing Machinery.

Dennis, J. and Van Horn, E. March 1966. Programming Semantics for Multiprogrammed Computations. *Communications of the ACM* vol. 9(3).

Donahue, J. and Demers, A. July 1985. Data Types Are Values. *ACM Transactions on Programming Languages and Systems* vol. 7(3).

Eckart, J. April 1987. Iteration and Abstract Data Types. *SIGPLAN Notices* vol. 22(4).

Embley, D. and Woodfield, S. 1988. Assessing the Quality of Abstract Data Types Written in Ada. *Proceedings of the 10th International Conference on Software Engineering.* New York, NY: Computer Society Press of the IEEE.

Ferber, J. October 1989. Computational Reflection in Class-Based Object-Oriented Languages. *SIGPLAN Notices* vol. 24(10).

Fisher, J. and Gipson, D. November 1992. *In Search of Elegance*. Computer Language vol. 9(11).

Gannon, J., Hamlet, R., and Mills, H. July 1987. Theory of Modules. *IEEE Transactions on Software Engineering* vol. SE-13(7).

Gannon, J., McMullin, P., and Hamlet, R. July 1981. Data Abstraction Implementation, Specification, and Testing. *ACM Transactions on Programming Languages and Systems vol.* 3(3).

Gardner, M. May/June 1984. When to Use Private Types. *Ada Letters* vol. 3(6).

Goguen, J., Thatcher, J., and Wagner, E. 1977. An Initial Algebra Approach to the Specification, Correctness, and Implementation of Abstract Data Types, in *Current Trends in Programming Methodology: Data Structuring* vol. 4. ed. R. Yeh. Englewood Cliffs, NJ: Prentice-Hall.

Goldberg, D. 1989. *Genetic Algorithms*. Reading, Massachusetts. Addison-Wesley Publishing Company.

Graube, N. October 1989. Metaclass Compatibility. *SIGPLAN Notices* vol. 24(10).

Gries, D. and Prins, J. July 1985. A New Notion of Encapsulation. *SIGPLAN Notices* vol. 20(7).

Grogono, P. and Bennett, A. November 1989. Polymorphism and Type Checking in Object-Oriented Languages. *SIGPLAN Notices* vol. 24(11).

Guttag, J. 1980. Abstract Data Types and the Development of Data Structures, in *Programming Language Design*. ed. A. Wasserman. New York, NY: Computer Society Press of the IEEE.

Hammons, C. and Dobbs, P. May/June 1985. Coupling, Cohesion, and Package Unity in Ada. *Ada Letters* vol. 4(6).

Harel, D. and Kahana, C. October 1992. On Statecharts with Overlapping. *ACM Transactions on Software Engineering and Methodology* vol. 1(4).

Harel, D., Lachover, H., Naamad, A., Pnueli, A., Politi, M., Sherman, R. Shtull-Trauring, S., and Trakhtenbrot, M. April 1990. STATEMATE: A Working Environment for the Development of Complex Reactive Systems. *IEEE Transactions on Software Engineering* vol. 16(4).

Harrison, G. and Liu, D. July/August 1986. Generic Implementations Via Analogies in the Ada Programming Language. *Ada Letters* vol. 6(4).

Hayes, P. 1981. The Logic of Frames, in *Readings in Artificial Intelligence*. ed. B. Webber and N. Nilsson. Palo Alto, CA: Tioga.

Hayes-Roth, F. July 1985. A Blackboard Architecture for Control. *Artificial Intelligence* vol. 26(3).

Hayes-Roth, F., Waterman, D., and Lenat, D. 1983. *Building Expert Systems*. Reading, MA: Addison-Wesley.

Haynes, C. and Friedman, D. October 1987. Embedding Continuations in Procedural Objects. *ACM Transactions on Programming Languages and Systems* vol. 9(4).

Henderson, P. February 1986. Functional Programming, Formal Specification, and Rapid Prototyping. *IEEE Transactions on Software Engineering* vol. SE-12(2).

Herlihy, M. and Liskov, B. October 1982. A Value Transmission Method for Abstract Data Types. *ACM Transactions on Programming Languages and Systems* vol. 4(4).

Hesselink, W. January 1988. A Mathematical Approach to Nondeterminism in Data Types. *ACM Transactions on Programming Languages and Systems* vol. 10(1).

Hibbard, P., Hisgen, A., Rosenbers, J., Shaw, M., and Sherman, M. 1981. *Studies in Ada Style.* New York, NY: Springer-Verlag.

Hilfinger, P. 1982. *Abstraction Mechanisms and Language Design.* Cambridge, MA: The MIT Press.

Hoare, C. October 1974. Monitors: An Operating System Structuring Concept. *Communications of the ACM* vol. 17(10).

Hoare, C. 1985. *Communicating Sequential Processes.* Englewood Cliffs, NJ: Prentice/Hall International.

Hogg, J. and Weiser, S. October 1987. OTM: Applying Objects to Tasks. *SIGPLAN Notices* vol. 22(12).

Jajodia, S. and Ng. P. 1983. On Representation of Relational Structures by Entity-Relationship Diagrams, in *Entity-Relationship Approach to Software Engineering.* ed. C. Davis et al. Amsterdam, The Netherlands: Elsevier Science.

Johnson, C., 1986. Some Design Constraints Required for the Assembly of Software Components: The Incorporation of Atomic Abstract Types into Generically Structured Abstract Types. *Proceedings of the First International Conference on Ada Programming Language Applications for the NASA Space Station.* Houston, TX: NASA Lyndon B. Johnson Space Center.

Kernighan, B. and Plauger, P. 1981. S*oftware Tools in Pascal.* Reading, MA: Addison-Wesley.

Knight, B. 1983. A Mathematical Basis for Entity Analysis, in *Entity-Relationship Approach to Software Engineering.* ed. C. Davis et al. Amsterdam, The Netherlands: Elsevier Science.

Knuth, D. 1973. *The Art of Computer Programming,* Vol. 1-3. Reading, MA: Addison-Wesley.

Kosko, B. 1992. *Neural Networks and Fuzzy Systems.* Englewood Cliffs, New Jersey: Prentice-Hall Incorporated.

LaLonde, W. and Pugh, J. August 1985. Specialization, Generalization, and Inheritance: Teaching Objectives Beyond Data Structures and Data Types. *SIGPLAN Notices* vol. 20(8).

Leeson, J. and Spear, M. March 1987. Type-Independent Modules: The Preferred Approach to Generic ADTs in Modula-2. *SIGPLAN Notices* vol. 22(3).

Lenzerini, M. and Santucci, G. 1983. Cardinality Constraints in the Entity-Relationship Model, in *Entity-Relationship Approach to Software Engineering.* ed. C. Davis et al. Amsterdam, The Netherlands: Elsevier Science.

Levesque, H. July 1984. Foundations of a Functional Approach to Knowledge Representation. *Artificial Intelligence* vol. 23(2).

Lindgreen, P. 1983. Entity Sets and Their Description, in *Entity-Relationship Approach to Software Engineering.* ed. C. Davis et al. Amsterdam, The Netherlands: Elsevier Science.

Lins, C. 1989. A First Look at Literate Programming. *Structured Programming.*

Liskov, B. May 1988. Data Abstraction and Hierarchy. *SIGPLAN Notices* vol. 23(5).

—— 1980. Programming with Abstract Data Types, in *Programming Language Design*. ed. A. Wasserman. New York, NY: Computer Society Press of the IEEE.

Liskov, B. and Scheifler, R. July 1983. Guardians and Actions: Linguistic Support for Robust, Distributed Programs. *ACM Transactions on Programming Languages and Systems* vol. 5(3).

Liskov, B. and Zilles, S. 1977. An Introduction to Formal Specifications of Data Abstractions, in *Current Trends in Programming Methodology: Software Specification and Design* vol. 1. ed. R. Yeh. Englewood Cliffs, NJ: Prentice-Hall.

Lowry, M. and McCartney. 1991. *Automating Software Design*. Cambridge, Massachusetts: The MIT Press.

Lucco, S. October 1987. Parallel Programming in a Virtual Object Space. *SIGPLAN Notices* vol. 22(12).

Maes, P. October 1987. Concepts and Experiments in Computational Reflection. *SIGPLAN Notices* vol. 22(12).

Mark, L. 1983. What is the Binary Relationship Approach?, in *Entity-Relationship Approach to Software Engineering*. ed. C. Davis et al. Amsterdam, The Netherlands: Elsevier Science.

Markowitz, V. and Raz, Y. 1983. A Modified Relational Algebra and Its Use in an Entity-Relationship Environment, in *Entity-Relationship Approach to Software Engineering*. ed. C. Davis et al. Amsterdam, The Netherlands: Elsevier Science.

Matsuoka, S. and Kawai, S. September 1988. Using Tuple Space Communication in Distributed Object-Oriented Languages. *SIGPLAN Notices* vol. 23(11).

McAllester, D. and Zabih, F. November 1986. Boolean Classes. *SIGPLAN Notices* vol. 21(11).

McCullough, P. October 1987. Transparent Forwarding: First Steps. *SIGPLAN Notices* vol. 22(12).

Merlin, P. and Bochmann, G. January 1983. On the Construction of Submodule Specifications and Communication Protocols. *ACM Transactions on Programming Languages and Systems* vol. 5(1)

Meyer, B. 1987. *Programming as Contracting*, Report TR-EI-12/CO. Goleta, CA: Interactive Software Engineering.

—— October 1992. Applying "Design by Contract." *IEEE Computer* vol. 25(10).

Minoura, T. and Iyengar, S. January 1989. Data and Time Abstraction Techniques for Multilevel Concurrent Systems. *IEEE Transactions on Software Engineering* vol. 15(1).

Murata, T. 1984 Modeling and Analysis of Concurrent Systems, in *Software Engineering*. ed. C. Vick and C. Ramamoorthy. New York, NY: Van Nostrand Reinhold.

Mylopoulos, J. and Levesque, H. 1984. An Overview of Knowledge Representation. *On Conceptual Modeling: Perspectives from Artificial Intelligence, Databases, and Programming Languages*. ed. M. Brodie, J. Mylopoulos, and J. Schmidt. New York, NY: Springer-Verlag.

Nakano, R. 1983. Integrity Checking in a Logic-Oriented ER Model, in *Entity-Relationship Approach to Software Engineering*. ed. C. Davis et al. Amsterdam, The Netherlands: Elsevier Science.

Newton, M. and Watkins, J. November/December 1988. The Combination of Logic and Objects for Knowledge Representation. *Journal of Object-Oriented Programming* vol. 1(4).

Nii, P. Summer 1986. Blackboard Systems: The Blackboard Model of Problem Solving and the Evolution of Blackboard Architectures. *AI Magazine* vol. 7(2).

Ohori, A. and Buneman, P. October 1989. Static Type Inference for Parametric Classes. *SIGPLAN Notices* vol. 24(10).

Pagan, F. 1981. *Formal Specification of Programming Languages.* Englewood Cliffs, NJ: Prentice-Hall.

Parent, C. and Spaccapieta, S. July 1985. An Algebra for a General Entity-Relationship Model. *IEEE Transactions on Software Engineering* vol. SE-11(7).

Parnas, D. 1977. The Influence of Software Structure on Reliability, in *Current Trends in Programming Methodology: Software Specification and Design* vol. 1. ed. R. Yeh. Englewood Cliffs, NJ: Prentice-Hall.

—— 1980. Designing Software for Ease of Extension and Contraction, in *Tutorial on Software Design Techniques.* Third Edition. ed. P. Freeman and A. Wasserman. New York, NY: Computer Society Press of the IEEE.

Parnas, D., Clements, P., and Weiss, D. 1983. Enhancing Reusability with Information Hiding. *Proceedings of the Workshop on Reusability in Programming,* Stratford, CT: ITT Programming.

Pattee, H. 1973. *Hierarchy Theory.* New York, NY: George Braziller.

Peckham, J. and Maryanski, F. September 1988. Semantic Data Models. *ACM Computing Surveys* vol. 20(3).

Pedersen, C. October 1989. Extending Ordinary Inheritance Schemes to Include Generalization. *SIGPLAN Notices* vol. 24(10).

Peterson, J. September 1977. Petri Nets. *Computing Surveys* vol. 9(3).

Reed, D. September 1978. Naming and Synchronization in a Decentralized Computer System. Cambridge, MA: The MIT Press.

Rich, C. and Wills, L. January 1990. Recognizing a Program's Design: A Graph-Parsing Approach. *IEEE Software* vol. 7(1).

Robinson, L. and Levitt, K. 1977. Proof Techniques for Hierarchically Structured Programs, in *Current Trends in Programming Methodology: Program Validation* vol. 2. ed. R. Yeh. Englewood Cliffs, NJ: Prentice-Hall.

Ross, D. July/August 1986. Classifying Ada Packages. *Ada Letters* vol. 6(4).

Ruane, L. January 1984. Abstract Data Types in Assembly Language Programming. *SIGPLAN Notices* vol. 19(1).

Rumbaugh, J. September 1988. Controlling Propagation of Operations Using Attributes on Relations. *SIGPLAN Notices* vol. 23(11).

Sedgewick, R. 1983. *Algorithms.* Reading, MA: Addison-Wesley.

Shankar, K. 1984. Data Design: Types, Structures, and Abstractions, in *Software Engineering.* ed. C. Vick and C. Ramamoorthy. New York, NY: Van Nostrand Reinhold.

Shaw, M. 1984. The Impact of Modeling and Abstraction Concerns on Modern Programming Languages. *On Conceptual Modeling: Perspectives from Artificial Intelligence, Databases, and Programming Languages.* ed. M. Brodie, J. Mylopoulos, and J. Schmidt. New York, NY: Springer-Verlag.

—— October 1984. Abstraction Techniques in Modern Programming Languages. *IEEE Software* vol. 1(4).

—— May 1989. Larger Scale Systems Require Higher-Level Abstractions. *SIGSOFT Engineering Notes* vol. 14(3).

Shaw, M., Feldman, G., Fitzgerald, R., Hilfinger, P., Kimura, I., London, R., Rosenberg, J., and Wulf, W. 1981. Validating the Utility of Abstraction Techniques, in *ALPHARD: Form and Content.* ed. M. Shaw. New York, NY: Springer-Verlag.

Shaw, M., Wulf., W., and London, R. 1981. Abstraction and Verification in ALPHARD: Iteration and Generators, in *ALPHARD: Form and Content.* ed. M. Shaw. New York, NY: Springer-Verlag.

Sherman, M., Hisgen, A., and Rosenberg, J. 982. A Methodology for Programming Abstract Data Types in Ada. *Proceedings of the AdaTEC Conference on Ada.* New York, NY: Association of Computing Machinery.

Siegel, J. April 1988. Twisty Little Passages. *HOOPLA: Hooray for Object-Oriented Programming Languages* vol. 1(3). Everette, WA: Object Oriented Programming for Smalltalk Application Developers Association.

Stefik, M., Bobrow, D., and Kahn, K. January 1986. Integrating Access-Oriented Programming into a Multiparadigm Environment. *IEEE Software* vol. 3(1).

Strom, R. and Yemini, S. January 1986. Typestate: A Programming Language Concept for Enhancing Software Reliability. *IEEE Transactions on Software Engineering* vol. SE-12(1).

Stubbs, D. and Webre, N. 1985. *Data Structures with Abstract Data Types and Pascal.* Monterey, CA: Brooks/Cole.

Swaine, M. June 1988. Programming Paradigms. *Dr. Dobb's Journal of Software Tools*, no. 140.

Tabourier, Y. 1983. Further Development of the Occurrences Structure Concept: The EROS Approach, in *Entity-Relationship Approach to Software Engineering.* ed. C. Davis et al. Amsterdam, The Netherlands: Elsevier Science.

Tanenbaum, A. 1981. *Computer Networks.* Englewood Cliffs, NJ: Prentice-Hall.

Tenenbaum, A. and Augenstein, M. 1981. *Data Structures Using Pascal.* Englewood Cliffs, NJ: Prentice-Hall.

Throelli, L. October 1987. Modules and Type Checking in PL/LL. *SIGPLAN Notices* vol. 22(12).

Tomlinson, C. and Singh, V. October 1989. Inheritance and Synchronization with Enabled-sets. *SIGPLAN Notices* vol. 24(10).

Toy, W. 1984. Hardware/Software Tradeoffs, in *Software Engineering.* ed. C. Vick and C. Ramamoorthy. New York, NY: Van Nostrand Reinhold.

Vegdahl, S. November 1986. Moving Structures between Smalltalk Images. *SIGPLAN Notices* vol. 21(11).

Walters, N. October 1992. Using Harel Statecharts to Model Object-Oriented Behavior. *SIGSOFT Notices* vol. 17(4).

Wasserman, A. 1980. Introduction to Data Types, in *Programming Language Design.* ed. A. Wasserman. New York, NY: Computer Society Press of the IEEE.

Weber, H. and Ehrig, H. July 1986. Specification of Modular Systems. *IEEE Transactions on Software Engineering* vol. SE-12(7).

Wegner, P. 6 June 1981. *The Ada Programming Language and Environment.* Unpublished draft.

Wegner, P. 1987. On the Unification of Data and Program Abstraction in Ada, in *Object-Oriented Computing: Concepts* vol. 1. ed. G. Peterson. New York, NY: Computer Society Press of the IEEE.

Wegner, P. 1987. The Object-Oriented Classification Paradigm, in *Research Directions in Object-Oriented Programming.* ed. B. Schriver and P. Wegner. Cambridge, MA: The MIT Press.

Wegner, P. and Zdonik, S. August 1988. Inheritance as an Incremental Modification Mechanism or What Like Is and Isn't Like. *Proceedings of ECOOP'88: European Conference on Object-Oriented Programming.* New York, NY: Springer-Verlag.

Weihl, W. and Liskov, B. April 1985. Implementation of Resilient, Atomic Data Types. *ACM Transactions on Programming Languages and Systems vol.* 7(2)

Weinberg, G. 1971. *The Psychology of Computer Programming.* New York, New York, Van Nostrand Reinhold Company.

Weller, D. and York, B. May 1984. A Relational Representation of an Abstract Type System. *IEEE Transactions on Software Engineering* vol. SE-10(3).

White, J. July 1983. On the Multiple Implementation of Abstract Data Types within a Computation. *IEEE Transactions on Software Engineering* vol. SE-9(4).

Wirth, N. December 1974. On the Composition of Well-structured Programs. *Computing Surveys* vol. 6(4).

—— January 1983. Program Development by Stepwise Refinement. *Communications of the ACM* vol. 26(1).

—— 1986. *Algorithms and Data Structures,* Second Edition. Englewood Cliffs, NJ: Prentice-Hall.

—— April 1988. Type Extensions. *ACM Transactions on Programming Languages and Systems* vol. 10(2).

Wolf, A., Clarke, L., and Wileden, J. April 1988. A Model of Visibility Control. *IEEE Transactions on Software Engineering* vol. 14(4).

Woods, W. October 1983. What's Important About Knowledge Representation? *IEEE Computer* vol. 16(10).

Zilles, S. 1984. Types, Algebras, and Modeling, in *On Conceptual Modeling: Perspectives from Artificial Intelligence, Databases, and Programming Languages.* ed. M. Brodie, J. Mylopoulos, and J. Schmidt. New York, NY: Springer-Verlag.

Zippel, R. June 1983. Capsules. *SIGPLAN Notices* vol. 18(6).

K. Tools and Environments

Andrews, T. and Harris, C. 1987. Combining Language and Database Advances in an Object-Oriented Development Environment. Billerica, MA: Ontologic

Corradi, A. and Leonardi, L. 1986. *An Environment Based on Parallel Objects.* Bologna, Italy: Universita' di Bologna.

Deutsch, P. and Taft, E. June 1980. *Requirements for an Experimental Programming Environment,* Report CSL-80-10. Palo Alto, CA: Xerox Palo Alto Research Center.

Diederich, J. and Milton, J. October 1987. An Object-Oriented Design System Shell. *SIGPLAN Notices* vol. 22(12).

Durant, D., Carlson, G., and Yao, P. 1987. *Programmer's Guide to Windows.* Berkeley, CA: Sybex.

Erman, L., Lark, J., and Hayes-Roth, F. December 1988. ABE: An Environment for Engineering Intelligent Systems. *IEEE Transactions on Software Engineering* vol. 14(12).

Ferrel, P. and Meyer, R. October 1989. Vamp: The Aldus Application Framework. *SIGPLAN Notices* vol. 24(10).

Fischer, H. and Martin, D. 1987. *Integrating Ada Design Graphics into the Ada Software Development Process.* Encino, CA: Mark V Business Systems.

Goldberg, A. 1984a. *Smalltalk-80: The Interactive Programming Environment.* Reading, MA: Addison-Wesley.

—— 1984b. The Influence of an Object-Oriented Language on the Programming Environment, in *Interactive Programming Environments.* ed. B. Barstow. New York, NY: McGraw-Hill.

Goldstein, I. and Bobrow, D. March 1981. *An Experimental Description-Based Programming Environment,* Report CSL-81-3. Palo Alto, CA: Xerox Palo Alto Research Center.

Gorlen, K. May 1986. *Object-Oriented Program Support.* Bethesda, MD: National Institute of Health.

Hecht, A. and Simmons, A. 1986. Integrating Automated Structured Analysis and Design with Ada Programming Support Environments. *Proceedings of the First International Conference on Ada Programming Language Applications for the NASA Space Station.* Houston, TX: NASA Lyndon B. Johnson Space Center.

Hedin, G. and Magnusson B. August 1988. The Mjolner Environment: Direct Interaction with Abstractions. *Proceedings of ECOOP'88: European Conference on Object-Oriented Programming.* New York, NY: Springer-Verlag.

Hudson, S. and King, R. June 1988. The Cactic Project: Database Support for Software Environments. *IEEE Transactions on Software Engineering* vol. 14(6).

International Business Machines. April 1988. *Operating System/2 Seminar Proceedings, IBM OS/2 Standard Edition Version 1.1, IBM Operating System/2 Update, Presentation Manager.* Boca Raton, FL.

Kant, E. 26 March 1987. *Interactive Problem Solving with a Task Configuration and Control System.* Ridgefield, CT: Schlumberger-Doll Research.

Kleyn, M. and Gingrich, P. September 1988. GraphTrace – Understanding Object-Oriented Systems Using Concurrently Animated Views. *SIGPLAN Notices* vol. 23(11).

Laff, M. and Hailpern, B. July 1985. SW-2 – An Object-Based Programming Environment. *SIGPLAN Notices* vol. 20(7).

MacLenna, B. July 1985. A Simple Software Environment Based on Objects and Relations. *SIGPLAN Notices* vol. 20(7).

Marques, J. and Guedes, P. October 1989. Extending the Operating System to Support an Object-Oriented Environment. *SIGPLAN Notices* vol. 24(10).

Minsky, N. and Rozenshtein, D. February 1988. A Software Development Environment for Law-Governed Systems. *SIGPLAN Notices* vol. 24(2).

Moreau, D. and Dominick, W. 1987. *Object-Oriented Graphical Information Systems: Research Plan and Evaluation Metrics.* Lafayette, LA: University of Southwestern Louisiana, Center for Advanced Computer Studies.

Nakata, S. and Yamazak, G. 1983. ISMOS: A System Based on the E-R Model and its Application to Database-Oriented Tool Generation, in *Entity-Relationship Approach to Software Engineering.* ed. C. Davis et al. Amsterdam, The Netherlands: Elsevier Science.

Nye, A. 1989. *Xlib Programming Manual for Version 11.* Newton, MA: O'Reilly and Associates.

O'Brien, P., Halbert, D., and Kilian, M. October 1987. The Trellis Programming Environment. *SIGPLAN Notices* vol. 22(12).

Open Look Graphical User Interface Functional Specification. 1990. Reading, MA: Addison-Wesley.

OSF/Motif Style Guide, Version 1.0. 1989. Cambridge, MA: Open Software Foundation.

Penedo, M., Ploedereder, E., and Thomas, I. February 1988. Object Management Issues for Software Engineering Environments. *SIGPLAN Notices* vol. 24(2).

Reenskaug, T. and Skaar, A. October 1989. An Environment for Literate Smalltalk Programming. *SIGPLAN Notices* vol. 24(10).

Rosenplatt, W., Wileden, J., and Wolf, A. October 1989. OROS: Toward a Type Model for Software Development Environments. *SIGPLAN Notices* vol. 24(10).

Russo, V. and Campbell, R. October 1989. Virtual Memory and Backing Storage Management in Multiprocessor Operating Systems Using Object-Oriented Design Techniques. *SIGPLAN Notices* vol. 24(10).

Scheifler, R. and Gettys, J. 1986. The X Window System. *ACM Transactions on Graphics* vol. 63.

Schwan, K. and Matthews, J. July 1986. Graphical Views of Parallel Programs. *Software Engineering Notes* vol. 11(3).

Shear, D. 8 December 1988. CASE Shows Promise but Confusion Still Exists. *EDN* vol. 33(25).

Sun Microsystems. 29 March 1987. *NeWS Technical Overview* Mountain View, CA.

Tarumi, H., Agusa, K., and Ohno, Y. 1988. A Programming Environment Supporting Reuse of Object-Oriented Software. *Proceedings of the 10th International Conference on Software Engineering,* New York, NY: Computer Society Press of the IEEE.

Taylor, R., Belz, F., Clarke, L., Osterweil, L., Selby, R., Wileden, J., Wolf, A., and Young, M. February 1988. Foundations for the Arcadia Environment. *SIGPLAN Notices* vol. 24(2).

Tesler, L. August 1981. The Smalltalk Environment. *Byte* vol. 6(8).

Vines, D. and King, T. 1988. *Gaia: An Object-Oriented Framework for an Ada Environment.* Minneapolis, MN: Honeywell.

Weinand, A., Gamma, E., and Marty, R. 1989. Design and Implementation of ET++, a Seamless Object-Oriented Application Framework. *Structured Programming* vol. 10(2).

Wiorkowski, G. and Kull, D. 1988. *DB2 Design and Development Guide.* Reading, MA: Addison-Wesley.

The *Rational Booch Reference Card* is a handy glossary of the complete Booch notation. For a free copy, contact Rational at any of the phone numbers below or by Internet booch-card@rational.com.

Software Engineering Solutions

Santa Clara, CA 800-767-3237 or 408-496-3600
France +33-1-47-17-41-77, Germany +49-89-797-021, U.K. +44-273-204733, Sweden +46-8-761-
Australia +61-3-521-0507, Taiwan +886-2-720-1938, Italy +39-2-264-0107, Spain +34-1-279-72-56

State Transition Diagram
Shows the existence of classes and their relationships in the logical view of a system.

State icon

name
actions

State transitions

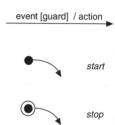

event [guard] / action

start

stop

Nesting

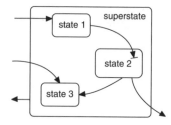

History

Object Diagram
Shows the existence of objects and their relationships in the logical view of a system.

Object icon

name
attributes

Link

order : message
object/value ◯──►

role
[key]
{constraint}

Synchronization

simple

synchronous

balking

timeout

asynchronous

Visibility

G	global
P	parameter
F	field
L	local

Interaction Diagram
Traces the execution of a scenario.

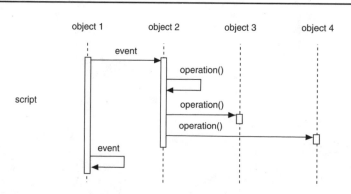

object 1   object 2   object 3   object 4

event

operation()

operation()

operation()

script

event